Frames, Fields, and Contrasts

FRAMES, FIELDS, AND CONTRASTS

New Essays in
Semantic and Lexical Organization

Edited by
ADRIENNE LEHRER
University of Arizona
EVA FEDER KITTAY
SUNY Stony Brook

LEA

LAWRENCE ERLBAUM ASSOCIATES, PUBLISHERS
1992   Hillsdale, New Jersey   Hove and London

Copyright © 1992 by Lawrence Erlbaum Associates, Inc.

Lawrence Erlbaum Associates, Inc., Publishers
365 Broadway
Hillsdale, New Jersey 07642

Library of Congress Cataloging-in-Publication Data

Frames, fields, and contrasts: new essays in semantic and lexical
organization / edited by Adrienne Lehrer, Eva Feder Kittay.
    p. cm.
    Based on a conference sponsored by the National Science Foundation
held in Tucson, Arizona, July 8-10, 1989.
    Includes bibliographical references and indexes.
    ISBN 0-8058-1088-9 (cloth). — ISBN 0-8058-1089-7 (pbk.)
    1. Semantics. 2. Lexicology. I. Lehrer, Adrienne. II. Kittay,
Eva Feder.
P325.F66   1992
401'.43—dc20   92-425
                                               CIP

Printed in the United States of America
10 9 8 7 6 5 4 3 2 1

Contents

To Sir John Lyons

This collection grew out of a conference sponsored by the National Science Foundation held in Tucson, Arizona, July 8-10, 1989.
Much to our regret, Sir John Lyons, who originally planned to attend, had to withdraw. He was the teacher and mentor of several of the participants—Keith Allan, Eve Clark, Mava Jo Powell, and Adrienne Lehrer, and he was instrumental in bringing semantic field theory to the attention of English-speaking linguists.
It is to him that we dedicate this volume.

Introduction

Eva Feder Kittay
SUNY Stony Brook

Adrienne Lehrer
University of Arizona

The chapters in this multidisciplinary volume reflect contemporary research into principles of lexical and semantic organization. Past years have seen much progress in the study of language in understanding the systems of phonology and syntax. The analysis of individual words has been undertaken by lexicography and philology, but the global organization of vocabularies of natural languages has not received comparable attention. Recently, there has been a surge of interest in the lexicon. The demand for a fuller and more adequate understanding of lexical meaning required by developments in computational linguistics, artificial intelligence, and cognitive science has stimulated a refocused interest in linguistics, psychology, and philosophy.

In linguistics, the earlier view was that the lexicon was an unordered list of words where information on the grammatical idiosyncracies of words was to be described. Recent syntactic theories ascribe a more significant role to the lexicon, some claiming that much of the syntax is projected from the lexicon (Bresnan, 1982; Chomsky, 1981). Work in these theories has revealed (or at least suggested) that many syntactic generalizations follow from the meaning of the words (Carter, 1988; Levin, 1985). If these generalizations hold up, then the semantic organization of the lexicon can predict and explain at least some syntactic regularities.

In psychology, there are at least two avenues of interest in the organization of the lexicon: One deals with studies in the relationship between the lexicalization of concepts—that is, how concepts are expressed—and broader knowledge structures; and the second involves studies of the mental lexicon, language processing, and lexical retrieval. Semantic relations and field or frame structures seem to be operative in the mental lexicon. Lexical substitution errors, for

1

example, show that speakers often substitute an intended word by one in the same semantic field (see Garrett, this volume).

In philosophy, lexical meaning has been confined to a small number of problems (e.g., synonymy and entailment), but, even where these concepts are recognized and valued, little work has been done on the details and implications. But principles of lexical organization bear on the very conception of meaning and mental content, and they challenge the adequacy of dominant theories of truth semantics and referentially based theories of word meaning.

Scholars in computer science, artificial intelligence, and computational linguistics are interested in the organization of the lexicon because lexical items are a convenient starting point for analyzing and parsing natural-language texts. How the lexicon is organized determines the nature of the access to those items. Moreover, if the relations among lexical items (whether semantic, syntactic, morphological, or phonological) are made explicit, text processing can be improved, since the connections among various parts of the text that might otherwise be overlooked can be processed in terms of those relations.[1] Finally, investigations into the requirements for lexical entry in a machine-readable language challenge the traditional dichotomy between dictionary and encyclopedic information.

Different disciplines have studied lexical structure from their own vantage points. Because scholars have only intermittently communicated across disciplines, there has been little recognition that there is a common subject matter. In the summer of 1989, we arranged a conference, sponsored by the National Science Foundation, to bring together interested thinkers across the disciplines of linguistics, philosophy, psychology, and computer science to exchange ideas, discuss a range of questions and approaches to the topic, consider alternative research strategies and methodologies, and formulate interdisciplinary hypotheses concerning lexical organization.

The problems which emerged and which are investigated in the chapters that follow are discussed briefly here. They include alternative and complementary conceptions of the structure of the lexicon; the nature of semantic relations; the relation between meaning, concepts, and lexical organization; the nature of polysemy; critiques of truth-semantics and referential theories of meaning; computational accounts of lexical information and structure; and the advantages of thinking of the lexicon as ordered. The conference and this volume are just the beginning of an investigation into the importance and consequences of taking seriously the idea of a structured lexicon—whether such structure be innate or a product of the configuration of knowledge reflected in a given language. As the editors of this volume, we wanted to reflect the conference participants' recognition of the exploratory nature of the work done so far, and so we end the

---

[1]We are grateful to Terry Langendoen for this point.

introductory chapter with a cursory look at some questions that remain un-answered.

Concepts of Organization:
Fields, Frames, and Contrasts

Semantic Fields.   We begin with the concept of a semantic field, which has the longest history and widest acknowledgment. The concept was introduced by Humboldt (1936), Trier (1931), Porzig (1950), and Weisgerber (1950), and more recently developed by Lyons (1963, 1977), Lehrer (1974), Kittay (1987), and Grandy (1987). The proposal that the lexicon has a field structure has shown up in many disciplines. Common to all is the idea that words applicable to a common conceptual domain are organized within a semantic field by relations of affinity and contrast (e.g., synonymy, hyponymy, incompatibility, antonymy, etc.). The concept has far-ranging significance. It proposes a theory of semantic organization, of categorization, and of word meaning—positing that semantic relations are at least partly constitutive of the meaning of a word. It has been widely used as a basis of descriptive work on linguistics and anthropological linguistics, and the term *semantic field* is often used without comment by many linguists. Nonetheless, much work remains in clarifying the concept, and meth-odological problems in delineating semantic fields persist.

A semantic field, especially as understood in this volume, consists of a lexical field—that is, a set of lexemes or labels—which is applied to some content domain (a conceptual space, an experiential domain, or a practice). Although some field theorists (e.g., Lutzeier, 1981) restrict the field to lexemes belonging to the same syntactic class, others, for example, Lehrer (1974) and Kittay and Lehrer (1981), see an important part of the lexical study to look at semantically related words belonging to various parts of speech. The content domain supplies the concepts that are labeled by the lexical items, although the application of a lexical set to a given domain may in fact generate the set of concepts. Elements of the semantic field are generally "words" or "lexemes."[2] However, some writers would permit elements to be phrases which could be but are not lex-icalized in the language (e.g., "the parents of the spouse of my child," a phrase which is lexicalized in some languages, as in Yiddish). A lexeme usually consists of a word-form and one or more related senses. Some sense may participate in other semantic fields.

Semantic field theory makes a meaning claim that the meanings of words must be understood, in part, in relation to other words that articulate a given content domain and that stand in the relation of affinity and contrast to the word(s) in

---

[2]A lexeme is a meaning-form unit which consists of at least one word, but which ignores allomorphy. Where a lexeme consists of more than one word, its meaning is noncompositional, as in idioms.

question. Thus to understand the meaning of the verb *to sauté* requires that we understand its contrastive relation to *deep fry, broil, boil,* and also to affinitive terms like *cook* and the syntagmatic relations to *pan, pot,* and the many food items one might sauté.

Frames.   The largest organizational unit is the frame. Fillmore wrote the seminal article (1985) proposing a "frame semantics." Within a frame semantics, a word's meaning is understood "with reference to *a structured background of experience, beliefs, or practices*" (Fillmore & Atkins, this volume). Frames are interpretive devices by which we understand a term's deployment in a given context. Frames can either be created by or reflected in the language. An example of a frame created by the language itself would be the case of grading terms for detergent packages. The framing device allows the consumer to properly interpret the label *large* on the package; knowing that the other sizes are *economy, family size,* and *jumbo,* the consumer is led to the correct conclusion that *large* signifies the smallest package (Fillmore, 1985, p. 227). Other frames reflect understandings encoded in the language. Interpretative frames can be invoked by the interpreter or evoked by the text itself; some frames are innate (e.g., knowledge of the features of the human face), while some are learned through daily experience or through explicit training. According to Fillmore (1985), the claim of frame semantics is that such knowledge structures are necessary "in describing the semantic contribution of individual lexical items and grammatical construction and in explaining the process of constructing the interpretation of a text out of the interpretation of its pieces" (p. 232).

The notion of a frame grew out of Fillmore's early work in case grammar. There the grammatical positions often marked in languages by the use of case inflections were understood to structure the semantic items that could collocate with a verb. So, for example, the verb *to fish* would be represented as taking an AGENT as subject, a PATIENT as object. Since one fishes at a given place, the verb can take the prepositional phrase as LOCATIVE, and since one fishes with something, it can take another prepositional phrase as INSTRUMENT. From what is literally a frame for a verb, the concept grew to include more background knowledge. In this volume, Fillmore and Atkins describe a portion of a research project in construction grammar which has grown out of the concept of a frame. Within construction grammar, semantic and syntactic elements are combined in order to reflect the meaning dependence between word and frame. Fillmore and Atkins illustrate the possibilities of creating a "frame-based dictionary," with an analysis of the term *risk.* Paul Kay (this volume), working within the same paradigm, provides another example of how semantic and syntactic considerations figure in construction grammar to give an adequate account of the lexical representation of *at least.* These contributions, as well as some others in the volume, (e.g., Clark, Ross, Lehrer) show how the direct encoding of various pragmatic forces and interpretive instructions into the grammar of lexical items and constructions pose special kinds of challenges to standard truth-conditional semantics, even at the sentence level.

Barsalou provides a further development of the concept of a frame as consisting of attribute value sets, relations between attributes, and constraints. Barsalou attempts to integrate a theory of semantic fields and componential representation with a frame theory. He regards frames as dynamic, flexible configurations that are built recursively and that are highly sensitive to context.

Contrasts.   Some writers, notably Grandy, base the concepts of fields and frames on the idea of contrast. Grandy has a relatively strong concept of contrast: If terms *A* and *B* contrast, then that which is denoted by *A* should not also be denoted by *B*. Clark also sees the notion of contrast as fundamental but works with a weaker sense: If terms *A* and *B* contrast, then there must be some appropriate applications of *A* that are not appropriate applications of *B*. But Clark's concept is primarily pragmatic; Grandy's is semantic. He proposes the *contrast set,* which contains two or more terms that contrast, a covering term and one or more relations specifying the contrast(s), as the building block for semantic fields and ultimately of semantic frames.

Writers on semantic fields generally accept that the relations of contrast and affinity which order a field are of two types: paradigmatic and syntagmatic. Paradigmatic relations, such as synonymy, hyponomy, meronymy, antonymy, etc., exist among terms that are substitutable for one another in a well-formed syntactic string, preserving well-formedness. Syntagmatic relations hold between words that collocate in a grammatical string and that have semantic affinities (e.g., one *kicks* with a *leg,* or *foot,* but not with an *arm*). Syntagmatic relations have been variously characterized. One account (Kittay, 1987; Kittay & Lehrer, 1981) builds on Fillmore's case grammar (Fillmore, 1968) and considers case relations such as AGENT, PATIENT, LOCATIVE, etc. as syntagmatic field relations. Most work in semantic field theory has used sets of paradigmatic contrasts such as color terms, kinship terms, and calendrical terms as exemplars, often underestimating the importance of syntagmatic relations. The syntagmatic relations seem to have pride of place in the construction of frames. In Barsalou's formulation, the paradigmatically related terms appear as variables in attribute sets.

Some writers have developed the notion of semantic relations or contrasts independently of fields or frames and essentially regard them as autonomous meaning structures. Cruse (1986) has provided perhaps the most comprehensive study of semantic relations. Ross' account (1981, and this volume) stresses the dynamic relations that are affinitive or oppositional and that emerge as words exert different "forces" on one another in given contextual frameworks. In the contribution to this volume, Ross tries to set the notion of linguistic force into a "general theory of linguistic relativity." Using the metaphor of the theory of physical forces, Ross attempts to place notions of opposition and affinity at the center of his dynamical and relativistic account of meaning.

We leave a detailed discussion of semantic relations for the section that follows, but we note here that a central concern when focusing on contrasts is whether the contrasting items are concepts, senses, or lexemes. In speaking of lexical fields the relata in many theories are lexemes, or in some theories, are lexemes after we disambiguate them. Cruse (1986) understands relations to stand between senses, while Chaffin (this volume) holds that relations, which are themselves concepts, can hold between either relations or words. The theory proposed by Ross is clearly a theory of word meaning, and the relata are polysemous words whose meanings get specified and disambiguated in their dynamic interactions with other words.

Comparing the Three Structures.   The three positions outlined may be seen as alternative or as complementary theories. Whereas Fillmore contrasts his view with that of field theorists, Barsalou, Grandy, and Lehrer (this volume) all argue that one needs both frames and fields to adequately discuss conceptual and lexical organization. Barsalou tries to show how fields emerge out of frames and how relations structure not only fields but frames as well. In short, he argues that all fields have frames implicit in them and that one could not have fields without frames. A question that remains is whether frames and fields are mutually derivable, or whether insisting on the one or the other would lead to different empirical predictions. In earlier work, Fillmore (1985) has argued that it would, but he used a conception of fields limited to paradigmatic notions. If one broadens the concept to include syntagmatic relations, can one eventually build enough into a field for it to incorporate everything accounted for by frames? A difference between frames and fields that may remain is noted by Barsalou, who suggests that frames allow for temporal, dynamic, script-like relations between the elements. Fields tend to be constructed like tableaus and not like scripts. Frames might better capture the temporal elements constitutive of many practices or domains. Other differences are evident. Whereas frame semantics has explicitly distanced itself from a truth semantics, that is, a semantics that asserts that the meaning of a sentence is given by the truth conditions of the sentence, semantic field theorists have not explicitly distanced themselves from such a position. And although frame semantics explicitly includes encyclopedic knowledge within a frame, taking some encyclopedic knowledge to be important as a precondition for understanding a term, field theorists have not determined what kind of information is to be included in a field. Instead, the criteria for what is included in a field has been the product of relationships of a specifiable kind among words. As *yellow* is a hyponym of *color* and a cohyponym of *red*, both *red* and *yellow* are part of the semantic field of color. Similarly with syntagmatic relations: We fish for fish and because *trout, carp, snapper* denote kinds of fish, they are all included in the semantic field of *fishing*. *Shark* also denotes a species of fish, but we more often speak of *hunting sharks* or refer to a catch of big fish as the result of *deep sea fishing*. These kinds of distinctions are clearly not analytic but they are guided by the relations rather than by a pregiven synthetic-analytic distinction.

Although most conceptions of fields emphasize the importance of structure and therefore of relations, at least one author views the significance of fields more as a heuristic. Wierzbicka argues that the meaning of a word is "a configuration of semantic primitives" and as such does not "depend on the meaning of other words in the lexicon." The value of semantic fields, she claims, lies in the grouping of words thought to be similar in meaning, for "to establish what the meaning of a word is one has to compare it with the meaning of other, intuitively related words" (this volume). Relations are for Wierzbicka just concepts, some of which are decomposable into primitives.

Semantic Relations

Most authors represented in this collection consider relations an integral part of the structure of the lexicon. A number of chapters query the nature of relations. Lyons (1963, 1977), Lehrer (1974), and Cruse (1986) have treated relations like antonymy, synonymy, hyponymy, etc. as primitives, in the sense that they cannot be further decomposed. But are semantic relations, in fact, primitive in this sense or derived from more elemental concepts or relations? In this volume, Cruse (on antonymy) joins Chaffin (on meronymy and hyponymy) in arguing that relations are themselves composed of more primitive notions (see Lehrer & Lehrer, 1982).[3] Cruse analyzes antonymy in terms of grading schemas and scale schemas, each of which depends on other concepts, such as directionality and intensification. Chaffin, with Wierzbicka (this volume), treats relations as concepts, but as complex ones. He decomposes meronymy into the features +/−FUNCTION, where a part has a function (as in the relation between *handle* and *cup* but not between *tree* and *forest*); +/−SEPARABLE (as in *cup* and *handle*, but not in *bicycle* and *aluminum*); +/−HOMEONEROUS (in *pie* and *slice*, but not in *forest* and *tree*); and +/−SPATIO-TEMPORAL EXTENT, which distinguishes processes and events from other relations. Another concern is whether relations can be dynamic and still capture the changing and contextually bound interactions between words. Although lexical semanticists all recognize that languages are continually evolving and that lexemes are always used in new ways (e.g., to fill lexical gaps where the language may lack an appropriate word, to make novel metaphors and metonyms), most scholars have treated semantic relations as fixed contrasts in the language. Ross, however, presents a dynamic model of the lexicon, in which word meaning is not static but

---

[3]Lehrer and Lehrer (1982) analyzed antonymy in terms of scales and directionality.

is always dependent on the textual and contextual environment, where changing relations among words are reflected in changing sense. Yet there are constraints as well, because word meanings adapt and adjust in principled ways.

Specific semantic relations receive an extended treatment in several chapters. Chaffin's discussion of hyponymy and meronymy helps elucidate puzzling features such as the apparent failure of transitivity in some but not all cases. He shows that we are dealing not with a uniform set of relations, but with complex configurations of concepts that exhibit a wide range of properties. Cruse's analysis of antonymy involves cross-linguistic comparisons, displaying intriguing cross-linguistic patterns of contrast involved in antonymous relations.

Synonymy is a traditional semantic relationship (and one of the few, along with antonymy, whose name is part of common English vocabulary). In the philosophy of language synonymy has been overemphasized—to the exclusion of more interesting other semantic relationships, such as antonymy. Goodman (1952) and Quine (1953), using a very strong characterization of synonymy as complete substitutability, have argued that there are no synonyms and therefore no principled basis for drawing a distinction between analytic and synthetic knowledge. Goodman has said that we must settle for a weaker notion—likeness of meaning.[4]

In the current volume, synonymy is discussed by Clark and Ravin. Clark, like Goodman and Quine, argues that there are no exact synonyms, but her conclusion is based on evidence from lexical innovations, historical change, and language acquisition. So-called synonyms have at least some differences in informational content—be they differences in dialect or register.[5] Children and adults assume that if two words are different in form, then there must be some difference in meaning. If necessary, they will invent differences!

Ravin describes techniques for on-line manipulation of synonyms extracted from thesauri. But if there are no synonyms, how can this be accomplished? Is there a contradiction in the two chapters? Not necessarily. Part of the problem concerns the definition of *synonymy*. If synonyms are by definition exactly equivalent in meaning and interchangeable in all contexts, then there may not be any. However, there is certainly similarity of meaning or an overlap of word

---

[4]One problem with similarity is that it is too general and too weak a notion. Antonymous pairs are similar in meaning, even though they are oppositions. *Hot* is more similar in meaning to *cold* than it is to *telephone*. *Answer* and *ask* are also similar in meaning, because they both involve speaking, but they are not synonyms.

[5]Clark calls these differences "meaning" differences. Although what constitutes a meaning component is theory dependent, it seems safe to say that lexemes that differ in dialect or register are not equivalent simpliciter and often convey different information. Even if one could find a half dozen exact synonyms in a language (with say 50,000 words), Clark's point would still be valid.

meaning, and if we use a weaker notion and call that *synonymy*, which is what Ravin does, then one finds considerable synonymy in languages.

Definitions, Semantic Primitives, and Concepts

Central to the conception of an organized lexicon is the understanding of the lexical, semantic, and conceptual unit. Interconnections within the lexicon have often been derived from the grouping of words with reference to shared primitive components. But we need to ask if words can be decomposed and defined in terms of primitives of some kind. Semantic decomposition has a long history in semantic description, with roots in European structuralism (e.g., Hjelmslev, 1953) and American linguistic anthropology (Lounsbury, 1956). One motivation was economy—to show how a small number of semantic components could be used to define a large number of words and allow for semantic comparisons across languages. Although decomposition has been widely used as a descriptive device, it has been attacked by Lyons (1977), Allan (1986), and Cruse (1986). At one extreme is the position advocated by Fodor (1987), who claims that no decomposition is possible and all words are learned and treated as wholes. At the other extreme is the research by Wierzbicka (this volume), who has tried to work out a radical decomposition of all the words in any vocabulary into a couple dozen primitives. In between is the position of Jackendoff, who advocates some decomposition but argues that some conceptual information must be represented in other modalities. Our representation of the difference between a duck and a goose is stored in terms of the different way they look, not in terms of any differentiating linguistic features.

Wierzbicka and Jackendoff both select (with differing metalanguages) several of the same components, for example, (SOME)THING, PLACE, (BE)CAUSE, HAPPEN, BECOME, UNDER. Their two chapters form an interesting dialectic even though the two scholars have analyzed different lexemes, making it difficult to compare them directly. They differ in several fundamental ways. Most important is the fact that Wierzbicka assumes and uses English syntax, whereas Jackendoff develops explicit formal rules for mapping semantic structure onto syntactic structures which are consistent with the program of generative grammar. Wierzbicka analyzes grammatical meaning with the same methods and concepts as lexical meaning. In addition, she has focussed on cross-linguistic universals and the possibility of composing concepts and lexemes from a common store of universal primitives.

Related to the problem of definition are those of polysemy and disambiguation. Should we aim for a single general and abstract meaning for each lexical item or should we provide a more specific definition for each sense? Polysemy interacts with syntactic, semantic, and pragmatic principles enabling the hearer to select the most appropriate sense. The chapters that contain extensive analyses of a given word or phrase, Kay's (on *at least*), Powell's (on *literal*), and Allan's (on "something that rhymes with rich"), as well as Fillmore and Atkins' (on *risk*), and Chaffin's (on *part of* and related terms), each use implicit or explicit criteria for distinguishing related word meanings. (Note that all this work presupposes the Principle of Contrast developed in Clark's chapter.)

Powell looks at the polysemy of *literal* by taking into account historical developments whose accretions are evident in the different ways we use the term. Allan points to the importance of nonliteral aspects of meaning to access the appropriate sense in certain contexts. In reconstructing the correct sense of the term that "rhymes with rich," Allan shows that phonological, syntactic, and encyclopedic knowledge are required and thereby throws into question the adequacy of an analysis in terms of a finite set of semantic primitives. Kay often resorts to subtle syntactic considerations in delineating differences in meaning. He argues that the various senses of *at least* have historical connections and semantic relationships that some speakers may be aware of, but that there are no principles that allow speakers to predict senses. Hence the speaker must learn each sense individually. In Ross's approach, where meaning is dynamic, polysemy plays a major role as contexts force the generation of new senses of words. The fragmentation of meaning evident in the argument for pervasive polysemy and the desire (as in Cruse, 1986) to make the unit of analysis a specific sense rather than a word with multiple senses still demands that we explain why multiple senses are lexicalized by the same phonological form.

Meaning, Truth, and Reference

We have suggested that principles of lexical organization have implications for word meaning. To see how this is the case, many of the chapters in this volume investigate textual units larger than the word or sentence. Dominant theories in semantic theory have been atomistic (with the focus on the word), molecular (with the focus on the sentence), or holistic (with the focus on the language as a whole). Some of the chapters advocate a "local holism" in which the focus of meaning must be sought in linguistic structures that simultaneously function to organize the individual words, structures such as frames, fields, or contrasts. This is to say that some elements of meaning are intralinguistic and that an entirely extralinguistic account is not adequate. Still other writers in the volume are interested in the relation of language and thought and see meaning not perhaps as dependent on linguistic structures as much as on mental structures. Writers who insist on the importance of intralinguistic and mentalistic analyses of meaning share a dissatisfaction with those dominant positions in semantic theory in which truth and reference are prominent.

Truth theories of meaning—the view that the meaning of a sentence is either explained or given by the conditions that make the sentence true or false—and referential theories of word meaning—the view that the meaning of a word is given by its referent—generally have nothing to say about the organization of the lexicon, and often little to say about how the meanings of individual words may be represented in the mind of the speakers and hearers of the language. A truth semantics, although a theory of sentence meaning, is compatible with atomistic theories of word meaning, the position that the meaning of every word in the language is independent of the meaning of every other word. Influenced by Quinean holism, Davidson (1985) proposes a truth theory of meaning that is holistic. According to this view, the meaning of a word is to be understood in the context of a sentence which receives its truth value when taken together with all the other sentences of the language. For example, we understand the word *snow* if we understand all the sentential contexts in which the word plays a role, and we understand these if we understand the conditions under which the sentences are to be counted as true or false. Whereas the meaning of the term *snow* may be determined through sentential contexts, the meaning of the word is context independent. And the meaning of the sentence is built up compositionally from the meaning of its parts (and the logical or syntactic structure). The idea of holism may suggest some organization of the lexicon, but Davidson and his followers are not committed to any such structure. The meanings of words could be given through a lexicon conceived only as a arbitrary list. The meaning of every word is in some way dependent on the meaning of every other word in the lexicon, in the sense that to understand the words in the language requires that we understand the language as a whole, but there is no discussion suggesting that some words may be more dependent on some other items in the lexicon than any other or that the dependence has any structural characteristics. In this volume, Jackendoff alludes to the limitations of a truth semantics by invoking Chomsky's (1981) distinction between an E-language ("external language, language as seen as external artifact") and an I-language ("internal language, language as a body of internally encoded information"). Essentially, a truth semantics treats language as an E-language. Meaning is given, not by representations in the mind of the speaker and hearer, but by the conditions by which the sentence is made true. (For a view of semantic fields as mediating between the internalist and externalist position, see Kittay, this volume.)

A semantics compatible with generative grammar, argues Jackendoff, must be one that looks toward the principles that are internalized by the speaker, an I-semantics. In thinking of language as a "vehicle for expressing concepts" rather than a set of sentences that are true or false, Jackendoff (this volume) sees the importance of semantics in its ability to give an account of "the mental resources that make possible human knowledge and experience of the world." In particular, he gives an account of meaning through concepts that are I-concepts, concepts as they are represented by the speakers and hearers of a language and as they are composed of a set of mental primitives and principles of combination. Only in this way, argues Jackendoff, can we account for the creativity and generativity of the conceptual aspect of language and for our ability to acquire during our lifetime an indefinitely large set of concepts. Distancing himself from Fodor, model theoretic semantics, and others who insist that "a theory of semantics must include a realist account of truth-conditions and inference," Jackendoff gives voice to many contributors in the volume, notably Wierzbicka, Fillmore and Atkins, Lehrer, Clark, Ross, and Barsalou (many of whom do not—or no longer—work explicitly within the generative grammar framework). Such scholars insist that the semantics they are engaged in "is concerned most directly with the form of the internal mental representations that constitute conceptual structure and with the formal relations between this level and other levels of representation" (Jackendoff, this volume).

Many of the chapters in this volume, then, work within a conceptual semantics (though not necessarily one identical to the Conceptual Semantics of Jackendoff). And whereas a truth and referentially based semantics has little or nothing to say about the organization of the lexicon, most conceptual semantics understand organization to pertain to the lexicon either through the interrelation of concepts composed of a common stock of primitives, or through the relational links between concepts organized through frames, fields, or contrasts. Both Wierzbicka and Jackendoff concentrate on lexical connections via what they take to be the compositional nature of words and concepts. Although both embrace the idea that the lexicon is not simply an arbitrary list, their accounts of meaning share with atomism the position that meaning can be given of lexical items singly, without reference to some larger whole. Other authors in the volume (especially Fillmore and Atkins, Kay, Ross, Kittay, Grandy, Chaffin, and Barsalou) find that the inadequacy of a truth semantics emanates from its inattention to semantic relations (other than synonymy and entailment). Theories of frames and fields replace the global holism of Davidson and Quine with a local holism, which provides a structured account of the way the meaning of one word is constrained by other words in the same conceptual domain. This constraining and contrastive effect of other terms (see Clark and Grandy) receives no recognition in the global holism of Davidson and those who conceive of meaning in truth theoretic terms. The assignment of meaning for them is essentially extralinguistic rather than internal to the structure of language and thought. Kittay suggests that supplementing a truth theory with the local holism of fields will be useful to resolving puzzles generated by a construal of meaning and mental content as either discrete definitions in the head of the speaker or as essentially external to the speaker.

Fillmore (1985) has proposed a frame semantics as a "semantics of understanding" rather than truth—that what it is to understand the meaning of a word or sentence is to understand much more than the conditions under which a sentence is true. The claim may be stated using the example of the term *orphan*. On a truth-theoretic and holistic account, the meaning of *orphan* will be given by all those sentences in which *orphan* plays a role in statements that are true or false. In a frame semantics, the meaning of the term will suppose a knowledge structure that includes an understanding of biological parenthood, the upbringing of a child within an essentially nuclear family consisting of the biological family, and those aspects of the legal and social structure that give biological parents a *prima facie* special status with respect to the child. To be orphaned would have an altogether different significance if, for example, the rearing of children were to be conducted primarily by those who had no biological link to the child and the biological parents had no special status with respect to the child. The epistemic links that tie a term to a set of beliefs and form an individual's understanding of that term are not arbitrary and do not depend on fortuitous circumstances of language acquisition but are structured by a general knowledge frame that serves as a set of default assumptions for the term. Similarly, within semantic field theory, the epistemic links are given by a set of contrasts and affinities: *orphan, biological mother, biological father, stepmother, stepfather,* etc.

A position associated with truth theoretic and referentially based semantics is the view that names do not have meanings—that proper names, at least, only refer. The results of Lehrer's study indicate that naming practices are not arbitrary, as they might well be if names are merely meaningless labels. Her study reintroduces the question of something like a Fregian claim that proper names have a sense. But Lehrer is not suggesting a Fregian sense insofar as a name directs us to the referent. Instead her work shows that in the case of names drawn from the common vocabulary, the common meaning of the words constrain what is to be named by the expression. Her claim is that names for a certain type of entity (e.g., cars, rock groups, beauty parlors, etc.) are drawn from a common semantic field. One may say that this is a pragmatic principle, but it also involves semantic considerations. Lexemes are not simply emptied of nor dissociated from their meaning when they are used as names. While the name does not have a sense that directs one to the referent, the meaning of the lexeme helps delineate the possible references of a name. And the reference might, in time, come to influence the meaning of the lexeme (e.g., if it becomes fashionable to call fancy shopping centers "lanes," part of the meaning of *lane* eventually may become "a street on which fashionable shops can be found").

Against referentially based theories, the analyses of individual terms by Powell, Allan, and Kay suggest the extent to which historically based considerations, nonliteral connotations, and syntactically related information are crucial to the correct understanding of a lexeme and even to the appropriate assignment of truth conditions to a sentence.

What are the Gains of Thinking About the Lexicon as Organized?

As many of the chapters in this collection demonstrate, there are multiple advantages to thinking of the lexicon as organized. It provides a principle of meaning which is, at the very least, complementary to a theory of reference and a truth theoretic semantics; it provides a way of looking at lexical universals; it can provide principles of lexicalization and translation; it has the potential to give an account of implications that are not entailments; it forms hypotheses about the psychological reality of an internal lexicon that are useful for explaining certain principles of retrieval and learning; it serves as a pragmatic principle; and it has practical application in the construction of machine-readable lexicons.

The local holism of an organized lexicon and hypotheses about the interrelation of concepts in the decomposition of meaning of a lexical item argue for a semantics that is concerned with psychological as well as logical principles, and with the expressive as well as the communicative potential of language. The concept of an organized lexicon provides a way of looking at the possibility of lexical universals by grouping together conceptually related words that may not have an exact translation (or at least an exact lexicalized counterpart) in another language. Whereas word-for-word translations may not be available, cross-linguistic comparisons can be made given a common conceptual space. The different articulations of that conceptual content can give us clues with respect to transcultural primitives (see Wierzbicka, this volume).

As Kittay, Fillmore and Atkins, Kay, Barsalou, Lehrer, Chaffin, Cruse, and Grandy all point out, there are numerous implications, which are short of entailment that come with sentences and that are based on the relations of certain sentential items to other words in the same field, or to the role of that sentential item in a frame. Grandy points to different implications that emerge by virtue of the ordering relation in a contrast set. Allan's study shows that implications can involve even phonetic considerations, such as rhyming schemes. In construing frames as attribute-value sets (that is, as a set of attributes that take certain values), Barsalou, for example, can show how certain values of an attribute may be constrained by the values of other attributes. In a vacation frame, if the value for the attribute LOCATION is BEACH, then values for the attribute activity would constrain a choice such as SNOW SKIING. The frame structure that Fillmore and Atkins propose can also explain curious syntactic features of terms. For example, in the risk frame that they develop in this collection, the difference between *run a risk* and *take a risk* can be explained insofar as the subject of the former expression is a VICTIM, whereas the subject of the latter is an ACTOR (this volume). Fillmore and Atkins note that they have found no dictionary that offers an account of the difference between the two phrases.

Garrett has collected intriguing data on the production of errors—errors that organize themselves along phonological and semantic lines. The hypothesis that the lexicon is organized and that this organization has a psychological reality provides a fine explanatory hypothesis for the production of many of the errors that Garrett has documented. If the internal mental lexicon is in fact organized, there should be interesting repercussions in making predictions about language acquisition. It should be easier to teach related terms than unrelated ones, and it should be easier to teach terms in a contextual frame rather than individually.

Clark has collected data which suggests that language acquisition grows through positing contrasts between words we know and those that are newly introduced. She suggests that, at the very least, a Principle of Contrast is in effect in the acquisition of language; that is to say, children and adults reject synonymy and presume that if there is already a word in the lexicon that means what the newly introduced word might mean, there is probably a meaning difference between the two words.

Clark treats the Principle of Contrast, and its accompanying Principle of Conventionality, as pragmatic principles, but ones that have semantic and lexical consequences. To think of the lexicon as organized, then, calls in pragmatic as well as semantic considerations. The confluence of these concerns is also evident in the work of Ross. Like Clark, Ross underscores the contrastive relations that emerge in language use. He discusses what he calls "craft-bound" discourse, discourse that develops "for the refined arts of survival, ornamentation, and peculiarly human expression" (this volume). Craft-bound discourses are particularly good "laboratories" for studying pragmatic principles implied by the organization of the lexicon.

Finally, conceiving of the lexicon as ordered has a number of practical applications that are quite independent of the psychological reality of such organization or any commitment to a theory of meaning. The on-line frame-based dictionary that Fillmore and Atkins are constructing will be of interest to anyone looking for effective ways to encode information pertinent to our understanding of a lexical item—whether or not we grant the importance of frames within a theory of semantics. The organization of semantic information that is accomplished by Ravin's study of synonyms is of interest to someone who is building lexicons that will contain information needed to be understood by machines. The development of computational linguistics is importantly moved forward by considering the lexicon as a thesaurus rather than a dictionary. Lexical grouping allows for the exploration of what Walker (this volume) calls *the ecology of language*. Those doing focussed research on lexical problems will have for the first time the data and tools necessary for work on a massive scale. Large corpora can provide examples that the linguist is likely to miss. Because judgments of acceptability are often too subtle for intuitions to be reliable, corpora can provide speech data on what utterances actually occur. In addition, computational linguistics can permit analysts to investigate hundreds of semantic, syntactic, and collocational features, in order to find which features predict or correlate with others. Finally, the work of those studying the lexicon can be considered in the context of what other scholars are doing and have done. The newly available electronic resources to which Walker directs us will, in turn, help reveal the ordered structure of the lexicon.

Unanswered Questions

Many questions that we had hoped to answer remain unanswered. First of all, how do we individuate fields or frames? This problem seems to be equivalent for both approaches. Fillmore (1985) analyzes *stingy, generous, thrifty,* and *profligate,* arguing that *John isn't stingy; he's just thrifty* involves a rejection of one frame (*stingy–profligate*) by another one (*thrifty–generous*). Field semanticists have the same option in saying that the words belong to different semantic fields. But how do we decide that terms belong to different semantic frames or fields, rather than saying that they have different meanings within one frame or field?

Barsalou shows that new categories (ad hoc categories) are easily created, but these are lexicalized phrasally, using ordinary principles of composition. What gets lexicalized are the conventional categories that have corresponded to traditional semantic fields. What are the conditions under which concepts become lexicalized monolexemically? Are there similarities across languages?

Both Grandy and Barsalou utilize the concept of a prototype in their semantic analysis. The notion of a prototype has played a major role in cognitive psychology, and a more limited role in linguistics, in the last two decades. How does prototype theory (or rather various versions of prototype theory) enter into issues relevant to the organization of the lexicon?

A related issue deals with basic words—a central feature of research stemming from Berlin and Kay's *Basic Color Terms* (1969), which showed that not all words in the lexicon are of equal value. Berlin and Kay showed that the concept of basic words enables us to make significant cross-linguistic comparisons that would not be possible if all the words in a vocabulary are given equal importance. Wierzbicka's chapter (this volume) utilizes and discusses this notion. In field semantics Lehrer (1974) argued that it is the basic words in a domain that define the semantic structure. What use does frame semantics make of the basic–nonbasic word distinction? How exactly do prototypes and basic words interact? Whereas we can assume that basic words are more prototypical than nonbasic ones, can one concept be derived from the other?

In the philosophy of language and its intersection with the philosophy of mind, problems have been formulated assuming either an atomistic or a global holism with respect to word meaning. Can the local holism advocated in several chapters in this volume throw light on some vexing problems in philosophy and cognitive science, such as the question of meaning change in scientific theories, the principle of compositionality, category formation, and the internalist–externalist debates about content?

Finally, how does the organization of the lexicon interact with syntax? Fillmore, Atkins, and Kay have been developing a theory which integrates the two, "Construction Grammar." Levin (1985) and Carter (1988), among others, have argued that there are significant syntactic generalizations that follow from the meaning of lexical items. Jackendoff, in working out the mapping between syntax and semantics, has shown how words belonging to the same fields tend to share the same or similar syntax. These approaches are promising and will hopefully lead to advances in our understanding of the interaction of syntax and lexical meaning.

We hope that this collection will stimulate others to consider the issues raised by the chapters, and we also hope that the approaches from various disciplines can be integrated into new research paradigms.

ACKNOWLEDGMENTS

The authors wish to thank the contributors to this volume for their valuable comments on earlier drafts of this introduction. We also wish to express our deep appreciation to the National Science Foundation for providing support to hold this conference, NSF Grant BNS 8816135. Our thanks also go to Diane Meador and Pat Perez for their help in preparing the manuscripts for publication, and Michele Svatos for preparing the index.

REFERENCES

Allan, K. (1986). *Linguistic meaning*. London: Routledge & Kegan Paul.

Berlin, B., & Kay, P. (1969). *Basic color terms*. Berkeley and Los Angeles: University of California Press.

Bresnan, J. (1982). *The mental representation of grammatical relations*. Cambridge, MA: MIT Press.

Carter, R. (1988). On linking: Papers by Richard Carter. In B. Levin & C. Tenny (Eds.), *Lexicon Project Working Papers* (Vol. 25). Cambridge, MA: Center for Cognitive Science, MIT.

Chomsky, N. (1981). *Lectures on government and binding*. Dordrecht: Foris.

Cruse, D. A. (1986). *Lexical semantics*. Cambridge: Cambridge University Press.

Davidson, D. (1985). *Inquiries into truth and interpretation*. Oxford: Clarendon Press.

Fillmore, C. J. (1968). The case for case. In E. Bach & R. T. Harmes (Eds.), *Universals in linguistic theory* (pp. 1–90). New York: Holt, Rinehart, & Winston.

Fillmore, C. J. (1985). Semantic fields and semantic frames. *Quaderni di Semantica, 6.2, 222–254*.

Fodor, J. A. (1987). *Psychosemantics*. Cambridge, MA: MIT Press.

Goodman, N. (1952). On likeness of meaning. In L. Linsky (Ed.), *Semantics and the philosophy of language*, Urbana: University of Illinois Press.

Grandy, R. (1987). In defense of semantic fields. In E. Le Pore (Ed.), *New directions in semantics* (pp. 261–280). New York: Academic Press.

Hjelmslev, L. (1953). *Prolegomena to a theory of language*. F. J. Whitfield (Trans.) Bloomington: Indiana University Press.

Humboldt, W. (1936). *Über der Verschiedenheit des Menschlichen Sprachbaues*. Berlin.

Jackendoff, R. (1987). *Consciousness and the computational mind*. Cambridge, MA: MIT Press.

Kittay, E. F. (1987). *Metaphor: Its cognitive force and linguistic structure*. Oxford: Clarendon Press.

Kittay, E. F., & Lehrer, A. (1981). Semantic fields and the structure of metaphor. *Studies in Language, 5, 31–63*.

Lehrer, A. (1974). *Semantic fields and lexical structure*. Amsterdam: North–Holland.

Lehrer, A., & Lehrer, K. (1982). Antonymy. *Linguistics and Philosophy, 5, 483–501*.

Levin, B. (1985). Lexical semantics in review. *Lexicon Project Working Papers* (Vol. 1). Cambridge, MA: Center for Cognitive Science, MIT.

Lounsbury, F. F. (1956). A semantic analysis of the Pawnee kinship system. *Language, 32, 158–94*.

Lutzeier, P. R. (1981). *Wort und Feld*. Tübingen: Niemeyer.

Lyons, J. (1963). *Structural semantics*. Oxford: Blackwell.

Lyons, J. (1977). *Semantics* (Vol. 1,2). Cambridge: Cambridge University Press.

Porzig, W. (1950). *Das Wunder der Sprache*. Bern: Francke.

Quine, W. v. O. (1953). Two dogmas of empiricism. *From a logical point of view* (pp. 20–46). Cambridge, MA: Harvard University Press.

Rosch, E. (1978). Principles of categorization. In E. H. Rosch & B. B. Lloyd (Eds.), *Cognition and categorization*. Hillsdale, NJ: Lawrence Erlbaum Associates.

Ross, J. F. (1981). *Portraying analogy*. Cambridge: Cambridge University Press.

Trier, J. (1931). *Der deutsche Wortschatz im Sinnbezirk des Verstandes*. Heidelberg: Winter.

Weisgerber, L. (1950). *Vom Weltbild der deutschen Sprache*. Düsseldorf: Schwann.

Wierzbicka, A. (1988). *The semantics of grammar*. Amsterdam and Philadelphia: John Benjamins.

PRINCIPLES OF ORGANIZATION

1 Frames, Concepts, and Conceptual Fields

Lawrence W. Barsalou
University of Chicago

In this chapter I propose that frames provide the fundamental representation of knowledge in human cognition. In the first section, I raise problems with the feature list representations often found in theories of knowledge, and I sketch the solutions that frames provide to them. In the second section, I examine the three fundamental components of frames: attribute-value sets, structural invariants, and constraints. Because frames also represent the attributes, values, structural invariants, and constraints within a frame, the mechanism that constructs frames builds them recursively. The frame theory I propose borrows heavily from previous frame theories, although its collection of representational components is somewhat unique. Furthermore, frame theorists generally assume that frames are rigid configurations of independent attributes, whereas I propose that frames are dynamic relational structures whose form is flexible and context dependent. In the third section, I illustrate how frames support a wide variety of representational tasks central to conceptual processing in natural and artificial intelligence. Frames can represent exemplars and propositions, prototypes and membership, subordinates and taxonomies. Frames can also represent conceptual combinations, event sequences, rules, and plans. In the fourth section, I show how frames define the extent of conceptual fields and how they provide a powerful productive mechanism for generating specific concepts within a field.

FEATURE LIST REPRESENTATIONS OF CATEGORIES

Before proceeding to a detailed discussion of frames, I first discuss their most obvious competitor—feature list representations. Later, we see that frames remedy the fundamental problems of feature lists. Many theories across the cognitive sciences adopt feature list representations of categories. For example, work on natural categories and semantic memory in the 1970s typically employed feature list representations. Figure 1.1 contains examples of feature lists from the 1975 technical report that preceded Rosch, Mervis, Gray, Johnson, and Boyes-Braem's (1976) paper on basic level categories. As can be seen, each category representation is a list of features that subjects typically produce for the category, where a feature is any characteristic that category members may possess. Rosch and Mervis (1975) similarly constructed feature list representations of categories, as did Ashcraft (1978), Glass and Holyoak (1975), and Hampton (1979). Many other researchers did not collect feature lists explicitly from subjects but nevertheless assumed feature lists in theoretical modeling. In the semantic memory literature, feature comparison models assumed that semantic decisions involve the comparison of feature lists, as in McCloskey and Glucksberg (1979), Meyer (1970), Smith, Shoben, and Rips (1974), and A. Tversky (1977) (see also Wyer & Srull, 1986, in the social cognition literature). Barsalou and Hale (in press) review the wide variety of forms that feature lists take in categorization models.

More recently, connectionist models have embedded feature lists in dynamic networks (e.g., McClelland & Rumelhart, 1986; Rumelhart & McClelland, 1986). Rather than being independent, features in a connectionist system become intercorrelated, with excitatory relations developing between features that typically cooccur, and inhibitory relations developing between features that do not. In Fig. 1.1, each feature would be related to every other feature in its list, with some relations being excitatory and others being inhibitory. During categorization, input features activate correlated features and inhibit all others. As input features vary, they activate different feature subsets. Whereas traditional models represent a category with its entire feature list on every occasion, connectionist models represent a category dynamically with different feature subsets in different contexts.

BIRD	APPLE	SOCKS
feathers	seeds	you wear it
wings	sweet	keeps you warm
beak	you eat it	heel
legs	stem	toe
feet	core	cotton
eyes	skin	wool
tail	juicy	multicolored
head	round	worn on feet
claws	grows on trees	come in pairs
lays eggs		
nests		
flies		
chirps		
eats worms and flies		

FIG. 1.1. Examples of feature lists for *bird, apple,* and *socks* from Rosch, Mervis, Gray, Johnson, and Boyes-Braem (1975). Copyright (1975) by the American Psychological Association. Reprinted by permission.

In principle, numerous theories in psychology and linguistics assume that representations contain more than feature lists. In many cases, however, the additional structure—which tends to be frame-like—remains implicit theoretically and receives little attention empirically. As a result, these representations essentially reduce to feature lists. Consider work on artificial category learning in cognitive psychology. Typically, this work assumes the presence of frames in category representations. As described in much more detail shortly, a frame includes a cooccurring set of abstract attributes that adopt different values across exemplars. To see this, consider the category structures in Fig. 1.2, adapted from artificial categories in Medin and Schaffer (1978, p. 213). Notice that each exemplar in a category has one value on each of four attributes: *color, form, size,* and *position.* The frame in each category is this cooccurring set of abstract attributes, which take different values across category members. Work on artificial categories almost always uses frames in this manner to define category structures, as in the work of Estes (1986), Gluck and Bower (1988), Hayes-Roth and Hayes-Roth (1977), Hintzman (1986), Homa (1978), McClelland and Rumelhart (1985), and Nosofsky (1984).

Although frames typically structure artificial categories, they have played little role empirically or theoretically. Empirically, frames are irrelevant because every exemplar in every category has values on the same attributes. As can be seen from Fig. 1.2, Categories A and B are not distinguished by attributes but instead by values of these attributes. Consequently, the focus of work on artificial categories has been on how subjects learn patterns of values that predict category membership. Although subjects must be learning the frame as well—the fact that all exemplars have values on the same attributes—this form of learning has generally remained unaddressed. Moreover, attribute learning must be important in category learning, because attributes often differ across categories. For example, *car* has attributes for *engine* and *transmission,* whereas *dog* has attributes for *fur* and *temperament.* Rather than categorizing entities solely on the basis of specific values, people often categorize them on the basis of more abstract attributes.

Theoretically, the frames that researchers use to define artificial categories

CATEGORY A				CATEGORY B			
ATTRIBUTES				ATTRIBUTES			
EXEMPLAR	COLOR	FORM	SIZE	POSITION	EXEMPLAR	COLOR	FORM	SIZE	POSITION
1	red	square	small	left	4	green	circle	large	right
2	red	square	small	right	5	green	circle	small	left
3	green	circle	large	left	6	red	square	large	right

FIG. 1.2. The presence of frames in artificial categories. Adapted from Medin and Schaffer (1978, p. 213) by permission.

have also received little attention. Theorists generally have nothing to say about the psychological status of these frames. Nor have researchers specified whether subjects view exemplar characteristics as attribute-value pairs or as a feature list. Figure 1.3 illustrates this distinction. In the upper left, prototype representations are essentially feature lists. Frames and the attribute-value sets that compose them are not represented explicitly but are only implicit in the representation. In contrast, the prototype representations in the upper right of Fig. 1.3 include an

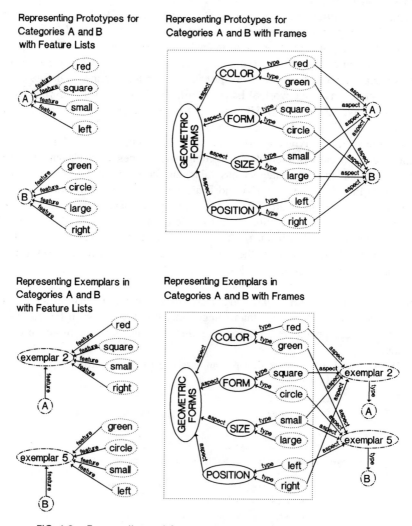

FIG. 1.3.   Feature list and frame representations of prototypes (top) and of exemplars (bottom). Frames are enclosed in boxes.

explicit frame (enclosed in the dotted box). The bottom half of Fig. 1.3 illustrates this distinction for exemplar representations. Because attributes are constant across artificial categories, and because attribute learning has not been of interest, the distinction between attributes and values has not been salient or explicit theoretically. As a result, representations in prototype and exemplar models have essentially been reduced to feature lists, such as those on the left of Fig. 1.3.

In exemplar models and multidimensional spaces that weight attributes differentially, the distinction between attributes and values is more salient (e.g., Medin & Schaffer, 1978; Nosofsky, 1984; Shepard, 1974). However, these models nevertheless fail to specify how subjects know that particular characteristics of exemplars are values of one attribute and not another (e.g., how subjects know that *triangle* is a *shape*). Because these models include no explicit representation of attributes and their values, the ability to weight characteristics the same amount because they are values of the same attribute remains unspecified. Such an ability could rely on abstracted representations of attributes and their values; or it could rely on an embedded level of exemplar processing for categorizing characteristics as values of attribute categories.

Finally, work on componential analysis and semantic fields sometimes reduces semantic representations to feature lists. All of these theories assume that entries within a semantic field have values on abstract, shared attributes (e.g., Grandy, 1987; Katz, 1972; Kittay, 1987; Lehrer, 1974; Lyons, 1977; Miller & Johnson-Laird, 1976). However, semantic representations sometimes seem to include only values of these attributes. For example, *bachelor* might be represented as *adult, male, human,* and *unmarried,* failing to specify the attributes of *age, sex, species,* and *marital status.* Although these attributes are implicit, not specifying them explicitly implies that semantic representations are feature lists.

Evidence Against Feature Lists

The current psychological evidence against feature lists can be described alternatively as evidence for two structural properties of human knowledge: attribute-value sets and relations.

Evidence for Attribute-Value Sets.   Rather than coexisting at a single "flat" level of analysis, the characteristics of exemplars typically form attribute-value sets, with some characteristics (values) being instances of other characteristics (attributes). For example, *blue* and *green* are values of *color; swim* and *fly* are values of *locomotion; six-cylinder* and *eight-cylinder* are values of *automobile engine.* Whereas features are independent representational components that constitute a single level of analysis, attribute-value sets are interrelated sets of representational components at two levels of analysis (at least). In this section, I review several sources of evidence that people encode exemplar characteristics as values of more abstract attributes, rather than as independent features.[1]

Extensive literatures offer compelling evidence that animals use attribute-value sets in discrimination learning (see Sutherland & Mackintosh, 1971, for a review). Consider intradimensional transfer. Animals receive stimuli that vary on two attributes and are conditioned to expect reward following a particular value on one of them. For example, animals might receive stimuli that vary in *color* (*blue* versus *yellow*) and *shape* (*circle* versus *oval*). In the process, they might learn that *blue* signals reward and that *yellow* does not, with *shape* being irrelevant. Once animals learn this first discrimination, they learn a second. The attributes remain the same, but their values are new. For example, the two attributes might still be *color* and *shape,* but their values might be *red* versus *black* and *triangle* versus *square.* When the second discrimination involves the same attribute as the first (intradimensional shift), learning is faster than when the discriminating attribute changes (extradimensional shift). For example, if *color* predicted reward for the first discrimination, learning is faster when the second discrimination involves *color* than when it involves *shape.* Even though all attribute values are new for the second discrimination, animals typically learn faster when the critical values are from the same attribute (but not always; Medin, 1975, 1976). Once animals learn that one attribute predicts reward, they continue attending to it, even when its values change. Such evidence suggests that animals encode the stimulus information as attribute values—rather than as independent features—and learn which attribute provides information about reward. Many other well-documented phenomena offer converging evidence, including reversal shift, overtraining on reversal shift, and transfer along a continuum. In addition, many such findings have been demonstrated with humans (e.g., T. S. Kendler & H. H. Kendler, 1970; Trabasso & Bower, 1968).

More recently, several new areas of work have further demonstrated the importance of attribute-value sets in human learning. Ross, Perkins, and Tenpenny (1990) found that an imaginary person with the characteristics, *buys wood* and *likes sherbet,* reminds subjects of another imaginary person with the characteristics, *buys nails* and *likes ice cream.* As a result, subjects place these two imaginary people in the same category and generalize that its members *buy carpentry supplies* and *like dessert.* These generalizations, in turn, function as frame attributes, such that later imaginary people belong to the category if their characteristics are values of these attributes. For example, someone who *buys a chisel* belongs to the category, whereas someone who *buys sunglasses* does not. Rather than representing the category with the simple features of exemplars, subjects represent it with more abstract attributes that take these characteristics as values. Thorndyke and Hayes-Roth (1979) reported a similar result (also see Watkins & Kerkar, 1985).

---

[1]My use of "attribute" is essentially equivalent to other theorists' use of "dimension," "variable," and "slot." I assume that all of these terms are at least roughly synonymous.

Wisniewski and Medin (1991) reported evidence for attribute-value sets in categories of children's drawings. Rather than representing these categories with features from visual images (e.g., concrete lines, shapes, squiggles), subjects instead represented them with abstract attributes. For example, subjects represent the category, *drawings by creative children,* with the attributes, *detailed* and *unusual.* When a drawing's visual characteristics provide evidence for these abstract attributes, it belongs in the category.

Finally, much work on story understanding shows that people use abstract attributes to code the specific components of stories (Stein, 1982; Stein & Trabasso, 1982). For example, people assign story components to attributes such as *setting, goal, protagonist, obstacle, plan,* and *outcome.* When a story presents values of these attributes in coherent patterns, understanding and recollection proceed smoothly. When values of these attributes are missing, not easily recognized, or organized incoherently, story processing is difficult and nonoptimal.

Evidence for Relations.   Contrary to feature lists, people do not store representational components independently of one another. Instead, people have extensive knowledge about relations between them. For example, Malt and Smith (1984) found that people's knowledge of *bird* contains a correlation between *sing* as a value of *sound* and *small* as a value of *size.* Medin, Altom, Edelson, and Freko (1982) found that people learn correlations of symptoms that define disease categories (e.g., the cooccurrence of *discolored gums* and *nosebleeds* defines *burlosis*). L. J. Chapman and J. P. Chapman (1969) and Murphy and Wisniewski (1989) showed that people readily learn relations that are consistent with background beliefs and intuitive theories. Billman and Heit (1988) demonstrated that learning a relation proceeds more rapidly when it is embedded in a system of relations than when it occurs in isolation. Gentner (1989) reviewed the importance of relations in constructing analogies. Medin, Goldstone, and Gentner (1990) and Goldstone, Medin, and Gentner (1991) demonstrated the importance of relations in similarity judgments. Finally, people do not encode the events within a story independently of one another but integrate them with causal relations (Trabasso & Sperry, 1985; Trabasso & van den Broek, 1985; Trabasso, van den Broek, & Suh, 1989).

Some of the aforementioned work assumes that relations are simply correlations between representational components. Connectionist models similarly view relations as various forms of correlation. However, people clearly represent many relations conceptually. Although *robin* and *feather* are both highly correlated with *bird,* people know that a robin *is* a bird and that a feather is *part* of a bird—people would never claim that a feather is a bird or that a robin is part of a bird. Fodor and Pylyshyn (1988) provided detailed and convincing arguments that relations between representational components are often conceptual and not just correlational.

Because connectionist nets typically do not represent conceptual relations, they have difficulty representing attribute-value sets, which require conceptual relations between attributes and values (e.g., *circle* is a *type* of *shape*, not a *part* of one). Rumelhart, Smolensky, McClelland, and Hinton (1986, p. 33) claim the opposite, proposing that attribute-value sets occur in a connectionist net when inhibitory relations exist between mutually exclusive features. For example, Rumelhart et al. argue that inhibitory relations between *small, medium,* and *large* in their "schema" for *room* produce an attribute for *room size.* Because a value for one attribute can have inhibitory relations with values of *different* attributes, however, inhibitory relations are not sufficient for defining attribute-value sets. Although an inhibitory relation exists between *shower* for *room fixtures* and *piano* for *room furniture, shower* and *piano* are not values of a common attribute. Nor are inhibitory relations necessary for attribute-value sets, because the values of many attributes are not mutually exclusive (e.g., *color* is simultaneously *brown* and *red* for *robin*). As a result, Rumelhart et al.'s schemata are simply dynamic feature lists. Features may suppress one another across contexts, but this only represents cooccurrence relations—not conceptually related attribute-value sets. Moreover, the notion of competing "values" provides no account of the more general attributes that integrate these values (but see Rumelhart et al., 1986, p. 25, for the hint of an intriguing possibility).

Frames

Because frames contain attribute-value sets and relations, they provide natural solutions to the problems of feature lists. The construct of frames is hardly new in the cognitive sciences. In classic work, Fillmore suggested that frames underlie people's syntactic knowledge of verbs (Fillmore, 1968; more recently, Fillmore, this volume; Jackendoff, 1987; Wilkins, 1988). The frame for *buy* specifies that an active sentence containing "buy" must include an *agent* and a *theme* and may optionally have a *source* and an *instrument,* as in:

> The *artist* (agent) buys *paint* (theme) at the *art store* (source) with a *credit card* (instrument).

Fillmore's account of frames focused primarily on the syntactic structure of verbs, although he frequently stressed the importance of underlying conceptual structure (e.g., Fillmore, 1977, 1984, 1985). Complementary to Fillmore's work, Norman and Rumelhart (1975) developed explicit accounts of the conceptual structures that underlie syntactic frames. Schank (1975, 1982) and Schank and Abelson (1977) developed the conceptual approach further. Minksy (1977) developed an account of frames relevant to vision, which, too, has received wide application. Bobrow and Winograd (1977), Lenat and Guha (1989), and Minsky (1985) provided additional accounts of frames. The technical definition of *frame* in artificial intelligence has evolved to mean something like a *fixed set of named slots whose values vary across applications* (e.g., Charniak & McDermott,

1985). Hayes (1979) argued that frames bear many deep resemblances to first-order predicate calculus.

In cognitive psychology, frames have received much attention in research on the essentially identical construct of *schema* (Bartlett, 1932). Theorists who have attempted to articulate the structure of schemata have generally identified the same structural properties proposed for frames (e.g., Cohen & Murphy, 1984; Rumelhart & Ortony, 1978). However, much undesirable baggage has become associated with "schema." Psychologists frequently demonstrate the ubiquity of schemata in human knowledge (for reviews, see Alba & Hasher, 1983; Brewer & Nakamura, 1984). Yet, their studies rarely attempt to provide evidence for the structural characteristics of schemata proposed in more theoretical analyses (e.g., attribute-value sets, relations). As a result, "schema" is often criticized as being vague and unspecified. Moreover, "schema" has come to mean many different things to many different people. Most problematic is the frequent use of "schema" to mean a feature list prototype (e.g., as illustrated in the upper left of Figure 1.3). Researchers sometimes assume that a schema is simply those features most common across a category's exemplars (e.g., Cohen, 1981; Markus, Smith, & Moreland, 1985; Posner & Keele, 1968). Because of these problems, I use "frame" to highlight the well-specified, structural properties common to formal analyses of frames and schemata.[2]

My interest in frames stems from encountering them frequently in my previous work. Frames play a central role in constructing ad hoc categories during planning (Barsalou, 1983, 1991). Frames play a central role in representing and organizing autobiographical memories (Barsalou, 1988). Frames offer a natural means of accounting for contextual variability in conceptual representations (Barsalou, 1987, 1989; Barsalou & Billman, 1989).

COMPONENTS OF FRAMES

I next examine three basic components of frames: attribute-value sets, structural invariants, and constraints. I assume that frames represent all types of categories, including categories for animates, objects, locations, physical events, mental events, and so forth. As we shall see, the representation of adjectives, adverbs, and quantifiers is feasible within the context of frames as well. In all cases, my examples of frames *greatly* underestimate their actual complexity. Although these simplified examples keep presentation tractable, it is important to remember that constructing a complete conceptual frame for a single category is a

---

[2]Some psychologists have provided evidence for structural properties of schemata. Examples include careful analyses of story schemata (Stein, 1982; Stein & Trabasso, 1982; Trabasso & Sperry, 1985; Trabasso & van den Broek, 1985; Trabasso et al., 1989) and careful analyses of verb frames (Tanenhaus & Carlson, 1989; Tanenhaus, Carlson, & Trueswell, 1989).

challenging and sobering experience. For examples of how complex frames can become, see Lenat and Guha (1989).

Attributes and Values

A cooccurring set of attributes constitutes the core of a frame. Consider the partial frame for *car* in Fig. 1.4, whose attributes include *driver, fuel, engine, transmission,* and *wheels.* Again, note that this frame is simplified considerably to facilitate presentation, with many attributes being absent (e.g., *color, seats*). As a frame represents different exemplars, its attributes adopt different values. When the frame for *car* is applied to one particular car, its attributes might adopt values of *Liz* for *driver, gasoline* for *fuel, four-cylinder* for *engine, standard* for *transmission,* and *alloy* for *wheels.* When applied to another car, the same attributes might adopt different values.

A fundamental task for frame theorists is to provide satisfactory definitions for *attribute* and *value.* I define an attribute as a concept that describes an aspect of at least some category members. For example, *color* describes an aspect of *birds,* and *location* describes an aspect of *vacations.* A concept is only an attribute when it describes an aspect of a larger whole. When people consider *color* in isolation (e.g., thinking about their favorite color), it is not an attribute but is simply a concept. Similarly, when people think about *location* in isolation (e.g., in geography), it is not an attribute. A concept is only an attribute when viewed as describing some aspect of a category's members. *Color* becomes an attribute when viewed as an aspect of *bird,* and *location* becomes an attribute

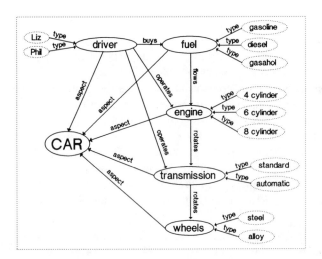

FIG. 1.4. A partial frame for *car* that illustrates attribute-value sets and relations in frames.

when viewed as an aspect of *vacation*. In this regard, the definition of *attribute* is extrinsic, depending on a concept's aspectual relation to a category.

By *concept* I mean the descriptive information that people represent cognitively for a category, including definitional information, prototypical information, functionally important information, and probably other types of information as well. In this regard, my use of *concept* vaguely resembles *intension* and *sense*. In general, I assume that frames represent all types of concepts, whether they are free-standing concepts, such as *bird* and *vacation,* or whether they are attributes, such as *color* for *bird* and *location* for *vacation.* Later sections address frames for attributes in greater detail.[3]

What aspects of a category can be attributes? Clearly, this depends significantly on a category's ontological domain (Keil, 1979, 1981). For physical objects, attributes are likely to include *color, shape,* and *weight;* whereas for *events,* attributes are likely to include *location, time,* and *goal.* Attributes are often *parts* of category members. As discussed by Chaffin (this volume) and Winston, Chaffin, and Herrmann (1987), *part* is a highly polysemous relation. According to their analysis, *part* can refer to a physical part of an object (*leg–chair*), the material of an object (*metal–ring*), a member of a collection (*flower–bouquet*), an action in an activity (*pitch–baseball*), an object in an activity (*food–eat*), a location in an activity (*destination–drive*), and so forth. However, I assume that attributes can represent many other aspects of category members beside their parts. For example, attributes include evaluations (*enjoyment–music*), quantities (*cardinality–family*), costs (*sacrifices–career*), benefits (*skills–education*), and so forth. As I argue later, people are highly creative in their construction of attributes, often producing new ones relevant to specific contexts.

The definition of *value* follows from the definition of *attribute:* Values are subordinate concepts of an attribute. Because values are subordinate concepts, they inherit information from their respective attribute concepts. In the frame for *car,* values of *engine* (e.g., *four–cylinder*) inherit properties of *engine* (e.g., *consumes fuel, produces force*). Values further inherit the extrinsic fact that they are an aspect of category members. Because *engine* is an aspect of *car,* its values are aspects of *car* as well. Values contain additional information not in their respective attributes, thereby making them more specific concepts. *Four-cylinder* and *six-cylinder* contain information that makes them more specific than *engine* and that differentiates them from each other.

---

[3]In previous papers, I have proposed that concepts are temporary representations of categories in working memory (Barsalou, 1987, 1989). Because the emphasis in the current chapter is on the structure of knowledge in long-term memory, I use *concept* more generally to mean any descriptive information about a category or attribute, either in long-term memory or working memory. I remain committed to the view that people use relatively stable knowledge in long-term memory to construct temporary representations in working memory, with these temporary representations exhibiting extensive flexibility and context sensitivity. I present numerous examples of how frames produce flexibility in later sections.

Attribute Taxonomies. Because values are concepts, they in turn can be attributes having still more specific values. For example, the frame for *animal* might include an attribute for *means of locomotion,* whose values include *legs, wings,* and *fins.* In turn, the frame for *land mammal* might include an attribute for *legs,* whose values include *human legs, horse legs,* and *dog legs.* Whereas *legs* is a value in the frame for *animal,* it is an attribute in the frame for *land mammal.* As Fig. 1.5 illustrates, the increasing specificity of values may produce an attribute taxonomy having many levels. For example, *human legs* can be an attribute whose values include *female human legs* and *male human legs.*

Attribute taxonomies exhibit many of the same properties as object taxonomies (e.g., *animals, fruit, clothing*). Like object taxonomies, attribute taxonomies exhibit typicality. For example, people may egocentrically perceive *legs* to be more typical of *means of locomotion* than *fins* or *wings.* Like object taxonomies, attribute taxonomies exhibit a basic level (B. Tversky & Hemenway, 1985). *Legs, wings,* and *fins* constitute the basic level for *locomotion,* because each is monomorphemic, constitutes a large information gain, shares a common shape, and exhibits a common action. Like object taxonomies, attribute taxonomies depend on nested sets of properties. *Legs* inherit the properties of *locomotion* but include additional properties that distinguish them from *wings* and *fins.*

These analogies between attribute and object taxonomies are perhaps surprising. On the one hand, attributes constitute the building blocks of object taxonomies. On the other hand, attributes form taxonomies just like those for object taxonomies. Attributes mirror the taxonomic structure they produce. The extent to which people represent attribute taxonomies explicitly is an open question. If people regularly process taxonomic relations between attributes and values across multiple levels, they may establish attribute taxonomies in memory. However, if people generally process attributes and values more locally, they may fail to integrate them into taxonomies. Although Barsalou and Ross (1986) provide evidence for this more local view, their Experiment 4 illustrates that people can compute new relations in attribute taxonomies. On the other hand, Hampton's

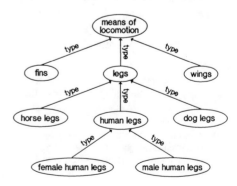

FIG. 1.5. Example of an attribute taxonomy for *means of locomotion.*

(1982) demonstrations of intransitivity in object taxonomies suggest that people may sometimes fail to integrate distant levels in attribute taxonomies.

Attribute Frames.   Not only do attributes mirror the taxonomies to which they contribute, they also mirror the frames that contain them. Within a frame, each attribute may be associated with its own frame of more specific attributes. In Fig. 1.6, consider the frame for *companion* embedded in the frame for *vacation* (Barsalou, 1991). Rather than being a simple unidimensional attribute, *companion* is an embedded frame containing a more specific set of attributes, such as *age, relation, free time,* and *preferred activities* (in this and all later figures, dotted boxes, such as those around *vacation* and *companion,* enclose frames). Similarly in our recent work on real estate planning, the frame for *house* has an attribute for *location,* which in turn is a frame whose attributes include *convenience, utilities, zoning,* and *security.* These secondary attributes often have frames as well. For example, *convenience* is a frame whose attributes include *proximity to employment, proximity to entertainment, proximity to educational facilities,* and *proximity to shopping.* Even these attributes continue to have frames. For example, *proximity to employment* is a frame whose attributes might include *driving duration,* which in turn is a frame whose attributes might include *traffic conditions.* Later figures provide many further examples of frames for attributes.

Attribute Construction.   People frequently create new attributes to achieve goals, much like they create ad hoc categories to achieve goals (Barsalou, 1991). Consider the frame for the *companion* attribute of the *vacation* frame in Fig. 1.6. One attribute of *companion* that subjects often mention is *free time,* because companions must be free at the same time to take a shared vacation. If we asked people to describe characteristics of *companion* in a neutral context, they might

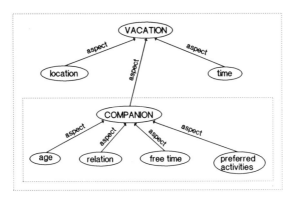

FIG. 1.6.   Example of an attribute frame for *companion* embedded in a frame for *vacation.*

never produce this attribute. When people consider *companion* in the context of *vacation,* however, they consider *free time* to coordinate the schedules of possible companions. Similarly, consider the frame for the *time* attribute of the *vacation* frame. Planners frequently consider the attribute *amount of work disruption* for each possible vacation time, preferring times that produce minimal disruption. If we asked subjects to produce attributes of *time* in isolation, they would probably never produce *amount of work disruption.* Instead, people produce this attribute because of its relevance to *time* in the context of *vacation.*

Do people construct these specialized attributes or retrieve them from memory? When new aspects of exemplars become relevant in novel contexts, people may construct new attributes to represent them. The extensiveness of highly idiosyncratic attributes in our planning data suggests that people readily construct new attributes as they need them. As a side effect of the construction process, however, these attributes are likely to become stored in memory, such that they can be retrieved later in similar contexts.

Clearly, an infinite number of attributes could be constructed for a category (Goodman, 1955). In this regard, the human conceptual system is highly productive, although no person constructs all or even many of these potential attributes. Experience, goals, and intuitive theories play important roles in constraining attribute construction. If people experience different exemplars of a category, they may represent different attributes for it. For example, if cars have smog devices in one country but not in another, only citizens of the former country may typically represent *smog device* as an attribute of *car.* If people have different goals while interacting with exemplars, they may represent different attributes for them. For example, a wine connoisseur may represent *wood used for aging* as an attribute of *wine,* whereas someone who counsels alcoholics may not. If people have different intuitive theories about a category, they may represent different attributes for it. For example, people who know scientific theories of biology may represent *genes* as an attribute of *animal,* whereas people who do not know these theories may not.

Once particular attributes become represented for a category, they determine relevance. If two people represent a category with different attributes, they encode its exemplars differently. Different aspects of the exemplar are relevant, because the perceivers' respective frames orient perception to different information.

Attribute Systematicity.   Frames often contain core attributes that cooccur frequently, what Barsalou and Billman (1989) call *attribute systematicity.* Whenever a frame applies, its core attributes are all usually relevant and considered in the current context. Consider core attributes in the frame for *buy: buyer, seller, merchandise,* and *payment.* When an instance of buying occurs, values for these attributes are usually known. If some are not known, perceivers often infer default values, thereby considering all attributes regularly across exemplars.

Because psychological cooccurrence produces associative strength, these attributes become integrated in memory to form an established structure, namely, the core of a frame.

Attribute systematicity is not all-or-none but varies continuously as attributes cooccur to different extents. Consider a country in which smog devices occur only in some cars. Because *smog device* does not cooccur with *engine* and *wheels* as highly as they cooccur with each other, it exhibits less attribute systematicity than they. Similarly, *loan source* exhibits low systematicity for *buy*, because not all exemplars have values for this attribute. Because the attributes associated with a frame vary in systematicity, frames are not rigid structures. Although many frame theorists assume that a frame *entails* the presence of its attributes (e.g., Hayes, 1979), I assume that the presence of attributes is probabilistic. Across contexts, different subsets of attributes are active in a frame, depending on the specific exemplar and the surrounding context (cf. Murphy, 1990, Experiments 3 and 4). Nevertheless, core sets of attributes may be active for most if not all exemplars.

Why do some attributes and not others constitute a frame's core? Certain attributes may have a value for every exemplar, such that encoding these values causes their attributes to be processed together frequently, thereby forming an experiential core. However, some attributes may be necessary conceptually, such that it is impossible to understand the concept without considering them, even when values are absent. For example, *buy* cannot be understood fully without considering *buyer, seller, merchandise,* and *payment.* Both frequency of occurrence and conceptual necessity probably contribute to the cores of frames.

Structural Invariants

Attributes in a frame are not independent slots but are often related correlationally and conceptually. As we saw in the previous section, a frame's core attributes correlate highly, often appearing together across contexts. As a result, correlational relations develop between them, somewhat like those in connectionist nets. However, the relations between frame attributes generally reflect more than cooccurrence, reflecting conceptual information as well (Barsalou & Billman, 1989, pp. 158–159). Consider the *car* frame in Fig. 1.4. The *operates* relation between *driver* and *engine* reflects people's conceptual understanding that the driver controls the engine's speed. Similarly, the *rotates* relation between *engine* and *transmission* represents the knowledge that the engine spins components of the transmission. Because such relations generally hold across most exemplars of a concept, providing relatively invariant structure between attributes, I refer to them as *structural invariants.*

Structural invariants capture a wide variety of relational concepts, including spatial relations (e.g., between *seat* and *back* in the frame for *chair*), temporal relations (e.g., between *eating* and *paying* in the frame for *dining out*), causal relations (e.g., between *fertilization* and *birth* in the frame for *reproduction*), and intentional relations (e.g., between *motive* and *attack* in the frame for *murder*). Miller and Johnson-Laird (1976) review the tremendous amount of work that has addressed these relations and others.

Most theorists view the relations that underlie structural invariants as primitives. However, Chaffin and his colleagues argue convincingly that these relations are not primitives but instead decompose into more specific attributes (Chaffin, this volume; Winston, Chaffin, & Herrmann, 1987; also see Cruse, this volume). On Chaffin's analysis, the *part* relation, which integrates a wide variety of attributes in frames, decomposes into attributes for *functionality, separability, homeomeronomy,* and *spatio-temporal extent. Functionality* reflects whether a part's function in the whole determines its location. *Separability* reflects whether a part can be separated from the whole. *Homeomeronomy* reflects whether all parts are the same kind of thing as the whole. *Spatio-temporal extent* reflects whether the position of a part in space or time is more salient. Consider:

A roof is *part* of a house.

Functionality has the value of *restricted,* because the roof's function determines its location in a house; *separability* has the value of *separable,* because the roof can be removed from the house; *homeomeronomy* has the value of *non-homeomeronomous,* because the entire house is not made of roofing material; *spatio-temporal extent* has the value of *spatial,* because the roof's spatial position in a house is salient. In contrast, consider:

Wood is *part* of a baseball bat.

Contrary to the previous example, *functionality* has the value of *unrestricted, separability* has the value of *inseparable,* and *homeomeronomy* has the value of *homeomeronomous.* Although it is unlikely that people label these attributes with terms such as *homeomeronomy,* Chaffin's findings suggest the human conceptual system distinguishes and represents them in some manner.

Clearly, this analysis assumes that a frame represents the *part* relation, where the frame's attributes are *functionality, separability, homeomeronomy,* and *spatio-temporal extent.* Different instances of the *part* relation take different values on these attributes, depending on the part and the whole. Once again we see recursion in frames representing frames. Just as frames represent the attributes of a frame, so too do they represent its structural invariants.

For the sake of simplifying presentation, I gloss over differences between various forms of *part* (and other relations) from here on. Also, to simplify presentation in all later figures, I omit structural invariants between attributes, such as *operates* and *rotates* in Fig. 1.4. Instead, I generally use *aspect* and *type* to integrate frame components in a simpler manner. If more complete representations were constructed for these frames, better articulated relations between attributes would be required, as would subtle distinctions among them.

Constraints

The structural invariants described in the previous section represent relatively constant relations between a frame's attributes. In Fig. 1.4, the relation of *flows* between *fuel* and *engine* is generally true of cars, as is the relation of *rotates* between *engine* and *transmission*. Such relations capture normative truths about relations between attributes.

Constraints, too, are relations but of a different type. Rather than being normative, constraints produce systematic variability in attribute values. The central assumption underlying constraints is that values of frame attributes are not independent of one another. Instead, values constrain each other in powerful and complex manners. In the following sections, I describe various types of constraints, including *attribute constraints, value constraints, contextual constraints,* and *optimizations.* Figure 1.7 illustrates examples of constraints in a partial frame for *vacation* (Barsalou, 1991). Note again that structural invariants between attributes are omitted for simplicity of presentation (e.g., *occurs* between *activity* and *location*).

Attribute Constraints.   Attribute constraints are rules that constrain attribute values globally. The *transportation* frame of Fig. 1.7 contains a negative attribute constraint (−) between *speed* and *duration:*

As a form of transportation becomes faster, its duration becomes shorter (over a constant distance).

Figure 1.7 also includes positive attribute constraints (+):

As a form of transportation becomes faster, its cost becomes higher.
As a location's distance from home increases, transportation becomes faster.

Note that these attribute constraints need neither be logical nor empirical truths. Although some are (e.g., the inverse relations between *speed* and *duration*), others are not (e.g., the requirement that long distances from home covary with fast transportation). Instead, attribute constraints often represent statistical patterns or personal preferences, which may be contradicted on occasion. For a change of pace, someone may want to travel slowly over a long distance to see beautiful scenery.

Value Constraints.   Whereas attribute constraints are general rules that constrain attribute values globally, value constraints are specific rules that relate

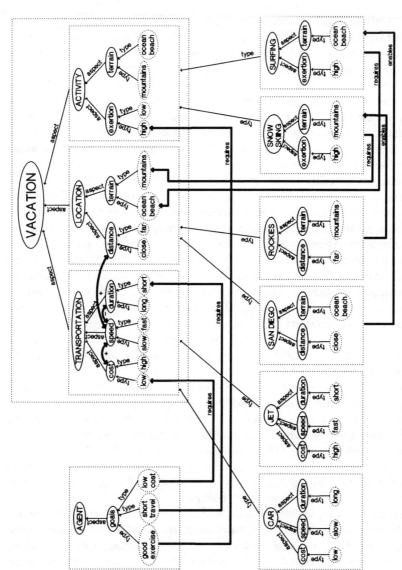

FIG. 1.7.   Examples of attribute constraints, value constraints, contextual constraints, and optimizations in a frame for *vacation*.

particular sets of values locally. Consider the *enables* relation between *San Diego* and *surfing* in Fig. 1.7. This relation specifies that a particular value of the *location* attribute constrains a particular value of the *activity* attribute. Another value constraint similarly relates *Rockies* and *snow skiing*. The *requires* relations between *snow ski* and *mountains* and between *surfing* and *ocean beach* illustrate somewhat more complex value constraints that cross levels within the frame representation. Similar to attribute constraints, value constraints may often represent statistical patterns and personal preferences, rather than necessary truths.

Contextual Constraints.   A distinction between contextual constraints and optimizations is orthogonal to the distinction between attribute constraints and value constraints. Contextual constraints occur when one aspect of a situation constrains another, such as physical constraints in nature. For example, *speed* of transportation constrains its *duration* over a fixed distance. Similarly, the activity of *surfing* requires an *ocean beach*. Contextual constraints also reflect cultural conventions. For example, people's *income* and the *taxes* they pay may bear a relationship to one another. Similarly, *swimming* as an *activity* may require a *swimsuit* as *clothing*. In general, the various aspects of a particular situation are not independent of one another. Instead, physical and cultural mechanisms place constraints on combinations of compatible attribute values. As the preceding examples illustrate, contextual constraints can either be attribute constraints or value constraints.

Optimizations.   Whereas contextual constraints reflect physical and cultural mechanisms, optimizations are constraints that reflect an agent's goals. Consider how the agent's goals in Fig. 1.7 constrain the values of various attributes. The agent's goal of *good exercise* constrains the value of *exertion* in the *activity* frame to be *high*. Similarly, the agent's goals of *short travel* and *low cost* constrain the *duration* and *cost* variables in the *transportation* frame to be *short* and *low*, respectively. Although all of the optimizations shown in Fig. 1.7 are value constraints, optimizations can also be attribute constraints. For example, the value of an agent's *desire* to achieve a goal generally constrains the value of the agent's *effort* in pursuing it.

Whereas contextual constraints typically require that values *satisfy* them, optimizations typically require that one value *excel* beyond all others. For example, just about any kind of *swimsuit* will satisfy the contextual constraint that clothing be worn while swimming. In contrast, the cheapest form of transportation optimizes the goal of *inexpensive travel*. Whereas people generally select values that satisfy contextual constraints, they generally seek values that excel when optimizing goals.

People often attempt to optimize multiple goals simultaneously for an attribute. For *transportation*, someone might optimize *cost*, *speed*, and *comfort* simultaneously—not just *cost* alone. As a result, the optimal value may not be optimal for any one goal in isolation. The optimal form of transportation may not be the cheapest, because a slightly more expensive form optimizes *cost, speed,* and *comfort* together.

Propagating Constraints Through Frames. Constraints often propagate themselves through frame systems in complex manners. To see this, consider how *low cost* propagates constraints in Fig. 1.7. To optimize *cost,* the agent first propagates *low cost* as a goal to *low cost* for *transportation.* Next, through the attribute constraint that relates *cost* and *speed, low* as the value of *cost* selects *slow* as the value of *speed.* In turn, the attribute constraint between *speed* and *distance* from home selects *close* as the value of *distance.* Once *close* has been selected, it constrains the instance of *location* to be *San Diego,* because a satisfactory instance of *location* must match values established in the *location* frame. Once *San Diego* has been selected, a value constraint selects *surfing* as the instantiation of *activity.* What began as an attempt to optimize the goal of *low cost* propagated constraints through the frame system to select *surfing.* Such reasoning appears to occur ubiquitously in human cognition (Barsalou, 1991). Although the preceding description of constraint propagation had a serial flavor, much constraint propagation may occur in parallel.

Constraint Frames. In previous sections, we saw that frames represent attributes and structural invariants. Frames, too, represent constraints. Consider the constraint:

Swimming *requires* swimsuits.

The *requires* relation in this constraint is actually a frame containing attributes such as *likelihood, source, conditions,* and so forth. *Likelihood* states the intuitive probability that the constraint applies. For the swimsuit requirement, the likelihood that it applies may be high, at least in some cultures. *Source* states the origin of the constraint. For the swimsuit requirement, the source is usually a government or its agents. *Conditions* specifies conditions under which the requirement holds. For the swimsuit requirement, conditions might be all contexts except for privately owned swimming areas and nude beaches.

Representational Primitives

Human conceptual knowledge appears to be frames all the way down. Frames are composed of attributes, structural invariants, and constraints, which in turn are represented by frames themselves. Such recursion and "self-similarity" bear an intriguing resemblance to the fractal structures found across a wide variety of physical systems (Gleik, 1987).

Does the representation of frames at some terminal level of analysis ever become grounded in perceptual, motor, and conceptual primitives as theorists often assume (cf. Miller & Johnson-Laird, 1976)? Are there terminal components out of which all frames are constructed? I suspect not, because of the following general principle: For any attribute, structural invariant, or constraint, people can always construct further attributes, structural invariants, and constraints that capture variability across instances. Although an attribute, relation, or constraint may start out as a holistic, unanalyzed primitive, aspects of its variability may subsequently be noted, represented with attribute-value sets, and integrated by structural invariants between attributes, and constraints between values. What was once a simple, unitary primitive becomes analyzed and elaborated, such that it becomes a complex concept.

To see this, consider a possible representational primitive *red,* which occurs across an enormous set of instances. Various animals, fruits, and artifacts are red, at least to some extent. People could represent *red* as a primitive in each of the concepts that represent these entities. Alternatively, people could isolate aspects of *red* through analysis and elaborate these aspects with attribute-value sets. For example, *intensity* could be identified as an aspect of *red* and be elaborated with a description of its values across known instances. Similarly, the *shape* of a red area, its *location,* and its *time* of occurrence could each be represented as attribute-value sets. As a result, *red* is no longer a holistic, unanalyzed, representational primitive but instead becomes a complex frame, taking different values across categories. In *robin,* for example, the frame could specify that *intensity* is *low, shape* is *oval, location* is *breast,* and *time* is *at maturity.* Or for *stop sign,* the frame could specify that *intensity* is *high, shape* is *hexagonal, location* is *front,* and *time* is *permanent.* As a result, no simple primitive represents *red* for all red things (cf. Halff, Ortony, & Anderson, 1976; Wierzbicka, this volume).

One can view Chaffin's analysis as demonstrating a similar point for structural invariants. *Part* could be viewed as a primitive relation that takes the same form across uses, but as we saw earlier, such relations appear considerably more complex, being represented by a frame whose attributes include *functionality, separability, homeomerony,* and *spatio-temporal extent.* Whereas these attributes take one set of values for a *roof as part of a house,* they take another set for *wood as part of a bat.* Because constraints are also relations, a similar argument applies to them. For both structural invariants and constraints, frames develop to represent the variability across their respective instances.

For any representational component—whether it be an attribute, structural invariant, constraint, or something else—people can always note a new source of variability across instances, and add further frame structure to capture it. Through the continuing process of analysis and elaboration, people transform what were once holistic, unanalyzed primitives into complex frames. As a result, primitives that serve as simple, elementary building blocks no longer exist. Note that this is not an ontological claim about the structure of the physical world but is instead a psychological conjecture about how people represent it.

If primitive building blocks do not exist psychologically, then what kinds of primitives might there be? Perhaps a primitive is a general, abstract, unanalyzed concept that typically appears initially at some point during early development. Through experience, it becomes analyzed and elaborated, acquiring the ability to spawn a wide diversity of more specific, complex concepts from which other concepts are built. These primitives might include ontological categories such as *location, object, event, person,* and *mental state;* semantic roles such as *agent, instrument,* and *source;* activities such as *see, move,* and *get;* qualities such as *color, intensity, shape,* and *size;* and relations such as *is, part, in, before, cause,* and *intend.* Wierzbicka (this volume) and Jackendoff (this volume) suggest a variety of other possible primitives.

Rather than being the elementary building blocks of knowledge, primitives may instead be larger wholes, the analysis of which produces an indefinitely large set of complex building blocks. Rather than lying at the representational "bottom," these primitives may lie at the representational "top." For example, *location* may begin as a primitive that simply means something like *region.* But with experience, it may be analyzed and elaborated to include attribute-value sets for *terrain, climate, altitude,* and so forth. As a result, the *location* frame acquires the ability to produce a wide variety of specialized *location* concepts. For example, the *location* frame might take *mountains, cold,* and *high* as values of *terrain, climate,* and *elevation* to produce a specialized *location* concept for *snow skiing.* Similarly, the *location* frame might take values of *beach, warm,* and *low* to produce a specialized *location* concept for *body surfing.* Once the *location* primitive becomes analyzed and elaborated with attribute-value sets, it develops the ability to produce a wide variety of more specialized *location* concepts that can be used to build new frames.

As the examples for *snow skiing* and *body surfing* illustrate, different values across a common set of attributes can represent different types of locations. But some locations differ so much that they may not even share attributes. Consider *location* in the frames for *fire hydrant, star,* and *electron.* Whereas *street* is an important attribute of *location* in the frame for *fire hydrant,* it is not an important attribute of *location* in the frames for *star* or *electron.* Instead, *galaxy* is an important attribute of *location* for *star,* and *distance from the nucleus* is an important attribute of *location* for *electron.* Because different entities often occur in very different spatial reference systems, the *location* frame must develop different attributes to capture the variability in each.

Perhaps the most difficult issue is: Which particular attributes, relations, and constraints become established in frames? This is indeed a deep and difficult issue upon which the success of this enterprise rests. Suffice it to say for now that perceptual salience, goal-relevance, intuitive theories, and memory entrenchment are all important (Barsalou, 1992). Just what the specifics of these factors might be continues to constitute one of the most significant challenges facing the study of knowledge (see Barsalou, in press, for further discussion).

Summary and Critique

At their core, frames contain attribute-value sets. Attributes are concepts that represent aspects of a category's members, and values are subordinate concepts of attributes. Because values are concepts, they in turn can be attributes by having still more specific values. People appear to construct new attributes and values as new aspects of categories become apparent or relevant. Unlike previous theories, frames are not rigid configurations of independent attributes. Instead, attributes vary in systematicity, with the relevant attributes varying across contexts. Frames further contain a variety of relations. Structural invariants in a frame capture relations in the world that tend to be relatively constant between attributes. Conversely, constraints capture systematic patterns of variability between attribute values. Because frames represent attributes, structural invariants, and constraints themselves, the mechanism that constructs frames builds them recursively. Frames for what were once primitive concepts produce complex concepts that are used to build new, more specific concepts.

Absent from this account is a coherent view of frame processing. Before a computational system can build the frames described here, it needs a powerful processing environment capable of performing many difficult tasks. This processing environment must notice new aspects of a category to form new attributes. It must detect values of these attributes to form attribute-value sets. It must integrate cooccurring attributes into frames. It must update attribute-value sets with experience. It must detect structural invariants between attributes. It must detect and update constraints. It must build frames recursively for the components of existing frames.

Another significant challenge concerns the power of frames. Hayes (1979) argues that frames are an implementation of first-order predicate calculus (also see Charniak & McDermott, 1985). In addition, Hayes entertains the possibilities that frames extend into higher order logics and that nondeductive procedures operate on frames (actually, such procedures often exist in other theorists' frame implementations). Given these properties, frames clearly have substantial expressive power, and it is difficult to see what constrains them.

One way to tackle this issue is to distinguish between the content and form of frames. Psychologically, the content of frames seems highly constrained in one regard and relatively unconstrained in another. Biologically, humans and other organisms have predispositions to perceive and represent certain attributes (cf. Jackendoff, this volume; Wierzbicka, this volume). In humans, there are clear biological bases for attributes such as *color, pitch, location,* and so forth. Similarly, some relations seem to have biological bases, including simple spatial relations, temporal relations, and causal relations. These attributes and relations appear privileged in many ways, including ease of perception, presence in early development, and so forth. Consequently, one way to constrain a frame theory is to limit the initial attributes and relations in frames to some set of primitives and then assess whether all subsequent frames can be derived from them.

Although early frames in human development may be relatively constrained to biological attributes and relations, later frames in adult knowledge seem relatively unconstrained. At least as far as we can imagine, people seem capable of constructing frames for any content (cf. Fodor, 1983). Consequently, the fact that the content of frames is formally unconstrained seems quite compatible with the observation that people's ability to conceptualize content seems relatively unconstrained. Perhaps surprisingly, the unconstrained content of frames is psychologically valid.

Regarding form, frames are constrained in important ways. According to my analysis, frames contain three basic components: attribute-value sets, structural invariants, and constraints. If this analysis is correct, then evidence for these components should be ubiquitous. Moreover, hypotheses about these components are falsifiable. We might find evidence for isolated features rather than for more structured, attribute-value sets. We might not observe structural invariants between attributes nor constraints between values. We might observe structural invariants and constraints to be correlational—as in connectionist models—rather than conceptual. Even if we obtain evidence for these three components, we might not observe them to be organized in the way I propose. Clearly, the properties of frames are distinct and testable. In addition, these properties can probably be constrained further. For example, the capacity of working memory might constrain the number of core attributes in a frame to around five. Similarly, capacity and performance limits in human cognition might limit the recursive depth of frames and the length of constraint chains. In principle, developing a constrained and falsifiable theory of frames appears quite feasible. What remains is to implement such a theory and acquire rigorous empirical evidence for its components.

REPRESENTING CONCEPTS WITH FRAMES

Frames support a wide variety of conceptual tasks that are fundamental for natural and artificial intelligence. In this section, I illustrate how frames can represent exemplars and propositions, prototypes and membership, subordinates and taxonomies. I also illustrate how frames can represent conceptual combinations, event sequences, rules, and plans.

Representing Exemplars and Propositions

Instantiated frames readily represent exemplars (cf. Brooks, 1978, 1987; Hintzman, 1986; Jacoby & Brooks, 1984; Medin & Schaffer, 1978). Consider

Fig. 1.8, which shows a subset of the attributes that a person might represent for *bird*. Exemplars of *bird*, such as *bird-1* and *bird-2*, are represented as cooccurring sets of attribute values. For example, *bird-1* has values of *small*, *brown*, and *straight* for the attributes of *size*, *color*, and *beak*. As each new exemplar is encountered, its values are integrated into the frame, similar to *bird-1* and *bird-2*. If exemplars have values for different attributes, they instantiate different subsets of attributes. For example, if the silhouette of a bird were perceived at dusk and *color* were imperceptible, values might be stored only for *size* and *beak*.

In most exemplar models, exemplars are stored independently of one another, not being stored together or associated in any way (as in the bottom left of Fig. 1.3). In contrast, frames provide a natural means of organizing exemplars. As Fig. 1.8 illustrates, exemplars that have values on the same attributes are integrated into the same frame, thereby being stored together. Because exemplars with values on other attributes would be stored elsewhere in memory, frames organize exemplars according to similarity. Exemplars with many shared attributes are stored closer to one another in memory than exemplars with few shared attributes. Integrating an exemplar into a frame does not necessarily lose exemplar information, because an exemplar's values remain interconnected. Nevertheless, integrating exemplars into frames provides natural mechanisms for forgetting exemplar information. Cooccurrence relations between an exemplar's values could become lost, leaving the values associated to attributes independent of any particular exemplar. Or values of an exemplar might become inaccessible from the frame's attributes, thereby precluding retrieval of the exemplar.

One can view an exemplar in a frame system as an existential proposition: There exists an entity *x* in category *C* that has values *p*, *q*, and *r* for attributes *P*, *Q*, and *R* (cf. Hayes, 1979). More specifically:

$$\exists x\ C(x)\ \&\ P(x,p)\ \&\ Q(x,q)\ \&\ R(x,r)$$

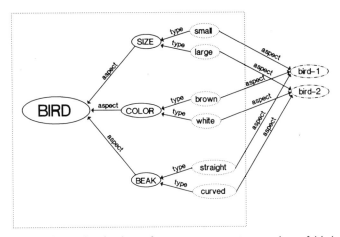

FIG. 1.8. Example of using a frame to represent exemplars of *bird*.

Applying this notation to *bird-1* in Fig. 1.10 produces:

$\exists x$ BIRD(x) & COLOR(x, brown) & SIZE(x, small) & BEAK(x, straight)

Following many philosophers, existential propositions could reflect purported claims about the physical world. Or, following many psychologists, existential propositions could simply be psychological representations, whose truth value is largely irrelevant.

Through the integration of existential propositions, frames can represent the complex propositional structure of discourse, as has been known for some time (Kintsch & van Dijk, 1978). Consider the following short discourse from Barsalou (1992):

Rick, feeling festive, rented a house near a tropical reef. He had recently built a house worth three million dollars. Rick had visited the reef long ago. The fish had been beautiful, and many divers were present (pp. 210–211).

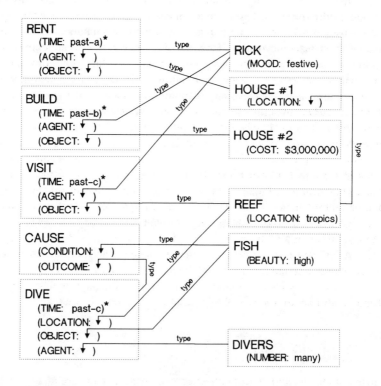

* time-c < time-b < time-a

FIG. 1.9.   Example of using frames to represent a discourse.

Figure 1.9 illustrates how frames for *rent, build, visit, dive, Rick, house, reef, fish,* and *divers* can represent this text.[4] As suggested in Barsalou (1992, chs. 8 and 9), activating and instantiating conceptual frames is the central process in language comprehension. As comprehenders encounter nouns, verbs, and prepositions, they activate frames, whose attributes may become instantiated through later text. Upon encountering *Rick* and *rented* in the aforementioned text, for example, readers activate a frame for each. Information about Rick's mood is integrated into the *mood* attribute in the frame for *Rick.* In turn, the frame for *Rick* is integrated into the *agent* attribute in the frame for *rent.* Barsalou (1992) describes the process of frame activation and instantiation in further detail (see also Just & Carpenter, 1987).

Representing Prototypes and Membership

Prototypes.   Frames not only provide a natural means of representing specific exemplars but also of representing general information across exemplars. We have seen already how frames represent general attributes that typically take values for a category. However, frames can also represent typical values and typical patterns of values across category members. Consider Fig. 1.10. As can be seen, one value for each attribute is more likely than the other value across exemplars (e.g., *brown* occurs for five exemplars, whereas *white* occurs for three). The prototype is simply the set of most frequent values across attributes. In Fig. 1.10, the prototypical *bird* is *small* in *size, brown* in *color,* and has a *straight beak.*

Prototypes can be computed in a number of ways. After integrating a new exemplar into a frame, a procedure could determine the most frequent value of every attribute and represent these values as an explicit prototype (e.g., as in Fig. 1.10). Or, this same procedure could update an explicit prototype only when needed, rather than after every new exemplar. Or, prototypes might not be represented explicitly at all. Instead, prototypes might only emerge implicitly when exemplars are used in category processing, because the most frequent values dominate across exemplars (Medin & Schaffer, 1978).

Regardless of how prototypes arise, frames naturally produce typicality effects: If an exemplar's values occur frequently across the exemplars integrated into a frame, then it is typical (e.g., *bird-1* in Fig. 1.10). In contrast, exemplars whose values occur infrequently are atypical (e.g., *bird-7*). Additionally, if exemplars vary in the attributes for which they have values, then an exemplar's typicality also depends on how frequently its attributes have values across exem-

---

[4]Figure 1.9 uses a somewhat different frame notation than the other figures, with attributes and values being represented in a more propositional manner (e.g., *LOCATION: tropics*). This difference in notation is not intended to convey any difference in structure. As in previous figures, rectangles enclose frames.

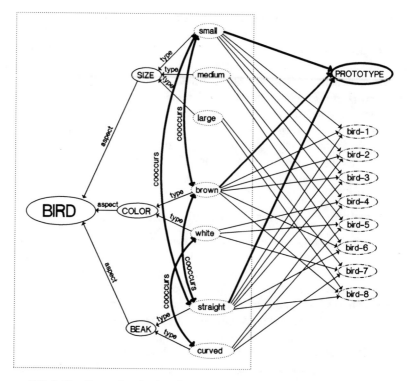

FIG. 1.10. Example of using frames to represent a prototypical *bird* and co-occurrence relations between attribute values.

plars. For example, if a talking parrot has values for *owner, language,* and *vocabulary,* it would be atypical, because most birds do not have values on these attributes. In general, an exemplar's typicality is an increasing function of how well its instantiated attributes and its specific values on these attributes approximate the most frequent attributes and values across exemplars.

Barsalou (1985) showed that typicality does not always depend on the frequency of attributes and values (i.e., central tendency). In some categories, an exemplar's proximity to an ideal attribute value determines typicality instead. In *things to eat on a diet,* proximity to the ideal of *zero calories* determines typicality, whereas proximity to the most frequent caloric value does not (see also Borkenau, 1990; Chaplin, John, & Goldberg, 1988; Lakoff, 1987; Lehrer, this volume; Loken & Ward, 1990; Read, Jones, & Miller, 1990). As we saw earlier for optimizations, frames readily represent ideals as constraints from a person's goals to attribute values. For example, the goal of *losing weight* projects a constraint to the value of *zero* for *calories,* such that a food's typicality reflects its proximity to this ideal.

Frames can also represent typical *patterns* of values, using the various constraints described earlier. In Fig. 1.10, a value constraint explicitly represents the correlation between *small size* and *brown color* across exemplars. As discussed in Barsalou (1990), cooccurrence information can be computed in many possible ways. Analogous to prototypes, cooccurrence relations could be updated explicitly with each new exemplar; they could be computed only when needed; or they could exist implicitly, emerging as frequent patterns of values across exemplars. Because exponential amounts of cooccurrence information exist, computing all of it is probably unrealistic. One reasonable approach is only to compute cooccurrence information that is relevant to the goals and background knowledge of the perceiver (Murphy & Medin, 1985). Another is to compute only cooccurrence information discovered during remindings (Medin & Ross, 1989; Ross & Spalding, 1991). Much cooccurrence information may generally be ignored and not become stored in a frame system. If ignored cooccurrence information should become relevant at a later time, it can be computed from whatever exemplars are currently accessible.

Prototypes and cooccurrence relations provide default information about a category when values for frame attributes are not specified explicitly. Consider the sentence:

When Hank came home, a *bird* was sitting on his porch.

Although this sentence does not describe any characteristics of the bird that Hank observed, a frame can produce inferences about it. First, the reader can infer that the bird has values on attributes such as *size, color,* and *beak,* given these attributes generally take values across birds. Second, the reader can infer default values for these attributes, based on prototypical values extracted from previous exemplars. If the reader's knowledge were similar to Fig. 1.10, he or she could infer that the bird is *small, brown,* and has a *straight beak.* To see how cooccurrence relations provide defaults, consider:

When Hank came home, a *white bird* was sitting on his porch.

Because *white color* cooccurs with *curved beak* in Fig. 1.10, the reader can infer that the bird has a curved beak. Note that *straight beak* is prototypical but is overridden by the correlation between *white color* and *curved beak* that occurs across *bird-4, bird-5,* and *bird-7.* Because *white* does not correlate with any value for *size,* the reader could use the prototype to infer that the bird is *small.*

Cooccurrence relations enable frames to generate defaults dynamically, as occurs in the norms described by Kahneman and Miller (1986). For example, if partial information about a bird is encountered, cooccurrence relations may generate defaults for attributes whose values remain unspecified. For any pattern of provided attribute values, a frame system can fill in the remaining attribute values (much like a connectionist net). As the provided attribute values vary, the inferred defaults can vary dynamically as well. Rather than being limited to values in the prototype, defaults are contextually sensitive, being determined by the particular pattern of cooccurrence relations that the input activates.

Membership. Frames provide a wide variety of mechanisms for representing category membership. First, possession of certain attributes can count as evidence for belonging to a category. For example, having any value on the attribute of *color* counts as evidence for being a *physical entity* (Keil, 1979, 1981). Second, possession of certain attribute values can count as evidence for category membership. For example, having the values of *human, female,* and *adult* for *species, sex,* and *age* counts as evidence for being a *woman.* Third possessing values within a certain range can count as evidence for category membership. For example, having values of *cost* that range from *$125,000 to $175,000* could count as evidence for someone's category of *potential houses to buy* (Flannigan, Fried, & Holyoak, 1986). Fourth, possession of values lying beyond a reference point can count as evidence for category membership. For example, *legal U.S. voters* are *18 years or older* (Medin & Barsalou, 1987).

Through the use of various constraints, frames can represent a wide variety of membership decision rules. For example, a *requires* constraint from a frame's root node to an attribute value specifies that the value is necessary for category membership (e.g., *man* requires *adult* as the value of *age*). Conversely, a *requires* constraint from a value to the root node of a frame specifies that the value is sufficient for membership. Typically, a joint set of values may determine sufficiency, as for *human, child,* and *female* being jointly sufficient for *girl.* To represent joint sufficiency, values must be integrated by a cooccurrence relation, from which a *requires* constraint projects to the root node. Frames can also represent disjunctive and biconditional categories. To represent the disjunctive category of *baseball strike,* three independent *requires* constraints must project to the root node: one from *swings* and *misses* for *hitter's action,* one from *swings and fouls* for *hitter's action,* and one from the cooccurrence of *in the strike zone* for *pitch location* and *hitter does not swing* for *hitter's action.* To represent the biconditional category of *gay relationship,* one *requires* constraint must relate *male* for *partner 1* and *male* for *partner 2,* and another must relate *female* for *partner 1* and *female* for *partner 2.*

All of the *requires* constraints in the previous categories produce well-defined categories. In the absence of such constraints, categories are fuzzy. Under these conditions, an exemplar's similarity to the attribute and value information stored in a frame may control categorization: As an exemplar's attributes and values increasingly match those in a frame, the frame becomes increasingly likely to provide the exemplar's categorization. Following Murphy and Medin (1985), constraints from background knowledge to frames may specify that some attributes and values in a frame are more relevant to similarity comparisons than others.[5]

Representing Subordinates and Taxonomies

Subordinate concepts emerge naturally in frame systems. Consider the representation of *fowl* as a subordinate of *bird* in Fig. 1.11. According to this much simplified example, birds are those entities that have the particular attributes and values in the frame for *bird*. In turn, *fowl* is the subset of *birds* whose values for *size, color,* and *beak* are typically restricted to *large, white,* and *large,* respectively. Subordinates are sets of exemplars whose values constitute a subset of frame information.[6]

Through the representation of increasingly specific subordinates, taxonomies emerge in frames. To see this, consider the representations of *water fowl* and *duck* in Fig. 1.11. *Water fowl* are those *birds* that typically have *large, white, large,* and *paddles* as values for *size, color, beak,* and *locomotion,* respectively. *Ducks* are those *birds* that typically have *large, white, large, paddles,* and *short* as values for *size, color, beak, locomotion* and *neck,* respectively. Because *water fowl* have all the values of *fowl* plus an additional value for *paddles, water fowl* are subordinates of *fowl.* Similarly, because *ducks* have all the values of *water fowl* plus an additional value for *short neck, ducks* are subordinates of *water fowl.* Through the representation of nested attribute values, taxonomies evolve naturally within frames.

Figure 1.11 represents taxonomic relations explicitly (i.e., the *type* relations from *fowl* to *bird,* from *water fowl* to *fowl,* and from *duck* to *water fowl*). If *type* relations were not represented explicitly, however, this taxonomy would still be represented implicitly, based on value nestings alone. By assessing whether one subordinate's attribute values are nested within another's, a procedure could identify taxonomic relations. Given such flexibility, frame systems can represent both prestored taxonomies and computable taxonomies (Smith, 1978).

---

[5]By further assuming that different attributes and values can underlie membership and typicality, frames readily account for the dissociation that sometimes occurs between typicality and membership. For *odd numbers,* membership requires that a number have *one* as its value of *remainder when divided by two.* In contrast, typicality may reflect an exemplar's value on *frequency of occurrence* or its proximity to the ideal of *minimal magnitude* (cf. Armstrong, Gleitman, & Gleitman 1983). When typicality and membership are directly related, the same attributes and values underlie both. For example, Barsalou (1985) found that typicality in *weapons* increases with *destructiveness,* which is clearly related to membership (also see Fehr & Russell, 1984, Experiment 5; Hampton, 1988).

[6]The examples in Fig. 1.11 are much simplified for the sake of presentation (e.g., some *fowl* are not *white*).

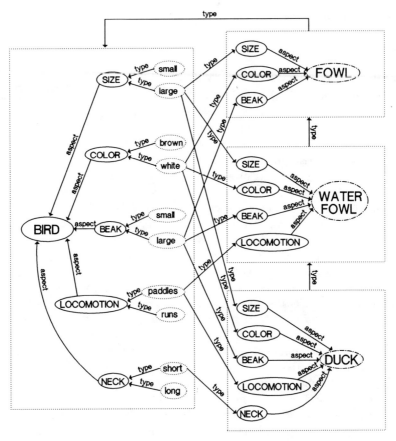

FIG. 1.11.   Example of using frames to represent subordinates in a partial taxonomy for *bird*.

Representing Conceptual Combinations

Frames readily represent conceptual combinations, which include adjective–noun compounds (e.g., *red bird*), noun–noun compounds (e.g., *bird house*), and more complex noun phrases (e.g., *birds from Canada that live in Florida for the winter*). Complex propositional representations for discourses, such as the one in Fig. 1.9, exhibit the ultimate in conceptual combination (Barsalou, 1992).

In their selective modification model, Smith, Osherson, Rips, and Keane (1988) represent conceptual combinations with frames. On their view, when an adjective modifies a noun, the adjective replaces the default value for the relevant attribute in the noun's frame. In *red bird,* for example, *red* replaces *color's* default of *brown* in the frame for *bird*. All other nonmodified attributes in the

noun's frame retain their defaults (e.g., *size* retains its default of *small*). However, selective modification fails to account for interactions that often occur
between modified and unmodified attributes (Medin & Shoben, 1988; Murphy,
1988, 1990). In *white bird,* for example, *size* as well as *color* is likely to be
modified, because white birds are generally *large,* thereby overriding the default
of *small* for *size.*

The examples in Fig. 1.12 illustrate how frames represent conceptual combinations and the interactions that often accompany them. As can be seen, one
meaning of *bird house* can be represented by integrating frames for *bird* and
house into the *agent* and *location* attributes in the frame for *live* (cf. Gleitman &
Gleitman, 1970). Constraints capture the interactive inferences that people are

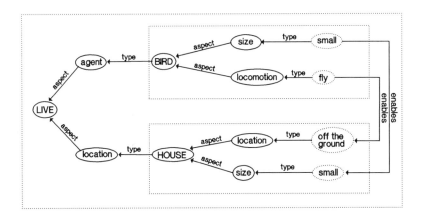

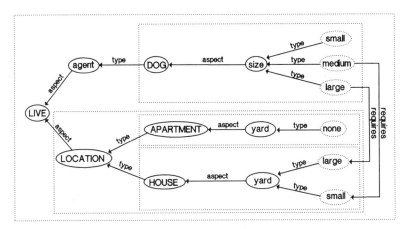

FIG. 1.12. Examples of using frames to represent conceptual combinations for *bird house* and *apartment dog.*

likely to make about *bird house*. Because the birds who typically live in such houses are *small* and *fly*, these defaults enable the *house* to be *small* and *off the ground*. As Fig. 1.12 also illustrates, constraints similarly capture interactive inferences that underlie *apartment dog* (cf. Murphy, 1988). Frames for *dog* and *apartment* are integrated into the *agent* and *location* attributes of the frame for *live*. The constraint that *medium* and *large* dogs typically require a yard enables the inference that *small* dogs tend to live in apartments. Because apartments do not have yards, they generally preclude dogs that are medium or large, with *small* remaining as the most plausible *size*.

Representing Event Sequences

So far, I have been using frames to represent timeless states of the world. Yet, frames also lend themselves to representing the dynamic flow of events over time, what many refer to as *scripts* (Schank & Abelson, 1977) and *mental models* (Johnson-Laird, 1983). Consider the partial frame for a simple four-stroke engine, which might include attributes for *carburetor, ignition system,* and *cylinder*. In an atemporal frame representation, the values of these attributes are the specific carburetors, ignition systems, and cylinders of particular engines. However, the values of frame attributes can be used in a much different way to simulate engine behavior.

To see how frames can represent event sequences, consider the much simplified frame for a one-cylinder, four-stroke engine in Fig. 1.13 (cf. Barsalou, Hale, & Cox, 1989). Instead of the frame's attributes taking values for the components of a specific engine, the attributes take values for *states of operation* (e.g., the *carburetor* can either be in the state of *forming fuel vapor* or of being *empty*). To see the difference, compare the values of engine attributes in Fig. 1.4 with the values of engine attributes in Fig. 1.13.[7]

Because the frame in Fig. 1.13 represents a four-stroke engine, the engine can be in one of four states, which are represented as the four strokes of the engine cycle. Each stroke in Fig. 1.13 is represented by a vertical line (i.e., a "stroke line"). Each horizontal line connected to a stroke line by a solid circle indicates a value of a frame attribute that occurs during that stroke. Those horizontal lines with "wickets" over a stroke line do not occur during that stroke. In *stroke 1*, for example, the *carburetor* is in the state of *forming fuel vapor*, the *ignition system* is in the state of *charging*, the *intake valve* is in the state of *open*, the *exhaust valve* is in the state of *closed*, the *piston* is in the state of *decompressing*, and the

---

[7]Simultaneous representation of particular engine components and states could be achieved by having particular components emanate directly from the attributes, with states being defined over these components instead of over the attributes. For example, *carburetor* could have *the carburetor in Phil's car's engine* as its component value, which could be in the state of either *forming fuel vapor* or of being *empty*.

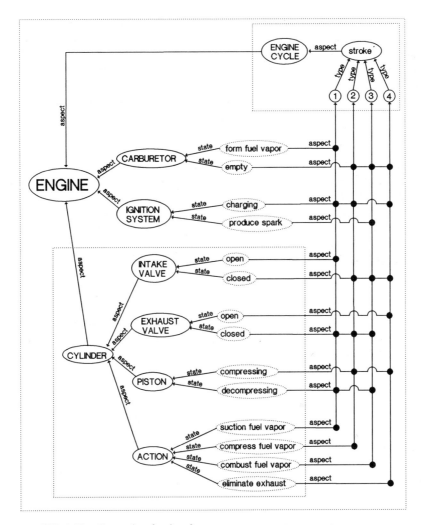

FIG. 1.13. Example of using frames to represent an event sequence for a physical device, *engine.*

action of the *cylinder* is to *suction fuel vapor* into the cylinder. The states of the engine's components on each of the remaining three cycles can be determined by noting the state values connected to each of the remaining three stroke lines. As can be seen, this event sequence is represented by crossing the frame for the *engine* with the frame for the *engine cycle* and noting all "intersections." As examples in Figs. 1.14, 1.15, and 1.16 illustrate further, crossing one frame for a

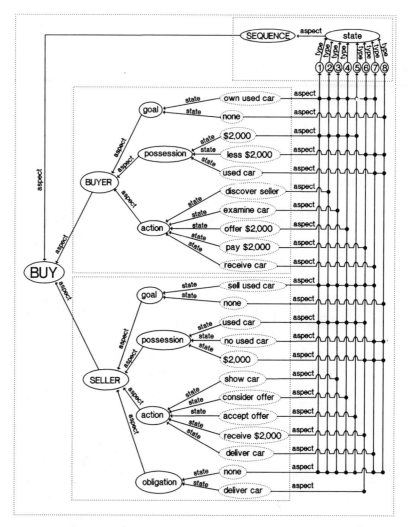

FIG. 1.14. Example of using frames to represent an event sequence for an event, *buy.*

physical domain with a second frame for time provides frames with a general means of representing event sequences.[8]

Figure 1.14 illustrates how frames represent the temporal sequence of states in an interpersonal event, namely, buying a used car for $2,000. Each vertical line

[8]The representation of engine states in Fig. 1.13 is formally identical to the representation of exemplars in Figs. 1.8 and 1.10: In each case, a state/exemplar is a collection of attribute values. The only difference is that the states in an event sequence are temporally related, whereas exemplars are typically not connected to each other in any manner (although they could be).

represents one state in the event sequence constituting the sale. This frame representation of an event attempts to account for the same type of information as Schank and Abelson's (1977) scripts, but in a somewhat different manner.

Representing Rules

Rules provide a common mechanism for producing event sequences. Applying a rule to an initial state transforms it into a subsequent state. In turn, applying a second rule (or perhaps the first rule again) produces a third state. Through a series of rule applications, an event sequence ensues, where each event is the transformation of one state into another. In production systems, production rules produce a wide variety of event sequences in this manner (Anderson, 1983). In theories of qualitative reasoning, rules propagate forces and substances over device topographies to produce device functions (de Kleer & Brown, 1984; diSessa, 1983; Forbus, 1984; Hayes, 1985). In story grammars, rules produce the plot transitions that form a story (e.g., Stein, Kilgore, & Albro, 1990; Stein & Levine, 1990; Trabasso & Sperry, 1985; Trabasso & van den Broek, 1985; Trabasso et al., 1989).

Frames for event sequences contain rules implicitly. Consider the stroke lines for *stroke 1* and *stroke 2* in Fig. 1.13, which can be integrated to form the following rule:

Rule 1: CAUSE (*condition:* stroke 1, *outcome:* stroke 2).

Three additional rules can be constructed for the engine cycle in Fig. 1.13:

Rule 2: CAUSE (*condition:* stroke 2, *outcome:* stroke 3).

Rule 3: CAUSE (*condition:* stroke 3, *outcome:* stroke 4).

Rule 4: CAUSE (*condition:* stroke 4, *outcome:* stroke 1).

Using frame notation, each rule could be represented as an independent production. Rule 1 would contain all of Fig. 1.13, excluding the stroke lines for strokes 3 and 4. In addition, a *cause* frame could be added, with its attributes for *condition* and *outcome* bound to *stroke 1* and *stroke 2*, respectively. Rules 2, 3, and 4 could be represented similarly. If the condition for a rule were met, then the rule would fire as a production, producing its outcome.

Rather than storing rules as separate productions, they can be stored more efficiently in a frame that integrates them. Consider Fig. 1.15, where the frame for the engine cycle contains four causal events, one for each rule. Note that the complete stroke lines and the frame for the engine from Fig. 1.13 are not shown but are assumed to be present. Each stroke line is the outcome of one causal event and the condition for the next causal event.

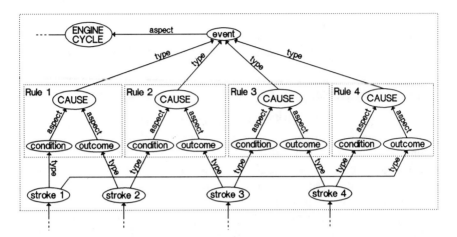

FIG. 1.15.   Using a frame to integrate the rules that produce the event
sequence for *engine cycle* in Fig. 1.13.

Representing Rules 1 through 4 in this manner differs in important ways from
production systems. Whereas these rules are integrated in a frame representation,
they would be independent entities in a production system. As a consequence,
the frame representation is more economical. Each stroke line is only represented
once in Fig. 1.15 but would have to represented twice in a production system:
once as a condition, and once as an outcome (similar to Rules 1 through 4
preceding). Moreover, the frame representation provides a more coherent and
global account of the engine cycle, because relations among the four rules are
shown explicitly. However, an individual rule can still fire separately of the
others. Rule 3 rule could fire, if its condition occurs, even if Rules 1 and 2 have
not. Additionally, automatic firing of rules could be represented as the extent to
which the relevant causal relations become strengthened in memory (Shiffrin &
Schneider, 1977), or as the extent to which exemplars are integrated with rules
(similar to Figs. 1.8 and 1.10; Logan, 1988). Nevertheless, the representation in
Fig. 1.15 suggests that rules embedded in frames should be harder to access than
isolated rules in production systems, if surrounding rules in an integrated frame
provide interference. Evidence from Carlson and Yaure's (1990) blocking condition demonstrates such difficulty.

Figure 1.16 illustrates two further examples of frames representing rules. At
the top, an intuitive view of *combustion* is represented as a causal relation
between two sets of states defined over *fuel, air,* and *heat source.* At the bottom,
the epitome of a rule, *modus ponens,* is represented as a relation between two
sets of states defined over $X \rightarrow Y$, X, and Y. As these examples illustrate, frames
can represent a wide variety of rules.

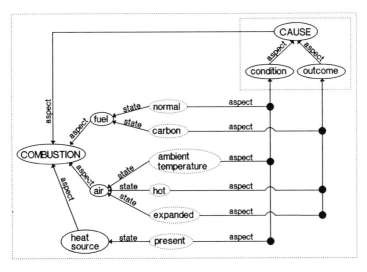

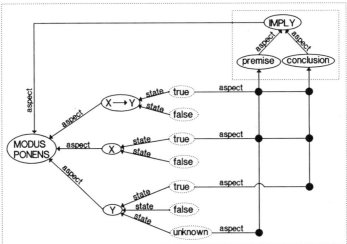

FIG. 1.16. Examples of using frames to represent intuitive rules for *combustion* and *modus ponens*.

Representing Plans

Frames are central to the initial planning of events (Barsalou, 1991). When people plan events such as trips, purchases, social events, and repairs, they often begin by partially activating a frame for the event being planned. In planning a vacation, people might activate the partial frame in Fig. 1.17.

The primary activity during the initial planning of an event is to instantiate frame attributes. As illustrated in Fig. 1.17, a planner might select *snow skiing* as

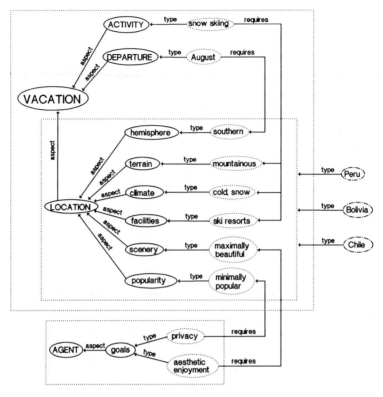

FIG. 1.17. Example of using frames to represent a contextualized category, *vacation locations,* in a plan for a *vacation.*

the value for *activity* and *August* as the value for *departure.* To instantiate attributes, planners often select exemplars from *goal-derived categories,* such as *activities to perform on a vacation* and *times to go on a vacation* (Barsalou, 1983, 1985, 1991; also see Dougherty & Keller, 1985). When such categories are stored in memory, planners retrieve them and search their exemplars, trying to find the optimal one(s) for the current plan. If such categories are not prestored, then *ad hoc categories* must be computed using a generate and test procedure. In computing *times to go on a vacation,* a planner might use temporal knowledge to generate seasons and months, testing their acceptability for a particular vacation.

Planners contextualize goal-derived and ad hoc categories to satisfy contextual constraints and optimization constraints. Consider contextual constraints first. As seen in Fig. 1.17, values for *vacation location* cannot be selected independently of values for *departure* and *activity.* If they were, a location might be selected that precludes snow skiing (e.g., a Caribbean beach). Instead, the values for *departure* and *activity* propagate constraints to the frame for *location.*

If a plan to snow ski in August is to succeed, satisfactory locations must be identified, such as *mountainous regions with ski resorts in the southern hemisphere*. If *departure* were changed to *January*, however, then new locations must be identified, such as *mountainous regions with ski resorts in the northern hemisphere*. Similarly, if *departure* and *activity* were changed to *March* and *sunbathing*, still new locations must be identified, such as *beaches near the equator*. In general, the already instantiated values of frame attributes contextualize the goal-derived categories used to instantiate later attributes.[9]

Optimizations of a planner's goals further contextualize categories. As can be seen from Fig. 1.17, the agent has goals of *privacy* and *aesthetic enjoyment,* which propagate additional constraints to the *vacation* frame in the form of *ideals* (Barsalou, 1985; cf. Lehrer, this volume). Specifically, the ideals, *maximally beautiful,* and *minimally popular,* become established in the frame for *location.* To optimize the planner's goals, locations should approximate these ideals as much as possible. In contrast, if the planner's goals were to *socialize* and *be warm,* a different set of locations would be ideal. As a planner's goals vary, they contextualize the categories used to instantiate frame attributes.

THE STRUCTURE OF CONCEPTUAL FIELDS

The previous section focused primarily on how frames structure concepts, including concepts for exemplars, prototypes, subordinates, conceptual combinations, event sequences, rules, and plans. This final section explores how frames structure large fields of concepts. In particular, it explores how frames define the implicit extent of a conceptual field, how specific concepts within a field come to be represented explicitly, and how frames support the adaptation of concepts within a field. As we shall see, a frame is a finite generative mechanism capable of producing a large field of related concepts.

Defining the Extent of Conceptual Fields

Every frame defines an implicit conceptual field. To see this, consider the partial frame for *animal* in Fig. 1.18. If someone knew only these attributes and values for *animal*, its field would have 100 potential concepts, each having 1 value on each of the 4 attributes (i.e., 5 species $\times$ 2 sexes $\times$ 5 ages $\times$ 2 states of neutering $= 100$ combinations). These concepts include *human–male–child–unneutered*

---

[9]As discussed earlier, constraints are often statistical patterns rather than logical necessities. As a result, exceptions to the constraints in Fig. 1.17 are possible. For example, an August departure does not necessarily require that the location be in the southern hemisphere, given summer skiing is possible in the European Alps. Statistically, however, most summer skiing locations may be in the southern hemisphere.

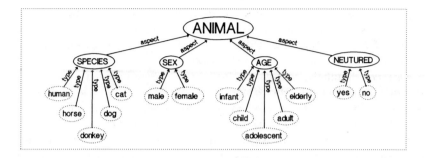

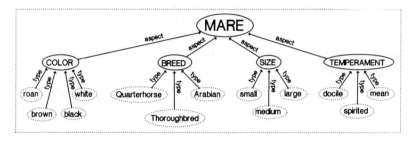

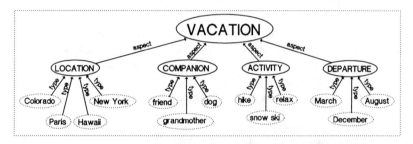

FIG. 1.18. Examples of frames for *animal, mare,* and *vacation* that produce conceptual fields.

and *cat–female–adult–neutered*. Additional concepts of fewer than four values are also possible, such as *horse–child–male, horse–child,* and *horse*. Concepts of more than four values are possible as well, such as *horse/donkey–female–adult–unneutered* for a subset of *mules*. If a frame contains all of the attributes and values possible within a conceptual field, then the frame defines the potential concepts that can be produced exhaustively.

The field for *animal* is much more complex than Fig. 1.18 implies. Because the frame for *animal* also contains frames for its values, relations, and constraints, the field of *animal* concepts is considerably larger. For example, frames could represent the value of *male,* a relation between *neutered* and *sex,* and so forth. Furthermore, frames could continue to represent frame components recursively at many levels. To see the potential explosion in growth, imagine that a frame of 5 attributes, each having 2 values, represents each of the original 14 values for *animal* in Fig. 1.18. Adding this level of embedded frames increases the total number of concepts in the field from 100 to 104,857,600.[10] If frames for relations and constraints are included as well, the field would continue to grow. Assembling frames in conceptual combinations, event sequences, and plans produces still larger conceptual fields. For example, *friend* can embed recursively within itself to form conceptual combinations for *the friend of a friend, the friend of a friend's friend, the friend of a friend's friend's friend,* and so forth. In principle, a frame that can take itself as an attribute value produces a conceptual field that is infinite in size. Obviously, such frames do not define their fields of potential concepts exhaustively.

As these examples illustrate, frames are highly generative mechanisms. From explicitly representing a small number of frame components in memory, a person develops the ability to represent an indefinitely large number of concepts in the frame's field. Although individuals may only represent a few of these concepts explicitly, they can construct any of the remainder by forming new combinations of values across attributes.

Semantic Fields.   Some of the concepts in a conceptual field become lexicalized to form a semantic field (Grandy, 1987; Kittay, 1987; Lehrer, 1974; Lyons, 1977; Miller & Johnson-Laird, 1976). In the semantic field for *animal,* the word "eunuch" means *human–male–adult–neutered,* "mare" means *horse–female–adult,* and "puppy" means *dog–infant.* Most research on semantic fields has addressed conceptual fields that are heavily lexicalized, as well as their most densely, lexicalized regions. When part of a field is unlexicalized, it constitutes a *lexical gap.* For example, no lexical item exists for *horse–female–adult–un-neutered* or *dog–male–infant–neutered.* References to these concepts require more complex clausal expressions, such as "unneutered mare" and "male puppy that has been neutered."

The partial frame for *mare* in Fig. 1.18 further illustrates the large space of lexical gaps often found within a field. As far as I know, none of the concepts in this field is lexicalized. People do not have lexical terms for a mare that is *roan–Arabian–small–spirited* or for a mare that is *white–docile.* Instead, people express these concepts in more complex linguistic constructions, such as "roan Arabian mare that is small and spirited." Lexicalized concepts in a semantic field only capture a small fragment of the concepts in the conceptual field.

---

[10]The number of forms that each of the original 14 values can take is 2^5 (i.e., 32 combinations of 5 attributes, each having 2 possible values). The number of forms that each of the original 100 combinations of 4 values can take is therefore 32^4 (i.e., 1,058,576). Because there were 100 original combinations, the total number of concepts possible in the extended field is 105,857,600.

The partial frame for *vacation* in Fig. 1.18 illustrates how a frame defines the conceptual field for an event, which includes the concepts described by "a vacation with a grandmother to relax in Hawaii in August" and "a vacation with a friend to ski in Colorado in December." Although none of the concepts in the field for *vacation* is lexicalized, lexicalization sometimes occurs in event fields. In the field for *cook*, "simmer" lexicalizes the concept of cooking with *water, gentle action, no oil,* and *no vapor* (Lehrer, 1974). Similar to "mare" in the field for *animal*, however, many unlexicalized concepts for *simmer* exist, such as the one described by "simmering mushrooms in vegetable stock and garlic over gas heat."

Constructing Specific Concepts within a Field

Frames are finite generative mechanisms. A modest amount of explicit frame information in memory enables the computation of a tremendously large number of concepts. By combining attribute values in new ways, people construct new concepts implicit within existing frame knowledge. Although all of these concepts are potentially computable, not even experts are likely to consider more than a small subset. This next section explores several factors that may lead to the construction of specific concepts within a conceptual field.

Experience and Concept Construction. As the result of experiencing particular exemplars, a person populates the respective conceptual field with exemplar representations. Each exemplar representation is the combination of attribute values that defines it as a particular point within the field. Figures 1.8 and 1.10 illustrate one form that exemplar representations can take.[11]

The combination of values used to code an exemplar depends on the content of the relevant frame. For example, a novice's frame for *horse* might contain fewer attributes and values than an expert's frame. In coding a particular horse, a novice might only encode *color, size,* and *stockiness*. In contrast, an expert might code additional attributes, such as *breed, sex, age, back sway,* and so forth. As a result, the expert's coding of a particular horse as a point in the conceptual field carries more information, in an information theoretic sense. Analogously, different cultures may have different frames for the same field that produce different codings of the same exemplar. In this way, frames define relevance with respect to particular perceivers.

The content of frames also determines the distinguishability of exemplars. Imagine that a novice's frame for *horse* only contains attributes for *color, size,* and *stockiness*. As long as different horses have different combinations of values

---

[11]In this section, I only discuss how exemplars instantiate points within a conceptual field. I do not discuss how states instantiate points within an event field, although the same proposals apply (Figs. 1.13, 1.14, 1.15, and 1.16).

for these attributes, no two horses are encoded identically, and exemplars remain distinguishable. However, to the extent that two or more horses are coded with the same set of values, they are not distinct. As multiple exemplars become coded identically, they may establish an increasingly entrenched representation of a subordinate concept of *horse,* as discussed earlier for Fig. 1.11.

Because experts encounter many more exemplars than novices, yet have richer frames, the key factor in expert knowledge concerns the relation between exemplar density and frame content. If exemplars are distributed evenly throughout a conceptual field, an expert may rarely code them identically, because so many possible attributes apply. As a result, an expert's frame system produces "deeper" processing of exemplars, thereby producing better memory (cf. Chiesi, Spilich, & Voss, 1979; Craik & Tulving, 1975; Ross, 1981; Spilich, Vesonder, Chiesi, & Voss, 1979). If exemplars populate a few small areas of a field densely, however, an expert may code many exemplars identically, such that poor memory results. A more likely possibility is that attribute-value sets are best articulated in the most densely populated regions of a field. Exemplars in these regions receive fine-grained codings that rarely overlap, whereas exemplars in less populated regions receive coarser codings. Densely populated regions of a field may also exhibited greater taxonomic depth (cf. Rosch et al., 1976).

Constraints on Exemplars.   Not all combinations of attribute values in a conceptual field are physically possible. Because exemplars exhibiting these combinations never occur, concepts for them may not develop. In the field of *cooking utensils,* for example, *frying pans* made of *paper* are impossible. Similarly, *vacations* with *Caribbean beach* and *snow skiing* as values of *location* and *activity* are impossible. Many other concepts are physically possible yet never occur. Although a *frying pan* made of *platinum* is possible, it may never occur. Similarly, a *vacation* to *Japan* with one's *grandmother* may be possible yet never occur. Because people never encounter such exemplars, they rarely consider the respective concepts, except perhaps in imagination. As a result, extensive "conceptual gaps" exist in conceptual fields, analogous to the lexical gaps in semantic fields.

Two factors appear central to the realization of specific concepts: natural forces and goal optimization. Natural forces constrain the patterns of attribute values that occur in zoological, botanical, and geological fields. For example, genetic mechanisms constrain patterns of phenotypic traits in organisms. Because the genes of *robins* cause *straight beaks* and *red breasts* to cooccur, people do not know them to have *curved beaks* and *red breasts.* Similarly, physical forces constrain the characteristics of inorganic substances. Because atomic mechanisms cause *gold* to be relatively *yellow* and *soft,* people do not know it to be *blue* and *soft.*

For artifacts, goal optimization constrains the patterns of attribute values that occur. In constructing tools, the patterns that people encounter are those that optimize their goals. For example, hammers generally have *wooden handles* and *steel heads.* Hammers typically do not have *solid steel handles,* because the added weight tires the arm. Nor do hammers typically have *platinum* heads, because the extra expense has little benefit in durability. Similarly, the plans that people construct for events are those that optimize their goals. In planning trips, people do not experience *limousine* and *grocery store* as values of *vehicle* and *destination,* because the benefits of taking a limousine to buy groceries do not outweigh the costs. Similarly in brushing, people do not experience *one hour* and *teeth* as values of *duration* and *object,* again because of low payoff.

Imagination and Concept Construction.   Experienced exemplars are not necessary for constructing concepts within a field. Clearly, people can imagine concepts for nonexistent exemplars. In evaluating typicality, people construct concepts of ideal category members, whose realization in experience would optimize a goal (Barsalou, 1985). In planning, people imagine events that do not exist (Barsalou, 1991). In decision making, people imagine possible choices (Kahneman, Slovic, & Tversky, 1982). In evaluating actual events, people imagine alternative events that might have occurred instead (Kahneman & Miller, 1986). The computational power of the human cognitive system reflects its ability to imagine concepts within conceptual fields. Through mental simulation, people develop insights into past events and predictions for future events. By comparing multiple possibilities, people identify optimal alternatives. By combining concepts in new ways, people invent new devices and procedures. Much of what is unique in human nature rests on the ability to combine conceptual information creatively.

Frames readily support the creative combination of information. As we saw earlier, frames define huge spaces of implicit concepts. Because most of these concepts are never considered but nevertheless computable, they provide extensive opportunities for creativity. By combining attribute values in new ways, people explore explicitly what were once implicit regions of a conceptual field. Moreover, every new attribute or frame added to memory offers further opportunities for creativity. When people learn about *genes,* learning does not end with this concept. Instead, people can combine *genes* with any plant or animal frame to construct a new conception of each. Furthermore, people can apply *genes* to other frames metaphorically, as did Holland (1975) in his conception of *genetic algorithms* for machine learning. Frames provide the combinatorics that support construing reality in myriad ways and conceiving of the possible worlds that lie beyond it.

Adapting Concepts within a Field

Frames readily allow people to adapt their knowledge to a changing world. Imagine that robins evolve to have *purple* instead of *red breasts.* To represent this, people simply have to change the value of *color* from *red* to *purple* in their frame for *robin*. Because all other values remain the same, nothing else in the frame need be altered. Similarly, imagine that people begin using hammers with solid steel handles to develop arm strength. The addition of *steel* as a value of *handle material* in the frame for *hammer* captures this change, along with an *enables* relation to *develops arm strength* as a value of *goal*.

Because people constantly experience new things in the world, and because the world is constantly changing, human knowledge should be of a form that adapts to change readily. Frames offer a type of flexibility that is "genetic" in character. Similar to the somewhat orthogonal structure of genes in organisms, attributes can function orthogonally in frames. Because values for attributes can vary independently—to the extent that they do not violate constraints—they can capture whatever orthogonal variation occurs in nature. If values of *hair color* and *eye color* vary independently in a species, frames can readily capture this variation, because the respective attribute-value sets can function orthogonally. On the other hand, when correlations exist in nature, frames can capture them with structural invariants and constraints.

Representing change in experience and evolution is much like representing event sequences: For each, a frame's attributes remain relatively constant, with changes in values capturing change over time (cf. Hayes, 1985). As we saw earlier, frames can represent the evolution of a system over a short time period, as in the successive states of a four-stroke engine. However, frames can also represent change over much longer time periods, as in the physical growth of a person over their life span, change in cultural convention over history, or change in a species over evolution.

CONCLUSION

Frames capture constancy and variability across exemplars and time. The same basic, frame-producing mechanism applies virtually to any domain. Moreover, it applies recursively, producing frames within frames at any point where new aspects of variability are noted. As a result, frames represent the attributes, values, structural invariants, and constraints that compose frames. What may begin as a relatively undifferentiated "primitive" domain becomes increasingly articulated as frames develop to represent it. So far, the evidence for a fundamental frame-producing mechanism in human cognition rests mostly on informal examples and intuition. A much stronger empirical case remains to be developed. In addition, much remains to be learned about the mechanisms that produce and process frames. Although frames may provide a fairly uniform representation across tasks and domains, a wide variety of processing mechanisms may underlie their utilization in human intelligence.

ACKNOWLEDGMENTS

Work on this chapter was supported by National Science Foundation Grant IRI-8609187 and Army Research Institute Contract MD A903-86-C-0172. I am grateful to Adrienne Lehrer and Eva Kittay for the opportunity to write this chapter and for their helpful advice over the course of its development. I am also grateful to Nancy Stein for much helpful discussion and to Roger Chaffin, Janellen Huttenlocher, Barbara Malt, Arthur Markman, Gregory Murphy, Douglas Medin, and Edward Smith for comments on an earlier draft. This chapter has benefitted considerably from their comments and suggestions. Address correspondence to Lawrence W. Barsalou, Department of Psychology, 5848 S. University Ave., University of Chicago, Chicago, IL 60637.

REFERENCES

Alba, J. W., & Hasher, L. (1983). Is memory schematic? *Psychological Bulletin, 93,* 203–231.

Anderson, J. R. (1983). *The architecture of cognition.* Cambridge, MA: Harvard University Press.

Armstrong, S. L., Gleitman, L. R., & Gleitman, H. (1983). On what some concepts might not be. *Cognition, 13,* 263–308.

Ashcraft, M. H. (1978). Property norms for typical and atypical items from 17 categories: A description and discussion. *Memory & Cognition, 6,* 227–232.

Barsalou, L. W. (1983). Ad hoc categories. *Memory & Cognition, 11,* 211–227.

Barsalou, L. W. (1985). Ideals, central tendency, and frequency of instantiation as determinants of graded structure in categories. *Journal of Experimental Psychology: Learning, Memory, and Cognition, 11,* 629–654.

Barsalou, L. W. (1987). The instability of graded structure in concepts. In U. Neisser (Ed.), *Concepts and conceptual development: Ecological and intellectual factors in categorization* (pp. 101–140). New York: Cambridge University Press.

Barsalou, L. W. (1988). The content and organization of autobiographical memories. In U. Neisser (Ed.), *Remembering reconsidered: Ecological and traditional approaches to the study of memory* (pp. 193–243). New York: Cambridge University Press.

Barsalou, L. W. (1989). Intra-concept similarity and its implications for inter-concept similarity. In S. Vosniadou & A. Ortony (Eds.), *Similarity and analogical reasoning* (pp. 76–121). New York: Cambridge University Press.

Barsalou, L. W. (1990). On the indistinguishability of exemplar memory and abstraction in category representation. In T. K. Srull & R. S. Wyer, Jr. (Eds.), *Advances in social cognition, Vol. 3: Content and process specificity in the effects of prior experiences* (pp. 61–88). Hillsdale, NJ: Lawrence Erlbaum Associates.

Barsalou, L. W. (1991). Constructing categories to achieve goals. In G. H. Bower (Ed.), *The psychology of learning and motivation: Advances in research and theory* (Vol. 27). San Diego: Academic Press.

Barsalou, L. W. (1992). *Cognitive psychology: An overview for cognitive scientists.* Hillsdale, NJ: Lawrence Erlbaum Associates.

Barsalou, L. W. (in press). Three properties of concepts: Flexibility, structure, and symbolic arbitrariness in concepts: Perceptual symbols grounded in a compositional system of perceptual knowledge. In A. C. Collins, S. E. Gathercole, M. A. Conway, & P. E. M. Morris (Eds.), *Theories of memory.* Hillsdale, NJ: Lawrence Erlbaum Associates.

Barsalou, L. W., & Billman, D. (1989). Systematicity and semantic ambiguity. In D. Gorfein (Ed.), *Resolving semantic ambiguity* (pp. 146–203). New York: Springer-Verlag.

Barsalou, L. W., & Hale, C. R. (in press). Components of conceptual representation: From feature lists to recursive frames. In I. Van Mechelen, J. Hampton, R. Michalski, & P. Theuns (Eds.), *Categories and concepts: Theoretical views and inductive data analysis.* San Diego, CA: Academic Press.

Barsalou, L. W., Hale, C. R., & Cox, M. T. (1989). *MECH: A computer interface for teaching and investigating mental models and troubleshooting.* Technical Report GIT-ICS-89/17, School of Information and Computer Science, Georgia Institute of Technology, Atlanta.

Barsalou, L. W., & Ross, B. H. (1986). The roles of automatic and strategic processing in sensitivity to superordinate and property frequency. *Journal of Experimental Psychology: Learning, Memory, and Cognition, 12,* 116–134.

Bartlett, F. C. (1932). *Remembering: A study in experimental and social psychology.* New York: Cambridge University Press.

Billman, D. O., & Heit, E. (1988). Observational learning from internal feedback: A simulation of an adaptive learning method. *Cognitive Science, 12,* 587–626.

Bobrow, D. G., & Winograd, T. (1977). An overview of KRL, a knowledge representation language. *Cognitive Science, 1,* 3–46.

Borkenau, P. (1990). Traits as ideal-based and goal-derived social categories. *Journal of Personality and Social Psychology, 58,* 381–396.

Brewer, W. F., & Nakamura, G. V. (1984). The nature and function of schemas. In R. S. Wyer & T. K. Srull (Eds.), *Handbook of social cognition* (Vol. 1, pp. 119–160). Hillsdale, NJ: Lawrence Erlbaum Associates.

Brooks, L. R. (1978). Non-analytic concept formation and memory for instances. In E. H. Rosch & B. B. Lloyd (Eds.), *Cognition and categorization* (pp. 169–211). Hillsdale, NJ: Lawrence Erlbaum Associates.

Brooks, L. R. (1987). Decentralized control of categorization: The role of prior processing episodes. In U. Neisser (Ed.), *Concepts and conceptual development: Ecological and intellectual factors in categorization* (pp. 141–174). New York: Cambridge University Press.

Carlson, R. A., & Yaure, R. G. (1990). Practice schedules and the use of component skills in problem solving. *Journal of Experimental Psychology: Learning, Memory, and Cognition, 16,* 484–496.

Chaplin, W. G., John, O. P., & Goldberg, L. R. (1988). Conceptions of states and traits: Dimensional attributes with ideals as prototypes. *Journal of Personality and Social Psychology, 54,* 541–557.

Chapman, L. J., & Chapman, J. P. (1969). Illusory correlation as an obstacle to the use of valid psychodynamic signs. *Journal of Abnormal Psychology, 74,* 272–280.

Charniak, E., & McDermott, D. (1985). *Introduction to artificial intelligence.* Reading, MA: Addison-Wesley.

Chiesi, H. L., Spilich, G. J., & Voss, J. F. (1979). Acquisition of domain-related information in relation to high- and low-domain knowledge. *Journal of Verbal Learning and Verbal Behavior, 18,* 257–273.

Cohen, C. E. (1981). Goals and schemata in person perception: Making sense from the stream of behavior. In N. Cantor & J. F. Kihlstron (Eds.), *Personality, cognition, and social interaction* (pp. 45–68). Hillsdale, NJ: Lawrence Erlbaum Associates.

Cohen, B., & Murphy, G. L. (1984). Models of concepts. *Cognitive Science, 8,* 27–58.

Craik, F. I. M., & Tulving, E. (1975). Depth of processing and the retention of words in episodic memory. *Journal of Experimental Psychology: General, 104,* 268–294.

de Kleer, J., & Brown, J. S. (1984). A qualitative physics based on confluences. *Artificial Intelligence, 24,* 7–83.

diSessa, A. A. (1983). Phenomenology and the evolution of intuition. In D. Gentner & A. L. Stevens (Eds.), *Mental models* (pp. 15–33). Hillsdale, NJ: Lawrence Erlbaum Associates.

Dougherty, J. W. D., & Keller, C. M. (1985). Taskonomy: A practical approach to knowledge structures. In J. W. D. Dougherty (Ed.), *Directions in cognitive anthropology* (pp. 161–174). Urbana: University of Illinois Press.

Estes, W. K. (1986). Array models for category learning. *Cognitive Psychology, 18,* 500–549.

Fehr, B., & Russell, J. A. (1984). Concept of emotion viewed from a prototype perspective. *Journal of Experimental Psychology: General, 113,* 464–486.

Fillmore, C. J. (1968). The case for case. In E. Bach & R. Harms (Eds.), *Universals in linguistic theory* (pp. 1–88). New York: Holt, Rinehart, & Winston.

Fillmore, C. J. (1977). The case for case reopened. In P. Cole & J. M. Sadock (Eds.), *Syntax and semantics, Vol. 8. Grammatical relations* (pp. 59–81). San Diego: Academic Press.

Fillmore, C. J. (1984). Lexical semantics and text semantics. In J. E. Copeland (Ed.), *New directions in linguistics and semantics* (pp. 123–147). Houston: Rice University Studies.

Fillmore, C. J. (1985). Frames and the semantics of understanding. *Quaderni di Semantica, 6,* 222–255.

Flannigan, M. J., Fried, L. S., & Holyoak, K. J. (1986). Distributional expectations and the induction of category structure. *Journal of Experimental Psychology: Learning, Memory, and Cognition, 12,* 241–256.

Fodor, J. A. (1983). *The modularity of mind.* Cambridge: MIT Press.

Fodor, J. A., & Pylyshyn, Z. W. (1988). Connectionism and cognitive architecture: A critical analysis. *Cognition, 28,* 3–71

Forbus, K. D. (1984). Qualitative process theory. *Artificial Intelligence, 24,* 85–168.

Gentner, D. (1989). The mechanisms of analogical learning. In S. Vosniadou & A. Ortony (Eds.), *Similarity and analogical reasoning* (pp. 199–241). New York: Cambridge University Press.

Glass, A. L., & Holyoak, K. J. (1975). Alternate conceptions of semantic memory. *Cognition, 3,* 313–339.

Gleik, J. (1987). *Chaos: Making a new science.* New York: Penguin.

Gleitman, L. R., & Gleitman, H. (1970). *Phrase and paraphrase: Some innovative uses of language.* New York: Norton.

Gluck, M. A., & Bower, G. H. (1988). Evaluating an adaptive network model of human learning. *Journal of Memory and Language, 27,* 166–195.

Goldstone, R. L., Medin, D. L., & Gentner, D. (1991). Relations, attributes, and the non-independence of features in similarity judgments. *Cognitive Psychology, 23,* 222–262.

Goodman, N. (1955). *Fact, fiction, and forecast.* Cambridge, MA: Harvard University Press.

Grandy, R. E. (1987). In defense of semantic fields. In E. Le Pore (Ed.), *New directions in semantics* (pp. 259–280). San Diego: Academic Press.

Halff, H. M., Ortony, A., & Anderson, R. C. (1976). A context-sensitive representation of word meanings. *Memory & Cognition, 4,* 378–383.

Hampton, J. A. (1979). Polymorphous concepts in semantic memory. *Journal of Verbal Learning and Verbal Behavior, 18,* 441–461.

Hampton, J. A. (1982). A demonstration of intransitivity in natural concepts. *Cognition, 12,* 151–164.

Hampton, J. A. (1983). Overextension of conjunctive concepts: Evidence for a unitary model of concept typicality and class inclusion. *Journal of Experimental Psychology: Learning, Memory, and Cognition, 14,* 12–32.

Hayes, P. J. (1979). The logic of frames. In D. Metzing (Ed.), *Frame conceptions and frame understanding* (pp. 46–61). Berlin: Walter de Gruyter.

Hayes, P. J. (1985). Naive physics I: Ontology for liquids. In J. R. Hobbs & R. C. Moore (Eds.), *Formal theories of the common sense world* (pp. 71–107). Norwood, NJ: Ablex.

Hayes-Roth, B., & Hayes-Roth, F. (1977). Concept learning and the recognition and classification of exemplars. *Journal of Verbal Learning and Verbal Behavior, 16,* 321–328.

Hintzman, D. L. (1986). "Schema abstraction" in a multiple-trace memory model. *Psychological Review, 93,* 411–428.

Holland, J. H. (1975). *Adaptation in natural and artificial systems.* Ann Arbor: University of Michigan Press.

Homa, D. (1978). Abstraction of ill-defined form. *Journal of Experimental Psychology: Human Learning and Memory, 4,* 407–416.

Jackendoff, R. (1987). The status of thematic relations in linguistic theory. *Linguistic Inquiry, 18,* 369–411.

Jacoby, L. L., & Brooks, L. R. (1984). Nonanalytic cognition: Memory, perception, and concept learning. In G. H. Bower (Ed.), *The psychology of learning and motivation: Advances in research and theory* (Vol. 18, pp. 1–47). San Diego, Academic Press.

Johnson-Laird, P. N. (1983). *Mental models.* Cambridge, MA: Harvard University Press.

Just, M. A., & Carpenter, P. A. (1987). *The psychology of reading and language comprehension.* Boston: Allyn & Bacon.

Kahneman, D., & Miller, D. T. (1986). Norm theory: Comparing reality to its alternatives. *Psychological Review, 93,* 136–153.

Kahneman, D., Slovic, P., & Tversky, A. (Eds.) (1982). *Judgment under uncertainty: Heuristics and biases.* San Diego: Cambridge University Press.

Katz, J. (1972). *Semantic theory.* New York: Harper & Row.

Keil, F. C. (1979). *Semantic and conceptual development: An ontological perspective.* Cambridge, MA: Harvard University Press.

Keil, F. C. (1981). Constraints on knowledge and cognitive development. *Psychological Review, 88,* 197–227.

Kendler, T. S., & Kendler, H. H. (1970). An ontogeny of optional shift behavior. *Child Development, 41,* 1–27.

Kintsch, W., & van Dijk, T. A. (1978). Toward a model of text comprehension and production. *Psychological Review, 85,* 363–394.

Kittay, E. F. (1987). *Metaphor: Its cognitive force and linguistic structure.* Oxford: Oxford University Press.

Lakoff, G. (1987). *Women, fire, and dangerous things: What categories reveal about the mind.* Chicago: University of Chicago Press.

Lehrer, A. (1974). *Semantic fields and lexical structure.* New York: American Elsevier.

Lenat, D. B., & Guha, R. V. (1989). *Building large knowledge-based systems: Representation and inference in the Cyc project.* Reading, MA: Addison-Wesley.

Logan, G. D. (1988). Toward an instance theory of automatization. *Psychological Review, 95,* 494–527.

Loken, B., & Ward, J. (1990). *Alternative approaches to understanding the determinants of typicality. Journal of Consumer Research, 17,* 111–126

Lyons, J. (1977). *Semantics (Vol. 1).* New York: Cambridge University Press.

Malt, B. C., & Smith, E. E. (1984). Correlated properties in natural categories. *Journal of Verbal Learning and Verbal Behavior, 23,* 250–269.

Markus, H., Smith, J., & Moreland, R. L. (1985). Role of the self-concept in the perception of others. *Journal of Personality and Social Psychology, 49,* 1494–1512.

McClelland, J. L., Rumelhart, D. E. (1985). Distributed memory and the representation of general and specific information. *Journal of Experimental Psychology: General, 114,* 159–188.

McClelland, J. L., Rumelhart, D. E., & the PDP Research Group (1986). *Parallel distributed processing: Explorations in the microstructure of cognition. Vol. 2: Psychological and biological models.* Cambridge: MIT Press.

McCloskey, M., Glucksberg, S. (1979). Decision processes in verifying category membership statements: Implications for models of semantic memory. *Cognitive Psychology, 11*, 1–37.

Medin, D. L. (1975). A theory of context in discrimination learning. In G. H. Bower (Ed.), *The psychology of learning and motivation: Advances in research and theory* (Vol. 9, pp. 263–314).

Medin, D. L. (1976). Theories of discrimination learning and learning set. In W. K. Estes (Ed.), *Handbook of learning and cognitive processes* (pp. 131–169). Hillsdale, NJ: Lawrence Erlbaum Associates.

Medin, D. L., Altom, M. W., Edelson, S. M., & Freko, D. (1982). Correlated symptoms and simulated medical classification. *Journal of Experimental Psychology: Learning, Memory, and Cognition, 8,* 37–50.

Medin, D. L., & Barsalou, L. W. (1987). Categorization processes and categorical perception. In S. Harnad (Ed.), *Categorical perception: The groundwork of cognition* (pp. 455–490). New York: Cambridge University Press.

Medin, D. L., Goldstone, R. L., & Gentner, D. (1990). Similarity involving attributes and relations: Judgments of similarity and difference are not inverses. *Psychological Science, 1, 64–69.*

Medin, D. L., & Ross, B. H. (1989). The specific character of abstract thought: Categorization, problem-solving, and induction. In R. J. Sternberg (Ed.), *Advances in the psychology of human intelligence* (Vol. 5, pp. 189–223). Hillsdale, NJ: Lawrence Erlbaum Associates.

Medin, D. L., & Schaffer, M. M. (1978). A context theory of classification learning. *Psychological Review, 85,* 207–238.

Medin, D. L., & Shoben, E. J. (1988). Context and structure in conceptual combination. *Cognitive Psychology, 20,* 158–190.

Meyer, D. E. (1970). On the representation and retrieval of stored semantic information. *Cognitive Psychology, 1,* 242–299.

Miller, G. A., & Johnson-Laird, P. N. (1976). *Language and perception.* Cambridge, MA: Harvard University Press.

Minksy, M. L. (1977). A framework for representing knowledge. In P. H. Winston (Ed.), *The psychology of computer vision* (pp. 211–277). New York: McGraw-Hill.

Minsky, M. L. (1985). *The society of mind.* New York: Simon & Schuster.

Murphy, G. L. (1988). Comprehending complex concepts. *Cognitive Science, 12,* 529–562.

Murphy, G. L. (1990). Noun phrase interpretation and conceptual combination. *Journal of Memory and Language, 29,* 259–288.

Murphy, G. L., & Medin, D. L. (1985). The role of theories in conceptual coherence. *Psychological Review, 92,* 289–316.

Murphy, G. L., & Wisniewski, E. J. (1989). Feature correlations in conceptual representations. In G. Tiberghien (Ed.), *Advances in cognitive science, Volume 2: Theory and applications* (pp. 23–45). Chichister: Ellis Harwood.

Norman, D. A., & Rumelhart, D. E. (1975). *Explorations in cognition.* New York: W. H. Freeman.

Nosofsky, R. M. (1984). Choice, similarity, and the context theory of classification. *Journal of Experimental Psychology: Learning, Memory, and Cognition, 10,* 104–114.

Posner, M. I., & Keele, S. (1968). On the genesis of abstract ideas. *Journal of Experimental Psychology, 77,* 353–363.

Read, S. J., Jones, D. K., & Miller, L. C. (1990). Traits as goal-based categories: The importance of goals in the coherence of dispositional categories. *Journal of Personality and Social Psychology, 58,* 1048–1061.

Rosch, E. H., & Mervis, C. B. (1975). Family resemblances: Studies in the internal structure of categories. *Cognitive Psychology, 7,* 573–605.

Rosch, E. H., Mervis, C. B., Gray, W. D., Johnson, D. M., & Boyes-Braem, P. (1975). *Basic objects in natural categories.* Working Paper No. 43, Language Behavior Research Library, University of California, Berkeley.

Rosch, E. H., Mervis, C. B., Gray, W. D., Johnson, D. M., & Boyes-Braem, P. (1976). Basic objects in natural categories. *Cognitive Psychology, 8,* 382–439.

Ross, B. H. (1981). The more, the better? Number of decisions as a determinant of memorability. *Memory & Cognition, 9,* 23–33.

Ross, B. H., Perkins, S. J., & Tenpenny, P. L. (1990). Reminding-based category learning. *Cognitive Psychology, 22,* 460–492.

Ross, B. H., & Spalding, T. L. (1991). Some influences of instance comparisons in concept formation. In D. Fisher & M. Pazzani (Eds.), *Computational approaches to concept formation.* San Mateo, CA: Morgan Kaufmann.

Rumelhart, D. E., McClelland, J. L., & the PDP Research Group (1986). *Parallel distributed processing: Explorations in the microstructure of cognition. Vol. 1: Foundations.* Cambridge: MIT Press.

Rumelhart, D. E., & Ortony, A. (1978). The representation of knowledge in memory. In R. C. Anderson, R. J. Spiro, & W. E. Montague (Eds.), *Schooling and the acquisition of knowledge.* Hillsdale, NJ: Lawrence Erlbaum Associates.

Rumelhart, D. E., Smolensky, P., McClelland, J. L., & Hinton, G. E. (1986). Schemata and sequential thought processes in PDP models. In J. L. McClelland, D. E. Rumelhart, & the PDP Research Group, *Parallel distributed processing: Explorations in the microstructure of cognition. Vol. 2: Psychological and biological models.* Cambridge: MIT Press.

Schank, R. C. (1975). *Conceptual information processing.* Amsterdam: North-Holland.

Schank, R. C. (1982). *Dynamic memory: A theory of reminding and learning in computers and people.* New York: Cambridge University Press.

Schank, R. C., & Abelson, R. P. (1977). *Scripts, goals, plans, and understanding: An inquiry into human knowledge structures.* Hillsdale, NJ: Lawrence Erlbaum Associates.

Shepard, R. N. (1974). Representation of structure in similarity data: Problems and prospects. *Psychometrika, 39,* 373–421.

Shiffrin, R. M., & Schneider, W. (1977). Controlled and automatic human information processing II: Perceptual learning, automatic attending, and a general theory. *Psychological Review, 84,* 127–190.

Smith, E. E. (1978). Theories of semantic memory. In W. K. Estes (Ed.), *Handbook of learning and cognitive processes. Vol. 6. Linguistic functions in cognitive theory* (pp. 1–56). Hillsdale, NJ: Lawrence Erlbaum Associates.

Smith, E. E., Osherson, D. N., Rips, L. J., & Keane, M. (1988). Combining prototypes: A selective modification model. *Cognitive Science, 12,* 485–528.

Smith, E. E., Shoben, E. J., & Rips, L. J. (1974). Structure and process in semantic memory: A featural model for semantic decisions. *Psychological Review, 81,* 214–241.

Spilich, G. J., Vesonder, G. T., Chiesi, H. L., & Voss, J. F. (1979). Text processing of domain-related information for individuals with high- and low-domain knowledge. *Journal of Verbal Learning and Verbal Behavior, 18,* 275–290.

Sutherland, N. S., & Mackintosh, N. J. (1971). *Mechanisms of animal discrimination learning.* New York: Academic Press.

Stein, N. L. (1982). What's in a story: Interpreting the interpretation of story grammars. *Discourse Processes, 5,* 319–335.

Stein, N. L., Kilgore, K., & Albro, E. (1990). The development of the story concept. Under review.

Stein, N. L., & Levine, L. J. (1990). Making sense out of emotion: The representation and use of goal-structured knowledge. In N. L. Stein, B. Levanthal, T. Trabasso (Eds.), *Psychological and biological approaches to emotion* (pp. 45–73). Hillsdale, NJ: Lawrence Erlbaum Associates.

Stein, N. L., & Trabasso, T. (1982). What's in a story: An approach to comprehension and instruction. In R. Glaser (Ed.), *Advances in instructional psychology* (Vol. 2). Hillsdale, NJ: Lawrence Erlbaum Associates.

Tanenhaus, M. K., & Carlson, G. (1989). Lexical structure and lexical comprehension. In W. D. Marslen-Wilson (Ed.), *Lexical representation and processing* (pp. 529–562). Cambridge: MIT Press.

Tanenhaus, M. K., Carlson, G., & Trueswell, J. C. (1989). The role of thematic structures in interpretation and parsing. *Language and Cognitive Processes*.

Thorndyke, P. W., & Hayes-Roth, B. (1979). The use of schemata in the acquisition and transfer of knowledge. *Cognitive Psychology, 11,* 82–106.

Trabasso, T., & Bower, G. H. (1968). *Attention in learning: Theory and research.* New York: Wiley.

Trabasso, T., & Sperry, L. L. (1985). The causal basis for deciding importance of story events. *Journal of Memory and Language, 24,* 595–611.

Trabasso, T., & van den Broek, P. (1985). Causal thinking and story comprehension. *Journal of Memory and Language, 24,* 612–630.

Trabasso, T., van den Broek, P., & Suh, S. Y. (1989). Logical necessity and transitivity of causal relations in stories. *Discourse Processes, 12,* 1–25.

Tversky, A. (1977). Features of similarity. *Psychological Review, 84,* 327–352.

Tversky, B., & Hemenway, K. (1985). Objects, parts, and categories. *Journal of Experimental Psychology: General, 113,* 169–193.

Watkins, M. J., & Kerkar, S. P. (1985). Recall of a twice-presented item without recall of either presentation: Generic memory for events. *Journal of Memory and Language, 24,* 666–678.

Wilkins, W. (Ed.) (1988). *Syntax and semantics, Vol. 21. Thematic relations.* San Diego: Academic Press.

Winston, M. E., Chaffin, R., & Herrmann, D. (1987). A taxonomy of part–whole relations. *Cognitive Science, 11, 417–444.*

Wisniewski, E., & Medin, D. L. (1991). Harpoons and long sticks: The interaction of theory and similarity in rule induction. In D. Fisher & M. Pazzani (Eds.), *Computational approaches to concept formation.* San Mateo, CA: Morgan Kaufmann.

Wyer, R. S. Jr., & Srull, T. K. (1986). Human cognition in its social context. *Psychological Review, 93,* 322–359.

2 Toward a Frame-Based Lexicon: The Semantics of RISK and its Neighbors

Charles J. Fillmore
University of California, Berkeley

Beryl T. Atkins
Oxford University Press

In these pages we present some initial results of a large-scale inquiry into a semantic field centered in the English lexeme RISK.[1] The kind of description we seek to justify could not easily be represented in a standard print dictionary, for reasons that soon become clear, but we imagine, for some distant future, an on-line lexical resource, which we can refer to as a "frame-based" dictionary, which will be adequate to our aims. In such a dictionary (housed on a workstation with multiple windowing capabilities), individual word senses, relationships among the senses of polysemous words, and relationships between (senses of) semantically related words will be linked with the cognitive structures (or "frames"), knowledge of which is presupposed for the concepts encoded by the words. A user's keying in of a word to be looked up will cause a window to appear that will display relationships between particular lexical meanings and specific lexico-syntactic patterns. Each of these lexico-syntactic patterns will have its components indexed with specific parts or aspects of the associated frame. The language used in the description of this indexing will contain category names founded on the characteristics of the relevant underlying frames. Accompanying each such description will be provided the means for giving the user access to descriptions of the associated conceptual frames, allowing the user who wishes to be reminded of the properties of the frames associated with a given word to open an additional window that presents information about it, and which identi-

---

[1]The main product of that larger work is Fillmore and Atkins (forthcoming). The authors are indebted to the computational facilities of the Institute of Cognitive Studies at the University of California, Berkeley; to IBM, Hawthorne, for providing the concordance lines, and the American Publishing House for the Blind for the use of the APHB corpus.

fies those categories derived from the frame that are used in the meaning descriptions.[2]

The frame descriptions will themselves contain pointers allowing access to other expressions in the language whose meanings are founded on the same schema, thus giving the system the character of a thesaurus as well.

The dictionary must be, in principle, capable of allowing its users access to *all* the information that speakers possess about the words in their language; that is, it will not be limited by the usual space and marketability concerns that constrain decision making in the production of traditional commercial dictionaries. Nor can the type of dictionary imagined here be constructed, directly or indirectly, from the information contained in even a very large collection of existing commercial dictionaries. One reason for this is that the necessary links to the background frames are generally not made available in print dictionaries. Another reason is that research into the lexicon inevitably uncovers much more information about words than standard dictionaries have room for.

FRAME SEMANTICS VERSUS SEMANTIC FIELD THEORIES

The methods and assumptions behind "frame semantics" are different in a number of respects from those associated with familiar theories of semantic fields. Semantic analyses within field theories posit systems of paradigmatic and syntagmatic relationships connecting members of selected sets of lexical items. A major activity for lexical semanticists influenced by the field notion is that of cataloguing the kind of interitem relations that can be defined for the elements of a lexicon, and characterizing the kinds of lexical sets that are structured in terms of such relationships.[3]

Semantic theories founded on the notion of *cognitive frames* or *knowledge schemata*,[4] by contrast, approach the description of lexical meaning in a quite different way. In such theories, a word's meaning can be understood only with reference to a structured background of experience, beliefs, or practices, con-

---

[2]The frame descriptions exemplified in this chapter are intuitive and informal, though the possibility of making them more precise, or of reducing them to a well-defined set of semantic primitives, is not ruled out. The purpose of the frame descriptions in the kind of practical dictionary we have in mind is to inform the user of the concepts needed for understanding the categories. It may not matter whether this is done through diagrams or animation, prose descriptions of states of affairs, or appeals to common human experiences.

[3]Perhaps the most detailed survey of such relationships can be found in D. A. Cruse (1986), *Lexical Semantics* (Cambridge Textbooks in Linguistics).

[4]Some writers make clear distinctions among such words as "frame," "schema," "scenario," "knowledge structure," and the like. For the use we put these notions to, such distinctions play no role.

stituting a kind of conceptual prerequisite for understanding the meaning. Speakers can be said to know the meaning of the word only by first understanding the background frames that motivate the concept that the word encodes. Within such an approach, words or word senses are not related to each other directly, word to word,[5] but only by way of their links to common background frames and indications of the manner in which their meanings highlight particular elements of such frames.

A Simple Example: Day Names

As an example of one such background frame, we can ask what is necessary for understanding the names of the days of the week. In a semantic field approach, one could say of the English words MONDAY, TUESDAY, WEDNESDAY, etc. that they comprise a closed class of words, related to each other by the *successor* relation, a relation that in this case defines a *cycle*. The terms in the set can then be said to be interdefinable, with reference to their position in the cycle as established by the relationship, and by means of the "part of" relationship that each of them holds to another word, WEEK, which names the entire cycle.

A frame-based description of these same words would concentrate on the manner of their fit into the complete system of *calendric terms.*[6] What holds such words together is the fact of their being motivated by, founded on, and costructured with a specific schematization of experience. In the case of the weekday names and other related words, we can appeal to a frame made up of knowledge about (a) the natural cycle created by the daily apparent travels of the sun, (b) the standard means of reckoning when one day cycle ends and the next one begins, (c) the conventional calendric cycle of 7 days, with a subconvention specifying the beginning member of the cycle, and (d) the practice in our culture of assigning different portions of the weekly cycle to work and nonwork.

An implicit awareness of this particular organization of our physical and social world provides the conceptual background for a fairly large body of lexical material, including common nouns like WEEK and DAY, their adjectival derivatives, the individual weekday names, and a small number of special categories such as WEEKDAY, WEEK-END, and FORTNIGHT. This particular subsystem articulates with other calendric structures such as that of the MONTH and the

---

[5]The discussion about "words" and "word senses" could be made more precise if we were to use the term *lexical unit* to refer to the pairing of a particular "lexeme" (a family of lexical variants) with a particular sense. We allow ourselves the risk of being occasionally misunderstood, because (1) for the most part readers will probably be able to understand our intentions, and (2) we do not wish to bring to the reader's mind Cruse's prejudices (1986, p. 80) about the irrelevance of polysemy structures to lexical semantic description.

[6]The discussion about calendric terms follows closely the language used in Fillmore's "Frames and the semantics of understanding," *Quaderni di Semantica* (1985, pp. 223f).

larger cycle, the YEAR, definable (in one way) as the cycle comprising a sequence of months. Any description of the structure and meaning of a phraseological unit such as as "Friday, February 23rd, 1990" must appeal to this whole set of interconnected notions.

Commercial Transaction Verbs

The frame semantic descriptions we seek to develop need to be integrated into a theory of the lexicon within which grammatical and semantic information come packaged together. Each lexical item, or idiomatized phrase, can be associated with what can be called its *valence description,* a description that specifies, in both semantic and syntactic terms, what the expression requires of its constituents and its context, and what it contributes to the structures that contain it. The most developed systems of valence descriptions concern the grammar and meanings of verbs. A clear example involving semantically related verbs with difference valences can be provided for the domain of commercial transactions.

We can characterize the *commercial transaction frame,* informally, by constructing a scenario in which one person acquires control or possession of something from a second person, by agreement, as a result of surrendering to that person a sum of money. The needed background requires an understanding of property ownership, a money economy, implicit contract, and a great deal more. This schema incorporates ("inherits") many of the structural properties of a simple exchange frame, but it adds to that base a number of further specifications regarding ownership, contractual acts, and the trappings of a money economy.

The categories derivable from the commercial transaction frame that are needed for describing the lexical meanings linked to it include, in the first instance, *Buyer, Seller, Goods,* and *Money,* the essential props and players in any commercial event scene. With respect to the simple category *Money,* we find it necessary, in a careful analysis, to distinguish the monetary value of the goods as determined by the Seller (or negotiated between Seller and Buyer) from the amount of money the Buyer actually transmits to the seller. From this we derive such secondary categories as *Cost, Tender,* and *Change.* (The difference between the Cost and the Tender is the Change.) Further elaborations of the scenario, for structurally more complex members of the lexical field, have to do with negotiations of the cost ("bargaining," "discount"), differences between the time of the Goods-transfer and the time of the Money-transfer ("credit"), the possibility of total or piecemeal transfer of money ("time payment"), the difference between price and value, the difference between the value of the tender and the actual physical currency that is tendered, and so on.

A display of some of the primary verbs in this lexical field, and the manner in which the grammar of active sentences built around them allows expression of the categories taken from the frame, is given in Table 2.1. For each verb or verb use (given as row headings), the table simultaneously shows (as column head-

TABLE 2.1
The Semantic and Syntactic Valence (Active Voice) of the Verbs from the
Commercial Transaction Frame

	Buyer	Seller	Goods	Money
BUY	Subj	(from)	D-Obj	(for)
SELL	(to)	Subj	D-Obj	(for)
CHARGE	(I-Obj)	Subj	(for)	D-Obj
SPEND	Subj	NULL	for/on	D-Obj
PAY	Subj	[I-Obj]	[for]	D-Obj
PAY	Subj	(to)	for	D-Obj
COST	(I-Obj)	NULL	Subj	D-Obj

ings) the elements of the commercial transaction frame that must or may be given linguistic realization, and (in the cells) the nature of such realizations.[7] The word "subject" in a cell indicates that, in the use of the verb represented by its row, the verb's subject represents the category labeled by its column. "D-Obj" means "direct object" and "I-Obj" means "indirect object" (i.e., the first member of a double-object construction). A preposition in a cell means that the indicated elements can be represented by a preposition phrase headed by that preposition. Parentheses signal optionality; square brackets signal omissibility under conditions of "definite" anaphora (i.e., in a context in which the identity of the object representing the category is "given" in the conversational context). Looking at the SPEND row in Table 2.1, we can construct a sentence of the type *Harry spent twenty dollars on a new tie.* The Buyer is represented as the subject, the Money as the direct object, and the optional mention of the Goods is marked with the preposition ON. The Seller cannot be introduced into the sentence (hence the entry NULL in the Seller cell for SPEND). (There is a difference (not revealed in the table) between FOR and ON, the former requiring the understanding that the exchange took place.)

THE RISK FRAME

Whereas our main concern in this chapter is the single word RISK, the family of words that are the object of the larger research effort are all of those English words whose semantic descriptions share some reference to *the possibility of an unwelcome outcome.* These are words that are understandable only to someone who is capable of realizing that the future is uncertain, and that among the alternative possible futures that one faces are some that one might not want.

---

[7]The table is intended as a simple demonstration of the kinds of information needed: The reality is a bit more complex; for example, the nominal complement of COST is not strictly speaking a direct object.

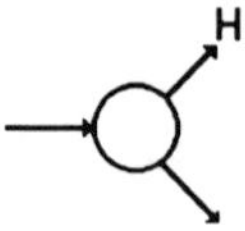

FIG. 2.1.   Risk-running.

The words in this set include: RISK, DANGER, PERIL, HAZARD, VENTURE, etc.; their neighbors in semantic space, words like GAMBLE, INVEST, EXPOSE, etc.; and derivatives of all of these, VENTURESOME, RISKY, INVESTMENT, PERILOUSLY, etc. The whole set includes verbs, nouns, adjectives, adverbs, and conventionalized phrases.

The vocabulary items considered here all fit into what we can call the RISK frame, as do the individual meanings of the polysemous word RISK. The RISK frame crucially involves two notions—Chance and Harm—that we can represent with diagrams borrowed from *decision theorists*.[8] The diagrams make use of nonlooping directed graphs with unidirectional paths whose nodes are circles or squares, each having two or more exiting paths. The circles represent *chance* and the squares represent *choice*. The circles, or chance nodes, are associated with possibilities, and for all the word meanings in our set, one of the paths leading from the chance node leads to an undesirable state of affairs, which we refer to as *Harm*, and the probability of entering this path is assumed to be greater than zero (i.e., there is a chance of encountering Harm) but less than one (i.e., there is a chance of avoiding it).

The RISK frame requires two subframes, depending on whether the language accessing it does or does not explicitly represent the state of being at risk as resulting from someone's action. When we need to represent the idea of simply being *in danger*, or *at risk*, we will only need a graph containing a chance node leading to Harm (represented by "H"), as in Fig. 2.1 ("Risk-Running"). But many of the words in our set involve somebody *making a choice*, with that choice leading to the possibility of Harm, as in Fig. 2.2 ("Risk-Taking"). Because Fig. 2.1 is a subpart of Fig. 2.2, it is shown that all instances of *taking* risks include instances of *running* risks. The "deciding actor" feature is "marked" in the case of risk-taking, unmarked in the case of risk-running.[9]

Within decision theory the person who is seen as choosing a path that leads to the possibility of harm has in mind a Goal, and the decision is one that opens a path for which there is both the possibility of achieving that goal and the possibility of encountering harm instead. We could represent that by putting "G" for

---

[8]We became aware of the notation through Daniel Kahneman. A standard reference on decision theory that uses this notation is Raiffa (1970).

[9]The labels have proved helpfully mnemonic, but the difference between the English phrases "run a risk" and "take a risk" appear to be somewhat more complicated than is suggested here. More details are available in Fillmore and Atkins (forthcoming).

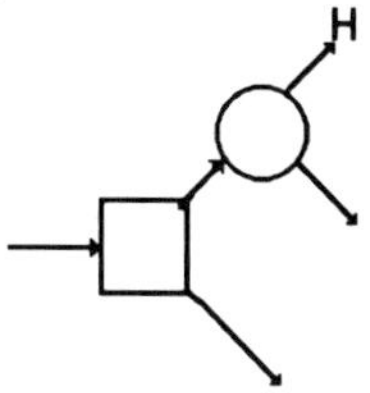

FIG. 2.2.   Risk-taking.

goal at the end of the second arrow exiting from the chance circle in Fig. 2.2.[10] In the semantics of RISK as an English word, however, the presence of a Goal is not a necessary component; hence it is not represented in Fig. 2.2.[11]

The choices and possibilities, and the negatively and positively valued alternative outcomes, make up part of the basic scenarios associated with RISK, somewhat analogously to the understandings we have of the basic outlines of the commercial transaction scenario. Corresponding to the categories defined within that scenario—Buyer, Seller, Money, Goods, Tender, Cost, Change, and the rest—we now describe the categories that will prove useful in a valence description of RISK and its semantic companions.

THE CATEGORIES

The categories that we propose for these purposes are the following:[12]

Chance: the uncertainty about the future (represented by the circles in Figs. 2.1 and 2.2). This notion can be expressed linguistically as a noun like CHANCE or POSSIBILITY, or, making it explicit that Harm is a possible outcome with the set of words under examination, the nouns RISK or DANGER.[13]

---

[10]In this description, the risk-taker's aims have been labeled *Goal*. Some further discriminations are introduced later, including *Gain* (what the risk-taker hopes to acquire), *Purpose* (what the risk-taker hopes to do), and *Beneficiary* (the person the risk-taker wishes to benefit).

[11]But see Fig. 2.3 later.

[12]We are not completely happy with the labels we have chosen for the categories. In several cases words were rejected so as not to duplicate initial letters, because we wanted to use single upper-case letters in our abbreviated notations. For *Deed* we might have preferred *Act*, but we need "A" for *Actor;* for *Harm* we might have preferred *Damage*, but we need D for *Deed*. *Valued Object* is inconvenient, but all the alternatives we could think of (Assets, Capital, Fortune, Property, Treasure and Wealth) brought their own difficulties.

[13]That the noun RISK is clearly associated with Harm can be seen by comparing the two sentences, "There's a possibility that the coin will come up heads" and "There's a risk that the coin will come up heads." In the latter sentence, the "coming up heads" possibility is presented as reason for worry.

Harm: a potential unwelcome development (the outcome labeled "H" in Fig. 2.1 and 2.2). The two categories Chance and Harm make up the core of our understanding of all the words in our set. The Harm can be linguistically expressed as a nominal object or gerundial complement of the verb RISK (e.g., RISK DEATH, RISK LOSING MY JOB), as a clausal complement to the nouns RISK and DANGER (e.g., THE RISK THAT SHE WILL LEAVE ME), or as a nominal of a gerundial object of the preposition OF complementing the nouns RISK and DANGER (e.g., THE RISK OF DEATH, THE DANGER OF LOSING MY JOB).

Victim: the individual who stands to suffer if the Harm occurs (the person who travels the path leading to the circle in Figs. 2.1 and 2.2).

This category can be introduced in a preposition phrase headed by TO (e.g., THE DANGER TO THE CHILDREN), as the object of certain verbs (e.g., PUT SOMEONE AT RISK, ENDANGER SOMEONE), or as the subject of certain verbs (e.g., HE RUNS THE RISK OF RUINING HIS REPUTATION).

Valued Object: a valued possession of the Victim, seen as potentially endangered. The most typical linguistic presentation of the Valued Object is as the direct object of RISK (e.g., HE RISKED HIS HEALTH IN TAKING THAT JOB), but in some environments it can be introduced as the object of the preposition WITH (e.g., YOU'RE TAKING RISKS WITH YOUR CHILDREN'S LIVES IN DRIVING LIKE THAT) and others in which it can be introduced by TO (e.g., THERE'S A CONSIDERABLE RISK TO OUR HEALTH IN LIVING IN THIS COMMUNITY; it should be noticed that for PUT X AT RISK, X may be either Victim or Valued Object, whereas with RISK, X may only be the Valued Object.).[14]

(Risky) Situation: the state of affairs within which someone might be said to be at risk (represented by the path leading to the circle in Figs. 2.1 and 2.2).

The Situation can be described by an adjective (LIVING NEAR THIS TOXIC WASTE DUMP IS RISKY / HAZARDOUS / DANGEROUS, etc.), or it can be the subject of a sentence expressing the presence of risk, with such predicates as (THIS ACTIVITY) OFFERS CONSIDERABLE RISK / HAS UNKNOWN HAZARDS / INVOLVES LITTLE RISK, etc.

The notions listed so far can all be seen as fitting either Fig. 2.1 or Fig. 2.2. Those that follow, all involving someone making a choice, specifically fit situations representable by Fig. 2.2.

---

[14]There appear to be dialectal differences regarding the use of the reflexive pronoun as the direct object of RISK. "I want the freedom to risk myself" is acceptable in British English but not in American English.

Deed: the act that brings about a risky situation (represented in Fig. 2.2 by the corner of the square connected with the path leading from the square to the circle).

The Deed—the "action" counterpart of the Situation—can be represented in the main clause of a sentence, its risky character represented in an adjunct phrase, as in HE CRITICIZED HIS BOSS AT THE RISK OF LOSING HIS JOB, or it can be subordinated as a gerundial clause, as in THEY RISKED DROWNING (BY) SWIMMING IN THAT PART OF THE RIVER. It can also be represented as a nominal or gerundial object of the verb RISK, as in WE DECIDED TO RISK A TRIP INTO THE JUNGLE and WE DECIDED TO RISK GOING INTO THE JUNGLE.

Actor: the person who performs the Deed that results in the possibility of Harm occurring (the person who makes the decision represented by the square in Fig. 2.2).

In most of the Actor-involved sentences in our collection, the Actor and the Victim are identical (when you "take a risk" you typically endanger yourself), but, as mentioned earlier, there are some expressions indicating situations in which what one person does endangers another: YOU (= Actor) PUT ME (= Victim) AT RISK. (The verb RISK, as noted, appears not to be used in such expressions.)

The following four categories are always secondary components of their clauses, and, because they all concern the Actor's intentions, they are closely related to each other and conceivably permit interparaphrasability (i.e., they may be instances of a single category). Nevertheless, they are included within the category list for the RISK frame because they fit into the RISK schema perfectly, and their presence must be taken as licensed by some but not all senses of the words in our set. They have been separated from each other because of the differences in the grammatical means of their expression; they are all subtypes of what we called *Goal* earlier—roughly, what an Actor has in mind at the time of performing the Deed.

(Intended) Gain: the Actor's hoped-for gain in taking a risk.

It is typically introduced as the object of the preposition FOR (e.g., YOU'VE RISKED YOUR HEALTH FOR A FEW CHEAP THRILLS).

Purpose: what an Actor intends to accomplish in performing the Deed.

In the examples given here, Purpose is represented mainly in the form of "purpose clauses": TO + VP or IN ORDER TO + VP (e.g., YOU RISKED ALL THAT JUST TO MAKE ONE POINT?).

FIG. 2.3. H = Harm, G = Goal,
D = Deed, VO = Valued Object,
V = Victim, A = Actor.

Beneficiary: the person for whose benefit something is done.

This category, too, is most often introduced by FOR (e.g., YOU RISKED YOUR LIFE FOR SOMEONE YOU DON'T EVEN KNOW).

Motivation: the psychological source of the Actor's behavior.

What we are calling Motivation can be expressed with FOR, OUT OF, etc. (e.g., HE RISKED LOSING OUR FRIENDSHIP OUT OF SPITE, SHE RISKED HER HEALTH FOR VANITY).

There is a brute force character to this list, to be sure; but we can at least be sure that the roster of categories needed for describing the meanings and the grammar of the words in our set go far beyond anything envisioned by current theories of thematic roles or deep cases.[15] Our claim is that in describing the meaning of a word we are necessarily engaged in describing the categories expressed by the phrases built up around that word, interpreted against a particular background frame.

Figure 2.3 is intended to give a simple visual representation of the main categories from the preceding list.

SOME RESULTS OF THE STUDY

Our aim was to survey a large corpus of attested uses of RISK in such a way as to be able to say something about the elements of every clause in the corpus in which RISK, as noun or verb, plays a role. The RISK citations used in this study were taken from a 25,000,000-word corpus provided to IBM, Hawthorne, by the American Publishing House for the Blind. The extraction of all the RISK sen-

---

[15]The point is that in a careful description of the semantic roles associated with predicates of most verbs we need "frame-specific" semantic role categories, thus going far beyond the familiar repertories of Agent, Patient, Experiencer, etc., found in much recent discussion of the semantics and grammar of verbs.

tences in the corpus, accomplished through the courtesy of IBM's Roy Byrd and Slava Katz, yielded 1,770 examples. We have recorded, for each sentence in the collection, certain grammatical facts about the target word and the categories from the RISK schema that are represented in the sentence, and the lexical and grammatical means of their representation.[16] The main observations reported later concern the verb, but we have also included certain observations about RISK as a noun.

Observations about Nominal RISK

Noun-phrases with RISK at their head can occur in all the usual syntactic positions (e.g., as subjects of their clauses, as direct or oblique objects of verbs, as prepositional objects in adverbial expressions, and so on). As subjects we found them (1) with predicates indicating the extent or seriousness of the probability of Harm (e.g., THE RISK WAS CONSIDERABLE), and (2) in existential sentences bearing quantifiers (e.g., THERE'S QUITE A BIT OF RISK IN THIS, THERE WAS NO RISK OF FAILURE).

RISK occurred in the predicate-phrase AT RISK (e.g., THESE CHILDREN ARE AT RISK) and in adverbial phrases of the kind AT THE RISK OF X, AT X RISK, WITHOUT RISK, WITHOUT X RISK (OF Y), etc. (e.g., HE INSULTED HIS FATHER AT THE RISK OF LOSING HIS INHERITANCE, YOU COULD WALK THROUGH THE YARD WITHOUT ANY RISK OF BEING NOTICED).

As the phrasal head of the direct object of a verb, the most common cases involved the verbs RUN (107 instances) and TAKE (170 instances). We have found no dictionary that offers an account of the difference between RUN A RISK and TAKE A RISK. (A careful examination of the semantic difference between the two will be given in Fillmore & Atkins, forthcoming.)

There were four main classes of verbs, other than RUN and TAKE, occurring with RISK as direct object. Verbs in the first group represent the Actor's cognitive awareness: *KNOW* THE RISK, *UNDERSTAND* THE RISK, *APPRECIATE* THE RISK, *CALCULATE* THE RISKS. The existence of such examples supports the idea that in some of its uses the noun represents something computable, the computation involving the negative value of the Harm, the positive value of the intended Gain, and the probabilities associated with each. In *BALANCE THE RISKS* we are comparing two such computations. Examples from the corpus are:

> But if, *knowing* the risks, you embark on this outing do you have a claim at all? ⟨427 1259⟩

---

[16]A final working method has not yet been worked out, but the early steps in the analysis were accomplished with dBaseIII on IBM equipment and with the Ingres relational database on a UNIX machine in Berkeley.

"You don't *understand* the risks a police officer takes." ⟨256 3904⟩

No one knows how to *calculate* the risk of a future catastrophe. ⟨224 391⟩

And you had to *balance* its risks against the hazards of pregnancy. ⟨208 677⟩

The verbs of a second group represent acts of avoiding or reducing, such as *AVOID* THE RISK, *MINIMIZE* THE RISK, *ELIMINATE* THE RISK, denoting decisions to select alternative paths to the one leading to Harm, or to reduce the probabilities of getting onto the Harm path. Buying insurance, or not standing under a lone tree in an electric storm, are ways of doing these things. Examples from the corpus are:

The investor who is morbidly preoccupied with *avoiding* risk should stay out of the market altogether. ⟨479 996⟩

Risks of accident at sea can be *minimized* by raising the standards of seamanship. ⟨181 1996⟩

Proceeding by stages, with extreme precautions, we try to *eliminate* the slightest risk of accident or even minor mishap. ⟨5 2587⟩

The verbs in the third class represent the relation between a Situation (as subject) and the probability of Harm, as in *INCURS* RISK, *ENTAILS* RISK, *OFFERS* LITTLE RISK, *INVOLVES* CONSIDERABLE RISK, etc. Examples are:

I recognized that an activist domestic program *involved* great political risks. ⟨313 8⟩

The leveling of incomes *offers* the risk that a comfortable middle class may supply no patrons interested enough in architecture to aspire to the best. ⟨33 107⟩

This manner of presentation *incurs* the risk of rationalizing on the one side and confusion and lack of perspective on the other. ⟨526 184⟩

Cogar realizes, of course, that starting out with so expensive a plant *entails* big risks. ⟨225 332⟩

And the verbs in a fourth group represent the relation between the Victim and the probability of Harm, as in *FACE* THE RISK, *ASSUME* THE RISK, *SHOULDER* THE RISK, *BEAR* THE RISK, and the like. Taking a high deductible on an insurance policy is a decision to face the risks for which the insurance is being purchased. Examples from the corpus:

The only people to remain exposed in the operation are, in theory, the tankers' owners *facing* the risk of Arab reprisals. ⟨154 470⟩

We must *assume* the risks, play according to the rules of the game; and, if it comes at last to that, lose with serenity. ⟨10 1263⟩

There is a growing consensus that the risks of life should not be *borne* by the individual but should be spread through the society. ⟨409 797⟩

RISK as a Verb

There is a great deal to say about RISK as a noun, but the portion of our study that is our main focus here involves the patterns we found with RISK as a verb.

The verb RISK always has either a nominal or a gerundial direct complement. For simplicity's sake, we refer to them both as (direct) objects, distinguishing between them as nominal objects and gerundial objects. There are three main RISK-schema categories represented grammatically as objects: Valued Object, Harm, and Deed. Because the Valued Object is always a "thing," it is represented only by nominal objects; because Harm is an "event" and Deed is an "act," these can be represented verbally (most commonly in gerundial form) or nominally (e.g., as a nominalization of a verbal notion or as a metonym of an event or an act).

Valued Object as Grammatical Object.   As noted, we find the Valued Object element realized only in nominal form (i.e., as a typical direct object). Possibilities for adding to such clauses adjuncts or circumstantial adverbial phrases expressing various other notions include the following:

The Situation can be introduced in a prepositional phrase with IN or ON:

RISK $VO_{\{NP\}}$ $Sit_{\{Prep\ NP\}}$

Valued Object as D-Object, Situation as PP

Examples:

He was being asked to risk
$VO_{\{his\ good\ name\}}$
$Sit_{\{on\ the\ battlefield\ of\ politics\}}$. ⟨14 1532⟩

Others had risked
$VO_{\{all\ \}}$
$Sit_{\{in\ the\ war.\}}$. ⟨344 3678⟩

It would be foolhardy to risk
$VO_{\{human\ lives\ \}}$
$Sit_{\{in\ the\ initial\ space\ flights\}}$. ⟨348 2516⟩

You may find yourself risking
  ^{VO}{ever-greater sums }
  ^{Sit}{*in* ever-more-ambitious campaigns}. ⟨479 3556⟩

The Beneficiary can be indicated with the preposition FOR, or with the phrasal preposition FOR THE SAKE OF:

RISK ^{VO}{NP} ^{Ben}{FOR NP}

Valued Object as D-Object, Beneficiary as PP

Examples:

Why did he risk
  ^{VO}{his life }
  ^{Ben}{*for* a man he did not know}? ⟨359 2583⟩

But specialists in the U.S. State Department . . . declared that there was no point in risking
  ^{VO}{a friendship with 80 million Arabs}
  ^{Ben}{for the sake of a few thousand Jews.} ⟨314 94⟩

The Actor's intended Gain shares with Beneficiary the ability to be marked by the preposition FOR, but it also can be marked by the phrasal preposition IN EXCHANGE FOR):

RISK ^{VO}{NP}^{G}{FOR NP}

Valued Object as Object, Gain as PP

Examples:

The men and women of the French resistance, who had fought the underground and risked
  ^{VO}{everything}
  ^{Gain}{*for* this day} . . . ⟨404 929⟩

It would always be worthwhile, for instance, to risk
  ^{VO}{the Apache}
  ^{Gain}{*in exchange for* a chance to destroy a light cruiser}. ⟨320 89⟩

The Actor's Motivation (in the sense defined earlier) can be marked with the preposition FOR, but also in a number of other ways:

RISK ^{VO}{NP} ^{Mot}{**FOR NP**}

Valued Object as D-Object, Motivation as PP

Examples:

> ready to risk
>> ^{VO}{everything }
>> ^{Mot}{*for* what he believes}. ⟨311 784⟩
>
> She had risked
>> ^{VO}{so much }
>> ^{Mot}{*for* the sake of vanity}. ⟨447 306⟩
>
> I have risked
>> ^{VO}{all that I have}
>> ^{Mot}{*for* this noble cause}. ⟨173 5279⟩
>
> A speculator is someone who has money and is willing to risk
>> ^{VO}{it}
>> ^{Mot}{*in hope of* making more}. ⟨479 3087⟩

A Purpose phrase can be added to a Valued-Object complement, in an infinitive phrase or in a variously marked THAT-clause:

RISK ^{VO}{NP} ^{Purp}{**Infinitive**}

Valued Object as D-Object, Purpose as Infinitival

Examples:

> Why should he risk
>> ^{VO}{his life}
>> ^{Purp}{to try to save Brooks}? ⟨179 851⟩

But he was willing to risk

VO{his neck}

Purp{to make up for fouling things up before}. ⟨301 1945⟩

They . . . considered it worthwhile to risk

VO{a large expeditionary force}

Purp{to get the hero out of the country}. ⟨448 702⟩

How could it be wrong to risk

VO{one's life}

Purp{in order that everyone should be equal}?. ⟨295 1981⟩

He pleaded with the council to send Ireland a bishop who could lead the men and women who were risking

VO{their lives}

Purp{so that their faith could continue to exist}. ⟨338 1589⟩

When the Deed is represented by a Gerund, this can be done either with or without a BY or IN subordinator, as shown in the following two groups:

RISK VO{NP} D{BY/IN Gerund}

Valued Object as D-Object, Deed as PP/Gerund

Examples:

He was unwilling to risk

VO{his newfound independence }

D{*by* invest*ing* in such a dubious concern}. ⟨97 1132⟩

Better be blamed for weak leadership than risk

VO{the cause}

D{*by* attempt*ing* too much}. ⟨344 3083⟩

He had risked

VO{two of his submarines }

D{*by* send*ing* them to the edge of the American beaches}. ⟨507 1894⟩

Never gain did Japan risk

VO{big ships}

D{*in* supply*ing* either New Guinea or cut-off garrisons in the Solomons}. ⟨504 2410⟩

RISK VO{NP} D{Gerund}

Valued Object as D-Object, Deed as Gerund alone

Examples:

No one could doubt his obvious chagrin at not being able to risk
VO{his neck }
D{ jump*ing* horses over fences}. ⟨143 432⟩

. . . the unknown ordinary people who risked
VO{their lives}
D{carry*ing* messages between the lines}. ⟨387 1078⟩

The corpus contained one example of the Deed expressed infinitivally.

RISK VO{NP} D{Infinitive}

Examples:

he had risked
VO{his life}
D{to guide them}. ⟨83 3308⟩

Harm as Grammatical Object.   The second major role expressible as a nominal or gerundial direct complement is Harm. With nominal expression, we have these:

RISK H{NP}

Harm as D-Object, no adjuncts.

Examples:

Not wanting to risk
H{any repetition of the Cuban crisis}, . . . ⟨60 750⟩

Leafy vegetables can be consumed without risking
H{a great weight gain}. ⟨184 137⟩

The board was risking
H{a liquidity crisis}. ⟨326 286⟩

Scholars were unwilling to risk
H{the loss of the benefits they were receiving from the Manchu invaders}. ⟨336 603⟩

Don't try to touch the kitten; you'll only risk
H{a bite}. ⟨499 1611⟩

The gerundial Harm complement of RISK can be either phrasal (its subject interpreted as the subject or RISK) or clausal.

RISK H{Gerund}

Harm as Gerundial Object, no adjuncts

Examples:

The paper is too successful and risks
H{becoming complacent}. ⟨46 875⟩

Any moderate risked
H{being called a traitor}. ⟨97 1765⟩

He could not risk
H{being discharged}. ⟨159 910⟩

He could not risk
H{Walters going over to Brady}. ⟨99 2077⟩

I would merely risk
H{the court making a mistake and finding me guilty}. ⟨393 244⟩

Adjuncts capable of accompanying the Harm-indicating complement include Deed, expressible as IN + Gerund, and Purpose, expressible as an infinitival verb phrase optionally introduced by the complex preposition IN ORDER TO.

RISK ^{H}{NP/Gerund} ^{D}{IN Gerund}

Harm as Object, Deed as IN-Gerund

Examples:

> Rather than risk
>
> ^{H}{wak*ing* Peggy}
>
> ^{D}{*in* search*ing* for my pajamas},
>
> I crept into bed in my underpants. ⟨339 2368⟩

RISK ^{H}{NP/Gerund} ^{Purp}{[IN ORDER] Infinitive}

Harm as Object, Purpose as Infinitival

In these cases, of course, the Subject will be interpreted as Actor rather than Victim.

Examples:

> Some of the large firms are willing to risk
>
> ^{H}{initial losses}
>
> ^{Purp}{*in order to* get into the field ahead of US steelmakers}. ⟨322 1655⟩

> Captain Prien risked
>
> ^{H}{treacherous tides and currents and a narrow passage}
>
> ^{Purp}{*to* penetrate British defenses and torpedo the battleship Royal Oak}. ⟨504 462⟩

> She risks
>
> ^{H}{the hazards of the highway }
>
> ^{Purp}{*to* catch a glimpse of him as he addresses wayside crowds}. ⟨410 384⟩

We are prepared to risk

H{a substantial increase in unemployment }

Purp{*in order to* bring inflation to an end}. ⟨521 2131⟩

RISK H{NP} B{FOR [the sake of] NP}

Harm as Object, Beneficiary as PP

Example:

Men were not inclined to risk

H{scalping}

Ben{*for the sake of* settlers they had never seen}. ⟨344 1918⟩

RISK H{Gerund} G{FOR NP}

Harm as Object, Gain as PP

Examples:

That they should risk

H{be*ing* murdered}

Gain{*for* their pleasure}

was too senseless and capricious altogether. ⟨306 2762⟩

Deed as Object.   The third type of direct complement is the Deed, representable as a nominal or as a gerundial direct object.

RISK D{NP}

Deed as NP Object, no adjuncts

Examples:

Paul decided to risk
^{D}{a reconnaissance in town}. ⟨5 798⟩

No skipper or fisherman would risk
^{D}{the crossing}. ⟨96 691⟩

Users were unwilling to risk
^{D}{any software changes}. ⟨234 195⟩

He walked away, not even risking
^{D}{a parting glance}. ⟨297 962⟩

Franklin decided to risk
^{D}{a desperate diplomatic maneuver}. ⟨371 557⟩

Hamburg risked
^{D}{an open break with the Hanseatic League}. ⟨408 1868⟩

RISK ^{D}{Gerund}

Deed as Gerundial Object, no adjuncts

Examples:

If he risks
^{D}{say*ing* something highly personal} . . . ⟨39 712⟩

We were happy and it seemed foolish to risk
^{D}{chang*ing* things}. ⟨68 3644⟩

I did not dare risk
^{D}{leav*ing* my vantage point}. ⟨204 1157⟩

Will would never risk
^{D}{turn*ing* up again}. ⟨204 3903⟩

In the Deed-as-object examples, the principal adjunct we found was a Purpose expression:

RISK ^{D}{NP} ^{Purp}{[IN ORDER] Infinitival}

Deed as NP Object, Purpose as Infinitival

Examples:

> I didn't dare risk
> D{a pause }
> Purp{*to* let that sink in}. ⟨172 1567⟩

RISK D{Gerund} Purp{[IN ORDER] Infinitive}

Deed as Gerundial Object, Purpose as Infinitival

Examples:

> We risked
> D{surfac*ing* }
> Purp{*to* race into a new attack position}. ⟨328 3449⟩

> Lance risked
> D{stay*ing* at the ridge alone}
> Purp{*to* watch}. ⟨397 2216⟩

> He couldn't keep up there much longer, not unless he wanted to risk
> D{show*ing* himself in the village
> Purp{*to* buy supplies}. ⟨281 3304⟩

The Residue: "Derivative Syntax."   On developing the preceding categorization of the segments of sentences built around the verb RISK, we found a number of examples that did not lend themselves to a direct interpretation in terms of what we took to be the RISK schema. These words, in these contexts, seemed to mean more than just RISK. Put differently, the meaning of these sentences seemed to involve more elements than what we could find in the otherwise fairly well-motivated RISK frame.

The solution seemed to lie in a theory of derivative syntax. In examining semantic relations between words, as well as the polysemy structure of a word, we will frequently find that in some of its secondary senses a word can have distributional and semantic properties that overlap the properties of certain other words (or word-classes). We might say it "inherits" some of its grammatical properties, in this use, from the associated word.

Examples of such *derivative syntax* are easy to find. For example, when "slipping" something can be seen as part of an act of "giving" something to someone, the verb SLIP can take on the syntax associated with GIVE, as in "he slipped me an envelope." When GIVE is used in the meaning "contribute," it enjoys the argument omission possibilities allowed by CONTRIBUTE, as in "I gave five dollars." And, to use even better known examples, when "smearing" something on some surface results in covering that surface, the verb SMEAR acquires the syntax of COVER, as in "I smeared the wall with mud," and when loading hay onto the truck results in filling the truck, LOAD can take on the syntax of FILL, as in "I loaded the truck with hay."[17]

To illustrate this last notion in the set of words we are exploring, we might want to say that when RISK or DANGER includes a meaning component shared by POSSIBILITY, it acquires some of the syntactic patterns associated with POSSIBILITY, as in "there is a slight risk/danger/possibility that such-and-such will happen." With verbal RISK, some of its observed syntactic behavior is associated with its possibility of occurrence in contexts involving *exposing* (something *to* danger), *investing* (*in* something), and *betting* (*on* something). All the derived-syntax version of RISK that we found involves the "Valued-Object as Direct Object" version.

Expose.   In one of these, we can paraphrase the sentence using the verb EXPOSE, and we find in the clause a secondary complement appropriate to EXPOSE, namely the TO-phrase representing the threat against which something is unprotected. The RISK phrase in these uses incorporates (and "inherits" some of the syntax associated with) the meaning of "expose."

RISK << 'expose' $\text{VO}_{\{NP\}}$ $^?\{\text{TO NP}\}$

We would have to reinforce it before risking
   $\text{VO}_{\{it\}}$
   $^?\{to$ the waves$\}$. ⟨75 1040⟩

He feared to risk
   $\text{VO}_{\{his\ two\ precious\ flattops\ \}}$
   $^?\{to$ enemy submarine or torpedo-bomber attacks$\}$. ⟨520 2266⟩

In the remaining two cases, the Valued Object is deliberately offered as

---

[17]A correct description would presumably not be one that mentioned FILL and COVER, but which recognized the semantic commonality of these two words and associated the grammatical realization pattern as fitting that meaning.

something capable of achieving the Goal. The first use fits the syntax of INVEST, the second fits the syntax of BET, WAGER, etc.

Invest. In this case, the "invested-in" object is introduced by the preposition IN.

RISK << 'invest' ^{VO}{NP} $^?${IN NP}

Roosevelt risked
   ^{VO}{more than $50,000 of his patrimony }
   $^?${*in* ranch lands in Dakota Territory}. ⟨6 5741⟩

Bet. The last case is one in which an act of risking is taken as superimposed (quite naturally) on the Gambling schema. An ON-phrase represents what is "bet on."

RISK << 'gamble, bet' ^{VO}{NP} $^?${ON NP}

He's likely to risk
   ^{VO}{a week's salary }
   $^?${*on* a horse}. ⟨439 791⟩

The unnamed categories in the preceding three types (the ones labeled "?") are categories that need to be named for the linked frames of exposing-to-danger, investment, and gambling. When we invest in something (nonmetaphorically), we encumber some portion of our resources in the knowledge that we stand the possibility of either losing it or receiving more in return. When we gamble on something, we predict some outcome related to that thing, in opposition with some other person or persons willing to predict a different outcome. When we expose something to danger, we make it possible that certain persons or properties (maybe not our own) will be damaged or lost. Because all these situations involve both uncertainty and danger, the notion of RISK fits into them well.

THE POLYSEMY SYSTEM OF VERBAL RISK

In this section we lay out what dictionaries might present as the various senses of RISK, as found in the corpus. It is our own view that a description of the meanings of this verb would be more perspicuously presented by displaying the frame and its categories, describing the manner of introduction of associated concepts within the frame, and adding whatever embellishments a given usage requires. In this section we also offer other words from the same semantic field that share the "senses" being described.

(S1) RELATION BETWEEN ACTOR AND HARM

to act in such away as to create a situation of (danger for oneself); "He risked death"

(S2) RELATION BETWEEN VICTIM AND HARM

to be in a situation of (danger to oneself); "You risk catching a cold dressing like that"

In the first two cases (S1 and S2), there do not appear to be other words that can show the same relationship.

(S3) RELATION BETWEEN ACTOR AND DEED

to perform (an act) which brings with it the possibility of harm to oneself; chance, hazard, venture; "He risked a trip into the jungle"

The class of RISK uses in which the verb encodes the relationship between the Actor and the Deed has near synonyms using the verbs CHANCE, HAZARD, and VENTURE, and, with somewhat different syntax, the verb DARE.

(S4) RELATION BETWEEN ACTOR AND VALUED OBJECT

to act in such a way as to expose (something) to danger; endanger, jeopardize, imperil; "He risked his inheritance"

The RISK verbs that encode the relationship between the Actor and the Valued Object permit paraphrases with verb-phrases headed by ENDANGER, JEOPARDIZE, and IMPERIL.

(S5) RELATION BETWEEN ACTOR AND VALUED OBJECT: DERIVATIVE

to act in such a way as to expose (something) to (danger); expose; "He risked his ship to torpedo attack"

The uses of RISK in which it is associated with EXPOSE shows a relationship between Actor and Valued Object. The TO-phrase represents a category available to the EXPOSE schema, representing a source of Harm.

(S6) RELATION BETWEEN ACTOR AND VALUED OBJECT: DERIVATIVE

to expose (something valuable) to loss by wagering it on (something capable of failing) in the hope of gain; bet, wager, stake, gamble; "He risked his inheritance on lottery tickets"

The uses of RISK in which it is associated with the verbs BET, WAGER, and STAKE show a relationship between Actor and Investment and permit adjunct phrases with the preposition ON, where the ON represents a chance-involved entity or event about which the outcome is a matter of contest (e.g., WE RISKED ALL THAT MONEY ON A HORSE).

(S7) RELATION BETWEEN ACTOR AND VALUED OBJECT: DERIVATIVE

to expose (something valuable) to loss by investing it in (some venture capable of failing) in the hope of achieving gain

And lastly, the use of RISK in which it is associated with the verb INVEST also shows a relation between Actor and Investment, its derivative adjunct designating the purchased element in an investment (e.g., Roosevelt risked more than $50,000 of his patrimony in ranch lands in Dakota Territory). ⟨20⟩

ON POLYSEMY

Semanticists studying the polysemy structure of individual lexical items are generally unable to find what they need by examining the "senses" laid out in a typical dictionary entry. The usual lexicographic practice is to identify as separate individual senses those uses for which separate paraphrases are required to fit particular grammatical environments. Thus, if the verb RISK is paraphrased as "put at risk" in one context but "face the risk of" in another context, these must be taken as evidence for different senses of the verb. Such differences founded on differences of grammatical pattern are altogether unlike the kinds of secondary semantic developments created by such general processes as metaphor and metonymy. (Thus, in "my car died," dying is taken as a metaphor for mechanical failure; and in "I wrote to Paul," an expression of the act of writing is taken as a metonym of communicating with a series of actions in which writing is one part.) It ought to be possible to recognize the difference between the kind of polysemy resulting from a transfer of a semantic frame to a new domain (through metonymy or metaphor, for example) and the kind that reflects merely the accommodation of a word to different syntactic patterns.

The concept of "frame" makes it possible to reconsider the notion of polysemy, and to develop the consequences of this reconsideration for lexicography. Once we see the relevance of the frame notion for understanding the meanings of words, we find ourselves actually seeing the naturalness of the so-called "when"—definitions that we learned to avoid in school. It is common and easy—and "wrong"—for a definition of (say) "disappointment" to take such a form as "Disappointment is when you really wanted something to happen but then it didn't happen, and so you feel bad." The objections we heard to such a definition were precisely because they did not make it possible to distinguish between the verb "disappoint," the adjectives "disappointed" and "disappointing," and the noun "disappointment"; that is, such a definition fails because its form does not match the *grammatical* characteristics of the word being defined. Proper definitions, we were taught, were phrases that could replace —however awkwardly—the word being defined, in the sentences in which it had the meanings we were trying to characterize, preserving that meaning. It is because of this tradition that a dictionary built along familiar lines has to regard each of the "senses" of RISK surveyed in the previous section as different.

Frame semantics makes it possible to separate the notion of the conceptual underpinnings of a concept from the precise way in which the words anchored in them get used. We need the means of associating a word (or a group of words, or a group of word uses) with particular semantic frames, and then to describe the varying ways in which the elements of the frame are given syntactic realization. We ought not to have to regard each of these varying mappings as different senses of the word.

We wish to say, for example, that in explaining uses of the verb RISK we merely need to specify the interrelations between two notions: semantic frame and syntax. There are two related frames associated with this verb—those suggested by Figs. 2.1 and 2.2—but the usage differences that need to be reported are best described, not necessarily in terms of lexical semantic differences as such, but as differences in the manner of syntactic realization of the elements of their common frame.

Standard dictionaries are not equipped to present polysemy organizations in the way suggested here, because they do not provide a means to access the details of given conceptual frames. A more appropriate representation can be provided in a frame-based dictionary-on-computer with properties outlined at the beginning of this chapter. We hope to be able to offer some somewhat less programmatica proposals on the structure and performance of such a dictionary at a later date.

ACKNOWLEDGMENTS

For discussion of earlier versions of this chapter, the authors are indebted to conversations with Jane Espenson, Daniel Kahneman, Paul Kay, Eva Kittay, Frank Knowles, George Lakoff, Adrienne Lehrer, and Laurel Sutton. Time pressure prevented us from acting on a number of very good suggestions from these friends.

REFERENCES

Cruse, D. A. (1986). *Lexical semantics, Cambridge textbooks in linguistics.* Cambridge: Cambridge University Press.

Fillmore, C. J. (1985). Frames and the semantics of understanding. *Quaderni di Semantica, 6,* 223f.

Fillmore, C. J., & Atkins, B. T. (forthcoming). *Starting where the dictionaries stop: The challenge of corpus lexicography.*

Raiffa, H. (1970). *Decision analysis: Introductory lectures on choices under uncertainty* (p. 309). Reading, MA: Addison Wesley.

3 Semantic Fields, Prototypes, and the Lexicon

Richard E. Grandy
Rice University

Unless some theory of eternal recurrence is true, every macroscopic object and event is unique. But if we are to use past experience as a guide to behavior, then we must make judgments about similarities between present objects and events and those experienced in the past. Because the past encounters are not contained in our heads, we must rely on those representations of them that remain. And "experience" should be understood broadly; it includes that acquired directly by an individual during their lifetime, or what has been painfully acquired by other members of the culture and transmitted by some means.

INFORMATION, PRAGMATICS, AND CONTRAST SETS

Many phenomena, especially the abilities to deal with metaphor, ambiguity, and the interpretation of spoken language in general, indicate the importance of knowledge of semantic fields in the performance of a competent speaker. It may seem nonetheless to skeptics that the presence of semantic fields is an accidental feature of natural language, unworthy of serious theoretical dissection; or at least not of semantic interest. For most of the phenomena cited might be argued to be either matters of pragmatics or, worse, of psychology.

One way to answer this challenge is to consider the explicitly pragmatic phenomena of Gricean conversational postulates. Whereas Grice (1989) formulated these postulates as governing conversation, I believe that appropriately interpreted they have far wider scope of application. Two of the significant and often conflicting maxims are: (a) Provide sufficient information; (b) be relevant (do not provide unnecessary information).

The motivation for both principles in plain conversation is evident. And that the principles are much stronger together than separately is of great importance. Sufficient information would be provided, eventually, by a lengthy monologue relating anything of the most remote possible interest. A selection of relevant information might stop far short of sufficiency.

Similar principles must guide memory. As a guide to future action we require sufficient relevant information. If we attempted to recall every detail of every event we saw or heard, our memories (cf. Cherniak, 1983; Miller, 1956) would be overwhelmed quickly, but if we do not recall enough, we act out of unnecessary ignorance. The process of selectively encoding aspects of the world of sufficient importance is a continuing process that is extremely similar in general form to conversation. And for most people a considerable portion of their memory is semantic in character rather than pictorial or auditory.

In short, for our own future benefit it is important that we selectively encode those aspects of our current experience that will be beneficial in guiding our future behavior. And an aspect of our current experience will be relevant and of interest only if its future occurrences will be sufficiently correlated with phenomena of interest. Thus, in coding our current experience for future reference we wish to retain those matters of sufficient salience, significance, and import that they will provide a beneficial guide to future action. But we also wish to use a coding scheme that is efficient (i.e., that incorporates the past experience in a way that is most useful for future applications and does not squander memory space or computational resources).

English is an historically evolved coding scheme for representing events, objects, and relationships of importance and interest. If one is set a particular coding task where a single level of information is to be represented, perhaps positions on a chess board, then a single level of coding representation can be efficiently designed. However, the demands of understanding, communicating, and remembering are quite various. Sometimes we care only that something is an animal, on other occasions we need to know that it is a dog, and on yet others we may need to know whether it is a corgi. Thus the most efficient coding system will have nested sets of distinctions at various levels. These mutually exclusive (and usually jointly exhaustive) sets of terms that are organized under an inclusive covering term are often called *contrast sets* and, at least in my own way of thinking, are fundamental to explicating the grander idea of semantic fields.

Although lexical contrast sets evolve slowly, it is important to emphasize the forward-looking aspect as well, for we hope that our coding scheme will provide an appropriate vehicle for predictions of the future. This is a strong constraint on the linguistic evolution of lexical items, which are, of course, subject to the influence of our interests and many other factors. To give one more precise example, contrast sets (under the name "families of predicates") played a major role in Carnap's (1950) work on induction and (again not by name) in at least one suggestion for resolving paradoxes of confirmation (cf. Grandy, 1967).

CONTRAST SETS

Although concepts similar to that of a contrast set are often used in philosophy and other fields, the notions are typically employed with little foundational thought as to the nature of the concept and how best to characterize it. Kay (1971) is one of the few rigorous attempts to give a definition, though he is primarily interested in the more specific concept of a taxonomy. His definition there was in terms of the extensions of the terms involved, so that two terms contrast if they never both apply to same object. This approach is problematic for two reasons; first it does not give a proper treatment of terms (unicorn, dragon) that apply to no actual objects unless the treatment is supplemented along the lines of Scheffler (1979). Furthermore, even when terms do extensionally contrast, his approach does not do justice to the linguistic necessities relating the extensions. It is not an accident that no instant during Monday is also an instant during Wednesday (although there is a common sense in which one speaks of the same time Monday and Wednesday, but these 'times" are recurring items). In typical contrast sets the contrasting terms are not only disjoint but are so nonaccidentally. In a later paper Kay (1975) expresses exactly this dissatisfaction and proposes that the matters of contrast and inclusion must hold necessarily.

My own suggestion is that the contrast set should be defined in terms of common linguistic beliefs that competent speakers have about the contrasts and inclusions. A statement is a **common linguistic belief** for a group just in case everyone in the group would regard someone who did not agree to the statement as evidencing an inadequate understanding of one or more of the words involved. (What is such a common linguistic belief will vary, of course, with the size and nature of the group analyzed.) If someone did not believe that Wednesday is a day of the week, or thought that Monday and Wednesday overlapped for a few hours, or thought that Wednesday was the day after Monday, we would regard their knowledge of the terms as at least incomplete. Common semantic beliefs represent a kind of semantic a priori, though with several differences. These a priori statements are not only not necessarily true but may turn out to be false when combined with other assumptions about how language applies to the world.

Note that I put the definition in terms of beliefs rather than knowledge, a deliberate choice I attempt to justify shortly. The concept of common linguistic belief is not entirely clear or well defined of course. There are questions about what the relevant size of the group is, who counts as competent speakers, and what to do about cases of disagreement. I should emphasize that the operative term is belief, and what a speaker utters is relevant but not conclusive evidence about what they believe. My goal is to offer a realistic account, not an artificially precise one. We can easily produce formal representations of the various sets of beliefs that one might argue should be included, but choosing one of these as the correct account of the contrast set is a difficult empirical question. For example, it might be argued that one does not understand any of the terms for days unless one also believes that they begin at midnight and last 24 hours. Or perhaps we should require the beliefs that they begin just after midnight, and that they typically last 24 hours, though occasionally leap seconds are inserted as correctives to keep conventional time synchronized with solar reality.

More formally, our first approximation to a definition of a contrast set will consist minimally of a covering term T, a contrast relation R and a set F of linguistic terms F_i (i = 1..n) such that (a) there are common linguistic beliefs that each $F_i \in T$, and (b) if i $\neq$ j then it is a common linguistic belief that F_i and F_j ($F_j \in T$) contrast in respect R.

In the simplest basic contrast sets, the terms are all monolexemic, the contrast relation is a simple one, and the same contrast relation holds between all the contrasting terms. Even in this situation there is a great deal of hidden complexity because of the variety of possible contrast relations (Lehrer & Lehrer, 1982) For example, if we accept Berlin and Kay's (1969) analysis of the basic color terms of English, then one contrast set consists of the covering term *color,* the covered and contrasting terms *black white red green blue yellow purple brown,* and the contrast relation *different (basic) color than.* (This is, of course, restricting attention to the most general sense of "color"—the senses in which it applies to colors of hair and of wine would have distinct contrast sets.)

On the other hand, many contrast sets have a complex structured set of contrast relations; for example, the contrast set covered by "day" in the sense of "day of the week" and including "Sunday" "Monday" etc. has as its fundamental contrast relation the "next day after" relation (i.e., Monday is the day after Sunday). Moreover, there is no time between them and no time belongs to both of them. This together with the same relation between Monday and Tuesday generates the different derivative contrast relation between Tuesday and Sunday of being the second day after, and so on. This illustrates the point allowed previously that the contrasts among the terms may be ones R^* that are derived from the fundamental contrast relation R.

Thus we need to revise condition (b) aforementioned to:

(b') if i $\neq$ j then it is a common linguistic belief that F_i and F_j ($F_j \in T$) contrast in respect R or some relation R^* derivable from R.

The "day after" relation is a cyclic relation of order seven (i.e., seven iterations brings you back to the starting point). Cyclic orders are very common in contrast sets involving time—seconds, hours, minutes, days, months, and (in many calendars) years are cyclic with various orders. This commonality is not noted in the individual contrast sets but would be in a larger semantic field that included all the temporal contrast sets.

Yet other contrast sets are multidimensional. For example, the contrast set of kin terms or family terms in English depends on at least three distinctions: the dyadic contrast between male and female, the generational contrast between

parent and child, and the dyadic distinction between blood and marriage relatives. Thus there are three fundamental contrast relations and a large number of
complex contrast relations that can be derived from them. Thus a sister of x is
someone distinct from x who has the same parents and who is female.

In view of these complexities, we need yet another revision of the definition
of contrast sets. Our final version is:

> A contrast set will consist minimally of a covering term T, a set R of fundamental
> contrast relations R_k (k = 1..n) and a set F of linguistic terms F_i (i = i..n) such that
>   (a) there are common linguistic beliefs that each $F_i \in$ T, and
>   (b″) if i ≠ j then it is a common linguistic belief that F_i and F_j ($F_j \in$ T) contrast
> either in one of the respects R_k or in some complex relation R derivable from R_k.

The particular relations that are lexicalized in English are somewhat arbitrary in
some cases; for example the term *uncle* includes both the brother of a parent and
the husband of a sister of a parent, whereas neither of those disjuncts is lexicalized, nor is the apparently more natural relation of sibling of a parent (i.e., a
blood uncle or aunt). Those concepts that are articulable by complex expressions
but not by monolexemes are sometimes called *lexical gaps* by linguists and
covert categories by anthropologists.

One reason that I have defined contrast sets in terms of belief rather than
knowledge, and one of the reasons I have not followed Kay (1975) in making the
contrasts matters of necessity, is that in some cases I believe that the matters that
are semantic a priori are not generally true. For example, it appears from a
moderate amount of not very careful sampling that speakers regard it as a semantic a priori principle that John's brother cannot be his uncle, but it is not impossible that his older brother could marry his mother's younger sister. The assumption of contrast between generations that is built into the contrast set does not
always correspond to reality.

These examples have all involved terms sufficiently familiar that almost all
adult speakers are competent in their use, but there are also a large (indeed,
larger) number of contrast sets where speakers are less competent. For example,
quizzed about the relations among the meanings of "swamp" "bog" "fen" and
"marsh," many speakers either believe them to be synonyms or believe that they
contrast but disclaim knowledge of the nature of the contrast (or, in some cases,
invent one). In this case as in many others, speakers have beliefs about the
general field relations among the terms without having precise or accurate knowledge of the specifics of the relations.

FROM CONTRAST SETS TO SEMANTIC FIELDS

Semantic fields are larger units of analysis that will include a number of contrast
sets. A first approximation to a definition of a semantic field would be that it is a

commercial set of contrast sets. However, we want to include more than that for terms in a semantic field that can be related in ways other than contrast or exclusion.

Writers concerned with semantic fields (Lehrer, 1974; Lyons, 1977) typically note that some lexical items are converses of each other: husband/wife, buy/sell. No one seems to have noted that these "converses" are actually instances of different relations. In the relevant sense husband/wife are two place relations such that

x is the husband of y if y is the wife of x

whereas the relationship for buy/sell involves a permutation of the first and third elements rather than first and second:

x buys y from z if z sells y to x.

Thus if we are to include information about "converses" in a semantic field, we should include information about which permutation occurs as well as the pair. Thus a permutation relation will be an ordered triple consisting of a specification of the permutation (e.g., $P_{i,j}$, which permutes the i-th and j-th argument places, and two linguistic items that are so related (e.g., $\langle P_{1,3}$, buy, sell$\rangle$).

Another semantic relation that merits inclusion is synonymy. In defining a semantic field we would want typically to include synonyms of those terms that are included. I should emphasize that the operative notion of synonymy is to be defined in terms of the linguistic beliefs of the relevant linguistic community, and thus the concept bears little epistemic or metaphysical weight.

Other semantic relations deserve consideration and inclusion. For example, in the middle ages, terms of venery and the associated relations ($\langle$pride, lion$\rangle$, $\langle$flock, sheep$\rangle$, etc.) were sufficiently salient in certain social classes that it would probably have been necessary to include knowledge of the term of venery with each species noun.

There are a number of other significant semantic relations as well as paratactic ones that should be included in a thorough discussion of semantic fields, but I hope that the sketch here indicates how I would attempt to include them.

WHAT SEMANTIC FIELDS ARE (PARTLY)

Although all were inspired by Saussure, the original definitions of semantic field (Bedeutungsfeld) by Ipsen (1924), Porzig (1934), and Trier (1934) were rather at odds with one another. I do not wish to attempt to recapitulate the history here. Rather I want to suggest an analysis that is clearer, less grandiose, and more pragmatic. It is certainly more tentative. If we are to be more pragmatic and clear, then it is desirable to define semantic fields in such a way that, as much as possible, we avoid appeal to meanings or to any specific conception of meaning. The point is to find a definition that remains relatively close to the phenomena and thus leaves the theoretical ramifications for a later stage. Thus, for a start, a semantic field for me will be a set of linguistic items and must include at least one contrast set. It is true that these are meaningful lexical items, but I stress that it is the meaningful lexical items and not their isolated abstract meanings that form the field. I choose the term *semantic field* rather than *lexical field,* for my concern is with the semantic relations among the expressions.

Thus my suggested definition of a semantic field is that it is a set including one or more contrast sets and possibly also including permutation relations such that:

1. at most one covering term does not occur as an element of a contrast set in the semantic field.

2. except for the covering term mentioned in (1), any expression that occurs in a contrast set with an element of the semantic field is also in the field.

Condition 1 requires the unity of the semantic field, that there is a single general expression that covers all other items; it rules out taking the natural semantic fields of mammals and of vehicles and declaring them a single un-natural semantic field. (They will both appear, of course, as part of some unified semantic fields, e.g., under the very general field of physical objects.) The requirement is parallel to Kay's (1971) requirement of a "unique beginner." Any other item that occurs as a covering term in one of the contrast sets must be itself a contrasting element in another contrast set if this condition is met. I require that there be a covering term because I am concerned about semantic fields that can be regarded as lexicalizations of conceptual structures that could be labelled *conceptual fields.* Barsalou (this volume) investigates conceptual fields that are not lexicalized.

Condition 2 requires a kind of horizontal completeness—the contrast set ⟨animal:dog,cat...⟩ qualifies as a semantic field on its own, but if we are to include "German shepherd" then we must also include all the contrasting terms ("poodle," "corgi," etc.). In other words, if a term is not the unique beginner of the field, then every term that contrasts with it must be included in the field. It should be mentioned that the same covering term may occur with more than one contrast set (e.g., Lehrer's (1974, p. 31) example of two distinct contrast sets covered by the term *methods of cooking,* but this is very atypical.

According to this definition, a semantic field can be as small as a single contrast set or could include a multitude of them together with permutation and other relations. This may seem to be evading a question alluded to earlier as to how large a semantic field is. I see no reason to legislate the matter—a semantic field is a unit of analysis that an investigator chooses to treat in relative isolation from the rest of a language. Depending on the purposes at hand and the degree of isolation, a given unit may be a good or bad choice. But it would be inappropriate to try to settle in general on the size of a semantic field just as it would have been to try to decide how large a closed system should be in classical mechanics. Semantic fields smaller than an entire language are units selected for analysis—if the phenomenon of interest on that occasion is impervious to terms outside the chosen boundaries, then the choice is a good one.

Thus far I have talked of semantic fields built around basic contrast sets, sets whose monolexemic members contrast as a matter of plain linguistic conditions. But there are also comparable sets of whose members are either not monolexemic or that contrast because of contextual factors. (Actually I am using context very broadly because it can include any factor such as shared dialect, shared perceptual orientation, shared family history, shared hobby, etc. that enriches the shared assumptions of the participants in the discourse either temporarily or permanently.) In the one case we must relax the condition of monolexemity; in the other case the condition that contrasts is a matter of semantic bizarreness. Kittay's (1987) notion of default assumptions may prove helpful here.

Barsalou (this volume) explores in considerable detail the psychological phenomenon of categorization with such nonbasic categories as "things to take on vacation" and finds the conceptual structure is very similar to that for monolexical categories. Whether the linguistic aspects are similar is a matter for exploration on another occasion.

SEMANTIC FIELDS AND COMPONENTIAL ANALYSIS

Componential analysis fares well in accounting for containment relations (a cat is an animal) and for pairs of antonyms, where one can postulate that one of the antonyms is simply (the other). But the approach fares less well when we ask about the largest contrast sets. For example, because (I claim) it is a part of the meaning of "dog" that it contrasts with "cat," an adequate componential analysis will have encoded that information. For a contrast set with n elements, it will be necessary to have $n(n - 1)$ components to encode the information about contrast. We can confine our attention mainly to the level of the most detailed information for the items, because "dog" and "cat" will share higher markers such as (ANIMATE) and (ANIMAL). There are three possible approaches to the contrast problem that come readily to mind.

The first is simply to add appropriate markers. Just as one introduces a special distinguishing marker (CANINE) to distinguish dogs from other animals, one will include (FELINE) as a marker. The trouble is that the list doesn't end there for it will have to include (BOVINE), (EQUINE), (URSINE), and dozens of others. And each of the other entries will have to contain a very similar list. So for a contrast set of n items, there will have to be $n(n - 1)$ entries to represent the information.

A second approach would be to introduce a single item (OTHER ANIMAL THAN DOG), which would appear in the entry for "dog," with a similar new item for each other lexical entry. This seems to me to amount to an ad hoc backhanded way of admitting the importance of contrast sets. Whereas even Katz is now rather less inclined to press the idea of the semantic components as simple primitive semantic atoms in a chemistry of meaning, the complex and derivative nature of these particular markers seem too far from the spirit of the enterprise to be appealing.

The third approach is to argue that the information is already implicit in the system of markers and that one needs only know how to find it. The idea would be that as a general principle if an item (e.g., "dog") shares a marker (ANIMAL) with another item "cat" but they also have different markers, then the two are automatically incompatible. This will not work, however, for the principle does not always hold. In its general sense (i.e., the one in which it includes birds and insects and contrasts with plants), the marker (ANIMAL) is shared by "bird" and "insect" but is is also shared by "herbivore" and "carnivore," and whereas "bird" and "insect" are incompatible, "bird" and "carnivore" are not. Although I have not given a general argument as to the impossibility of representing the information contained in contrast sets in componential analysis, none of the obvious suggestions seem acceptable.

Even if this problem could be solved, another serious one arises when we consider the relations among contrasting terms. As illustrated earlier, many contrast sets are internally ordered—⟨days: Monday, . . . Sunday⟩—in a way that the competent speaker knows. In this particular case one might avoid introducing markers mentioning other items at the same level (e.g., IMMEDIATELY SUCCEEDS WEDNESDAY) by regarding the order as derivative from numerical order so that "Monday" would have a marker (FIRST DAY OF WEEK). For other cases, however, it is very difficult to see how the appropriate markers can be found without embedding reference to other elements of the contrast set within them (e.g., ⟨east, west, north, south⟩ or ⟨port, starboard, fore, aft⟩).

I suspect that componential analysis seems most appealing when it is believed that a relatively short universal set of components can be identified (Wierzbicka, 1980). Whether this can be done is a quasi-empirical question for which I believe there is considerable negative evidence. In the case cited earlier, the differences between a marsh and swamps, bogs, and fens is that the marsh is only seasonally under water whereas the others are normally underwater; swamps are demarcated from bogs and fens by the fact that the former have smaller quantities of decaying vegetable matter, and the last two are differentiated by the relative acidity of the water. It is implausible that these contrasts can be reduced to simple atomic universals.

This is not to deny that componential analysis is aimed at an important facet of language, namely the recurrence both within and across languages of many significant concepts. To do justice to both the contrasting character of lexical items, their relations, and the recurring components, we may think of describing the structures in quasi-axiomatic ways at the level of somewhat larger fields. For example, the semantic field of mammals is governed by some general principles even though not all items are lexicalized:

1. kinds   no mammal is of two different kinds
            the number of kinds is large and not completely specified
            mammals do not change kinds
2. sex   no mammal is of more than one sex
            there are two sexes
            mammals do not normally change sex
3. stage   no mammal is at two different stages
            mammals change stage irreversibly over time

This is obviously incomplete but perhaps indicates the way in which, with a listing of lexical items and other relations, this approach would capture some of the important facts from componential analysis in a way that does justice to the field aspects of semantics.

In summary, componential analysis emphasizes the atomic view of word meaning, whereas consideration of contrast sets points out the relational aspects of word meaning. This is not to deny that componential analysis can have value, especially in discerning the recurrent elements of meaning that appear in various contrast sets. Nonetheless, the main function of contrast sets in elaborating a portion of a speaker's knowledge is at best obliquely served by componential analysis.

PROTOTYPES AND SEMANTIC FIELDS

In a series of experiments and papers, Rosch (1973, 1974, 1975a, 1975b, 1978) brought into prominence the role of prototypes in various memory and classification tasks. This conception of categorization was originally proposed for perceptual categories by Wertheimer (1938) and generalized by Attneave (1957) but was only systematically explored in the 1970s, probably under the stimulus of Berlin and Kay (1969), Posner and Keele (1968), and Reed (1972). An informal intuitive characterization of a prototype for a category would be an item that would be a "good example" of the category.

Indeed, one of the experiments consisted of asking subjects to rank various members of various categories in terms of the appropriateness of the use of that member in teaching or explaining the category. The concept, prototype, however, is best seen as a cluster concept, for prototypes are characterized by the repeated occurrence of the same items in different experimental settings. For example, in a reaction time task where subjects are asked to judge whether an object is or is not in a category, prototypes are more quickly classified. Furthermore, being shown either a picture or name of a prototype just before the task (the technical term is *priming*) facilitates classification of other items more than priming with nonprototype. When subjects are asked to list items in a category, prototypes are more frequently mentioned.

Many exaggerated claims have been made (not by Rosch) about the significance of prototypes and of Rosch's work. I do not think, for example (contrary to Lakoff, 1972), that there is any indication that the phenomena in question show that nonprototypical members of a category are members to a lesser degree or that we require a fuzzy set theory to account for the phenomena. Nor does Rosch's work show that all categories have the structure associated with prototypes.

Her work, however, reinforces an intuitively plausible idea about how many of our categories are internally represented for speakers, how these internalizations are acquired, and how they are applied in categorization tasks. The intuitive idea is that we learn many words by being shown examples and then generalizing to similar objects. Of course, a defender of an alternative view, perhaps the view that the representation of a mature language speaker consists of a set of features requisite for the category, might grant that an early stage of learning would involve prototypes but would claim that eventually the set of features is abstracted and provides the ultimate form of representation.

The two views suggest different results, but I do not here intend to review the experimental evidence concerning this continuing dispute. Instead, I want to address a conceptual argument against the prototype-based theory. Let us make explicit the *Naive Prototype Theory of Categories* as:

> "For many categories C, for any x, x is a member of C just in case it is similar to the prototype p for C. Speakers of a language have internal representations of the prototype and judge membership by similarity."
>
> There are two obvious objections to this proposal: Similar in what regard (Vide Goodman (1972)? How similar?
>
> I see no way to answer these objections if one persists in formulating the theory in terms of individual categories. I suggest it be replaced by the
>
> *Contrast set with prototype theory:* For many contrast sets, speakers competent with regard to the contrast set have internal representations of a particular kind of similarity (associated with the covering term) and prototypes of the members. An object is categorized as E_i just in case it is more similar to the E_i prototype than to any E_k prototype.

For example, an object is classified as red just in case it is more similar in color to the prototypical red than to prototypical green, blue, etc. One would anticipate that a category that was prototypically learned and represented would differ in some important respects from one where the members were independently characterizable in terms of characteristic features. For example, in the case where they are independently characterizable, one would expect that the members could be learned independently and at different times, whereas for a prototypically organized category, one would expect the acquisition of all members to (more or less) coincide because it would depend on acquiring the conception of "similarity$_L$." Colors seem to fit the prototype model and ⟨geometric figures: triangle, square, . . . ⟩ the independent features one (cf. Kelly & Keil, 1985).

It is important to emphasize the importance of the similar$_L$ relation. Many critics of prototype theory assume that the similarity relation must be defined in terms of perceptual features of the objects, but there is no reason to make such an assumption. The similarity relations can be informed by either folk or scientific theories as well as utilizing perceptual aspects (Medin, 1989; Murphy & Medin, 1985).

On a slightly more abstract level, naive prototype theories question the assumption that a category (one-place predicate) is always definable using only nonrelational expressions (one-place predicates). It offers instead an analysis in terms of a two-place relation (similarity$_L$) and a prototypical object. The field + prototype view that I have just advocated requires even more complication, for the definition has to be formulated in terms of the three-place relation: x is more similar$_L$ to y than to z!

A contrast set is strongly cohesive just in case for each i any two members of E_i are more similar$_L$ to each other than to any member of E_k. Geometrical shapes (circle, square, triangle) and perhaps vehicles would be examples of strongly cohesive contrast sets.

A contrast set is prototypical just in case it is not strongly cohesive and for each i one can find a member (the prototype of E_i such that any member of E_i is more similar$_L$ to the prototype P_i of E_i than it is to the prototype P_k of any other E_k. Colors, as mentioned earlier, would probably be an instance of a prototypical contrast set.

The differences among these kinds of contrast sets would lead one to expect differences with regard to how easily they are learned and with regard to the frequency of problematic borderline cases and intersubjective disagreements.

CORES, CONCEPTS, AND MEANINGS

Smith and Medin in their reviews discuss three main objections to the prototype approach. One, the problem of compositionality, of how prototype theory accounts for complex categories, is an area where more work certainly needs to be done, but most of the criticisms of prototype theories are criticisms of those that postulate degrees of membership (Osherson & Smith, 1981, 1984). The second criticism, that the theory has no serious account of the constraints on category formation, is a just criticism but the reply ought to be more work on the problem rather than giving up.

The third, and most serious criticism, depends on Smith and Medin's (1981) distinction between the core of a category and identification procedure for the category. The core is to be understood as giving the necessary and sufficient conditions for membership in the category, the identification procedure would include whatever heuristic devices involved in actual judgments that something is in the category. This parallels fairly closely some of Putnam's views (1975) according to which the meaning of a word is not to be found in the minds of the average speakers but in the minds of the scientists who will eventually someday reach a complete understanding of the kind of item in question.

It is certainly possible to give an explanation of how prototypicality phenomenon might exist even if categories satisfy the Classical View, but this is not a defense of the Classical View against the most serious objection to it, namely the prolonged inability to find any significant number of categories that can be shown to fit the model, except in mathematics. At this point it is important to consider a distinction between what ought to interest psychologists and what ought to interest philosophers. If the classical view cannot be defended as a view of what concepts people actually operate with, then psychology must attend to alternative models.

However, it might be argued that philosophers of language, at least, can ignore the entire debate because what is in the head is irrelevant to meaning, as Putnam has argued. This seems wrong to me. Even if we supposed Putnam is correct (a BIG assumption) and the ultimate verdict on the extension of a category and thus on the truth of various contemporary assertions must await the final and ultimate scientific developments, we need to understand how people learn, use, and understand language while they are waiting for the millennium. Putnam's is another worldly view of philosophy of language.

Let me give a down to earth illustration. One example that is often cited as showing that categories are fuzzy or that their membership comes in degrees is that many speakers of English are very hesitant in answering the following question, and when they do give answers the answers tend not to be at all uniform:

Are tomatoes fruit or vegetable?

But I have a different interpretation of what is happening. I believe that "fruit," like almost every word of English, is polysemous, that is, has multiple closely related meanings (Vide Ross, this volume).

On one meaning, the technical biological one, a tomato is a kind of fruit because it contains the seeds of the plant. By this criterion other examples of fruit are pumpkins, zucchini, cucumbers, eggplants, and beans! But on the second meaning, the technical grocery one, tomatoes are vegetables. If you want to find tomatoes in the grocery store or it you want to buy tomato seeds, you need to know that they are vegetables.

AGREEMENT AND VARIATION

Rosch's studies reported intersubjective agreements on typicality that were surprisingly high, in most cases a correlation greater than .9. A subsequent reconsideration of her statistical methods revealed that her measure of agreement was biased in that the larger populations automatically tended to produce a higher degree of agreement. Barsalou performed comparable studies of his own to gather further data on the issue of agreement and found considerably less. He also investigated various other aspects of the stability of typicality judgments, such as the consistency of judgment for individuals over time and in judging typicality from the points of view of others.

From these studies Barsalou (1989) produced intersubjective agreements ranging from about .3 to .6. In his experiments in which the same subject was asked to re-do the same task at various intervals, the correlations were .92 when the interval was an hour, around .87 after a day, and about .80 for any interval of a week or longer. A related study by McCloskey and Glucksburg (1978) found that subjects not infrequently changed their minds about whether an item was or was not in a category with a 1-month interval between trials.

The variation in individual's typicality rankings was not, however, uniform across the range of possibilities. The most typical and least typical items had stabler scores than those in the middle of the scale. This means, for example, that robins and sparrows would be consistently judged high in typicality, ostriches and penguins low, and that the highest degree of variability would be among items of medium typicality, such as eagles and chickens.

One explanation of this would be that most categories involve several different dimensions on which members can vary in typicality. The most typical items in a category will be those that rank high in typicality on each dimension, whereas the least typical will be those that rank low in typicality in each individual dimension. Thus for those items it does not matter what relative weight is given to each dimension because any weighting will produce the same result. However, for other intermediate items, which may be typical on some dimensions (e.g., size) but atypical on others (e.g., being predators), how the composite ranking turns out hinges very substantially on how the dimensions are weighted.

This resembles the phenomenon of student admissions. Those who have high grades at excellent institutions, high test scores, and very positive letters of recommendation will be ranked high by everyone on an admissions committee, and, if the same committee member were asked to rank the candidates again at a later time, those candidates would again emerge at or near the top. Similarly, the candidates who fare poorly in all those respects will be consistently ranked low. The candidates where decisions are difficult, variable over time, and contentious in a committee are those who have intermediate credentials or who have a mixture of high- and low-quality credentials.

The change-of-category type of phenomenon observed by McCloskey and Glucksberg is somewhat different. The examples for which subjects changed their minds over time were those that were least typical of a category (e.g., a number of subjects changed their mind about whether yeast is an animal). One further complication that is difficult to experimentally determine is the extent to which the subjects changed their minds about which of several definitions of "animal" they were using. In one sense of "animal," we are included in that category (at least by the scientifically minded), whereas in another sense we are just as clearly excluded. When a university sets guidelines for animal experiments, these are in contrast with experiments on human subjects as well as with those involving the inanimate.

What implications these results have depend on whether typicality phenomena are merely ancillary or heuristic aspects of categorization, or whether prototypes are definitive of (many) categories. If the former, then we would expect to find considerable disagreement about what objects are in various categories, but this would not show that there was any vagueness or variability about true category membership. On the other hand, if categories are defined by sets of contrasting prototypes, then we must either accept that there is potential vagueness or inconsistency in our system of categories or push the problem back by arguing that, although our speakers of a language disagree about prototypicality, there is a single, true, correct prototypicality ranking that they are groping toward.

But the problems of vagueness and potential inconsistency need not lead to actual inconsistency for an individual or disagreements within a group of speakers. Graphically, the strongly cohesive contrast sets are clusters with large open areas between; more exactly, the crucial consideration seems to be that the open areas between clusters exceed the width of the clusters. The prototypical contrast sets are represented by clusters where the spaces between them are less than the widths of the categories and the widths of the categories are fairly uniform. In the last case the gap need only exceed the distances between adjacent outlying members of the same category.

If the world is cooperative and the gaps between clusters are sufficiently large, or if our perception of matters is conditioned to make the gaps large, or if the inhabitants of the fuzzy areas are sufficiently infrequent or unimportant, then the characterizations of the terms in the contrast set will suffice for our practical purposes.

All this assumes metricization of the similarity space that may well raise philosophical skepticism—those doubts are addressed on some other occasion. Note here that the similarity space is a psychological one, and that the mapping f from a corresponding physical dimension (if any) will not usually map pairs of equal distances x and y into equal instances $f(x)$ and $f(y)$, and the process of learning and using categories can change the psychological space.

PROTOTYPES AND MEANING

A number of philosophical objections have been raised against the claims that prototype theories have philosophical significance. One, originally suggested by

Smith, Shoben, and Rips (1974) and amplified by Smith and Medin (1981), is that prototypes are heuristic devices used to provide rough and ready guides to categorization, but that they have nothing to do with true membership.

A considerable degree of unclarity about what a prototype or prototype theory is complicates matters further. It is possible to discuss the phenomena of typicality and the informational aspects of categories without being precise about what a prototype is, but, if we are to directly compare prototype theories of categorization with others, we have to probe deeper into what the theories are. I will still ignore the differences among the origins of prototypes (e.g., the fact that some represent central tendencies whereas others are ideal cases; Barsalou, 1985; Lakoff, 1987).

Prototype theorists often speak of the prototype as the "best example" of the category and discuss the process of making category judgments in terms of having the prototype in mind or using the prototype in making comparisons. The actual best example is either a specific individual, in all of its almost infinite detail, which is not in the subject's head, or else a type (e.g., sparrows are often said to be the prototype of birds) in which case the prototype is itself abstract. In either case we have to consider how the item is represented in the subject who is making the judgment. And either the representation would seem to be in terms of values of features and dimensions, in which case the prototype seems superfluous and we have only a more complex version of the classical theory, or else the prototype is represented in some as yet unexplained theory, in which case we have a mystery and not an explanation or theory.

In other words, if the prototypical bird is a sparrow, then the subject must have a representation of a sparrow in his or her mental warehouse. (English nicely allows just the needed ambiguity so that the phrase "a sparrow" hides the type/instance question.) To attempt to say what a prototype is would involve me in matters that are more empirical than I care to venture into at present. However, I think that some progress can be made in contrasting two kinds of theories, starting with a version of the classical theory and a version of the more radical prototype theory, and then working through more sophisticated versions toward greater adequacy and clarity.

The simplest classical theory is the Conjunctive, which postulates that for each category in question membership is an all or nothing matter, and that there is a conjunction of positive and negative features that is decisive for membership. The most radical prototype theory postulates that membership is a matter of degree that is a direct reflection of similarity to a prototype for a category. A weaker version of the classical view is the Boolean, which postulates that there is a disjunction of conjuncts of positive and negative features. A less radical version of the prototype view is the one I advanced earlier, that membership is all or nothing (with some tough borderline cases), but that membership was decided in terms of which prototype of the contrasting categories the item in question was most similar to. A weakness of the Boolean view is that it can only operate on binary features, whereas it seems plausible that in at least some cases dimensions are relevant to membership as well.

This leads naturally to the Weighted Features and Dimensions view suggested by Smith, Shoben, and Rips (1974). On this view, membership is decided by weighting the various features and dimensions so that instead of a Boolean combination one has something like:

$$W_{1,1}F_1 + W_{1,2}F_2 + \ldots + W_{1,n}F_n, + W_{1,n+1}D_1 \ldots + W_{1,n+m}D_{n+m},$$

where weight $W_{i,j}$ is the weight assigned to the j-th feature of dimension for category i. Membership is then decided by whether the weighted score for the category meets a designated cutoff criteria. Thus, as in the modified prototype theory, the scores are continuous, the membership decision is binary. The suggestion, as originally articulated, was that the weighted score provided the information about typicality whereas the cutoff score preserved binary membership results, and the weights were a classical adaptation of the point that not all features count exactly the same amount. Note that, as least in the version I have given, the weights are not only not the same for all features, but the weight of a feature can vary depending on the category in question as well, so that the same feature can have different weights for different categories.

Although this definition is at some conceptual distance from the classical starting point, it still has at least one important property in common with the conjunctive view—for each feature or dimension and each category, the feature (or dimension) is either uniformly positively or negatively relevant to that category; that is, either having or not having the feature is relevant, or having more or less of the quantity measured by the dimension contributes to membership regardless of the values of any other feature of dimension value. Technically, this is known as linear separability because we can separate the contribution of each dimension and feature and represent the total value as a simple sum. But there are many intuitive cases where typicality, at least, does not work so simply. Being large may be more typical for a bird if it is a predator, but less typical if it is not (cf. Medin, 1989, and Rips, 1989).

A further complication of the Boolean approach can continue the spirit of the neo-classical weighted fuzzy features approach, but I do not prolong that avenue here. Instead, I want to direct attention to whether any essential difference will remain after we make reasonable revisions of the classical and prototype approach. I believe that the one aspect that divides the two significantly even when they produce very similar results is whether the categorization decision is local or global. By this I mean the difference between deciding whether x is in category Ci by applying an evaluation procedure to x and comparing it to the necessary standard on the weighted fuzzy and whatever scale, or whether we compute a rating for each Cj and then judge x as in the category on which it scores highest (i.e., in the first case, if it is rated .4312 or greater, it is in Ci, and otherwise it is not). In the second case we cannot in general decide whether it is in Ci without computing all the Cj values.

CONCLUSION

I have attempted to clarify the related concepts of contrast set and semantic field and have argued that in combination with prototypes they present a significant alternative to more traditional views of how categories are defined and represented. Much further work remains to be done to articulate more clearly the differences between the two styles of characterization, and to investigate the extent to which each is the optimal portrayal of:

1. how concepts are represented in the minds of speakers (a question of cognitive psychology);
2. how concepts ought to be represented in semantic theories, understood as accounts of ideal speakers knowledge (a question of linguistics);
3. how concepts are best represented for machine processing of natural language speech, reasoning, and memory (a question of artificial intelligence).

More specifically, I have argued that knowledge about contrast relations and field relations generally are part of the knowledge that ordinary speakers have and deploy, and that such information ought to be incorporated into the linguistic description of the abstraction that is identified as the language that they speak. It seems very likely that such knowledge will have to be included in any artificial intelligence programs that deal with language with any sophistication.

On the other hand, prototypes loom large in individual processing and in the actual classification of objects by speakers, but there is a great deal of individual variation and probably less is required for artificial intelligence purposes than is required for explanations of specific speaker behavior. And it is not clear that any specific information about prototypes ought to be included in the linguists' account of the lexicon because it appears mainly relevant to psychological and referential issues.

What I am suggesting is that it may well be a serious mistake to assume that it makes sense to discuss **the** structure of **the** lexicon. The lexicon is a theoretical construct, and there may be good reasons for different disciplines to construct it somewhat differently, especially in that they may require more or less inclusive theories. The articulation of nonstandard theories will require much further work, particularly because it is difficult to provide rigorous accounts of holistic phenomena. We should be particularly careful not to make the task more difficult by conflating the uses to which various disciplines may want to put the results.

REFERENCES

Attneave, F. (1957). Transfer of experience with a class-schema to identification-learning of patterns and shapes. *Journal of Experimental Psychology, 54,* 81–88.

Barsalou, L. W. (1985). Ideals, central tendency, and frequency of instantiation as determinants of graded structure in categories. *Journal of Experimental Psychology: Learning, Memory and Cognition, 11,* 629–54.

Barsalou, L. W. (1989). Intraconcept similarity and its implications for inter-concept similarity. In *Similarity and analogical reasoning.* S. Vosniadou & A. Ortony (Eds.), Cambridge: Cambridge University Press.

Berlin, B., & Kay, P. (1969). *Basic color terms.* Berkeley, CA: University of California Press.

Carnap, R. (1950). *The logical foundations of probability.* Chicago: University of Chicago Press.

Cherniak, C. (1983). Rationality and the structure of human memory. *Synthese, 57,* 163–86.

Goodman, N. (1972). Seven strictures on similarity. Reprinted in *Problems and projects.* Indianapolis: Hackett.

Grandy, R. E. (1967). Some comments on confirmation and aselective confirmation. *Philosophical Studies, 18,* 19–24.

Grice, H. P. (1989). *Studies in the ways of words.* Cambridge, MA: Harvard University Press.

Ipsen, G. (1924). Der alte Orient und die Indogermanen. *Stand und aufgaben der Sprachwissenschaft: Festschrift für W. Streitburg.* Heidelberg: Winter.

Kay, P. (1971). "Taxonomy and semantic contrast." *Language, 47,* 866–887.

Kay, P. (1975). A model-theoretic approach to folk taxonomy. *Social Science Information, 14*(5), 151–166.

Kelly, M., & Keil, F. C. (1985). The more things change . . . : Metamorphoses and conceptual structure. *Cognitive Science, 9,* 403–16.

Kittay, E. (1987). *The cognitive force of metaphor.* Oxford: Oxford University Press.

Lakoff, G. (1972). Hedges. *Papers from the Eighth Regional Meeting CLS* (pp. 183–228).

Lakoff, G. (1987). *Women, fire and dangerous things.* Chicago: Chicago University Press.

Lehrer, A. (1974). *Semantic fields and lexical structure.* Amsterdam: North-Holland.

Lehrer, A., & Lehrer, K. (1982). Antonymy. *Linguistics and Philosophy, 5,* 483–502.

Lyons, J. (1977). *Semantics.* Cambridge: Cambridge University Press.

McCloskey, M. E., & Glucksburg, S. (1978). Natural categories: Well defined or fuzzy sets? *Memory & Cognition, 6,* 462–472.

Medin, D. L. (1989). Concepts and conceptual structure. *American Psychology, 44,* 1469–1481.

Miller, G. A. (1956). The magical number seven, plus or minus two: Some limits on our capacity processing information. *Psychological Review, 63,* 81–97.

Murphy, G. L., & Medin, D. L. (1985). The role of theories in conceptual coherence. *Psych. Rev., 92,* 289–316.

Osherson, D. N., & Smith, E. E. (1981). On the adequacy of prototype theory as a theory of concepts. *Cognition, 9,* 35–58.

Porzig, W. (1934). Wesenhafte bedeutungsbeziehungen, *beitrage zur geschichte der deutschen sprache und literatur, 58,* 70–79.

Posner, M. I., & Keele, S. W. (1968). On the genesis of abstract ideas. Journal of *Experimental Psychology, 77,* 353–63.

Putnam, H. (1975). The meaning of meaning. In K. Gunderson (Ed.), *Language, mind and knowledge. Minnesota studies in the philosophy of science V. VII.* Minneapolis: University of Minnesota Press.

Reed, S. K. (1972). Pattern recognition and categorization. *Cognitive Psychology, V, 3,* 382–407.

Rips, L. (1989). Similarity, typicality, and categorization. In S. Vosniadou & A. Ortony (Eds.), Similarity and analogical reasoning. Cambridge: Cambridge University Press.

Rosch, E. (1973). On the internal structure of perceptual and semantic categories. *Cognitive devel-*

opment and the acquisition of language. (pp. 111–44) T. E. Moore (Ed.), New York: Academic Press.

Rosch, E. (1974). Universals and cultural specifics in human categorization. In R. Breslin, W. Lonner, & S. Bochner (Eds.), *Cross-cultural perspectives on learning.* London: Sage.

Rosch, E. (1975a). Cognitive reference points. *Cognitive Psychology V, 7,* 532–47.

Rosch, E. (1975b). Cognitive representations of semantic categories. *Journal of Experimental Psychology: General V, 104,* 192–233.

Rosch, E. (1978). Principles of categorization. In E. Rosch & B. B. Lloyd (Ed.), *Cognition and categorization.* Hillsdale, NJ: Lawrence Erlbaum Associates.

Scheffler, I. (1979). *Beyond the letter: A philosophical inquiry into ambiguity, vagueness, and metaphor in language.* London, Boston: Routledge & Kegan Paul.

Smith, E. E., & Medin, D. L. (1981). *Categories and concepts.* Cambridge, MA: Harvard University Press.

Smith, E. E., Shoben, E. J., & Rips, L. J. (1974). Structure and process in memory: A featural model for semantic decisions. *Psychological Review, 81,* 214–241.

Trier, J. (1934). Das sprachliche feld. *Neue Jahrbucher fur Wissenschaft und Jungenbilden, 10,* 428–449.

Vosniadou, S., & Ortony, A. (Eds.). (1989). *Similarity and analogical reasoning.* Cambridge: Cambridge University Press.

Wertheimer, M. (1938). Numbers and numerical concepts in primitive peoples. In W. D. Ellis (Ed.), *A source book in gestalt psychology.* New York: Harcourt Brace.

Wierzbicka, A. (1980). *Lingua mentalis: The semantics of natural language.* New York: Academic Press.

4 Names and Naming: Why We Need Fields and Frames

Adrienne Lehrer
University of Arizona

INTRODUCTION

An important question that arises with respect to the organization of the lexicon is what the best theoretical framework is for showing (a) how lexical items are related to one another and (b) how concepts are lexicalized, that is, expressed in words. In particular, is there an empirical difference between the claims of semantic field theory and semantic frames? If there is a difference, is one approach superior, or does each have advantages in handling information that the other does not? This chapter addresses these issues by examining proper names in English.

A common basic distinction in noun subclasses is between proper and common nouns. Often little more is said about the difference, as in contemporary generative grammar, where the difference is characterized by the feature $+/-$ Proper. However, if we look at a wide range of names and at the processes for naming, we discover that the difference between common and proper nouns is anything but clear-cut; and moreover, the vocabulary is not neatly divided. Instead we see that names are productively drawn from the common word classes and that not only nouns are used. Finally, words that are traditionally classified as proper nouns, such as *John,* are often used as nonreferring expressions.

Philosophical accounts of proper names, though interesting and important, have focused too narrowly on personal and place names, which in turn have led to a limited perspective on names. Moreover, philosophers have been interested primarily in names as referring expressions (insofar as they refer). The principal philosophical conflict has been between the causal theory and the descriptive theory, each of which is best suited to a different range of cases.[1]

But personal and place names are a small part of the phenomenon of naming. John Carroll (1985) has called our attention to the fact that people name all kinds of other things—buildings, streets, companies, computer files, events, and pets. Carroll does not distinguish between proper and common names, but the English language does not either. So we say equally naturally:

1. Phoenix is the name of the capital city in Arizona;
2. red is the name of a bright color.

The common grammatical distinction between common and proper nouns, which is partially correlated with capital and small letters in contemporary English orthography, fails to correspond to any important philosophical distinction, such as the difference between referring to an individual or a class. *General Motors* refers to an individual company, whereas *Buick* refers to a class of cars, with numerous time-indexed models. Therefore, we can talk about a Buick or Buicks, using the normal patterns for articles and plurals with count nouns. *Christmas* and *Passover* denote cyclical holidays, whereas *Monday* and *January* denote cyclical time periods, and thus each denotes a class rather than a unique event.

Algeo (1973), who provides an extensive discussion of the various kinds and uses of proper names, demonstrates that there is no single definition of proper name that will serve all purposes. The syntactic division between proper and common nouns, the distinction between count and mass nouns, the semantic and pragmatic aspects of names, and referential functions of names are all distinct (though overlapping) aspects of names, and it is not possible to reduce everything to a single distinction or definition.

For the purposes of this chapter I follow Huddleston (1988), who draws a distinction between proper nouns and proper names. A proper noun is a grammatical noun subclass. A proper name is "the institutionalized name of some specific person, place, organization, etc.—institutionalized by some formal act of naming and/or registration" (p. 96). A proper name may have the form of a

---

[1]The causal theory, which is most closely associated with Mill (1936) and Kripke (1980), sees proper names as referring to individuals, and thereby as having no meaning. This account works very well for people we know or know of and can identify, and for whom we can imagine a different life history (e.g., Richard Nixon, President of the United States from 1968 to 1974). The descriptive theory of names, associated with Russell (1905) and Searle (1969), which associates proper names with descriptions (but in Searle's version, with no unique description), is best suited to cases like Jack the Ripper, the referent of which has not been identified, and where the name is associated with particular actions and properties. Names of historical figures, such as Moses or Homer, whose existence has been questioned, are in between.

proper noun, such as *London* or *Jack,* but it need not. "Thus *The Open University* is a proper name but not a proper noun: what distinguishes it from, say, *the older university* is precisely that it is the official name of a particular institution."

It is important to distinguish between names as referring expressions and name inventories. The female name inventory in English contains *Mary, Joan, Susan,* and *Ann* among others. In the case of inventories there is no reference to any particular individual in a decontextualized sentence. That explains why these names can so easily be treated like common count nouns, as in sentences like *I know three Marys* or *the tall Mary you met in France.* These names are available for reference, and, in normal context-based utterances, the speaker usually employs the name to refer. Names such as *John F. Kennedy,* used for the former president of the United States, refers to a particular unique individual.[2]

Linguists normally draw a distinction between closed and open classes. The class of name inventories is extremely open, much more so than classes of common nouns and verbs, because new items are frequently added. Moreover, among some groups of speakers, parents frequently make up new names for children. However, at least the commonest items in name inventories will be recognized as names, and new ones will be identified as names on syntactic grounds. In the case of traditional names, we can often identify the referent on the basis of the name. Consider the following:

3. John is hungry;
4. Fido is hungry.

Although *John* could refer to a dog or cat or specific car, it probably "refers" to a human male, whereas (4) "refers" to a dog.[3] Personal surnames are even more open than first names.

Just as a competent speaker of a natural language is expected to know the basic vocabulary, so he is expected to know the common names. As Algeo (1973) pointed out, someone who did not recognize *John* and *Mary* as personal names or *London* and *New York* as place names could hardly be considered completely competent in English.

In this chapter I am concerned with a variety of names—some of them for individuals (persons and things) and some trade names, especially with names for things and events which are drawn from the common vocabulary (e.g., names that correspond to descriptions, such as the *Grand Canyon* and *World War Two*).

---

[2]Of course, we can always imagine situations with several individuals named John F. Kennedy, and in this case the name does not guarantee unique reference.

[3]"Refers" is in quotes because in these examples no reference to any particular individual is intended. But in linguistics examples, the use of such names carries with it information, for example, sex. Therefore, if a reflexive is used, as in *John hurt himself,* in contrast to the starred **John hurt herself,* it is unnecessary (and would be pedantic) to add that *John* is male.

I confine this study to proper names, not common nouns. The reason for including proper names and trade names together is that they both result from some "baptismal" process, that is, they are deliberately selected and applied.

Unlike philosophers, whose main interests involve reference, along with associated metaphysical and ontological issues, my focus is on the appropriateness in selecting names for a variety of entities: concrete things (house pets, race horses, streets, university buildings, beauty shops), semiabstract entities (rock bands, opera companies), and events (festivals and wars). Since names often involve naive metaphysics and folk beliefs, these notions are invoked where necessary. But when I discuss names like *Mary,* my concern is not with any particular referent of that name but rather of the kinds of entities that can appropriately be called *Mary.*

There are two ways of attacking the problem: (1) We can look at kinds of things to be named and ask what names are given, and (2) we can look at inventories of names and ask what kinds of things the names can be attached to. I use both approaches in this chapter.

The main thesis of this chapter is that speakers of any language make judgments about the appropriateness of names for things that are analogous to judgments about grammaticality, semantic well formedness, and pragmatic acceptability. Corporations and business establishments have long known this fact, but it has been ignored by linguists and philosophers, perhaps because it is either too obvious to bother about, or perhaps because naming seems somewhat unpredictable. However, I try to show that there is a great deal of systematicity in names.

A central question in the philosophical controversy on names is whether names have meaning. The question is theory laden, because it depends on what is meant by "meaning." If any kind of cultural, historical, or pragmatic information is included, then names have meaning. On the other hand, if meaning is restricted to words that can be defined by a set of necessary and sufficient conditions (or a comparable prototypical definition), then names do not have meaning. Lyons (1977) holds the view that names have no sense, although he discusses aspects of naming, such as conditions of appropriateness, culture practices, uses of names as predicates, and other phenomena to which "name meaning" has been attached.

My position on this point is somewhat of a hybrid. With respect to name inventories, such as *Paul, Evelyn, George,* they have no meaning, although their application to individuals (persons, animals, and things) is strongly constrained by cultural norms. In the case of referring expressions, my position is sympathetic to that of Mill (1936), who argued that names directly denote—they have no sense. Mill's criterion was that a name based on a description can be detached from that description without any loss of meaning—because it has no connotation in Mill's terminology—or without leading to any contradiction. Consider Mill's example of *Dartmouth,* which was so named because it was located at the mouth of the Dart River: "If sand should choke up the mouth of the river, or an earthquake change its course, and remove it to a distance from the town, the name of the town would not necessarily be changed" (p. 20). Actually, Mill's example is not the best one, since the phonological reduction of /mawθ/ to /məθ/ has already obscured the etymology. A better example is one of a dance company that was named the *Tenth Street Dance Works,* because the group originally had a small studio on Tenth Street. When a more suitable performance space became available (and which was not on Tenth Street), the company did not change its name. The London Bridge, currently located in Lake Havasu, Arizona, retains the name appropriate to its origin. Notice that Mill does not rule out the possibility that a name might be changed, if the description on which it is based is no longer appropriate. (Below I present examples where changes were made because a change in circumstances make the names inappropriate.)

Proper names like the *Tenth Street Dance Works* or *the Social Sciences Building* appear to have meaning because the names (or at least parts of them) are drawn and/or constructed from the common vocabulary, and *those* words do have meaning. The line between a pure description and a proper name based on a description is subtle and difficult to draw, but I hope that a theory could draw that line.

Most names, whether based on descriptions or not, provide some information about the referent. In other words, if one knows the name for someone or something, one can usually make reasonable inferences about the referent. Even the proper nouns that are used as first names in English and many other cultures enable one to predict the sex of the bearer.[4] Therefore, most speakers of English would feel that *Sally* is an unsuitable name for a boy and *Samuel* a poor choice for a girl. A few names are androgynous, but sometimes when a name is commonly given to girls, parents stop using it for boys. This happened with the name *Shirley.* Some names (both first and last) may enable one to make predictions about ethnicity, but such predictions are likely to be weaker than those for sex.[5] My position is close to that of Allan (1986), who argues that although proper names do not have a sense, they must be listed in the lexicon of a language because they carry information with them.

The current study, motivated by Carroll's *What's In A Name?* (1985), calls attention to the large variety of names for things besides personal and place names. Carroll introduces the notion of rule-scheme, which is characterized as follows:

> A rule-scheme differs from a linguistic rule in being less complete, less permanently a part of the language, and more discretionary from a speaker's point of view. . . . Violating linguistic rules makes speech ungrammatical. In contrast,

---

[4]Exceptions come to mind, of course. There are a few androgynous names, like *Lynn,* and masculine noms de plume for female writers, like George Sands.

[5]Stan Lieberson (1984) uses first names as an index of ethnic integration into mainstream society.

rule-schemes are relatively flexible; they narrow down the space of possibilities instead of making a single prediction. . . . And rule-schemes can be violated with impunity; if someone really wanted to name a new type of cookie *Ronald Reagan,* they could. Nevertheless, rule-schemes have structure. People don't mechanically grind out new names, but surely they don't start completely from scratch each time either. (p. 16)

Rule-schemes consist of a morphosyntactic part and a semantic part, although Carroll does not stress this difference, and for the domains he has examined, he tends to lump them together. The morphosyntactic part would deal with whether the name was simple (consisting of one word, for example), a compound, a noun phrase with a prenominal modifier or a postnominal prepositional phrase (which could be further specified by a specific preposition), or a morphologically complex expression, or some constructed word, such as a blend or acronym. Although these categories are rather simple, they do in fact correlate loosely with categories of names for things. A *by*-NP following a head noun is more likely to appear as the name for a beauty salon than for a restaurant. For example, *Coiffures by Jacques* is a better name than *Cuisine by Jacques* for their respective categories. Even a difference in the number of words in a name can differentiate schemes. House pets typically have one-word names, whereas race horses are more likely to have names with two or three words. However, the semantic considerations are more interesting and more to the point of this chapter, and I concentrate on these.

Personal Names

Personal names not only name persons but can also serve as a source of many other kinds of names. There's a wealth of data on naming practices among different groups of people at different times, the popularity of certain names, etc. but this will not be dealt with here.

First of all, names that refer to specific individuals, such as *Abraham Lincoln* or *Martin Luther King, Jr.,* can serve as the basis for names for many kinds of things: streets, towns, buildings, parks, schools, and objects whose names are selected to commemorate one of these individuals. Such names can also be given names for other individuals or used as a part of a name, as in *George Washington Carver.* In these commemorative cases, it is the surname which is important and which will be selected if only a part of the name is used. Chains can occur, so that a street might be named Lincoln Street, and at a later time a bridge that is connected to Lincoln Street might be called *Lincoln (Street) Bridge,* not directly to commemorate Lincoln but because of the location of the bridge vis-a-vis the street.

Personal names can be the source of most business establishments, and in such cases the genitive form of either the first or last name can be used. So *Ellen*

Jefferson can name her restaurant or boutique *Ellen's* or *Jefferson's*. And of course personal names can combine with common nouns to produce very ordinary-looking noun phrases, like *Ellen's Diner or Jefferson's Beauty Salon.*

Pet Names

Although pet names must vary from culture to culture, just as attitudes toward pets do, there are three principle schemes for naming house pets (cats and dogs) in contemporary American culture. First of all, names can be selected from the personal first name inventory, and I have met cats and dogs named *Jack, Tex,* and *George.* Sometimes a name with ethnic associations will be selected for a particular breed. For example, a German Shepherd is more likely to be called *Ludwig* and a Russian Wolfhound *Vladmir* than vice versa. Also an Arabian horse may receive an Arabic name, whereas an American quarterhouse will not (see Taggart, 1962). Secondly, house pets can be named after famous individuals, with names like *Cleopatra, Rembrandt,* or *Maximillian.* Thirdly, they can be given descriptive names, such as *Stripes, Fluffy, Smoky,* or *Pepper.* Although there are generic dog names like *Rover* and *Fido,* and cat names like *Felix,* these names are more likely to be used for comic strip animals than for real house pets.

Automobiles

Aronoff (1981) has described the relationship of lines and models of American automobiles with respect to their place in the system. He points out that the common practice was to introduce a new line and model at the top of the hierarchy, thereby devaluing the others and eliminating the lowest rank.

But another aspect of automobile naming involves looking at the names selected for makes, models, and lines, because these are taken from a rather limited number of domains, and some names fit into several categories. The lists that follow show that most of these names can be classified into the following domains:

Animals

Impala	Jaguar	Mustang	Rabbit	Pinto
Stingray	Falcon	Cobra	Cougar	Road runner
Firebird	Ram	Spider	Gazelle	Bobcat
Lark	Skylark	Superbee	Superwasp	Golden Hawk
Taurus	Sable	Cuda <Barracuda		(Bug/Beetle)
Thunderbird				

Most of the animals are associated with speed, strength, agility, cunning, or some combination. The list also includes the mythological Firebird and Thunderbird, and as we see later, mythological references are common in this name domain. Although the VW Bug/Beetle is listed and these creatures do not fit into the characteristics of speed, grace, and power, it should be noted that these are, as far as I am aware, unofficial names, not those originally conferred by the company.

A second popular domain for cars is taken from place names:

Places

Malibu	Montclair	Eldorado	Bel Air	Seville
Biarritz	Calais	Granada	Riviera	Versailles
Torino	Belvedere	Montego	Windsor	Monte Carlo
Hollywood	Catalina	De Ville	Grandville	Fairlane
Corsica	Cordoba	Ventura		

We could add a few more items, like *Victoria,* which could be classified as a place or personal name, and also items like *New Yorker* and *Continental,* which add suffixes to places. Many of these places are famous as resorts and vacation spots where the rich and famous hang out (or did so in the past) or as places where the rich and famous live or work.

Another common domain for car names is drawn from astronomical objects. (Compounds with one astronomical morpheme are included.):

Astronomical Objects

Vega	Pulsar	Taurus	Nova	Mercury
Comet	Meteor	Astro	Apollo	Galaxie
Satellite	Starfire	Sunliner	Skyliner	Starchief

Another small class of natural objects is taken from meteorology, giving us the following:

Meteorological Objects (Winds)

Tempest   Cyclone   Tornado   Duster

Personal names do not usually serve as a basis for car names (except for companies, such as Ford). The main exceptions are *Edsel* and *Brougham. Victoria, Lafayette,* and *Lincoln* could be treated as personal names, but they could also be treated as the places named after those individuals. *Tudor,* a family name, is a counterexample but is probably used because of its association with royalty. *Victoria* may also enter the domain because its most salient referent is *Queen Victoria.* However, nouns denoting roles and types are common as a source for names. In some cases an adjectival derivative is used, or some metonymic object associated with royalty.

Royalty and Nobility

Monarch	Regency	Crown	Imperial	LeBaron	Marquis
Coronet	Cavalier	(Tudor)	Windsor	(Victoria)	
White Prince					

Roles associated with masculinity and power are popular for four-wheel drive vehicles and trucks:

Macho Types

Matador	Samurai	Ranger	Scout	Champ	Challenger
Corsair	Chieftain				

Other roles include high status items such as *Ambassador* and *Judge.* A few others are *Blazer, Nomad,* and *Maverick,* with connotations of adventure, daring, and risk.

There are a number of other nouns and adjectives, but they can be classified into emotions and feelings (*Fury, Caprice, Esprit*), words associated with power and victory (*Triumph, Conquest, Elite, Valiant, Citation*), and items associated with adventure (*Safari, Horizon, Ventura, Blazer*).

Racetracks provide a source of automobile names, as in the following:

Racetracks

Grand Prix	LeMans	Sebring	Grand National
Gran Torino	Daytona	Bonneville	Baja

Another popular type of automobile name is to take one that sounds Italian (for a car that does not come from Italy), no doubt based on the high status of a few Italian cars:

Italian Sounding

Avanti	Camaro	Fiero	Quattro	Volare
Allante	Ventura	Beretta		

A few names are based on weapons (*Dart, Javelin, Cutlass, Laser, Corvette,* and *Cruiser*). There is also a miscellany of names loosely associated with roads and travel: *El Camino, Fleetliner, Speedster, Dasher, Roadster, Cruiser.* Another category is one that sounds hi-tech, containing *Turbo, Delta 80,* and *Laser.*[6] Finally, numbers and letters are frequently used in automobile names.

Although there are a few items not classified, we see that automobile names fall into distinct categories. Even some of the items not categorized can be

---

[6]This category was suggested by Paul Saka.

lexically associated with some of the traditional classes. *Geo,* for example, can be analyzed as contrasting with *Astro.*

Generalizations among the semantic fields can be made, combining powerful things (some animals, weapons, and storms) and fast things (some animals and racetracks).

One of the striking things about automobile names, of course, is that the class is necessarily open, because new models and lines will get new names. And, of course, new categories may be called on for name sources. One new class is names of fashionable streets, such as *Park Avenue* and *Fifth Avenue.* If this turns out to be a trend, we can expect names like *Champs Elysée* and *Wilshire Boulevard.*

Rock Bands

Names for rock bands, especially heavy metal rock, are interesting, because one criterion for a name in this domain is that it be outrageous, even offensive. In this respect, the naming practices fall in place with other unconventional practices associated with rock musicians, such as dress and hair styles.

There are a variety of scheme classifications, but the one proposed here accounts for a large number of names. The largest single category I found was names involving death:

Death

Grateful Dead	Dead Kennedys	Megadeath	Suicidal Tendencies
Creeping Death	The Stranglers	Overkill	Skull and Tophat
Slayer	D.O.A.	Styx	Dead or Alive
Killer Dwarfs	Dead Tongues	S.O.D.	

Other popular categories as a source of names are dangerous animals, drugs (and other unhealthy substances), and weapons:

Drugs and Unhealthy Substances
Pot Leaf   Poison   Alcoholica   Venom

Dangerous Animals

King Cobra	Scorpions	Great White	White Snake
White Lion	W.A.S.P.		

Weapons

Guns N' Roses	Iron Maiden	L. A. Guns
Sex Pistols	U 2	Bulletboys
Kick Axe	B-52s	

In addition, there are a variety of other names with connotations of disease, abnormality, and social deviance: *Anthrax, Misfits, Twisted Sister, Motley Crüe, 10,000 Maniacs, Atrophy,* and *Public Enemy.*

Another fairly popular source category involves religious associations, usually without pious connotations:

Religious Associations

Kingdom Come	Exodus	Black Sabbath
Leviticus	Heathen	Genesis

One aspect of the unconventionality of rock band names can be seen in ones with unusual syntactic combinations, or even outright syntactic violations: *The Who, Faster Pussycat,* and *Frankie Goes to Hollywood.* Names consisting of whole clauses are common in titles of literary works, but otherwise they are highly unusual.[7]

Some groups are named after their leader (Alice Cooper, Elvis Costello, Randy Rhoads, Ozzy Osbourne). Sex does not seem to be a major category source, though there are a few names: *Sex Pistols, Kiss, The Slits* (a female group), *AC/DC,* and possibly *The Kinks.*

Some of the names involve language play of certain kinds, such as puns (*Kick Axe, Little Feat, Beatles*), incongruent combinations (*Guns N' Roses, Skull and Tophat*) and oxymorons (*Quiet Riot*). The pun in *Dead Tongues* rests on the fact that the leader is a linguist.

Beauty Salons

Names for beauty salons have been described by Wilhelm (1988), based on listings in the Denver telephone directory (yellow pages). Similar results can be found in other American cities, and in fact many shops are national chains.

In addition to names based on the owner's first or last name and location (devices common to many kinds of business establishments), names for beauty salons make extensive use of alliteration (*Crystals Cut and Curl*), rhyme (*Loxy Locks, Swirl and Curl*), and consonance (*Scissor Wizards*). Puns are common in names, with the most frequent ones based on *shear, mane, cut,* and *hair: Shear Genius, Mane Street Hair Stylists, A Head of Our Time, Hair It Is,* and *A Cut Above. Hairport* is the name of a barber shop in the Minneapolis–St. Paul Airport. One of my favorites is *Curl Up and Dye.*[8]

---

[7]I have been told that there is a hair product called *Gee Your Hair Smells Terrific.*

[8]It has been pointed out to me that class differences are relevant. Cute names are principally found among the lower priced establishments. This might also explain why such naming practices are not found for the next category, theater and opera company names, because the clientel is upper and middle-upper class.

The word play associated with names for beauty salons and rock groups can be contrasted with names for civic opera, dance, and theater companies, which tend to be serious and descriptive, although theater companies sometimes select names that give the acronym ACT.[9]

Streets

Names for streets are interesting, and quite a lot of variety is permitted.[10] Streets are often named for famous people, geographical features, trees (in the United States), presidents, and places (cities, U.S. states, islands). In the United States important dates are not used, whereas they are common in some countries (e.g., Mexico). Another common source for street names is numbers and to a lesser extent letters. Whenever numbers are used (which are almost always positive integers[11]), the number names must follow the numerical sequences. Whereas there is no particular requirement to group *Fir Street* one street over from *Spruce Street*, it is completely inappropriate to shift around numbers by putting *Fifth Street* between *Third Street* and *First Street*. The same principle of sequence holds for letters, which must be alphabetical.[12]

Algeo (1978) compares the old and recent streets names in Athens, Georgia,

---

[9]The local company was formerly named Arizona Civic Theater when it performed only in Tucson. However, when it became a statewide group, it changed its name to Arizona Theater Company.

[10]The naive ontology of what constitutes an individual street is interesting. In the United States, at least, streets should be continuous, preferably straight, although some curving is permitted to follow natural contours (e.g., when following a lake or cliff contour). Using the same name for 90° shifts is alright when it would be impossible to go straight or when the road must go around some barrier, but then it is expected that the "same" street will continue, following a roughly straight path. Discontinuous parts of the "same" street are acceptable if they can be connected by an imaginary straight line on a map (e.g., if there is a barrier or park that interrupts the flow of through traffic) or, in a new community, if the parts of the same street are not completely built, but it would be expected that at some future time they would be. In the case of cities that are laid out in strict grids, where a street corresponds to a hypothetical straight line, the same street name may be used. It seems inappropriate to change the name of a street when there is no deviation from a straight line or when two (or more) noncontinuous parts that cannot be connected by a hypothetical straight line are given the same name.

[11]Occasionally, a half may name a street, such as *Seven and a Half,* between *Seventh Street* and *Eighth Street,* but one does not find a street named *Square Root of Minus One.*

[12]There are some exceptions, such as the fact that what would be expected to be Sixth Avenue in Manhattan is Avenue of the Americas. Sometimes a named street will lie between two numbered streets. In other domains involving numbers and letters, exceptions occur. For example, hotels often omit calling a floor the 13th floor because 13 is considered an unlucky number. In some theaters in which the rows are letters, *i* is sometimes omitted because it could be confused with *j*. Also, as Keith Allan points out, highway numbers do not work in a regular way, although there is some loose correlation between geography and U.S. highway and interstate numbers, even though the numbering is not consecutive. Interstate numbers tend to be multiples of 5; the gaps were no doubt left so that new interstates could be built and that appropriate new numbers could be used.

and his results are mirrored in many American cities, especially those with recent rapid growth. Whereas most old street names were named after local people of prominence or after descriptive features adjacent to the street (e.g., *Broad Street, College Avenue,* or *Factory Street*), modern streets are laid out and named by developers of housing developments with dominant themes. Plantation Estates uses a pioneer theme, with names like: *Plantation Drive, Homestead Drive, Frontier Court,* and *Doe Run.* Moreover, street names contain words like *spring, lake,* and *hill,* even though there are no such geographical features in the area. But note that the names are drawn from limited semantic fields. Many new developments use the same first part for many street names, relying on the category for complete identification, such as *Oahu Circle, Oahu Lane,* and *Oahu Place.*

In addition to studies like that of Algeo, street names are often the subject of journalistic feature stories in the popular press, for example, one in *The Arizona Republic* August 20, 1989, which lists unusual street names in the Phoenix area, such as *Cow Track Drive, Meander Way, Mosquito Range Drive,* and *Shootout Plaza.*

More important for the purposes of this chapter, however, is the other part of the street names—the semantic category of street, avenue, boulevard, lane, court, freeway, highway, or alley. It is expected that there be some correlation between the use of these words in names and their decontextualized meanings. Moreover, in some cases, it is expected that parallel streets share the same category. This is especially true with numbered and lettered streets, where often numbered *streets* contrast with numbered *avenues.* For example, in Tucson numbered streets run east–west whereas numbered avenues run north–south. In Phoenix numbered streets run north–south to the east of Central Avenue whereas numbered avenues run north–south to the west of Central.[13]

To what extent do the descriptive parts of the name correspond to their meanings? Consider just a few possible terms: *court, circle, boulevard, avenue,* and *drive.* Although a complete study of denotation would require on-site inspections, I did not do this, but I did look at a Tucson map to get some idea of the way in which these terms were applied to streets. On the whole, *court* is used for cul-de-sacs only. But of course many cul-de-sacs are called other things (*drive, lane*). Most things called *circle* have some curving in the path of the street, but relatively few *circles* are complete loops. (Even fewer approximated circles at all!) Many things that do make complete loops were not called *circles* but have various names (e.g., *drive, calle,* Spanish for "street"). *Boulevard* and *avenue* tend to be reserved for relatively major thoroughfares, but many wide streets are called other things, such as *way* or *road,* and *street* and *drive* seem to be usable

---

[13]Of course, if there is no contrast, and a speaker mistakenly uses *Central Street* for *Central Avenue,* reference may still succeed. This case is exactly like Donellan's example of using the expression *man with a martini* to pick out a man with water in a martini glass.

for anything. In addition, Tucson uses a number of Spanish loans, such as *calle,*
paseo, camino, and *avenido,* but there is no evidence that any attention is paid to
the Spanish meanings.

The question for the semanticist and psycholinguist is whether the language
learner is in any way influenced by the names for streets and the decontextualized
meanings. Does our concept of *lane* come from experiences we have with streets
having *lane* as part of the name or do we treat these categories as rather opaque?
In the former case, we might expect semantic shifts to result from a casual (read
careless) use of categories in street names. But in the latter case, we would not
expect any change. In many cases (e.g., *circle*), the more salient meanings for
the term would probably keep the senses together, in spite of anything street
names might do. In other cases, such as *lane* or *boulevard,* our concepts might be
formed through linguistic contexts (e.g., stories of children walking down lanes,
or narratives that involve boulevards that are vividly described as being wide and
tree lined).

University Buildings

The next category is names for university buildings. There are two popular
naming schemes: The first is to name a building after some person who was
important in the history of the institution, such as a past president or a generous
benefactor. The other is to name the building after some discipline for which the
building is used. Both types are used at the University of Arizona. The problem
with the latter strategy is that when a department moves out of a building with the
department name, the building name is no longer appropriate. At Arizona when a
new psychology building was constructed, the old one was called *Old Psych* for
awhile and then renamed after an person. The former *Liberal Arts Building* was
renamed *Social Sciences* after most of the tenants were social science departments, and the *Humanities Building* was changed to *Center for English as a
Second Language* when the function of the building changed. These changes
required considerable expenditures, because the stone lettering on the outside of
the building had to be redone, new maps constructed, etc. Moreover, when the
Linguistics Department was located in the Mathematics Building (because there
was space for it there), many people would look puzzled about its being located
there and expected an academic justification.

Numbers as Names

The final topic briefly mentioned is numbers as names. Numbers (often in
conjunction with other names and letters) can be used as names for many things:
streets (as we have seen), aircraft types (Boeing 727, Lockheed 1011), appliance
models, biological varietals, cars (Mazda RX–7), stone tool types, and stars.

However, people I have talked with are resistant to accepting numbers as names of individuals in the current world. Although they will admit that in a science fiction context numbers could well be names, they do not accept social security numbers as names, even though such numbers may well be superior to names as a means of identifying people. Numbers are too impersonal and are therefore used in situations in which people are deliberately depersonalized, such as prisons.

Discussion

Having looked at a variety of naming schemes in several domains, the main question is: How does this contribute to a theory of names and naming or to anything else in semantics?

One consequence is that although the concept of semantic fields is relevant, it is not sufficient. We must deal with names in terms of something larger, for example, frames or domains. At the same time, it is not particularly useful to talk about names and naming practices in general, since each frame (domain, class of entities) has different schemes. What counts as a good name for one kind of object is bad for other kinds. Even closely related categories like house pets and race horses utilize different kinds of name schemes. At the same time, semantic field analyses that deal only with lexemes are also not sufficient, because many names are larger than lexemes. Therefore, a theory of good naming must have access to compositional processes in semantics to evaluate a name properly. For example, *Over the Edge* is a good name for a race horse, but no current semantic field approach can deal with such phenomena. As Barsalou shows (this volume), relatively few complex concepts are lexicalized monolexemically.

A second reason for requiring frames in addition to fields (pointed out by Scott DeLancey, personal communication) is that not everything in semantic fields would make a good name. For example, not every animal name is appropriate for a car, only those that denote speed, strength, and other qualities desirable for automobiles. This would make a car name like *Turtle* or *Slug* highly unlikely.

Third, although the stock of names in any domain is quite open—far more so than even the open syntactic classes—it is not the case that "anything goes" any more so than in applying common names to things. Just as I can stipulate that my car is to be called "your table" and your table is to be called "my car," to do so without a compelling reason is to violate maxims of conversational cooperation. I suggest that calling a baby girl "Someone is Listening" or "Mouse" (except perhaps as a nickname) is equally inappropriate, in this case violating cultural norms. This is not to say that people do not behave inappropriately at times. The Hogg family named their daughters Ima and Eura. But many people feel that this practice is weird, if not downright cruel.

Fourth, the names for many kinds of things are created from the common word class (that is, those words that have meaning). And the meaning of the word is relevant to the name. In the more straightforward categories (where irony is seldom used), the common noun (adjective, verb, etc.) provides a constraint. Carroll (1985) wrote that "while it is not a contradiction to say that *Dartmouth* is not at the Dart's mouth, it *is* a contradiction to say that *the Willis Avenue Bridge* is not a bridge, or is not named after Willis Avenue" (p. 167). Although I am sympathetic to Carroll's position, I would prefer to say not that it would be a contradiction for *the Willis Avenue Bridge* to be something else but rather that this name might be inappropriate. I use the weak "might be" because *bridge* in a name could be extended to things that are marginally bridges (e.g., pedestrian overpasses). Calling a pedestrian overpass that spans the Marshall Freeway *the Marshall Freeway Bridge* might not be analytic. It depends on one's semantic theory and semantic analysis: whether an overpass counts as a bridge. However, the meanings of words in the common vocabulary severely constrain the use of such words in names. *Shady Lane* might be given to an avenue but not to a freeway.

Fifth, in many naming domains, such as car names (models, makes, and lines), new names are selected from a relatively small set of semantic fields (extending the term *semantic field* to include place names). Although not all car names can be fit into these categories, most can be. And I would predict that when new source domains are added, they will be productive. In other words, if an automobile company decides to name a line after famous movie stars or winning race horses, a whole set of names from these domains will be selected, not just one name from each new set.

Words in the common vocabulary enter into a variety of lexical relationships, such as synonymy, hyponymy, antonymy, etc. (see Chaffin, this volume). Are there lexical relationships among names? Although I have not investigated this topic yet, it seems that some names do exhibit something like synonymy, in that alternative expressions can denote the same entity. For example, *World War II* can also be referred to as *The Second World War,* although *Second Street* cannot be called *Street II*. There are also conventional nicknames for many personal names, such as *Dick* for *Richard* and *Sandy* for *Sandra*. Although not every Richard or Sandra uses the nickname, they are conventional enough so that in situations where first names are used, a speaker may well call someone *Dick* after that person is introduced as *Richard*.

Building on ideas of Paul Saka (1989), I propose that the "meanings" associated with proper names actually belong to the pragmatic component of the language, not the semantic component. Therefore, the information associated with certain proper names (e.g., personal and place names) is an important and often conventional part of its representation. Consider the car names that are based on places and recall that they are associated with glamourous places, such as resort areas where the "beautiful people" go (or went at the time that the name was selected). I predict it unlikely that an automobile manufacturer would select a name like *Gary, Indiana,* or *Watts* as a name.

As Kripke (1980) would no doubt stress, it is not necessary that Monte Carlo, a source for a fancy car name, be an attractive resort area and Gary, Indiana, not, and we can well imagine a future time where Monte Carlo becomes ugly due to increased crowding, pollution, urban decay, and where a complete renovation of Gary along with neighboring communities turns the south shore of Lake Michigan into one of the beauty spots in North America. If that were the case, and automobile manufacturers were still basing model names on attractive places, then perhaps *Gary* might be selected as a car name.

There are naming domains where irony is considered appropriate, such as pet names, especially names for dogs and cats. One of my colleagues had a cat named *Dog*. A panel of subjects (see Appendix) considers *Mouse* to be a good name for a dog or cat. However, the notion of irony in naming depends on the semantics of the ironical terms chosen, and irony often involves selecting an "opposite" in some sense, where "opposite" is construed as a significant contrast. This makes *Dog* or *Mouse* an appropriate ironical name for a cat. Although I do not know if *Screwdriver* or *Cantaloupe*[14] are good names for a cat, I do not think that they would be judged ironic. Bestowing pets with names like *Aristotle, Cleopatra,* and *Napoleon* also involves irony because a nonhuman creature is endowed with a name associated with a great person. Even in street naming, there is irony. Herb Caen reported in his column that the Bolton (England) Council lost a battle with a developer, but it had the right to choose the street names and has selected *Chernobyl Cresent, Salman Rushdie Avenue, Auschwitz View,* and *Ayatollah Khomeini Road.*[15] (These last cases involve pragmatic principles rather than semantic ones.)

In any case, the point is that words in the common lexicon (that is common nouns, verbs, etc.) are available for use as proper names. It has also been often pointed out that proper nouns can serve as a source for creating new common nouns. So we see that there are interactions between the two sets.

Finally, as Saka pointed out (1989, p. 2) by associating content with names, we are able to show the similarity between utterances in which proper names refer to specific individuals and metaphorical predicates (cf. Jespersen, 1929);

5. He's another Napoleon,

requires a similar kind of interpretation as

6. He's a wolf (where *he* refers to a man).

---

[14]One could well imagine a situation in which *Cantaloupe* was selected as a pet name for an animal that loved to eat cantaloupe or who (which?) had an amusing experience (from the owner's point of view) with a cantaloupe.

[15]I wish to thank Paul Kay for pointing out this column.

In both cases for the hearers to figure out the interpretation, they must draw on their commonplace beliefs about Napoleon and wolves, respectively. Or consider:

7. Bill is a pansy.

There are at least two interpretations: The first is that Bill refers to a human male and the predicate must be reinterpreted metaphorically to mean that Bill is a weakling or is gay. In the second interpretation, the sentence is interpreted literally, but the flower referred to has a proper name, a somewhat unusual, but not unheard of situation.

To test the main hypothesis that speakers have strong intuitions on the appropriateness of names for various classes of objects, I submitted a questionnaire to students in beginning linguistics classes. One group was asked to consider a set of names and decide for which objects the names would be appropriate, and the other group was asked to consider a set of objects and decide which names would be good for them.

The null hypothesis would be that any name would be equally good or bad for any of the objects. However, I prefer to state a positive hypothesis: Speakers' judgments about the appropriateness of names is strong and rule governed. They will accept new names for things that are drawn from semantic fields or name inventories that pattern like existing names for such objects.

The most general hypothesis is confirmed: namely, that subjects have intuitions about appropriateness of names for various objects. However, in some cases, more specific predictions were not confirmed. For example, I predicted that *Milano* would be judged to be a good car name, because it refers to an Italian place. However, maybe Milan is not considered an attractive enough city, or maybe the subjects did not know where Milano is or even that it is a city in Italy. When we turn to personal given names, it can be seen that naming children is highly restricted. Although only appropriate names for baby girls were requested, it is mainly conventional names for girls that are acceptable. Appropriate names for rock bands are quite diverse, but there are still restrictions. In a pilot study the category for book titles was included, but apparently the name of a literary title can be anything at all. So there is at least one domain with unrestricted naming, though it is expected that most titles will have something to do with the literary work in question.

The normal situation is that naming, though creative, is highly constrained. Moreover, the preceding considerations suggest that semantic fields and semantic frames are not equivalent. In the case of names, semantic fields (or something like them) seem necessary to explain why whole sets of words from the common vocabulary can be drawn on for proper names and why they must retain at least some characteristics of their semantics. But because many names are constructed from phrases, and because they utilize pragmatic information such that not everything in a field is appropriate, fields are not sufficient, and for this reason, semantic frames are necessary as well.

ACKNOWLEDGMENTS

I wish to thank Keith Allan, Eva Kittay, Keith Lehrer, Laurell McLain, Diane Meador, Duane Roen, Paul Saka, and conference participants for comments on an earlier draft. I am also indebted to linguists from the University of Oregon for many insightful comments.

REFERENCES

Algeo, J. (1973). *On defining the proper name.* Gainsville: University of Florida Press.

Algeo, J. (1978). From classic to classy: Changing fashions in street names. *Names, 26,* 80–95. Reprinted in Harder (pp. 230–45).

Algeo, J. (1985). Is a theory of names possible? *Names, 33,* 175–44.

Allan, K. (1986). *Linguistic meaning.* New York: Routledge & Kegan Paul.

Aronoff, M. (1981). Automobile semantics. *Linguistic Inquiry, 12,* 329–47.

Askanas, M., & Kittay, E. F. (1979). What's in a name? *Philosophia, 8,* 689–99.

Barnhart, C. L. (1975). The selection of proper names in English dictionaries. *Names, 23,* 175–9. Reprinted in Harder (pp. 305–9).

Bach, K. (1987). *Thought and reference.* Oxford: Oxford University Press.

Carroll, J. M. (1985). *What's in a name?* New York: W. H. Freeman.

Harder, K. B. (1986). *Names and their varieties.* Boston: University Press of America.

Huddleston, R. (1988). *English grammar: An outline.* Cambridge: Cambridge University Press.

Jespersen, O. (1929). *The philosophy of grammar.* London: Allen & Unwin.

Jockey Club. (ND). *Names currently not available in the American stud book.* Lexington, KY.

Kripke, S. (1980). *Naming and necessity.* Cambridge, MA: Harvard University Press.

Landau, R. M. (1967). Name or number—which shall it be? *Names, 15,* 11–20.

Lieberson, S. (1984). What's in a name? . . . Some sociological possibilities. *International Journal of the Sociology of Language, 45,* 177–87.

Lockney, T. M., & Ames, K. (1981). Is 1069 a name? *Names, 29,* 1–35.

Lyons, J. (1977). *Semantics* (Vol. 1). Cambridge: Cambridge University Press.

Millward, C., & Millward, R. (1984). Ski-trail names: A new toponymic category. *Names, 32,* 191–217.

Mill, J. S. (1936). *A system of logic.* London: Longman's Green (Originally published, 1843).

Olson, G. (1989). Easy St.? No Way! *Arizona Republic,* August 20. Section S, p. 1.

Russell, B. (1905). On denoting. *Mind, 59,* 479–93.

Saka, P. (1989). *The architecture of proper meaning.* Tucson: MS.

Searle, J. (1969). *Speech acts.* Cambridge: Cambridge University Press.

Sloat, C. (1969). Proper nouns in English. *Language, 45,* 26–30.

Stewart, G. R. (1954). A classification of place names. *Names 2,* 1–13. Reprinted in Harder (pp. 23–35).

Sullivan, W. J. S. (1977). Review of *On defining the proper name* by John Algeo. *Forum Linguisticum, 2,* 79–92.

Taggart, J. E. (1962). *Pet names.* New York: Scarecrow Press.

Wilhelm, A. E. (1988). Pretty is as pretty says: The rhetoric of beauty salon names. *Names, 36,* 61–68.

APPENDIX

Questionnaire on Appropriateness

The figures to the left of the slash are in response to the question: Can the objects presented be appropriately given the names listed? (N = 50). The figures to the right of the slash are in response to the question: Can the names presented be appropriately used for the objects listed? (N = 45).

	Cat or Dog	Race Horse	Baby Girl	Rock Band	Beauty Salon	Clothing Store	Car Model	Street	Festival
Butch	46/40	12/14	1/1	9/18	8/10	7/5	1/1	4/9	1/1
R.S.V.P.	3/5	18/14	0/0	38/36	18/12	21/19	4/3	1/0	3/1
Mouse	17/30	6/10	1/2	8/7	1/1	3/1	7/1	3/8	1/1
Acapulco	11/7	24/22	2/4	20/23	7/15	13/22	12/9	31/30	14/17
John	17/19	7/10	0/0	3/0	4/11	7/13	0/2	5/13	0/3
Chez Pierre	10/10	22/18	0/0	15/11	31/30	28/29	7/5	8/10	4/7
Winter wonder	4/4	37/31	0/0	12/17	8/6	20/18	4/5	6/8	40/35
Promise	8/13	30/29	4/11	28/29	10/15	12/15	12/11	9/15	1/4
Ella	19/18	12/13	50/35	3/6	12/24	9/19	2/2	13/19	0/0
I 500	1/2	10/14	0/0	12/21	3/2	3/5	43/39	10/11	8/2
Happy Pacer	5/7	40/37	1/2	8/8	4/2	2/2	13/12	2/1	3/1
Tulip	22/28	10/16	9/8	7/6	4/11	6/9	0/2	24/27	4/3
Guaymas Fair	1/2	24/15	0/0	20/15	9/4	14/10	1/1	11/5	45/38
Ten	3/14	11/20	0/0	24/28	14/21	14/16	14/12	18/19	12/1
Gary Indiana	2/4	15/9	1/0	7/4	2/2	5/4	3/2	6/12	11/11
Lucky Winner	4/5	47/45	1/1	4/12	4/2	6/5	3/2	6/12	6/3
Aristotle	35/31	23/30	0/2	15/18	7/18	5/6	5/5	20/16	3/5
Marion	15/14	15/15	39/35	15/18	14/22	16/21	4/4	15/24	1/0
James Johnson	8/7	13/11	0/0	9/8	2/6	9/16	2/3	10/12	1/0
Silky	36/19	15/26	5/1	7/8	27/17	15/26	4/1	5/6	1/0
Milano	20/23	16/19	6/4	12/13	11/15	11/26	18/9	23/28	8/7
Over the Edge	0/2	26/22	0/0	40/37	14/9	18/19	2/1	3/0	14/9
Trendy	7/13	15/13	2/0	9/9	20/22	40/28	5/4	4/4	14/9
Stripes	28/23	17/21	1/0	17/30	5/2	19/25	3/2	3/4	2/3
Tahiti	15/17	16/19	3/1	12/18	8/8	7/18	11/3	21/20	16/20
Southern Exposure	2/2	13/18	1/3	37/33	23/10	31/25	6/2	6/0	20/12
L	13/8	5/6	4/1	15/18	12/8	11/9	36/17	17/25	2/0
Susan Mills	5/6	10/5	43/36	5/2	31/25	30/24	1/0	13/7	2/1
World War III	2/2	17/7	0/0	37/28	6/1	5/2	1/3	1/0	4/3
Someone is Listening	2/2	12/8	0/0	36/34	6/3	5/3	1/0	1/0	4/1
Thomas Jefferson	23/14	17/12	0/1	5/6	2/1	3/2	4/3	30/31	10/6

5 Semantic Contagion

James Ross
University of Pennsylvania

I: INTRODUCTION: THE PROBLEM OF "THE ORGANIZATION OF THE LEXICON" WITH A NEW APPROACH

Lexical Fields do not Organize the Lexicon; Something Else Does

Lexical field theories[1] were thought to display the organization of the lexicon at least at the level of contrastive word selection.[2] But no generalized theory of networking lexical fields (semantic fields)[3] was proposed for the overall organization of natural languages lexically, or to explain the similarity of lexical fields (with somewhat divergent members) across noncognate languages (e.g., words for kinship), or to explain field differences among languages (e.g., differences of words for weather, or time). Lexical field theory was developed unpretentiously and may have untested potentialities. Yet, those versions that postulate parallel

---

[1]A remote product of de Saussure's structuralism (and holistic contrast-dependence) and of earlier German scholars (see Lyons, 1977, Vol. 1, pp. 230–269). Lyons adapted the lexical field idea as "a paradigmatically and syntagmatically structured subset of the vocabulary" (the lexicon. cf. 13.1). Lyons' thrust was developed by Lehrer, (1974) and by Kittay (1987). (See also, Cruse, 1986.)

[2]Lyons (1977, Vol. 2, p. 412 and pp. 512–569) discusses lexical organization in terms of polysemy, hyponymy, compounding, and paronymy—the same principles I discuss. Lyons points out that Trier (1934) had considered lexical fields to be dynamic: "fields are living realities intermediate between words and the totality of the vocabulary." I disapprove, as I think Lyons does, of postulating abstractions, "realities" intermediate between words and another abstraction, "the vocabulary."

[3]Jackendoff (this volume) seems to offer a categorical organization of the lexicon of the kind I am proposing here to replace.

verbal and "mental" lexicons will suffer most from accumulating evidence that our conceptual competence, in various respects, subsists in our linguistic competence and is not separate from it, even though it can in some cases survive damage to the word-producing portions of the brain.

There are reasons of principle limiting what lexical fields can explain. As will emerge, they are not just the limitations that have encouraged "frame" semantics, or an emphasis on the "belief elements of meaning" peculiar to the lexicon of a given language, but reasons concerned with the combinatorial adaptation of words in all languages. An example of combinatorial adaptation, which I call *semantic contagion,* is the italicized pair: *"look down* / on art; *look down* / at the floor."[4]

Consequently, I go in a different direction, to develop an account of lexical organization that has lexical fields (semantic fields) as nonexplanatory but observable outcomes. My account has two explanatory dimensions: (a) *semantic contagion* (meaning-adaptation of words to their verbal contexts), on which this chapter concentrates, and (b) *pragmatic traction*[5] (the engagement of talk with action, that, for instance, generates symbol distinctions, yet with commonalities across cultures; e.g., words for body parts, kinship, boatparts, or disorders of the human spirit, etc.). The energy that drives both the "software" of semantic contagion and the development of new words comes from the engagement of talk with action; pragmatic traction. Both explanatory dimensions are especially prominent and easily distinguished in *craft-talk* (e.g., the professional talk of lawyers, doctors, boatbuilders, iron workers, newspapermen, etc.), and particularly visible, there, are the subcategories of semantic contagion (like analogy, metaphor, homonymy, figurative discourse, and denomination). It is on the enormous and luxuriantly varied subcorpus of craft-talk that I propose my accounts of "semantic contagion" and a related notion, *semantic relativity* (see later), should be tested and compared to other accounts of lexical organization.

---

[4]People who think that kind of difference is only "in the head" and not "on the page" will find little of interest in what follows.

[5]I mention a number of features of pragmatic traction, the mutual *grip* of discourse and action, but do not propose a general explanation of the notion (see Wittgenstein, 1968). For example, in the simple discourse used as part of some activity, say building with stones, where helpers are given a few commands, and where there are practices like leveling, positioning, etc. in very little time, "up" as a command to hand slabs or mortar to the builder will differentiate into "up" as command to climb up to join the builder, and a command to haul something up to the builder and a command to lift the end of a stone somewhat, for leveling; and so on, for every word in the discourse. Far from ever having to learn every sense of every word individually, talk in action makes the senses out of the activity. Thus you could start with *any* meaning (arbitrarily chosen from the lexicon as the "first" one learned for any word), and in a very brief time, in an activity that employs the other senses, a newcomer who learns the activity will know all the other senses.

My hypotheses can be confirmed or falsified by experiment and also approximated easily in second-grade games. Further, craft-talk is rapidly taught in just this way in law school and in medical school, by practice: "talk like a doctor!," "talk like a lawyer!"

Semantic contagion is a phenomenon, that is, a regular happening: Words adapt in meaning to other words—and word surrogates—which combine with them or are within syntagmatic reach: He *swallowed* /his water, /the insults, /his rage, /the lies, /his pride, /his enemies. Contrasting completion words differentiate susceptible frame words. That is the phenomenon to be explained, not just at the surface of events, but with a conception of the semantic cosmos.

The explanation discloses what I call the underlying *general semantic relativity*. According to this notion, widely accepted views of the componentiality of utterance-meaning have to be rejected, as well as standard notions of what compositionality consists in (see part IV). That is because we are not combining fixed meaning-values (like fixed quantities) under a single structural syntax, but are combining varying values in a syntax-affecting way. Instead of the notion of units of meaning combined by insertion into syntactical slots to make sentential wholes (see Davidson, 1984a, 1984b; Dummett, 1978), we have meaning units whose IDENTITY depends reciprocally on which meaning-units they combine with, so as to determine a semantic whole that has a definite syntactic structure as a RESULT of the semantic adjustment. Thus, the explanatory order is exactly the reverse of what is usually supposed.

Lexical organization, even among the items in a particular utterance, follows principles of "general semantic relativity," analogous to the physics of general relativity.[6] Moreover, the analogy with physics holds for a considerable depth, even to the component forces (of meaning contrast) and the roles they play (see part III). Furthermore, like physical relativity, lexical organization is dynamic. It is virtually the same across languages, so that the "laws" of semantic relativity are the same regardless of the frame of observation from which they are projected, as is the case with cosmic physics. Thus, there is a *dynamic* lexical organization for natural languages,[7] one that explains many phenomena hitherto unexplained.

This project relies upon something observable: that refined behavior requires refined distinctions, which need multiple meanings and enriched vocabulary. In a word, talk is *part* of our activities, shaping, extending, fitting, and changing

---

[6]I realize that most philosophers and linguists have slight familiarity with the general theory of relativity. Geroch (1978) may help. Maybe, even the two principles that "mass determines space" and "space determines motion" (with adaptation of Newtonian "gravity," "inertia," and "force") will convey what I want. If relative mass is the "size" of an object's "dent" in space, compared to any other such "dent," and if the motion of objects has to follow the "surface," dents and all, then the path any object follows will, perhaps, corkscrew, depending on what objects it "passes."

[7]In fact, this is the first dynamic semantic organization I know of. None of the recent accounts of semantic organization or any account of sentence meaning (especially Davidson's (1984a, 1984b, and Dummett's, 1978) can account for semantic contagion.

I offer further details on the subclassification of semantic contagion, on figures of speech, on the meaningfulness of craftbound discourse, on the limitations of philosophical analysis, and on analogy of meaning in legal discourse, as well as a comparison of semantic organization to classical diatonic harmonic organization, in Ross (1981).

what we do, and talk undergoes reshaping, extensions, and fittings of its own to what we do. In fact, in many craft-activities, the talk is part of what we are doing, from shamanism, to psychiatry, to law, to philosophy, to governing, even to sailing, as in, "Ready, about! Hard alee!" Survival skills (hunting, fishing, farming, feeding, and fasting), ornamentation (e.g., the arts), and expressive excellence (literature, music, dance, science, and philosophy) evolve galaxies of words in variously geometrized semantic spaces but under universal semantic forces, the same regardless of the local geometry.[8] I mean that particular contrasting practices, for instance, kinds of canoe paddling or steering, or kinds of sowing seeds, have associated verbal oppositions that create a verbal *geometry* of what to say and what not to say, a subspace, shaped by the particular kinds of action. The features of a local space are exhibited in "affinity," "proximity," and many kinds of "opposition" and other semantic relations (see Cruse, 1986), just as Lyons postulated, among distinct words (but coapplicable in the very utterance)[9] and in the constant *polysemy* of "utility" words, and of every word upon occasion—a condition that results when a given word is dominated by contrasting completion words, as in: *look for:* trouble/ money/ men/ advice/ help/ support/ death/ victory/ release/ freedom. In fact, recurring words tend to differentiate in meaning. The relativity hypotheses explain that.

In all crafts, practices, and rituals modified by discourse—and all are— *discourse is symbiotic with the activity it modifies.* That observation is the foundation of this inquiry. The results are both polysemy and multiplicity of symbols, both of which are in constant change, like an expanding universe, as our forms of life grow and diverge. And, though I concentrate on how semantic contagion produces polysemy, and how that is accounted for by general semantic relativity, let me emphasize that the energy for semantic relativity, as well as for symbol proliferation, is from the traction between discourse and action.

Objectives

I move from lexical fields to broad explanatory principles of semantic relativity and, then, to describe craft-talk, where we can test hypotheses like these, in five steps. First, I explain why lexical fields do not explain semantic contagion, or lexical organization generally. Second, I explain how we can treat semantic

---

[8]The order of the overall space is one of general relativity, as I will explain. The meaning relations of the whole language are like a net that is in constant internal and external deformation (from the movement of fish in it). Meaning adjustments are net-fiber deformations (stretchings and narrowings); the demands of action are what change the bends and bumps in the net, like movements of fish and water.

[9]The conditions of coapplicability are stated in the discussion of "predicate schemes" and differ enough from those Lyons had in mind to distinguish predicate schemes from lexical fields. See the further elaboration of the distinction in Ross (1981).

contagion, neatly, as the *display of continuous forces* causing polysemy (of classifiable kinds) by fitting single words or phrases to contrasting verbal contexts (e.g., *to sponge/* a stain; *to sponge/* a living). I develop an analogy with cosmic physics to describe the semantic forces and their interactions as general semantic relativity, even with analogous component principles (part III).

What explains differentiation of meaning for the same word synchronically also explains the development of a language's expressive capacity diachronically. For if you explain how words get different meanings from being combined in different ways, you explain how the language varies its expressive power as it is used, including the effects of introducing new words, which ripple through the language, creating new affinities and oppositions of meaning to words "already" there. Having a systematic story to tell about developing expressive power is one of the most important "payoffs" of a general account of semantic contagion.

Third, I remark, and illustrate now, that lexical organization is evolutionary,[10] *adaptive:* Talk changes with the activity it modulates,[11] making, selling, and using computerese, trading narcotics, building space shuttles, selling junk bonds. Words like "cause" or "entail" become *semantically captured* in the practice of law; "store" is semantically captured in computerese; "balance," in banking. Old crafts and practices (whale oil processing; New England spinning mills; puritan predestinarianism), and their ways of talking, sometimes the very words dry out, while the language is still "capable" of them, as historic recreations (Williamsburg, Plymouth) and historical plays and novels show; yet gradually such usage becomes "archaic," no longer part of linguistic competence. New ideas, activities, and appraisals find expression in "new life forms," with new meanings for old words and new words as well, in a drug culture with "hash," "stash," and "narcowar," or in a money-culture with corporate "takeovers," "greenmail," "poison pills," "junk bonds," and "insider trading," and in the calmer talk of "ecosystems," "ozone holes," "global warming," and "the biosphere."

Just by standing in various affinity, opposition, and other combinatorial relationships with old words, new words differentiate the old ones (because the old ones now have different antonyms, synonyms, hyponyms, etc.). A new form of

---

[10]I speak of "the organization of the lexicon" and of "the lexicon" as a shorthand for "lexical organization of a given language" where I do not mean anything like a tree-structured dictionary, but a structured space (e.g., as if it had a local physical geometry), which is under an outside force (see footnote 7).

[11]This most important and fundamental conviction I find confirmed by Wittgenstein's own analyses, ranging from the talk about "language games" through his notebooks, on into *Philosophical Investigations,* and in all the later work.

Language is a cognitive integration (by public symbols) of understanding with action (of which there are others: music, dance, drawing, and so on). Our cognitive processes are so densely interwoven with our animal activities in a physical environment that using language is a way of acting materially.

life—cold war, corporate raiding, or computer literacy—makes a new semantic space with a local geometry of affinities, oppositions, congruities, and unacceptabilities for words both old and new. Linguists, as far as I know, regard that as obvious, even trivial; but they cannot explain how, when new words are made or captured, old words shift around, making room, accommodating them like a crowd at a cocktail party, as I propose to do.

One consequence of semantic relativity is that certain philosophical accounts are in "big trouble" because typical compositional analyses of utterance meaning (as well as certain views of componentiality) are in principle mistaken (see part IV). Finally, I explain what is so special about craft-talk (part V): there, semantic contagion, and pragmatic traction visibly gear together to make forms of life in which *meaning* and *experience are inextricable* (as with a medical student's finding out what ascites *is* by poking the swollen belly of an alcoholic and *feeling* the difference from someone who is pregnant, obese, or has peritonitis); so it is in farming, fishing, house-building, cabinetry, goldsmithing, air traffic control, philosophy, news reporting, banking, law, medicine, ballet, music, painting, and every refinement of life. Of course, the two explanatory features of semantic organization are everywhere in discourse; but in craft-talk, they are prominent, like an aristocratic nose or authoritative height, and, so, easily distinguished from one another; they afford the separate testing of my hypotheses without a confusion of results, or a confusion with other theories. Further, besides making purely formal models (see part III, following), we can do dynamic experiments, by making certain kinds of games (that are like craft-talk), by altering activity and observing the effect on discourse and by altering discourse and observing the effect on activity.[12]

II. SEMANTIC CONTAGION MAKES LEXICAL ORGANIZATION

Semantic Fields are Consequences, not Explanations of Semantic Organization

There are several reasons. (i) Lexical fields are idealizations. They can only be said, metaphorically, to realign, regroup, or recalibrate when a member changes completion words, as in "*black* American" versus "*black* Irish." Rather, the difference of lexical field is the result of the difference of meaning, not the

---

[12]For instance, we can "prohibit" a certain class of warning expressions and see what practitioners, in the experimental action situations, do to get around the prohibition, to adapt other words or gestures, to alter the activity, or what. So, too, we can change the activity and observe what discourse becomes unused. Of course, all these experiments have actually been "run" in our society by its own cultural–industrial–social–legal history in the last two centuries, and more and more rapidly in the present one.

explanation of it. Color words ("black" or "red") contrast for people (who can be brown and still black and can be brownish and still "red"), whereas the color contraries and intermediates are quite different for cows; yet, it is not that any lexical field changed but that the relevant fields are different, having different members. The difference, again, is the result of the difference of meaning, not the explanation of it. When the same word recurs ("black mood"), in a distinct lexical field ("black Irish"), something has to explain the SELECTION[13] of its lexical field in the particular context. That has to be dynamic and causal. Lists or ranges of words will not do.

Thus we have several lexical fields for "color" words, some where "black" includes "brown" (in some racial classifications), some where "fuschia" is not a relevant contrary to any other word (e.g., as a color for people or chickens) or where "white" includes "pink" and is never pure (as in skin tones); we also have distinct fields of color words for paints, pigments, stone, chromatic shades, and light, etc. Yet nothing about the fields *explains* why the same word in one context has a different meaning (say different contraries) than in others. Neither will the difference in the kinds of *objects* referred to, as is commonly supposed, because they are not linguistic entities. But if one appeals to thoughts or *concepts* for explanation, one acknowledges (though looking in the wrong place for the explanation) the very phenomenon I am discussing: semantic contagion—adaptation of meaning caused combinatorially by words, or word surrogates.[14] Because such combinatorial differences are causal and constant, they require semantic software: "She grabbed the handle."; "She grabbed the limelight." Thought alone will not do; the semantic software FORMS the thought by organizing the expression of thought.

We can get closer to the explanatory realities by noticing that the same word, when differentiated (e.g., *to block* / a road / a scenario / a proposal), belongs to different *predicate schemes*. (see Ross, 1981, pp. 63–70, 76–8, 129–131.) For now, simplify the idea of "predicate schemes" into

---

[13]There's a case of stealth contagion: "Select" has to belong to computerese to convey the full effect of what is meant and what needs explaining.

[14]I, of course, do not think the introduction of "concepts" or "thoughts" adds anything helpful; just the opposite; the differences of word meaning do not depend on anyone's present concepts, they are right on the page. The thought has been *expressed* and partly formed by its expression.

See a remark of Katherine Dunn on reading George Elliot: "And then George Elliot—I can remember reading the first page in a bookstore and just kind of standing there with my chin on my chest because it was just this **mind** beating up off the page. Utterly genderless, you know, just intelligence" (Interview with Kellner, *Philadelphia City Paper,* "Book Report," p. 9, June 15, 1990).

There are also "belief-elements of meaning" (a phrase that comes from Wilfred Sellars via Churchland, 1979) that function in the explanation of why "necessity" cannot be explained by analyticity or any other meaning-inclusion, and why some analytic statements can be false because the belief-elements of the meaning are false (e.g., "whales are fish"). The "belief-elements" have other functions not covered here. (See Ross forthcoming).

differences of what *other words* can be replacements for a given word in otherwise the very same utterance [and action context] (a) to convey "nearly the same idea", or (b) a contrary idea, or (c) an appropriately modified idea, where "replacement" is measured by speakers familiar with the acceptable discourse (e.g., film, electronics, waste disposal) as if they were a "qualified jury of speakers."

So, "he flinched" has different cognitive content among detectives explaining a bullet's trajectory, from its content among psychologists explaining physical signs of one's being insulted. We can map and mark the differences of meaning at the level where causation is obvious in the differences of coapplicable (as aforementioned) words. They are a kind of "on the ground" lexical field.

One reason for saying lexical fields are abstracted from predicate schemes is that differences of predicate schemes are both more and less than field differences. Predicate schemes are, as I said, roughly the "alternatives" for one word in a *given* sentence that will yield an acceptable sentence close in meaning or in suitable contrast to "this" one. Such alternatives can be idealized, simplified, augmented, smoothed out, and clumped into lists called "lexical fields" (like cooking or kinship or sailing or walking or running terms). The appropriate substitutions (the predicate scheme) for a given case are often only a small portion of a lexical field because of syntagmatic exclusions, and, yet, may include antonyms, contraries, or other words not in the lexical field either because they are not often *enough* alternatives,[15] or because the custom is not to include bungling and failure words in the lists, though they are genuine verbal (and behavioral) alternatives. "He burned it," "He trashed it," "He cremated it," are appropriate contraries, sometimes, for most people's "broiling," "baking," etc., but not in the field of COOKING terms. Further, not every cooking term applies acceptably when any one of them does (e.g., poaching fish and eggs is an alternative to broiling, but not for a saddle of lamb). And the exclusion is not just syntagmatic, either. Smoothing out contextual incongruities and ignoring syntagmatic restrictions (e.g., that "He is her . . ." excludes "her aunt") and omitting failure and misadventure words amounts to idealizing abstraction, a project not illicit, provided licitly understood, and not applied where it mixes up causes and effects.

Paradoxically, the very fact that the same word recurs in distinct lexical fields shows that something *besides* lexical fields has to explain lexical organization. For something dynamic has to explain why a word belongs to the one of its lexical fields (say people colors vs. primary colors) rather than another in the particular case. That cannot be the fact that it *does*. The difference of fields is an EFFECT of semantic contagion.[16]

---

[15]As predicate schemes do, for, after all, a predicate scheme is nothing but the other words substitutable in a given case, with restrictions.

[16]See the preceding qualification, that the observed effect is actually in a *representation* of discourse (in a lexical field) but has a real correlate in the worldlines of the words.

Lexical fields are like the constellations, practical groupings of objects into recognizable patterns (with some "common conceptual content") that allow us to tell "where we are," the way a sailor can stay at a certain latitude by sailing along under the Little Bear. Such groupings are not arbitrary in the sense of "without rational basis"; they may, in fact be pragmatically *compelled* by the necessities of action, the way bluewater sailing requires a dependable measure of "where we are" for success and survival. Besides, lexical fields have more contact with reality than do the *obtuse abstractions* of propositional calculus or of first-order quantification.[17] Not so much has been smoothed out and *replaced* with made-up features. Navigation by the stars, by the constellations, was our way to explore the world before the refined sextant and satellite navigation. Without the earlier success, the more daring deep-space vantage would not be accomplished.

If you take lexical fields seriously, you may think the "lexicon" is the domain of fields. But "the lexicon" as a range of items is only an idealization, an obtuse abstraction[18] from working words under a load of action, and not the explanation of anything.[19] Nevertheless, there has to be a general explanation of lexical organization, even if there is no such domain as "the lexicon" to be organized; for there is evident semantic organization in natural languages. In fact, studies not directed to explanation convincingly exhibit semantic organization even in the name patterns for hairstyles, cosmetics and boutiques, street names and housing developments, and automobile models, as well as trendy restaurants and nightspots (see Lehrer, this volume). Two explanatory dimensions are evident in those cases, though one is more prominent than the other; for the effect is evidently one of pragmatic traction: Things that are supposed to be attractive get names connoting attraction; things associated with success, social leadership, and snobbery get names to attach those associations to the things (and that includes fads in baby-names). But another dimension is needed to explain exactly how "Knock Knees" (a club name) comes to mean intimacy rather than awkwardness; that requires another story besides, a story of semantic contagion.

---

[17]*Obtuse abstractions* (see Ross, 1989) do more than leave features out; they **substitute** made-up features of the formality that have neat formal behavior for messy, untidy features of the reality. Thus all propositions are treated as determinately true or false, and all in one plane: having the same or opposed truth values. That kind of abstraction, which marks propositional and first-order quantificational logic, is thought by some influential philosophers to be the formal structure of English; for example, see Davidson (1984a) and (1984b). However, Kripke (1982) seems as suspicious of Davidson's view, as I am unbelieving.

[18]Idealizations that substitute formally well-behaved features for messier features of reality, for example, treating a list of words as if they were determinates under a determinable (that is, where any *one* applies, the others must, in principle) when utterances only *roughly suggest* such a notion.

[19]Words cannot be prior to their uses, like platonic forms, for the very obvious syntagmatic dependence in meaning that they display (see Lyons, 1977, and Cruse, 1986). See Davidson's (1984a, 1984b) assumption to the contrary where, from linguistic holism, the meaning of words, as components of individual sentences, are a result of the truth-conditions for *all* sentences in the language that use those words, as well as all others.

ii) We can do with a few words, variously adapted, what we can do with many different ones; we can have the *meaning* equivalent of many lexical contrasts, without many distinct symbols. So a surly sea captain's saying, "Coffee," can range from questioning whether there is some (on board, cooked, in the pot, in the cup, or offered for shipment), to a command to find it, to cook it, to pour it out, to wipe it up, to watch out not to spill it, or, even to throw it. Furthermore, we can have homonymy by contagion, the equivalent of unrelated words: *charge* / battery; *charge* / account.[20] So, symbol complexity is not explained merely by meaning complexity or vice versa. Now the fact that there are two kinds of meaning plurality (polysemy, and many words), where neither explains the other, signals a deeper mechanism. A striking display of both points is that polysemy in one language is a string of symbols in another. Furthermore, that holds pairwise over a wide domain of languages.

(iii) The lexicon[21] evolves by semantic contagion[22] at least as much as by "field additions" (like the invention of new word groups for computerese). That is displayed everywhere in the writing of this chapter, and by the analogous application of words like "display," "read," "print out," "screen," "memory," "recall," along with new words like "hard drive," "floppy drive," "byte," "megabyte," and "nanosecond" in computerese. So there is at least as much demand to explain meaning proliferation by combination (semantic contagion) as there is by addition of words.[23] Something has to explain both.

(iv) The same lexical items, (a field of tree names, say), taken as a group, adapt in meaning by belonging to contrasting craft-talk: "walnut," "oak," "maple," "birch," and "cherry," as WOOD names differ in truth-conditions and conditions of warranted application from PLYWOOD names, VENEER names, COLOR names, FINISH names, and TREE names, though the general "shape" of the contrast is maintained. The words keep their general geometry of contrasts but acquire local differences of meaning: different conditions of application. So semantic fields can migrate, pretty much unchanged in membership, through domains of discourse, as the kind of activity differs: logging, carpentry, cabine-

---

[20]In Ross (1981) I explain, with examples, that mere equivocation can be the result of diverging lines of contextual adaption for a word, as well as come about by distinct word origins. Mere equivocation can, like nonsense (see chap. 7 for that), be the fallout of contrasting adaptations.

[21]Here I mean the meaning-structured vocabulary of a language and not some idealization of it. Words can be regarded as patterns of semantic energy (positive and negative) around a conventional mark or sound, in contrast to other, similar items.

[22]Pragmatic traction, as mentioned, is the deforming force, whereas general relativity is the space geometry that manifests as semantic contagion.

[23]In fact, careful analysis will show that you could not even have plurality of meaning by multiple words, in a natural language (a language embedded in action), without the semantics of contagion. That is because anyone able to understand "Slab" to mean "give me one" when a builder needs the next stone will, after awhile, also understand "Slab" to mean "grab hold of it," when the builder's grasp is slipping. So we might mark the second verbally, making the word "Slabit" in fact, a command.

try, counter-making, furniture-finishing, and milling; thus, "maple" differs in sense in: "maple trees," "maple stain," "maple patterns," maple plywood." That suggests that meaning-distinction by adaptation may be more basic than by symbol distinction. Thus the stage is set for finding semantic software that explains how words adjust in meaning.

Polysemy in One Language Needs a Lexical Field for Translation into Another

A few words, variously adapted, can do what many words can do (like a few bent wires opening a lot of locks that need a lot of keys). That has to be true if polysemy in one language is lexical plurality (many distinct words) in another,[24] *dare* in Italian is a lexical field (or several) in English: "give/ grant/ permit/ commit/ appoint/ announce/ produce/ yield/ show/ tell/ strike." This case, *dare,* is particularly convincing because the English words so obviously belong to several linguistic fields, yet the Italian word is not used homonymously. Similarly, *"see"* in English can be: "vedere/ comprendere/ connoscere/ osservare/ scopire" in Italian; and *"vedere"* in Italian can be: "to see/ perceive/ observe/ notice" etc. in English, which may not amount to distinct fields but surely amounts to a whole field. Thus, if we can explain polysemy, there will be no point in assigning lexical fields semantic software of their own, because the fields will be consequences of the contagion (and of pragmatic traction multiplying symbols as practice demands).

Polysemy Requires Semantic Contagion

We are so used to differentiated meanings we do not even notice them:[25] He *collected* friends/ coins/ debts/ a pension/ the interest/ specimens/ invitations/ wives; he *looked for* peace/ progress/ a dollar/ his car/ a new car/ his wife/ a wife. Thus we tend not to look for an explanation of why and how the meaning-contrast of "debts" and "pension" can account for a meaning difference in two occurrences of "collected." Even more subtle is the difference in "understands" in "He understands Italian" and "He understands music," and between "commands" in "He commands my respect," and "He commands my attention." Yet

---

[24]So too, paronymy in one language is denominative analogy in another and vice versa (see Ross, 1981, chap. 5). For example, *"sanus"* in Latin means both "healthy/healthful"; whereas in English *"healthy* woman/*healthy* man" is *"sanus* homo," *"sana* femina" in Latin, a difference of grammatical form. So a difference of meaning that is represented by two different grammatical forms in one language is represented by one grammatical form in another: Paronymy in one language may be adaptation in another.

[25]We do not *notice* that to make friends, make appointments, make war, make opportunities, make faces, make words, and make a difference are all different. We are perfect at adaptation from childhood: "Fix my lunch"; "fix my wagon"; "fix Johnny"; and "fix Johnny's pants."

something has to explain how that happens; it does *not* depend on the thinking of the utterer or hearer. The difference would be there, even if the utterance were composed by a computer malfunction and printed out in a part of the daily paper that no one read.

Adjustment of meaning to context is displayed, comparatively, as analogy of meaning: analogy of *proportionality* (*see/* the color; *see/* the point), *denominative* analogy (*brilliant/* writer; *brilliant/* book), and *metaphor* (*blacken/* shoes; *blacken/* his name), and the figures of speech as well.[26] The fact that one word adapts so differently in webs of other words as to belong to distinct lexical fields (e.g., "see" = "perceive/ sense/ observe/ notice/ grasp/ understand/ comprehend/ espy/ sight") is semantically fundamental. We have to explain it and explain it by some constant causation, some *force,* that makes semantic contagion automatic, that is, not requiring thought or intention, just utterance (use) as part of some action (which, of course, is also some kind of thought). Differentiation of recurring words is the norm. For that, a constant cause, a force, so general and so regular as to be before our eyes, unseen, adjusts word-meanings to one another in the context; that is the *universal linguistic force:* "the syntactically coherent tends to make a semantic whole." That there should be such a force is quite natural when you consider that the function of syntactical unities is to express thought, to have semantic content, where the thought content expressed is part of what we DO, not in isolation but as practices.

Infants internalize semantic contagion. We learned to talk that way. We learned to think that way. Parents talk to children with a simplified grammar and semantics and by using utility words in many senses: "*See* daddy; *see,* mommy is putting peas on the spoon; *see,* here comes grandma"; and so forth for almost all the words that are used, and children's primers reinforce this by also using utility words in many senses: "get sick," "get home," "get paid"; "fix dinner," "fix the wagon," and so forth. (See the adaption of "way," aforementioned; there was no thought required, beyond my saying, and your seeing, what I meant to say.) We do not, therefore, notice that differences of meaning for the same word in contrasting verbal neighborhoods must be the result, in part, of a *tendency* of grammatically well-formed (or approximately well-formed) utterances to have semantic unity (as far as each can), to be something we understand to be said (whether or not we understand what is being said). "Making sense" (a semantic unity), whether or not we get "the sense," turns out to be a universal linguistic force. "He's blanketing our sails" makes sense whether or not you know enough about sailing to know what the maneuver consists in. So too "He chamfered the stone before polishing it." You can recognize semantic integration even though you may not know enough about stone-cutting to know what cham-

---

[26]In Ross (chap. 6), the myth that figurative discourse always contains metaphor is falsified, and where figurative discourse is, constructively, stepwise adaptation, typically involving metaphor and paronymy from admittedly prosaic uses.

fering is. Consider this well-formed sentence (Drabble, 1989): "All things out of abstraction sail, and all their swelling canvas wear" (p. 125). Integration of meaning, like gravity in nature, is a constant force "downward" from utterance, embedded in its action-role, on the component words to go together so as to fill that role (with limitations mentioned later).

Even linguists tend to suppose that we have learned to "put the pieces down in the right order," like Lego blocks or dominos, to make semantic unities of what we say. But that cannot be right; WHAT piece has been put down is a function of pieces a long way away and sometimes quite a long time afterward, or supposed, in an activity. Semantic unity is not straightforward, like explaining a brick wall from the placing and mortaring of the bricks. Nor is it like Newtonian billiard balls, a mere product of initial force. It is like the unity of galaxies in space formed by their very passage.

The component meaning-units are dependent, for their semantic "values" or "mass," on the "resultant" meaning. If we have trouble explaining what looks like "backwards" causation, so much the worse for the poverty of our analogies. Pieces often take shape from what follows (and at some distance)—like history: "Thus, he toppled the Saracen Empire with one attack." Words often gain identity from neighbors ("They cheated their way closer to the wind") and from what has gone by a while before or belongs to the discourse as a whole. So the unity of the utterance is *not* explained by the mere sequence of the pieces; change goes backwards, too, as in "He challenged himself and his enemies." Semantic unity of utterance has to involve a constant cause (a force); in fact, several.[27]

Even a constant force toward "making sense" will not explain the differences of recurrent words without something that functions like mass, to be subject to gravity (the force downward from resultant meaning that causes adaptation); for it is mass under force(s) that makes some words *dominant,* relatively, over others. The only way we can get adaptation, fit (relatively) to context, is (a) for a word to display a *different* pattern of affinities and oppositions to other words, and (b) for another word to be, relatively, intransigent in *maintaining* its pattern of affinities and oppositions to other words, and (c) for the difference in the adapting word and the intransigent word to be required by the utterance-meaning in its role in action.

The same general structure explains the simple differences of "She *dropped/* a friend, her jaw, her eyes, her glasses" and the more subtle ones like "He *engineered/* the new submarine;/ the peace treaty in the East;/ the indictment of every one of his friends." In brief, adaptation is the outcome of *differential* resistance to "giving up" relations of affinity and opposition to other words in

---

[27]If a cause is constant, mathematizable and differentiated from others, I call it a force; if it has "spatiality" as well, I can call it a force-field. There is the hypothesis that all matter is fundamentally force-fields; maybe, analogously, word-meaning, too, is given "spatiality" by the sound or mark that is the medium.

order to make a semantic unity that performs the expression's role in action. Thus, the *action* counts: "Fire! The forward gun!" versus "Fire! In the forward hold!" To explain differential resistance, we need the semantic analogue of relativistic mass in General Relativity (see III).

Predicate Schemes are Abstractions, too

They are a map of the substitutions one *might* have put in, say, to distinguish "He saw her car" from "He saw her home"; they are a counterfactual map of meaning differences, and so, only better than lexical fields because less abstract and less "made up" but still made up. And they are always incomplete. Such a map only marks what needs explaining. We need something that explains *why* the substitutions in contrasting cases *would* have been different, by explaining why there is a difference of meaning in the first place. Yet, we do have some progress: We see that whatever makes meaning "fit" context is done to attain "acceptability" of the utterance, given its role in action.[28]

Semantic Contagion is Contrastive Adaptation

Semantic contagion is *observable* by the "method of difference" (J. S. Mill, 1936): synchronically as differentiation of same-word meaning,[29] and diachronically as *change* of same-word meaning[30] triggered by the contrasting contexts. Contagion is the *fit* of words to one another like people crowded on a bench, with give and take; give is indifference; take is dominance. Difference of meaning displays itself as comparative rearrangements of oppositions and affinities to other words, for instance, ones that might be substituted in the very sentence but to different effects: You could *see* an invisible point but not, in the same sense, an invisible cat. You can *miss* me with an ax, or with a sigh, or in the crowd.

Dominance

Here is the nub of it. Unity of meaning is achieved if it can be (see linguistic force). To attain that, indifferent expressions adapt to dominant ones. But *what* is indifferent and *what* is dominant is entirely relative, partly to how the words are

---

[28]In comparison to its other occurrences, of course. Now that might seem circular, but acceptability is actually a feedback system, like a servo-mechanism (say cruise control on a car).

[29]For example, "cancelled": "The dentist cancelled my appointment"; "I cancelled my plans for writing two papers"; "The check was cancelled within ten days"; "The governor cancelled his appointment."

[30]Consider the successive utterances in a child's language learning. They will look as if a word, say "fix" or "take," gets new meanings or uses: "Take a picnic," "take your lunch," "take the dog," "take a train," "take too long."

used elsewhere, and partly to what the words are being used to DO (both in an illocutionary and perlocutionary way). For, as I mentioned, the equivalent of gravity is the force downward, from the perlocutionary role of the utterance in the context, upon the component words to adjust so as to perform that role. (A hint of that is our consternation when by mistake we say something with quite the opposite effect from what we intend.)

A word becomes dominant when pushed "to the edge of the bench," to the edge of unacceptability and can "give" no more, say, because it has an antecedent or a syntagmatic link, or a tie to the subject matter, and so, "has its foot down." Thus, the equivalent of mass is entrenchment in a subject, anchoring to a case, or syntagmatic ties to another anchored expression. Words also adapt to avoid semantic uncompletability, and to avoid commonplace falsity or public offensiveness and various equivalents (the latter are defeasible conditions of unacceptability, the former, are not).[31] Those are the other forces (see later). It is *resistance* under the linguistic forces (1) to make illocutionary sense in the perlocutionary roles of the utterance in action; (2) to avoid (a) uncompletability, (b) commonplace falsehood, and (c) other kinds of unacceptability that makes a word dominant in an utterance.

Some words resist adjustment to a context when others do not; those that resist, *dominate*. Dominance is the resistance of the, relatively, definite units (whether anchored or entrenched)[32] to concatenating unacceptably, as long as something else *can* "give" so as to avoid unacceptability. That makes dominance relative to other words and to context. Being dominated comes down to "giving up" affinities and oppositions to other words (in *this* context, as compared with various other contexts) to compose an acceptable utterance. (Notice, in an arbitrarily chosen utterance, by itself, neither dominance nor adjustment is discernable.) The dominant words fit the context without adaptation.[33] Adaptation is relative.

No word is always dominated, or always dominates (see Ross, 1981). They all get their turns. Dominance is relative, like physical mass (or size), depending on

---

[31]The context has to be disambiguating in order to make the kinds of examples we need. The reader can make them. The contexts should include a pragmatic environment because words fit environments of *action*, not by mere reference.

Zeugma depends on contagion. "He governed himself and his province" or "He cheated himself and his employer." Contagion not only disambiguates among meanings already within the corpus, it refines meanings, as when Dylan Thomas wrenches words into a new armor-plated metaphor. "Furiously, he melted words into shells."

[32]The difference is that anchored expressions are tied to cases that determine when they apply, like the *case* of the patient with ascites or law cases; whereas, words are entrenched when a subject-matter determines their significance (unless that is defeated by something): thus, "pitch" in baseball disambiguates from "pitch" in road engineering, meaning "angle," and in construction, meaning "tar" or "asphalt," just by the discourse environment—what I later call "neighborhood."

[33]Strictly, that is too simple: For words dominate *after* adaptation too. See Ross (1981, pp. 51–52) "double dominance."

what is in the *neighborhood,* the discourse environment. The semantic cosmos is just a distribution of neighborhoods. There is no absolute semantic mass. The relative mass of an expression is a function of whether it tends to be indifferent to other words or intransigent. That depends on the neighborhoods it frequents and upon its entrenchment in a subject or its anchoring to benchmark cases of *what* it is.

Why do "eyes/ books/ friends/ jaw" all dominate "dropped" in the sentence frame "She *dropped* her eyes/ books/ friend/ jaw" but only conditionally dominate "burned" in "She *burned* her eyes/ books/ friend/ jaw," because several senses of "burn" will do? Whereas, some of these, "She *sold* her eyes/ books/ friend/ jaw" need a "saving" context to avoid unacceptability? Why isn't "cut" dominated in "She *cut* her eye/ books/ friend/ jaw," though it could be? Here is clear dominance: He *commanded* a submarine/ respect/ a thousand dollars a day/ attention/ a regiment/ more and more of my attention. No adaptation of "cut" is needed for the completed sentence to make a definite and acceptable sense (in context). In other words, when the same sense will do,[34] nothing dominates a common word. This is the principle of *inertia,* that words recur in the same meaning unless something makes a difference in meaning (for any n-tuple of recurrences).

III. LINGUISTIC GENERAL RELATIVITY

1. What is Linguistic General Relativity? **Every meaning element depends synchronically on every other.** And the "value" of a meaning-element (its particular meaning) depends on what it is combined with and in what perlocutionary role. Yet, effects diminish with distance. So, degree of dependence depends.

Word meaning in natural language is dynamically organized, like the distribution of matter in space-time. Everything affects everything else semantically, with the "biggest" effects being caused by the, relatively, most massive lexical items on "less" massive words that appear frequently nearby (utility words). Over time, meaning seems to become "more" diversely organized because adaptation tends to increase expressive variety (though, nonsense is a by-product of semantic contagion too.)[35]

Although there are synchronic *slices* of discourse (even very big ones), the *language (la language)* does not *exist* atemporally. English exists only in what

---

[34]As in any other arbitrarily given occurrence. When the same sense won't do, the completion words dominate (see earlier, on kinds of unacceptability). Notice, "do," right here, is a case in point. There are varying kinds of unacceptability, corresponding to "strong" and "weak" forces.

[35]See Ross (1981, chap. 7) on "nonsense" created by differentiation: bad metaphors like "Thisness evokes essential being."

was said and written during seven centuries, or so. Nevertheless, slices, without regard for time order, reveal explanatory structures (that I call software), the way cell-slices do to a cell biologist; some of the structures are localized geographically, historically, and by social class; but there are underlying universal features; for example, the adaptation of a "utility" word to categorically contrasting completion words, as happens with "used" in "He *used* language/ ointment/ exercise/ surgery/ railways/ deceptions/ flattery/."

Diachronically, in the semantic as well as the physical universe, *mass determines space and space determines motion*[36]—where "mass" is "dominance" and "space" is "locus of semantic adaptation" and "motion" is actual adaptation. Besides the two basic principles of linguistic inertia[37] and universal linguistic force, there are four component forces, paralleling (1) gravity (the force on component words to achieve the meaning required by the utterance's role in action), (2) electromagnetic force (the force of semantic inclusions,[38] the way "man" involves "male"), (3) weak force (the force of the defeasible unacceptabilities, like commonplace falsehood, impropriety, and public offense), and (4) strong force, like the force binding the nucleus of an atom, the binding force of *combined* semantic and syntagmatic ties within discourse.[39] The overall idea is that to fit one context, say, "He *used* English," the word "used" adds or drops no more of its relations to other words than exactly those needed to differentiate its meaning from its fit in "He *used* patience," and *vice versa,* and so on for any other occurrence of "used" in a complete context.

There is no absolute, only relative semantic mass, indicated by how much contextual modification, especially by explicit phrases, it takes to dominate an expression so that it adapts in meaning to fit the context. That varies with context and with completion expression. Thus semantic mass is equivalent to resistance (potential).

---

[36]In the solar system, the mass of the sun "dents" the space (already dented by the Milky Way), so that the planets, like marbles under great propulsion, fly around the sides of the dent, kept in place by the gravity of the sun (the *slope* of the dent) and kept in motion by their propulsion, like cycle-riders on the walls of (Elvis Presley's) cycletron (my word). Thus, the shape of the space determines what paths there are from one place to another, like knees under a blanket, determining paths along the outside slopes.

[37]"Words recur univocally unless something makes a difference of meaning." "Same meaning unless something makes a difference": Inertia. "Words adjust to make what sense they can in the context of our actions": linguistic force.

[38]Semantic inclusions and exclusions are like the polarity of electromagnetic force. So, adjustments are minimal, by stepwise "on" and "off" of inclusions or oppositions of other words. The weak force is the resistance of words to the defeasible unacceptabilities.

[39]That yields a quantum principle: stepwise adaptation (see Ross, 1981, chap. 6). Meaning adjustments are, compared to other same-word occurrences in complete contexts, comparatively minimal and stepwise by the shortest route of distinct "on" and "off" steps of dropping (or taking up) inclusion and opposition to other words—the way electrons change orbits a jump at a time. That feature allows the process to be simulated with digitalized formal models (see part III).

Overall, (1) grammatically well-formed expressions adapt their words to one another[40] to "fit" the action to which the talk belongs, and (2) HOW the "fit" is achieved varies, though under detectable forces. That IS general semantic relativity ("mass determines space; space determines motion"). Diachronically, relativity, displayed as adaptations, expands expressive capacity. Poetry not only shows it up, it shows it off.

2. The principle of inertia is observable, "there is no difference of word meaning without something that makes a difference of meaning." Construct several sentence frames: "She *shot . . .* " and complete two with the same word, "pictures," *twice.* "She shot pictures." "She shot pictures." If "shot" has a different meaning in the two cases, something has to make a difference, the way something does in "She shot *rapids*" and "She shot *rustlers.*"

3. In "She *shot* pictures, rapids and rattlers and rustlers," something has to cancel, turn off and turn on, the affinities and oppositions of "shot" to other words (in other contexts). That requires several other elements, the first and most important being resistance to unacceptability, *universal linguistic force* (namely that "grammatically well-formed sentences make what sense they can"). Another formulation of linguistic force is: "grammatically well-formed utterances resist concatenating unacceptably until forced." The logical consequence of universal force is linguistic gravity, a constant causation exerted downward from the meaning of the whole (from its role in our *actions*) upon the meanings of the parts to adjust to one another.

Linguistic force manifests itself when the same sense (as any arbitrarily given one) will result in unacceptability for *failure* of semantic unity (or for certain defeasible reasons).[41] In such a case, each element of the expression is under "pressure" to adjust. Comparatively, the subdominant word adapts. This is universal: Utterances avoid unacceptability unless forced.[42] So the meaning of "dropped" and "burned" and "cut" adjusts selectively, in the examples I gave earlier, just as "shot" does in the examples just preceding. Why does the contrast of "pictures," "rapids," and "rustlers" make a difference of meaning of the word "shot"? (Of course, it doesn't automatically make a difference; it depends on the order in which the sentences occur.) Because the differential adjustment of "shot" avoids unacceptable concatenations, which cannot be avoided by any

---

[40]There is no absolute dominance and no absolute semantic mass, yet there is adaptation of word meaning to word environment (and to word surrogates in the context, e.g., references, antecedents, disambiguations).

[41]Resistance to commonplace falsehood, triviality, incongruity, public offense, taboo are a defeasible and *weak* force, but still one that affects meaning everywhere. That is why I call it a star builder, because though it works locally on its near neighbors, just as does the "weak force" in physics, it has its effects everywhere. For example, "That's a dumb idea" does not mean "incapable of speaking," which it might mean because that has no cognitive point: It is too dumb.

[42]See Ross (1981, pp. 10, 57, 78, 81) for cases where unacceptability is forced, and other cases where unacceptability is avoided by semantic exsanguination, nonsense (chap. 7).

available adjustment of the other words; "failure of semantic unity" (incongruity in the sense of "failure of meaning") is the most powerful of the forms of unacceptability. "Making no sense at all even to the speaker" is not a discourse function; for making no sense at all is not really *talk* (but only an echo of it).

4. There is *weak force,* as I said: "words resist concatenating to commonplace falsehoods, public offense, etc. unless forced." That has enormous "nearby" effects. Local resistance to commonplace falsehoods, offense, impropriety, stupidity, silly puns, etc. is a semantic star builder like the weak force in physics. It tends to stabilize meaning, eliminating double meanings, for instance (see footnote 41). For "weak force" builds craft-talk directly out of neologisms, etymological derivatives, verbal inventions, and utility adaptations. The force is called "weak" because the resistance to commonplace falsehood, or pointlessness, is easily defeated. So, for example, "everything is garbage" would not be taken literally; yet, it could quite easily be meant literally by someone who says to the garbageman that everything on the curb should be taken away.

5. Further, there is a *quantum* principle. The strong force of semantic and syntagmatic inclusions combines with the "on/off" form of adjustments to other words ("affinity," "opposition," "congruence," "consequence,") to make stepwise adjustments, so that "meaning adjustments are comparatively minimal."[43] For instance, consider figurative discourse. Relatively to a given, nonfigurative statement with the required words, any figure of speech can be generated by a short sequence of steps, by changing the dominant words in the sentence frame until the figurative sense is produced. There is a discussion of figurative discourse in Ross (1981, chap. 6), in which it is argued that "complex meaning-relatedness can be decomposed into stepwise atomic adaptations (proportionality, simple metaphor, denomination, and paronomy) . . . Figurative occurrences can similarly be decomposed into stepwise adaptations whose salient feature is double differentiation, at least one of which is metaphorical and the other of which involves paronymy" (p. 147). There is a method of hypothetical construction offered by which one can confirm, or disconfirm, this hypothesis.

6. Adjustment is quantized; it consists in the comparative addition or loss, a whole step at a time (or several in a clump), of affinity or opposition to other words. An example of this is the fact noted earlier that, among color words that apply nowadays to people, "brown" is not opposed to "black," and "white" has only "black," "yellow," "red," and a few others as contraries. The list, however, is quite different for the skin tones of cosmetics and different again for the skin colors used by painters.

Because adjustments are by *whole steps* (usually taken in clumps), of giving up opposition or affinity, they are digitalized rather than continuous. Adjustments

---

[43]Comparatively to any arbitrarily chosen same-word occurrence in a complete context. And by "minimal" one means by the shortest chain of differences (by contextual dominance) in affinities and oppositions to other words.

ratchet, rather than glide, even though the semantic fit seems as seamless as a movie. (The constructive method I described in Ross (1981, chap. 6) can be used to demonstrate this point, I think.)

The stepwise feature of adaptation makes modeling feasible. First, we can devise a computational model in which each semantic unit has "experiential anchors"[44] (that might in advanced systems change over time), where the semantic value of each term (at a given occurrence) is a small number of pluses and minuses and "neutrals" (zeros), to every other semantic unit, where only certain patterns make utterance-sense. As you combine units, the anchored ones resist changing values until the unanchored (or distantly anchored ones) run through the shortest, next shortest, etc. paths of adjustments of pluses and minuses (and replacements for zeros), until a shortest path into a semantic unity is found. That gives the compositional unity of the whole (subject to various overriding rules and priorities that can be invented, to taste). Thus, you can say of everything that it is not *whatever you like*.[45] But in "March's storms are Spring's nurse," "nurse" has to drop "human" as a hypernym. A formal dynamic model of adjustment to context can be made, especially using the oversimplified structural principle that semantic incompatibilities will not compute. We of course have no such principle in natural languages; incompatibilities can make semantic unities. Our principles of nonassembly, nonunity have yet to be discovered.

Secondly, less formal models, models for craft-talk well known to the model-maker (models made by experts sampling the talk in which the sampler is an expert) can be used to examine inertia, linguistic force, strong force, and weak force, to see whether semantic contagion really is the visible manifestation of general semantic relativity. That is what I describe in section V, below.

7. *Semantic Software.* There is (a) a *dynamic semantic software* of natural languages, that is (b) *embedded synchronically* in any large slice from the corpus of actual discourse,[46] that (c) *explains* the *adaptations*[47] of word-meaning to contrasting contexts and (d) *produces multiple semantic fields* from the *same* (or overlapping and regrouped) word members and (e) expands expressive capacity with new meaning.

Rearranging lexical fields (like color words for cows and people) is as startling as a scar. But it is a mere product (along with new words) of the simple

---

[44]It is not the reference, say, to a particular patient that gives a medical student the signification (*sense* meaning) of the word "ascites" over and beyond the verbal meaning; it is the *experience* the medical student has of feeling and poking the swollen abdomen of the patient.

[45]Though we cannot *simply* do that in English because grammatical forms must change (e.g., "storm is not run" is incoherent without a rehabilitating context).

[46]Regardless of how the corpus is selected (e.g., chronologically, or from the same place and near in time, or all scrambled together over time and place). To be synchronically embedded is to be "extractable," just as the grammar can be said to be embedded synchronically.

[47]As in "The storm swept the coast"; "the clouds swept the sky"; "fear swept the subway"; even the *metaphors* are polysemous. Kittay (1987) makes the same point.

adaptation that slides by, in silent computation, like envy, yet recalibrates words, like temperature words, as we drive through another linguistic neighborhood. So hot days and cool nights give way to hot shades and cool colors, to hot trumpets and cool saxes (hot saxes and cool flutes), to hot eyes and cool glances, hot spots and cool stances. The silent adaptation (contagion) is invisible. Look at "recalibrates"; look at "slides by"; look at "rearranging lexical fields"; they are low on the semantic horizon and as dun colored as stealth planes, but they have adapted.[48]

Adapted utility words, along with special words dictated by the demands of action,[49] make galaxies of craft-talk that dot the semantic space of the language; the common structure of the space *is* the organization of the lexicon. That structure, cosmically, is general relativity. That, in precis, is my message.

The meaning-space forms under general relativity, constantly, locally where a singer sings "Every lover is a thief, all want, no friend. . . . No wonder every love, with want, will end." Items far apart lexically, say, "lover" and "thief," get closer in meaning, whereas "lover" and "friend" move apart a little, and "love" and "loyal" separate, and "love" and "want" get closer, whereas "want" and "love" and "am interested in" pull apart. But quote St. Paul, *Romans,* 13:10: "Love is the one thing that cannot hurt your neighbor," and space reshapes. The worldline of "love" veers toward that of "friend" and streams along near "want," wobbles relatively to "loyal" and sharply veers toward and away from "ends," time after time.

It is as if culture moved its knee in bed and the blanket of meaning reshaped. With big life changes (atomic war and power; cancer and pollution; jets and takeovers), there are big meaning changes: Linguistic dust is sucked into new galaxies of craft-talk. Old star clusters burn out like radio tubes. Old words and neologisms congeal like gasses into new spiral nebulae, fiery blue and red (the further and faster), into discourse that IS our thought for new and beautiful, bad and sad things: holes in the ozone layer; chemicals killing fish; binaural sound; acid rock, interferon, crack.

The same "software" explains (a) the meaning-adjustment (*teeming/* rain; *teeming/* crowds) as if it were reorganization of lexical fields to fit distinct subjects; (b) the polysemy of the "utility" words of natural languages, (like "give/ take/ run/ cut/ hit/ fix/ learn/ read/ see/ drive/ . . ."), and (c) the transfer of those unbound utility words into the craftbound discourse, where some of the words are *semantically captured,* the way "cause" is in tort law, "run" is in baseball, and "drive" is in golf, and where other utility words remain adapted to unbound contexts to provide the "bridging" facts between unbound

---

[48]That is why, before, I call differential adaption "analogue semantic speed" in contrast to digitalized computation.

[49]Some of which are as simple as the need for disambiguation where life is at stake, and some of which are political, like preserving the power of esoteric knowledge.

and craftbound talk. Thus "I have a stomachache" has both an unbound and a craftbound use each with different truth conditions.

IV. COMPOSITIONALITY?

Compositionality as previously understood through this century has been falsified. There are many forms of compositionality, but basically all are as Cresswell (1985) reasoned, required because the complexity and multiplicity of what we say could not be learned "one by one." Thus, utterance meanings have to be composed (put together) and also understood by our working them out from the utterance structure and the meanings of the individual words. It is a Lego theory of utterance meaning, however it is packaged. Moreover, it invites the errors of translation that Latin students quickly abandon (I hope). If what the components are depends on how they are assembled, as I say it does, then compositionality as now understood is false. You have to understand the whole to know how to translate the words: *Cimini sectores* are not barbers, or scissiors, but hair splitters.

Davidson (1984a) dragged the semantics of natural languages behind the grammar: that the language must be axiomatizable formally, and that there must be a finite number of meaning primitives, from which all utterances are made. I agree that a learner has to begin with a finite number of meaning units. The rest, in particular Davidson's conclusion that otherwise the language would be unlearnable, seems gratuitous—as is Chomsky's claim that unless we have a hardwired language-learning machine or grammar-induction machine, we could never learn the grammar of a natural language because it has infinite potential sentences. (In a few minutes one can learn patterns of piano or singing notes that have equal variety, and just by hearing a few.) For instance, Davidson (1984a) argued:

> Suppose that a language lacks this feature; then no matter how many sentences a would-be speaker learns to produce and understand, there will be always others whose meanings are not given by the rules already mastered. Such a language is unlearnable. (p. 10)

Natural languages *are* unlearnable in Davidson's sense. There will always be sentences whose meanings are *not given* by any rules already learned for the production and understanding of sentences. That is not so much because we cannot compute the grammar of new sentences, as that we cannot break into the meaning network from our base of experience. That holds for everyone, and for extremely large samples of the well-formed utterances in the language. No matter how much you learn, you will be a stranger in so many areas of human expertise as to be unable even to understand what is being said by those familiar with the subject. Probably, most of what is said in English nowadays is semantically inaccessible to most speakers because it is craftbound. And it is a deep misunderstanding to regard that missing element as a matter of not knowing the "references" of words. Rather, in C. I. Lewis' (1947) terms, it is a case of not knowing the *sense meaning* (e.g., how a broken femur *feels* to an orthopedist's hands; what the *sense* of "collateral estoppel" is in law, as distinct from "equitable estoppel"). We are not just short on the words; we are short on experience.

You cannot, because of craft-talk, learn any natural language as a whole. There always WILL be well-formed utterances whose meanings we cannot compute, whose truth-conditions and conditions of warranted-assertability escape us. The talk is inaccessible from our experiential base.

It seems that there is one thing that must be jettisoned for sure; that is Davidson's (1984b) notion of compositionality functioning as follows:

> If sentences depend for their meanings on their structures, and we understand the meaning of each item in the structure only as an abstraction from the totality of sentences in which it features, then we can give the meaning of any sentence (or word) only by giving the meaning of every sentence (and word) in the language. (p. 22)

Not that words are not components, or that they do not contribute individually to utterance meanings. They do. But what they contribute depends on what the other words contribute as they resolve their resistances.

V. FROM UNBOUND DISCOURSE TO CRAFT-TALK

Once we understand some principles that explain the general relativity of word-meanings within a language[50] (e.g., the opposition between "boy" and "girl," but the relative affinity of "boy" and "girl" in contrast to "cat" and "dog"; and their affinity, in contrast to "philosophy" and "religion," and so on—to use an oversimplified example), we can look at the lexicon as a cosmos of word clusters, looking for (a) an internal "software" for meaning adaptations in utterances

---

[50]Internal relationships of opposition, affinity, dominance, indifference, etc. are like the internal harmonic relationships *within* a composition among the "notes" in diatonic music. Harmonic relationships are law-governed in detail but suppose a relativity of tonic / dominant / subdominant / leading tone, etc.; for any sound can be the tonic, provided all others are regarded in the appropriate tonal relationships (and there are no quarter-tones or not many anyway to worry about). The harmonic structure of a Bach violin concerto is perfectly determinate (I skip special cases here), but entirely relative. You can "start" anywhere, on any tone. So too with meaning taken internally. But taken externally, referentially and pragmatically: That is quite another matter. Nor can you, as Putnam suggested, "skolemize" natural language; but you *can* skolemize diatonic music (provided "references" are tones not frequencies).

and for (b) interferences, deformation of word clusters by the demands of action (the pragmatic traction of talk that is [part of] doing something). For the necessities of action are to meaning what mass is to space.

The lexicon *is* ordered, but not hierarchically. It is ordered adaptively to action. We make "new" (multiple) symbols for exactitude at the expense of analogue semantic speed (differentiation by context) where the payoff rewards it; otherwise we use analogy, analogue meaning, as "payoff" and "rewards" in the previous clause display, and as "look at" and "look for" in the preceding paragraph do, too.

There really is an explanation for why we have many words, when a few words with many meanings might also do. There really is an explanation of why many meanings are lexicalized by a single morphophonological form. (That turns out to be a necessary consequence of dominance.) The explanatory structure in both cases is basically the same (general relativity and pragmatic traction). And HOW a meaning contrast is lexicalized (by a new word or by adaptation of a word in service) almost entirely depends on what is at *stake*. In fact, we often use both for different objectives, as ". . . am aquainted with . . ." and ". . . know of . . . ," and, other times, simply "know."

Something is at stake in the talk that might be lost without distinct symbols, and even special phrases and sounds (as in airplane talk, "niner"). Often, the need to avoid ambiguity (in matters of life and death, and money and marriage, too) or the demands of elegance and the display of power count on different words to mark the meanings. Vanity, precision, and a thousand frailties and virtues motivate marking distinct meanings with distinct sounds (not the least social factor being the power of esoteric knowledge protected by the craft-talk of insiders: doctors, financiers, shamans, and lawyers). Just as importantly, the revelatory power of metaphor and the emotive force of figurative discourse motivate the silent assault of semantic contagion.

Semantic contagion and pragmatic traction steam, groan, and boil over in *craft-talk,*[51] the talk "insiders" know (with its many faces), and in its apes and impersonations, right down to the jargon of hang-tough executives and con-artists, and to "street talk" and "rap." That's where the "linguistic action" is: where the doing is.

We can use craft-talk as an experimental laboratory (a) to find craft-talk to be (partially) a product of the semantic organization of the *unbound* lexicon, (b) with a distinct arena of *experience* that, by pragmatic traction, makes its special vocabulary; and (c) to show how general relativity is taught by linguistic *practice* from infancy (e.g., "Mommy *loves* you," "Johnny *loves* ice cream"; *See* Daddy," "*See* the ball"; "*See* the red?" "*Fix* lunch," "*Fix* my wagon," "*Fix* my

---

[51]Moreover, "the lexicon" is ordered like waves crisscrossing in the storm. The more violent the semantic waves, the more importantly talk modifies the action. Dynamic, evolutionary principles, rather than static hierarchy, explain waves.

pants."), so that children have *a general purpose semantics* that unfolds into the many domains of adult craft-talk, mastered even by the greatly disadvantaged.

The general purpose semantics and pragmatics of infants is the very same software for the craft-talk of adults, and for the meanderings of the deranged. The differences lie in the experience base and the contexts of action. So, only part of the story is in general relativity, the semantics. The rest is the distinct experiences of crafts, and in pragmatic traction, the mutual molding between talk and doing. Among dairymen there cannot be an argument as to whether a heifer is a cow; but in law there can be; and in law as to whether a train engine is a railroad car[52] or an airplane, a motor vehicle.

You can tell when you have craft-talk for an activity, not just by the sudden blossoming of bunches of words associated with the activity but, more importantly, by what insiders MUST NOT SAY; that is, by restrictions on the acceptability of utterances that are otherwise well formed and acceptable in "unbound discourse," our general purpose discourse. So a sailor says "throw me the line," not "throw me that rope." A person may ask "can I sue him?" In legal parlance, the answer is "you can sue anybody for anything." But that is not what the craft-outsider is really asking; he is asking "can I probably win?" Craft discourse is more *regimented*, more full of *rank* and restriction of meaning than unbound discourse, in particular, by excluding expressions that are semantically well formed and close in meaning to what is required in the craft: So "that's robbery" is acceptable in unbound discourse when you are overcharged but is a solecism in law if violence or a threat of imminent violence is not involved.

There are not neat boundaries among related crafts (e.g., between tax law and tort law). Classifications often migrate, are appropriated, distorted, and augmented for use in related crafts, as I illustrated with a family of wood names, earlier. Some crafts are more or less "close" to others. Others are unrelated: Stonewall-building is nothing like cannon law; goldsmithing, nothing like flight-control; policework is nothing like currency arbitrage, or electronic design. Unrelated crafts are so distant that their lexical changes, short of supernovae (like the introduction of computer analogies), don't have an apparent impact on the others, even though everything is subtly and often imperceptibly (at short range) changing relative semantic position (opposition and affinity), like the fixed stars, and all word worldlines travel subtle corkscrews of semantic space.

The two key features of lexical organization, semantic contagion and pragmatic traction, are consequences of the **engagement of discourse with endeavor.** When you put talk into gear ("put your mouth in gear") to DO SOME-

---

[52]See *Erie R. Co. v. Tompkins*, 304 U.S. 64 (1938) for legal argument on whether a train engine is a railroad car. Also, Justice Holmes says, in *McBoyle v. United States*, 283 U.S. 25 (1931), it is a matter of law, not a matter of fact, whether an airplane is a motor vehicle for purposes of a federal law making it a crime to take a stolen motor vehicle across state lines. (Does it make a difference whether you fly it, drive it, or truck it?)

THING, from simply lying, sighing, or crying, to "telling how it happened," to talking a nonpilot down to a safe landing, or an enraged friend out of a walk-out—and everything we do is far more complicated than those words display— *the necessities and niceties of the task explain the ramification* (and often the simplification)[53] *of the vocabulary,* including the polysemy, just as they do in the real crafts like cabinetry, masonry, boating, and instrument flying. To see the gears and levers working, look at some case of craft-talk, a planetarium for the whole language.[54]

VI. CONCLUSION

One thing I take to be beyond doubt, already displayed, is that there is, comparatively, adaptation of meaning (of the same words) to varying semantic contexts—namely, semantic contagion—and that it is everywhere in discourse and is principled. Whether I have sketched the principles minutely enough or accurately is another matter. Further, the examples make it plain, I think, that the identity of the lexical components of a sentence is dependent on what items are combined.

That dynamic feature of semantics cannot be explained by any account presupposing a fixed basic vocabulary, or a fixed categorical nesting of lexical fields, or even a finite innate stock of lexical markers that maintain their "original" affinities and oppositions regardless of how they are combined.

But once you allow that there are principles of semantic combination, you have recognized general relativity of meaning; that is, the simple change in assumption that has to be made to revolutionize semantics. I suggest, even urge, that we attend to the complexity of craft-talk that both displays and proves these claims and is the place to turn general speculation into manageable empirical hypotheses.

The whole of the data, the rioting waves of opposition, overlap, contrast, and clash of meaning, are whipped around by the winds of our doings, shaping discourse to action and making acts out of talk, in a sea of semantic relativity explained by harmonious and beautiful symmetries.

---

[53]It is widely recognized that adults, regardless of education or social status, simplify and streamline both grammar and vocabulary to talk to small children; they even have common and special *tone* practices.

[54]Our unbound discourse is like craftbound discourse, but without the craft-specifying restrictions *on otherwise well-formed utterances.* It is not as if unbound discourse is verbally impoverished. Not at all; it is general-purpose talk. For one thing, you can apply any craftbound expression in unbound discourse, though you can't guarantee understanding without explaining it, because the requisite *experience* cannot be generally supposed.

REFERENCES

Churchland, P. (1979). *Scientific realism and the plasticity of mind.* Cambridge, England: Cambridge University Press.

Cresswell, M. J. (1985). *Structured meanings: The semantics of propositional attitudes.* Cambridge, MA: MIT Press.

Cruse, D. A. (1986). *Lexical semantics.* Cambridge, England: Cambridge University Press.

Davidson, D. (1984a). Theories of meaning and learnable languages. *Inquiries into truth and interpretation.* Oxford: Oxford University Press. Originally published in the *Proceedings of the International Congress for Logic, Methodology, and Philosophy of Science* (1965) Amsterdam: North-Holland.

Davidson, D. (1984b). Truth and meaning. *Inquiries into truth and interpretation.* Oxford: Oxford University Press. Originally published in *Syntèse, 17,* 304–23, (1967).

Drabble, M. (1989). *Natural curiosity.* New York: Viking.

Dummett, M. (1978). *Truth and other emigmas.* Cambridge, MA: Harvard University Press.

Geroch, R. (1978). *General relativity.* Chicago: University of Chicago Press.

Kellner, A. (1990). Philadelphia City Paper. "*Book Report*" (p. 9).

Kittay, E. (1987). *Metaphor: Its cognitive force and linguistic structure.* Oxford: The Clarendon Press.

Kripke, S. (1982). *Wittgenstein on rules and private language.* Cambridge, MA: Harvard University Press.

Lehrer, A. (1974). *Semantic fields and lexical structure.* Amsterdam: North-Holland.

Lewis, C. I. (1947). *An analysis of knowledge and valuation.* La Salle, IL: Open Court.

Lyons, J. (1977). *Semantics* (Vol. 1, 2). Cambridge, England: Cambridge University Press.

Mill, J. S. (1936). *A system of logic.* London: Longman's Green (Originally published, 1843).

Ross, J. (forthcoming). *Truth and impossibilities.*

Ross, J. (1981). *Portraying analogy.* Cambridge, England: Cambridge University Press.

Ross, J. (1989). The crash of modal metaphysics. *Review of Metaphysics,* 251–279.

Trier, J. (1934). Das sprachlich Feld. *Eine Auseinandersetzung. Neue Jahrbücher für Wissenschaft und Jugendbildung, 10,* 428–49.

Wittgenstein, L. (1968). *Philosophical investigations.* Oxford: Blackwell.

6 Conventionality and Contrast: Pragmatic Principles with Lexical Consequences

Eve V. Clark
Stanford University

Language use is regulated in part by pragmatic principles. Speakers adhere to such principles in order to make language work for them effectively in conveying their intentions to others. Two of these principles are Conventionality and Contrast. In this chapter, I explore some of the consequences of these principles for the lexicon. These two principles are central to language use because they (a) govern use of the well-established lexicon, the stock of words accrued to the language over time, and (b) place constraints on what speakers can do by way of coining new words on particular occasions. I begin with a brief account of Conventionality and Contrast, and how they act together in governing lexical usage, and then look at where we can see these principles at work, both in everyday adult speech and in child acquisition.

CONVENTIONALITY AND CONTRAST

When speakers choose words to convey the meanings they intend, they rely in large part on the conventional lexicon—the stock of words with already established meanings that can be assumed to be known to most speakers in the language community. They rely on established words to express the meanings they intend unless they wish to convey some meaning for which there is no conventional expression already available. This principle of Conventionality can be expressed as "For certain meanings there is a form that speakers expect to be used in the language community."

Conventionality is to be taken in the sense of Lewis' (1969) account of convention—that it constitutes an agreement on the part of members of a group about the accepted meanings of particular form-meaning pairs, words or expressions. The group in this case is a speech community, and any one speaker may be a member of several different speech communities, where each of these is defined by dialect either geographically or socially, by age, by sex, and by technical expertise, and thus in each instance by specialized vocabulary and expressions peculiar to each such group of speakers. The agreement in every instance is as to the established meaning of a word or expression within that specific speech community. The utility of such agreements or conventions for speakers comes from the mutual understanding they create and the consistency they provide over time: A term like *book* designates books for all speakers who use this term in English-speaking communities, and the conventional meaning associated with this word remains consistent over time. (Meanings can change, of course, but any change must be sanctioned by the speech community itself.) Mutual understanding and consistency over time appear to be two general design features necessary for a communication system such as language to work. Without conventionality, it is unclear how speakers and their addressees could reach mutually agreed on interpretations of what the speakers were trying to convey. Conventionality smooths the path for communication.

Conventionality alone is not enough. It needs to work hand-in-hand with Contrast, the principle that different forms in a language have different meanings. This principle can be stated as "Every two forms contrast in meaning." Different forms in a language typically have different meanings, a fact that has long been recognized (e.g., Bolinger, 1977; Bréal, 1897; Paul, 1898; de Saussure, 1919/1968). The reverse, though, does not hold: Different meanings are not necessarily carried by different forms; they may be and often are expressed by the same form.

Conventionality and Contrast together place constraints on the possibilities speakers make use of in conveying their intentions to their addressees. Speakers assume that the expression they have chosen on a particular occasion, for their addressees, denotes a situation, object, property, or relation their addressees can compute readily on that occasion. In using a verb, for instance, a speaker assumes he is denoting "(a) the kind of situation (b) that he has good reason to believe (c) that on this occasion the listener can readily compute (d) uniquely (e) on the basis of their mutual knowledge" (Clark & Clark 1979, p. 787). Conditions (a) through (e) of this contract capture general pragmatic conditions on the use of language, whether conventional or innovative. This contract is close kin, as Clark and Clark (1979) pointed out, to Grice's (1975) Co-operative Principle.

By Conventionality, if there is a conventional term already available, the speaker must make use of it, and not of something else, if he is to make sure he will be understood by his addressee. If the speaker doesn't use the conventional, established term for the meaning he intends, he runs a strong risk of being misunderstood. This is because the conventional terms for particular meanings *pre-empt*, or take priority over, any innovative expressions devised to express those same meanings. As Clark and Clark (1979) put it:

The rationale [for pre-emption] can be illustrated for *hospital,* an innovative verb intended to mean 'put into a hospital'. By conditions (b)–(d), the speaker must have good reason to believe the listener can readily compute the intended sense uniquely. Thus the listener would 'reason' as follows: Suppose my interlocuter had intended to convey the sense 'put into a hospital'. If he had, he would have used the well-established verb *hospitalize,* which means precisely 'put into a hospital', because then he would have had good reason to think I would compute the intended sense uniquely. Since he used *hospital,* he must have meant something distinct from 'put into a hospital'. Yet the only reasonable sense I can come up with is 'put into a hospital', which I already know to be impossible. Thus I find *hospital* to be uninterpretable, and therefore unacceptable. (p. 798)

Pre-emption applies wherever there is some already established term that carries just the meaning an innovative expression is intended to have, such that the established term's meaning is the only one computable by the addressee of that utterance.

If there is no conventional term available, the speaker may then have to construct a new word or expression for his meaning and must then do so in such a way that his addressee will be able to compute the intended meaning of the innovation. This can be illustrated for innovative denominal verbs in English such as *to porch the newspaper, to Houdini one's way out of a prison, to wrist a ball over the net* (in tennis), or *to cannonball someone's idea.* Such verbs can only be interpreted if they contrast in meaning with conventional, established verbs already familiar to speaker and addressee. If the innovations do not contrast with conventional verbs, they are typically rejected as uninterpretable because the established meanings pre-empt them, as we just saw in the case of *hospital* versus *hospitalize.*

The requirement that innovative expressions contrast in meaning with established, conventional expressions is sometimes called differentiation. Whenever a speaker uses an innovation that is a potential synonym of an established term, he must use it with a different meaning, one that is computable on that occasion. For example, *to palm someone's face* is acceptable provided it contrasts with *to slap* (for instance, by meaning "brush with one's palm"), as is *to sweeper the floor* provided it contrasts with *to sweep the floor* (for instance, by meaning "clean by means of a carpet-sweeper"). For the addressee, therefore, the meaning of such an innovation must be readily computable: The innovative expression must pick out a situation or entity that is currently salient for the speaker or addressee. It can either be "on stage" right at that point in the conversation or be highly salient and so accessible in memory. Part of this computability depends on the specificity of the situation warranted by the speaker's choice of innovative term. Typically, the more specific the situation, the easier it should be for the addressee to arrive at the intended interpretation. The degree of specificity in turn depends on the speaker's and addressee's mutual knowledge (see further, H. Clark, 1983; Clark & Carlson, 1981; Clark & Marshall, 1981).

The "contract" proposed by Clark and Clark (1979) to account for uses of innovative denominal verbs also holds for other kinds of lexical innovations. A partial list might include innovative COMPOUND NOUNS (as in *Ferrari-woman* "woman who wanted to be buried in her Ferrari"), EPONYMOUS VERBS (as in *do a Napoleon for the camera* "stand with the right hand tucked inside one's coat"), GENITIVE CONSTRUCTIONS (as in *my street voted Democrat in the last election* "the people who live on my street. . ."), CONTEXTUAL *do* (as in *do the lawn* "seed/mow/trim/weed/water the lawn," with the intended meaning computable only on the occasion of the utterance), and EXTENSIONS OF IDIOMS (as in *the police car sirened the daylights out of them* "the police car scared them badly by sounding its siren"; see Clark & Clark, 1979; H. Clark, 1983; Clark & Gerrig, 1983).

In short, *pre-emption by synonymy* is a major consequence of Conventionality and Contrast. This consequence has been summarized as follows (Clark & Clark, 1979): "If a potential innovation would be precisely synonymous with a well-established term, the innovative term is normally pre-empted by the well-established one, and is therefore considered unacceptable" (p. 798).

Some common instances of pre-emption among nouns and verbs in English are listed in Tables 6.1 and 6.2. Note that innovative forms are only pre-empted if they have the same meaning as an existing, conventional form. Otherwise speakers are free to make use of any innovative form to express a particular meaning. They are constrained only to make sure that their addressees can arrive at their intended meanings.

Pre-emptions by synonymy can be classified under several headings. In earlier work (Clark & Clark, 1979), we identified three main types in the domain of verb formation: (a) *Suppletion,* where an existing form pre-empts formation of a verb that would otherwise be the regular form to fill the paradigmatic "slot" for that

TABLE 6.1
Preemption in the Lexicon—Nouns

curious	curiosity	
tenacious	tenacity	
glorious	*gloriosity	glory
furious	*furiosity	fury
polish$_V$	polisher	
sweep$_V$	sweeper	
drill$_V$	*driller	drill$_N$
bore$_V$	*borer	bore$_N$
ride$_V$	rider	
drive$_V$	driver	
cook$_V$	*cooker	cook$_N$
spy$_V$	*spyer	spy$_N$
apply	*applier	applicant
inhabit	*inhabiter	inhabitant

Note. Preempted forms are marked with an asterisk (*).

TABLE 6.2
Preemption in the Lexicon--Verbs

to bicycle	
to jet	
*to car	to drive
*to airplane	to fly
to knee	
to shoulder	
*to foot	to kick
*to palm	to slap
to stable	
to jail	
*to hospital	to hospitalize
*to prison	to imprison
to salt	
to pollen	to pollinate
to butcher meat	
to chauffeur	
*to baker bread	to bake
*to banker money	to bank

Note. Preempted forms are marked with an asterisk (*).

meaning. For instance, although most verbs in English rely on the same base in forming the past tense, as in *jump/jumped, brush/brushed, fit/fitted*, the verb *go* calls on a suppletive form, *went*. Equally, although vehicle names are readily made into verbs in English (e.g., *to taxi, to truck, to sled, to bus*), the potential verb *to airplane* meaning "to go by plane" is pre-empted by the already established, suppletive verb form *to fly*.[1] (b) *Entrenchment*, where an existing form derived from the pertinent noun is already entrenched in the lexicon with the requisite meaning. So verbs like *to imprison* (from the noun *prison*), *to enthrone* (from *throne*), or *to pollinate* (from *pollen*), pre-empt the formation of *to prison, *to throne*, and *to pollen* with those same meanings. (c) *Ancestry*, where existing terms like the verbs *to bake, to bank*, or *to drive* themselves provide the source from which the nouns *baker, banker*, and *driver* are derived. These nouns cannot then be used as the source of further verbs—*to baker, *to banker, *to driver*—with the very same meaning as their ancestors, namely *to bake, to bank*, and *to drive* (see further, Clark & Clark, 1979).

Another form of pre-emption is driven by homonymy rather than synonymy. In the case of innovative denominal verbs, pre-emption by homonymy can be stated as follows (Clark & Clark, 1979): "If a potential innovative verb is homonymous with a well-established verb and could be confused with it, the innovative verb is normally pre-empted, and therefore is considered unaccept-

---

[1]If *to airplane* or *to plane* contrasts in meaning with *to fly*, of course, it is no longer pre-empted. The same applies to any other innovative verb: As long as they *contrast* in meaning with their neighbors, they are acceptable and so readily computable.

able" (p. 800). For instance, although the names of specific vehicle types can generally be made into verbs in English, certain vehicle names are pre-empted. So while *Jan Chevied to New York* (from the noun *Chevy*) is unexceptional, both *Jan *Forded to New York* and *Jan *Dodged to New York* are generally avoided. The established verbs *to ford* and *to dodge* are too readily accessible and so pre-empt the meanings that would be attached to the vehicle names *Ford* and *Dodge* used as verbs. The same principle of pre-emption by homonymy appears to account for the unacceptability of **to spring* and **to fall*, meaning "spend the season of spring/fall," alongside the unimpeachable *to winter* and *to summer*, both meaning "spend the season of." In this case, the existing verbs *to spring* and *to fall* take priority. (Notice that the innovations sound even worse when inflected for the past tense, as in *They springed and falled in France*.) Homonymy, then, is a further source of pre-emption that appears to apply when the established term is much more accessible or salient than the other and so makes comprehension of the innovation excessively hard to compute.

Of these forms of pre-emption, the major one is pre-emption by synonymy. Conventionality and Contrast work together to eliminate SYNONYMS, and this has immediate effects on how speakers use both established and innovative lexical items. First, speakers avoid coining words with meanings that are already represented in the conventional or well-established lexicon, and second, when they do coin new words, they make them contrast in meaning with terms already in the lexicon. The effects of Conventionality and Contrast show up in other ways too—in the process of historical change in a language and in the fact of speakers' repairs to their utterances. The effects are also highly visible in language acquisition—in children's repairs, in their lexical innovations, and in the strategies they rely on for assigning meanings to unfamiliar words.

CONVENTIONALITY AND CONTRAST AT WORK

The pre-emption of potential synonyms by established terms is nothing new. Speakers have probably always relied on Conventionality and Contrast together in shaping their language use. This would account in large part for many patterns of change in language. For example, Bréal (1897) noted that speakers typically eliminated synonyms by assigning a new meaning to one of a pair of terms. In doing so, he attributed to speakers a general rejection of synonymy as running counter to the general purpose of language and argued that, as a result, synonyms in general either vanished through differentiation of meanings, or through the dropping of one of the terms (Bréal, 1897): "Ayant le sentiment que le langage est fait tout pour servir à l'échange des idées, à l'expression de sentiments, à la discussion des intérêts, [le peuple] se refuse à croire à une synonymie qui serait inutile et dangereuse. Or, comme il est tout à la fois le dépositaire et l'auteur du langage, son opinion qu'il n'y a pas de synonymes fait qu'en réalité les synonymes n'existent pas longtemps: ou bien ils se différencient, ou bien l'un des deux termes disparaît" (p. 30). One striking example of such differentiation of meanings is very familiar to English speakers: The series of terms for animals on the hoof versus animals on the plate. After the Norman Conquest, English speakers at court found themselves faced with two sets of terms—one from English, as in *sheep, cattle, calf, pig, deer,* and one from French, *mouton, boeuf, veau, porc, venaison.* So as more French words were assimilated into English, speakers were faced with apparent synonyms among terms for animals. Instead of accepting such synonyms, speakers differentiated the meanings of each pair, with the term borrowed from French assigned for the food meaning, and the English term retained for the live animal. The result was the series familiar today in such pairs as *sheep/mutton, cattle/beef, calf/veal, pig/pork,* or *deer/venison* (Jespersen, 1930; Ullmann, 1962).

Differentiation of meaning may also arise as a result of speaker regularizations. When a word form is regularized to fit into a common paradigm, existing irregular forms may be retained with a new meaning alongside newer regularized forms. Speakers readily regularize forms to fit larger paradigms. And speakers of Modern Hebrew are no exception. Children regularize the plural of a feminine noun like /simla/ "dress" to /*simlot/ instead of using the normative Hebrew /smalot/, or give a masculine noun like /gamad/ a regular plural in /*gamadim/ instead of normative /gmadim/ (Berman, 1981). Adult speakers make direct use of similar regularizations in reforming the singular of nouns to "fit" the plurals. They may go even further and assign a new meaning to the old singular form as well. One such case has been documented recently by Ravid (1988). In Classical Hebrew, the word for "shell" was the segolate noun /cédef/, with stress on the first syllable in the singular, and a stem change in the plural to /cdafim/ (with final stress). In recent years, many speakers have formed a new singular for this noun, /cdaf/, from the plural, for a more transparently related singular/plural pair: /cdaf-cdafim/. With this change in form has come a differentiation in meaning for the two existing singular noun forms: /cdaf/ now denotes a shell on the beach (the old singular meaning) and is used as a count noun, and the old singular /cédef/ is used as a mass noun with the meaning "mother-of-pearl."

The loss and reassignment of meanings over time offer extensive evidence that speakers resist synonymy in language. They drop synonymous forms when they arise as a result of language contact, and they assign distinct meanings to words that would otherwise be synonyms. These patterns of use over time suggest that speaker attitudes to synonymy haven't changed. Synonyms never enter a language to stay. They have to move on, their meanings differentiated, or else be lost.

Conventionality and Contrast also play a role in the domains of utterance repair and lexical innovation. Speakers make repairs to their utterances, for example, whenever they perceive that their production has gone astray in some way (Levelt, 1989). When they make repairs to their lexical choices on such occasions, the motivation for their repairs is to contrast what was actually produced with what was intended. The repair itself typically reinstates the intended form. Consider the examples of repairs shown in Table 6.3 (from Jefferson, 1982, p. 58). In the first, Hannah corrects her initial production of "his own paintings" to "his own frames," in talking about a painter. In the second example, the addressee offers a repair to the speaker (the name of the politician being talked about), and the speaker takes the proffered repair and repeats it herself. In the third, the addressee is again the source of the repair, which is repeated by the speaker who then queries the need for it. These types of lexical repair are typical. They become motivated only if the speakers are assuming Contrast, such that what they actually produced missed its target in some way and therefore contrasted with what was intended. Repairs reinstate speakers' intended meanings.

In lexical innovations, speakers systematically contrast their new terms with what is already available in the conventional lexicon. Such innovations fill lexical gaps but may also have additional functions—to provide shortcuts in talking about complex events or objects and to achieve certain rhetorical effects (Clark & Clark, 1979). Lexical innovations on the part of speakers are probably much more frequent than we realize. Provided speakers take care to provide enough information, their addressees take no longer to process innovations than they do established words (Gerrig, 1989). In Table 6.4, I list some typical examples of innovations—denominal verbs like *to medal, to journal, to black-sheep,* and newly derived nouns like *assister* or *operathon.* Compound nouns in English are also frequent among lexical innovations, and I have included two typical examples at the end of Table 6.4. These are novel because their interpretations in context do not fit the conventional interpretations that might otherwise be associated with *elephant ride* (a ride on an elephant) or *homeless hotel owners* (hotel owners who are homeless).

TABLE 6.3
Lexical Repairs

Hannah:	And he's going to make his own paintings.
Bea:	Mm nm,
Hannah:	and—or I mean his own frames,
Bea:	Yeah.
Milly:	...and then they said something about Krushchev has leukemia so I thought oh it's all a big put on.
Jean:	Brezhnev.
Milly:	*Brezhnev* has leukemia. So I didn't know *what* to think.
Pat:	...the Black Muslims are certainly more provocative than the Black *Muslims ever* were.
Jo:	The Black Panthers.
Pat:	The Black *Panthers.* What'd I
Jo:	You said the Black Muslims twice.

Based on Jefferson (1982, p. 58).

TABLE 6.4
Typical Examples of Lexical Innovations

Announcer at the Olympics (diving): "Do you think Louganis is gonna medal in this event?" (meaning 'win a medal in this event')

Cartoon (the neighborhood): Woman writing in a journal at breakfast, opposite her spouse who's talking.
Caption "Elizabeth journals her way through another relationship" (meaning 'writes a journal')

A Presidential aide talking about Reagan's son Michael, on hearing that he was planning a book: "He hasn't black-sheeped us, but, apparently, he's back." (meaning 'acted as a black-sheep to')

Radio ad: "operathon-30 hours continuous" (meaning 'non-stop opera')

An IRS assister (meaning 'someone who helps the public with income tax forms'; compare *assistant*)

SF Chronicle headline: "Homeless hotel owners may get $1 million bill" (meaning 'owners of hotels with rooms for homeless people')

Cartoon: Below a board advertising 'Elephant rides 25 cents', man with a cart, to small girl: "I'm sorry, little girl, but you're not an elephant" (meaning 'rides *for* elephants')

Among items that are already in the lexicon, speakers are careful to differentiate between near synonyms when they customarily make use of both terms. For example, although such pairs as *oblige* and *obligate, medicine* and *medication,* and *flammable* and *inflammable* are often regarded as synonyms, they do not have identical meanings, and dictionaries follow speakers in differentiating them in denotation (e.g., in the *American Heritage* Usage Notes), as in (1)–(3), in dialect, or in register:

1. a. oblige "indebtedness for a favor"
   b. obligate "indebtedness for a favor; legally bound to do"
2. a. medicine "art of healing; internal treatment"
   b. medication "external treatment"
3. a. flammable—used in warnings and technical writing
   b. inflammable—applied to objects and states, common in nontechnical writing

Dialects are a major source of apparent synonyms, but individual speakers typically use only one of such competing forms as their basic, everyday term. They may be familiar with the terms from several dialects and even adjust to speakers of other dialects by choosing on occasion to use a term other than their own, but that does not make the terms synonymous (Clark, 1988). For example, one speaker may use *haystack* where another uses *haymow,* and a third *hayrick.* All three terms have the same reference, but they each belong to a different dialect of English and so contrast with each other. The same goes for terms like *milkshake, frap,* and *cabinet* (for a malted milk drink), or for *Danish, honey bun,*

TABLE 6.5
Contrasts Associated with *Receive*

receiver	sender
receptor	emittor
recipient	(sender) giver
donee	donor
receptionist	
reception	

and *sweet roll* (for a sweet breakfast roll). One finds technical as well as regional dialects where the same observation holds. For example, philosophers favor *semantical* and *syntactical*, while linguists use *semantic* and *syntactic*. Essentially, terms from different dialects should no more be considered complete synonyms within a language than analogous terms drawn from two distinct languages.

Speakers also contrast terms in register, with some terms reserved for less formal uses than others, as in the following pairs where the first is informal, the second more formal in tone: *gas/gasoline, PC/personal computer, try/attempt, many/numerous,* and so on (see further Cruse, 1986, Nunberg, 1978). In each instance, the members of a pair or set of terms contrast in meaning.

At the same time, speakers make extensive use of the fact that a difference in form connotes a difference in meaning by exploiting a range of different patterns in word formation over time to set up the range of contrasts available in words related to the verb *receive,* as shown in Table 6.5. In addition to *receiver* (the listening end of a telephone, the receiving mode on a ham radio), one finds *receptor* (the receiving element in the nervous system), *recipient* (the person to whom something has been given), *receptionist* (the person who receives clients, patients, or visitors), and *reception* (a party or gathering to welcome or congratulate someone). These terms in turn are linked in meaning to *sender, emittor, giver, donor,* and *donee.* Speakers of English make use of alternative means of deriving nouns from verbs, for example, to elaborate the set of pertinent meanings that are linked to a specific stem, marking their differences in meaning through differences in form.

CONVENTIONALITY AND CONTRAST IN CHILDREN

Children give evidence of observing Conventionality and Contrast too, and they do so from an early age (Clark, 1980, 1983). Like adults, they repair what they say. They too make extensive use of lexical innovations to fill lexical gaps. And they also give evidence of observing Contrast when they assign meanings to unfamiliar words.

Children make spontaneous repairs to their own utterances from a very early age, and do so frequently. In one study of 2- and 3-year-old repairs, the children produced between 30 and 50 repairs per half-hour of recording (Clark, 1982b). Up to 50% of these repairs were lexical repairs, repairs to the choice of words actually produced in the first version of the utterance. For example, one 2-year produced the word *shoe* for talking about what he was wearing and then promptly repaired it to *sandal,* a more specific label. Another child changed his utterance of *ship* (usually for large vessels) to *boat* in talking about a smallish boat, and yet another appropriately repaired the verb *come* to *bring.* Just as in adult speech, self-initiated repairs are much commoner than other-initiated ones. Children attempt to choose the right words for what they wish to convey, and when they realize they haven't produced the right word, they change their utterance by substituting a different word for what they are talking about. (Their other repairs are repairs to phonology, to morphology, and to syntax.) Lexical repairs are common from the age of 2 or even earlier (e.g., Scollon, 1976). Some typical examples are listed in Table 6.6.

Children also make extensive use of coinage. Their lexical innovations serve to fill gaps in their current vocabulary when they want to talk about things for which they have not yet acquired the conventional term (Clark, 1981a, 1982a). These innovations contrast in meaning with terms already in their vocabulary. Children as young as 1½ or 2 may produce some coinages, and by age 4 they often control many of the options for word formation available in their language. Some typical examples of innovations from young children acquiring English, French, and Dutch, respectively, are given in Tables 6.7, 6.8, and 6.9. Similar innovations have been observed in children acquiring many other languages, including German, Hebrew, Hungarian, Icelandic, and Italian.

In a more direct assessment of how much children attended to Conventionality, Amy Neel-Gordon and I asked young children to make judgments about which of two puppets was "right" in how he talked about various activities. The choices were between the conventional verb for a pictured action and an innovative verb, where the innovations were all attested coinages from young children. Sample verb pairs judged included *row* versus *oar* for talking about a picture of a small

TABLE 6.6
Lexical Repairs from Children

Kate (2; 8, 7): What–who's that?

Kate (2; 9, 0): You have to squeak–squeak–scrape it.

Zoe (2; 11, 21): Not the–I don't mean the *new* one.
The *old* one.

Kate (3; 0, 5): Dey have *little*–I mean *big* turtle hands.

Zoe (3; 2, 0): *These animals* are– *all these animals* are small.

From Clark (1982 b, p. 185).

TABLE 6.7
Typical Spontaneous Coinages in English

Nouns

I want a plate-egg, not a cup-egg (2;0) = fried/boiled egg
the car-smoke (2;6) = the car exhaust
my butterfly-shirt (2;8) = T-shirt with a butterfly on it
a fix-man (3;0) = mechanic
the plant-man (3;0) = gardener
a driver (3;0) = ignition key
a lessoner (4;0) = teacher

Adjectives

---

hay-y (3;3) = covered in hay
it needs to be salter (3;6) = saltier
this one is gooder (3;7) = better
a windy parasol (4;0) = a parasol blown by the wind
and about what time will they be flyable? [cocoons] (4;0) = able to fly

---

Verbs

---

you have to scale it (2;4) = to weigh
I monstered that towel (2;8) = to roar at
string me up, mommy (3;2) = to do up the string (of a cowboy hat)
I'm darking the sky (2;6) = making it dark/darkening it
how do you sharp this? (3;0) = to sharpen
we already decorated our tree (4;11) = to put decorations on/to decorate
I'm sticking it (5;7) = to hit with a stick

---

boy rowing a dinghy, *weigh* versus *scale* for someone weighing fruit, and so on. Up to age 3½ or so, children's choices were at chance, but soon after that, they began to show strong preferences for the conventional verb over the innovative one for the scenes they saw pictured (see Clark, Neel-Gordon & Johnson, 1991). In other words, as they got older, they preferred the conventional verb for an action over an innovative verb for the same action. This pattern of choices offers evidence that the conventional verbs pre-empted other options but only did so once children had realized that the innovative verb would mean the same thing as the conventional verb and was therefore pre-empted.

But could one be sure that younger children really assigned distinct meanings to such pairs of verbs? To look more closely at this question, we asked 2- and 3-year-olds to follow act-out instructions with a manipulable doll and various props. The instructions consisted of a randomized list of verb pairs, where one verb denoted the conventional action of a body part such as the foot (e.g., *to kick*), and a second verb was intended to designate some other action of the same body part (e.g., *to foot*). Our question was whether children would assign distinct actions to the verbs of each pair, even though they did not hear the two verbs next

TABLE 6.8
Typical Spontaneous Coinages in French

Nouns

une roule (1; 10, 27) < rouler 'to roll' = a ball (un bal)
une fume (2; 10) < fumer 'to smoke' = a pipe (une pipe)
une fauche (2; 11) < faucher 'to scythe' = a scythe (une faucille)
le cersonnier (3; 0) < cerceau 'hoop' = a person who repairs hoops
le poutrier (3+) < poutre 'beam' = carpenter (le charpentier)
le preneur (3; 8, 11) < prendre 'to take' = a person who takes something
le crêmeur (3; 8, 20) < crême 'cream' = person who's eating cream

Adjectives

enoeuffé (6; 8) < oeuf 'egg' = covered in egg
enconfituré (7; 0) < confiture 'jam' = covered/spread with jam
entartée (7; 3, 19) < tarte 'pastry' = decorated with pastry
eautée (9; 3) < eau 'water' = [procession] on the water

Verbs

métrer (3+) < metre 'metre, ruler' = to measure (mesurer)
pianer (3+) < piano 'piano' = play the piano (jouer du piano)
piper (4; 8, 15) < pipe 'pipe' = to smoke (fumer)
rater (4; 10, 6) < rateau 'rake' = to rake (ratisser)
dégrandir (2; 6) < grandir 'to grow' = to shrink (rétrécir)
débagager (3; 0) < bagage 'luggage' = to return from on holiday
démonter (3; 5) < monter 'to climb' = to climb down (descendre)
déprocher (3; 6) < proche 'close' = to go away (s'éloigner)

to each other. Even the youngest children appeared very consistent in assigning different meanings to different forms. The verb pairs were not treated as synonyms but consistently differentiated in some way. For example, children might make the doll kick a pebble or small ball in response to *kick* and stand on the ball in response to *foot*.

This preference for assigning different meanings to different forms has been explored in some detail for children presented with words that are unfamiliar. Dockrell (1981) showed that 3- and 4-year-olds readily inferred that unfamiliar words labeled unfamiliar categories. For instance, when children were presented with several familiar toy animals with known labels (cow, sheep, and pig) and one unfamiliar, as-yet unlabeled animal (tapir) and were asked for one of them with an unfamiliar word, *the patas*, they consistently assigned *patas* as the label for the tapir and not for any of the animals with already-known labels. Children made similar inferences about novel terms for locomotion, color, and shape.

Two-year-olds also make use of Contrast in similar tasks. Golinkoff and her colleagues (1985) showed that children as young as 2:4 made systematic inferences about the referents of unfamiliar words when shown objects with known

TABLE 6.9
Typical Spontaneous Coinages in Dutch

Nouns

zingetjes (5; 0) < 'to sing' = little songs (adult: liedjes)
een timmer (5; 6) < 'to hit' = a hammer (adult: hamer)
doekspel (3; 6) < 'cloth + game' = blindman's buff (adult: blindemannetje)
vleesman (3; 6) < 'meat + man' = butcher (adult: slager)
engeltjemuis (4; 4) < ' little angel + mouse' = a mouse that flies
stapvoeten (4; 6) < 'step + feet' = little notches (on skates)
boshakken (5; 9) < 'woods + cut up + er' = woodcutter (adult: houthakker)

Adjectives

ruikerig (4; 9) < ruiken 'to smell' = scented, smelling
jagerig (5; 0) < jagen 'to hunt, shoot' = huntery, hunter-ish
raperig (5; 0) < rapen 'to pick up' = picky
donderig (7; 0) < donder 'thunder' = thunder-ish

Verbs

otoen (4; 0) < auto 'car' = drive (adult: rijden)
een kindje melken (4; 6) < melk 'milk' = to nurse (adult: de borst geven)
afdoeken (2; 6) < doek 'cloth' = to towel off, to dry (adult: met een doek afdrogen)
de lantaan is opgebrand (3; 0) < brand 'fire' = is fired up, lighted (adult: opgestoken)
afbouwen (4; 8) < bouw 'building' = to knock down, demolish (adult: afbreken)
aanvlammen (5; 4) < vlam 'flame' = to flame, light (a match)

labels alongside unfamiliar objects for which they lacked labels. They chose appropriate referents for known labels over 90% of the time, and novel objects for novel labels. And they consistently chose a second type of unfamiliar object as the referent for a second novel label, after having assigned the first one.

Moreover, if children already have a label for an object, they readily infer that additional labels must contrast with any label already known. Two- and 3-year-olds, in fact, typically infer that a further label can denote a part (see Markman & Wachtel, 1988), or that it can stand in a subordinate or superordinate relation to terms already acquired (Taylor & Gelman, 1989). Contrast doesn't predict which meanings children are likely to assign to additional terms, only that they will assign meanings that contrast with any already mastered.

When do children arrive at the Principle of Contrast? I suggest that a likely route would be through their grasp of rational behavior, as early as during their first 12 months of life. As I have argued previously (Clark, 1988):

To discover Contrast as a pragmatic principle, children would first have to see the underpinnings of rational behaviour—that people do things intentionally, and they always have a reason for choosing one word, **x**, on a particular occasion, rather than another, **y**. From this it would follow that **x** could not be equivalent to **y**, and so must contrast with it in some way (p. 324).

In this way, then, Contrast would be available to help guide children's interpretations of words in the input they hear as soon as they begin to assign meanings to words and parts of words.

Much the same goes for Conventionality. Again, children make use of the input they hear from adults, and by 1:6 or 2:0 years clearly act as if they assume there **are** conventional words for many (perhaps all) events, objects, and relations. The stumbling block for acquisition is learning just what those conventional terms are and how precisely they map onto the kinds of events, objects, and relations the child has identified so far. This learning can take a long time and also depends to a considerable extent on what input the child receives about different topics and domains (Clark, 1987).

Lastly, Contrast and Conventionality together make some general predictions about children's uses of established versus innovative words. These predictions are essentially equivalent to the predictions we would make for adult speakers: (a) Contrasting meanings exclude synonyms; (b) established words have priority over innovative ones with the same meaning; and (c) lexical innovations can be used to fill gaps. Each of these three predictions has received strong support from research on children's assignments of meanings to unfamiliar words (e.g., Dockrell, 1981; Markman & Wachtel, 1988; Taylor & Gelman, 1989) and their assignments of meaning to innovative words (e.g., Clark, 1980, 1983, 1987; Clark & Berman, 1984; Clark, Gelman, & Lane, 1985; Clark & Hecht, 1982; Clark, Hecht, & Mulford, 1986). Children consistently reject synonyms and assign contrasting meanings to potential synonyms; they opt for the established conventional word once they discover that an innovative and an established form have the same meaning; and they readily construct new lexical items out of elements already known to them, to fill lexical gaps (see Tables 6.7, 6.8, and 6.9; also Clark, 1981a).

Contrast and Conventionality together also offer children a way to recover from earlier over-regularizations they may have made. For example, children who have generalized the paradigm of English verbs to include irregular forms typically produce such regularized pasts as *breaked, bringed, comed, goed,* and *digged.* Yet in the input they hear, they never get these past forms but only the conventional *broke, brought, came, went,* and *dug.* As children check on these forms and their own, they find out that wherever they produce the regular form (e.g., *breaked*), adult speakers produce only the irregular *broke.* Eventually (and this may take a long time), they realize that there is no difference in meaning between their own form, *breaked,* and the adult form, *broke.* And because they do not tolerate synonyms, they must at that point choose just one of the forms and drop the other. Since the majority of speakers around them use *broke,* they too opt for the conventional form and so get rid of *breaked* (see further, Clark, 1987). In fact, Contrast also plays a basic role in the acquisition of morphology more generally (Clark, 1990), as children sort out what different affixes mean and how many allomorphs they have. And the role of these principles in getting rid of over-regularizations—even where this may take many years—extends beyond words and affixes to larger structures too. For example, part of the meaning of a verb lies in the kinds of arguments it takes, but the array of verb and accompanying noun phrases may also be treated as syntactic rather than lexical. Yet here too, these principles play a basic role in getting rid of unwanted gener-alizations as children learn to distinguish, for example, between such verbs as *give* and *donate,* or *pour* and *spill* (Gropen, 1989, Gropen, Pinker, Hollander, Goldberg, & Wilson, 1989, Mazurkewich & White, 1984).

CONCLUSIONS

These are just a few of the consequences of two pragmatic principles, Conven-tionality and Contrast, but there are many details for which there is no space here. What makes an expression "readily computable," as demanded by the Gricean contract for dealing with innovative lexical expressions (Clark & Clark, 1979)? And, related to that question, how does one decide that an innovative meaning is "specific enough" in context? There are also numerous questions of implicature that require more detailed analysis. For example, because direct causation is normally expressed with a single lexeme, uses of other, periphrastic, expressions to express notions of causation typically *implicate* less direct forms of causation (e.g., McCawley, 1976; see also Horn, 1989). This follows in part from Contrast (a difference in form marks a difference in meaning) and in part from Conventionality (the "direct causation" meaning is already taken by the single lexeme that therefore pre-empts that meaning being carried by some other form). Compare, for instance, the different types of causation expressed in (a)–(c): (a) dress the child, (b) make the child dress, and (c) put a dress on the child. In short, speakers—whether adult or child—observe Conventionality and Con-trast in their uses of the lexicon. These two principles place constraints on how the established lexicon is used, and on how word formation is deployed in the coining of new words. They also motivate many of the repairs speakers make to word choice. And, in addition, they also make predictions about how children will use words, coin words, and get rid of unwanted generalizations in the lexicon. Conventionality and Contrast play an invaluable role not only for the adult speaker but also for the child learning what the lexical resources of his language offer.

ACKNOWLEDGMENT

Preparation of this chapter was supported in part by a grant from the Sloan Foundation to the Cognitive Science Group, Stanford University.

REFERENCES

Berman, R. A. (1981). Children's regularizations of plural forms. *Papers & Reports on Child Language Development* (Stanford University). *20*, 34–43.

Bolinger, D. (1977). *Meaning and form*. London: Longman.

Bréal, M. (1897). *Essai de sémantique*. Paris: Hachette.

Clark, E. V. (1980). Convention and innovation in acquiring the lexicon. (Keynote Address, Twelfth Annual Child Language Research Forum, Stanford University.) *Papers & Reports on Child Language Development* (Stanford University). *19*, 1–20.

Clark, E. V. (1981). Lexical innovations: How children learn to create new words. In W. Deutsch (Ed.), *The child's construction of language* (pp. 299–328). New York: Academic Press.

Clark, E. V. (1982a). The young word-maker: A case study of innovation in the child's lexicon. In E. Wanner & L. R. Gleitman (Eds.), *Language acquisition: The state of the art* (pp. 390–425). Cambridge, England: Cambridge University Press.

Clark, E. V. (1982b). Language change during language acquisition. In M. E. Lamb & A. L. Brown (Eds.), *Advances in developmental psychology* (Vol. 2, pp. 171–195). Hillsdale, NJ: Lawrence Erlbaum Associates.

Clark, E. V. (1983). Meanings and concepts. In J. H. Flavell & E. M. Markman (Eds.), *Handbook of child psychology, Vol. 3: Cognitive development* (pp. 787–840). (P. H. Mussen, Gen. Ed.). New York: Wiley.

Clark, E. V. (1987). The principle of contrast: A constraint on acquisition. In B. MacWhinney (Ed.), *Mechanisms of language acquisition: The 20th Annual Carnegie Symposium on Cognition* (pp. 1–33). Hillsdale, NJ: Lawrence Erlbaum Associates.

Clark, E. V. (1988). On the logic of Contrast. *Journal of Child Language, 15*, 317–335.

Clark, E. V. (1990). On the pragmatics of Contrast. *Journal of Child Language, 17*, 417–431.

Clark, E. V., & Berman, R. A. (1984). Structure and use in the acquisition of word formation. *Language, 60*, 547–590.

Clark, E. V., & Clark, H. H. (1979). When nouns surface as verbs. *Language, 55*, 767–811.

Clark, E. V., Gelman, S. A., & Lane, N. M. (1985). Compound nouns and category structure in young children. *Child Development, 56*, 84–94.

Clark, E. V., & Hecht, B. F. (1982). Learning to coin agent and instrument nouns. *Cognition, 12*, 1–24.

Clark, E. V., Hecht, B. F., & Mulford, R. C. (1986). Coining complex compounds in English: Affixes and word order in acquisition. *Linguistics, 24*, 7–29.

Clark, E. V., Neel-Gordon, A., & Johnson, J. (1991). *Contrast and Conventionality in the acquisition of verb meanings*. Unpublished manuscript.

Clark, H. H. (1983). Making sense of nonce-sense. In G. B. Flores d'Arcais & R. J. Jarvella (Eds.), *The process of language understanding* (pp. 297–331). New York: Wiley.

Clark, H. H., & Carlson, T. B. (1981). Context for comprehension. In J. Long & A. Baddeley (Eds.), *Attention and performance* (Vol. 9, pp. 313–330). Hillsdale, NJ: Lawrence Erlbaum Associates.

Clark, H. H., & Gerrig, R. J. (1983). Understanding old words with new meanings. *Journal of Verbal Learning & Verbal Behavior, 22*, 591–608.

Clark, H. H., & Marshall, C. R. (1981). Definite reference and mutual knowledge. In A. Joshi, B. Webber, & I. Sag (Eds.), *Elements of discourse understanding* (pp. 10–63). Cambridge, England: Cambridge University Press.

Cruse, D. A. (1986). *Lexical semantics*. Cambridge, England: Cambridge University Press.

Dockrell, J. E. (1981). *The child's acquisition of unfamiliar words: An experimental study*. Unpublished doctoral dissertation, University of Stirling, Scotland.

Gerrig, R. J. (1989). The time course of sense creation. *Memory & Cognition, 17*, 194–207.

Golinkoff, R. M., Hirsh-Pasek, K., Lavallee, C., & Baduini, C. (1985, October). *What's in a word? The young child's disposition to use lexical contrast.* Paper presented at the Boston University Conference on Child Language, Boston.

Grice, H. P. (1975). Logic and conversation. In P. Cole & J. L. Morgan (Eds.), *Speech acts* (pp. 41–58). *Syntax & Semantics* (Vol. 3). New York: Academic Press.

Gropen, J. H. (1989). *Learning locative verbs: How universal linking rules constrain productivity.* Unpublished doctoral dissertation, Massachusetts Institute of Technology.

Gropen, J., Pinker, S., Hollander, M., Goldberg, R., & Wilson, R. (1989). The learnability and acquisition of the dative alternation in English. *Language, 65,* 203–257.

Horn, L. R. (1989). *A natural history of negation.* Chicago: University of Chicago Press.

Jefferson, G. (1982). On exposed and embedded correction in conversation. *Studium Linguistik, 14,* 58–68.

Jespersen, O. (1930). *Growth and structure of the English language* (6th ed.). Leipzig: Teubner.

Levelt, W. J. M. (1989). *Speaking: From intention to articulation.* Cambridge, MA: MIT/Bradford Books.

Lewis, D. K. (1969). *Convention: A philosophical study.* Cambridge, MA: Harvard University Press.

Markman, E. M., & Wachtel, G. F. (1988). Children's use of Mutual Exclusivity to constrain the meanings of words. *Cognitive Psychology, 20,* 121–157.

Mazurkewich, I., & White, L. (1984). The acquisition of the dative alternation: Unlearning over-generalizations. *Cognition, 16,* 261–283.

McCawley, J. D. (1976). Conversational implicature and the lexicon. In P. Cole (Ed.), *Pragmatics* (pp. 245–259), Semantics & syntax (Vol. 9). New York: Academic Press.

Nunberg, G. (1978). Slang, usage conditions, and l'arbitraire du signe. In D. Farkas, W. M. Jacobsen, & K. W. Todrys (Eds.), *Papers from the parasession on the lexicon* (pp. 301–311). Chicago: Chicago Linguistic Society.

Paul, H. (1898). *Prinzipien der Sprachgeschichte* (3rd ed.). (Originally published in 1880.) Halle: Niemeyer.

Ravid, D. D. (1988). *Transient and fossilized phenomena in inflectional morphology: Varieties of spoken Hebrew.* Unpublished doctoral dissertation, Tel Aviv University.

Saussure, F. de. (1968). *Cours de linguistique générale.* W. Baskin (Trans.) (Originally published in 1919). New York: Philosophical Library.

Scollon, R. (1976). *Conversations with a one year old: A case study of the developmental foundation of syntax.* Honolulu: University of Hawaii Press.

Taylor, M., & Gelman, S. A. (1989). Incorporating new words into the lexicon: Preliminary evidence for language hierarchies in two-year-old children. *Child Development, 60,* 625–636.

Ullmann, S. (1962). *Semantics: An introduction to the science of meaning.* Oxford: Basil Blackwell.

II CONCEPTS AND RELATIONS

7 What is a Concept?

Ray Jackendoff
Brandeis University

E-CONCEPTS AND I-CONCEPTS

Pretheoretically, there is a fundamental tension in the ordinary language term *concept*. On one hand, it is something out there in the world: We speak of "the Newtonian concept of mass" as though it exists independently of who actually knows or grasps it. Likewise, "grasping a concept" evokes comparison to grasping a physical object, except that we somehow do it with our minds instead of our hands. On the other hand, we speak of a concept as an entity within one's head, a private entity, a product of the imagination that can be conveyed to others only by means of language, gesture, drawing, or some other imperfect means of communication. How should a theory of concepts confront this tension?

As it happens, precisely the same tension has been discussed by Chomsky (1986) with respect to the term *language*. He differentiates the two poles as "E-language" (external language, the language seen as external artifact) versus "I-language" (internal language, the language as a body of internally encoded information). I adopt Chomsky's terminology and speak of E-concepts versus I-concepts.

For Chomsky's purpose—the characterization of the mental resources that make possible human knowledge of language—the notion of I-language rather than E-language is the appropriate focus of inquiry. Chomsky argues this point at length in Chomsky (1986), and he has in fact been quite explicit on this point at least since Chomsky (1965). The new terminology only helps make clearer an old and forceful position.

However, the choice of I-language as the focus of Chomsky's linguistic theory does not rest on a priori argumentation alone. Rather, it rests primarily on the

191

suitability of this notion to support scientific investigation of language. To the extent that generative linguistics has indeed been successful in increasing our understanding of the human language capacity, the choice of I-language as the object of inquiry has been vindicated. (And notice that disagreement, even violent disagreement, among its practitioners does not diminish the fact that progress has been made. It stands to reason that, at any particular moment, the most time and energy is being spent at the frontiers of understanding, not in the areas that have been settled. Any linguist will acknowledge that the frontiers have expanded considerably over the past three decades.)

The goal of my own work since the mid-1970s has been to characterize the mental resources that make possible human knowledge and experience of the world. I conceive of this enterprise as an extension of Chomsky's goals. Accordingly, an important boundary condition on my enterprise is that it must be in all respects compatible with the world view of generative linguistics.

In particular, if we think very roughly of language as a vehicle for expressing concepts, an integrated theory of language and thought must include a way for linguistic expressions to be related to concepts. If, for my purposes and Chomsky's, the notion of I-language rather than E-language is the suitable focus of inquiry, then on the face of it one should also choose I-concepts rather than E-concepts as the focus for a compatible theory of knowledge.

In this chapter I hope to accomplish two things. First, I ground a theory of I-concepts called Conceptual Semantics in first principles parallel to those of generative syntax. Second, I briefly demonstrate some empirical results that flow from adopting my approach. (Most of the arguments are elaborated in much greater detail in Jackendoff, 1983, 1987, 1990.)

FIRST PRINCIPLES OF CONCEPTUAL KNOWLEDGE

The fundamental motivation behind generative syntax is of course the creativity of language—the fact that a speaker of a language can understand and create an indefinitely large number of sentences that he or she has never heard before. It follows from this observation that a speaker's repertoire of syntactic structures cannot be characterized just as a finite list of sentences. Nor, of course, can it be characterized as an infinite set of possible sentences of the language, because it must be instantiated in a finite (albeit large) brain. Rather, the speaker's potential repertoire of syntactic structures must be mentally encoded in terms of a finite set of primitives and principles of combination that collectively describe (or generate) the class of possible sentences. In speaking or understanding a sentence, then, a language user is taken to be creating or invoking a mental information structure, the syntactic structure of the sentence, which is organized in conformance with the principles of syntactic structure.

Parallel arguments obtain for conceptual knowledge, in two different ways.

First, a language user presumably is not gratuitously producing and parsing syntactic structures for their own sake: A syntactic structure expresses a concept or idea. On the basis of this concept, the language user can perform any number of tasks, for instance checking the sentence's consistency with other linguistic or extralinguistic knowledge, performing inferences, formulating a response, or translating the sentence into another language. Corresponding to the indefinitely large variety of syntactic structures, then, there must be an indefinitely large variety of concepts that can be invoked in producing and comprehending sentences. It follows that the repertoire of concepts expressed by sentences cannot be mentally encoded as a list, but must be characterized in terms of a finite set of mental primitives and principles of combination that collectively describe the set of possible concepts expressed by sentences. For convenience, I refer to these two sets together as the "grammar of sentential concepts."

It is widely assumed, and I take for granted, that the basic units out of which a sentential concept is constructed are the concepts expressed by the words in the sentence, that is, *lexical* concepts. It is easy to see that lexical concepts too are subject to the argument from creativity. For instance, consider the concept expressed by the word *dog*. Someone who knows this concept will be able to judge of an indefinitely large variety of objects whether they are dogs or not. Thus the concept cannot be encoded as a list of the dogs one has previously encountered; nor, because the brain is finite, can it be a list of all dogs there ever have been and will be, or the set of all possible dogs. Rather, it must be some kind of finite schema that can be compared with the mental representations of arbitrary new objects to produce a judgment of conformance or nonconformance.

Two immediate qualifications: First, there may well be objects for which people's judgments disagree. This does not entail that there is no concept *dog* or that people do not know the meaning of the word. Rather, because my concern is with people's internalized schemas, I conclude that people may have schemas for *dog* that differ in various details, and that these differences too may bear examination.

Second, there may be novel objects such that one cannot judge clearly whether they are dogs or not. ("It's sort of a dog and sort of a wolf.") Again, this does not necessarily challenge the idea that one has an internalized schema for *dog*. Rather, from such examples—of which there are many—we conclude that there is a potential degree of indeterminacy in the lexical concept itself, or in the procedure for comparing it with mental representations of novel objects, or in both.

To sum up so far: Paralleling the argument from creativity to the necessity for principles or rules in syntactic knowledge, I have argued (a) that sentential concepts cannot be listed but must be mentally generated on the basis of a finite set of primitives and principles of combination; (b) that lexical concepts cannot consist of a list of instances but must consist of finite schemas that can be creatively compared (i.e., in rule-governed fashion) to novel inputs.

The second major issue in the foundation of syntactic theory flows from the problem of acquisition: How can a child acquire the rules of syntax on the basis of the fragmentary evidence available? In particular, how does the child induce *rules of grammar* from *instances* of well-formed sentences? The problem of language acquisition motivates the central hypothesis of generative linguistics: that the child comes to the task of language learning equipped with an innate Universal Grammar that narrowly restricts the options available for the grammar he or she is trying to acquire. The driving issue in generative linguistics, then, is to determine the form of Universal Grammar, consonant both with the variety of human languages and also with their learnability.

A parallel argument can be made for the logical problem of concept acquisition, in both the sentential and lexical domains. For the former case, consider that the language learner must acquire not only the principles for constructing syntactically well-formed sentences, but also the principles for constructing the corresponding sentential concepts. Like the rules of syntax, these principles must be acquired on the basis of some combination of linguistic experience, non-linguistic experience, and innate constraints on possible principles. As in syntax, then, an important part of our task is to determine what aspects of the grammar of sentential concepts are learned and what aspects are innate. The boundary condition imposed by learnability is that the innate parts must be sufficiently rich to make it possible to acquire the rest.

Turning to lexical concepts, consider that one is capable of acquiring during one's lifetime an indefinitely large number of concepts, each of them on the basis of rather fragmentary evidence. Again, because lexical concepts must be encoded as unconscious schemas rather than lists of instances, lexical concept acquisition too presents a problem parallel to the acquisition of syntax. As in syntax, we adopt the hypothesis that lexical concepts are constructed from an innate basis of possible concepts, modulated by the contribution of linguistic and nonlinguistic experience.

But now the argument from creativity applies in a new way. If there is an indefinitely large stock of possible lexical concepts, and the innate basis for acquiring them must be encoded in a finite brain, we are forced to conclude that *the innate basis for concepts must consist of a set of generative principles*—a group of primitives and principles of combination that collectively determine the set of lexical concepts. This implies in turn that most if not all lexical concepts are composite, that is, that they can be decomposed in terms of the primitives and principles of combination of the innate "Universal Grammar of lexical concepts." Learning a lexical concept, then, is to be thought of as constructing a composite expression within the grammar of lexical concepts, associating it with phonological and syntactic structures, and storing them together in long-term memory as a usable unit.[1]

---

[1]This contrasts sharply with the view of Fodor (1975) and Fodor et al. (1980), that lexical concepts are cognitively primitive monads linked with each other by meaning postulates. This view,

Given the parallelism in first principles, I therefore believe that the central issue of the theory of conceptual knowledge ought to parallel that of the theory of syntax: What are the innate units and principles of organization that make human lexical and sentential concepts both possible in all their variety and also learnable on the basis of some realistic combination of linguistic and nonlinguistic experience?

THREE MODELS FOR THE DESCRIPTION OF MEANING

The idea that a concept or meaning is a kind of mental representation is, of course, not universally accepted. Perhaps the most prestigious tradition in the study of meaning grows out of Frege's "Sense and Reference" (1892), where he very carefully disassociates the "sense" of an expression—which he takes to be an objective, publicly available entity—from the "idea" that a user of the expression carries in his head, which is subjective and variable. Frege's notion of "sense" underpins the approach to meaning in truth-conditional and especially model-theoretic semantics. To be sure, both generative grammar and truth-conditional semantics treat language as a formal system. But they differ radically in the goals they wish to accomplish through such treatment. The purpose of truth-conditional semantics is to explicate Truth, a relation that is supposed to obtain between language and reality, independent of language users. In turn, the truth conditions of sentences can be treated as speaker-independent only if both reality *and* the language that describes it are speaker-independent as well. Hence a truth-conditional semantics in the Tarskian or Davidsonian sense requires a theory of E-language, of language as an abstract artifact extrinsic to speakers.

As stressed earlier, the purpose of generative grammar has always been to explicate I-language, the principles internalized by speakers that constitute knowledge of a language. A compatible theory of meaning must therefore concern the principles internalized in the speaker that permit him or her to understand sentences, draw inferences from them, and judge their truth: It must be a theory of I-semantics, not E-semantics.

It is sometimes suggested to me that there is no inherent conflict between the two approaches. One is about the way the world *is*, and the other is about the way we *grasp* the world. They might lead to altogether different, though hopefully complementary, insights. I see nothing wrong with this conclusion in principle: You go your way, I'll go mine. The difficulty is one of terminological imperi-

---

though it has been influential in certain circles, denies the possibility of doing lexical decomposition and hence the value of any of the work presented in this volume. As Fodor has worked out no alternative analyses for any nontrivial phenomena discussed in the tradition of lexical semantics, and as I have shown in detail (Jackendoff, 1983, 1987) where his arguments go astray, we can safely dismiss his position here.

alism, as exemplified by Lewis' (1972) widely quoted slogan to the effect that the study of "Mentalese"—in effect I-semantics—isn't *really* semantics. Along with this goes the implication that what an I-semanticist does isn't really worth doing. My own feeling is that one can't decide whether it's worth doing until the results are in. Toward the end of this chapter, I offer some results that suggest there is considerable interest to this enterprise, whatever one cares to call it. (The rest of this volume, of course, also gives the lie to such assertions that the study of the mental lexicon is not of interest; and it represents only a small sample of a large and flourishing tradition.)

It is also sometimes suggested that I have been unfair to model-theoretic semantics: It is in principle neutral between E-semantics and I-semantics. Even if Davidson and Lewis designed the theory with E-semantics in mind, we are always free to choose a model that conforms to psychological constraints and thereby to produce a model-theoretic I-semantics. Again I agree in principle. But to my knowledge, all model-theoretic semantics, other than a few exceptions such as Bach (1986a) and Verkuyl (1989), has in practice been E-semantics. Moreover, it seems to me that the project of determining a psychologically defensible model theory is equivalent to the enterprise of Conceptual Semantics, that is, finding out how human beings actually encode their construal of the world. Again, I don't want to make heavy weather of the terminology. If some readers are more comfortable thinking of Conceptual Semantics as a very particular and eccentric brand of model-theoretic semantics, I have no objection. It is the *psychological* claim, not the name of the theory, that is crucial. (See Jackendoff, 1983, chap. 2, 3, 5, and Jackendoff, 1987, chap. 7, for amplification of these points.)

It is next necessary to differentiate Conceptual Semantics from Fodor's "Language of Thought" Hypothesis. On the face of it, Fodor's position seems closer to mine. His purpose is to understand the character of mind. Unlike the model theorists, he is committed to a combinatorial mental representation in terms of which language users make inferences and formulate responses. But in addition to mental representation, Fodor insists (especially in Fodor, 1987) on "Intentional Realism," the idea that the mental representations over which computations take place have further semantic content—that they are representations of propositions with real-world reference and truth value.

But let us look at the representations of, say, generative phonology. It makes little sense to think of the rules of phonology as propositional, *true in the world independent of speakers of English*. In generative phonology as it is conducted by its practitioners, phonological rules are regarded as principles of internal computation, not as facts about the world.

The question at issue, then, is whether conceptual structure is somehow different from phonology and syntax—whether, when we enter the domain of meaning, the rules of the game should be changed, so that propositional content rather than computational form ought to be the focus of inquiry. What Fodor appears to require is a marriage between the realism of truth-conditional semantics and the mentalism of generative grammar—that is, a unified theory of E-semantics and I-semantics, mediated by the relation of intentionality, which for him gives content to mental representations. One immediate difficulty with this approach is that this relation is highly mysterious—even to Fodor. If an understanding of intentionality is necessary in order to just get started on a theory of semantics, it seems to me one's theory is in deep trouble.

Conceptual Semantics, by contrast, is concerned most directly with the form of the internal mental representations that constitute conceptual structure and with the formal relations between this level and other levels of representation. The theory of conceptual structure is thus taken to be entirely parallel to the theory of syntactic or phonological structure.

For Fodor, as for the model theorists, such an inquiry does not count as semantics: A theory of semantics must include a Realist account of truth conditions and inference. Once again, I don't care too much about terminology. I would rather that the enterprise be judged on its merits than dismissed because it doesn't address issues that someone calls the True Issues of Semantics. If one prefers to call the enterprise logical or conceptual syntax, or the "Syntax of Thought" Hypothesis, that's fine with me. We should be clear, though, that it is in principle as different from "straight" syntax (the grammar of NPs, VPs, etc.) as straight syntax is from phonology.

Given the meager positive empirical results of Fodor's approach, which has been largely devoted to showing what else won't work, I submit that the merits of the Language of Thought Hypothesis over the Syntax of Thought Hypothesis have yet to be demonstrated.

I should also mention the relation of Conceptual Semantics to a program of research called Cognitive Grammar or Cognitive Semantics (e.g., Fauconnier, 1984; Herskovits, 1986; Lakoff, 1987; Langacker, 1986; Talmy, 1978, 1980, 1983, 1985). This work, like Conceptual Semantics, is concerned with the mental representation of the world and its relation to language. It shares with Conceptual Semantics a concern with the encoding of spatial concepts and their extension to other conceptual fields. Some work in this tradition, especially that of Talmy, has provided important insights and analyses to the present framework. Conceptual Semantics differs from Cognitive Grammar, however, in that (a) it is committed to an autonomous level of syntactic representation rather than its abandonment; (b) it is committed to rigorous formalism, insofar as possible, on the grounds that formal treatment is the best way of rendering a theory testable; (c) it makes contact with relevant results in perceptual psychology rather than leaving such relationships tacit; (d) it is committed to exploring issues of learnability and hence to the possibility of a strong innate formal basis for concept acquisition.

ORGANIZATION OF LANGUAGE

Next I must spend a little time sketching the relation of the putative level of conceptual structure to language. For concreteness, I assume an overall organization of the information structure involved in language as diagrammed in Fig. 7.1.

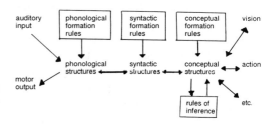

FIG. 7.1. Overall organization of the information structure involved in language.

This organization includes three autonomous levels of mental representations: phonological, syntactic, and conceptual. Each of these has its own characteristic primitives and principles of combination, characterized as a set of *formation rules* that generates the well-formed structures of the level.

The grammar also contains sets of *correspondence rules* that link the levels, indicated by arrows between the levels. The correspondence of phonological structure to syntactic structure is specified by one such set. This is, for instance, the locus of "readjustment rules" such as cliticization. The correspondence of syntactic and conceptual structures is specified by what used to be called *projection rules* (Katz & Fodor 1963), which determine the relation of syntactic structure to meaning.

Figure 7.1 also includes correspondence rules between the linguistic levels and nonlinguistic domains. On one end, there must be a mapping from the acoustic analysis provided by the auditory system into phonological structure; this mapping is the subject matter of acoustic phonetics. There must also be a mapping from phonological structure into motor commands to the vocal tract, the domain of articulatory phonetics. On the other end, there must be mappings between conceptual structure and other forms of mental representation that encode, for instance, the output of the visual faculty and the input to the formulation of action. I have discussed these mappings, especially the connection to vision, in Jackendoff (1987).

Because conceptual structure is the domain of mental representation over which inference can be defined, Fig. 7.1 also includes a component called "rules of inference," which maps conceptual structures into conceptual structures. As argued in Jackendoff (1983, chap. 5 and 6), I include in this component not only rules of logical inference but also rules of invited inference, pragmatics, and heuristics: Whatever differences there may be among these categories of principles, they are all defined over the same level of mental representation. In other words, there is no proprietary level of "semantic representation" at which only logical properties of sentences are encoded, with other "pragmatic" properties reserved for a different level.

It should be pointed out that, under the view being laid out here, the level of conceptual structure is not language dependent, because it serves as an interface between linguistic information and information germane to other capacities such as vision and action. I assume, on grounds of evolutionary conservatism, that nonlinguistic organisms—both higher animals and babies—also possess a level of conceptual structure in their mental repertoire, perhaps not as rich as ours, but formally similar in many respects.

Figure 7.1 as it stands contains no explicit lexical component. Where is the lexicon in this picture? Under the standard view of the lexicon, a lexical item establishes a correspondence between well-formed fragments of phonological, syntactic, and conceptual structure; that is, the lexicon is a part of the correspondence rule component. Thus we can regard each component in Fig. 7.1 as divided into lexical principles (those that apply within words) and extralexical principles (those that apply to domains larger than the word level). However, the basic alphabet of primitives and principles of combination is shared by the two subcomponents.

It is an ancient observation that the semantic combinations that can be expressed through syntactic phrases can in many cases also be incorporated into lexical conceptual structures. For instance, to the extent that *two times* paraphrases *twice*, or *cause to die* paraphrases *kill*, or *break violently* paraphrases *smash*, or *give away in exchange for money* paraphrases *sell*, the extralexical conceptual structures expressed by the paraphrases must be reproduced internal to unitary lexical items. That is, the grammars of sentential concepts and of lexical concepts interpenetrate in much the same way as do the grammars of, say, sentential and lexical stress; they share many of the same primitives and principles of combination, even if they differ in details. In short, the division of the overall grammar into three independent levels linked by correspondence rules is crosscut by a subsidiary division in each component into lexical versus extralexical principles.

FEATURE-BASED ASPECTS
OF CONCEPTUAL STRUCTURE

I argued earlier that the central issue of a theory of I-conceptual knowledge ought to be the innate units and principles of organization that underlie human lexical and sentential concepts. I have now presented enough background to be able to sketch out two major subsystems within conceptual structure. The first involves the major category system and argument structure; the second involves the conceptualization of boundedness and aggregation.

Ontological Categories and Argument Structure

Jackendoff (1983, chap. 3 and 4) proposes a basic organization of major conceptual categories that in many ways parallels X-bar theory in syntax. Recall the major point of X-bar theory: Although none of the syntactic categories N, V, A, P can be reduced to any of the others, they project complement and specifier structure in highly similar fashion. Their similarities and differences are expressed in terms of a feature system. A similar organization obtains in the major conceptual categories. Instead of a division of formal entities into such familiar logical types as constants, variables, predicates, and quantifiers, each of which has nothing in common with the others, Jackendoff (1983) argues that the major units of conceptual structure are *conceptual constituents,* each of which belongs to one of a small set of major ontological categories (or conceptual "parts of speech") such as Thing, Event, State, Place, Path, Property, and Amount. These are obviously all quite different in the kind of reference they pick out, but formally (algebraically) they have a great deal in common. Here are six formal characteristics that cut across the categories.

(a) Each major syntactic constituent of a sentence (excluding contentless constituents such as epenthetic *it* and *there*) maps into a conceptual constituent in the meaning of the sentence. For example, in *John ran toward the house, John* and *the house* correspond to Thing-constituents, the PP *toward the house* corresponds to a Path-constituent, and the entire sentence corresponds to an Event-constituent.

Note that this correspondence is stated very carefully. In particular, the converse mapping does not hold—not every conceptual constituent in the meaning of a sentence corresponds to a syntactic constituent, because (for one thing) many conceptual constituents of a sentence's meaning are completely contained within lexical items. In addition, note that the matching is by *constituents,* not by *categories,* because the mapping between conceptual and syntactic categories is many-to-many. For instance, an NP can express a Thing (e.g., *the dog*), an Event (*the war*), or a Property (*redness*); a PP can express a Place (*in the house*), a Path (*to the kitchen*), or a Property (*in luck*); and S can express a State (*Bill is here*) or an Event (*Bill ran away*). However, each of these examples matches a syntactic *constituent* to a conceptual *constituent,* in accordance with the preceding claim.

(b) Each conceptual category supports the encoding of information not only on the basis of linguistic input, but also on the basis of the visual (or other sensory) environment; that is, each category supports extralinguistic reference. For example, (2a) points out a Thing in the environment; (2b) points out a Place; (2c) accompanies the demonstration of an Action; (2d) accompanies the demonstration of a Distance, independent of the object whose length it is.

(2) a. **That** is a robin.
     b. **There** is your hat.

c. Can you do **this?**

d. The fish was **this** long.

(c) Many of the categories support a type-token distinction. For example, just as there are many individual tokens of the Thing-type expressed by *a hat,* there may be many tokens of the Event-type expressed by *John ate his hat,* and there may be many different individual Places of the Place-type expressed by *over your head.* (Properties and Amounts, however, do not so clearly differentiate tokens and types.)

(d) Many of the categories support quantification.

(3) a. Every dinosaur had a brain. (Things)

b. Everything you can do, I can do better. (Actions)

c. Anyplace you can go, I can go too. (Places)

(e) Each conceptual category has some realizations in which it is decomposed into a function-argument structure; each argument is in turn a conceptual constituent of some major category. The standard notion of "predicate" is a special case of this, where the superordinate category is a State or Event. For instance, in (4a), which expresses a State, the arguments are *John* (Thing) and *tall* (Property); in (4b), also a State, both arguments are Things; in (4c), an Event, the arguments are *John* (Thing) and *(PRO) to leave* (Event or Action).

(4) a. John is tall.

b. John loves Mary.

c. John tried to leave.

But unlike standard predicate logic, this function-argument organization extends to other categories, just as complement structure in syntax occurs with other categories besides Verb. For instance, a Thing also may have a Thing as argument, as in (5a) or (5b); a Path may have a Thing as argument, as in (6a), or a Place, as in (6b); a Property may have a Thing (7a) or an Event/Action (7b) as argument.

(5) a. father of the bride

b. president of the republic

(6) a. to the house

b. from under the table

(7) a. afraid of Harry

b. ready to leave

(f) The conceptual structure of a lexical item is an entity with zero or more open argument places. The meanings of the syntactic complements of the lexical item fill in the values of the item's argument places in the meaning of the sentence. For instance, the verb *be* in (4a) expresses a function that maps a Thing (the subject) and a Property (the predicate AP) into a State; *love* in (4b) expresses a function that maps two Things (the subject and object) into a State; *try* in (4c) expresses a function that maps a Thing (the subject) and an Event (the complement clause) into an Event; *father* and *president* in (5) express functions that map a Thing (the NP complement) into another Thing; *from* in (6b) expresses a function that maps a Place (the complement PP) into a Path; *afraid* in (7a) expresses a function that maps a Thing into a Property.

These observations, though slightly tedious, should convey the general picture: Though none of the major conceptual categories can be insightfully reduced to the others, they share impoortant formal properties. Thus a basic formation rule for conceptual categories can be stated along the lines in (8).

$$(8)\ \ \text{Entity} \rightarrow \begin{bmatrix} \text{Event/Thing/Place/}\ldots \\ \text{Token/Type} \\ F\ (<\text{Entity}_1,\ <\text{Entity}_2,\ <\text{Entity}_3>>>) \end{bmatrix}$$

(8) decomposes each conceptual constituent into three basic feature complexes: the category feature, the token/type feature, and the argument structure feature. The last of these allows for recursion of conceptual structure and hence an infinite class of possible concepts.

In addition, observation (a) above—the fact that major syntactic phrases correspond to major conceptual constituents—can be formalized as a general correspondence rule of the form (9); and observation (f)—the basic correspondence of syntactic and conceptual argument structure—can be formalized as a general correspondence rule of the form (10). (*XP* stands for any major syntactic constituent; X° stands for any lexical item whose complements are (optionally) *YP* and *ZP*.)

(9) *XP* corresponds to Entity

$$(10)\ \begin{bmatrix} X^0 \\ \underline{\hspace{1em}} <YP <ZP>> \end{bmatrix} \text{corresponds to} \begin{bmatrix} \text{Entity} \\ F\ (<E_1>,\ <E_2,\ <E_3>>) \end{bmatrix}$$

where *YP* corresponds to E_2, *ZP* corresponds to E_3, and the subject (if there is one) corresponds to E_1.

The examples in (a)–(f) show that the values of $\pm$N, $\pm$V, and the conceptual n-ary feature Thing/Event/Place, etc. are irrelevant to the general form of these rules. The algebra of conceptual structure and its relation to syntax is best stated cross-categorially, very much like X-bar theory in the theory of phrase structure.

Aggregation and Boundedness

The phenomena discussed in the previous subsection involve an area where the syntactic category system and the conceptual category system match up fairly well. In a way, the relation between the two systems serves as a partial explication of the categorial and functional properties of syntax: Syntax presumably evolved as a means to express conceptual structure, so it is natural to expect that some of the structural properties of concepts would be mirrored in the organization of syntax.

On the other hand, there are other aspects of conceptual structure that display a strong featural or X-bar character but that are not expressed in so regular a fashion in syntax (at least in English). One such aspect (discussed in Bach, 1986b, Declerck, 1979, Dowty, 1979, Hinrichs, 1985, Link, 1983, Mourelatos, 1981, Platzack, 1979, Talmy, 1978, Vendler, 1967, Verkuyl, 1972, among others) can be illustrated by the examples in (11).

(11) $\left\{ \begin{array}{l} \text{For hours,} \\ \text{Until noon,} \end{array} \right\}$

    a. Bill slept.
    b. the light flashed. [repetition only]
    c. lights flashed.
    d. *Bill ate the hot dog.
    e. Bill ate hot dogs.
    f. *Bill ate some hot dogs.
    g. Bill was eating the hot dog.
    h. ?Bill ran into the house. [repetition only]
    i. people ran into the house.
    j. ?some people ran into the house. [repetition only]
    k. Bill ran toward the house.
    l. Bill ran into houses.
    m. Bill ran into some houses. [repetition only]
    n. Bill ran down the road.
    o. *Bill ran 5 miles down the road.
       [ok only on reading where 5 miles down the road is where Bill was, not where 5 miles down the road is how far he got.]

The question raised by these examples is why prefixing *for hours* or *until noon* should have such effects: Sometimes it leaves a sentence acceptable, sometimes it renders it ungrammatical, and sometimes it adds a sense of repetition. The essential insight is that *for hours* places a measure on an otherwise temporally unbounded process, and that *until noon* places a temporal boundary on an otherwise temporally unbounded process. *Bill slept,* for instance, inherently expresses an unbounded process, so it can be felicitously prefixed with these expressions. On the other hand, *Bill ate the hot dog* expresses a temporally bounded event, so it cannot be further measured or bounded.

In turn, there are two ways in which a sentence can be interpreted as a temporally unbounded process. One is for the sentence to inherently express a temporally unbounded process (as is the case in 11a, c, e, g, i, k, l, n). We return to these cases shortly. The other is for the sentence to be interpreted as an indefinite repetition of an inherently bounded process (as in 11b, h, j, m). (*Bill ate the hot dog,* like *Bill died,* is bounded but unrepeatable, so it cannot be interpreted in this fashion.) This sense of repetition has no syntactic reflex in English, though some languages such as Hungarian and Finnish have an iterative aspect that does express it.

How should this sense of iteration be encoded in conceptual structure? It would appear most natural to conceive of it as an operator that maps a single Event into a repeated sequence of individual Events of the same type. Brief consideration suggests that in fact this operator has exactly the same semantic value as the plural marker, which maps individual Things into collections of Things of the same type; that is, this operator is not formulated specifically in terms of Events but should be applicable in cross-categorical fashion to any conceptual entity that admits of individuation. The fact that this operator does not receive consistent expression across syntactic categories should not obscure the essential semantic generalization.

Returning to the inherently unbounded cases, it has often been observed that the bounded/unbounded (event/process, telic/atelic) distinction is strongly parallel to the count/mass distinction in NPs. An important criterion for the count/mass distinction has to do with the description of parts of an entity. For instance, a part of *an apple* (count) cannot itself be described as *an apple;* but any part of a body of *water* (mass) can itself be described as *water* (unless the part gets too small with respect to its molecular structure). This same criterion applies to the event/process distinction: A part of *John ate the sandwich* (event) cannot itself be described as *John ate the sandwich.* By contrast, any part of *John ran toward the house* (process) can itself be described as *John ran toward the house* (unless the part gets smaller than a single stride). These similarities suggest that conceptual structure should encode this distinction cross-categorially too, so that the relevant inference rules do not care whether they are dealing with Things versus Substances or Events versus Processes.

It has also been often observed that plurals behave in many respects like mass nouns, and that repeated events behave like processes. (Talmy suggests the term *medium* to encompass them both.) The difference is only that plural nouns and repeated events fix the "grain size" in terms of the singular individuals making up the unbounded medium, so that decomposition of the medium into parts is not as arbitrary as it is with substances and processes. Thus the structure of the desired feature system is organized as in (12).

(12)
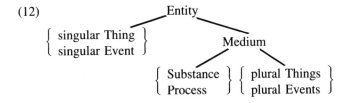

That is, the features that distinguish Things from Events are orthogonal to the features that differentiate individuals from media, and within media, homogeneous media from aggregates of individuals.

The examples in (11) provide evidence that Paths also participate in the feature system shown in (12). For instance, *to the house* is a bounded Path; no subparts of it except those including the terminus can be described as *to the house*. By contrast, *toward the house* and *down the road* are unbounded Paths, any part of which can also be described as *toward the house* or *down the road*. *Into houses* describes multiple bounded Paths, one per house. Thus the cross-categorial feature system in (12) extends to yet another major ontological category. (See Jackendoff, 1992 for more detail of this system.)

A general conclusion emerges from these two brief case studies. Beneath the surface complexity of natural language concepts lies a highly abstract formal algebraic system that lays out the major parameters of thought. The distinctions in this system are quite sharp and do not appear to be based on experience. Rather, I would claim, they are the machinery available to the human mind to channel the ways in which all experience can be mentally encoded—elements of the Universal Grammar for conceptual structure.

Significantly, the primitives of this system cannot appear in isolation. Rather, they are like phonological features or the quarks of particle physics: They can only be observed in combination, built up into conceptual constituents, and their existence must be inferred from their effects on language and cognition as a whole. This result militates against Fodor's Intentional Realism, in that one should not expect constant counterparts in reality for every aspect of the conceptual system. Roughly speaking, concepthood is a property of conceptual *constituents,* not conceptual *features.*

I should conclude this section by mentioning three characteristics in Conceptual Semantics that do not conform to classical feature decomposition. First, a lexical item can be associated with something like a 3D model structure in the sense of Marr (1982)—a spatial representation that is the counterpart in the present theory of an image of a stereotypical instance. Second, features can be specified as focal values in a continuous cognitive space. Color and temperature words are paradigmatic cases where such features are necessary. Third, features can be combined not just by simple conjunction, as in the aforementioned cases, but also by a different relation that creates a *preference rule system,* a set of conditions none of which is necessary and each of which may be sufficient for categorization.

These mechanisms (developed in Jackendoff, 1983, 1987) lead to a multitude of semantic field effects and to categories with fuzzy boundaries and family resemblance properties à la Wittgenstein and Rosch. However, these enrichments of the theory's descriptive power are still within the gambit of a thoroughly mentalistic semantics, and the same questions about creativity and learnability apply as in the more categorical cases discussed earlier. It is perhaps important in the context of this volume to mention that these devices play a much greater role in lexical semantics than in the combinatorial semantics of phrases. This is one reason why phrasal definitions are largely impossible—the expressive power of phrasal combination is in some respects less than that of individual lexical items.[2]

CONCLUSION

So what is a concept? I have shown here that for the purpose of understanding the mind, the apposite focus of inquiry is the notion of I-concept, a species of mental information structure. The program of Conceptual Semantics provides a theoretical realization of this notion that unifies it in many ways with a mentalistic theory of the language faculty. In particular, I have identified the notion of *I-concept* with the formal notion of *conceptual constituent* as developed in Conceptual Semantics. Furthermore, I have sketched a few of the major elements of the internal structure of concepts, showing how the approach accounts for some basic phenomena in the semantics of natural language.

What I find appealing about the present approach is that it leads one into problems of richer and richer articulation: What are the ontological categories, and do they themselves have internal structure? What kinds of fundamental functions are there that create Events, States, Places, and Paths? How are various semantic fields alike in structure, and how do they diverge? How do conceptual features interact with each other in phrasal combination? What are the conceptual primitives underlying social cognition and "folk psychology"? How are conceptual systems learnable? And so forth. The fact that Conceptual Semantics begins to provide a formal vocabulary in which such questions can be couched suggests

---

[2]Fodor et al. (1980) argue from the impossibility of formulating phrasal definitions to the conclusion that *no* lexical decomposition is possible. There is an alternative, though, simply that English is not a rich enough formal language for stating definitions of English words; that is, the Syntax of Thought is richer than (or at least different from) English syntax.

to me that, despite its being at odds with much of the recent philosophical tradition on meaning, it is a fruitful framework in which to conduct scientific inquiry.

ACKNOWLEDGMENTS

This chapter is excerpted from chapter 1 of my monograph *Semantic Structures,* a different version of which appeared under the title "What is a Concept, that a Person Can Grasp It?" in *Mind and Language.* I am grateful to Noam Chomsky, John Macnamara, James Higginbotham, and Jerry Fodor for comments on an earlier version of the chapter. I do not, however, intend to imply by this that they endorse my approach; in particular, Fodor doesn't believe a word of it. This research was supported in part by National Science Foundation Grants IST 84-20073 and IRI 88-08286 to Brandeis University.

REFERENCES

Bach, E. (1986a). Natural language metaphysics. In R. Barcan-Marcus, G. Dorn, & P. Weingartner (Eds.), *Logic, methodology, and philosophy of science* (pp. 573–595). Amsterdam: North-Holland.

Bach, E. (1986b). The algebra of events. *Linguistics and Philosophy, 9*(1), 5–16.

Chomsky, N. (1965). *Aspects of the theory of syntax.* Cambridge: MIT Press.

Chomsky, N. (1986). *Knowledge of language: Its nature, origin, and use.* New York: Praeger.

Declerck, R. (1979). Aspect and the bounded/unbounded (telic/atelic) distinction. *Linguistics, 17,* 761–794.

Dowty, D. (1979). *Word meaning and Montague grammar.* Dordrecht: Reidel.

Fauconnier, G. (1984). *Mental spaces: Aspects of meaning construction in natural language.* Cambridge, MA: Bradford/MIT Press.

Fodor, J. (1987). *Psychosemantics.* Cambridge, MA: Bradford/MIT Press.

Fodor, J., Garrett, M., Walker, E., & Parkes, C. (1980). Against definitions. *Cognition, 8,* 263–367.

Frege, G. (1892/1975). On sense and reference. In E. Davidson & G. Harman (Eds.), *The logic of grammar.* Encino, CA: Dickenson.

Herskovits, A. (1986). *Language and spatial cognition.* Cambridge: Cambridge University Press.

Hinrichs, E. (1985). *A compositional semantics for Aktionsarten and NP reference in English.* Unpublished doctoral dissertation, Ohio State University.

Jackendoff, R. (1983). *Semantics and cognition.* Cambridge, MA: MIT Press.

Jackendoff, R. (1987). *Consciousness and the computational mind.* Cambridge, MA: MIT Press.

Jackendoff, R. (1990). *Semantic structures.* Cambridge, MA: MIT Press.

Jackendoff, R. (1992). Parts and boundaries. *Cognition, 41,* 9–45.

Katz, J. J., & Fodor, J. A. (1963). The structure of a semantic theory. *Language 39*(2), 170–210.

Lakoff, G. (1987). *Women, fire, and dangerous things.* Chicago: University of Chicago Press.

Langacker, R. (1986). *Foundations of cognitive grammar* (Vol. 1). Stanford, CA: Stanford University Press.

Lewis, D. (1972). General semantics. In D. Davidson & G. Harman (Eds.), *Semantics of natural language* (pp. 169–218). Dordrecht: Reidel.

Link, G. (1983). The logical analysis of plurals and mass terms: A lattice-theoretic approach. In R. Bauerle, C. Schwarze, & A. von Stechow (Eds.), *Meaning, use and interpretation of language* (pp. 302–323). Berlin: de Gruyter.

Marr, D. (1982). *Vision.* San Francisco: W. H. Freeman.

Mourelatos, A. P. D. (1981). Events, processes, and states. In P. J. Tedeschi & A. Zaenen (Eds.), *Syntax and semantics* (Vol. 14, pp. 191–212). New York: Academic Press.

Platzack, D. (1979). *The semantic interpretation of aspect and Aktionsarten.* Dordrecht: Foris.

Talmy, L. (1978). The relation of grammar to cognition—a synopsis. In D. Waltz (Ed.), *Theoretical issues in natural language processing—2.* New York: Association for Computing Machinery.

Talmy, L. (1980). Lexicalization patterns: Semantic structure in lexical forms. In T. Shopen (Ed.), *Language typology and syntactic description (Vol. 3).* New York: Cambridge University Press.

Talmy, L. (1983). How language structures space. In H. Pick & L. Acredolo (Eds.), *Spatial orientation: Theory, research, and application.* New York: Plenum Press.

Talmy, L. (1985). Force dynamics in language and thought. In *Papers from the Twenty-First Regional Meeting, Chicago Linguistic Society,* Chicago: University of Chicago. Also in *Cognitive Science, 12*(1), 49–100 (1988).

Vendler, Z. (1967). Verbs and times. *Linguistics in philosophy* (pp. 97–121). Ithaca, NY: Cornell University Press.

Verkuyl, H. (1972). *On the compositional nature of the aspects.* Dordrecht: Reidel.

Verkuyl, H. (1989). Aspectual classes and aspectual composition. *Linguistics and Philosophy, 12, 1,* 39–94.

8 Semantic Primitives and Semantic Fields

Anna Wierzbicka
Australian National University

There can be many different approaches to the study of the lexicon. It would seem to me, however, that ultimately the value of these approaches must be demonstrated not in abstract discussions but in empirical investigations. It is true, of course, that large-scale empirical investigations cannot be undertaken without some initial methodological assumptions. But the value of such assumptions must prove itself in the fruit they bear in the actual description of linguistic facts. There would seem to be little point in debating, decade after decade, the perennial question of which approaches to lexical analysis are the most "promising." To my mind, at some point we have to simply look at the results.

This chapter presents and briefly illustrates views that are supported by a large body of empirical investigations. Limitations of space prevent the presentation here of any detailed report of these studies, and for justification of the claims made here I must refer the reader to those other, more empirically and descriptively oriented studies, such as, in particular, Wierzbicka (1985, 1987, 1988, 1989a, 1989b, 1990a, 1991a, 1991b, and 1992).

My basic assumptions can be stated as follows:

1. The lexicon of any language can be divided into two parts: a small set of words (or morphemes) that can be regarded as indefinable, and a large set of words that can be regarded as definable and that in fact can be defined in terms of the words from the set of indefinables.

2. For any language, its indefinables can be listed and the other words of this language can be defined in terms of these language-specific indefinables.

3. Although the set of indefinables is in each case language specific, one can hypothesize that each such set realizes, in its own way, the same universal and

innate "alphabet of human thoughts." (For example, *this* is an English word, and *hic*, a Latin one, but both can realize the same "atom" of human thought. We could say, therefore, that the set of indefinables is universal, although every language has its own, language-specific "names" for them.) Consequently, the number of indefinables is probably the same in all languages, and the individual indefinables can be matched cross-linguistically. Of course the indefinables of different languages cannot be expected to be equivalent in all respects; they can, nonetheless, be regarded as SEMANTICALLY equivalent. (For discussion and justification of this point, see in particular Wierzbicka, 1980 and 1989, a and b.) In this sense (and only in this sense), semantic primitives can be identified with lexical universals.

The list of postulated indefinables has expanded in the course of two decades from 14 (cf. Wierzbicka, 1972) to something like 30. The current list includes the following elements (cf. Goddard, 1989a, 1989b; Wierzbicka, 1989a, 1989b, and forthcoming): *I, you, someone (who), something (what), this, the same, two, all, think, say, know, want, feel, do, happen, good, bad, big, small, can, place (where), time (when), after, under, kind of, part of, like (how), because, if (imagine), more, very,* and *no (I don't want)*.

These elements have their own language-independent syntax. For example, the verb-like elements *think, know, say, feel,* and *want* combine with "nominal" personal elements *I, you,* and *someone* and take complex, proposition-like complements. The "nominal" element *someone* combines with the determiner-like elements *this, the same, two,* and *all* (whereas *I* and *you* do not combine with *them*), and so on (for a fuller discussion, see Wierzbicka, 1991a).

Generally speaking, the minilexicon of universal semantic primitives can be thought of as a minilanguage. It is a model not just of the innate "alphabet of human thoughts" but of the innate "language" of human thoughts; or rather, of the "language" of subconscious mental operations and of subconscious cognitive processes.

The meaning of a word is, so to speak, a configuration of semantic primitives; therefore it doesn't depend on the meaning of other words in the lexicon. The meanings of different words can overlap (as *abc* overlaps with *bcd*), and the meaning of one of the overlapping words can change without a concomitant change affecting the other (e.g., *abc* may change to *acd*, with *bcd* remaining as it was). But although the meaning of a word does not depend on the meanings of other words, to establish what the meaning of a word is one has to compare it with the meanings of other, intuitively related words. By comparing a word to other words that intuitively are felt to be related to it, we can establish what each of these words really means; having done this, we can compare them again, this time more precisely, being able to identify the elements that are different. Proceeding in this way, we can often discover remarkable symmetries and regularities in the semantic structure of many words—as well as unexpected asymmetries and irregularities. We can discover self-contained fields of semantically related words with analogous semantic patterning. We can also discover irregular and open-ended networks of interlacing networks.

The idea that words form more or less natural groupings, and that at least some of these groupings are nonarbitrary, is intuitively appealing, even irresistible. But if we couldn't decompose meanings into components, we couldn't really investigate this possibility in a systematic and methodical way. If we do, however, have a list of hypothetical indefinables, and if we learn how to discover configurations of indefinables encapsulated in individual words, we can reveal the hidden structure of these words and ipso facto we can reveal the structural relations linking different words together. For example, if we establish that the meaning of one word is "abc," of another, "bcd," and of a third, "bcf," we will know that their common core is "bc." Consequently, we can reveal nonarbitrary semantic fields, and we can investigate their nature. Thus, semantic primitives offer us a tool for investigating the structure of semantic groupings or fields. In particular, they can show us how to distinguish nonarbitrary semantic groupings from arbitrary ones; and how to distinguish discrete, self-contained groupings from open-ended ones.

In what follows, I illustrate the preceding tenets with a number of examples pertaining to several different areas of the lexicon. Before doing so, however, I must clarify the notion of "configuration," which was just illustrated (perhaps somewhat misleadingly) with combinations of letters such as *abc* or *bcd*. In fact, meanings are very complex structures, built not directly from simple elements such as "someone," "want," or "this," but from structured components such as "I want something," "this is good," or "you did something bad."

Components of this kind are ordered, and because they often contain the temporal element "after," or the causal component "because," sequences of such components can be often regarded as "scripts" or "scenarios" (cf. Abelson, 1981 and Schank & Abelson, 1977). This applies, for example, to words designating emotions or to words designating speech acts. (I return to this point later.) "Concrete" nouns (i.e., names of natural or cultural kinds) will usually exhibit a more static semantic structure, but, here too, many different components are usually involved, and these components refer not only to certain inherent features of the referents, but also to the "external frames"—such as habitat, behavior or typical interaction with people in the case of animals, or the typical situation of use in the case of artefacts (cf. Fillmore, 1975, 1977). Here too, the components have to be seen as ordered (see Wierzbicka, 1985).

The general assumptions stated in this section are now illustrated with three sections devoted to specific semantic domains: (1) the names of "natural kinds" and "cultural kinds"; (2) speech act verbs; (3) color words. All these domains have been explored in considerable detail elsewhere (cf. Wierzbicka, 1985, 1987, 1990a); for reasons of space, the present discussion must be brief, sketchy, and selective.

"NATURAL KINDS" AND "CULTURAL KINDS"

Names of animals (in the everyday sense of the word, not in the scientific sense), of birds, fishes, flowers, or trees embody, I believe, taxonomic concepts, that is, concepts based on the idea of "kind." It is reasonable, therefore, that they are usually referred to as "natural kind" words. For example, *dog* or *lion* can be defined as "a kind of animal"—plus, in each case, a long sequence of components, specifying the habitat, appearance, behavior, relation to people, and so on (for illustrations, see Wierzbicka, 1985).

Words such as *dog, lion, tiger, squirrel,* and so on can be said to form a well-defined, discrete semantic field because they all have definitions headed, so to speak, by the same component "a kind of animal." Similarly, words such as *swallow, eagle, penguin,* or *emu* can be said to form a well-defined, discrete semantic field because they all have definitions headed by the same component "a kind of bird"; and words such as *oak, willow, birch,* or *palm* can also be said to form a well-defined, discrete semantic field because they all have definitions headed by the same component "a kind of tree."

Furthermore, the conceptual supercategories on which the names of "natural kinds" are based have also a taxonomic character. For example, *animal, bird,* or *fish* can all be justifiably defined as "a kind of creature" (plus of course a number of additional components), whereas *tree* or *flower* can be justifiably defined as, roughly, "a kind of thing growing out of the ground" (plus, again, a number of additional components).

On the other hand, it is an illusion to think that words such as *doll, ball, tricycle, rattle, swing,* and *teddy bear* can be similarly defined in terms of one nonarbitrary supercategory such as *toy.* As I have tried to show in my *Lexicography and conceptual analysis* (Wierzbicka, 1985), words such as *toy, vehicle, container,* or *weapon* embody functional concepts, not taxonomic concepts; and they are not related to cultural kind words (such as *tricycle, bottle, cup,* or *knife*) in the same way in which taxonomic supercategories (*animal, bird, fish, flower,* or *tree*) are related to their subordinates (such as *dog, canary, fruit, rose,* or *oak*). For example, *toy* doesn't stand for any particular, describable, and recognizable KIND of thing; rather, it stands for things of ANY KIND made by people for children to play with. Therefore "toys," "weapons," and so on are not taxonomic supercategories, in the sense that "animals," "birds," or "trees" are. Consequently, one cannot speak of "semantic fields" of "toys," "vehicles," or "weapons" in the same sense in which one can speak of semantic fields of "animals," "birds," "trees," and so on.

If one wishes to, one can of course group words such as *doll, ball, tricycle,* and *rattle* together, and for certain purposes this may be useful (for example, as a list of various kinds of objects that can be bought in a toy department of a department store). But a grouping of this kind would not have a semantic basis.

This is not to imply that words such as *doll, ball, tricycle,* and so on are not all "headed" (in their semantic structure) by the same semantic component. They are. But the component in question is not "a kind of toy"; rather, it is a much more general one, subsuming a vast number of names of human artefacts: roughly "a kind of thing made by people." There is no reason, of course, why one should not speak of all the words headed by this component as forming one discrete, nonarbitrary semantic field. But it is a huge field, which itself is not hierarchically structured: It is not divided, semantically speaking, into "toys," "vehicles," "weapons," and so on, because these are functional categories, not taxonomic ones. Of course if we want to we can classify "cultural kinds" into toys, weapons, instruments, kitchenware, and so on, but this classification would be arbitrary from the point of view of semantic structure. From the point of view of "folk categorization" reflected in the semantic structure, *cups* are not "a kind of kitchenware," *bicycles* are not "a kind of vehicle," *balls* are not "a kind of toy," and *knives* are not "a kind of weapon."

I suggest, therefore, that names of "cultural kinds" do not form nonarbitrary, discrete fields, whereas names of "natural kinds" do. It seems to me that it is a mistake to speak, for example, of "the field of containers" (cf. Lehrer, 1974) as if there were a nonarbitrary, self-contained field of "names of containers." Of course, words such as *cup, mug, bottle, jar, jug, bucket,* or *barrel* ARE mutually closely related, and in fact their full explications reveal a degree of symmetry even greater than one might have expected (see the explications of these words in Wierzbicka, 1985). But *bucket* is also felt to be related to *bowl* or *tub, bottle* is related to *carafe, carafe* is related to *vase, pot* is related to *pan,* and so on; and tubs, vases, or pans would not be naturally described as "containers." Pace Lakoff (1972), birds do not fade off similarly into bats, fishes into animals (in the everyday sense of the word), or flowers into trees (for example, magnolias are thought of as a kind of tree, whereas roses are thought of as a kind of flower; emus are thought of as a kind of bird, whereas bats are not; and so on). Thus, semantically, *pots* and *pans, buckets* or *bowls* are not "a kind of container," whereas *sparrows* are "a kind of bird," and roses, "a kind of flower."

The popular current view that human cognition is "fuzzy," and that words are linked by "family resemblances," not by specifiable semantic relations, is due, I believe, to the fact that empirical investigations of lexical categorization undertaken by psychologists have often been carried out in a theoretical vacuum, that is to say, that they have not been grounded in any linguistically based semantic theory (for further discussion and exemplification, see Wierzbicka, 1990b).

"Category membership" of words and meanings cannot be established by asking informants simple questions, or giving them simple "sorting" tasks. It can only be established by methodical semantic analysis. In the absence of such an analysis, different schemes of "semantic" and "conceptual" categorization proposed in recent literature, particularly in psychological literature, often reflect the pretheoretical ideas of the researchers rather than results of valid, well-conceived empirical investigations.

SPEECH ACT VERBS

In English, and in other European languages, there are hundreds of verbs that can be said to form, together, one coherent, self-contained field; these are verbs referring to "different things that one can do with words," that is, to different types of speech acts. I have investigated some 250 such words in my *English speech act verbs: A semantic dictionary* (Wierzbicka, 1987), and I have found a very high degree of patterning.

What gives coherence to the field of "speech act verbs" is the presence of some well-defined semantic components. These components underlie what is usually called the "illocutionary force" (cf. Austin, 1962; Searle, 1976) of the speech act described by a given speech act verb. This illocutionary force comprises components that spell out the speaker's intentions, assumptions, or emotions, expressed in speech. For example, the verbs *ask* and *order* describe an attitude that includes the following component:

(I say:) I want you to do it

In addition, *order* includes the component:

(I think:) you have to do it because of this
whereas *ask* contains the opposite assumption:
(I think:) you don't have to do it because of this

Forbid is in some ways symmetrical with respect to *order*, and it includes the component:

(I say:) I don't want you to do it

as well as a similarly confident assumption:

(I think:) you can't do it because of this

Complain includes the components:

(I say:) something bad is happening to me
I feel something bad because of this

Reproach, rebuke, scold and *reprimand* include the component:

(I say:) you did something bad

Thank and *apologize* include, respectively, the components:

(I say:) you did something good to me
(I say:) I did something bad to you

And so on. It is not my purpose to provide here exhaustive explications of any speech act verbs. (The interested reader can find such explications in Wierzbicka, 1987.) Rather, I am trying to show here how the "field" of speech act verbs can be delimited in a nonarbitrary way.

The class of verbs that I am talking about does not coincide with the class of "performative" verbs. For example, whereas *ask, order, forbid,* or *apologize* can all be used performatively, *reproach, threaten,* and *boast* cannot:

I ask/order/forbid you to do it
I apologize for what I have done
*I reproach you: you shouldn't have done it
*I threaten you: I will do something bad to you if you do it
*I boast: I am the best

Nonetheless, all these verbs exhibit the same kind of semantic structure: They attribute to the speaker a certain attitude that can be portrayed in terms of first-person illocutionary components such as:

(I say:) you did something bad [*reprimand*]
(I say:) I will do something bad to you [*threat*]
(I say:) I am good (better than other people) [*boast*]

I believe that components of this kind, all framed, explicitly or implicitly, by "I say," do allow us to identify a class of words in a nonarbitrary way; and that this class does constitute a "real," relatively self-contained part of the English lexicon.

It is particularly interesting to note that the phrasing of components of this kind can be supported not only with semantic but also with syntactic evidence, as different speech act verbs that share certain semantic components (or combinations of components) can be shown to also share certain syntactic frames (or combinations of frames). Consider, for example, the component:

you did something bad/good

which is associated with the following frame:

X V-ed Y for doing Z.

For example, the following verbs share this component and this frame: *reproach, rebuke, reprove, reprimand, admonish, scold.* Utterances such as:

X reproached/rebuked/reprimanded/scolded/thanked Y for Z

imply that X said to Y something that included the semantic component "you did something bad (good)" (cf. *X rebuked/reproached/scolded Y, Z).

The frame "X V-ed Y for Z" is also used with verbs such as *criticize* or *praise,* which describe acts that can be performed, so to speak, behind the back of the target person: One cannot *reprimand* or *rebuke* people behind their backs, but one can *criticize* or *praise* them to a third person. However, the two groups of verbs can be distinguished in terms of another syntactic frame: "X V-ed Y's Z":

X criticized/praised Y for Z
X criticized/praised Y's Z
*X rebuked/reprimanded Y's Z

Thus, speech act verbs that imply the component:

person Y did something bad/good

allow both of the syntactic frames in question:

(1). X V-ed Y for doing Z
(2). X V-ed Y's Z

whereas speech act verbs that imply the component

you did something bad

allow only the first of these two frames.

As a second example, compare the syntactic possibilities of verbs such as *order, command, instruct, urge, ask,* and *beg,* all of which can be said to imply the semantic component:

I want you to do this

and all of which can occur in the syntactic frame:

X V-ed Y to do Z.

Some of these verbs, however, have an additional frame:

X V-ed Y for Z
(e.g., X asked/begged Y for Z)

which the others don't have:

> * X ordered/commanded/urged Y for Z.

This additional syntactic frame links *ask* (for) and *beg* (for) with verbs such as *plead* (for), *apply* (for), or *wish* (for)—all verbs that imply that the speaker cannot expect to have control over the outcome, that is to say, verbs that attribute to the speaker the intention to convey (among others) the following combination of components:

> I say: I want you to do Z
> I don't think: you will do it because of this

On the other hand, verbs such as *order, command,* or *urge,* which take the frame "X V-ed Y to do Z" but not "X V-ed Y for Z," imply, as mentioned earlier, a more confident attitude on the part of the speaker:

> I say: I want you to do Z
> I think: you will do it because of this

The interested reader is likely to raise at this point some objections pointing to apparent asymmetries and idiosyncrasies. For example, why can't *demand,* which should be similar to *order* and *command,* occur in the frame "X V-ed Y to do Z"? Or why can *plead* and *apply* occur with *for* (like *ask* or *beg*) but (unlike *ask* or *beg*) cannot occur in the frame "X V-ed Y to do Z"?

> *X demanded Y to do Z
> X allowed/forbade Y to do Z
> *X pleaded for Z
> X applied for Z
> *X pleaded Y to do Z
> *X pleaded Y for Z
> *X applied Y to do Z
> *X applied Y for Z

At first sight, differences of this kind may seem idiosyncratic and semantically arbitrary. But if one studies them more closely, one discovers that far from being arbitrary, they, too, point to very real semantic differences and thus confirm the reliability of syntactic clues in semantic analysis. For example, one *pleads* WITH a person, as one *argues* or *reasons* WITH a person, because *plead,* like *argue* or *reason,* involves an exchange of arguments rather than a direct appeal to the addressee's will. One *demands* SOMETHING, not SOMEONE, because what the person who *demands* something wants is, above all, a certain outcome (which may be brought about by somebody's action), not a specific action by a particular addressee. For the same reason, one *applies* for SOMETHING, and one doesn't apply SOMEONE, because what the *applying* person wants is, above all, a particular outcome, not a specific action of a particular addressee. At the same time, the attitude of a person who *applies* for something is less confident than that of a person who *demands* something; and this is why one *applies* FOR something, as one *hopes* or *asks* FOR something, whereas one *demands* SOMETHING, not FOR SOMETHING (for evidence and justification, see Wierzbicka, 1987).

Certainly, this method of verification cannot be applied to all areas of the lexicon. (Generally speaking, it is more applicable to verbs than to nouns.) It can, however, be reliably applied to speech act verbs; and for this reason alone, speech act verbs constitute a particularly fruitful domain for semantic experimentation. In particular, they offer a golden opportunity to investigate the structure of a large and highly patterned "semantic field"; and to explore, on an empirical basis, the very notion of a "semantic field."

COLOR WORDS

Color is not a universal human concept. There are languages that don't have a word for "color" in general and that don't have words for any individual colors. Some scholars who have written about colors and color words appear to be confused on this point, and to believe that all languages have at least two color terms, corresponding to the English words *black* and *white*. But there is plenty of evidence showing that this belief is mistaken. For example, in the Australian Aboriginal language Gidjingali, the two would-be "color words," *gungundja* and *gungaltja*, stand in fact for something like "dark–dull–lightless" and "light–shining–sunlike–firelike," which means that they embody concepts quite different from those embedded in color words such as *black* and *white* (cf. Jones & Meehan, 1978).

Berlin and Kay (1969) have claimed that English (like many other languages) has a self-contained set of 11 words that can be described as "basic color words": *black, white, red, yellow, green, blue, brown, pink, orange, purple,* and *grey.* I find the claim that these 11 words have a special status in the English lexicon quite convincing (see, however, Moss, 1989). At the same time, however, it seems clear that these color words belong to a much larger "field" whose boundaries are not well defined. This wider field also includes words such as *beige, maroon, off-white, magenta, turquoise, scarlet, violet, milky, khaki, bottle green, sky blue, navy blue, gold, golden, silver, ashen, mauve, olive, apricot, peach, rosy, blond, tan, pepper-and-salt,* and so on.

Do words of this kind have analyzable, definable meanings? In some cases, it seems quite obvious that they do. Many of the words just listed are clearly based on a comparison with a prototype and can be described, roughly, in terms of the semantic structure: "It looks like X." This applies, for example, to *gold, golden, silver, olive, apricot, pea, violet, rosy,* and so on. Words of this kind do not all represent the same degree of "emancipation" from the prototype (in terms of aspects other than color). For example, paper can be described as *gold* or *silver,* but not as *rosy* or *khaki* (not to mention *blond*). Blueberries can hardly be described as *navy blue,* and it would be odd to describe kiwifruit or beans as *khaki.*

   *She bought some rosy/khaki/apricot envelopes.
   *The cakes were decorated with some navy-blue berries.

Why can paper be described as *gold* or *silver* but not as *khaki* or *apricot*? Presumably, because the semantic structure of adjectives such as *khaki* or *apricot* does not specify: "It looks like X in color"; rather, it leaves the dimension of similarity open: "It looks like X." But it is odd to imply that blueberries or envelopes look like navy uniforms, roses, or apricots, or that kiwifruit or beans look like army uniforms. On the other hand, it is not similarly odd to imply that some piece of paper looks like gold or silver, because these prototypes (gold and silver) do not specify form, shape, size, and so on.

   It should also be noted that *gold* and *silver* as color terms imply not only certain kinds of color but also a shining appearance of the referents. In this respect, they are rather like the Gidjingali word *gungaltja.* All this suggests that even in English the field of "color words" is not strictly separated from words describing other aspects of appearance: *Gold* and *silver* imply the presence of a shine, *rosy* suggests something living, fresh and lovely (like roses), *blond* suggests a certain kind of texture (characteristic of human hair), and so on.

   We have established, then, that a number of English words describing color (and possibly other aspects of appearance) is based on the "look-like" paradigm. But not all words regarded as "color terms" have this kind of semantic structure. For example, *grey, pink, purple,* or *beige* do not refer to any exemplars. Rather, they are conceptualized in terms of imaginary mixtures: a "mixture" (or simultaneous presence in the same place) of red and white in the case of *pink,* of black and white in the case of *grey,* of blue and red in the case of *purple,* and of brown and white in the case of *beige.*

   But again, this kind of semantic structure characterizes only a certain subset of "color words": If *grey* or *pink* are conceptualized as "imaginary mixtures," *black, white,* or *red* are not. This suggests that not even the small set of the "basic 11" is semantically uniform.

   But what kind of semantic structure can be attributed to the most fundamental color words such as *black, white, red, yellow, green,* or *blue*? Can their meaning be analyzed (i.e., verbally defined) at all? Many scholars believe that it cannot, and that (scientific explanations aside) words of this kind can only be defined ostensively, rather like proper names: "This is Harry"; "this is blue"; "this is black" (cf. Burling, 1970, p. 80; Russell, 1948, p. 78).

Moreover, as pointed out by Frumkina (1984), "definitions" of this kind fail to account for the intuitively felt relations between different color words. In particular, they fail to account for the fact that *white* and *black* are felt to be the opposites of one another, rather like *long* and *short,* or *hard* and *soft* are.

Furthermore, ostensive definitions fail to account for the intuitively felt relations between certain color words and words describing other aspects of appearance, such as the relation between *black* and *dark,* or between *white* and *light.* The reality of these relations is clearly manifested in the following contrasts in acceptability:

dark blue, light blue
*dark black, *light black
*dark white, *light white

To account for facts of this kind, we simply have to analyze further all the words involved.

Consider also the relations between different words describing colors such as "blue" or "green" in different languages of the world. For example, Russian has two words corresponding to *blue,* both distinctly different from the English *blue* in their range of use: *goluboj* (roughly, "sky blue") and *sinij* (roughly, "deep blue" or "dark blue"). Polish also has two words, whose range does not coincide, however, with that of the Russian words: *Niebieski* (from *niebo,* "sky"), stands for light blues, medium blues, and even some dark blues, but not for very dark blues (such as, for example, navy blue, or the color of "blue jeans"), and *granatowy,* which stands for an imaginary mixture of blue (or rather of *niebieski*) and of *black.* If we refuse to define words such as *blue,* and if we insist that *blue* is simply *blue, goluboj* is *goluboj,* and *niebieski* is simply *niebieski,* we will not be able to show how these words are semantically related. What is more, we will not be able to explain how native speakers of the different languages in question know how far they can extend the application of a given word.

Of course, the boundaries of color words are "fuzzy." Nonetheless, the boundaries of *blue, goluboj,* and *sinij* are clearly very different (although they can all be said to be fuzzy). If the concept of *blue* were simply biologically determined, that is, if it were the result of precultural "wiring" (as it has been claimed, for example, by Kay and McDaniel, 1978), one would expect that it would be culture independent. But, in fact, it is not culture independent: Boundaries, and sometimes even the foci of "basic" color words such as *blue,* can differ from language to language. For example, the focus of *goluboj* corresponds to the English *sky blue,* not to the English *blue;* and the focus of the Dani *mola,* "white," corresponds in fact to the English *red* (cf. Heider, 1972).

Furthermore, even when the foci do coincide it should be remembered that it is not only the foci that have to be accounted for, but also the boundaries. I am not sure whether the focus of the Polish *niebieski* is the same as that of the

English *blue* or slightly different; but even if it were the same, we still have the problem of why *niebieski* is so much narrower in range than *blue.* At first, the solution to this problem may seem simple: Polish also has another "basic" color word, *granatowy,* which competes with *niebieski* for a part of the range of the English *blue.* But, in fact, this solution is more apparent than real, because basic color terms do not have to be semantically exclusive.

For example, Japanese has only one basic color term corresponding to *blue,* namely *ao,* and only one basic color term corresponding to *green,* namely *midori,* and yet the range of use of *ao* is much wider than that of *blue;* in particular, *ao* can be applied to "green" traffic lights, to wet grass or trees after rain, to "green" (e.g., Granny Smith) apples, and so on—that is, to referents that can also be described as *midori.*

In addition to overlaps, there are also gaps between color terms. For example, in Polish many shades lying, roughly speaking, between red and brown can be called neither *czerwony* ("red") nor *brązowy* ("brown"), even though there is no other color word that could be applied to these shades. According to Gedda Aklif (p.c.), the same applies to German. On the other hand, in English, informants appear to be quite willing to extend the words *red* and *brown* in such a way as to cover the entire area between the foci of these two words.

Similarly, in urban Thai there are two color words corresponding to *blue. Fá:* means literally "sky," and *nám-ngoen* means "silver tarnish" and is used for the deep blue of the Thai national flag. But the medium blue, that is, what is regarded in English as the focal blue, is seen by Thai speakers as lying in a kind of no-man's land: They refuse to describe it as either "sky" or "silver tarnish," and in fact they say that it is "hard to describe" (Diller & Juntanamalaga, forthcoming).

But if the range of application of a given basic color word is culture specific and therefore is not determined by "biological wiring," what does determine it in the speakers' tacit knowledge of their native language?

I conjecture that it is determined—like the range of application of other kinds of words—by the word's semantic structure. Native speakers may or may not have access to this structure on a conscious level, but they control it on a subconscious level; often they can bring it to the surface of their consciousness by methodical introspection; and in any case, it is reflected in common collocations, metaphors, set phrases, and other direct linguistic and ethnographic evidence.

My hypothesis is this. The most basic "color concepts" (that is, the first seven in Berlin and Kay's sequence) are based on certain universal prototypes that play a fundamental role in human experience. These prototypes don't have to be conceived of as "exemplars" or "models," that is, as something that a given object "looks like." Rather, they are conceived of as points of reference—as something that a given object can make people think of.

For example, if we are looking for the most "natural" and most widely occurring exemplar of black (that is to say, the model of what black things "look like"), we will probably agree on charcoal; and indeed, in many languages, the closest equivalent of *black* is derived from the word for charcoal. But if we are looking for the most natural point of reference for black, we may well find it elsewhere—not in charcoal but in the idea of "night." In particular, the overwhelming contrast between night and day may well provide the most natural point of reference for the contrast between dark and light, and also, between black and white. This would explain, incidentally, the link between *white* and *light,* and between *black* and *dark,* noted earlier; and also, the link between the adjective *light* (as in *light blue*) and the noun *light*.

If in a given language the word for "black" is identical with, or is derived from, the word for charcoal, we can suspect that the meaning of this word is based on an exemplar: "It looks like charcoal." If, however, the word for "black" is related to the word for night (as, for example, in the Australian Aboriginal language, Luritja; Ian Green, p.c.), we can suspect that this word has a rather different semantic structure: not "it looks like night" but "it can make people think of night." This semantic structure, too, refers to a certain prototype, but this prototype constitutes a point of reference rather than an exemplar.

Consider, for example, the Thai word *fá:* (lit. "sky") and the Polish word *niebieski* (from *niebo* "sky"). Clearly, both these words somehow involve the concept of sky. Why is it, then, that the Polish color word based on the word for sky can be extended to keep darkish blues whereas the Thai word cannot? I suggest that the reason lies in the different kind of semantic structure. Speaking loosely, one can say that both words are based on a prototype. But to account for the different ranges, one has to posit something a little more precise. I suggest the following:

fá: =   things like X look like the sky
           (when one can see the sun)
niebieski = when one sees things like X
           one can think of the sky

I believe that if the English word *blue* has a focus similar to that of the Polish word *niebieski* it is because *blue,* too, involves the same prototype: the sky. But again, *blue* has a range of use wider than that of what is called *sky blue*. This suggests that *blue,* too, involves the sky as a point of reference, not as an exemplar (whereas *sky blue* involves the sky as an exemplar).

But if both *blue* and *niebieski* are thought of as colors that "can make people think of the sky," why is it that the range of *blue* is wider than that of *niebieski*? To account for this difference, I propose that *blue* involves more than one point of reference: not only the sky but also water—not water from the tap, but naturally occurring water, that is, the water of seas, lakes, rivers, and so on. Roughly:

X is blue
when one sees things like X
one can think of the sky
or of places (not made by people)
where there is water

Generally speaking, I propose that the seven basic color terms that are not thought of as an imaginary mixture are all based on universal features of human life and human environment: The concepts of "dark" and "light" (and, indirectly, of "black" and "white") utilize as their frame of reference the contrast between night and day; the concept of "red" involves, as its basic point of reference, the concept of blood (and, possibly, the concept of fire); "yellow" refers to the sun, "green" to things growing out of the ground, "blue" to the sky (and perhaps to water), and "brown" to what is perceived as the color of the ground.

The universal presence, and salience of these prototypes explains, in my view, the striking similarities in the location of the foci of color words in the languages of the world. The hypothesis that these prototypes play a crucial role in human conceptualization of color explains also, I believe, the evolutionary sequence, established by Berlin and Kay (1969), and otherwise largely mysterious, despite some attempts at explanation in terms of neurophysiology (cf. Kay & McDaniel, 1978). As far as I know, no neurophysiological explanation has been found for the fact that, for example, "brown" emerges universally before "orange" (perceptually a much more salient color); why it also explains in languages with only two basic color terms "red" is universally categorized with white rather than with black; or why in those languages that distinguish four basic categories, "macro-white," "macro-black," "macro-red," and "macro-green," yellow is usually categorized with red rather than with green. The hypothesis advanced here explains all this (and much more). The essence of my explanation for the evolutionary sequence can be expressed by a diagram (see Table 8.1).

As Table 8.1 shows, the first, most basic distinction has to do with the presence versus absence of light. Light is associated with day, sun, and fire, which is why "macro-whites" include not simply white and "light" colors but also yellow and red, even deep red, like the red of glowing embers, and also why brilliance is an important aspect of this category. The absence of light is associated with the idea of night (black and "dark" colors), but also with the absence of sun and the absence of fire ("dull" colors, "cool" colors, "dark" colors). "Macro-red" emerges as a separate category when fire starts to be thought of as a separate prototype (apart from other sources of light). When the sun starts to be thought of as a separate prototype, apart from daylight and apart from fire, "yellow" emerges as a new distinct category.

The absence of light underlies the category of "macro-black." This category becomes differentiated when night becomes conceptually separated from sky and

TABLE 8.1
The Evolutionary Sequence

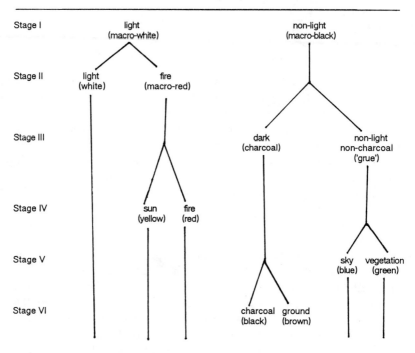

Stage VII ['mixed colors' added to those above]

vegetation (the two perceptually most salient and most stable features of the environment other than the two sources of light, sun and fire).

"Brown" emerges as a separate category when the ground (visually less salient than fire, sun, sky, or vegetation) receives attention as a separate environmental prototype.

The last identifiable universal prototype appears to be blood, which underlies the idea of "pure red," as distinct from other fire-related shades (for detailed discussion, see Wierzbicka, 1990a).

I am not suggesting that speakers of a language like modern English are consciously aware of any links between *blue* and sky, *green* and growing things, *yellow* and sun, or *red* and blood (and/or fire). There is plenty of evidence, however, that they do make these links on a subconscious level. For example, the very expression *sky blue* demonstrates that speakers of English do link *blue* with sky; the semantic extension from "green" (in color) to "immature" points to a link between *green* and growing; and so do words and expressions such as *green belt, greenery, greenies, greenhouse, greengrocer, greens, greenwood,* and so on. The link between sun and *yellow* can be supported with ethnographic evidence of children's drawings, in which the sun is invariably yellow. The word *blood-red* points to an intuitive link between *red* and blood, as do, moreover, other words and expressions such as *bloody Mary, bloodstone,* or *bloodworm.* The link between *red* and the concept of fire can be documented with expressions such as *red coals, red hot,* or *red iron.*

The hypothesis advanced here also explains why, as pointed out by Moss (1989), "the focus of "green," alone among the chromatic primary colour terms, is not located towards the saturated end of the dimension" (p. 316): Fire and the sky provide examples of vivid, pure colors, whereas, as Moss herself points out (on the same page), "the natural background also includes many dull greens."

Above all, the present hypothesis explains why the evolutionary sequence proposed by Berlin and Kay (1969) allows for deviations and exceptions; for example, why some languages may have such unorthodox basic color words as the Ainu *hu* "red–green" and *siwnin* "blue–yellow" (MacLaury, 1987; McNeill, 1972). If the basic sequence were determined, in essence, by human biology, one would expect it to be exceptionless. If it is, however, determined by the human conceptualization of our shared earthly environment, one would expect both commonalities and variation—which is exactly what we do find.

I propose, then, that even the most basic color words such as *white, black, red, yellow, blue,* and *green* in English do have an analyzable semantic structure. This structure is based on one recognizable semantic scheme: when one sees things like X one can think of Y, where Y is the sky (for *blue*), things growing out of the ground (for *green*), the sun (for *yellow*), blood and fire (for *red*), and the ground (for *brown*). This type of semantic structure is different from that characteristic of less basic color words, such as *gold, silver, violet, turquoise,* or *khaki,* which are all based on the "looks like" model: when one sees things like X, one can think: it looks like Y. It is also different from the semantic structure of the semibasic and nonbasic color words that correspond to imaginary mixtures, such as *grey, pink, purple,* or *beige.*

Do color words constitute a self-contained, sharply delimited semantic field? Not really. They are not sharply delimited from words describing other aspects of appearance, and they are not internally homogeneous. Nonetheless, they do exhibit pockets of words with analogous semantic patterning. But neither the degree of internal coherence of the domain of color words nor their external relations with other words in the lexicon can be explored without careful semantic analysis of the individual words—an analysis that necessarily involves decomposing them into simple semantic elements (and ultimately, into universal semantic primitives).

CONCLUSION

If we want to establish what the meaning of a word is, and if we want to demonstrate the validity of our analysis, comparisons with other words are virtually necessary. But the MEANINGS of individual words do not have to be dependent on "whatever other lexical items may be available in the inventory"; and ultimately, a definition, too, has to stand on its own: A definition expresses a hypothesis about the meaning of a particular word, and it is valid if it accounts correctly for the range of use of this particular word. The boundaries of this range may be "fuzzy," but even this fuzziness can and should be predicted by a well-phrased and well-researched definition.

Fodor, Garrett, Walker, and Parkes (1980) put forward the destructive slogan *Against definitions,* which soon enough led them to the conclusion that semantic analysis in general is impossible and must be abandoned. It is time to recognize the self-defeating nature of this slogan and to proclaim once again its opposite: *Back to definitions!* But not to old-style definitions, ad-hoc, circular, and devoid of predictive power. Meanings can be rigorously described and compared if they are recognized for what they are: unique and culture-specific configurations of universal semantic primitives. When the configurations of primitives conceptualized in individual words are revealed, the relations between different words also reveal themselves. I think, therefore, that the semantic primitives' approach to semantic analysis also offers a necessary firm ground for the study of semantic fields.

REFERENCES

Abelson, R. (1981). Psychological status of the script concept. *American Psychologist, 36(7), 715–729.*

Austin, J. L. (1962). *How to do things with words.* Oxford: Clarendon Press.

Berlin, B., & Kay, P. (1969). *Basic color terms: their universality and evolution.* Berkeley: University of California Press.

Burling, R. (1970). *Man's many voices: Language in its cultural context.* New York: Holt, Rinehart, & Winston.

Diller, A., & Juntanamalaga, P. (forthcoming). *An introduction to Thai grammar.*

Fillmore, C. J. (1975). An alternative to checklist theories of meaning. *Proceedings of the First Annual Meeting of the Berkeley Linguistic Society* (pp. 123–31).

Fillmore, C. J. (1977). Topics in lexical semantics. In R. W. Cole (Ed.), *Current issues in linguistic theory.* Bloomington: Indiana University Press.

Fodor, J. A., Garrett, M. F., Walker, E. T., & Parkes, C. (1980). Against definitions. *Cognition, 8(3), 263–367.*

Frumkina, R. (1984). *Cvet, smysl, sxodstvo.* Moscow: Nauka.

Goddard, C. (1989a). Issues in natural semantic metalanguage. *Quaderni di Semantica, 10(1), 51–64.* (Round table on semantic primitives, 1).

Goddard, C. (1989b). The goals and limits of semantic representation. *Quaderni di Semantica, 10(2), 297–308.* (Round table on semantic primitives, 2).

Heider, E. (Rosch). (1972). Probabilities, sampling, and ethnographic method: The case of Dani colour names. *Man, 7(3), 448–466.*

Jones, R., & Meehan, B. (1978). Anbarra concept of colour. In L. R. Hiatt (Ed.), *Australian Aboriginal concepts* (pp. 20–29). Canberra: Australian Institute of Aboriginal Studies.

Kay, P., & McDaniel, C. (1978). The linguistic significance of the meaning of basic colour terms. *Language, 54(3), 610–646.*

Lakoff, G. (1972). Hedges: A study in meaning criteria and the logic of fuzzy concepts. *Chicago Linguistic Society, Papers, 8, 183–228.*

Lehrer, A. (1974). *Semantic fields and lexical structure.* Amsterdam: North-Holland.

MacLaury, R. E. (1987). Color-category evolution and Shuswap yellow-with-green. *American Anthropologist, 89(2), 107–124.*

McNeill, N. B. (1972). Colour and colour terminology. *Journal of Linguistics, 8, 21–33.*

Moss, A. E. (1989). Basic colour terms: problems and hypotheses. *Lingua, 78, 313–320.*

Russell, B. (1948). *Human knowledge: Its scope and limits* (p. 78). New York: Simon & Schuster.

Schank, R., & Abelson, R. (1977). *Scripts, plans, goals, and understanding: An inquiry into human knowledge structures.* Hillsdale, NJ: Lawrence Erlbaum Associates.

Searle, J. R. (1976). A classification of illocutionary acts. *Language in Society, 5, 1–23.*

Wierzbicka, A. (1972). *Semantic primitives.* Frankfurt: Athenäum (Linguistische Forschungen, 22).

Wierzbicka, A. (1980). *Lingua mentalis: The semantics of natural language.* Sydney: Academic Press.

Wierzbicka, A. (1985). *Lexicography and conceptual analysis.* Ann Arbor, MI: Karoma.

Wierzbicka, A. (1987). *English speech act verbs: A semantic dictionary.* Sydney: Academic Press.

Wierzbicka, A. (1988). *The semantics of grammar.* Amsterdam: John Benjamins.

Wierzbicka, A. (1989a). Semantic primitives and lexical universals. *Quaderni di Semantica, 10(1), 103–121.* (Round table on semantic primitives, 1).

Wierzbicka, A. (1989b). Semantic primitives: The expanding set. *Quaderni di Semantica 10(2), 309–332.* (Round table on semantic primitives, 2).

Wierzbicka, A. (1990a). The meaning of colour terms: Semantics, culture, and cognition. *Cognitive Linguistics, 1(1), 99–149.*

Wierzbicka, A. (1990b). 'Prototypes save': On the uses and abuses of the notion of 'prototype' in linguistics and related fields. In S. L. Tsohatzidis (Ed.), *Meanings and prototypes: Studies in linguistic categorization* (pp. 347–367). London: Routledge & Kegan Paul.

Wierzbicka, A. (1991a). Lexical universals and universals of grammar. In M. Kefer & J. van der Auwera (Eds.), *Meaning and grammar.* Berlin: De Gruyter.

Wierzbicka, A. (1991b). *Cross-cultural pragmatics.* Berlin: Mouton de Gruyter.

Wierzbicka, A. (1992). *Semantics, culture, and cognition.* New York: Oxford University Press.

Wierzbicka, A. (in press). The search for universal semantic primitives. In M. Pütz (Ed.), *Thirty years of linguistic evolution.* Amsterdam: John Benjamins.

9 Semantic Fields and the Individuation of Content

Eva Feder Kittay
SUNY Stony Brook

The notion of a semantic field, the idea that both lexical items and the concepts associated with them come not singly but in groupings defined by specifiable relations of contrast and affinity, has had a limited but important influence among many who study language and thought. In particular, the concept has been important for some linguists, linguistic anthropologists, and semioticians. Among philosophers, the idea has scarcely been noticed.[1] It has not often seemed to join with the sorts of concerns had by philosophers of language and mind. For one thing, semantic field theory is concerned with meaning and the subject of meaning has itself been on the defensive in the recent history of analytic philosophy of language, often relinquishing pride of place to a theory of reference. For another, semantic fields are about the meaning of words, and, where meaning is readmitted, it is sentence meaning that is at issue. Nonetheless, there have been a number of central problems in contemporary philosophy of language and mind that raise questions about word meaning in a way that semantic field theory can illuminate. Most notable of these are concerns about how we individuate psychological content, that is, about the conditions under which we assert the existence and identity of mental contents.

The question of how mental content is individuated is the problem of how we are to differentiate two objects of beliefs (or desires and other intentional states), assuming that they exist. The object of an intentional state is generally taken to be a proposition, which is the mental content of some individual's mental state. The question of individuating content is usually cast in a form that makes problematic a particular concept within a proposition, a concept that is lexicalized. Semantic fields are clusterings of lexicalized concepts. Moreover, semantic

---

[1]There are exceptions. Aside from Kittay (1987), with Lehrer (1981), there is also work by Richard Grandy (1988), L. Jonathan Cohen (1981), Keith Lehrer with A. Lehrer (1982), and Alvin Goldman (1988/89). Semantic fields also play a role in the work of Daniel Rothbart (1984). James Ross (1981) uses the notion to some extent.

fields do not only group together semantically close terms, they also encode the differentiations that individuate concepts and terms. If one is asking about problems of individuation of concepts, appeal to semantic fields may be useful to resolve some puzzling questions about content. In this chapter, I suggest that recourse to semantic fields will help us understand why it is both correct to insist that mental content be accountable to norms that are independent and outside of the individual, and to insist that it be specifiable with respect to concepts, or more precisely to differentiations among concepts, made by the speaker. Semantic fields can explain and unify both wide content, that is, mental content that is specifiable with respect to factors that are not "within the head" of the speaker, and narrow content, that is, mental content that can be represented as a state of the individual to whom the content is attributed.

Because this chapter brings together ideas from areas that are generally far afield, the argument I present follows the exposition of the configurations of concerns I am trying to marry. I first discuss the issues surrounding the individuation of content, then present the outlines of a theory of semantic fields, showing how they occupy a position intermediate between atomism and holism, and finally argue for the particular resolution offered to the puzzles of the individuation of content by semantic field theory in virtue of this intermediate position.

Throughout the discussion keep in mind that crucial to the enterprise is the idea that contrast and affinity are organizing principles for the lexicon and for mental content. I intend to use the idea of contrast and affinity to address the problem of the individuation of concepts as they function in the words of our public language and within our individual mental states. In the process I look at the familiar pairs of distinctions, intentional/nonintentional and narrow/wide, and enquire how these may be illuminated using semantic field theory. And finally, I want to tie in facts about semantic fields with considerations of holism and of intellectual and social norms.[2]

The Problem of Individuation

The importance of mental content is, arguably, to provide explanations of our linguistic and nonlinguistic behavior. For example, I hold a belief that reading the writings of feminists promotes respect for women, and I have a desire that my son become a man who treats women as equals. Knowing this, a person could explain why I encourage my son to read feminist authors. The propositions *that* reading feminist literature promotes respect for women and *that* my son become a man who treats women with equal regard are contents of my mind. As the objects of my intentions they are *about* states that need not be *in the head* or *in*

---

[2]I want to thank Neil Tennant for helping me clarify the nature of my project. I also want to thank Richard Grandy, Adrienne Lehrer, Keith Lehrer, Jonathan Adler, and Peter Ludlow for their useful comments.

my head. It may well be a true fact about the world that those who read feminist literature tend to become more respectful of women because of their exposure. And the sort of man my son becomes will be something others can judge as well as I. But nonetheless, my beliefs and my desires do seem to have to be *in the head* and even more precisely *in my head.*

In his article "The Meaning of Meaning," Hilary Putnam (1975) set forth a challenge to the notion that the meanings expressed in the *that* clauses (my belief *that* reading the writings of feminists promotes respect for women, my desire *that* my son become a man who treats women as equals, etc.) were "in my head." His argument concerning Twin Earth is by now familiar even outside of philosophy circles, so the briefest retelling should suffice. We imagine a Twin Earth in which everything remains identical to our own earth except that water does not have the chemical composition H2O but XYZ. When I request water I am requesting H2O, whether or not I know that water is H2O; my Twin is requesting XYZ, again irrespective of her scientific sophistication. What I mean when I request water is then not merely determined by my physical state or by what is *in my head,* argues Putnam, but by an external fact about my world and my linguistic community, namely, that what we call water is H2O. What is in the head of my twin is identical, her physical state is identical, but what she requests when she requests water is determined by her external circumstances and her linguistic community, namely a liquid whose chemical composition is XYZ. Meanings, Putnam concludes, are not *in the head.* And if differences in our mental states cannot be reflected in differences in our physical states, then we cannot say that mental states reduce to (or even that they supervene on) physical states.

Tyler Burge, in a series of articles relating a number of thought experiments, has raised a related point, and it is Burge's formulation of the problem that will most concern us. Burge argues that not only are meanings not in the head, the contents of our mental states cannot be individuated by reference only to what is in our heads. Since the first of these thought experiments will take up most of our time, let me begin by recounting it.

Burge discusses the situation of Bert, an individual who thinks that he has arthritis in his thigh. Bert also thinks that he has had a touch of arthritis in his wrist; that is, he has some correct understanding of arthritis, but also some important misunderstanding. We are asked to imagine Bert in a counterfactual situation, one in which he belongs to a community where arthritis is, as a matter of course, understood to lodge in the thigh. That is to say, in the counterfactual community in which we are to imagine Bert, the disease that we distinguish as an inflammation of the joints is not distinguished from other rheumatoid diseases. Burge's claim is that, whereas all nonintentional states of Bert in the actual and the counterfactual situations remain the same, the intentional content of his belief that his arthritis has now lodged itself in his thigh is different. Bert in the actual situation believes that arthritis is the cause of his discomfort; Bert in the counterfactual situation believes that something else, we can call it *tharthritis,* is what he experiences in his thigh. The mental content of Bert, both in the actual and in the counterfactual situation, is determined in part by the theories held by the two communities. This seems to be the case, even though everything else about him, all his nonintentional states, remain the same. If confronted by his misconception, Bert would most likely agree to being corrected. He would agree that his ailment is not arthritis but some other rheumatoid problem. But Bert, as we imagine him in the counterfactual situation, could not justifiably acquiesce to a similar challenge. The two beliefs held by Bert in the two situations cannot be individuated individualistically, but only by reference to the linguistic practices and medical theories of the respective societies in which the beliefs took hold.

The thought experiment just described lends itself to both a linguistic and social interpretation[3]; that is, the nonindividualistic claims for the individuation of content lend themselves to an understanding of content that is mediated by the linguistic medium of thought and of content as socially determined. It is these considerations that are the focus of the arguments here.[4]

Another set of concerns can be found in Burge (1986c). Burge adduces another doppelganger thought experiment—this time one in which we are asked to individuate the mental state of the protagonist at once anti-individualistically and yet not socially. There we are asked to imagine someone, we will call her Alice, who comes to believe that sofas are not really furniture for sitting but are *really* articles of religious significance. Alice's doppelganger, we'll call her Alice in Wonderland, also believes sofas are really articles of religious significance but thinks that everyone thinks that they are pieces of furniture meant for sitting. When Alice confronts people with her view, she meets with expected resistance. When Alice in Wonderland confronts people with her view, she meets no resistance at all, only surprise that she didn't already see that this was the accepted understanding of sofas. Burge argues that in the actual situation Alice would not agree to a correction. She knows that most people think sofas are pieces of furniture, but she no longer believes this to be *true.* In the name of the intellectual norm of truth, she holds sofas not to be furniture but ritual articles. Her doppelganger, Alice in Wonderland, argues Burge, holds beliefs not about sofas but about some other article that everyone accepts *is* a religious article, a *safo,* let's say. (Although like her twin, Alice in Wonderland also expects resistance to her view as she is not aware that everyone in Wonderland believes safos to be religious articles.) Once again the nonintentional states of the hypothetical twins are identical, but the mental content varies—not because of the individual's responsibility to a social norm (i.e., the socially accepted beliefs concerning

---

[3]These arguments can be found in Burge (1979, 1982b).

[4]In a series of other articles Burge (1982a, 1986a, 1986b) found the nonindividualistic claim on other factors, namely, the nature of the nonsocial environment. These arguments I do not rehearse because they do not present the kinds of problems that can be illuminated by semantic fields. But they introduce decidedly nonlinguistic external considerations that argue against the individuation of belief by reference to nonintentional states.

the nature of sofas), but because of her responsibility to an intellectual norm (her beliefs about the *true* nature of sofas). Burge claims that, in essence, the individuation still does not take place with reference to nonintentional states. Instead, he says that the individuation takes place with respect to norms of an intellectual sort. In this argument, Burge undermines the nonindividualistic basis of his externalism with respect to content but still insists on the need to individuate content with reference to factors other than nonintentional states.

If we want to give a naturalistic account of intentionality, then Putnam's and Burge's thought experiments are disturbing, for we are confronted with the possibility of individuals in identical nonintentional states to whom we must attribute two distinct intentional states. And in the first set of cases, the Bert cases, there is an element of paradox in the conclusion that we cannot individuate the content of our own mental states without reference to something outside the individual mind. But, claims Burge, if we disabuse ourselves of the misleading view that our intentional states are reducible to, or supervene on, our nonintentional states, and accept the role of external and often social factors, in the individuation of the contents of our mental states, the paradox dissolves. We simply cannot determine the mental contents individualistically, and therefore we can formulate no adequate theories about the mind—or for that matter about language and linguistic competence—without appeal to nonindividualistic factors, external factors.

A number of writers have claimed that by drawing a distinction between narrow and wide content, when narrow content captures just what is in the head and wide content encompasses the externalist factors, you could simply set aside all but the narrow content for the purposes of psychological explanation. But if we require external factors to individuate content, then this route seems unacceptable. The problems can be understood in terms of psychological explanation or in terms of self-knowledge. Jerry Fodor (1991) has recently put the problem in the form of an antinomy:

Argument *A:*
1. My twin and I are molecular duplicates.
2. Therefore our (actual and counterfactual) behaviors are identical in relevant respects.
3. Therefore the causal powers of our mental states are identical in relevant respects.
4. Therefore my twin and I belong to the same natural kind for purposes of psychological explanation and "individualism" is true.

But on the other hand, there is argument *B:*

Argument *B:*
1'. My twin and I are molecular duplicates.
2'. Nevertheless, our (actual and counterfactual) behaviors are different in relevant respects.

3'. Therefore the causal powers of our mental states are different in relevant respects.

4'. Therefore my twin and I belong to different natural kinds for purposes of psychological explanation and "individualism" is false. (p. 5)

Fodor (1991) argues that externalism is independent of individualism; that is, we can argue for individualism as the basis for psychological explanation, while admitting that beliefs and desires be individuated broadly. And furthermore that such a position would still permit us to be intentional realists, that is, to affirm the reality of intentional states as long as "an individualistic notion of 'intentional state' suitable for the purposes of psychological explanation can be constructed" (p. 7). His argument hinges on the unacceptability of the move from 2' to 3'. This dissolves the antinomy in favor of argument A. I do not argue against this position. I too want to maintain that an externalism is compatible with a conception of individualism with respect to psychological explanation. But I want to make the case with respect to a stronger claim than the mere compatibility between an externalist semantics and an individualist psychology. The idea of a semantic field serves both the externalist semantics and the individualist psychology and thereby forges a link between the two.

Furthermore, the difficulty of maintaining an externalist semantics and an individualist psychology can be expressed in terms of the issue of self-knowledge. If I am to have a direct awareness of my mental contents, then I must be in a position to individuate them well enough to know what I am thinking. Put crudely, the intuition is that these are *my individual* mental states. I know what I mean by the term *arthritis,* and so I must be the one determining the content of that term as it occurs in oblique positions in ascriptions of *my* intentional states. Again, I argue that a translation of the problem into a semantics using semantic fields will offer a resolution to this apparent paradox.

We need to note that Burge (1979) resists a purely linguistic determination of the thought experiments. Surely an individual could claim to *mean* by arthritis the pain that is lodged in his thigh. But claims Burge, Bert's is not a problem to be resolved by some Humpty Dumpty-like resolution. His case, unlike Putnam's, is not about the meaning of arthritis but about what Bert *thinks* of the two situations postulated in the thought experiment. Nonetheless, the thought experiment suggests that Burge's problem must be linguistic, in some broad sense, as well as mentalistic.[5] For language is just that environmental factor by which mental contents lose their individualistic caste and acquire a social one. When we use a bit of sound upon which linguistic significance has been conferred, we use demarcations and distinctions that we have not made but that are made for us by

---

[5]Paul Boghossian (1989), writing on meaning scepticism, writes that given the intimate relation of language and thought there can be no way to confine scepticism only to language, that "content and meaning must stand or fall together" (p. 510). The point holds with respect to the issues raised here as well.

our language. We may be unable to distinguish an oak tree from a plane tree, and take the two labels "oak" and "plane" to be regional dialects designating the same tree. But when a botanist or a landscape gardener explains to us that these are different trees, we defer to experts because they establish the distinctions relevant to the definition of an oak or a plane tree. What Putnam (1970) called the linguistic division of labor is, of course, at once a conceptual division of labor.[6]

In general discourse, as well, distinctions and demarcations deemed important by our linguistic community are marked by distinctions in meaning. When we misunderstand the scope of a term, so that we think that arthritis can lodge itself in the thigh, we have not only failed to grasp the defining properties of arthritis but have also failed to grasp the distinctions the language embodies. We may, for example, have believed the salient distinction to be between joint and muscle pain caused by an injury and that not directly caused by injury. This is a reasonable axis about which to make distinctions. But it does not result in discriminations sufficiently fine for the purposes of a language that articulated the medical theory which treats muscles and joint pathology differently.

When Burge claims, rightfully, that we would not say that the counterfactual Bert does not have a concept of arthritis (that the mental contents of his intentions do not include the content of arthritis), we presume that this is because the defining properties of arthritis differ from those of tharthritis. But even before we give defining properties for the two concepts, we can see that the counterfactual concept tharthritis marks a different set of distinctions—plausible or implausible—from that of arthritis. The two language communities have chosen their terms in such a way as to make appeal to different sets of discriminations. The choice of pertinent discriminations mark the boundaries of the concepts, boundaries by which we individuate the two concepts. We need not be in possession of defining properties of either term to see this.

Note that on this view, definition via properties is but the outcome of the salient differentiations that determine them. A brief digression to defend against an appearance of circularity is necessary. In this account and in the account of semantic fields that follows, I use notions such as similarity, contrast, affinity as apparent primitives; and I use terms such as *pertinent, salient, related,* which seem to do a lot of foundational work. The obvious objection arises: " 'Similar,' 'contrasting,' and 'affine' relative to *what properties?* similar *qua what?* Does not one come full circle back to defining concepts/properties?"[7] True, similarity, contrast, and affinity are all relative notions. Terms that are similar are similar

---

[6]In a similar vein, James Ross (1981; also see Ross, this volume) speaks of craftbound discourses, discourse in which the meaning of terms is intimately tied in with a given activity, whether it be plumbing or metaphysics. Within craftbound discourses, distinctions and demarcations suit the needs of the given craft and evolve with the craft, generating meanings that mark these contrasts.

[7]I owe this point to Neil Tennant in correspondence.

with respect to certain properties or concepts and differ with respect to different properties or concepts. But the virtue of understanding the terms in the fashion suggested by semantic fields is that the properties that adhere to terms by virtue of their membership in a field need not adhere to them in a fixed manner. Change context, change field, and you change the set of properties or concepts that you affix to a term. Semantic fields are discerned through contexts that provide the differentiations that determine properties. The claim of semantic field theory is not that one cannot give a characterization of a term via defining concepts and properties. Rather it is that these defining properties are determined through contrasts and affinities that become salient in a given context, or in a given grouping in which comparisons are drawn.

Empirical support for this view is provided by Amos Tversky (1977). He has shown that, in the case of many comparative statements, the properties, which are diagnostic for grouping certain items and judging that one is more similar to a target than another, are ones that emerge by virtue of the items available for the grouping. This is because the relevant feature space emerges implicitly in context. Features of a term often become salient by virtue of contextual considerations, a functioning of what Tversky has called the *diagnosticity principle* (1977, p. 342.) When judging the similarity of three countries to Austria, Sweden was thought *most* like Austria when the two other countries were Poland and Hungary, but *least* like Austria when Norway was substituted for Poland. When the group of countries compared to Austria included two Slavic countries, subjects conceived of Austria as a non-Slavic country, as is Sweden. But when Norway was substituted for Poland, Austria was attributed the characteristic of being a non-Scandinavian country. Tversky's experimental results indicate that, given a cluster of figures, names, and terms, subjects will determine the basis of comparison not according to fixed properties, but according to the properties that the clustering makes salient.

The answer to the charge of circularity is that in order to make differentiations one need not antecedently define a similarity space, that is, a set of properties with reference to which the entities or terms are compared. Rather the context that brings a set of terms (or entities) together implicitly defines a similarity space, which then becomes diagnostic for salient similarities and differences. That is to say, our understanding of a term or a concept is dependent not simply on fixed and determinate properties, but on those that become salient in a given context. (The theory of semantic fields, as I understand it, is a theory that incorporates this relational understanding of content.)

To think of the difference between the two concepts not in terms of inherent defining properties that adhere atomistically to the concepts, but in terms of the choice of relevant distinctions that mark out the boundaries of the concept, underscores the extent to which the individuation of a concept takes place with respect to other related concepts. For example, in the case of arthritis we have a contrast drawn with respect to other rheumatoid and nonrheumatoid diseases or injuries that affect joints and muscle tissue. The specification of some content—whether we mean the content of our intentional states or the content of a term (a concept)—is thereby dependent on interconnections with other contents as the latter get articulated by terms used within a particular language community. Whereas Burge's concerns are with mental content and not linguistic usage, it seems, at least on the face of it, that there is a reasonable argument for insisting on the pertinence of decisions made by the social community as a linguistic community. Having made linguistic factors pertinent, it may now be appropriate to shift the discussion to semantic field theory.

Semantic Field Theory

Semantic field theory maintains that the meaning of a term is partially determined by terms that apply to a similar domain and to which the term stands in relation of contrast or affinity. It is a development of the notion of linguistic value, a notion introduced by Ferdinand de Saussure (1968). The idea of linguistic value is one of Saussure's most important contribution to linguistics, a contribution all but lost sight of in Anglo–American philosophy of language. The Saussurian insight is that language can perform its referential function only through the mediation of a set of discriminations he called *value*. Saussure (1968) took value to arise from the social fact of language. When I say that this insight has been lost sight of, I do not mean that the importance of the interrelations among terms and among concepts has not been recognized. Within the thesis of holism we certainly have an important acknowledgement of such a view. What has not been explicitly recognized is the role of contrast in the assignment of meaning and content. And it is this role of value that I bring forward by applying it to the Putnam and Burge doppelganger thought experiments.

I argue that to individuate is just to be capable of differentiating a concept from other similar concepts, that the individual who is a member of a language community is in possession of just such a capacity, and that, whereas learning the concept involves learning the pertinent contrasts, the individual may draw the lines of demarcation differently from the social group, either out of a misconstrual or out of thoughtful considerations. But insofar as the understanding of the term is bound up with the way the term is differentiated from other related terms in the language, the individual risks holding inconsistent beliefs with respect to the domain in question. There is another question of individuation that comes up when we, standing outside of two contexts, compare two similar contents and ask how we individuate these. There we illegitimately place into one semantic field two terms that are never considered by the agents in the thought experiments to be in a relation of contrast.

Before proceeding, we need an exposition of the concept of value. Saussure distinguished value from signification. Signification is roughly what we speak of as the denotation of a term. Value is what a sign has by virtue of its relation to other related terms, both the terms it collocates with in a sentence and the terms that may substitute for it in a sentence. Saussure understood value to apply not only to terms as such, but also to concepts insofar as these contents could be understood as constituting a system of differences. The marking or registering of these differences requires another system of differences, which in the case of language is a system of acoustic sound images. Saussure asserted (unfortunately, with too little argument) that the social community fixes the mutual articulations provided by the two systems of differences. I think the claim can be bolstered by Wittgensteinian arguments against private language. Except for some criteria exterior to us, what would justify the repeated application of a given sound to a given content? Even a causality of external objects would not suffice, for the causal efficacy still has to work through our representations, mediated as these are by our concepts. Therefore, Saussure took it to be evident that language could not be a private matter.

An individual alone, he claimed, was incapable of fixing the value of a term; only a social community could do that because the individual alone was only natively endowed with a system of conceptual differentia and a system of linguistic differentia but without the resources to decide what bit of sound to anchor on to what bit of conceptual content. I do not attempt to argue this point; but to fix our ideas with respect to the social aspect of value, I consider another domain in which the concept of value figures and which provided Saussure himself with an analogy to language: economics. The point that an individual alone cannot fix a single linguistic value is akin to the fact that an individual alone, outside of an economic community, would be in no position to fix an economic value on some goods. Outside of an economic community, the individual alone could not even fix on the unit of an economic good, for economically speaking what would be the salient criteria by which to make the distinctions necessary to individuate an item as an economic good. To decide water is valuable, for example, is one thing. But to decide that it has an economic worth requires a medium of exchange to determine even what will constitute water. Only the clear stuff? Or muddy stuff as well? Water by the droplet? Or by the bucket? How we determine the object of economic value will depend on how fine-grained our economic units are, on the properties of water that are salient given the various properties of entities we subject to our economic exchanges, and on how these properties are assessed relative to other items priced within a given economic system.

What now is the analogy between economic and linguistic value? Just as the cost of water does not merely signify its intrinsic worth but depends, among other things, on the price of potatoes (or yams or rice or wheat), so a term signifies not some concept independently delineated but that concept as it functions within an interrelated system of concepts. A paradigmatic example of a semantic field is the domain of color terms. As perceptually salient as the color green appears to us, not all languages have a term for green. Some languages have only two or three terms for color, and the array of hues we call green will not retain their unity as one color under a scheme with only three color terms. A dull green, for example, will be signified by the term for *black,* whereas a yellowish bright green will be signified by the term for *white.* Within our own language scheme, given a classification of objects into primary colors, a deep orange may not be differentiated from a red or a dark pink, but in looking at the spectrum in a more fine-grained way, these objects would not be thought to be the "same color."

Another example: If we recognize only signification (either denotation or reference or extension), then *father* means male parent. Within our own linguistic community the relation between a father and his child is biological. We have the term *step-father* to mark a similar, but nonbiologically based relation. Imagine, now, a society in which the biological relation is not marked by any term in the language and the analogous term for father marks the difference between persons who are a generation apart and who could plausibly be parent and child—we'll say that such a concept or term is *generational.* Consider our word *uncle.* The term denotes a male who is the sibling of a biological parent. Given the cultural strictures on the intermarriage of siblings, *father* contrasts with *uncle* (i.e., if a man is my father, then he is not my uncle, and if he is my uncle, he is not my father).[8] Given the very same strictures in our conjured society, *father* would not contrast with *uncle* in the same way—a man could be at once my father and my uncle; if *son* were equally a generational concept, then a man could be at once my son and my uncle, but not my son and my father. Notice that the contrasts pertain not only to words but also to the concepts and hence to mental contents into which these enter. Now it is these kinds of interconnections between concepts and between terms that figure in the notion of value.[9] I've developed Saussure's economic and linguistic analogy because it seems to me to have real

---

[8]With one exception. Since our term *uncle* also denotes (or more accurately, has as its extension the set of) husbands of parent's sisters, it is conceivable and neither illegal nor socially sanctioned that a widower may marry one of the sisters of his deceased wife, thus becoming an uncle to his children. Since it is certainly conceivable that our term *uncle* be restricted so as not to include the husbands of our parents' sisters, and that there be another term for these men, the counterexample need not affect the argument here. We simply assume such a restricted use, counterfactual as it may be. This point was made to me by Richard Grandy in a personal communication.

[9]Fodor (1991, p. 12) writes that the properties that distinguish the twins in Putnam's Twin Earth example are properties that have to do with the causal connection between the Earthling and the Twin Earthling and water and twater, respectively. Notice that the considerations that I remark on in the text concern the way in which social factors mediate that very causal connection. These considerations suggest that even a causal theory of reference can't stay clear of mediating concepts, *senses,* if you will, because, as in the case of economic value, we need to discern what the stuff that we are causally connected to is: Again, is it only the clear stuff or the muddy stuff as well? Liquid by the droplet or *en masse*? When discussing the causal connection between Earthling and water and Twin and twater, we have somehow presumed that the causal relations are such that the *stuff* that we are connected to in each case is of a certain sort, although we have not given any description of what that stuff is. It is just that stuff that we refer to when we refer to water. It happens of course that that stuff is

bearing on the individuation problem raised by Burge. For consider a dop-pelganger example in which these two different understandings of the term *father* occur. In the actual case, I think that my uncle is in the kitchen cooking dinner. And as a matter of fact it is my paternal uncle of whom I am thinking. In the counterfactual world, I think that my uncle is in the kitchen cooking dinner. And again, it is the same paternal uncle of whom I think. But if the two societies are such that they are otherwise identical except that father is a concept that applies only to a biological male parent in the actual case but is a generational term in the counterfactual case, then the content of my thoughts are different in the two cases. In the actual case I can say with certainty that the uncle of whom I speak is not my father, whereas in the counterfactual case I would most likely say that the uncle who is in the kitchen and of whom I speak is my father. Furthermore, if I owe a certain form of address when speaking to my father, which I do not owe to my uncle, then if I think of what I will say to the man in the kitchen will differ in the two cases. And if certain behavior is due my father which is not due my uncle, I will have different thoughts about what I am to do in the two cases. Mental content about the man in the kitchen, my paternal uncle, will differ depending on how *uncle* is defined relative to *father*. What has distinguished the content of the two thoughts is not the denotation of the two occurrences of uncle in the mental content, but the value of the concept given the different treatment of the term *father*. In the actual case, *father* and *uncle* stand in a relation of antipodal contrast (assuming that incest is not a factor, Y is a father of X, only if Y is not an uncle of X); in the counterfactual case, they are orthogonal (again on the same assumption, Y may be a father and an uncle of X or son and uncle of X, although in both cases Y cannot be both a father of and a son of X). The contrasts between *father* and *uncle* are different in the two cases and therefore issue in different sets of mental content employing these notions.

Psychological Content Again

With this reflection, let's look back at the case of arthritis. In Burge's example, *arthritis* in the actual and counterfactual cases have different extensions, although the actual Bert takes the extension to be identical to what pertains in the counter-factual situation. Burge concludes that we need to individuate the mental content

---

H2O. But this presumes that our differentia for what constitutes water is its chemical composition, whatever that might turn out to be. And once that is established it becomes the defining characteristic. But the choice of the differentia, the constraints that these impose, is just the pertinent mediating schema that picks out the referent (or perhaps more correctly, delineates the possible referent). If the stuff we refer to when we refer to water is identifiable by means of its chemical composition—and that this is the case is dependent on a larger schema by which physical stuff is identified by its chemical composition—then stuff that has the chemical composition of XYZ cannot be water—no matter how similar it is to water in every other regard. A causal theory of reference is not incompati-ble with a socially mediated set of implicit constraints as to what it is that we are causally related to.

Furthermore, the price of insisting that there need be no social mediation in respect to reference, causally understood, is the acceptance of the whole-scale nativism of Fodor, a price I find too high.

differently in the two situations. In response to efforts to understand the thought experiment in a way that would allow us to individuate the content of Bert's thought with reference only to what is happening in his own head, Burge points out that Bert would concede were he corrected. An important and relevant question is "why would he concede?" Why does he need to be responsible to nonindividualistic norms—to the norms of his linguistic community? If we don't hold Bert responsible, then there seems to be no obstacle to individuating content individualistically. The evident answer would be that only by such accountability is communication possible. This answer will not do, for then Bert could simply say, "Look, what I mean by *arthritis*—or alternatively, what I think of when I think of arthritis—is simply an inflammation whose proximate cause is not an injury, but an inflammation of a rheumatoid type that can just as well lodge itself in the thigh as in the wrist." And sometimes this is just what someone in Bert's position would say.

Still, Burge is correct in pointing out that we do allow ourselves to be corrected and consider deviant uses mistakes. Why? Because the misalignments that characterize the Burge example are not just misalignments between the beliefs of the individual and those of other language speakers. The misalignments may be internal to a speaker with the result that one finds oneself holding inconsistent beliefs. Another example may make this clearer. Let us say of Mary that she believes that unsaturated fats are fats that are not animal products and that only fats that come from animals are saturated fats. She therefore does not think that corn oil margarine is a saturated fat. She also believes eating unsaturated fats is healthy and eating saturated fats is unhealthy, on the assumption that a diet with unsaturated fats does not raise cholesterol levels and that saturated fats do, and that a diet of the latter sort is healthy and one of the former sort is not. Hence one can attribute to Mary the belief that eating corn oil margarine is healthy and eating any saturated fat is unhealthy. But this belief is inconsistent insofar as margarine is a saturated fat, and if Mary believes all saturated fats are unhealthy, then she should believe that eating corn oil margarine is unhealthy. Mary's doppelganger, Mary Contrary, lives in a world where the term *unsaturated fats* designates all fats that do not come from animal products. Mary Contrary does not hold inconsistent beliefs regarding corn oil margarine, although she has the incorrect belief that eating any unsaturated fats will help keep down cholesterol blood levels. The theory of Mary Contrary's world is less accurate and the terminology doesn't serve her and her compatriots well because the class of things they identify as unsaturated cannot be generalized in a manner that will identify the relation between disease and fat intake.[10] Let us say further that Mary learns that using corn oil margarine will not help reduce cholesterol levels,

---

[10]Of course it would also be incorrect according to our scientific theory, but we need not suppose that they maintain the same chemical theory that we do, at least with respect to saturated and unsaturated fats. Still it is interesting how quickly we come to the interconnectedness of the concepts with the whole body of chemistry, and how difficult it is to imagine the interconnections away.

whereas using corn oil will. At the same time, her mistaken understanding of unsaturated fats persists. Mary herself is then aware of an inconsistency, indeed a contradiction among her beliefs. On the one hand she believes eating corn oil margarine is healthy (because it is an unsaturated fat), and on the other hand she believes that eating corn oil margarine is not healthy (because that is what the medical reports inform her).[11]

The misalignment in the beliefs of Mary and Bert are not merely between the social and the individual but also between the beliefs held by the individuals themselves. That misalignment in the case of Mary is due to the acceptance of certain beliefs concerning saturated and unsaturated fats and the holding of certain beliefs incompatible and directly in contradiction with the other accepted beliefs. Mary's case is just one of many. The inconsistent beliefs are easily generated when a concept we employ is used divergently from that of the main linguistic community or by those who are the experts in a division of linguistic labor.

The preceding propositions no doubt sound familiar. They sound very much like the thesis of holism. But holism is far stronger a thesis than is necessary to capture the relevant insights. The theory of semantic fields does not commit one to a global holism à la Quine or Davidson. The interrelations are localized to the conceptual domain (and perhaps some pertinent adjacent domains) to which a term belongs.[12] What is of importance is that we must identify the content of arthritis with that given by its position in a semantic field because to individuate its content otherwise would have implications for, would force revisions in the ascriptions of, a set of beliefs covering a certain domain. We can think of the lexicon as structured into small interconnected but separable wholes—a sort of local holism. In order to understand the term *electron*, I may need to know related terms such as *proton, atom, charge*, etc., but I don't need to know the difference between an elm and a maple—I may not need to know what either a maple or an elm is. And even revolutionary changes in dendrology need not affect a correct understanding of the concept of or the term *electron*. Still the syntactic and conceptual structures are in place to make statements about possible predication of electrons in terms of elms or elms in terms of electrons.

These local holistic meaning structures encapsulate distinctions that speakers

---

[11]Notice first, if we subscribe to the idea of semantic fields, we subscribe not to holism per se, but to a local holism (see following). The contradiction need not infect all Mary's beliefs but only those that pertain to this conceptual domain, and of course any reasoning that involves utilizing the contradictory belief. Second, although Mary holds two contradictory beliefs, we need not regard her as irrational, nor need we be violating the principle of charity when we attribute these two contradictory beliefs to her. She knows that there is a contradiction, and she is puzzled. Not knowing the source of her problem she is not willing to withhold assent from one or the other, even if she is not willing to affirm their conjunction. This is not irrational behavior.

[12]For a related discussion of "globally separable local holisms," see Tennant (1987a, pp. 45–65) and Tennant (1987b, pp. 31–58).

of the language have deemed important—the ways in which speakers have formed contrasts and affinities between terms. I take it that the relatedness is given either through the experience we, as part of a social group, have with the world or (and perhaps and) with some elemental conceptual structure inherent in our species. Our theories, folk or scientific, and our practices, craft-like or not, determine what conceptual demarcations get linguistically marked. When we have to deal with trees, we may need to know the difference between a maple and an oak if we wish to tap a tree for a sweet edible sap. Or if we want to plant trees that give good shade but are relatively resistant to disease in our geographical location, we will want to tell a beech from an elm, but the difference between a beech and a plane tree may not interest us. If we are botanists studying the properties of trees, we will want to distinguish each of the species, make still finer distinction, and make them on a different basis than the lay person. The finer distinctions will precipitate out a set of properties worthy of study and codification. Each set of distinctions applied to referential, experiential material will generate concepts or properties (though it may well be that we also need the most elemental concepts upon which to build concepts and generate properties). But these properties are at best provisionally definitive of a term.[13]

These last remarks can be brought to bear on an interesting pragmatic fact that doubtless has semantic ramifications. I speak of what Eve Clark (1987) has called the *Principle of Contrast*. According to this principle, speakers of a language do not accept two terms as true synonyms. Where the language provides two terms that apparently denote the same thing, speakers will try to find a contrast, and in time a set of contrasting properties does develop that pertains to the two terms. Terms such as *mutton, pork, veal, beef,* for example, were initially foreign borrowings (*mouton, porc, veau, boeuf,* respectively) that had a register difference from *lamb, pig, calf, cow.* The foreign terms were used by the aristocracy that spoke French, especially to designate the animal as food. But rather than remain synonymous with their English counterparts, they were contrasted with the native terms so that eventually the native terms were used only to designate the domestic animal whereas the foreign terms were used exclusively for comestibles.[14]

The principle of contrast is the flip side of the notion of value—its pragmatic functioning, if you will. What both deliver is the idea that a semantic field gets generated by those contrasts that terms display among themselves. The further

---

[13] The reader may have noted that I sometimes speak of contrasts between terms, between concepts, and even between objects—at least as they are experienced differentially. The linguistic contrasts bespeak conceptual contrasts, which in turn bespeak differentially experienced things falling under the concepts. These relations between differences in terms, concepts, and things are heuristic, not definitive. Yet the notion of contrast has the virtue that it can be applied in each of these ontological categories, although a contrast has to be made within a given ontological category.

[14]*Lamb* is used for both the cut of meat and the animal, but it is still contrasted with *mutton,* which designates the meat from an older lamb.

claim is that these contrasts and affinities are just as important, if not more so, than sets of inherent properties in the determination of meaning and content. If these contrasts and affinities are understood as representing semantic and epistemic links a concept has to other concepts, then the claim is just the familiar claim of holism. But what fields adds is an understanding of these interdependencies that localizes the working of value and contrast to a portion of the lexicon. Why is the localization of interest to the question at hand the individuation of content, and the breadth of the contents individuated? I address this more fully shortly.

Let me first indicate how the issue of internalism versus externalism touches on the question of holism. To argue for an externalist conception of content, that is, according to Bilgrami (1987), for one that insists that "contents are constituted by the linguistic norms of the others in the community" (p. 201), raises the question of the importance of the epistemic links among concepts to the content of a concept; that is to say, it raises the question of holism. In the case of Mary and Mary Contrary, we saw that the misalignment of beliefs between an individual and her community can result in inconsistent, arguably contradictory beliefs. That is why (or at least that is the deep reason why) the nonexpert will defer to the expert, and why people will obey what Eve Clark has called the *Principle of Conventionality,* that is, that where there is a conventional meaning in place, speakers will defer to it.

The Principle of Conventionality not only assures consistency in communication between language speakers; it also assures a relative consistency within our own beliefs, given the interconnections in our beliefs captured by the interrelatedness amongst our concepts. At times the beliefs of the language community in fact yield important inconsistencies or discrepancies with the empirical. When these inconsistencies can no longer be tolerated, linguistic norms must give way to other norms—intellectual norms, for example. The conception of externalism and the notion of meaning holism hang together by two threads. The meanings we attribute to propositions and to the terms within propositions depend on concepts that are interrelated with other concepts within our language (some sort of meaning holism). The meanings and concepts of the terms within our language are determined not by the individual assignment of meanings, but by a collective process that becomes normative for our own usage (linguistic division of labor, for example). The sociality of language in this way comes into the web of our beliefs and the web of our concepts. For any given concept, and therefore for any given mental content, one cannot individuate content only with reference to the individual (externalism and the thesis of anti-individualism).

But if meaning holism were the whole story, we as individual speakers would be in no position to have any autonomy with respect to the meanings of the terms we use. Because the network of concepts are of one fabric, social factors with respect to one part would infect all parts. The localistic holism of fields allows an alternate course.

Previously I have indicated what it is to say that contents are individuated by reference to semantic fields. Contents are individuated with respect to other terms or concepts that are allied with them in a semantic field. The different contrasts and affinities that a semantic field encodes enable us to determine whether we have, in any given case, one content or a plurality of contents. If we grant this claim, the question remains: How are we to conceive of semantic fields? Are we to say that semantic fields exist in the heads of individual speakers? The answer is Yes! and No! Semantic fields are in general a communal result and a communal property. To understand a language each member of the language community must have some grasp of the semantic fields to which terms in the sentences of the utters/hearers belong—as well as the understanding that the field is so articulated for other members of the linguistic community. A semantic field theory then seems to be a theory that endorses the understanding of content as wide content. But the available distinctions in the fields—the contrasts and affinities that mark out relations among terms and concepts—are individualistically available—that is as content narrowly understood.

And here is where the localization of holism by virtue of semantic fields becomes useful. The relatedness of terms within a semantic field is not the outcome of some forces distributed throughout the whole of language or the totality of beliefs, such that shifts in one place in the network have repercussions, however mild everywhere else. Rather the interrelations are the result of rather crisp and definable relations of contrast and affinity: relations such as graded antonymy, scalar relations, hyponomy, mereological relations, contraries, contradictories, etc. Terms that bear these relations to one another contrast and belong to the same field. A shift in meaning of one such term will affect the meaning of the other terms in that field. Surely terms belong to more than one field and there are relations among fields, so that in some cases a shift in meaning will have larger repercussions.

What is most important for our considerations is that the individual, equipped with the ability to make contrasts, a variety of contrasts at that, is equipped with the wherewithal to create distinctions not currently available in the language. Distinctions so made would count toward narrow content. Consider the idiosyncratic contrasts that Bert might be employing: The pain in my thigh can't be the result of an injury (I've not injured my thigh); it must be arthritis. In the counterfactual world, the semantic field of arthritis individuates arthritis in just this manner. Not so in the actual world, where muscle and joint pain or inflammation caused by injury is contrasted with rheumatoid diseases wherein the cause may be infection or constitutional factors, and *arthritis* is a hyponym of *rheumatoid* diseases, specifying joint rather than muscle disease. The narrowness of content is given in the individualism of the distinction Bert draws. If you will, he alone is privy to that mental act (even though there is nothing private about it—that distinction can always be publicly displayed or articulated). But the content of his thought is wide insofar as the distinctions of a semantic field have not only to obey the Principle of Contrast, but also the Principle of Conventionality.[15] And we fail to adhere to such a principle on the pain of being misunderstood and finding ourselves with inconsistent beliefs, not throughout the network of beliefs, but locally.

We can think of the semantic relations as the semantic analogues of the syntactic features of a universal grammar. The particular relations given in semantic fields are analogous to the particular syntactic structure of a given language. The semantic variations one finds in smaller communities are again analogous to syntactic variations one finds in dialects and ideolects. What variations are possible are constrained, at least in part, by the semantic fields of the larger community, just as syntactic variations are constrained by the grammatical structure of the homologous language groups. As there is an interplay in the case of syntax between the individualistic contribution to syntactic structure and the constraining influence of the public language, so there is an interplay in the individualistic and social contribution of content, which, incidentally, is all that I think Burge has set out to show. The social contribution is the particular semantic field in which the term designating a pertinent content is situated. The semantic fields of the actual and the counterfactual worlds in which the thought experiment places Bert are distinct. To the extent that they are, and to the extent that Bert is using the term *arthritis* in an oblique position in the two worlds, his beliefs in the two worlds have a different content. But the distinctions that Bert and his doppleganger make are the same distinctions.[16]

The distinctions that Bert and his doppleganger make are "in the head," although the semantic field to which arthritis belongs is a field that is publicly accessible and not "in the head." A semantic field, consisting as it does of a level of content and a level of expression, is, and must be, publicly accessible; that is, it must be available to either the whole of, or some significant part of, the linguistic community. But I have argued that, when we identify a mental content as that content, we differentiate it from some similar but saliently distinct content. The content gets individuated against a background of relevant contrasts. These may or may not be encoded in a semantic field. The repertoire of contrasts are individualistically available.[17] For the individuation of content what we

---

[15]Alternatively, one can speak here not of adhering to the Principle of Conventionality, but of being responsible to norms. For the inconsistency in our beliefs may turn out to result from mistaken beliefs enshrined in the language. In 12th-century Europe one might suppose that it would be peculiar to speak of going around the world, whereas today we have to understand "going to the ends of the earth" metaphorically or else be thought to hold (1) false beliefs, if we are also prepared to assent to the proposition that the earth has ends, or (2) inconsistent beliefs, if we are prepared to assent to the proposition that the earth is round. It is considerations such as these that, I believe, drive Burge (1986c) to a seemingly more individualistic stance made in "Intellectual Norms."

[16]And we can add, these are what have a causal efficacy vis-a-vis the subject's actions, although not necessarily on the outcomes of these actions.

[17]And if we accept that they are individualistically available, then we are less tempted by the full-blown nativism of Fodor.

require are a set of contrasts and affinities against which the content is identified as such. As a rule, the relational character of the discriminations requires a socially codified set of contrasts, such as those given in a particular semantic field of some language, and one to which the individual is committed by virtue of her membership in the linguistic community. Therefore, that which regularly gets identified as a given content depends on the linguistic community. But because the repertoire of contrasts and affinities are individualistically available, individuals are in a position to make discriminations that are not simply identical to those of the social norm, with the result that the individual either makes mistakes or innovates; either one errs or one becomes accountable to extrasocial norms such as intellectual norms.

The case described in "Intellectuals Norms and the Foundations of Mind," the case described earlier with the protagonists, Alice and Alice in Wonderland, is one in which the mental content is individuated with reference to a set of contrasts and affinities, set within a theory about sofas, religious objects, and pieces of furniture, which the individual has specified—in opposition to the understandings of the social group. Burge, in this example, gives priority to the relations individuating content that are initiated by the individual who reconceptualizes sofas with respect to a theory that she believes is more truthful than the theory inscribed in the linguistic conventions. The argument for the necessity of norms for the individuation of content is an old one that goes back at least to Plato. It reappears in Wittgenstein's argument against a private language. The importance of intellectual norms is stressed by Plato; the importance of social norms is insisted upon by Wittgenstein—especially in the interpretation of the private language argument provided by Kripke. The Saussurian insight, as I would wish to adopt it, urges that the relevant norms are those contrasts and affinities that get taken to be authoritative within a linguistic community. Whether the authority is vested in the social, or the intellectual, or even the perceptual will be decided with reference to the commitments to interrelated beliefs. The protagonist of Burge's new thought experiment decides that the concept *sofa* is a hyponym of *religious object* and not of *furniture*. That decision is made with reference to beliefs pertinent to the domains of beliefs concerning furniture and religion. It is also made with regard to the commitments that these beliefs command. This means that the decision to defy the general social understanding regarding sofas is made for the same reason that Bert makes the decision to acquiesce to the social understanding of arthritis: In both cases the set of interlocking beliefs and commitments appear to the speaker to demand a particular understanding of the concept in question. These beliefs and commitments are "in the head."

This is not meant to challenge the nonreductionist thesis that Burge's examples purport to establish. What appears paradoxical in the results of Burgian thought experiments is that we can have mental contents not adequately specifiable in terms of what is "in our heads." But if we understand that content is always individuated to some extent with respect to other concepts, other contents—that the intentionality of content requires a notion of value just as the reference of a term requires a notion of value—then Burge's pill seems less bitter. The contrasts necessary to individuate a term or a content may be determined socially or individually, but they must be internalized if the term or content is to be used correctly and to have explanatory power with respect to our behavior. The related terms or concepts, which are involved in the individuation of content, are implicated in a set of beliefs that carry epistemological (and other) commitments. These beliefs and commitments must be carried "in the head," but what contrasts and differentiations will comport with the accepted beliefs and affirmed commitments may not be "in the head" of the individual. The semantic fields—in which terms are located and which serve to individuate content— encode beliefs and interdependencies among beliefs locally. They are more or less imperfectly taken up by language speakers, but they can remain an abstract reference point for all speakers (or all parties to a dialect or subcommunity of language speakers). They are at once social and individualistic, at once concrete (in a speaker) and abstract (a reference point for multiple speakers).

At this point one may ask: But how much has the idea of contrasts and fields done for us in considering the problem of individuating content? What have we gained over a characterization of the problems in terms of some idiosyncratic definitions on the one hand and conventional definitions on the other? Bert in the actual situation has an idiosyncratic definition that he willingly gives up when subjected to the conventional definition. What has been gained by speaking of contrasts rather than definitions; of fields rather than sets of beliefs? In fact, could one not argue that something has in fact been lost?

To get at the latter accusation, consider the Putnam Twin Earth case. It appears that both I and my Twin make all the same distinctions with respect to water. I wish to drink water rather than let us say milk, juice, or any other potable liquid. So does my twin. I wish to bath in water rather than any other substance that I might be submerged in; so does my twin. The semantic field of water in English is indistinguishable from the semantic field of twin water in Twin English. By posing the question of meaning in terms of semantic fields, the meaning difference between water and twin water seems to get lost. But if it is a loss, it's the right kind of loss. Putnam's thought experiment is in this regard different from the Burge cases. The difference between earth and twin earth is in the nature of that to which the semantic fields get applied. The difference, if you will, is pragmatic, not semantic.[18] It looks as if the difference must be semantic because we are cognitively situated so that we can entertain both the concept of water and the concept of twin water.[19] We can, so to speak, put them into the *same*

---

[18]This is a point that I have long suspected, but it has only been in conversations with Keith Lehrer, who shares this view, that I have begun to have confidence in its viability.

[19]The Burge examples differ from the Putnam case. In the Putnam case what remains invariant across contexts are the semantic fields; in the Burge case it is the domain to which the semantic fields

semantic field and draw a distinction between them: the distinction being that one applies to H2O whereas the other applies to XYZ.[20]

The claim is that without field differences there are no meaning differences, assuming that the field of applicability remains invariant. We understand that appearances to the contrary are mistaken just as it is an error to think that the sequence of phones [sis] when uttered by a French speaker and an English speaker, is homonymous because in the latter case it means "stop" and in the former *six*. While the phonetic point may be fairly easy to concede, the Burge examples show that this is no less true of individuating mental content. The intracontextual individuation can be construed differently by individual and society, but only because both the individual and society articulate content via a shared repertoire of contrasts.

Conclusion

Having argued that semantic fields provide an intermediate position between semantic atomism and holism and between narrow and wide content, I want briefly to indicate how such a position, which bears on the organization of the lexicon, and the organization of our concepts may be helpful for several of the discussions engendered by the problem of individuating content. These are puzzles concerning, first, the explanation of human behavior; second, the possibility that we are not privy to the content of our own minds; and third, the relation between meaning, the mental, and the very picture of the mind itself.

With respect to the causal efficacy of mental contents, we can explain an individual's actions on the basis of how s/he draws contrasts and of the concepts thereby generated. The actions of an individual will sometimes look irrational because explanations by a third party will be based on the social criterion, the contrasts made by the society at large as these are encoded in the semantic fields

---

are applied—different fields are applied to the same domain. If the contrasts available to us are more or less the same and the physical world we experience is in important respects the same, then the choice of how to apply the contrasts remains open, and that is on the whole a social decision.

We ought distinguish two relevant ways in which we may individuate content. One is with respect to the criterion of identity needed to pick out a concept (and the content into which the concept enters) from other concepts within a semantic field. The other is with respect to the criteria of identity across contexts. To meet the criteria of cross-context identity, we need to keep both the domain (which is often, but not always the physical world) and the relevant contrasts invariant.

[20]Fodor makes a similar point when he notes that the relevant taxonomy of causal powers in the Twin Earth example must be generated by considering each actor in her respective context. Cross-context comparison is analogous to trying to compare the causal power of two sets of biceps where one person is asked to lift a chair that is not nailed to the floor and the other is asked to lift a chair that is nailed to the floor (1988, p. 35f. Also see Fodor, 1991, in which he elaborates on the question of cross-context identity of causal powers). Just as one cannot compare causal powers of biceps or mental contents across contexts, so one cannot compare meanings across contexts. What is being assessed is so assessed comparatively. Hence the context of comparison must remain stable. This, however, is precisely Saussure's point with respect to value. The meanings of words are assessed with respect to one another, and so they too must be considered within a relatively stable context.

of the language. Furthermore, inconsistent behavior may result from the maintenance of conflicting beliefs. Witness the puzzlement of Mary in our previous example. But within semantic field theory, narrow and wide content come together in the fields shared by individuals within the society, and with respect to the physical and cultural environment in which they function. It is surely possible that two individuals whose understanding of some concepts are at odds can coordinate their behaviors in a relatively coherent fashion. But it is difficult to imagine two individuals with very different semantic fields being able to coordinate their behaviors. Our concepts really could be as different as we like, as long as they issue forth in actions and behaviors that make the same relative distinctions. These distinctions, again as they pertain locally and not globally within a network of concepts, are made public in semantic fields. The individuation of content must depend on such distinctions and not on whatever else may be "in the head."

We can now address the puzzle concerning self-knowledge that the doppelganger thought experiments incur. For if mental contents are to be the contents of our minds, then surely we should be able to individuate those contents individualistically—after all, these are *our* contents. What we can say is that I should be able to articulate the contrasts and distinctions I was after when I identified my ailment as arthritis. And about this I could not be wrong, on familiar Cartesian grounds (see Burge, 1988). But I could certainly be wrong in thinking that what I thought I had was arthritis, because arthritis is differently individuated in its semantic field.

Davidson (1987) has argued that the real lesson to be learned from the Putnam and Burge examples is that the picture of mind as holding contents that are open to our inspection, contents that we "behold" or "grasp" as objects before the mind, is in error. He writes: "the source of the trouble is the dogma that to have a thought is to have an object before the mind." The problem as Davidson diagnoses it is that the object must be partly identified with respect to external relations, to the environment, or to the social identification, and that the mind may be ignorant of that external relation. If the object is connected to the world in a relevant way, then it cannot be fully "before the mind." "Yet" he concludes, "unless a *semantic* object can be before the mind *in its semantic aspect,* thought, conceived in terms of such objects, cannot escape the fate of sense data" (p. 455). The remedy is to give up the idea of the subjective and in its stead to recognize that mental states are identified in part by their natural history.

This is not the place to argue for or against Davidson's positive position, but whatever stance one takes to his prescriptions, one can endorse his diagnosis. The approach to a resolution in terms of a causal theory is a diachronic one. But there is a synchronic approach as well. To think of both the lexicon and content itself as organized into semantic fields eschews the idea of an object of thought to be grasped or held before the mind no less than does a causal theory. What is in the mind is not an object, but a capacity: a repertoire of contrasts and affinities by which to articulate experience and thought. We need not reify concepts or contents. The distinctions are drawn on what presents itself to the thinking organism, generally as mediated by the social distinctions, formations, and constructions.[21] They are inherently semantic and they are for the most part social.

The Saussurian insight that language is used not only to refer but to differentiate—that without differentiations, reference would grope blindly—prompts us to see that the problem of individuation to which Burge draws attention is a problem of understanding the importance of value for both reference and intentionality.

REFERENCES

Bilgrami, A. (1987). An externalist account of psychological content. *Philosophical Topics, 15,* 191–226.

Boghossian, P. (1989). The rule-following considerations. *Mind, 98,* 507–549.

Burge, T. (1979). Individualism and the mental. *Midwest Studies, 4,* 73–121.

Burge, T. (1982a). Other bodies. In A. Andrew (Ed.), *Thought and object* (pp. 97–120). Oxford: Clarendon Press.

Burge, T. (1982b). Two thought experiments reviewed. *Notre Dame Journal of Formal Logic, 23,* 284–293.

Burge, T. (1986a). Individualism and psychology. *The Philosophical Review, 95,* 3–47.

Burge, T. (1986b). Cartesian error and the objectivity of perception. In P. Pettit & J. McDowell (Eds.), *Subject, thought, and context* (pp. 117–136). Oxford: Clarendon Press.

Burge, T. (1986c). Intellectual norms and the foundation of mind. *Journal of Philosophy, 83,* 697–720.

Burge, T. (1988). Individualism and self-knowledge. *Journal of Philosophy, 85,* 649–65.

Clark, E. (1987). The principle of contrast: A constraint on language acquisition. In B. MacWhinney (Ed.), *Mechanisms of language acquisition.* Hillsdale, NJ: Lawrence Erlbaum Associates.

Cohen, J. L. (1981). Chess as a model of language. *Philosophia, 11,* 51–87.

Davidson, D. (1987). Presidential address. *Proceedings and addresses of the American Philosophical Association, 60,* 441–458.

Davidson, D. (1988, December). *Symposium: Individuation and Self-knowledge.* American Philosophical Association, Eastern division, 85th Annual Meeting.

Fodor, J. A. (1988). *Psychosemantics: The problem of meaning in the philosophy of mind.* Cambridge: MIT Press.

Fodor, J. A. (1991). A modal argument for narrow content. *Journal of Philosophy, 88,* 5–26.

Goldman, A. (1988/89). Psychology and philosophical analysis. *The Aristotelian Society, Proceedings, 89,* 195–209.

Grandy, R. (1988). In defense of semantic fields. In E. LePore (Ed.), *New directions in semantics* (pp. 261–280). London: Academic Press.

---

[21]Let me just suggest here, harkening back to the opening discussion of Saussure and the social nature of value, that even how we determine what is causally responsible for our mental content must involve social considerations. I take it that Davidson himself is sympathetic to such a view from the brief comments he made at the "Symposium: Individuation and Self-Knowledge" at the American Philosophical Association, Eastern division, 85th Annual Meeting, December 1988, where he suggested that meaning and reference involve a triangulation between self, society, and the world (Also see Davidson, 1988.)

Kittay, E. F. (1987). *Metaphor: Its cognitive force and linguistic structure.* Oxford: Oxford University Press.

Kittay, E. F., & Lehrer, A. (1981). Semantic fields and the structure of metaphor. *Studies in Language, 5,* 31–63.

Lehrer, A., & Lehrer, K. (1982). Antonymy. *Linguistics and Philosophy, 5,* 483–501.

Putnam, H. (1970). Is semantics possible? In H. E. Kiefer & M. K. Munitz (Eds.), *Language, belief, and metaphysics* (pp. 50–63). Albany: State University of New York Press. Reprinted in H. Putnam (1975). *Mind, language and reality* (pp. 139–52). Cambridge & New York: Cambridge University Press.

Putnam, H. (1975). The meaning of "meaning." In K. Gunderson (Ed.), *Language, mind, and knowledge, Minnesota Studies in the Philosophy of Science, 7,* 131–93. Minneapolis: University of Minnesota Press. Reprinted in H. Putnam, *Mind, language and reality* (pp. 215–71). Cambridge and New York: Cambridge University Press.

Ross, J. F. (1981). *Portraying analogy.* Cambridge: Cambridge University Press.

Rothbart, D. (1984). The semantics of metaphor and the structure of science. *Philosophy of Science, 51,* 595–615.

Saussure, F. de. (1968). *Course in general linguistics* (Eds.), C. Bally et al. (Trans.) W. Baskin. New York: Philosophical Library. (Originally published in 1919).

Tennant, N. (1987a). *Anti-realism and logic.* Oxford: Oxford University Press.

Tennant, N. (1987b). Holism, molecularity, and truth. In B. Taylor (Ed.), *Michael Dummett— Contributions to philosophy. Nijhoff International Series* (Vol. 25, pp. 31–58). Nijhoff: The Hague.

Tversky, A. (1977). Features of similarity. *Psychological Review, 84,* 327–52.

10 The Concept of a Semantic Relation

Roger Chaffin
Trenton State College

Semantic relations have long played an important role as explanatory constructs in psychological and linguistic theories. This use of relations as theoretical primitives has obscured the fact that semantic relations are themselves concepts with interesting properties that are in need of explanation. The representation of semantic relations in memory must be explained, in the same way as the representation of other concepts, in terms of more basic meaning elements that are common to a variety of different concepts (Lyons, 1977, p. 317). In this chapter I examine two types of evidence for these claims. First, semantic relations are like other concepts in exhibiting a typicality gradient, in permitting similarity comparisons, in being lexicalized, and in being instantiated by context. Second, logical properties of particular semantic relations derive from the relation elements of which they are composed. Whereas the logical properties of semantic relations seem to set relations apart from other concepts, I argue that the complex patterns of transitivity found among inclusion relations can only be explained in terms of the more basic relational elements of which the relations are composed.

The ability to perceive relations between ideas has long been taken to reflect fundamental mechanisms of the mind. Aristotle explained the sequence of ideas in recall in terms of contiguity, similarity, and contrast (Aristotle, 1928–1952, chap. 2, 451b.19). Locke used relations between ideas to account for the formation of complex from simple ideas and for the ability to reason (Rapaport, 1974, pp. 68–85). The early experimental psychologists such as Wundt, Kraeplin, and Jung used relations between ideas as their basic explanatory construct and proposed a variety of taxonomies of relations (Warren, 1921). More recently, cognitive psychologists have used relations to explain such phenomena as the clustering of words in free recall (Bousfield, 1953), the representation of concepts in memory (Smith & Medin, 1981), and the role of inference in comprehension (Schank & Abelson, 1977). Semantic field theory belongs to the same tradition of using relations as explanatory constructs. Relations between words provide a starting point of inquiry and explanation (Lehrer, 1974, p. 22). Lyons (1977) stated: A semantic field is a set of "lexemes and other units that are semantically related . . . ; and a field whose members are lexemes is a lexical field" (p. 268).

Current theories represent concepts in terms of properties, prototypes, attributes, or networks. All these approaches rely on semantic fields in that they characterize meaning in terms of relations between concepts (Fillenbaum & Rapoport, 1971; Lehrer, 1974; Lyons, 1977). Feature models (e.g., Katz & Fodor, 1963; Osgood, 1970) assume that word meanings are represented by a limited number of conditions or features that are collectively necessary and sufficient to distinguish related words and to pick out the appropriate reference (Jackendoff, 1985, p. 112). Prototype theories (e.g., Rosch, 1978) focus on the graded structure of taxonomic categories but resort to features or attributes when faced with the need to describe intensional meanings in order to account for conceptual combination (Osherson & Smith, 1982). Attribute theories are similar to feature theories except that they make use of attributes that are features shorn of the claim that they are necessary or sufficient (Hampton, 1987; Tversky & Hemenway, 1984). Network and schema theories represent each concept as a node linked to other concepts by pointers that are labelled with the names of standard relations (e.g., ISA, HASA; Anderson, 1983; Minsky, 1975; Norman, Rumelhart, & the LNR Group, 1975; Rumelhart & Ortony, 1977; Schank & Abelson, 1977). In network models each node thus plays a double role as a concept defined by the network and as an attribute defining other concepts.

In all these approaches the key to representing meaning is the idea of a semantic field in which meaning arises from relationships between concepts. Semantic relations function, more or less explicitly, as theoretical primitives. Relations between concepts or between words are then used to explain other phenomena, such as word meaning, recall, comprehension, or inference, but are not themselves further explained. Semantic relations function as the unanalyzed and undefined primitive terms of these theories (Chaffin & Herrmann, 1987, 1988a; Johnson-Laird, Herrmann, & Chaffin, 1984).

The widespread use of relations to explain other phenomena has often led theorists to treat semantic relations as if they were thoroughly understood. This is not the case. There is no consensus on many basic questions about the nature of semantic relations. How many different semantic relations are there? How should we classify the numerous instances that do not fit into the handful of relations that appear in most discussions (i.e., antonymy, synonymy, hyponymy, and meronymy)? What is the psychological and linguistic status of relations? A measure of the lack of consensus on these questions is the number of new terms that Cruse (1986) found it necessary to coin in the most thorough account of lexical relations to date.

When we look closely at semantic relations, they lose the aura with which their long use as explanatory terms has imbued them and look much like other concepts. Semantic relations have many characteristics in common with other concepts. I consider four of them. First, semantic relations exhibit a typicality gradient (Herrmann, Chaffin, Conti, Peters, & Robbins, 1979; Rosch, 1978). Second, like other concepts, relations can be compared with one another; some relations are more similar to each other than others (Chaffin & Herrmann, 1984, 1988a). Third, the main semantic relations have been lexicalized (e.g., "opposite of," "same as," "kind of," "part of"), and, like other lexical items, these are subject to selection restrictions; they can be used appropriately in some contexts and not others (Katz, 1972; Winston, Chaffin, & Herrmann, 1987). Fourth, like other general terms (e.g., "container"), relation terms can be used to refer to a variety of different kinds of cases and are instantiated or elaborated by their context (Anderson & Ortony, 1977; Chaffin, Herrmann, & Winston, 1988).

In the following section I examine these four characteristics of semantic relations in order to see to what extent they are similar for semantic relations and other kinds of concepts. A theory of relation elements is then described that accounts for the four characteristics. In the second half of the chapter we see how relation elements account for the patterns of transitivity and intransitivity within and between inclusion relations. Because it has been the focus of my own work, the relation of meronymy is the focus of the discussion throughout most of the chapter. The analysis is, however, intended to apply to other relations and I use a variety of relations as examples whenever possible.

THE SIMILARITY OF RELATIONS AND OTHER CONCEPTS

Typicality Gradient

Exemplars of a category vary in the degree to which they are typical of the concept (Rosch, 1978). For example, a robin is a very typical bird, a crow is less typical, and an ostrich is not very bird-like at all. The gradient continues for nonmembers of the category; a *bat* is rather like a *bird* but is not a bird, whereas a *rock* is nothing like a *bird*. As Barsalou (1987) and Medin (1989) point out, this kind of graded structure has been found for every kind of category that has been studied: taxonomic categories (Rosch, 1978), formal categories (Armstrong, Gleitman, & Gleitman (1983), goal-derived categories (Barsalou, 1991), ad hoc categories (Barsalou, 1983), and linguistic categories (Lakoff, 1987), and for every kind of domain: artistic style (Hartley & Homa, 1981), chess (Goldin, 1978), emotion (Fehr & Russell, 1984), faces (Langlois & Roggman, 1990), medical diagnoses (Arkes & Harkness, 1980), and personality traits (Cantor & Mischel, 1977).

Semantic relations exhibit the same kind of graded structure. *Antonyms* is a category, just as *birds* is. Just as some birds are more typical birds than others, so some antonyms are more typical antonyms than others, some synonyms are more typical synonyms, and some parts are better examples of meronymy than others. As Table 10.1 illustrates, examples of standard semantic relations are graded in terms of how typical they are of the relation. *Wet:dry* is a good example of antonymy, *stable:frantic* is less antonym-like. *Popular:shy* are rather like antonyms but are not, whereas *sandy:smart* do not look like antonyms at all. Synonyms and meronyms also vary in how good they are as examples of their respective relationships, and nonexamples vary in their similarity to each relationship. This property has been called relation similarity (Hermann et al., 1979; Chaffin & Herrmann, 1987). Hyponymy is also included in Table 10.1. Typical members of a category are apparently higher in relation similarity than less typical members.

Typicality has been measured directly by asking subjects, usually college students, to rate how good an example a concept is of a category (e.g., "How good an example is an apple of a fruit?"). The same characteristic can be measured for semantic relations in a similar fashion by asking subjects to rate how good an example a word pair is of a target relation (e.g., "How good an example is *wheel:car* of the part–whole relation?"; Chaffin & Herrmann, 1988b, or "How good an example is *hot:cold* of antonymy?"; Herrmann, Chaffin, Daniel, & Wool, 1986). In this case the relation, meronymy or antonymy, is the category and the word pair is the exemplar whose typicality is being judged. It is this characteristic of typicality with respect to a particular relation that is called *relation similarity* (Herrmann et al., 1979).

Typical members of a category are those that are most similar to the prototype of the category. For example, the prototypical bird has feathers and wings, is about 9 inches long, and hops around on lawns. Robins have all these attributes and so are similar to the prototypical bird and are judged to be high in typicality. Likewise, word pairs that are highest in relation similarity are those that are most similar to the prototype for the relationship. The prototypical part is attached to

TABLE 10.1
Typicality Gradient of Exemplars of Relational Concepts

Relations	Examples Typicality		Nonexamples Relation similarity	
	High	Low	High	Low
ANTONYMY	WET:DRY	STABLE:FRANTIC	POPULAR:SHY	SANDY:SMART
SYNONYMY	CHEERY:MERRY	MODEST:SHY	SACRED:RARE	SALTY:FRANTIC
MERONYMY	BED:SPRINGS	BED:PILLOW	BED:CUSHION	BED:GASOLINE
HYPONYMY	BIRD:ROBIN	BIRD:OSTRICH	BIRD:BAT	BIRD:ROCK

its whole in a functional relationship, can be detached from the whole, and is different from other parts of the same whole. (These and other elements of meronymy are described in more detail later). Prototypical meronyms (e.g., *car:wheel*) are high in relation similarity and are thus similar to the prototype for meronymy. Likewise, high typicality antonyms (e.g., *hot:cold*) are similar to the prototype for antonymy (Chaffin & Herrmann, 1987, 1988a).

Tasks that are sensitive to typicality are also sensitive to relation similarity. One such task is the relation verification task. The most common version of this task involves the verification of hyponymy and is often referred to as category verification. Subjects are typically presented with pairs of words, a target category, and a stimulus word (A:B) and asked to decide whether B is member of target category A. "Yes" responses are faster to high typicality members (*furniture:chair*) than to low typicality members (*furniture:bench*), whereas "no" responses are slower when the nonmember is similar to the target category (*furniture:banister*) than when the nonmember is dissimilar (*furniture:water*).

Parallel results are found in relation verification tasks in which subjects are asked to decide whether word pairs exhibit relations other than hyponymy. "Yes" decisions are faster for good examples of the target relation than for poor examples, and "no" decisions are faster for pairs whose relation is very dissimilar to the target relation than for pairs whose relation is similar (Chaffin & Herrmann, 1988b; Herrmann et al., 1979; Herrmann & Chaffin, 1986). Table 10.2 provides

TABLE 10.2
Response Time (msecs) and Error Rate (%) Vary as a Function of Typicality in
Four Relation Identification Tasks

| Relations | Examples | | Nonexamples | |
| | Typicality | | Relation similarity | |
	High	Low	High	Low
ANTONYMY				
RT	1445	2255	1655	1257
%	2.0	18.3	22.3	0.8
SYNONYMY				
RT	1190	1390	1743	1385
%	6.0	12.0	26.2	0.4
MERONYMY				
RT	1217	1576	1623	1364
%	3.5	21.0	22.7	6.4
HYPONYMY				
RT	632	912	809	689
%	5.8	13.9	4.2	18.5

Note. Data for antonymy and for the nonexamples of synonymy are from Herrmann, Chaffin, Conti Peters, and Robbins (Expt. 3, 1979). Data for positive examples of synonymy are from Herrmann, Papperman, and Armstrong (1978). Data for meronymy are from Chaffin and Herrmann (1988). Hyponym are from Chaffin (1981).

mean response times and error rates from representative experiments in which subjects identified examples and nonexamples of the relations illustrated in Table 10.1. The data show that for each of the relations illustrated high typicality examples of the target relation are identified faster than low typicality examples, whereas nonexample pairs high in similarity to the target relation are identified slower than pairs low in relation similarity.

The effects of relation similarity shown in Table 10.2 can be explained by a Baysian-type decision model similar to those proposed to account for typicality and similarity effects for category membership (e.g., Gellatly & Gregg, 1977; McCloskey & Glucksberg, 1979). In these decision models evidence for and against a decision is accumulated until a decision can be made. Responses are faster for typical than for atypical cases because evidence of a match is accumulated more rapidly for typical examples. Nonexamples that are similar to the target are rejected more slowly because evidence of their difference accumulates more slowly.

Decision models of this kind were originally proposed to account for effects of typicality on the latency of category verification (Gellatly & Gregg, 1977; McCloskey & Glucksberg, 1979). Evidence for or against category membership was based on a comparison of the attributes of the stimulus concept with those of the prototype for the category. Evidence is more consistently positive for high typicality than for low typicality category members and more consistently negative for dissimilar than for similar nonmembers. Decisions are faster when evidence, positive or negative, is more consistent. The model explains the typicality/similarity effect for category verification: "Yes" responses are facilitated by typicality, "no" responses are impeded. The results for hyponym decisions in the last line of Table 10.2 are representative of the effect.

The effect of typicality and similarity on hyponym decisions in the last line of Table 10.2 are paralleled by effects of relation similarity on antonym, synonym, and meronym decisions in the same table. These parallels suggest another interpretation of the category verification effects, one that captures the way in which category verification is similar to other relation identification tasks. In all these tasks the subject is asked to identify or verify the presence of a particular relationship between two stimulus words (e.g., *hot:cold, robin:bird*). What the subject must compare is the relation of the two stimulus words with the target relation that the subject has been asked to identify. When told to identify antonyms, synonyms, part–whole, or category-member pairs, the subject retrieves from memory a representation of the target relation (i.e., the subject's concept of the target relation). This representation serves as a criterion against which each stimulus relation is judged. As each stimulus pair is presented, it is examined to see if the relation of the two words exemplifies the target relation. The stimulus pairs vary in how clearly they do or do not exemplify the target relation (Herrmann & Chaffin, 1986). Responses are faster for typical than for atypical examples of a relation because evidence of a match is accumulated more rapidly for typical examples. Nonexamples of the relation that are similar to the target relation are rejected more slowly because evidence of their difference accumulates more slowly.

Semantic relations thus appear to function like other categories. Just as the category *birds* has members that vary in how typical they are of the category, so the category *meronyms* varies in *relation similarity*. Relation similarity and typicality appear to have similar effects in relation verification tasks.

Similarity

As noted before, concepts have generally been viewed as composed of more basic components. One indication of this is that people are able to compare concepts. It is, for example, easy to decide that an apple and an orange are more similar than an apple and a mushroom. Comparison requires the identification of ways in which the things compared are similar and different (e.g., shape, size, color). The concepts to be compared must be decomposed into distinct attributes or dimensions (Tversky, 1977). This is recognized in the aphorism "You can't compare apples and oranges." The aphorism is true if apples and oranges are treated as unanalyzable wholes. But apples and oranges can be compared if they are decomposed into attributes or dimensions (e.g., texture and taste). Attributes of this type have been generally seen as providing the constituents out of which the concepts are built, whether the constituents are viewed as features, attributes, or nodes in a network.

Semantic relations can also be compared and ordered in terms of similarity. This suggests that relations, like other concepts, are composed of more primitive constituents. For example, the reader will have no trouble in deciding whether the relation of *car:wheel* is more similar to the relation of *tree:branch* or *lawyer:attorney*. It is this ability to evaluate the similarity of relations that is tested in multiple choice analogy items of the kind found on the SAT and GRE aptitude tests (Bejar, Chaffin, & Embretson, 1991).

Because people can easily make similarity judgments about relations, their judgments can be used to identify the elements that are used in comparing relations. In a study of meronym relations, Chaffin et al. (1988) asked subjects to sort examples of 31 different relations. Subjects were given 31 cards on each of which was five examples of a single relation. The instructions were to sort the cards into piles so that the same or very similar relationships were in the same pile. The 31 relations included 23 different kinds of meronymy, and 8 other relations, such as hyponymy, that have some similarity to the meronym relation. The relations, with an example of each, are listed in Table 10.3, which also includes data that is discussed in the following section.

A hierarchical clustering solution of the sorting data is shown in Fig. 10.1. Roman letters indicate groups of relations that were identified in an a priori taxonomy. The letters are included to aid inspection of the figure because, in

TABLE 10.3
Examples of 31 Relations with the Name Chosen Most Frequently, its Frequency, the
Number of Different Names Agreed on by Three or More Subjects (N), and Agreement.
Order and Classification of Relations Reflects Empirical Taxonomy

	Relation	Example	Name	Freq	N	Agreement
	I. PART-WHOLE					
i.	Dramatic event-section	book-chapter	section	7	5	.32
i.	Dramatic event-content	joke-punchline	feature	9	5	.33
i.	Functional loc.-component	kitchen-'fridge	component	10	4	.43
i.	Living thing-component	ivy-leaf	component	7	3	.38
i.	Complex artifact-component	telephone-dial	component	19	3	.65
i.	Simple artifact-component	cup-handle	component	12	5	.17
v.	Event-actor	rodeo-cowboy	member	14	3	.42
v.	Event-prop	banquet-food	feature	7	5	.48
v.	Object-topological part	room-corner	section	8	4	.40
ii.	Organization-unit	U.N.-Delegation	division	10	4	.39
ii.	Collection-member	forest-tree	member	13	4	.36
ii.	Group-member	fraternity-brother	member	20	1	.49
vi.	Natural area-place	desert-oasis	area	6	5	.64
vi.	Named area-place	Washington-Capitol	section	6	6	.30
v.	Named time-occasion	summer-July 4th	period	8	4	.25
iii.	Measure-unit	mile-yard	fraction	9	6	.38
iii.	Mass-natural tiny piece	salt-grain	fraction	8	3	.39
iii.	Mass-measured portion	pie-slice	portion	13	4	.48
	II. OBJECT-STUFF					
	Mass-stuff	trash-paper	element	7	4	.34
	Object-stuff	bike-aluminum	ingredient	10	3	.48
	III. HYPONYMY					
	Kind of artifact	vehicle-car	type	10	4	.45
	Kind of state	disease-polio	type	10	5	.41
	Kind of natural object	animal-horse	member	11	5	.49
	Kind of activity	sport-football	type	10	3	.37
	IV.REPRESENTATION					
	Activity-plan	meeting-agenda	component	5	4	.37
	Object-representation	wiring-diagram	feature	9	3	.42
	I. TEMPORAL INCLUSION					
iv.	Process-stage	growing up adolesence	phase	14	3	.47
iv.	Continuous activity-stage	cycling-pedaling	aspect	12	2	.49
iv.	Discrete activity-stage	shopping-buying	aspect	12	2	.54
	V. ATTRIBUTION					
	Object-attribute	tower-height	aspect	11	5	.49
	Disposition-stuff	burn-coal	phase	5	4	.39

PROXIMITY LEVEL

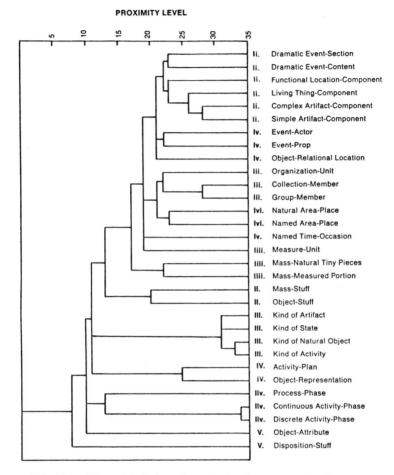

FIG. 10.1.   Hierarchical clustering solution for sorting data for 31 inclusion relations. From Chaffin et al. (1988).

many cases, the subjects' sortings agreed with the a priori taxonomy. Relations that were sorted together by more people are connected lower in the figure.

The subjects sorted similar relations together. There are seven major branches in the figure. Most of the meronym relations, part–whole (I) and stuff (II), are clustered in the right two-thirds of the figure. Hyponymy (III, *bird:robin*) is to the left of the stuff relations, followed by representation (IV, *diagram:wiring*). The activity-phase (I-iv, *cycling:pedaling*) relations, which were distinguished from other meronym relations, come next. Finally, two attribution relations are on their own on the right (V, *tower:height*).

Returning to the right side of the figure, the meronym relations were divided into six clusters. There were also three relations that were not grouped with any of the others. The right-most cluster includes components of objects (I-i, *cup:handle, telephone:dial, ivy:leaf, kitchen:refrigerator, book:chapter,* and *joke:punch line*). The next group includes features of events (I-v, *banquet:food* and *rodeo:cowboy*). The third grouping contains members of collections (I-ii, *fraternity:brother, forest:tree,* and *U.N.:delegation*); the fourth grouping contains parts of places (I-vi, *Washington:White House* and *desert:oasis*); the fifth group contains portions of masses (I-iii, *slice:pie, salt:grain*); and the sixth group included stuffs (II, *bike:aluminum*).

A set of relation elements that accounts for the distinctions subjects made between meronym and nonmeronym relations is shown in Table 10.4. The meronym and nonmeronym relations are distinguished by three elements: inclusion, connection, and similarity. The first three relations listed in the table were not included in the sorting study but have been included in the table because they help to characterize the nature of the three elements. The element of ⟨INCLUSION⟩ is present in a simple form in spatial inclusion (*bottle:milk*) and is also present in meronymy, and in an abstract form in hyponymy. The element of ⟨CONNECTION⟩ occurs in a simple form in the relation of attachment (*ear:earring*) and is also present in meronymy, and in an abstract form in hyponymy. The element of ⟨SIMILARITY⟩ is present in synonymy (*car:auto*) and is also present in hyponymy (Chaffin & Herrmann, 1987; Stasio, Herrmann, & Chaffin, 1985). These elements are sufficient to describe the distinctions between meronym and nonmeronym relations made by subjects in the sorting task.

Subjects' distinctions between different types of meronymy can be characterized by four elements of meronymy listed in Table 10.5. These elements characterize the nature of the connection between part and whole: (1) whether the part is separable from the whole, (2) whether the parts are spatial or temporal, (3) whether the part plays a specific functional role with respect to the whole, (4) whether the parts are homeomeronymous. Separable parts form a perceptual unit

TABLE 10.4
Relation Elements that Distinguish the Meronymic from the Nonmeronymic Relations
Included in the Sorting Tasks

		Elements of Inclusion Relations		
Relation	Examples	Inclusion	Connection	Similarity
Spatial inclusion+	bottle:milk	+	-	-
Connection+	ear:earring	-	+	-
Synonymy+	car:auto	-	-	+
Meronymy	car:engine	+	+	-
Class inclusion	bird:robin	+	+	+
Class membership	dog:Fido	+	+	+
Representation	agenda:meeting	-	+	-

+These relations were not included in the sorting study but are presented to clarify the nature of the elements proposed.

TABLE 10.5
Relation Elements that Distinguish the Types of Meronymy Included in the Sorting Task

			Elements of Meronymy		
Meronymic Relation	Examples	Separability	Spatio-temporal	Function	Homeo-meronmy
OBJECT:COMPONENT	CUP:HANDLE	+	+	+	-
EVENT:FEATURE	RODEO:COWBOY	+	-	+	-
COLLECTION:MEMBER	FOREST:TREE	+	+	-	-
MASS:PORTION	PIE:SLICE	+	+	-	+
PROCESS:PHASE	GROWING UP: ADOLESCENCE	-	-	-	-
AREA:PLACE	FOREST:GLADE	-	+	-	+
OBJECT:STUFF	LENS:GLASS	-	+	-	-

or gestalt so that they are seen as distinct from other parts of the same whole (e.g., *cup:handle*), whereas inseparable parts are not perceptibly distinct (e.g., *bicycle:aluminum*). Body parts are separable because they are perceptibly distinct from their wholes although they cannot be physically separated.[1] Spatial parts can be distinguished from one another by spatial location and are typically present at the same time in different locations (e.g., *car:wheel*), whereas temporal parts typically occur at different times and these differences in time are salient in distinguishing them (e.g., *growing up:adolescence*)[2]. Functional parts are restricted by their function to a particular location and configuration (e.g., *car:wheel*), whereas nonfunctional parts are less restricted (e.g., *forest:tree*). Homeomeronymous parts are the same kind of thing as the whole (e.g., *pie:slice*), whereas nonhomeomeronymous parts are different kinds of things than their wholes (e.g., *lens:glass*).

The different types of meronymy are organized in a way that reflects the description of their similarities and differences provided by the relation elements in Table 10.5. First, the stuff relations (II, *bicycle:aluminum*) were clearly separated from the other part–whole relations. Stuff relations have different values from the prototypical object:component relation on three of the four elements of meronymy. The difference is captured primarily by the relation element of separability; stuffs are not perceptibly distinct from each other in the way that, for example, components are. Second, the remaining part–whole relations were divided into five main clusters. The differences between these groups of relations can be described in terms of the elements ⟨HOMEOMERONYMY⟩ and ⟨FUNCTION⟩.

---

[1]An earlier account of this element (Chaffin et al., 1988) described separable parts as being separable "in principle" from the whole.

[2]The spatial/temporal feature differs from the "contemporaneous" element used by Chaffin et al. (1988) and has a different value for process:phase relations.

The role of homeomeronymy and function can be seen in the clustering of the large group of part–whole relations on the right of Fig. 10.1. The highest level distinction was between the mass-portion relations (I-iii, *salt:grain*) for which parts are homeomeronymous (i.e., each part is the same kind of thing as the whole), and the other part–whole relations for which the parts are non-homeomeronymous (i.e., each part is a different kind of thing than the whole, like *tree:leaf*). The nonhomeomeronymous relations were in turn divided on the basis of whether the location of the parts is determined by their function or not. For members of groups and parts of areas the location of the parts is not constrained by function (e.g., to be part of a forest a *tree* does not have to be in any particular location in the *forest*). For components of objects and features of events, location is important (e.g., the *handle* of a *cup* must be in the right place to serve its function).

One distinction that is not adequately accounted for by the relation elements is the wide separation of the activity-phase relations (I-iv, *cycling:pedaling*) from the other types of meronymy. This distinction was not made in the a priori taxonomy but is in agreement with the view of Fellbaum and Miller (1990), who call this relation between verbs "proper inclusion" and distinguish it from meronymy for nouns.

To provide a measure of how well the elements in Tables 10.4 and 10.5 describe the similarities perceived by the subjects in the sorting task, the elements were used to predict proximity in the clustering solution. For each element a 10×10 similarity matrix was constructed for the 10 types of relations in the a priori taxonomy; "1" indicated that the two relation had the same value on the element, "0" indicated different values. A similarity matrix was also constructed from the clustering solution using the proximity with which each pair of relation types was connected in the clustering solution. The location of the 10 relation types was identified by the main cluster for a relation in Fig. 10.1; isolated relations were ignored. Multiple regression analysis was used to evaluate the degree to which the elements succeeded in predicting proximity. The elements accounted for over 80% of the variance in the clustering solution, multiple $R =$ .91, $p < .0001$[3] indicating that the elements provide a good account of the similarities and differences between relations that were most salient to the subjects.

The results of the regression analysis are summarized in Table 10.6. The standardized regression coefficients indicate the weight given to each element. The tolerances indicate that the elements were adequately independent of one another. The element that accounted for the most variability was 〈SEPARABILITY〉. It appears that a very salient characteristic of meronymy for the subjects was whether or not the part formed a gestalt that was perceptibly separable

---

[3]Chaffin et al. (1988) reported a more conservative analysis of this data that yielded a lower value.

TABLE 10.6
Standardized Regression Coefficients for Prediction of Proximity in Clustering Solution from
Similarity in Terms of Relation Elements, with Tolerances, t and p Values

Relation Elements	Regression Coefficient (Beta)	Tolerance	t	p
Separability	.61	.58	7.84	.0001
Space/time	.29	.45	3.32	.002
Function	.23	.48	2.74	.009
Homeomeronymy	.16	.54	2.05	.05
Similarity	-.17	.50	2.02	.05
Function	-.20	.36	2.02	.05

$p < .001.$
$p < .01.$
$p < .05.$

from other parts. ⟨SPATIO/TEMPORAL⟩ was second in importance, followed by ⟨FUNCTION⟩ and ⟨HOMEOMERONYMY⟩. ⟨INCLUSION⟩ and ⟨SIMILARITY⟩ received negative weights. This may be because the majority of the relations were meronyms; ⟨INCLUSION⟩ and ⟨SIMILARITY⟩ do not distinguish between different types of meronymy but do distinguish meronymy from the small number of nonmeronym relations that were included in the sorting task.

In summary, the coherence of the sorting solution demonstrates that the subjects were able to make subtle judgments about the similarity of relations. To make these judgments it was necessary for them to identify elements that some relations had in common and others did not. The elements that the subjects used can be identified by a careful inspection of the sorting solution.

Relation comparison need not be the effortful process required by a large sorting task such as the one just described. Comparisons that do not involve fine discriminations can be made rapidly and effortlessly. For example, the reader probably will have no trouble in deciding that the relations of *arsenal:weapon* and *library:book* are more similar to each other than to *lawyer:attorney*. Relation identification typically takes between 1 and 2 seconds and, as described in the previous section, is affected by relation similarity. Relation comparison appears to occur rapidly and effortlessly as part of the process of identifying a relation.

Lexicalization

Unlike other concepts, most semantic relations are not lexicalized by terms that allow us to talk *about* them. Metalinguistic terms like *hyponymy* and *meronymy* are not part of the vocabulary of most people, even those with a higher education. The terms *antonym* and *synonym* are exceptions. These relation names are taught in school in the United States, although they are probably not part of the active vocabulary of many people. The important lexical items for semantic relations are not, however, these low frequency, metalinguistic expressions. For most people it is more important to be able to express the fact that "The wheel is part of the car" than to express the metalinguistic fact that "*Car:wheel* are meronyms." There are high-frequency relational expression for the standard semantic relations. Hyponymy can be expressed as "X is a kind of Y," meronymy by "X is part of Y," antonymy by "X is the opposite of Y," and synonymy by "X is the same as Y."

Relation terms are subject to the same kind of selection restrictions as other words. For example, when part terms are used inappropriately, bizarre relationships are suggested (Winston et al., 1987). One can say, "Simpson is a member of the Linguistics Department." "The carburetor is a component of the engine." But not, "*Simpson is a component of the Linguistics Department." "*The carburetor is a member of the engine." This kind of selection restriction can be accounted for in terms of the semantic features of the lexical items. For example, Osgood (1970) was able to account for the way in which interpersonal verbs and adverbs could combine by using 10 bipolar features to represent the meanings of the words. Combinations were anomalous when the two words had opposite values on the same feature. Thus *help selfishly* is odd because the two words have opposed codings on an ASSOCIATIVE/DISSOCIATIVE feature that represents the intent to form a positive or negative affective relation. A similar kind of account can be given of the oddness of the two aforementioned sentences. They are odd because the values of *component* and *member* on the ⟨FUNCTION⟩ element do not match the values of this element for the relations referred to. The relation of *carburetor:engine* is subject to functional constraints that are not characteristic of *members,* and the relation of *Simpson:Linguistics Department* is not subject to the constraints on function and location that are characteristic of *components.*

A relation term like *part of* expresses a wide range of relations. Are these more specific relations lexicalized? In the case of meronymy it seems that many of them are. Roget's Thesaurus (1962) lists approximately 400 terms meaning "part of." Many of these seem to be names for parts of very particular kinds of objects rather than names for general kinds of meronymic relations (e.g., "shard"). But there are about 40 terms that appear to have a fairly wide range of application. For example, parts of complex artifacts are *components;* groups have *members;* masses are divided into *portions;* activities and processes have *phases;* events have *features;* places can be divided into *areas.*

Do the kinds of meronymy that have been lexicalized correspond to the clusters of meronymic relations identified by the subjects in the sorting task described earlier? There was a close correspondence. After completing the sorting task, subjects were asked to express the relation illustrated on each card by completing a sentence of the form, "A is _____ of B" where A and B were the two words of each example pair on a card. Subjects were instructed not to use the word *part.* A list of 22 relation terms (e.g., *component, feature, aspect, phase*) was provided as examples, but subjects were encouraged to also generate their own terms.

The results of the naming task are summarized in Table 10.3, which lists for each relation the most frequent name, the frequency of this name, the number of different names given by three or more subjects, and a measure of agreement about the relation for which "1" represents complete agreement and "0" complete disagreement between subjects. There was moderate agreement on the names of the different relations (the mean was .42). The agreement was reflected in the small number of terms used frequently for each relation; a mean of 3.9 terms were given for each relation by three or more subjects. The most frequently given name for each relation accounted for 30% of all responses. On this measure, agreement was comparable to that for categories in the Battig and Montague (1969) category norms in which, for example, the most frequent response accounted for 37% of all responses for the category "bird" and 20% for the category "musical instruments." Agreement was not, however, the result of the same few relation terms being selected for all relations; 15 different relation terms occurred as the most frequent response to the 31 relations. Some of the names that subjects chose most frequently were used before in naming the relations (e.g., the *collection:member* relation).

Relations clustered together in the sorting task tended to be named in the same way. For example, the most frequent name for integral object–component relations was *component;* for area–place relations it was *section;* for hyponymy it was *type.* The degree of agreement with the empirical taxonomy was quantified by correlating the frequencies of production of relation terms for relations that were clustered together in the empirical taxonomy. (The clusters used for this analysis are indicated in Table 10.3 by the Roman numerals; i.e., integral objects [I-i], events [I-v], collections [I-ii], areas [I-vi], masses [I-iii], stuffs [II], hyponymy [III], representation [IV], and activities [I-iv].) The mean correlation of relations in the same cluster was $r = .63$. In contrast, the mean correlation between relations in adjacent clusters was lower, $r = .11$. Relations within a cluster were given the same name more often than relations in different clusters.

The sorting task identified different concepts of meronymy. The naming task identified names for those concepts. The correspondence of relational concepts and relation expressions demonstrates that the relation expressions are lexicalizations of relational concepts. The use of relation expressions is subject to selection restrictions that have to be accounted for by decomposing the meaning of the expression. The relation elements listed in Table 10.5 provide a way of describing the meaning of meronymic expressions that explains selection restrictions. Relation expressions are used appropriately when the values of their elements match those of the relations being characterized.

Although relation terms were used most frequently of similar kinds of relations, most terms were also used infrequently of a wide variety of different kinds of relations. For example, *portion* was used of measured parts of masses (*pie:slice*), times (*week:day*), and objects (*telephone:dial*) The mean number of different relations to which each relation term was applied was 12.0 (sd = 8.3). In the absence of a context, the relation of a particular word pair can usually be interpreted in a variety of ways (Chaffin & Herrmann, 1988a; Winston et al., 1987). For example, a refrigerator might be viewed as a *component* of a kitchen if one focuses on its contribution to the function of the room, as a *section* if one focuses on the available floor space, or as a *feature* if the refrigerator is notable in some way. Context may emphasize some elements of a relationship over others and different contexts may emphasize different elements. The role of context is discussed in more detail in the following section.

Instantiation

General terms are normally understood in terms of specific examples (Barsalou, 1982; Greenspan, 1986). For example, in a study by Anderson and Ortony (1977) subjects read a list of sentences that included one of the following: "The container held the apples." "The container held the cola." Later the subjects were given a cued recall test. The cue *basket* produced better recall for people who had seen the sentence about *apples,* whereas the cue *bottle* produced better recall for those who had seen the sentence about *cola.* The authors concluded that when the sentences were read, *container* was understood as a basket or bottle, depending on what it was holding. It was this more detailed instantiation that was stored in memory. In understanding the sentence, the subjects went beyond the information given to draw conclusions about the specific type of container used. This is an example of the "semantic contagion" discussed by Ross (this volume).

General terms for semantic relations are also subject to instantiation. For example, we have seen that *part of* is a general term that is superordinate to a relatively large number of more specific terms for meronymic relations. This suggests that *part of* might be understood differently in: "The wheels are part of the car." "The tuba is part of the brass section." In the first case *part of* would be understood as meaning *components of* and in the second case as meaning something like *member of.* The suggestion is that in understanding the meaning of *part of* people go beyond the information given to draw conclusions about the precise kind of meronymic relation involved.

Evidence for the instantiation of "part of" in a relation identification task comes from a study by Chaffin et al. (1988, Expt. 2). Subjects were given a relation identification task in which they were shown pairs of words, one pair at a time, and asked to decide for each pair whether "A is part of B." Meronym, hyponym, and synonym pairs were randomly interspersed. Here I focus on the results for meronyms. The meronym pairs were presented in blocks of five so that all the examples of meronymy in a block were of one type. Each block contained a different kind of meronymy. The nonmeronyms in each block were selected from the same semantic domain as the meronyms (e.g., *orches-*

tra:conductor was matched with the nonmeronym pairs *singer:vocalist* and *actor:comedian*). So that the subject would not know when a new block would begin, blocks were surrounded by filler items, and there was an opportunity to rest in the middle of each block. Each switch to a different kind of meronymic relation was unexpected.

In each block the new kind of meronymy was alternately close to and distant from the kind of meronymy in the previous block in the taxonomy of meronym relations shown in Fig. 10.1. Thus, for some subjects the block of group:member pairs (e.g., *brother:fraternity, cow:herd, don:Mafia, senator:legislature, bee: swarm*) was followed by a close jump to a block of collection:member pairs (e.g., *tree:forest, ship:fleet, book:library, mob:person, letter:alphabet*). This in turn was followed by a distant jump to, e.g., a block of artifact:component pairs (e.g., *handle:cup, eraser:pencil, prong:fork, blade:knife, flap:envelope*). The particular types of meronymy used and a sample order of presentation are given in Table 10.7.

The question was whether the jump to a new type of meronymy would slow down the decisions. If the subjects did only what they were told and simply decided if "A is part of B," they would use exactly the same criteria for identifying meronymy throughout the experiment. In this case, jumping from one kind of meronymy to another would have no effect. If, on the other hand, the subjects did more than was asked of them and identified not just the generic meronym relation but specific kinds of meronymy, jumping from one kind of meronymy to

TABLE 10.7
Kinds of Meronymy and a Sample Order of Presentation Showing One Sequence of Distant and Close Jumps in Chaffin et al. (1988)

1.	Actor:event	COWBOY:RODEO	distant
2.	Prop:event	BANQUET:FOOD	close
3.	Mass:natural tiny piece	SALT:GRAIN	distant
4.	Mass:measured portion	PIE:SLICE	close
5.	Component:location	REFRIGERATOR:KITCHEN	distant
6.	Component:living thing	LEAF:IVY	close
7.	Stuff:object	ALUMINUM:BIKE	distant
8.	Stuff:mass	PAPER:TRASH	close
9.	Member:group	BROTHER:FRATERNITY	distant
10.	Member:collection	TREE:FOREST	close
11.	Component:simple artifact	HANDLE:CUP	distant
12.	Component:complex artifact	DIAL:TELEPHONE	close
13.	Place:named area	WHITE-HOUSE:WASHINGTON	distant
14.	Place:natural area	OASIS:DESERT	close
15.	Content:dramatic event	PUNCHLINE:JOKE	distant
16.	Section:dramatic event	CHAPTER:BOOK	close

Note. Blocks were presented in the order listed. Block 1 was treated as a distant-jump block because it was preceded by practice items that made use of a different type of meronymy.

another would slow them down. At the beginning of a new block after a distant jump, the kind of meronymy the subjects were looking for would not exactly match what they saw. The poorer the match, the slower the response. Responses should, therefore, be slower after a distant jump.

Whether responses are slowed by both close jumps and distant jumps depends on how detailed the subjects' expectations are. If subjects have very detailed expectations about the kind of relation, then even a close jump to a slightly different relation will slow responding. If expectations are less detailed, then close jumps will make no difference. From the subjects' point of view it would be as though the same relation were presented for two complete blocks. In either case, distant jumps should produce a larger slow down than close jumps.

Table 10.8 shows the response times and error rates for the beginning and end of distant and close jump blocks. The table can be read from left to right as a sequence, starting at the beginning of a block after a distant jump, and continuing through to the end of the close jump block that followed each distant jump block. A distant jump to a different kind of meronymy resulted in slow responses and a high error rate at the beginning of the block. By the end of the block, after seeing three examples of the new kind of meronymy, responses were faster by .23 secs and errors had decreased by 12%. Close jumps did not significantly affect latency or error rate; latency decreased and error rate rose slightly. Over the course of the close jump block, latency continued to decrease (by 154 msecs) and error rate to fall (by 5.0%). The jump effect was due to the change in the type of meronymy and was not a general effect of changing semantic field. Nonmeronym pairs,

TABLE 10.8
Mean Latencies for Correct Responses (in msecs) and Error Rates (%) as a Function of Distance of Jump and Position in Block for Meronym, Synonym, and Hyponym Pairs

	Jump Distance			
	Distant		Close	
	Start	End	Start	End
MERONYMS: "YES" RESPONSES				
Latency	2335	2105	2039	1885
Errors	26.89	14.69	17.50	12.50
SYNONYMS: "NO" RESPONSES				
Latency	2029	1984	1951	1871
Errors	4.37	5.63	8.41	5.31
HYPONYMS: "NO" RESPONSES				
Latency	2105	2131	1989	1902
Errors	6.25	7.19	4.69	5.94

which were from the same semantic domain as the meronyms in each block, showed a much smaller jump effect. Error rates were unaffected by jumps and the effect on latency was less than half that for meronyms.

These results show that instantiation of the term *part* occurred. Identification of meronym relations was less accurate and slower after a distant jump than after a close jump and was more accurate and faster at the end than at the beginning of each pair of blocks. This *jump effect* shows that subjects were sensitive to differences between the major types of meronymy. Subjects were not sensitive to the small differences represented by close jumps.

Subjects were asked only to identify cases of meronymy, not to look for specific types of meronymy. The instructions for the task were simply to answer the general question, "Is A part of B?" The jump effect shows that subjects inferred a more precise definition of the relation they were looking for from the examples they saw. The examples of meronymy that subjects saw in each pair of blocks changed and, in response, subjects modified their idea of the relation they were looking for. After close jumps the meronym pairs closely fit the definition created during the previous block, and responding was accurate and fast. After a distant jump, however, the new meronym relation did not fit the definition well, and responding was less accurate and slower until the definition was adjusted once more on the basis of the new examples.

Instantiation occurs in the comprehension of general terms that cover a variety of different types of cases (Anderson & Ortony 1977; Barsalou, 1982; Green-span, 1986, Ross, this volume). The jump effect shows that *part of* is a general term that is subject to instantiation by context (i.e., is subject to semantic contagion). "Part of" can refer to a wide variety of relations, but the mental representation that is actually used in a part–whole decision task is specific to a particular type of meronymy.

Summary

We have now examined four respects in which semantic relations are like other concepts. Semantic relations exhibit a graded structure, can be compared in terms of elements that they have in common and on which they differ, are lexicalized and are subject to selection restrictions, and are instantiated by context. These similarities suggest that relations are represented in memory by more primitive meaning elements in the same way as other concepts.

RELATION ELEMENTS

A satisfactory account of the meaning of relation terms such as *part, kind,* and *opposite* would represent the characteristics of the different relations in terms of some more basic meaning elements that have the following characteristics. First, the elements should be simpler than the relations that they make up. The metric of simplicity is not obvious, but one approach would be to use elements rooted in sensory-motor experience (Miller & Johnson-Laird, 1976). Second, the elements should be general, so that the same element would contribute to more than one relation. Third, the elements should account for the properties of semantic relations described earlier. Fourth, the logical properties of the relations should emerge in a straightforward way as a consequence of their elements. Cruse's account (this volume) of the varieties of antonymy in terms of five properties appears to fit these prescriptions. He accounts for different types of antonymy in terms of five elements that appear to be based on a simple spatial model.

Relation element theory assumes that relational concepts are represented in memory by relation elements (Chaffin & Herrmann, 1987, 1988a; Herrmann & Chaffin, 1986; Winston et al., 1987). These take the form of dyadic rules expressing conditions that must be satisfied for two concepts to be related by the element. Some elements are hierarchically organized so that the presence of one element requires the presence of another. We refer to elements at the head of a hierarchy as *independent* elements, and to subordinate elements as *dependent*. Relations may share one or more elements. The relation between two words is constructed by locating common and complimentary structures in the meanings of the two words that support relation elements. For example, the relation element of ⟨CONTRAST⟩, which is characteristic of antonymy, is supported by two concepts sharing an attribute with values that lie on opposite sides of a mid-point (Herrmann et al., 1979). When relation elements supported by two concepts have been activated, the relation of the two words is identified by comparing the elements of the two words with sets of elements representing relational concepts (e.g., *part, kind, opposite*) that are stored in memory.

Three elements that distinguish different kinds of inclusion relations have already been described and are listed in Table 10.4. These elements, ⟨INCLUSION⟩, ⟨CONNECTION⟩, and ⟨SIMILARITY⟩, are independent elements. Each can be further specified by dependent elements that characterize the various forms in which the independent element can be manifested in more detail. Dependent elements for the ⟨CONNECTION⟩ element were listed in Table 10.5. These further characterize the nature of the connection of part to whole and distinguish the different kinds of meronymy. Dependent elements for the ⟨INCLUSION⟩ element specify whether the inclusion is spatial, temporal, or set inclusion. Dependent elements for ⟨SIMILARITY⟩ that distinguish different kinds of hyponymy are described later.

The four characteristics of semantic relations described previously can be readily explained in terms of relation elements. First, relations, like other concepts, exhibit a typicality gradient because they are represented in memory by prototypes. Prototypes specify typical values for elements or attributes that distinguish similar concepts from one another. In relation identification tasks elements of the target relation for the task serve as the criterion against which stimulus relations are evaluated. Evidence for the presence of the target relation is more consistently positive for typical examples of the target relation than for less typical examples and is more consistently negative for nonexamples whose relation is dissimilar than for nonexamples whose relation is similar to the target relation. Relation similarity (typicality) ratings and the latency of relation identification decisions are both a function of consistency of the evidence.

Second, relations vary in similarity to one another because relations vary in the number of elements that they have in common. The more elements two relations have in common, the more similar they are. The ability to compare relations was used earlier to identify elements of meronymy.

Third, relation terms may be used to express the relation between two words. Relation terms are used appropriately when the elements of the relations being expressed match the elements of the relation term. Relation terms vary in the felicity with which they can be used to characterize the relation between word senses. A relation term is anomalous in a context if it possesses an element that is not present in the relation that is being described (e.g., *Simpson is a component of the Linguistics Department*).

Fourth, relation terms are instantiated by context. When a relation term (e.g., *part*) is appropriately used to characterize the relation of two things (e.g., *car:wheel*), there is a match between the elements of the relation term and the relation described. The relation described may also support elements in addition to those possessed by the relation term. In this case, elements of the relation being expressed may be added to the current representation of the relation term to produce a more specific representation. Instantiation of this kind is a normal part of the process of relation identification. The criteria used in relation identification tasks are modified by the stimuli that are presented during the task. For example, if subjects are told to look for examples of the part–whole relation, then they retrieve their concept of a part from memory to serve as the initial criterion. As the experiment proceeds, the criterion is modified to fit the kinds of relations that are actually encountered.

Relation elements thus provide an account of the four psychological characteristics of relations between concepts that were described in the first part of this chapter. I now turn to the question of whether relation elements explain the logical properties of the relations that they represent. I show that the elements of inclusion relations account for the transitivity (and cases of apparent intransitivity) of meronymy, hyponymy, and spatial inclusion.

TRANSITIVITY

The elements of meronymy provide a solution to a persistent puzzle about whether meronymy is transitive or not and also explain how meronymy interacts with other transitive inclusion relations. A number of authors have noted that some cases of meronymy appear to be transitive whereas others do not (Cruse, 1979, 1986, pp. 165–168; Lyons, 1977, pp. 311–317; Miller & Johnson-Laird, 1976, p. 240). Some syllogisms involving meronymy are valid, such as:

(1a) The carburetor is part of the engine.

(1b) The engine is part of the car.

(1c) The carburetor is part of the car.

whereas others are invalid:

(2a) Simpson's head is part of Simpson.

(2b) Simpson is part of the philosophy department.

*(2c) Simpson's head is part of the philosophy department.

The transitivity of hyponymy has been widely noted (Lyons, 1977, p. 292), for example:

(3a) Camembert is a kind of cheese.

(3b) Cheese is a kind of food.

(3c) Camembert is a kind of food.

The fact that hyponymy sometimes appears to be intransitive has received less attention. Hampton (1982) provides a variety of examples:

(4a) Car seats are a kind of chair.

(4b) Chairs are a kind of furniture.

*(4c) Car seats are a kind of furniture.

Winston et al. (1987) show that the apparent intransitivity of meronymy can be accounted for in terms of relation elements by a single principle.

> The principle of element matching: A syllogism is valid if and only if the relation in the conclusion contains those relation elements and their values that are common to both premises.

Transitivity in Meronymic Syllogisms

A corollary of the principle of element matching is that the premises of a valid merological syllogism cannot contain different types of meronymy. Different types of meronymy were distinguished in Table 10.5 by assigning to each type a different set of values on the subordinate elements that specify the nature of the ⟨CONNECTION⟩ of part and whole. Each type of meronymy consequently has different values for the subordinate elements. A mixed syllogism that contains two different types of meronymy in its premises cannot, therefore, obey the principle of element matching. The principle requires that the relation elements in the conclusion take the same values as the premises. This condition cannot be met when the premises contain two different values for the same element.

> Corollary 1. *Meronymic syllogisms are valid if and only if the same type of meronymy occurs in both premises.*

On this analysis the falsehood of (2c) is due to the use of "part of" in the premises (2a) and (2b) to refer to two different kinds of meronymic relation. The nature of the equivocation becomes clearer if a specialized part term is substituted to make it clear which kind of meronymy is expressed in each premise:

(2a') Simpson's head is a component of Simpson's body.

(2b') Simpson is a member of the philosophy department.

*(2c') Simpson's head is a component/member of the philosophy department.

"Part of" in (2a) is understood as a component–object relation and in (2b) as a member–collection relation. The ⟨FUNCTION⟩ element has different values for these two types of meronymy. The arms, like other body parts, play a specific functional role that requires them to be in a particular spatial configuration with specific physical connections to the body. The relation of faculty members to their departments, in contrast, does not have these kinds of physical, functional constraints. ⟨FUNCTION⟩ thus takes different values in the two premises (2a) and (2b). Because both values cannot be present simultaneously in the conclusion (2c), the principle of element matching cannot be satisfied and the conclusion is invalid (cf. Cruse, 1979, p. 30). Equivocation between the component–object and the member–collection senses produces an invalid conclusion.

The conclusion (2c and 2c') is not only invalid, it is also strange. The principle of element matching and its corollary predict invalidity for cases like (2), but not strangeness. The strangeness of (2c) is independent of the invalidity of the syllogism. (2c) is strange as an isolated sentence without (2a) and (2b). It is possible for a syllogism to be invalid without its conclusion being strange. Example (5) seems to be parallel to (2):

(5a) The head is part of the statue.   COMPONENT

(5b) The statue is part of the Etruscan collection   MEMBER

?(5c) The head is part of the Etruscan collection.   ?

"Part of" in (5a) is component–object, whereas in (5b) it is member–collection;

yet there is nothing strange about the conclusion expressed in (5c). The reason (5c) is not strange is that it is possible to regard the head of a statue as "part" (in the member–collection sense) of a museum's collection whether or not it is attached to a torso. The head in (5c) can be part of a museum collection, but Simpson's head in (2c) cannot be part of a department. Strangeness is a characteristic of the individual sentences (2c) and (5c) and they differ in this property.

Validity, on the other hand, is a property of the whole syllogism. Syllogism (5) is invalid for the same reason that (2) is invalid. Although the head of the statue might be regarded as a member of the collection in its own right, this does not follow logically from the premises. If we interpret (5c) as expressing the member–collection relation, then we must also assume that the head is separated from the statue and hence individuated as a separate item in the collection. Because this assumption is not warranted by any information supplied by the premises, the conclusion expressed by (5c) does not follow. Alternatively, we may interpret (5c) in the component–integral object sense by appealing to a metaphorical use of the term *component,* in which the head is understood as the centerpiece or prominent example of a collection that has been organized around it. Again, this assumption is not warranted by the premises and the conclusion does not follow.

A similar kind of equivocation on the meaning of "part" occurs in (6):

(6a) Fingers are part of the hand.

(6b) The hand is part of the arm.

?(6c) Fingers are part of the arm.

As Cruse (1979, 1986, pp. 165–168) notes, on one interpretation (6c) suggests a deformity. The equivocation here is between "part of" and "attached to." Attachment is not transitive. The fingers are attached to the hand, and the hand to the arm, but the fingers are not attached to the arm. Attachment is the dominant interpretation of the relation expressed in (6b). The interpretation given to (6b) is another example of the instantiation of a relation term by its context. As just demonstrated, relation terms take on the relation elements provided by the context (Chaffin et al., 1988). In (6b) the relation term is *part,* but the most salient relation of *hand:arm* is attachment, and this is how the sentence is understood in Cruse's reading of the syllogism in (6). The shift in meaning here is larger than the shift from "member of" to "component of" that was occurred in (2). Evidence of an even larger effect of context can, however, be found in an experiment by Herrmann and Chaffin (1986), in which subjects were asked to rate the similarity of parts of the foot. Multidimensional scaling of the ratings produced a picture of a foot, indicating that subjects had rated proximity the most salient relation among the parts, rather than similarity.

Although the most salient relation in (6b) is attachment, it is possible to understand (6b) as expressing a component relation similar to that in (6a). On this interpretation we have to think of "the arm" as referring to both the arm and the hand. On this reading (6c), fingers are part of the arm, and the argument is valid. Thus when *part* is given a consistent interpretation throughout the syllogism, the argument is valid, and the relation is transitive. When we equivocate on the meaning of *part,* allowing the context to dictate a different meaning for "part" in the two premises, the argument is invalid and it appears that meronymy is intransitive.

An apparent exception to Corollary 1 is the collection–member relation. The set membership relation, as it occurs in set theory and in mathematics, is intransitive (Iris, Litowitz, & Evens, 1988). However, the intransitivity of set membership occurs because the relation is defined with respect to a hierarchy of classes, and the requirements for membership are different at each level of the hierarchy.

When the same level of membership relation is used throughout a syllogism, the syllogism is valid and the relation transitive. Consider:

7a. Lucy is a member of the Simpson family.

7b. The (members of the) Simpson family are members of the country club.

7c. Lucy is a member of the country club.

Here the relation throughout is that of membership of individuals in larger groups and the conclusion (7c) is valid. The requirements for membership in the Simpson family involve a history of social and biological relations between an individual and other members of the family. The requirements for membership in the country club likewise involve social relations between an individual and other members of the club. The collection–member relation is transitive in cases of this kind in which the membership is between the same two levels in a hierarchy of sets in both premises and conclusion.

Membership is intransitive when membership in the two premises involves different levels of a hierarchy of sets, as in:

8a. Simpson is a member of Trenton State College.

8b. Trenton State College is a member of the Middle States Association of Colleges and Universities.

*8c. Simpson is a member of the Middle States Association of Colleges and Universities.

The conclusion (8c) is both invalid and strange. It is strange because Simpson is a person and Middle States is an association of colleges and universities. Simpson is the wrong kind of entity to be a member of Middle States. The relations in (8) are the set membership relations of set theory. Imagine a hierarchy of sets in which each level of the hierarchy is composed of sets of sets from the next level down, as illustrated in Fig. 10.2. An entity that is a member of a set at one level is, by definition, the wrong kind of thing to be a member of a set at another level.

One way to capture the intransitivity in (8) is to treat membership as intransitive and as an exception to Corollary 1 (Iris et al., 1988). This approach does not, however, explain why (7) is transitive. An alternative approach is to treat the membership relations in (8a) and (8b) as different kinds of membership. In (8a) the membership is of a person in a group of people; in (8b) the membership is of an institution in a group of institutions. Generalizing, membership at each level of the hierarchy of sets is a different kind of membership because the conditions for membership are different at each level. The latter approach is to be preferred because it permits Corollary 1 to account for both the transitivity of (7) and for the intransitivity of (8).

The different kinds of membership relation can be represented in terms of relation elements by dependent elements that are subordinate to the element of homeomeronymy, which distinguishes relations in which the parts are the same kind of thing as the whole (e.g., *salt:grain*) from relations, such as membership, in which the parts are different kinds of thing from the whole (e.g., *orchestra:oboist*). The most important distinction for membership is whether members are individuals or larger units such as groups or institutions. In principle, however, there could be an infinite hierarchy of sets as envisioned by set theory. In this hierarchy only membership relations at the same level would have exactly the same elements, and so only these would be able to obey the principle of element matching and yield transitive inferences as in (7).

Transitivity in Hyponymic Syllogisms

Meronymy is not the only inclusion relation whose transitivity has been called into question. Hampton (1982) has demonstrated that some cases of hyponymy also appear to be intransitive, for example:

(9a)   A husky in a sled team is a kind of dog.

(9b)   A dog is a kind of pet.

(9c)   ?A husky in a sled team is a kind of pet.

Level		
1. Individuals	a,b c,d e,f g,h ...	
2. Sets of individuals	(a,b) (c,d) (e,f) (g,h) ...	
3. Sets of sets of individuals	[(a,b) (c,d)] [(e,f) (g,h)] [...]	
. .	. . . .	
. .	. . . .	
N. Sets of sets of sets ...	{...[(a,b) (c,d)] [(e,f) (g,h)] [...] ...}	

FIG. 10.2.   A hierarchy of tests. Conditions for set membership differ at each level of the hierarchy.

Hampton's subjects assented to (9a) and (9b), but not to (9c). The conclusion (9c) does indeed appear to be both invalid and false.[4] Hampton proposed that category statements are viewed as true on the basis of intensional similarity, the similarity of prototypes of the two concepts, rather than on the basis of extensional overlap, the existence of counterexamples. Thus the fact that some dogs are not pets is not viewed as incompatible with the truth of (9b).

The cases of intransitivity Hampton identifies appear to provide further support for the principle of element matching. The apparent intransitivity of hyponymy can be explained in the same way as apparent cases of intransitivity for meronymy. Hyponymy is a transitive relation that appears to be intransitive if different types of hyponymy occur in the two premises of a hyponymic syllogism. This gives rise to a second corollary of the principle of element matching.

Corollary 2. *Hyponymic syllogisms are valid if and only if the same type of hyponymy occurs in both premises and conclusion.*

Wierzbicka (1984) has identified five types of categories, and thus five types of categorical inclusion relation. These are listed in Table 10.9 together with five relation elements that I derived from Wierzbicka's descriptions of category types. Hyponymy is distinguished from meronymy, and from the collection:member relation in particular, by the fact that members of categories are similar to each other. This was represented earlier in Table 10.4 by attributing the element of ⟨SIMILARITY⟩ to hyponymy. Wierzbicka's five kinds of categories differ principally in the kinds of similarity required of category members. The elements of hyponymy in Table 10.9 describe the kinds of similarity and are subordinate to the ⟨SIMILARITY⟩ element.

Members of *taxonomic supercategories* (e.g., *bird, tree, knife, hammer*) are physically similar, so that it is possible to draw a picture of a typical member (Rosch, Mervis, Gray, Johnson, & Boyes-Braem, 1976). Members of *functional categories* (e.g., *vehicle, pet, weed, weapon*) are not necessarily physically similar but share a similar function or use (Tversky & Hemenway, 1984). Members of *singular collectives* (e.g., *furniture, underwear, vermin, crockery*) also share a common function and, in addition, are typically kept or occur together in a single place at some point in their history. This is particularly apparent in cases in which the name of the common location appears as part of the category name (e.g., *underwear, kitchenware, bed linen*). Singular collectives are heterogeneous, consisting of different kinds of things. What unites them is their common function and a history that has, at some time, brought them to the same location in the exercise of that function. Members of *heterogeneous classes of*

---

[4]Hampton (1982) presented subjects with pairs of words in random order and asked them to make category-subset judgments.

TABLE 10.9
Relation Elements that Distinguish Five Types of Hyponymy

| Type of Category | Elements of Hyponymy | | | |
	Physical Similarity	Functional Similarity	Same Location	Separability
I. Taxonomic (bird, tree, ball, cup)	+	-	-	+
II. Functional (toy, weapon, pet, weed, vehicle)	-	+	-	+
III. Collective:singular (furniture, crockery, underwear)	-	+	+	+
IV. Heterogeneous stuffs (drugs, herbs, cereals)	-	+	-	-
V. Collective: plural (leftovers, groceries, contents)	-	-	+	+

"*stuffs*" (e.g., *medicines, vegetables, cosmetics, spices*) do have a common function or purpose, do not have to occur in the same place together, and are masses (e.g., aspirin, pepper) rather than discrete entities (e.g., birds). Members of *plural collectives* (e.g., *leftovers, contents, groceries, refreshments*), like singular collectives, occur in the same place together. Unlike singular collectives, they do not share a common function but simply have a common origin or history. Unlike the other types of categories, members of plural collectives do not need to be similar either physically or functionally; also the relation is not readily expressed by "kind of." The relation of plural collectives and their members may perhaps be better viewed as a type of meronymy and is not included in the discussion following.[5] Wierzbicka (1984) provides more detailed descriptions of the five types.

When the type of hyponymy is the same in both premises, the relation is transitive and the inference is valid, as in (10):

(10a) A husky in a sled team is a kind of dog.   TAXONOMIC

(10b) A dog is a kind of mammal.   TAXONOMIC

(10c) A husky in a sled team is a kind of mammal.   TAXONOMIC

---

[5]Plural collectives overlap with collections that were described previously as a type of meronymy. Hyponymy and meronymy are not clearly distinguishable in these cases. This overlapping of relations at their fuzzy boundaries is another characteristic that relations share with other concepts (Chaffin & Herrmann, 1988).

Other types of hyponymy are also transitive, for example:

(11a)	A sedan is a kind of car.	FUNCTIONAL
(11b)	A car is a kind of vehicle.	FUNCTIONAL
(11c)	A sedan is a kind of vehicle.	FUNCTIONAL

and,

(12a)	Forks are a kind of cutlery.	SING. COLLECTIVE
(12b)	Cutlery is a kind of kitchenware.	SING. COLLECTIVE
(12c)	Forks are a kind of kitchenware.	SING. COLLECTIVE

and,

(13a)	Barbiturates are a kind of tranquilizer.	HETEROG. STUFF
(13b)	Tranquilizers are a kind of drug.	HETEROG. STUFF
(13c)	Barbiturates are a kind of drug.	HETEROG. STUFF

When different types of hyponymy appear in the two premises, the inference is invalid and the relationship appears to be intransitive. All Hampton's cases of intransitivity combine categories of two different types. For example, in (9), which is repeated here, *dog* is a taxonomic category, whereas *pet* is a functional category:

(9a)	A husky in a sled team is a kind of dog.	TAXONOMIC
(9b)	A dog is a kind of pet.	FUNCTIONAL
(9c)	*A husky in a sled team is a kind of pet.	?

In (14) taxonomic is combined with collective hyponymy.

(14a)	A car seat is a kind of chair.	TAXONOMIC
(14b)	A chair is a kind of furniture.	COLLECTIVE
(14c)	*A car seat is a kind of furniture.	?

Hampton (1982) found that for examples of this kind his subjects were willing to subscribe to the truth of the two premises but did not accept the truth of the conclusion.

The conclusions in (9c) and (14c) are both invalid and strange. Corollary 2 predicts invalidity but not strangeness. It is possible for the conclusion of a hyponymic syllogism to be invalid without being strange just as it is for meronymic syllogisms, e.g., (5):

(15a) A spaniel is a kind of dog.   TAXONOMIC

(15b) A dog is a kind of pet.   FUNCTIONAL

(15c) A spaniel is a kind of pet.[6]   ?FUNCTIONAL

Here the conclusion (15c) happens to be true; spaniels are generally pets. The truth of the conclusion does not, however, follow from the premises (15a) and (15b). The case parallels that in (5) for meronymy in which the conclusion that the Etruscan head was part of the museum's collection was also true but did not follow from the premises. The conclusions in each case appear to follow simply because we know the conclusion to be true. This is demonstrated for (15) by replacing "spaniel" by "husky in a sled team." When this was done in (9) the conclusion was clearly false, and we can readily appreciate that the argument is invalid. The form of the argument in (9) and (15) is the same and so both are invalid. The conclusion of (15) happens to be true, whereas that of (9) happens to be false.

The transitivity of hyponymy provides further support for the principle of element matching. So far it seems that hyponymy and meronymy are transitive only if exactly the same kind of relation appears in the two premises and the conclusion of the syllogism. I now describe Winston et al.'s (1987) application of the principle of element matching to cases of transitivity in which different kinds of inclusion relation appear in the two premises.

Transitivity in Mixed Inclusion Relation Syllogisms

So far, the only valid syllogisms we have seen have been those in which the premises and conclusion contain exactly the same relation. Valid syllogisms can, however, be constructed with different relations in the two premises. Syllogisms in which one premise contains meronymy and the other hyponymy can yield valid conclusions. It is also possible to combine either hyponymy or meronymy with spatial inclusion in a valid syllogism. Mixed inclusion relation syllogisms can be valid because, unlike syllogisms in which different types of meronymy or hyponymy are combined, they can obey the principle of element matching. When different types of inclusion relation occur in the two premises of a syllogism, it is possible for the conclusion to contain only the relation elements and values that are common to both premises.

The relation elements of spatial inclusion, meronymy, and hyponymy are listed in Table 10.4. The three inclusion relations can be ordered on a scale of complexity, in terms of the number of independent elements they contain. Spatial inclusion is the simplest, with the single element of inclusion. Meronymy adds

---

[6]I thank Alan Cruse for providing this example.

the element of connection. Hyponymy is the most complex with the additional element of similarity.

Spatial inclusion	⟨INCLUSION⟩
Meronymy	⟨INCLUSION, CONNECTION⟩
Hyponymy	⟨INCLUSION, CONNECTION, SIMILARITY⟩

Because the conclusion of a valid syllogism may contain only those elements common to both premises, when different kinds of inclusion relations are combined in the premises of a syllogism, the conclusion must contain the simpler of the two relations.

> Corollary 3. *A syllogism containing two different kinds of inclusion relations in its premises is valid if and only if the relation in the conclusion is the simpler of the two relations.*

Consider first what happens when premises containing meronymy and hyponymy are combined:

(16a)	Wings are parts of birds.	MERONYMY
(16b)	Birds are a kind of creature.	HYPONYMY
(16c)	Wings are parts of creatures.	MERONYMY
*(16d)	Wings are a kind of creature.	HYPONYMY

When the conclusion expresses the simpler of the two inclusion relations contained in the premises, meronymy, the syllogism is valid, as in (16c). In contrast, when the conclusion expresses the more complex of the two relations, the syllogism is invalid, as in (16d).

When the premises contain meronymy and spatial inclusion, the valid conclusion again contains the simpler of the two relations, spatial inclusion, as in:

(17a)	The wheel is part of the bike.	MERONYMY
(17b)	The bike is in the garage.	SPATIAL INCL.
(17c)	The wheel is in the garage.	SPATIAL INCL.
*(17d)	The wheel is part of the garage.	MERONYMY

A conclusion containing meronymy, the more complex of the two relations, is invalid (17d). Note that the relation of the valid conclusion can come from either the major or the minor premise when the syllogism is in standard form. In (16) the valid conclusion (16c) comes from the major premise, whereas in (17) the valid conclusion (17c) comes from the minor premise.

When we mix hyponymy with spatial inclusion, the valid conclusion contains the simpler of the two relations, spatial inclusion, as in:

(18a) Fish live in water.	SPATIAL INCL.
(18b) Water is a kind of liquid.	HYPONYMY
(18c) Fish live in liquid.	SPATIAL INCL.
*(18d) Fish are a kind of liquid.	HYPONYMY

The examples of meronymy used so far have all involved the object–component relation. Other types of meronymy follow the same rule. When the premises contain hyponymy and the stuff relation, the valid conclusion must contain the simpler stuff relation, as in:

(19a) Pies are a kind of dessert.	HYPONYMY
(19b) Desserts are partly sugar.	MERONYMY
(19c) Pies are partly sugar.	MERONYMY
*(19d) Pies are a kind of sugar.	HYPONYMY

When other types of meronymy are combined with hyponymy, the result is the same; the conclusion is valid only with the meronymy relation. Similarly, when various types of meronymy are combined with spatial inclusion, the conclusion is valid only with spatial inclusion, as in:

(20a)	The bird's nest is in the tree.	SPATIAL INCL.
(20b)	The tree is part of Sherwood Forest.	MERONYMY
(20c)	The bird's nest is in Sherwood Forest.	SPATIAL INCL.
(20d)	*The bird's nest is part of Sherwood Forest.	MERONYMY

The principle of element matching accounts for the transitivity of mixed inclusion relation syllogisms and predicts which relation must appear in the valid conclusion. It also accounts for the transitivity of meronymic and hyponymic syllogisms and explains why these relations appear to be intransitive when different kinds of meronymy or hyponymy are combined.

The utility of the principle of element matching is consistent with the view that the decomposition of relations into elements is part of the normal process of understanding relations. Relation elements play an essential role in the transitivity of inclusion syllogisms. Understanding such inferences appears to be an immediate and spontaneous product of understanding the relations. The role of elements in transitivity suggests that relation elements are involved in the immediate understanding of semantic relations.

CONCLUSION

Semantic relations have been widely used in psychology as explanatory primitives and in linguistics as the starting point of field theories of meaning. Although the value of using relations as theoretical constructs is clear, their status as primitives should not lead us to the conclusion that they are unitary constructs. They are not. Everyday relations, such as hyponymy and meronymy, are composed of simpler relation elements. These elements may be the real primitives, perhaps based on perceptual and haptic experience (Miller & Johnson-Laird, 1976). Alternatively, as Barsalou (this volume) suggests, there may be no primitives, no terminal level upon which the representational system is built. Barsalou envisages a system in which any relation or relation element is capable of variation and thus can be further articulated. An initial, undifferentiated associative relation may become increasingly differentiated through experience.

Semantic relations are no more primitive than other concepts with which they have much in common. Relations exhibit a typicality structure, with some cases being better examples of the relation concept than others. Good examples of a relation are rated as more characteristic of the relation and are identified more rapidly in relation identification tasks than less typical cases. Relations can be compared in terms of their similarity, and these comparisons used to identify dimensions on which the relations are seen as different. Some relations are lexicalized by common relations expressions that are subject to the same kind of selection restrictions that govern other lexical items. The acceptability of a particular relation expression in a context reflects the correspondence between its elements and the elements of the relation being named. The final similarity of relations and other concepts that we considered is that relation expressions are instantiated by their context. The meaning of a relation term in a particular context is interpreted more specifically than the same expression out of context.

Perhaps one reason for the attractiveness of relations as explanatory primitives is their logical characteristics, such as transitivity and reflexivity. These appear to distinguish relations from other concepts. The account of transitivity given here suggests, however, that the logical characteristics of relations are a product of the way relations are represented. In the case of inclusion relations, the ways in which relations can be combined to produce transitive inferences is determined by the relational elements of which the relations are composed.

ACKNOWLEDGMENTS

I would like to thank Larry Barsalou, Mary Crawford, Alan Cruse, and Mort Winston for their helpful comments on an earlier version of this chapter. The writing of this chapter was supported in part by a faculty research grant from Trenton State College.

REFERENCES

Anderson, J. R. (1983). *The architecture of cognition.* Cambridge, MA: Harvard University Press.
Anderson, R. C., & Ortony, A. (1977). On putting apples into bottles—A problem of polysemy. *Cognitive Psychology, 7,* 167–180.

Aristotle (1928–1952). De parva naturalia: De memoria et reminiscentia. In W. D. Ross (Ed.), *The works of Aristotle translated into English* (Vol. 3). Oxford: Oxford University Press. Reprinted in D. J. Herrmann & R. Chaffin (1988). *Memory in historical perspective: The literature before Ebbinghaus* (p. 68). New York: Springer–Verlag.

Arkes, H. R., & Harkness, A. R. (1980). Effect of making a diagnosis on subsequent recognition of symptoms. *Journal of Experimental Psychology. Human Learning and Memory, 6*, 568–575.

Armstrong, S. L., Gleitman, L. R., & Gleitman, H. (1983). What some concepts might not be. *Cognition, 13*, 263–308.

Barsalou, L. W. (1982). Context independent and context dependent information in concepts. *Memory & Cognition, 10*, 82–93.

Barsalou, L. (1983). Ad hoc categories. *Memory and Cognition, 11*, 211–227.

Barsalou, L. (1987). The instability of graded structure: Implications for the nature of concepts. In U. Neisser (Ed.), *Concepts and conceptual development: Ecological and intellectual factors in cognition*. Cambridge: Cambridge University Press.

Barsalou, L. (1991). Constructing categories to achieve goals. In G. H. Bower (Ed.), *The psychology of learning and motivation: Advances in research and theory* (Vol. 27). San Diego: Academic Press.

Battig, W. F., & Montague, W. E. (1969). Category norms for verbal items in 56 categories: A replication and extension of the Connecticut category norms. *Journal of Experimental Psychology Monographs, 80*(3, Pt. 2).

Bejar, I. I., Chaffin, R., & Embretson, S. (1991). *Cognitive and psychometric analysis of analogical problem solving*. New York: Springer-Verlag.

Bousfield, W. A. (1953). The occurrence of clustering in the recall of randomly arranged associates. *Journal of General Psychology, 49*, 229–240.

Cantor, N., & Mischel, W. (1977). Traits as prototypes: Effects on recognition memory. *Journal of Personality and Social Psychology, 35*, 38–48.

Chaffin, R. (1981). Context effects in the categorization task. *Journal of General Psychology, 104*, 293–302.

Chaffin, R., & Herrmann, D. J. (1984). Similarity and diversity of semantic relations. *Memory and Cognition, 12*, 134–141.

Chaffin, R., & Herrmann, D. J. (1987). Relation element theory: A new account of the representation and processing of semantic relations. In D. Gorfein & R. Hoffman (Eds.), *Memory and learning: The Ebbinghaus Centennial Conference*. Hillsdale, NJ: Lawrence Erlbaum Associates.

Chaffin, R., & Herrmann, D. J. (1988a). The nature of semantic relations: A comparison of two approaches. In M. Evens (Ed.), *Relational models of the lexicon: Representing knowledge in semantic networks* (pp. 249–294). New York: Cambridge University Press.

Chaffin, R., & Herrmann, D. J. (1988b). Effects of relation similarity on part–whole decisions. *Journal of General Psychology, 115*, 131–139.

Chaffin, R., Herrmann, D. J., & Winston, M. E. (1988). An empirical taxonomy of part–whole relations: Effects of part–whole relation type on relation identification. *Language and Cognitive Processes, 3*, 17–48.

Chaffin, R., Russo, A., & Hermann, D. (1981). An effect of relationship similarity on categorization latency. *Journal of General Psychology, 104*, 305–06.

Cruse, D. A. (1979). On the transitivity of the part–whole relation. *Journal of Linguistics, 15*, 29–38.

Cruse, D. A. (1986). *Lexical semantics*. Cambridge, England: Cambridge University Press.

Fehr, B., & Russell, J. A. (1984). Concept of emotion viewed from a prototype perspective. *Journal of Experimental Psychology: General, 113*, 464–484.

Fellbaum, C., & Miller, G. A. (1990). Folk psychology or semantic entailment? Comment on Rips and Conrad (1989). *Psychological Review, 97*, 565–570.

Fillenbaum, S., & Rapoport, A. (1971). *Structures in the subjective lexicon*. New York: Academic Press.

Gellatly, A. R. H., & Gregg, V. H. (1977). Intercategory distance and categorization times: Effect of negative probe relatedness. *Journal of Verbal Learning and Verbal Behavior, 16,* 505–518.

Goldin, S. E. (1978). Memory for the ordinary: Typicality effects in chess memory. *Journal of Experimental Psychology: Human Learning and Memory, 4,* 605–616.

Greenspan, S. L. (1986). Semantic flexibility and referential specificity of concrete nouns. *Journal of Memory and Language, 25,* 539–557.

Hampton, J. A. (1982). A demonstration of intransitivity in natural categories. *Cognition, 12,* 151–164.

Hampton, J. A. (1987). Inheritance of attributes in natural concept conjunctions. *Memory and Cognition, 15,* 55–71.

Hartley, J., & Homa, D. (1981). Abstraction of stylistic concepts. *Journal of Experimental Psychology: Human Learning and Memory, 7,* 33–46.

Herrmann, D. J., & Chaffin, R. (1986). Comprehension of semantic relations as a function of the definitions of relations. In F. Klix & H. Hagendorf (Eds.), *Human memory and cognitive capabilities* (pp. 311–319). New York: North–Holland.

Herrmann, D. J., Chaffin, R., Conti, G., Peters, D., & Robbins, P. H. (1979). Comprehension of antonymy: The generality of categorization models. *Journal of Experimental Psychology: Human Learning and Memory, 5,* 585–597.

Herrmann, D. J., Chaffin, R., Daniel, M. P., & Wool, R. S. (1986). The role of elements of relation definitions in antonym and synonym comprehension. *Zeitschrift für Psychologie, 194,* 134–153.

Herrmann, D. J., Papperman, T. J., & Armstrong, A. C. (1978). Synonym comprehension and the generality of categorization models. *Memory & Cognition, 6,* 150–155.

Iris, M. A., Litowitz, B. E., & Evens, M. (1988). Problems of the part–whole relation. In M. Evens (Ed.), *Relational models of the lexicon.* Cambridge: Cambridge University Press.

Jackendoff, R. (1985). *Semantics and cognition.* Cambridge, MA: MIT Press.

Johnson-Laird, P. N., Herrmann, D. J., & Chaffin, R. (1984). Only connections: A critique of semantic networks. *Psychological Bulletin, 96,* 292–315.

Katz, J. J. (1972). *Semantic theory.* New York: Harper & Row.

Katz, J. J., & Fodor, J. A. (1963). The structure of semantic theory. *Language, 39,* 170–210.

Lakoff, G. (1987). *Women, fire and dangerous things.* Chicago: University of Chicago Press.

Langlois, J. H., & Roggman, L. A. (1990). Attractive faces are only average. *Psychological Science, 1,* 115–121.

Lehrer, A. (1974). *Semantiic fields and lexical structures.* Amsterdam: North–Holland.

Lyons, J. (1977). *Semantics* (Vol. I). London: Cambridge University Press.

McCloskey, M., & Glucksberg, S. (1979). Decision processes in verifying category membership statements: Implications for models of semantic memory. *Cognitive Psychology, 11,* 1–37.

Medin, D. L. (1989).. Concepts and conceptual structure. *American Psychologist, 12,* 1469–1481.

Miller, G. A., & Johnson-Laird, P. N. (1976). *Language and perception.* Cambridge: Cambridge University Press.

Minsky, M. (1975). A framework for representing knowledge. In P. H. Winston (Ed.), *The psychology of computer vision.* New York: McGraw–Hill.

Norman, D. A., Rumelhart, D. E., & the LNR Group (1975). *Explorations in cognition.* San Francisco: W. H. Freeman.

Osgood, C. E. (1970). Speculation on the structure of interpersonal intentions. *Behavioral Science, 15,* 237–254.

Osherson, D. N., & Smith, E. E. (1982). Gradedness and conceptual conjunction. *Cognition, 12,* 299–318.

Rapaport, D. (1974). *The history of the concept of association of ideas.* New York: International Universities Press.

Roget's International Thesaurus of English Words and Phrases (3rd ed.). New York: Crowell, 1962.

Rosch, E. (1978). Principles of categorization. In E. Rosch & B. L. Lloyd (Eds.), *Cognition and categorization.* Hillsdale, NJ: Lawrence Erlbaum Associates.

Rosch, E., Mervis, C. B., Gray, W. D., Johnson, D., & Boyes-Braem, P. (1976). Basic objects in natural categories. *Cognitive Psychology, 8,* 382–439.

Rumelhart, D E., & Ortony, A. (1977). The representation of knowledge in memory. In R. C. Anderson, R. J. Spiro, & W. E. Montague (Eds.), *Schooling and the acquisition of knowledge.* Hillsdale, NJ: Lawrence Erlbaum Asssociates.

Schank, R. C., & Abelson, R. P. (1977). *Scripts, plans, goals, and understanding.* Hillsdale, NJ: Lawrence Erlbaum Associates.

Smith, E. E., & Medin, D. L. (1981). *Concepts and categories.* Cambridge, MA: Harvard University Press.

Stasio, T., Herrmann, D. J., & Chaffin, R. (1985). Predictions of relation similarity according to relation definition theory. *Bulletin of the Psychonomic Society, 23,* 5–8.

Tversky, A. (1977). Features of similarity. *Psychological Review, 84,* 327–352.

Tversky, B., & Hemenway, K. (1984). Objects, parts, and categories. *Journal of Experimental Psychology: General, 113,* 170–197.

Warren, H. C. (A 1921). *A history of association psychology.* New York: Scribner.

Wierzbicka, A. (1984). Apples are not a "kind of fruit": The semantics of human categorization. *American Ethnologist, 11,* 313–328.

Winston, M. E., Chaffin, R., & Herrmann, D. J. (1987). A taxonomy of part–whole relations. *Cognitive Science, 11,* 417–444.

11

Antonymy Revisited: Some Thoughts on the Relationship Between Words and Concepts

D. A. Cruse
University of Manchester

In this chapter I want to re-examine some of the structural characteristics of certain types of lexical fields, with a view to formulating a number of possible cross-linguistic generalizations, and at the same time drawing some tentative conclusions concerning the nature of the associated conceptual structures. The lexical fields in question are those whose members denote gradable properties such as length, weight and temperature, within which antonymy (in the narrow sense defined by Lyons, 1963) is a major operative relation.

Any adequate lexical semantics must take explicit account of the notions of concept and concept network, which are the stock-in-trade of cognitive psychologists; it is not sufficient, in my opinion, to treat word meaning exclusively in terms of relations between lexical items. (My views on this have hardened since I wrote *Lexical Semantics*. Although it is true that in that book I adopt an explicitly relational approach, certain sections—particularly those dealing with antonymy—can be seen as "crypto-cognitive," in that they do not really make sense unless one assumes an independent conceptual structure.) The fact that one must take account of concepts does not necessarily imply that all word meanings can be exhaustively described in terms of concepts, or that the connections between words and concepts are always straightforward. Nor does it imply that the conceptual system is fully independent and would subsist in its entirely even if language did not exist; on the contrary, there is undoubtedly a close interdependence between language and cognition. But it does mean that concepts are a necessary ingredient of the lexical-semantic cake.

It hardly needs to be pointed out that the nature of the human conceptual system is currently a matter of conjecture and controversy. However, for present purposes, we may, at least to begin with, adopt a relatively simple picture, which combines elements from the prototype approach to concepts with the notion of a concept network. My picture of the latter owes much to the diagrams in Collins and Loftus (1975), which show circles representing concepts, and lines joining them together in a highly interconnected network. The lines joining the circles can be thought of as representing different kinds of semantic relation between concepts, such as *-is-*, *-is a kind of-*, *-is a part of-*, *-is used for-*, etc. Much of what is thought of as the structure of a concept is thus represented in terms of linkages with other concepts, of varying strengths, the strengths reflecting degree of centrality/prototypicality according to some appropriate measure or measures.[1] However, there must be more to it than this: I do not believe that a concept can be entirely relational in nature. I assume that there must be some kind of substantive core—perhaps, in the case of concrete concepts, for instance, a complex of sensory-motor images. A prototypical concept also has an inner coherence—it forms a unified gestalt; it is not clear to me how this is to be modelled.

A natural language possesses an inventory of lexical forms, and these are mapped onto the concept network. In the simplest cases, a word serves only to activate a concept (together, of course, with all its connections), and this can be thought of as the whole of its meaning. I assume that this is what, for instance, basic level vocabulary items do. So, for instance, the form *horse* will take us straight to the concept [HORSE]. The semantic relations between [HORSE] and other concepts such as [ANIMAL], [MARE], [COW], [MANE], and [HOOF] will be represented in the concept network, and there will be no direct connections between these and the word *horse*. This means that many sense relations, such as taxonymy, cotaxonymy, and meronymy, on this view are primarily conceptual relations, and only secondarily lexical relations.

The mapping relations from lexical forms to concepts are not always one-to-one (perhaps they are rarely so). Obviously, many forms will map onto more than one concept: for instance, *bank*. The links between the form *bank* and the concepts [SLOPING MARGIN OF RIVER] and [INSTITUTION FOR THE CUSTODY OF MONEY] will need to be organized in such a way that only one of them can be operative at a given instant.

Another possibility that must be catered to is the mapping of several lexical forms onto the same concept. I do not mean by this that some concepts can only be accessed by a string of words, although that possibility must also be allowed for: I am thinking of alternative lexical access routes to a single concept. An

---

[1]One of the ways in which the picture I have just sketched is an oversimplification is that it ignores the fact that in some sense the linkages between concepts are themselves concepts (see Chaffin & Herrmann, 1988, and Chaffin, this volume). However, I am not fully convinced that we should equate the ordinary everyday "overt" concepts associated with words like *part, kind,* and *opposite* with the corresponding links in the conceptual network, which I see as more "covert"; but I am unable to throw any light on what the connection between the two might be.

example of this would be *die, kick the bucket, pass away,* and *snuff it;* as a rule of thumb, I assume that cognitive synonyms map onto identical concepts. The stable meaning properties that differentiate the members of a pair of cognitive synonyms like *neonate* and *newborn baby,* or *pass away* and *snuff it* can then be viewed as properties of the individual lexical units, as distinct from properties of the common concept. Word-specific semantic properties will include such things as emotive coloring, and various kinds of contextual affinities (see Cruse, 1990, for a more detailed discussion of word-specific semantic properties).

If we allow the possibility of word-specific semantic properties, then this creates the possibility of lexical as opposed to conceptual semantic relations. For instance, if *die* serves to activate the concept [DIE] directly, without modulatory effect, whereas *snuff it* activates the same concept, but with a modulatory effect, then *snuff it* stands in a meaning relation to *die,* which has some resemblance to hyponymy but is not truth-conditional in nature (in Cruse, 1986, this relation is called *nano-hyponymy*). According to the view being developed here, the whole meaning of a word is the associated concept (together with its pattern of connections within the concept network) plus any word-specific properties. It would be useful to have terms to distinguish words that do not have any word-specific properties from those that do: I refer to the former as "plain" words, and the latter as "charged" words.

The picture of word meaning that has just been sketched out has some plausibility insofar as it applies to words associated with concrete concepts, but it is less clear how well it can model, for instance, the meanings of antonymous adjectives. I would now like to consider, through a detailed examination of a particular problem in antonymy, what kind of conceptual structures seem to be necessary to account for the behavior of antonyms.

The specific problem that I want to discuss is how to account for the pattern of "uncommitted" or "impartial" uses of members of antonym pairs (in the sense in which these terms are used in Cruse, 1986). A pair of adjectives partition some dimension between them, and when they occur in their most basic uses—uninflected and unmodified, and in attributive or predicative position—neither will trespass into the territory of the other. So, for instance, in sentences like *The film was long, That was a short film,* we obviously would not use *short* in connection with a film that we judged to be long, or vice versa. But if we put *long* or *short* into the comparative form, they become as it were liberated from these restrictions and can range over all the possible values for length, so that *This week's film was longer than the one we saw last week* can be used irrespective of whether the film in question was long or short, and likewise with *shorter.* We can even combine the two normally contrasting terms into one statement without contradiction:

1a. This week's film was quite short, but it was longer than last week's.

1b. This week's film was quite long, but it was still shorter than last week's.

(As K. Allan, 1988 points out, many speakers feel they need something like *still* or *nevertheless* in (1b) to make it fully natural, although it is not necessary in (1a); this difference is presumably a reflection of some kind of structural asymmetry between *longer* and *shorter*, but the exact semantic mechanism remains obscure.) The power of the comparative to liberate a term from its own part of the underlying scale does not extend to all antonyms, as least not in English, nor in the majority of the languages that I have examined. To simplify the following discussion I refer mainly to only three pairs of antonyms: *long:short, good:bad* and *hot:cold* (or their most natural equivalents in other languages). Each pair is meant to stand for a more-or-less numerous group of similarly behaving pairs. In the following table I have marked a "+" where impartial use is possible, and a "−" where it is not:[2]

	longer	*shorter*	*better*	*worse*	*hotter*	*colder*
English	+	+	+	−	−	−
French	+	+	+	−	+	+
Turkish	+	+	+	−	+	−
Macedonian	+	+	+	+	+	+
Arabic	+	+	+	−	−	−
Chinese	+	+	+	−	−	−

Nominalizations and certain types of questions also have the ability to liberate terms from their own part of the scale, as in (2a) and (b):

2a. The width of the car is 1.7 metres.

2b. How long is your garden path?

French and Turkish have impartial degree-questions based on derived nominals, but none using the bare adjective on the pattern of *How long . . ?:*

3a. Quelle est la longueur de votre voiture?

3b. Arabanızın uzunluğu ne kadar? (lit. "your-car its-length what degree?")

The also have something that does not seem to occur in English with antonyms, namely, impartial yes/no questions (these are discussed in Cruse (1986, pp. 244–246) under the heading of "weak impartiality"):

---

[2]I would like to thank the following people for acting (sometimes unwittingly) as informants: Ciğdem Balım, Kersti Börjars, Isabel Carvalho, Paule Cruse, Gürkan Doğan, Xudong Sun, Barry Tay, Sylvie Wanin, and Ghesoun Ward. Other sources of language data that I have used are German: Durrell (1988); Arabic: Zikri (1979); and Macedonian: Marsh-Stefanowska (1982).

4a. Il est bon, ce livre?

4b. O kitap iyi mi? (lit. "that book good [interrog.]")

The following table indicates the possibilities or otherwise of impartial nominals or degree questions:

	long	*short*	*good*	*bad*	*hot*	*cold*
English	+	−	+	−	−	−
French	+	−	+	−	−	−
Turkish	+	−	+	−	+	−
Macedonian	+	−	+	−	−	−
Arabic	+	−	+	−	−	−

It is noteworthy, firstly, that the possibilities for impartial use are more restricted than with the comparative, and secondly that there is much less variation between languages. There are also possibilities of impartial use with expressions of comparison other than the comparative. The following table shows which adjectives can occur impartially in the expressions indicated (NB: there is no Turkish equivalent for *less X than*):

	English	*French*	*Turkish*	*Arabic*
as X as	long,good	long,good	long,short, good,hot	(none)
not as X as	long,good	long,good	long,good, hot	(none)
less X than	good	long,good	Ø	(none)

This concludes the data for which I attempt to give a coherent account. Basically what I suggest is that impartiality is not scattered at random across expression types and languages; rather, its occurrence appears to be constrained by two implicational rules. I further suggest that in order to express these rules, account must be taken of the conceptual representation of antonymous adjectives. But first, mention must be made of certain other facts concerning impartiality in nominals and/or degree questions that it might be felt ought to be included in the aforementioned data, but that I exclude on the grounds that their explanation does not arise directly from the conceptual representation.

The first point is the fact that for instance *thickness* and *hardness* as in *the thickness of the material* and *the hardness of the water* can be impartial, whereas for instance *quickness, heaviness,* and *longness* cannot be impartial. Is this difference to be attributed to the conceptual structures underlying *thick* and *hard* on the one hand, and *quick, heavy,* and *long* on the other? I think not: In all the cases where the *-ness* nominal cannot be impartial, there exists an alternative nominal that can be impartial: in the preceding cases, *speed, weight,* and *length,* respectively. Furthermore, this impartial alternative seems always to be morphologically irregular. The existence or otherwise of a morphologically irregular nominal is to some extent a historical accident; but if such a form does exist, then there is automatically a potential regularly formed alternative. That two competing forms should become semantically differentiated is not a surprise (see the chapter by Eve Clark in this volume). But a couple of facts do seem to require explanation: (a) Why are no forms restricted to the impartial reading, and (b) why is it always the regular form that is restricted?

The second point concerns the difference between, for example, *How long is it?* and *How clean is it?* The former has two possible interpretations: It can mean either "What is its length?" or it can mean "Is it long or short?" These are quite distinct, and the question sometimes gets the wrong response:

5. A: How wide is the Toyota Carina?
    B: One point six four metres, madam.
    A: Oh, I see. Is that wide or narrow?

How clean is it?, on the other hand, has only one interpretation. Once again I would argue that the difference between the two questions is not due to differences in the conceptual structures underlying *long* and *clean:* It is more directly correlated with the existence of a familiar objective scale calibrated in conventional units. The existence or otherwise of conventional units for some property is a contingent fact about the world that is liable to change; my intuitions are that the coming into common use of a set of conventional units where none existed before would cause previously univocal degree questions to become ambiguous.

The ambiguity of *How long is it?* is not matched by any question in French; *Quelle est la longueur de votre voiture?* asks only for a length, like its English structural equivalent *What is the length of your car?* The most usual way of asking the other question is *Elle est longue, votre voiture?* This is ambiguous in another way, between an impartial interpretation: "Is your car long or short?" and a committed one: "Is it the case that your car is a long one?" There is a genuine problem here of how to represent the difference between these two readings, especially in view of the fact that on both interpretations the question must be answered with *Non* if the car in question happens to be short. Also interesting is the fact that *Est-ce que votre voiture est longue?,* for my informants at least, has only a committed reading. I do not offer solutions to either of these problems here. The Turkish *Uzunluğu ne kadar?,* although it is structurally parallel to *What is its length?,* shows the same ambiguity as *How long is it?*

The final point under this heading concerns the interpretation of nominals in the frame *Its (Nom) surprised me.* If I say of something *Its length surprised me,* it is possible that I was surprised that it was so short; but if I say *Its cleanness surprised me*, this can hardly mean that I was surprised by how dirty it was. According to my intuitions, the incidence of impartiality is as follows:

Impartial use possible	*Impartial use impossible*
length	cleanness
weight	politeness
speed	prettiness
width	kindness
depth	lightness (vs. darkness)
breadth	loudness
temperature	difficulty
strength	

Two regularities can be observed in the preceding data. First, there is an excellent correlation between the possibility of impartial use and the presence of suppletion or at least phonetic distortion of the root morpheme in the nominal; second, there is a slightly less good correlation between the possibility of impartial use and the existence of familiar conventional units of measurement (*strength* is the exception here; however, some speakers put *strength* in the other column, making the second correlation perfect). In French, impartiality is possible only in suppletive nominals, and the distribution is different from that in English:

Impartial use possible	*Impartial use impossible*
poids	longueur
température	largeur
	hauteur
	épaisseur
	profondeur
	vitesse
	propreté

The most natural translation of *Its weight surprised me* into Turkish does not contain a nominal form, but a bare adjective: *Onun ne kadar ağır olduğu beni şaşırttı* (lit. "its what amount heavy being me surprised"); all adjectives are committed in this construction. However, when I asked my informants to respond to the less natural construction containing the nominal—*Uzunluğu beni şaşırttı*—they provided some weak evidence for the "familiar conventional unit" factor in Turkish:

Impartial use possible	*Impartial use impossible*
uzunluk (length)	genişlik (width)
hız (speed)	yükseklik (height)
sıcaklık (temperature)	derinlik (depth)
	iyilik (goodness)
	güzellik (beauty)
	temizlik (cleanness)
	zeka (intelligence)

In view of the much more coherent behavior of antonyms in other respects, I assume that in each of the three types of case just described the distribution of impartiality is not determined by the conceptual structure of the adjective but by factors that are extrinsic to this, and at least to some extent accidental.

I now return to the main set of data to see what sense can be made of it in terms of words and concepts. A difficulty that emerges right away concerns the nature of concepts such as [LENGTH] and [TEMPERATURE]. The kind of picture suggested for concrete concepts like [BIRD] does not seem illuminating here. I find it useful to think of antonym-related concepts in terms of two levels of structure. The first is an area of conceptual "purport" (to borrow a term from Hjelmslev). For instance, *long, short, concise, length, lengthy* all map onto the same area of conceptual purport, whereas *hot, cold, warm, cool, lukewarm, temperature* map onto a different area. I do not think of conceptual purport as abstract, but as fairly concrete, and relatively unstructured. It is structured at the second level of structure by conceptual schemas of various kinds. These are abstract, rigid, limited in number, and they recur in connection with a wide variety of areas of purport.

In order to explain the patterns of occurrence of impartiality in connection with antonymous adjectives, I propose two types of conceptual schema: grading schemas and scale schemas. Of the former type, two appear to be necessary: a gradable schema and a nongradable schema. These operate in conjunction with one or more scale schemas—these are introduced later. We can represent the possible arrangements of grading schemas as in Fig. 11.1: A single (unbroken) arrow in the diagram indicates a schema that presents the property abstracted from some area of purport as a "more-or-less" one, whereas a rectangle indicates a schema that presents the property as a "yes–no" one. The gradable schemas point in a particular direction with respect to some underlying scale (which is indicated in Fig. 11.1 by the dotted arrow on the left) and locate themselves in a particular part of the scale relative to their partners. The schemas I have attributed to the lexical items in Fig. 11.1 are those that I take to be their basic ones; this does not mean, however, that they cannot operate with other schemas. For instance, I assume that when we say of something *It's clean* we are using *clean* nongradably, as opposed to *long* in *It's long*, which is essentially a graded use (for a justification of this claim regarding the nature of *clean*, see Cruse, 1980, pp. 16–19). However, in *It's fairly clean* or *It's very clean*, we require a

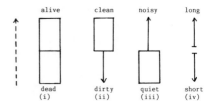

FIG. 11.1. Combinations of grading schemas.

different schema for *clean*. Type (i) are complementary opposites, type (iv) are antonyms (in the narrow sense), and types (ii) and (iii) are intermediate types. I discuss mainly type (iv), but type (ii) behave in most respects like type (iv). There is however a difference between them that should be mentioned. The gradable schema may be thought of as having as it were a slot for a value of the degree of the relevant property, which may be filled by items like *slightly, fairly, rather, very, extremely,* and so on: If none of these is present, a default value comes into play. This default value normally corresponds to a noteworthy degree of the property in question. This is the case with *dirty:* We would hesitate to say a blunt *It's dirty* of something that was only slightly dirty, even though we would be equally reluctant to describe it as clean. Hence, most informants find *It's neither clean nor dirty* perfectly well formed, just like *It's neither long nor short.* However, whereas there is a definite no-man's-land between *long* and *short*, there is not so much as a sliver of conceptual space between *clean* and *dirty,* and this shows up in the fact that everyone finds **It's neither clean, nor even the slightest bit dirty* logically anomalous. (Doubly nongradable pairs like *dead:alive* and *true:false* have this property, too.) This is a very robust property: I have found no dissenters among native speakers of English. Also, it is possessed by the equivalent terms in French, German, Dutch, Swedish, Spanish, Arabic, Turkish, and Chinese. Marsh-Stefanowska (1982) was unable to demonstrate it in Macedonian, although she found evidence that the word for "clean" is basically nongradable, whereas its partner is gradable, just as in English. However, I am still not convinced—I feel her problem was that she was unable to construct a suitable test frame.

Grading schemas work in conjunction with scale schemas.[3] I believe that a satisfying explanation can be achieved of most of the facts concerning impartiality if we assume three basic patterns for the scales underlying a pair of antonyms. These different patterns do not seem to be reflected in different behavior of antonyms under simple intensification; that is to say, modifiers like *slightly, fairly, rather, very,* and *extremely* do not cause any change in the scale schema activated by the bare adjective. They produce their effect most clearly in nominalizations, degree questions, and expressions of comparison.

The first pattern is exemplified by *long:short:* Here we see just a single scale encompassing all the possible values for length. The scale has a definite direction. This does not simply mean that it indicates high values of something at one end and low values at the other—if such were not the case, it would not be a scale: It means that "more" on the scale correlates with certain features of purport, and "less" with other features. Logically, the scale could have been oriented in the other direction. However, there must be a strong innate predisposition to arrange things the way they appear in English, that is, with a scale

---

[3]The "scales" referred to in this chapter are basically psychological scales and do not necessarily bear a simple relationship to any parallel technical or scientific scales.

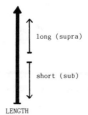

FIG. 11.2. Scale and grading
schemas for *long* and *short*.

of length rather than a scale of "shorth." Intuitively, I would judge the likelihood
to be small of discovering a language in which the most basic terms denoting
extension gave a high value to short things and a low value to long things.

Of the two grading schemas associated with a pair of antonyms, one will be
oriented in the same direction as the scale, that is to say, an intensifier such as
very will cause a move towards a higher value on the scale, whereas the other
schema will be oriented in the other direction. I borrow (or perhaps misappropri-
ate) an item of terminology from K. Allan (1988) and call the lexical item
associated with the schema that is co-directional with the underlying scale the
"supra" term, and its partner the "sub" term. The sub/supra distinction is rather
important for my purposes, so a way is needed of distinguishing one from the
other. This can be quite difficult in some languages. It is not too difficult in
English and can be intuited once one knows what one is looking for. A good test
in English is provided by test sentences of the form *A is twice as X as B* (where X
is the adjective being tested), or better still, *A is only half as X as B*. Compare the
items in the following table: Column A contains supra antonyms, column B their
sub partners, and column C contains adjectives semantically similar to those in
B, but sub rather than supra:

A	B	C
only half as long	?only half as short	only half as concise
only half as fast	?only half as slow	only half as leisurely
only half as big	?only half as small	only half as compact
only half as thick	?only half as thin	only half as slender
only half as safe	?only half as unsafe	only half as dangerous

For me, *less X* also seems to discriminate subs and supras, being fully normal
only with the latter:

A	B	C
less long	?less short	less concise
less fast	?less slow	less leisurely
less large	?less small	less compact
less safe	?less unsafe	less dangerous

Unfortunately, it is not possible to use analogous tests in French or Turkish; neither of these languages has an equivalent for *half as X,* whereas in both, *twice as X* is fully normal for all adjectives. As for *less X,* Turkish has no equivalent, whereas *moins X* in French does not appear to be discriminatory. For these languages I have had to rely on native speaker intuitions, although in certain crucial cases, other less general tests can be used.

One fairly safe generalization that can be made regarding subs and supras is that we will not find a sub term without a supra partner, although supras not infrequently occur alone. Two slightly less safe generalizations (because of the small data base), but ones that are more interesting in the present context, are (a) that a sub term has the same possibility of impartial occurrence as its supra companion in the comparative (but not necessarily in any other expression of comparison), and (b) that derived nominals and degree questions involving sub terms are invariably committed. So, for instance, *heavier* and *lighter* are both impartial, but whereas *How heavy is the suitcase?* is impartial, *How light is the suitcase?* is committed.

The information that we now have concerning length terms in English is summarized in Fig. 11.3. The thick arrow represents the scale schema, the thin arrows represent grading schemas, and the dotted arrows indicate the range and orientation relative to the scale of the forms to which they apply. Using the terminology introduced in Cruse (1986), we may refer to this complex as the "polar" pattern. Every language of which I have knowledge has examples of this pattern. I can go further and hazard a semantic generalization: Among the antonym pairs that exhibit this structure, we always find the vast majority of those that denote objective physical characteristics like height, weight, speed, strength, and so on. In many languages—English, French, Turkish, and Arabic, for instance—polar antonyms are almost exclusively of the objective physical kind. But this is not necessarily true for all languages: Macedonian, for instance, appears to have a wider semantic range in its polar group.

The second pattern is exhibited by *hot* and *cold* in English: Here we have two quasi-independent scales laid end to end, and pointing in opposite directions;

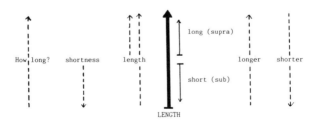

FIG. 11.3. Summary of committed and impartial uses of *long* and *short.*

they are not really independent, because in some sense they are felt to lie on the same continuum. This arrangement is referred to as the "equipollent" pattern. Both *hot* and *cold* are supra terms:

6a. A is only half as hot as B.
6b. A is only half as cold as B.
6c. A is less hot now.
6d. A is less cold now.

The characteristic feature of terms exhibiting this pattern is that they are symmetrical in all their properties. In English, *heat, cold, hotness, coldness, hotter, colder, How hot is it?*, and *How cold is it?* are all committed. Several languages of my acquaintance have temperature terms with an equipollent organization; this is presumably not unconnected with the fact that our basic temperature sensations have a high range, a qualitatively different low range, and a kind of zero in the middle. One such language is French (despite claims to the contrary in Cruse, 1986). Unlike their English equivalents, the comparatives of *chaud* and *froid* are impartial:

7a. Aujourd'hui il fait chaud, mais il fait plus froid qu'hier.
7b. Aujourd'hui il fait froid, mais il fait plus chaud qu'hier.

At first I was misled by this fact into thinking that *chaud* and *froid* were polar antonyms. However, many aspects of their behavior point to their being equipollents. For instance, the nominals *chaleur* and *froid* are both committed, and in all expressions of comparison other than the strict comparative, both are committed:

8a. ?Aujourd'hui il fait chaud, mais il fait aussi froid qu'hier.
8b. ?Aujourd'hui il fait chaud, mais il ne fait pas aussi froid qu'hier.
8c. ?Aujourd'hui il fait chaud, mais il fait moins froid qu'hier.

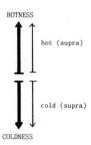

FIG. 11.4. Scale and grading schemas for *hot* and *cold*.

Also, neither of the yes/no questions *Il fait chaud?, Il fait froid/?* has a weakly impartial reading corresponding to that of *Il est long?* The situation in Macedonian appears to be the same as that in French, with impartial comparatives, but everything else committed; Arabic, on the other hand, is more like English, with committed comparatives. The information concerning *hot* and *cold* in English is summarized in Fig. 11.5:

The third pattern is shown by *good* and *bad* in English. It has some similarities with the equipollent pattern, in that there are two supra terms in the basic opposition. However, the scales are not arranged end to end but partially overlap: It is characteristic of antonyms with this type of organization—in English they all have an evaluative polarity—that although both are supras they are asymmetrical in the comparative, with the evaluatively positive term being impartial, and the evaluatively negative term committed:

9a. John's exam results were bad, but they were better than Bill's.

9b. ?John's exam results were excellent, but they were worse than Bill's.

I assume that *better* operates over the longer of the two scales, which we can call the MERIT scale, whereas *worse* operates over the shorter BADNESS scale. This would also explain why *How good is it?* is impartial and *How bad is it?* committed. An interesting feature of this system is that "inherently bad" items, by which I mean those that it is paradoxical (or even perverse) to describe as "good"—*accident, shipwreck, earthquake, epidemic, toothache, headache, drought, famine,* etc.—cannot be compared on the MERIT scale and therefore collocate oddly with *better*. The only items that can be compared on the MERIT scale are those that in principle could have occurred anywhere along the scale, including the "good" region. Inherently bad items can only be compared on the BADNESS scale:

10a. John's accident was worse than Bill's.

10b. ?Bill's accident was better than John's.

Furthermore, *how*-questions concerning inherently bad items are odd with the

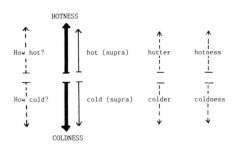

FIG. 11.5. Committed and impartial uses of *hot* and *cold.*

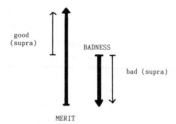

FIG. 11.6. Scale and grading
schemas for *good* and *bad.*

evaluatively positive term: *?How good was your accident?*, but normal with the negative term: *How bad was the famine last year?* I have evidence for similar inherentness phenomena in French, German, Turkish, Arabic, and Macedonian.

As it happens, *bad* is not the only antonymous partner that *good* possesses: There is also *poor,* as in *a poor exam result, a poor harvest, a poor performance.*[4] It is clear from the sentences in 11 that *poor* is sub and *bad* supra:

11a.   John's performance was only half as good as Bill's.

11b.   ?John's performance was only half as poor as Bill's.

11c.   John's performance was less bad than Bill's.

11d.   ?John's performance was less poor than Bill's.

Notice also that the sub term forms a paradoxical collocation with inherently bad items: *a poor toothache, a poor accident, a poor famine?*

It is interesting to compare the English basic evaluative terms with the German ones. In English, as we have seen, both members of the basic antonym pair are supra, whereas the sub term *poor* has a more restricted usage. In German, the basic opposition is between *gut* and *schlecht,* which are supra and sub, respectively. The nearest equivalent in German to a supra negative term is *schlimm.* *Schlecht* has all the signs of a sub term: The comparative *schlechter,* like *besser,* is impartial, and it gives a paradoxical effect with inherently bad items such as *Unfall* ("accident"): *ein schlechter Unfall.* Nouns of the *Unfall*-type will only collocate normally with the supra term: *ein schlimmer Unfall.* However, whereas

---

[4]The following discussion of *poor* is based on my own intuitions. It has been suggested to me that *poor* does not have a privileged status vis-a-vis *good,* that it is no more an antonym of *good* than, say, *awful* or *unpleasant.* It is just conceivable that there is a difference between British and American usage in this respect. However, I am persuaded that my intuitions are by no means idiosyncratic; while following up a number of references in the psycholinguistic and aphasiological literature recently, I noticed that in this context *good* is almost exclusively paired with *poor.* For instance, the *British Journal of Disorders of Communication, 23,* 3 (1989) yielded many examples: *good* vs. *poor* performance on the Peabody Test; *good* vs. *poor* comprehension of abstract nouns; *good* vs. *poor* agreement between different tests of fluency. Not only do these usages conform to my intuitions as to what is appropriate, but I am unable to think of an acceptable alternative to *poor.* For me this constitutes strong evidence for a privileged relationship.

bad can be used for inherently or contingently bad items (and as far as I can tell, without polysemy)—*a bad accident, a bad exam result*—*schlimm* can only be used for inherently bad things; that is to say, *schlecht* is less contextually specialized than *schlimm*. This is presumably not unconnected with the fact that German speakers feel *schlecht* to be the "real" opposite of *gut*. I have illustrated the relationships between the English and German evaluative terms in Fig. 11.7:

Turning now to French, if we ask a speaker bilingual in French and English to give the nearest French equivalent for *a poor result*, s/he will reply with *un mauvais résultat*. As we have seen, French is quite difficult to test for sub and supra; however, remembering that sub terms do not collocate normally with inherently bad items, I obtained informant reactions to *un mauvais accident*. It was immediately rejected as anomalous. This caused me some consternation, because it seemed to indicate that *mauvais* was a sub term. On the other hand, the comparative *pire* is committed; also, it is possible to say (12a), but not (12b):

12a. Cet accident était pire que l'autre.

12b. ?Cet accident était meilleur que l'autre.

These facts point to *mauvais* being supra. This dilemma was resolved when I discovered that *un mauvais accident* was not paradoxical like *ein schlechter Unfall* or *a poor accident,* but tautologous, more like *a bad catastrophe*. One difference between *mauvais* and *bad* is therefore that *mauvais* cannot shift its reference point when it is applied to inherently bad nouns in the way that *bad* does (a bad accident is not one that is bad rather than good; it is one that is relatively bad for accidents). French therefore has basically the same system as English but lacks a sub partner for *bon*. Turkish, too, exhibits the partially overlapping pattern for the basic evaluative terms *iyi* ("good") and *kötü* ("bad"); unlike its French equivalent, however, *kötü* can apply indifferently to inherently and contingently bad items—*kötü bir netice* ("a bad result"), *kötü bir kaza* ("a bad accident")—shifting its reference point with inherents, in the way that *bad* does. Turkish is however unique (in my experience so far) in that the temperature terms *sıcak* ("hot") and *soğuk* ("cold") display the partially overlapping pattern, rather than the more usual equipollent pattern. Figure 11.8 illustrates the overlapping pattern exemplified by *good:bad:*

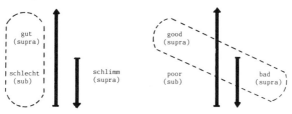

FIG. 11.7. Evaluative antonyms in German and English.

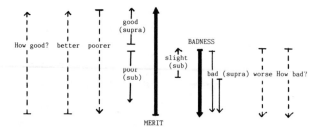

FIG. 11.8. Summary of committed and impartial uses of *good, bad* and related words.

CONCLUDING REMARKS

It appears that fairly complex mapping relations hold between the words comprising an antonym pair and their associated conceptual structures, which have been pictured here as areas of conceptual purport structured by conceptual schemas. These mapping relations are highly sensitive to context, particularly grammatical context, and vary from language to language. All antonymous adjectives have a committed reading; some, but not all, and only under certain conditions, also have an impartial reading. The committed–impartial alternation can be viewed as a kind of polysemy, and we can ask what generalizations can be made concerning the appearance or nonappearance of this type of polysemy. There is as yet no evidence of any typological groupings among languages, but there is evidence suggestive of three generalizations, two with cross-language validity, and one valid for English but not yet checked cross-linguistically. A revealing way to look at the data is to think, on the one hand, in terms of the power of various types of context to activate the impartial reading of an antonym, and on the other hand, in terms of the resistance of different types of antonym to such activation. Consider first the different types of context. The following table shows, for different expressions of comparison, which antonyms can have an impartial interpretation. Notice that the ordering is consistent across the four languages in that no expression allows more impartiality than one ranked above it:

	English	French	Turkish	Arabic
comparative	long,short, good	long,short, good	long,short, good,hot	long,short, good
as X as	long,good	long,good	long,short, good,hot	—
not as X as	long,good	long,good	long,good, hot	—
less X than	good	long,good	Ø	—

If we express the general form of a comparing expression as *A - Comp(X) - B,* meaning "A is compared to B with respect to X," then we can say that the more positive the relative value of X attributed to A by Comp, the more likely X is to be impartial.

Turning now to the question of the resistance of antonyms to impartiality, it appears that two species of regularity can be identified. The first has to do with structural type. The following ordering is shown consistently by the data at hand:

1. overlapping: whole scale (e.g., *good*)
2. polar: supra
3. polar: sub
4. equipollent
5. overlapping: half scale (e.g., *bad*)

Different activators of impartiality in different languages differ only in how far down this list they operate: Resistance increases as one goes down the list, so that for any given activator, if a particular type of antonym responds, then so do all those above it in the list. The second factor involved in resistance to polysemy concerns the distinction between "plain" and "charged" words that was introduced earlier. Although the mapping from words to concepts in the case of antonyms is more complex than for concrete nominal concepts such as [HORSE], it is still possible to distinguish plain words like *long, heavy, fast,* and *thin* from related charged words like *lengthy, weighty, speedy,* and *slender,* whose meaning contains word-specific elements. It seems to be generally the case that charged words are more resistant to impartiality than their plain counterparts.

The conceptual model of antonymy developed in this chapter has the merit that it allows the regularities described previously to be stated, but unfortunately it provides no plausible explanation for them. Clearly there is still some way to go before a satisfying account of antonymy can be provided. There are many other puzzles concerning the facts reported here. One might ask, for instance, whether the observed differences among adjectives have any communicative function, or whether they are, as it were, an accidental by-product of something more fundamental. It would also be interesting to know how and when the differences are acquired, and whether they show up in any other cognitive activity or are purely linguistic in nature. But perhaps the most urgent task is to investigate a wider range of languages, and a wider range of data within each language.

REFERENCES

Allan, K. (1986). Interpreting English comparatives. *Journal of Semantics, 5,* 1–50.
Chaffin, R., & Hermann, D. J. (1988). The nature of semantic relations: A comparison of two approaches. In M. W. Evens (Ed.), *Relational models of the lexicon.* Cambridge, England: Cambridge University Press.

Collins, A. M., & Loftus, E. F. (1975). A spreading-activation theory of semantic processing. *Psychological Review, 82,* 407–428.

Cruse, D. A. (1980). Antonyms and gradable complementaries. In D. Kastovsky (Ed.), *Perspektiven der lexikalischen Semantik.* Bonn: Bouvier Verlag Herbert Grundmann.

Cruse, D. A. (1986). *Lexical semantics.* Cambridge, England: Cambridge University Press.

Cruse, D. A. (1990). Prototype theory and lexical semantics. In S. L. Tsohatzidis (Ed.), *Meaning and prototypes: Studies in linguistic categorization* (pp. 382–402). London & New York: Routledge.

Durrell, M. (1988). Some problems of contrastive lexical semantics. In W. Hüllen & R. Schulze (Eds.), *Understanding the lexicon: Meaning, sense and world knowledge in lexical semantics.* Tübingen: Niemeyer.

Lehrer, A. (1985). Markedness and antonymy. *Journal of linguistics, 21,* 397–421.

Lehrer, A., & Lehrer, K. (1982). Antonymy. *Linguistics and Philosophy, 5,* 483–501.

Lyons, J. (1963). *Structural semantics.* Cambridge, England: Cambridge University Press.

Marsh-Stefanowska, P. J. (1982). *A contrastive study of some morphologically related opposites in English and Macedonian.* Unpublished masters dissertation, University of Manchester.

Zikri, M. S. (1979). *A comparative study of lexical relations in English and Arabic.* Unpublished doctoral thesis, University of Manchester.

III SPECIFIC ANALYSES

12 At Least

Paul Kay
University of California, Berkeley

Research in linguistic semantics may be roughly divided into two broad traditions.[1] Students concerned with lexical fields and lexical domains ("lexical semanticists") have interested themselves in the paradigmatic relations of contrast that obtain among related lexical items and the substantive detail of how particular lexical items map to the nonlinguistic objects they stand for. "Formal semanticists" (those who study the combinatorial properties of word meanings) have been mostly unconcerned with these issues, concentrating rather on how the meanings of individual words, whatever their internal structure may be and however they may be paradigmatically related to one another, combine into the meanings of phrases and sentences (and recently, to some extent, texts). Combinatorial semanticists have naturally been more concerned with syntax, especially as the leading idea of formal semantics has been the specific combinatorial hypothesis of Fregean compositionality.

A contribution that the Construction Grammar (CG) approach[2] hopes to make to the study of the lexicon is to furnish a conceptual and technical framework in which the two sets of problems can be treated in an integrated fashion. The semantic part of a lexical entry in a construction grammar connects the morphosyntactic object in question to a schema or frame, which presents a conceptual analysis of (the linguistically encoded aspects of) some area of extralinguistic experience—not excluding the experience of using language. Aspects of the conceptual schemata that constitute linguistic meanings are represented in the grammar, both in lexical entries and in nonlexically tagged constructions when appropriate, in the same attribute-value unification format as is the morphosyntactic information. Unification of constructions integrates information on both formal and meaning planes simultaneously.

---

[1]I would like to acknowledge the valuable comments of Claudia Brugman and Charles Fillmore on several of the matters discussed in this chapter.

[2]See Fillmore (1988) for a succinct exposition.

309

This chapter presents an initial description of the word *at least*, or perhaps better the three (different) words *at least*, within the CG framework. Questions are raised that do not receive answers. I hope, however, that the description goes far enough to indicate the delicacy with which formal and meaning properties of lexical items can be related and the potential of a constructional approach for providing a framework in which some of the problems arising from this delicacy can be profitably discussed.

The CG approach supposes a grammar to consist of a repertory of conventional associations of lexical, syntactic, semantic, and pragmatic information called constructions. Familiar grammar rules are simply constructions that are deficient in not containing any lexical information except for the specification of rather gross syntactic categories—and, in some cases, in lacking pragmatic values as well. Effectively, the constructions of Construction Grammar are much like the constructions of traditional grammars except that simple and complex lexical items and all kinds of grammatical rules are also viewed by CG as constructions; that is, as conventional associations of form and meaning elements. Every such conventional association that must be learned or recognized separately by the speaker of a language is a construction.[3] This includes all idioms and partially productive lexico-grammatical patterns. The principle operation that allows constructions, including lexical constructions, to be combined into sentences is the operation of unification. Two patterns can unify just in case they don't conflict.[4]

We will be concerned with mapping out some of the syntactic and meaning properties of three distinct usages of *at least*. I will try to get you to believe that it is useful to think of these as three distinct constructions, each with its own complement of syntactic, semantic, and pragmatic properties, though I do not provide any formal representations in the language of feature-structures. I will not lay great stress on the fact that some of the meaning properties we consider rather blur the traditional distinction between semantics and pragmatics, but you may want be on your guard for that.[5]

The different *at least* constructions we will be concerned with are illustrated by (1), (2), and (3), respectively.

---

[3]The network of constructions that constitutes a grammar may be given structure by an inheritance hierarchy, but consideration of this issue is beyond the scope of this chapter.

[4]In the unification-based implementation under development at Berkeley, the formal objects on which unification is defined are tree structures whose nodes are feature structures, and unification is defined on feature structures in the same way as in Functional Unification Grammar (M. Kay, 1979, 1984, 1985), LFG (Bresnan, 1982), HPSG (Pollard & Sag, 1987), and so on: Two feature structures can unify unless they specify different values for the same attribute. Unlike some of the other unification-based theories on the market, CG feature structures can contain semantic and pragmatic information. The constituent structure skeleton will be called upon to do more work in a language like English or French than in one like Japanese, Latin, or Warlpiri.

[5]The standard assumption of one tradition of linguistic semantics that sentence meaning = "what is said" = truth conditions = literal meaning = *semantics*, while *pragmatics* covers everything else

1. Mary received calls from at least three soldiers.
2. At least, this one's cooked.
3. I see her every day, at least when I'm in town.

The next three sections of the chapter are devoted to each of these usages/constructions in turn. The final section treats some cases in which more than one of these constructions may be employed in the analysis of a sentence containing *at least*.

IMPLICATURE SUSPENSION

The usage of *at least* that comes to mind first includes the cases in which *at least* precedes a numeral and has the semantic effect of requiring that the numeral be interpreted as the lower bound of an open interval, as in

4. Mary has at least three children.

We should note at the onset, however, that this construction deserves a broader characterization. This usage of *at least* does not require that the constituent modified by *at least* be numerical or even necessarily quantitative. It requires rather that the constituent modified by *at least* be the focus of a scalar sentence.[6] Thus, in (5) the constituent focussed by *at least*, i.e., *worry (him)*, is nonquantitative but is nevertheless the focus of a scalar sentence.

5. That's going to at least worry him [if not make him utterly distraught].

Thus, in the usage of *at least* illustrated in (1), (4), and (5), the constituent immediately containing *at least* need be neither notionally quantitative nor formally nominal, as long as it is interpreted as a scalar focus. Examples (6–9)

---

involved in the interpretation of utterances (sometimes modulo indexicals) has been subject to sufficient challenges that an attempt to acknowledge them all would require a text the length of the this chapter. My views on these matters, including the acknowledgment of many intellectual debts are expressed in Kay (1983, 1984, 1987, 1989) and Fillmore, Kay, and O'Connor (1988; hereafter, FKO).

[6]A scalar sentence is one that is interpreted in each context in which it is uttered in a scalar model. The notion of scalar model is introduced by Fillmore, Kay, and O'Connor (1988). Very roughly, a scalar model is a lattice of propositions related to one another by unilateral entailments in such a way as to explicate the intuition of one statement's being stronger or more informative than another along a certain dimension or, in the case of multiple foci, along several dimensions simultaneously. Scalar models represent systems of background assumptions shared (presumably) by speaker and addressee; they are thus inherently contextual. Scalar operators such as *at least* require that each utterance of a sentence in which they occur be interpreted in a scalar model, but the operator does not provide that model. For further discussion, see Kay (1990).

illustrate maximal phrases of a variety of syntactic categories modified by *at least* and serving as the foci of scalar sentences.

6. She's going to flunk at least YOU AND ME [and perhaps others].
7. He's going to be at least IRRITATED [if not outraged].
8. You'll at least SCRATCH IT doing that [if not shatter it completely].
9. I'm afraid I've at least PARTIALLY alienated her.

The four preceding examples illustrate nonquantified noun phrases, adjective phrases, verb phrases, and adverb phrases, respectively. (Capitals indicate semantic focus. These semantic foci will include a major prosodic prominence, often properly.) In each case, we can compare the sentence as given, call it S, with the relevant comparison sentence that is created by removing *at least;* let's call the latter C, for Comparison. For example the C sentence for (7) would be

10. He's going to be irritated.

An expected conversational implicature of (10) is the suitable epistemic qualification of

11. He's going to be no more than irritated [e.g., He won't be outraged].

Altering the C sentence (10) by adding *at least* to produce the S sentence (7) has the effect of suppressing the upper bounding scalar implicature of (10) that is given in (11).

Thus, the primary semantic effect of this usage of *at least* is the suppression of the upper bounding quantity implicature that attaches to scalar statements in ordinary contexts. Let us call this particular construction "Scalar *at least.*" Scalar *at least* is the *at least* construction that contrasts directly with *at most.* Whereas Scalar *at least* in (12) blocks the upper bounding quantity implicature of a scalar sentence like (13), to the effect that Mary has no more than three children, *at most* in (14) has the contrary effect of making Mary's having no more than three children an entailment.

12. Mary has at least three children.
13. Mary has three children.
14. Mary has at most three children.[7]

---

[7]There has to be more to the story of *at most* than this. *At most n* does not merely upper bound the interpretation of a scalar predicate *n* at n but also adds to the interpretation of *n* the interval that descends from n. *He got at most a B* is not only false if he got an A but also true if he got a C.

Intuitively, *at most* does the "opposite" of what Scalar *at least* does. It is not apparent how to represent this symmetry within the standard view, adopted here, according to which numerical and

When in examples (6–9) we implicitly compared S sentences containing *at least* with C sentences not containing *at least*, there was in each case a particular constituent focussed by *at least* whose interpretation was affected. For example, in (7) it was the AP *irritated*. More generally, Scalar *at least* always focusses a constituent and affects the interpretation of the sentence by affecting the interpretation of this constituent. The syntactic side of this semantic property is that, as one might expect, Scalar *at least* is always in construction with the constituent it focusses. More particularly, it may occur either as a left sister with no special intonational marking or somewhere to the right of its focus with parenthetical intonation. In (7), repeated as (15) to follow, we see Scalar *at least* as left sister of the constituent it focusses. In the slightly altered examples (16a–16c) we find Scalar *at least* as a right parenthetical.

15.   He's going to be at least IRRITATED.

16-a.   He's going to be IRRITATED, at least.

16-b.   He's going to be IRRITATED—at least—that I didn't call.

16-c.   He's going to be IRRITATED that I didn't call—at least.

But Scalar *at least* cannot focus at a distance (from the left). For example, in sentence initial position Scalar *at least* can only focus the subject. Thus in

17.   At least he's going to be irritated that I didn't call.

unless *he* receives special stress, indicating that it is the focus, the only possible interpretation is one requiring a different *at least*. In this interpretation, discussed in the next section, it is a necessary part of the context that his getting irritated is a good thing.

---

other scalar predicates are lower bounded by entailment and upper bounded only by generalized conversational implicature. (For a recent discussion of this view and references to earlier literature, see Horn, 1985). That is, if the inherent (linguistic, literal, truth conditional, etc.) meaning of *three* were taken to be '3' rather than '3 or more' as in currently standard doctrine, then it would be easy to say that putting (Scalar) *at least* before *three* adds to "3" the interval lower bounded by 3 just as putting *at most* before *three* adds to "3" the interval upper bounded by 3.

I drop this matter now and continue to treat Scalar *at least* as a suspender of the upper bounding implicature of scalar predicates; that is, for present purposes I confess inability to explicate the meaning of Scalar *at least* in a way that captures the intuition that it is the "opposite" of *at most*. (I put "opposite" in scare quotes because of the notorious elusiveness of that notion, if in fact there is a single such notion.)

Kempson (1980 and elsewhere) and her associates have argued that *three* is inherently ambiguous between "3" and "3 or more." These arguments have, however, suffered persuasive counterarguments (Horn, 1984). It remains possible that the standard story (in which the truth condition of a scalar predicate is the corresponding rising interval) could be wrong and yet the conflicting Kempson story (according to which each such predicate is ambiguous between a rising interval and a punctual reading) also could be wrong.

It is interesting to note that the very similar expression *at the (very) least* does not have this limitation. Thus, there is no problem with (18) under standard assumptions that we don't like to irritate people.

18. At the (very) least he's going to be IRRITATED that I didn't call.

That is, whereas Scalar *at least* must occur no further to the left of its focus than as sister to that focus, this restriction does not hold for *at the (very) least,* which as far as I can tell means the same thing as Scalar *at least.*[8]

A final syntactic property of Scalar *at least* should be briefly noted. The constituent with which Scalar *at least* is in construction, and which it modifies, is a maximal constituent, or in the familiar X-bar terminology a "maximal projection." There is a general tendency for scalar operators and for focus operators (significantly overlapping but not coextensive categories) to appear in construction with and as modifiers of maximal categories, often maximal categories of several different kinds, and not infrequently with any maximal category that can serve as a predicate.[9] Other focus and/or scalar operators that semantically modify and syntactically appear in construction with maximal categories include those italicized in (19).

19-a. John is *quite* the ideal spouse for Mary.

19-b. That was *sort of* the best he could do under the circumstances.

19-c. She's *too* ready to trust anyone to be trusted herself.

19-d. He's *too much* the bureaucrat for her to like him.

19-e. *Absolutely* the last person I wanted to see walked through that door.

---

[8]I am indebted to Charles Fillmore for example (18). It demonstrates nicely that although sometimes the conventions that tie a certain semantic form to a corresponding syntactic form are general, these conventions can also at times be highly specific. Insofar as the conventions are general we tend to think of them as productive rules, while the narrower the conventions associating meaning to form become the more likely we are to think of them as minor rules, collocations, idioms, or the like. In construction grammar the constructions simply are these conventional associations, whatever their degree of generality or particularity. In this framework, consequently, questions such as whether or not syntax is autonomous or whether or not syntax is determined by semantics do not naturally arise.

[9]Statements about tendencies of this kind are best viewed as meta-grammatical. The constructions that collectively account for the form meaning correspondences of a language constitute the grammar of that language. (There may be abstract constructions and an inheritance hierarchy according to which several concrete constructions can be shown to have features in common.) Additional statements of tendency and partial correlation across constructions are statements *about* the grammar. For example, the hedges *kind of* and *sort of* are focus operators but not scalar operators and occur in construction with, not only maximal categories, but categories of any "bar" status (Kay, 1984).

EVALUATION

The distinction between Scalar *at least* and the *at least* construction discussed in this section is recognized by Anscombre and Ducrot (1983, p. 139) with regard to the French expression *au moins*. A & D contrast the use of *au moins* in (20), which they call a quantitative use with that in (21), which they call, as they say arbitrarily, a modal use.[10]

20. Ça vaut au moins 30 F.
    That costs at least thirty francs.

21. J'aime bien ce restaurant: au moins, on sait ce que l'on y mange.
    I like that restaurant; at least you know what you're eating there.

A & D present an analysis of the use of *au moins* within Ducrot's theory of linguistic argumentation, which while differing in some detail from that presented here, encompasses the major intuition that this usage of *au moins/at least* has the two semantic properties of indicating positive evaluation and of indicating a less than maximal scalar degree: hence, putting these two together, of indicating a less than maximal degree of positive evaluation.

To establish the contrast between Scalar *at least* and the construction utilizing *at least* under consideration here, consider the following paradigm.

22-a. In that big trainwreck at least several people were saved.
22-b. In that big trainwreck at least several people were killed.
22-c. At least in that big trainwreck several people were saved.
22-d. At least in that big trainwreck several people were killed.

In example (22-d) an unusual set of background assumptions is necessary for the sentence to be pragmatically usable. It is clear that the function of *at least* in (22-c,d) is not to produce an interpretation of *several* as "several or more." In fact, try as one may one cannot get an interpretation for (22-d) parallel to that of (22-b). In initial position *at least* requires that the sentence be viewed as describing an event that is positively evaluated. In the scalar model framework of FKO, we would say that the abcissa of the scalar model at work represents events (real or hypothetical) with which the described event contrasts while the ordinate represents degrees of positive evaluation. With regard to (22-c), two relevant hypothetical events contrasting with the one described in the sentence might be the case in which no one was saved in the wreck and the case in which many people were saved (or all the people, and so on). In this particular case the alternative

---

[10]The analysis of A & D is based on the earlier analysis of Ducrot (1980, p. 104ff).

hypothetical events involve variations in a quantitative variable, but this is not necessary. For example, if Fred wants to marry a Norwegian mathematician who likes folk dancing, he could say about Helga

23. Unfortunately she's Danish, but at least she has a Ph.D. in math and adores folk dancing.

Let us call this kind of *at least* "Evaluative *at least*." (We should bear in mind that Evaluative *at least* is a scalar operator, just as Scalar *at least* is, but that the two are distinct scalar operators.) In initial position, *at least* cannot be of the Scalar variety unless the subject bears marked focus prosody. For example, in (17) we noted that unless *he* bears focus prosody the sentence must be interpreted as containing Evaluative *at least*. We return to the syntactic specification of the Evaluative *at least* construction presently. For the moment, having established the semantic property of evaluation for this construction, we turn our attention to the semantic property of nonmaximality.

A & D (1983, p. 140) make the point about the positive evaluation aspect of *au moins 'modale'* with the following examples, in which *au moins* is translated by *at least*.

24. Stay in that hotel; it's noisy but at least it's comfortable.
25. *Don't stay in that hotel; it's calm but at least its uncomfortable.

In earlier work, Ducrot (1980, p. 105) had come very close to the point about nonmaximality. He comments on the use of *au moins* in an analogous example in the following terms: "[The example sentence] means that [the hotel described], as against [a hypothetical alternative], is in the desirable category but at a lower level [of desirability]. (It is usual for *au moins* to yield this kind of argumentative effect: in asking, 'Has Pierre at least [*au moins*] read Chomsky?' one gives his hearer to understand that having read Chomsky is a desirable but minimal condition.)"

However, in considering the matter of degree of positive evaluation, A & D present an analysis that relies too closely on the structure of the particular example chosen, generalizing from sentences like (24) and (25) to a paradigm with 16 possibilities in which each of two properties (e.g., noise, comfort) is predicated positively or negatively of each of two subjects (e.g., the hotel we're talking about, a hypothetical alternative). They conclude that in saying about some individual O, *O at least has P* (where P is a desirable property), a speaker presents P as the single desirable property O has as compared to the contextually relevant alternative, O'.

This is wrong within its chosen universe of discourse, as indicated by example (23), where O (Helga) has two desirable properties: being a mathematician and liking square dancing. The correct limitation on positive evaluation is not limitation to a single property, but, as we will see, envisioning a contextually relevant event that is even more favorable than the one reported.

The A & D analysis is also overly restricted in supposing that there have to be precisely one pair of alternative individuals (subjects) and two pairs of possible properties (predicates). For example, zero-adic (argumentless) predicates are perfectly comfortable in Evaluative *at least* sentences such as (26), in which no semantic element plays the role of A & D's O; that is, (26) has no semantic subject.

26. Well, at least it's not snowing.[11]

But the A & D analysis is by no means entirely awry. It is concerned to explain that this use of *at least/au moins* requires that the event described be viewed by the speaker as (1) good; that is, better than some contextually relevant neutral or bad event and (2) not as good as some other relevantly imaginable event. The insight is that you can't say (27), but you can say (28).

27. *This hotel's quiet, and at least it's comfortable.
28. This hotel's noisy, but at least it's comfortable.

That is, an Evaluative *at least* sentence not only has to describe an event that is better than a contextually relevant alternative but it also has to describe an event that is not so good as a (different) contextually relevant alternative. The noisy but comfortable hotel described in (28) is immediately comparable both to an inferior alternative, which is noisy and uncomfortable and to a superior alternative, which is quiet and comfortable.[12] In the terms of the scalar model analysis of FKO, Evaluative *at least* (1) requires interpretation in a two-dimensional scalar model in which alternative events to the one described constitute the abcissa and

---

[11]This is a standard view, but not the only one. Bolinger (1977) has argued that weather *it* is part of a perhaps more general ambient *it* that has semantic content. But even if we were to grant that weather *it* is semantically contentful, it is hard to see what the alternative semantic subject, the O' that is required by the A & D analysis, could be; that is, even if we were to grant that (26) means something approximately like 'The weather is not snowing,' it would still be hard to imagine an alternative semantic subject for this sentence.

[12]In the oral presentation of this chapter, some auditors were distracted by the contrasting presence of *and* in (27) and *but* in (28). This alternation is, to be sure, connected with the fact that whereas *quiet* and *comfortable* are pragmatically cooriented here (both desirable properties) *noisy* and *comfortable* are contrastive. But the overt presence of *and* versus *but* has nothing to do with acceptability of *at least*. Consider the slightly altered versions

(27') A: This hotel's quiet.
 B: *At least it's comfortable.
(28') A: This hotel's noisy.
 B: At least it's comfortable.

degrees of desirability or goodness constitute the ordinate, and (2) there are two context propositions required (either explicitly stated or furnished by pragmatic accomodation): one representing a less desirable event than the one described and one representing a more desirable event.[13]

Returning now to the syntactic characterization of the Evaluative *at least* construction, we note that what we have described on the semantic level is an operator that takes a sentential argument without any particular sentence internal comparative focus. We are therefore not surprised to find that Evaluative *at least* appears syntactically as an unfocussed parenthetical, having essentially no role in the structure of the sentence. Initial, final, and preverbal position are favorite places for parenthetical insertions in English, though they are not the only such positions available.[14]

29. At least I passed!
30. I at least passed!
31. I passed, at least!

We have observed that sentence final position with parenthetical intonation is open to both Evaluative *at least* and to Scalar *at least*. In a later section this matter will come up again.

RHETORICAL RETREAT

The third and final usage or family of usages of *at least* to be described here is exemplified by quite a range of syntactic forms.

32. Mary is at home, at least John's car is in the driveway.
33. Mary is at home, at least I think so.
34. Mary is at home, at least that's what Sue said.
35. Mary will help me, at least {intermitently, for a short time, on the preliminary draft, to get started, if it doesn't rain, when I've finished the outline}.

Let us consider the unity of semantic function that binds these diverse examples together before attacking the problem of the diversity of syntactic forms they display. Actually, providing a satisfying analysis of the seeming semantic unity will alone provide a greater challenge than I am equal to. Taking examples (32–

---

[13]See Kay (1990) for elaboration of the notions of context proposition and pragmatic accommodation with regard to scalar operators.

[14]This would not be the appropriate place to attempt a full description of the syntax of English parentheticals.

34) first, we see that in each case the clause introduced by *at least* functions to provide the speaker with authority for asserting the clause to which it is appended. John's car being in the driveway is offered as an observation that, because it provides evidence for the truth of the proposition that Mary is at home, provides authority to the speaker for so asserting. Note particularly that with respect to example (32), even presented as it is here without supporting context, one can deduce from the sentence itself that an utterance of it will be appropriate only in a context in which the presence of John's car in the driveway can be counted on to provide evidence of Mary's being at home. To a first approximation then, our hypothesis regarding the semantic value of this form of *at least* will be that *at least* introduces a clause or fragment that provides the speaker with authority for an accompanying assertion.

But if examples (35) are to be covered under the same semantic description, the function of *at least* in examples (32–34) must be something more general than the introduction of a proposition that provides authority for a proposition already on the floor. Examples (35) add a qualification to the **content** of the proposition already asserted and do not address the issue of the speaker's warrant for its assertion. I would like to suggest that the appropriate generalization of our first-order hypothesis, which was based only on examples (32–34), to cover the full set of examples including (35), is captured intuitively by the notion of a **rhetorical retreat,** something that will include but not be restricted to the provision of authority function displayed in examples (32–34).

Note first that in (32–34), the clause introduced by *at least* is understood as doing more than merely providing authority for the clause that precedes it: Rather the statement of the authority for asserting that Mary is at home is taken to replace, as the assertion of record, the statement that Mary is at home. Thus (32) may be roughly paraphrased by

36. John's car is in the driveway and that suggests/confirms/gives some degree of authority for the assertion/ . . . that Mary is at home.

In the examples considered so far in this section, in which the clause or fragment introduced by *at least* comes at the end of the sentence, the effect is that of an afterthought qualification. We suppose the speaker first asserts that Mary is home and then qualifies this assertion by saying, in effect, well, I shouldn't really assert that Mary's home—I retract my bald assertion—but I do have the following authority to support such a claim: John's car is in the driveway. Let us call this construction, or family of constructions, "Rhetorical *at least.*"

We may note in passing that in examples (33) and (34), unlike (32), the authority comes, not in the form of a report about facts in the world directly, but in the form of a report about the speaker's or someone else's belief, claim, etc. Example (33), in addition, seems to have a metalinguistic flavor: the speaker cites his own belief that P is true as authority for asserting P and in so doing conveys the content of P with a lowered level of commitment than would have accrued from the straightforward assertion of P.

In considering examples (32–34), we have established that the kind of rhetorical retreat we are considering can involve the speaker's displaying the basis of his authority for making an assertion in place of simply making that assertion as a means of exposing the **content** of the target assertion with a lower level of illocutionary commitment. This may be accomplished, we have seen, either by directing attention to the evidence on which the assertion would be based or in some other way. The examples in (35) seem to involve rhetorical retreats as well, but these do not involve the authority status of a given statement: rather a comparison of the content of two distinct though related statements, one of which seems to be rhetorically 'stronger' than the other. The problem is that it is difficult to explicate what the intuition of relative strength here is based on. In certain cases this notion of strength seems explicable in terms of entailment or truth conditions, but not in all.

An example where the set of truth conditions pertinent to the qualified and unqualified statements appears relevant is the part of example (35) given in

37. Mary will help me, at least if it doesn't rain.

We may analyze this sentence in terms of the two propositions:

38. Mary will help me.
39. Mary will help me if it doesn't rain.

It seems fair to say that the truth conditions of (39) are a proper subset of the truth conditions of (38): the set of relevant worlds in which it doesn't rain is a proper subset of the set of all relevant worlds, which is by definition the set of worlds relevant to the unadorned sentence (38).

Consider, however,

40. Mary will help me to get started.
41. Mary will help me for a short time.

In neither case does it seem accurate to say that the truth set of the sentence in question is a proper subset of the truth set of (38). For example, the relevant reading of (38) in the context where (41) is relevant is something like what we find in

42. Mary will help me for as long as I need her to.

In any case it seems that it is from something like (42) that

43. Mary will help me, at least for a short time.

is a retreat. But (41) and (42) seem to be simply contradictory. In what sense then does the utterance of (43) represent a retreat from (42) to (41); that is, in what sense is (41) rhetorically weaker than (42)? I do not know the answer to this question, and it would seem that finding the answer to this question is a prerequisite to finding the answer to the more general and interesting question regarding the nature of the general concept of rhetorical strength that underlies the concept of retreat in our characterization of this use of *at least*.[15]

As we see in a later section, the Rhetorical reading can represent a rhetorical retreat from a statement about an event or situation evaluated positively and so reveal itself as pragmatically compatible with the Evaluative reading. But the rhetorical reading can also represent a retreat from an assertion denoting a negatively valued event, showing that the Rhetorical reading is semantically distinct from the Evaluative reading just as the Scalar reading is. For example, the rhetorical retreat reading of (44) does not require the unusual background assumptions of the Evaluative reading of (45), the latter being forced by the Evaluative *at least* syntax (initial position without sentence focussing prosody.)

44. She's going to ruin me, at least she has threatened to.
45. At least she has threatened to ruin me.

Turning now to the syntax of Rhetorical *at least,* my comments will be even sketchier than those regarding its semantics. Generalizing from the examples we have seen so far, we can say that Rhetorical *at least* (1) accompanies a main clause and (2) introduces a clause or fragment. It is clear from example (32) that, when the introduced constituent is a full clause, it need bear no syntactic relation at all to the main clause, including the relation of anaphora, although frequently, as in (33) and (34), the subordinate clause will bear an anaphoric relation to the main clause.

A fragment Y introduced by Rhetorical *at least* into a sentence of the form 'X, at least Y' seems always to be a possible constituent of a sentence whose segmental material is exhausted by X and Y jointly. Frequently, if not always, this will take the form "X Y." Thus, corresponding to the Rhetorical *at least* sentence (43), we have the sentence (41). Sometimes though this fragment will interrupt parenthetically, rather than follow the main clause, as in

---

[15]It is argued in Kay (1983) that distinct folk theories of reference are evoked by the hedges *loosely speaking* and *technically,* these theories, incidentally, bearing resemblances to the philosophical theories of reference associated with the names of Frege in the former case and Kripke and Putnam in the latter. One direction in which to seek what is meant by 'rhetorical retreat' in our gloss of this use of *at least* might involve the hypothesis that there is a folk theory of rhetorical strength evoked by the use of this lexical item (and perhaps others) that might (or might not) find echoes in some consciously elaborated philosophical or linguistic doctrine.

46. Mary will help us, at least temporarily, with the foreign exchange problem.

Mapping out the constraints on where these parenthetical insertions can occur is beyond the scope of this chapter.

Whether or not to consider the fragment phenomenon in general as a case of zero anaphora is a question I will not investigate here. For example, in

47. Mary caught a shark, and with her bare hands.

Is *with her bare hands* really a clause that begins with an inaudible anaphor for *Mary caught a shark?* Answers to such questions will no doubt vary with one's theoretical framework and in the current state of the art tell us more about the framework than the phenomenon. For example, in Construction Grammar the answer is No because the framework does not countenance empty categories. Hence from the CG point of view, the fragments introduced by Rhetorical *at least* are just that and not clauses containing fat empty categories. However, whereas CG has some good stories to tell about standard control phenomena and long distance dependencies, as well as superior stories to tell about optional arguments (Fillmore, 1986). CG, like every other going framework, has no satisfying theory of fragments. Lacking such an overall mapping of the domain of syntactic fragments, it is impossible for me to say what range of the variation observed in fragments introduced by *at least* is attributable to general principles or constructions. But even that modest statement is cheating, because I have not mapped out the full range of the data with regard to the kinds of fragments accepted by Rhetorical *at least*.

Finally, to complicate matters just a bit further, we find that Rhetorical *at least* can occur with the "parenthetical" syntax of Evaluative *at least* when the assertion from which it represents a retreat is expressed by a possibly nonadjacent sentence of the preceding discourse. For example, (48) can be followed by any of (49-a, -b, or -c) and the speakers of (48) and (49) can be either the same or different.

48.   They're going to invade us. (I'm sure that's what's going to happen.)
49-a.   At least there are strong indications to that effect.
49-b.   There are—at least—strong indications to that effect.
49-c.   There are strong indications to that effect, at least.

Ambiguities and Unified Interpretations

The syntax of our three varieties of *at least* has been discussed only briefly. Nevertheless, we have been able to establish that each of the three types has environments in which only it can occur, leading to univocal sentences. Thus

(50), (51), and (52) are univocal cases of Scalar, Evaluative, and Rhetorical *at least*, respectively.

50. Her trout weighed at least four pounds.
51. At least she caught a fish.
52. She fishes all day, at least on weekends.

We have also noted that the syntactic environments specified by our three *at least* constructions overlap. This leads to the possibility of *at least* occurring in a syntactic environment where more than one of the three semantic interpretations is possible.

Because we have three *at least* constructions, there are three cases of possible pairwise semantic ambiguities to consider: Scalar–Evaluative, Scalar–Rhetorical and Evaluative–Rhetorical. All three occur and we consider each in turn.

Scalar–Evaluative

It is noted by A & D (1983, p. 139) that final position is possible for both the Scalar and Evaluative *au moins* constructions: "On peut d'ailleurs imaginer des suites où l'introduction de *au moins* serait ambiguë—en particulier en position final—si l'on ne tenait pas compte de l'intonation et des pauses." A & D here state that prosody may disambiguate final *au moins* sentences and suggest that it must. Whatever the facts of French, it seems that in English an *at least* sentence such as (53), pronounced with the primary prosodic peak on *most* and with a level tone throughout the last three words, *right, at,* and *least,* can have either a Scalar interpretation as illustrated in (54), or an Evaluative interpretation as illustrated in (55).[16]

53. I got móst of the answers right, at least.
54. I got móst of the answers right, at least, and maybe áll.
55. I got móst of the answers right, at least, so I'm contént.

The Scalar and Evaluative interpretations, illustrated by (54) and (55), respectively, are not only distinct but incompatible. The Scalar interpretation specifically leaves open the possibility that I got all the answers right, but the Evaluative interpretation requires the conclusion that I did not get all of the answers right in order to satisfy the part of the semantics of the Evaluative *at least* construction which specified a **nonoptimal** outcome; that is, the context proposition for (53) which describes an event more highly evaluated than the one reported in (53) is

---

[16]Recall that Evaluative *at least* is a scalar operator though it is entirely distinct from the construction which suppresses an upper bounding implicature that we have christened the Scalar *at least* construction.

the proposition that I got (not just most of the answers right but) more than most of the answers right. Thus, *most of the answers right, at least* in (53) can't mean "most, and maybe more than most, of the answers right."

Scalar–Rhetorical

In Section 3 we noticed that, while the most usual place for a Rhetorical *at least* fragment is after the main clause to which it is attached, it can also be inserted parenthetically within this clause. When so inserted, the fragment probably has to receive parenthetical prosody, but this does not necessarily distinguish audibly the parenthetical insertion from a normal sentence constituent of the same shape occupying the same spot in the sentence. Thus, (56) can receive either the Scalar reading illustrated in (57) or the Rhetorical reading illustrated in (58).

56. He has, at least temporarily, fixed the leak.
57. He has, at least temporarily, fixed the leak—and possibly permanently.
58. He has, at least temporarily, fixed the leak. So we can catch our breath before we have to start bailing again.

Again, the two possible semantic interpretations are incompatible. The rhetorical retreat interpretation (58) requires that we understand him to have solved the problem **only** temporarily, while it is precisely this limitation that *at least* serves to block in the implicature suspension (Scalar) interpretation (57).

Evaluative–Rhetorical

With regard to the Evaluative–Rhetorical case, whenever *at least* occurs with parenthetical syntax it can be syntactically interpreted in either way.

59. My life is over. At least the most interesting part of my life is over.
60. We're making progress. At least the most difficult part of our job is finished.

In (59) the second sentence exemplifies Rhetorical *at least* while in (60) the second sentence exemplifies Evaluative *at least*.

Before proceeding to consider ambiguous examples, involving both Evaluative and Rhetorical readings, it would perhaps be advisable to review certain facts that establish that these are in fact two independent readings.

First, we established the independence of the Evaluative reading from the Scalar reading with examples like (22-d). Note that this kind of example shows that the Evaluative reading can be **imposed** by the utterance of an *at least* sentence with the appropriate syntax upon a context in which it does not naturally arise. This demonstrates that the Evaluative reading is indeed part of the relevant *at least* construction or lexical entry; that is, part of the grammar of (one lexical entry for) *at least* and not merely a contextual effect.

Secondly, let us recall examples like (44), which show that the Rhetorical reading can arise in a context that blocks the Evaluative reading, or, more precisely, show us that the grammar of the Evaluative *at least* construction would force us to accept bizarre background assumptions that are not required by the grammar of Rhetorical *at least;* that is, examples like (44) and like

61. Your dress will be ruined, at least if you don't wash the spot out right away.

show us that the Evaluative and Rhetorical interpretations are also distinguished by the grammar and do not result merely from contextual influences.

The reason I have considered it important to review these matters is that for some speakers, not all as far as I can tell, the Evaluative-Rhetorical *at least* ambiguities have an intuitive effect distinct from the other two kinds. Let us first consider a pair of sentences, both of which have the Rhetorical reading, but only one of which is ambiguous between this reading and the Evaluative one. Such is the case with (62) and (63). Only the former is construable as also Evaluative (under normal background assumptions.)

62. He's a nice boy, at least when things are going his way.
63. He's a nasty boy, at least when things aren't going his way.[17]

For some speakers, it is difficult to experience the ambiguity of a sentence like (62) as such; rather, these informants report either that they "get both readings at once" (or words to that effect) or that they "can't tell the readings apart" (or words to **that** effect); that is, while some speakers report the usual kind of "one thing or the other" effect like the familiar Necker cube, vase-face, or duck-rabbit illusions, these speakers report something involving a kind of mixture or unification of the Evaluative and Rhetorical readings for a sentence like (62). From the point of view of the grammar, these sentences are simply ambiguous: Both readings are possible. But perhaps this phenomenon, according to which compatible semantic interpretations that arise from different lexical selections seem,

---

[17]The possibility for (62) but not (63) to take the Evaluative reading is demonstrated by the following:

(62') At least he's a nice boy when things are going his way.
(63') *At least he's a nasty boy when things aren't going his way. [where the * assumes normal background assumptions]

according to the introspective reports of some speakers, to "unify" in some yet to be specified sense, might be worthy of psycholinguistic investigation.[18]

Multiple Meanings

It is apparently a fact that the several senses of *at least* identified here add up to a polysemous lexical item, rather than to three semantically unrelated, homophonous expressions.

Evaluative *at least* shares with Scalar *at least* the property of scalarity, as has been mentioned, although we have seen that Evaluative *at least* adds to the idea of attaining one contextually available alternative the additional notion of not attaining another. Evaluative *at least* places the proposition with which it is associated on a scale of evaluation by the speaker in a way that is partially, but not entirely, parallel to the way scalar *at least* places the proposition with which it is associated on a scale defined by the content and context of what is said. The relation of these two senses is not as arbitrary as it would be if alongside scalar *at least* there were a second sense meaning, say, "frankly" or "according to rumor." Without actually carrying out the historical research to prove the case, we may plausibly speculate that there is a historical connection between the scalar and evaluative senses of *at least*.

Rhetorical *at least* can be notionally related to its evaluative cousin. Rhetorical *at least* might be thought of as indicating a retreat on a scale of rhetorical commitment or assertive force. As such, if this is an appropriate characterization, this sense shares with Evaluative *at least* the property of indicating a lower value on the appropriate scale than some contextually available alternative, this time the scale in question being one of illocutionary commitment rather than evaluation. Again, it seems a reasonable conjecture that this overlap in the notional content of the two current usages of the form reflects something about the history of their co-evolution.

Some recent studies (e.g., Brugman, 1988; Lindner, 1982; Lakoff, 1987 [see especially index entries for "radial categories"], Sweetser, 1990) have implicitly or explicitly imputed all such notionally identifiable relations among word senses to the contemporary speaker's knowledge of the language; that is, to grammar. Although such studies are of undoubted linguistic interest, in the view of grammar adopted here some of them fall outside its purview. If we restrict our notion of the grammar of a language to those things a speaker must learn (or—if there is innate linguistic knowledge—know already) in order to speak and understand the language, many apparent relations like these among senses remain outside of grammar. There is no established principle of English from which, knowing the

---

[18]Similar phenomena are discussed by Norvig (1988, pp. 194–200) from the point of view of strategies for parsing and interpretation.

scalar use of *at least*, we could predict the evaluative use of this form. The two must be learned separately. Some speakers may notice the connection at the relevant level of (un)consciousness and others may not; the grammarian per se has no way to find this out.

I do not exclude all cases of polysemy from grammar. There might, for example, be a productive rule governing such cases as

64.   The air is warm/cold—I am warm/cold—This room is warm/cold.

The point is that the grammatical rule (or generalization or construction) has to specify all the cases in its domain and apply to all of them. Partial similarities, recognizable only after the fact, such as those relating the various senses of *at least*, do not qualify—until they are incorporated into an explicit principle which covers precisely those cases defined to be within its scope, a principle the speaker could learn instead of learning separately each of the items that can be predicted from it.

For the student of grammar, the descriptive job is to characterize each bit of knowledge that a person must possess in order to speak a particular language, no less and no more. (Grammatical theory then extracts the commonalities of these descriptions and attempts to express them perspicuously, within and across languages.) The bits may be as particular as the fact that the aspectual verb *stop* does not allow marked infinitive complements

65.   *He stopped to insist.

although its close relatives *start, begin, continue, cease,* etc. do. (*He continued/ceased to insist*). Or they may be as general as the fact that tensed auxiliaries precede subjects in non-subject Wh-questions (*Where he went?*). It is the grammarian's job to catalogue and make sense of all these bits, particular and general. Until they are all in, the job isn't done. Indefinitely many particular facts can be predicted from some of the general bits. For example, we don't have to have a special generalization about the fact that Wh-questions referring to past events exhibit inversion; this is included in the general rule governing Wh-inversion. (Of course, the phenomenon of inversion is itself more general than the domain of Wh-questions.)

The suggestive and historically interesting relations between word senses like those displayed by *at least* do not fall under the scope of a predictive generalization. These are separate bits that the speaker must learn severally, perhaps—or perhaps not—ultimately noticing the historically motivating relations among them. As such they do not fall within the scope of grammar, though they are of interest to the student of language history. They may also ultimately be revealed to play a role in the way some speakers access knowledge of their language in forming or interpreting utterances.

In the case of *at least,* the relations among senses considered, Scalar–Evaluative and Evaluative–Rhetorical, are—as far as I know—isolated examples. Thus, the content-scale-to-evaluative-scale relation displayed by *at least* does not appear to apply to any other scalar operator. The pattern showed in (66 a,b) does not extend to (67 a,b) nor, as far as I have noticed, to any other scalar operator; that is, (67b) is not a possible gloss of (67a).

66. a. At least John passed the test.
    b. 'John passed the test and that's a pretty good thing'
67. a. Even John passed the test.
    b. 'John passed the test and that's a good thing'

But the distinction of import here is not that between isolated instances of intersense relations and those in which several pairs of senses exhibit the same pattern. It is rather between cases in which the pattern of relations is explicit and productive and cases in which the domain of application of the generalization can be specified only by an arbitrary list of the forms to which it applies.

The best candidate for a genuinely productive pattern of polysemy of which I am aware is the case of the root and epistemic senses of the English modals, as described by Sweetser (1990, pp. 58–65). Sweetser argues that *every* root sense of a modal is related to a corresponding epistemic sense via a metaphor according to which voluntary action and belief are both subject to "forces" (Talmy, 1988). An explicit grammar of English might contain a generalization expressing the content of Sweetser's analysis, perhaps in the form of a lexical rule, because the domain of Sweetser's generalization is specified; that is, the generalization applies to every member of a class that has to be identified in the grammar for independent reasons. Sweetser's analysis of a similar systematic polysemy in the causal and adversative conjunctions of English (1990, pp. 76–86) also covers all the cases in its scope, although the independent function in the grammar of this particular class of words ({*because, since, although, despite*}) is not argued for by Sweetser—and is perhaps less self-evident than in the case of the modals.

Such analyses as Sweetser's are to be distinguished from, for example, that of Lindner (1982) regarding polysemy in the verbal particles *up* and *out. Up,* for example, can often be added to an activity verb to indicate something like 'to completion'. But not always, and no principle seems to be available to partition the potential domain of application of the generalization—something like: verbs denoting a purposeful activity with an intended result—into those to which the generalization applies and those to which it doesn't. No independent principle is offered to segregate verbs such as those appearing in the a versions of (68)–(71) from those appearing in the b versions.

68 a. He tallied up the figures.
   b. *He copied up the figures

69. a. He cut up the fish.
    b. *He scaled up the fish.
70. a. He polished up the car.
    b. *He waxed up the car
71. a. He finished up the job.
    b. *He completed up the job.

One further factor needs to be considered. As long as a linguistic generalization covers a merely finite domain, we cannot know whether the instantiation of the generalization in the behavior of a speaker reveals knowledge of a principle or merely memory of each individual instance. In the case of a generalization over a finite domain, even the application of the pattern observed by the linguist to novel cases, as in extension of phonological patterns to nonsense-word stimuli, does not present knockdown evidence for the psychological reality of the pattern. As Ohala (1974) has pointed out, such experimental results are susceptible of other explanations, including on-the-spot analogy from existing forms. Moreover, some experimental results indicate that speakers may differ amongst themselves in the degree to which they abstract from finite subcorpora of their internalized representation of the language those generalizations that the linguistic analyst has found. See, for example, Zimmer (1969) on the variation among speakers regarding the degree to which they will extend to nonsense forms the generalizations regarding Turkish vowel harmony.

Nonetheless, a reasonable goal for the grammarian would appear to be to describe every generalization that a speaker *could* abstract from the data of his or her language, leaving to the psycholinguist the hard task of determining which generalizations actually are abstracted by which speakers. We could think of this as the minimal, psychologically real grammar of the language. A speaker so equipped would be a perfect speaker, but we would bear in mind that such a speaker's behavior would be indistinguishable from that of a putative speaker whose mental representation of English, for example, contained no generalization covering the "dative" alternation, one who had merely learned separately in the case of each three-argument verb the facts about whether or not it occurs in the prepositional object and double object patterns.

Suppose we accord this broadest of possible licences to the hunter of linguistic generalizations. We put in the grammar any generalization the linguist can extract from the language data, putting aside the question of the psychological reality of generalizations that cover only a finite set of cases. Our grammatical generalizations must still do some work. They must still represent a *potential* savings over rote memorization of the cases to which they apply. Accounts of polysemy relations that do not specify their domain of application—unlike the cases of English modals and, perhaps, causative/adversative conjunctions—do not qualify as grammatical generalizations, even under this broad mandate. The notional observations we can make relating the various usages of *at least* to each other belong to the ad hoc, nonproductive family of polysemy relations. By the criterion just suggested, that a grammar needs to contain everything, but only such things, as a speaker can't figure out about his language from the other things he already knows about it (cf. Fillmore, Kay, & O'Connor, 1988, p. 502), the apparent notional relations among the three uses of *at least* do not qualify as grammatical observations.

REFERENCES

Anscombre, J., & Ducrot, O. (1983). *L'argumentation dans la langue*. Brussels: Mardaga.

Bolinger, D. (1977). *Meaning and form*. New York: Longmans.

Bresnan, J. (Ed.). (1982). *The mental representation of grammatical relations*. Cambridge, MA: MIT Press.

Brugman, C. (1988). *Story of* over: *Polysemy, semantics and the structure of the lexicon*. New York: Garland.

Ducrot, O. (1980). *Les mots du discours*. Paris: Minuit.

Fillmore, C. J. (1986). Pragmatically controlled zero anaphora. *Proceedings of the Twelfth Annual Meeting of the Berkeley Linguistics Society*, 95–107.

Fillmore, C. J. (1988). The mechanisms of 'Construction Grammar.' *Proceedings of the Fourteenth Annual Meeting of the Berkeley Linguistics Society*, 35–55.

Fillmore, C. J., Kay, P., & O'Connor, M. C. (1988). Regularity and idiomaticity in grammar: The case of *Let Alone*. *Language, 64 (No. 3)*, 501–538.

Horn, L. (1984). In defense of privative ambiguity. *Proceedings of the Tenth Annual Meeting of the Berkeley Linguistic Society*, 141–154.

Horn, L. (1985). Metalinguistic negation and pragmatic ambiguity. *Language, 61 (No. 1)*, 121–174.

Kay, M. (1979). Functional grammar. *Proceedings of the Fifth Annual Meeting of the Berkeley Linguistic Society*, 142–158.

Kay, M. (1984). Functional Unification Grammar: A formalism for machine translation. *Proceedings of Coling*, 75–78.

Kay, M. (1985). Parsing in functional unification grammar. In D. R. Dowty, L. Karttunen, & A. Zwicky (Eds.), *Natural language parsing: Psychological, computational and theoretical perspectives* (pp. 251–278). Cambridge, England: Cambridge University Press.

Kay, P. (1983). Linguistic competence and folk theories of language: Two English hedges. *Proceedings of the Ninth Annual Meeting of the Berkeley Linguistic Society*, 157–171.

Kay, P. (1984). The *kind of/sort of* construction. *Proceedings of the Tenth Annual Meeting of the Berkeley Linguistic Society*, 128–137.

Kay, P. (1989). Contextual operators: *Respective, respectively*, and *vice versa*. *Proceedings of the Fifteenth Annual Meeting of the Berkeley Linguistic Society*, (to appear).

Kay, P. (1990). EVEN *Linguistics and Philosophy, 13*, 59–111.

Kempson, R. M. (1980). Ambiguity and word meaning. In S. Greenbaum, G. Leech, & J. Svartvig (Eds.), *Studies in English linguistics for Randolph Quirk* (pp. 7–16). London: Longman.

Lakoff, G. (1987). *Women, fire, and dangerous things*. Chicago: University of Chicago Press.

Lindner, S. (1982). What goes up doesn't necessarily come down. *Papers from the eighteenth regional meeting of the Chicago Linguistic Society*, 305–323. Chicago: Chicago Linguistics Society.

Norvig, P. (1988). Interpretation under ambiguity. *Proceedings of the Fourteenth Annual Meeting of the Berkeley Linguistic Society*, 188–201.

Ohala, J. (1974). Experimental historical phonology. In J. Anderson & C. Jones (Eds.), *Historical linguistics* (Vol. 2, 353–389). Amsterdam: North–Holland.

Pollard, C., & Sag, I. A. (1987). *An information-based syntax and semantics* (Vol. 1). Stanford, CA. Center for the Study of Language and Information, Stanford University.

Sweetser, E. (1990). *From etymology to pragmatics*. Cambridge, England: Cambridge University Press.

Talmy, L. (1988). Force dynamics in language and cognition. *Cognitive Science, 2,* 49–100.

Zimmer, K. (1969). Psychological correlates of some Turkish morpheme structure constraints. *Language, 45,* 309–321.

13

Folk Theories of Meaning and Principles of Conventionality: Encoding Literal Attitude via Stance Adverb

Mava Jo Powell
The University of British Columbia

Although lexical theorists agree that a lexical entry provides a principled account of a literal rendering of meaning, theory types differ not only with respect to an appropriate formalism in which to represent this meaning, but also with respect to the way in which literalness itself is conceived. These two issues are intimately related; but in examining the latter of the two, one sees that differences typically turn on such issues as whether cognitive (descriptive) meaning is taken as an equivalent to literal meaning, on how narrowly cognitive meaning is conceived, on how sharply a line is drawn between semantic and pragmatic meaning, and on whether some aspects of pragmatic meaning are also constituents of literal meaning.

For example, one of the differences between semantic field theory and frame semantics is the extent to which each theory type encourages incorporation of socially determined attitudes within semantic description. Semantic field theorists specify the relations of sense that one lexeme incurs with others in a semantic or lexical field, the term *sense* being taken as closely equivalent to cognitive/descriptive meaning. Although other dimensions of lexical meaning, such as social and expressive meaning—subsumed under the rubric of interpersonal meaning—are recognized as aspects of lexical meaning and have been incorporated in the work of Lehrer (1983) and Lyons (1977), these latter aspects of meaning have not figured prominently in other field theoretical studies. Of course, one may maintain that interpersonal meaning is not semantic meaning; rather it is pragmatic in type and so legitimately falls outside the scope of a semantic lexical study. However that may be, the result is that, in semantic field theory, principles of conventionality are predominantly, if not exclusively, linked with definitions of sense; and through this connection, cognitive meaning, conventional meaning, and literal meaning are used interchangeably.

Within frame semantics, this set of equivalences is explicitly not maintained. Fillmore (1985) states that where "particular words or grammatical constructions appear to be dedicated to given pragmatic purposes" (pp. 233–234), aspects of meaning that are generally taken as pragmatic are regarded as part of conventional, literal meaning. In addition, because frame semantics derives from a tradition akin to ethnosemantics and is similarly committed to providing a motivating context of background conditions for understanding a word's meaning, aspects of lexical meaning that are linked with interpersonal relations and with cultural and social institutions occupy a prominent place within semantic description. Thus, in this theory type, when one defines the literal meaning of a word, one may draw on social and expressive values that would not ordinarily appear in the specification of sense relations comprising the lexical meaning of a word in semantic field theory. The consequences for a conception of literalness are marked. When compared with semantic field theory, literal meaning in frame semantics is a less restrictive conception for a number of reasons, one of which is that it may include not only descriptive but also social and expressive dimensions.

The main purpose of this study is to show that an ordinary speaker's conception of literalness, as it is revealed in uses of the lexeme, *literally,* incorporates more than a cognitive/descriptive dimension of meaning; crucially involved is an attitude of aptness. That is, an ordinary speaker's conception of literalness not only specifies the type of linguistic fit but also conventionally conveys a speaker's attitude that a particular encoding is the appropriate or correct one to use in a given instance. Moreover, this attitude reveals a speaker's close commitment to this choice. I believe that this dimension of meaning of *literally* reflects a normative attitude toward literal use in general.

Anticipating these results, one might conclude that a frame semantical conception of literal meaning is closer to one held by an ordinary speaker than is a conception formulated within field theory. However, my point is not to argue for the greater adequacy of one theory type over another on grounds of a single criterion, but to point to the differences between them and then to maintain that any lexical theory that does not include an attitudinal dimension within a theoretical definition of literalness fails to represent faithfully an ordinary speaker's conception of it. In the case of semantic field theory, this dimension of meaning needs a place either in a complementary pragmatic theory or in a less restricted notion of *sense.* In frame semantics, the condition is met within a continuing research commitment.

That a characteristic literal attitude should be a constituent of global, literal use should not be surprising since it is now generally accepted, as a result of research stimulated by speech act theory, that conventionally determined attitudes help to define not only the literal and nonliteral uses of individual speech acts but also of more global linguistic behavior. Concerning the latter of these, Gricean pragmaticists have explored to great effect the nature of a cooperative attitude as it is expected and expressed in the structure of ordinary conversation.

And if one were to seek further corroboration for global attitudinal expectations in English, one would find it in the words we have coined throughout the centuries to criticize people who ineptly or abusively misuse them. In the 14th century, *strait* (precurser to ME *strict*) characterized someone who was severe in nonlinguistic and linguistic behavior; and in the 17th century, a precisian was someone who was precise, especially in the interpretation and application of religious language and observance, often a Puritan. Although *strait* is now obsolete, both words are relevant to our present purposes because *strict* and *precise* are closely related in meaning to *literal*. Since the 17th century, *literalist* may be used to describe someone who unimaginatively insists on literal uses of language, and *literal-minded* to describe someone who not only has the literalist's habit, but who also misunderstands, typically deliberately misunderstands in obstructionist ways. Hence one can perceive from these unflattering names that speakers develop a sense for what constitutes an appropriate literal attitude.

It is the nature of this attitude that I shall characterize by explicating the stance adverb, *literally*, and also by taking into account a number of other lexemes with which *literally* incurs relations of substitution.[1] All of these lexemes perform the adverbial semantic role of modality (Quirk, Greenbaum, Leech, & Svartvik, 1985, pp. 484, 566 ff.). Their general function is to encode metalinguistic comment and attitudinal perspective on an utterance or on parts of it.

By linking literal attitude with folk theories of meaning and with principles of conventionality, my title is intended to establish two initial connections and acknowledgments. In an ethnosemantic investigation of *technically speaking* and *loosely speaking,* Kay (1983) defines two folk theories of reference that comprise ordinary speaker beliefs about the ways in which words fit the world. This study led me to see that *literally* is also used to encode an attitude not only toward the ways in which words connect with the world but also toward ways in which words connect with other words. I draw on Kay's data to construct two general correlations between attitude toward language and linguistic fit.

As for the link with principles of conventionality, these tell us: (1) If a word already exists to express a meaning, use it; don't construct another one; (2) if a word lexicalizes a meaning (concept), don't use it to mean something else, even if that meaning would fit the pattern of the language.[2] These principles were

---

[1]The set is sometimes called hedges (Brown & Levinson, 1978; Kay, 1983; Lakoff, 1972), speaker-oriented adverbs (Jackendoff, 1972), evidentials (Chafe, 1986), adverbial subjuncts and style/content disjuncts (Quirk et al., 1985) or stance adverbials (Biber & Finegan, 1988). Biber and Finegan (1988) explain: "A broad range of functions falls under the umbrella of 'stance,' including expression of certainty, generalization and actuality. All of these express some aspect of a speaker's (or writer's) attitudes toward their messages, as a frame of reference for the messages, an attitude toward or judgment of their contents, or an indication of the degree of commitment towards their truthfulness" (p. 2).

[2]I have taken these principles from Lehrer (1990), where they figure centrally. She, in turn, acknowledges Aronoff (1976), Clark (1987), Esau (1973), Kiparsky (1981), Lehrer (1983), and Paul (1889). See also Clark (this volume).

formulated to explain how speakers restrain, without wholly restricting, word formation and polysemy. Moreover, when these principles are operative, they act as strategic maxims which ensure an identifiable degree of consistency in the application of lexemic meaning. *Literally* signals that these principles are in play and that the meaning that is being applied is not only appropriate but also apt for the occasion. These principles, in turn, relate to folk theories of reference by conferring survival capacity on them. Irrespective of theory of reference, the principles will facilitate its efficient execution by perpetuating the use of an established link between word and object.

IDENTIFYING A LITERAL ATTITUDE: A LEXICAL ANALYSIS OF LITERALLY

The following examples in which a literal, linguistic intention is explicitly cued by *literally* are taken from speakers/writers who are not theorists of language. An explication will show that an ordinary speaker associates with explicitly signalled literal uses of expressions the normative stance of using the literal resources of the language with self-conscious attention to accuracy and aptness. This is not to claim that all literal uses of language are accurate and apt uses, but rather to maintain that, when a speaker reflects on literal uses and these reflections emerge as metalinguistic comment, the attitude conveyed is a normative one.[3]

Because nothing in the nature of communication itself forces the pairing of this set of attitudes with literal uses of language, one must assume that the attitudes were conferred as values appropriate to the linguistic occasions when speakers needed to make a literal/nonliteral distinction. The earliest attested use, 1382, is ecclesiastical: "Holy scripture hath iiij vndirstondingis; literal, alle-gorik, moral, and anagogik" (*O.E.D.*, 1971, s.v. "literal"). Moreover, because the source of English *literal* is either Old French *litéral* or late Latin *lit(t)erālis,* our first ecclesiastical uses may have been motivated by an earlier, four-fold biblical exegetical method of reading codified by Cassian (*Collationes*) and developed by St. Thomas Aquinas. In this method, three mystical or spiritual senses were derived from the historical or literal: "That signification whereby things signified by words have themselves also a signification is called the spiritual sense, which is based on the literal and presupposes it" (*Basic Writings,* ed. Anton C. Pegis, 1944, I, pp. 16–17; quoted by Taylor, 1979, pp. 223–24 n. 4). In this register, literal exegesis and literal construal had serious moral and

---

[3]Eva Kittay (p.c.) has remarked that theorists of language are used to thinking of attitude as constitutive of ironic, but not of (global) literal use. I believe, however, that just as lexical senses operate on principles of contrast, so do attitudes. An ironical attitude is distinctive in virtue of differing from a literal attitude.

ethical consequences.[4] This being the case, it is plausible to assume that an attitude of due care with respect to literal use became pragmatically paired with literal meaning construals.

The *O.E.D.* maintains that, by extension, this use had transferred by 1597 to one in which *literal* designated the etymological or relatively primary sense of a word, or the sense expressed by the actual wording of a passage. Both of these uses are connected with scholarly pursuits in which attitudes of due care and aptness are requisite. It may be that the Latin source affected this extension as well, since the plural form could mean "learning, scholarship, 'letters,' " and since an early but now obsolete English use of *literally* was to denote letters of the alphabet. One can see that a concern for applying literal meaning in apt and accurate ways was appropriate to very early English uses. In addition, all these early uses may be associated with socially prestigious English registers; therefore, any speaker who accepted the distinction and the attitudes would not be stigmatized or otherwise disadvantaged. How these attitudes came to be associated with all literal uses would take us into an examination of the ways in which traditional school grammars, the rise of printing, and the introduction of dictionaries helped to perpetuate and prescribe normative literal uses. An explication of *literally* will show, however, that attitudes which were conferred as values plausibly linked with early historical contexts now accompany all explicitly signalled literal uses.

We shall examine five categories of contemporary use. In the first, an examination of folk definitional uses and a consideration of a prototypical set of folk definitional conditions show that *literally* characteristically signals accuracy of fit in an all purpose register. Two attitude-to-fit correlations that bear on a number of metalinguistic locutions also show that closeness of fit is correlated with closeness of commitment and that *literally* encodes these dimensions. Four other categories of use, *literally* with lexemes which denote extreme cases; with dual readings; with formulary constructions; and with nonresonant, nonliteral expressions reinforce the claim that a normative attitude of aptness accompanies all uses. Of these categories of use, the last is the most interesting because in it *literally* is used to comment on a nonliteral reading. Contrary to what one might expect, this use is neither odd nor paradoxical; rather it illustrates that the lexeme exhibits great continuity of function in both literal and nonliteral environments. A concluding section considers the implications of a strengthening of subjectivity in the meaning of *literally* for polysemous extension and the role of attitude in defining speech styles.

---

[4]By "register" I mean "a configuration of semantic resources that a member of a culture typically associates with a situation type" (Halliday, 1979, p. 11). Cruse (1986) further explains: "Registers are varieties of language used by a single speaker, which are considered appropriate to different occasions of use" (p. 283).

Literally in Folk Definition

In the first category of use, the examples are expressly concerned with giving a definition. Because the speakers are nonlinguists who are directing their definition to a general audience, I call these folk definitions. This definitional context of use is preeminently metalinguistic, and so it provides an optimal linguistic frame for substituting Kay's adverbs for *literally*. To compress this procedure and summarize data from this category of use, I shall use the following three examples to construct a prototypical folk definition in which to show how each of the stance adverbs affects its conditions.

In sentence (1) the speaker is a Russian geneticist who has emigrated and now writes to a Western audience:

(1) The persecutors operated on the principle of the rigid determinism of human consciousness based on social conditions. Literally translated, this meant that if you or your parents had lived well before the Revolution, you were an enemy of the Revolution and should be destroyed (Berg, 1988, p. 25).

Here the speaker explains the meaning of a principle from the early postrevolutionary period of Soviet political ideology. She does not give the meaning via synonyms; rather she gives an example of the application of the principle in words that a Western reader not familiar with the ideology will understand. Moreover, the example is chosen to reveal the euphemistic phrasing of the principle. Here, the expression *literally translated* is closely paraphrasable by such expressions as *in reality, in practice,* and *actually.* Thus the literal attitude not only carefully fits words from one official register to words in another unofficial one but then fits words to world in order to expose an ideologically sanctioned violation of human rights. The evaluative dimension of the definitional illustration is an integral part of it.

In the next example, sentence (2), no evaluational dimension is highlighted:

(2) The word "inhibit" literally means to stop, prevent, prohibit, restrain (Maltz, 1960, p. 169).

The word being defined, *inhibit,* is a technical term in psychology; the writer, who is explaining its meaning in a popular account, chooses words from among those he assumes a nonspecialist reader will know. But unlike in example (1), the semantic relationship that is established is between a word in its technical sense and close synonyms in a nontechnical register.

In sentence (2), the closest lexical contrast with *literally* is *technically,* a lexeme that Kay (1983) roughly glosses as "stipulated by those persons in whom society has vested the right so to stipulate" (p. 134). Kay explains that this folk theory of reference is in rough agreement with Putnam's (1975) claims that, in a division of linguistic labor, a society of speakers will invest certain specialists with the authority to legislate in cases where technical uses are required and especially where referents must be identified as legitimate, natural kind exemplars. When *literally* is used contrastively with *technically,* as in examples (1) and (2), the folk theory maintains that the expert can explain the technical use in terms which nonexperts can understand and that the fit between the two will be careful, unless we are told otherwise.

One way that a speaker might signal that a careful fit is not being observed is to qualify the definition with the expression, *loosely put.* As Kay (1983) explains, its use signals a "laxness in obedience to the rules of language" or "looseness with respect to stylistic canons" (p. 132). As we shall see in a summarizing prototypical folk definition, *loosely speaking* relieves a speaker of finding the closest possible similarity of meaning between the word being defined and the defining word or example.

All the uses of *loosely speaking* that Kay (1983) examines lead him to posit a folk theory of reference that is distinctly Fregean: "In this framework words may refer to or represent world objects because the former have intensions that maybe matched by the actual properties of the latter" (p. 136). And because, as scientific theories of language, Putnam's theory expressly rejects Frege's intensional assumptions (Putnam, 1975, pp. 218–219), Kay (1983) concludes that folk theories of reference are locally consistent but globally inconsistent (p. 137). So far as I have been able to discover, explicitly signalled literal uses do not help one to choose between the two folk theories of reference; instead, irrespective of folk theory, *literally* encodes an attitude of self-consciously careful choice and narrowness of fit.

The next example (3) concludes the set that illustrates utterances expressly concerned with definition and completes the data for making a generalization about folk definition.

(3) What is potpourri? Simply, it is a mixture of aromatic and decorative flowers, herbs, and spices. Literally, the word comes from the French and means 'rotten pot' (Harley, 1980, p. 88).

Notice that this example contains two definitions. The first, which follows the lexeme *simply,* is a definition via properties of the noun being defined, and it is not lexically marked for explicit, literal construal. However, the second definition is. In this case, *literally* signals that the word itself comes from another language in which it bears the meaning "rotten pot." *Literally* thus means roughly both "originally" and perhaps "word-for-word." *Literally* forces the closeness of fit from the word in French to the meaning in French, but it makes no claim respecting the closeness of fit from the French meaning to the English meaning.[5]

---

[5]Alan Cruse (p.c.) has pointed out that the contemporary French meaning of *potpourri* is not "rotten pot," but, like the contemporary English meaning, may denote a jar filled with an assortment of flowers and herbs. Harley has given the meaning, not of contemporary French *potpourri*, but of the noun *pot* ("pot") and the adjective *pourri* ("rotten").

In summarizing the folk definitional function of *literally,* I shall take as a prototypical case one that is not qualified by stance adverbs and that consists of three conditions. One can then see how each of the stance adverbs, *literally, technically, strictly,* and *loosely* affect it.

Condition 1: The word being defined and the defining words come from the same natural language.
Literally, technically and *strictly* may override this condition to signal a different language.
Loosely is uninformative if used to specify change from one language to another.
Condition 2: The defining words come from a stock of vocabulary items that are not particular to a specialist use.
Literally and *loosely* may confirm this condition.
Technically and *strictly* override this condition to signal a specialist use.
Condition 3: Conventionally established, close similarities of meaning hold between the word being defined and the defining words.
Literally, technically, strictly confirm this condition.
Loosely overrides this condition.

Thus, one can see that *literally, technically,* and *strictly* pattern together in opposition to *loosely* in two of the three conditions. *Strictly* and *technically* signal a specialist's use; *literally* and *loosely* do not.

On a continuum with severity at one end and laxness at the other, *strictly* and *technically* fall toward the severe end, *loosely* toward the lax end, and *literally* in between. This patterning appears in both definitional and nondefinitional uses. Where selection of register is involved, however, the narrower the fit, the more likely it is that a specialized register is involved. *Literally* characteristically signals accuracy in an all-purpose register, one that is available to specialists and nonspecialists alike.

What now of attitude? Within any register, a speaker may express attitudinal commitment to a proposition, to an illocutionary force, or to an individual lexical item (Stubbs, 1986, p. 4). The syntactic mobility of stance adverbs greatly facilitates this variety of scope.[6] Moreover, if one collocates information from a number of studies (Brown & Levinson, 1978; Kay, 1983; Lakoff, 1972; Quirk et al., 1985; Stubbs, 1986), one may arrive at the following systematic attitude-to-fit correlations that characterize all uses:

---

[6]Lyons' (1977, p. 749 ff.) extension of Hare's speech act theory provides for the theoretical encoding of variations in semantic scope in that neustic, phrastic, and/or tropic may or may not be modally qualified. Both Lyons (1977, 1981) and Halliday (1970) have emphasized the interpersonal function that modality serves.

Correlation 1: The looser the fit of word-to-word or word-to-world, the greater is the speaker's attitudinal distance or detachment from what is said or the way in which it is said.

(*Loosely speaking, so-called, so-to-speak, quote unquote, roughly* exhibit this correlation.)

Correlation 2: The closer the fit of word-to-word or word-to-world, the greater is the speaker's attitudinal commitment to or responsibility for what is said or the way in which it is said.

(*Strictly speaking, technically speaking,* and *literally* exhibit this correlation.)[7]

We will see now that Correlation 2 is characteristic of *literally* not only in definitional but in all uses.

Literally with Lexemes that Denote Extreme Cases

A second category of use of *literally* is illustrated in examples in which it precedes some lexeme that denotes an extreme case. The lexeme may not be contiguous with *literally,* but it is in its scope. This use is motivated by a speaker's own astonishment at an outcome or by anticipation that the hearer will be surprised by or doubtful of the extreme case. Sometimes both reactions are operative. *Literally* affirms the claim and the choice of words that encodes it. In sentence (4), *literally* precedes a universal quantifier:

(4) Suddenly, in late September, the vice president's lead melted literally to nothing in Bob Teeter's polls (*Newsweek,* Nov. 21, 1988, p. 118);

in (5), it precedes a number denoting an exceptionless quantity:

(5) And I literally hadn't one day without a cigarette in 20 years (Foley, 1986, p. 102);

and in (6), it precedes a description of desperation and emotional intensity:

(6) He began to swear blasphemously, horribly, foully. All that he had learned of vileness among the vile with whom he had consorted, he poured over us. He literally and actually foamed (Wren, 1924, p. 309.)

---

[7]As Fillmore, Kay, and O'Conner (1988) show, the negotiation of speaker commitment may be made through subtle linguistic interaction of conjoined clauses. The function of the idiom *let alone* also illustrates how the notion of fit must include not only what is said but how it is said. See especially their discussion of the pragmatics of this idiom (pp. 432–533).

In each of these examples, the presence of *literally* is intended to force a non-hyperbolical—that is, a literal—meaning. It is also used to increase rhetorical emphasis on the extreme case. The emphatic effect is particularly noticeable in (6), where the partially synonymous *actually* is conjoined with *literally*. In each of these three sentences, the speakers try to pre-empt a hearer's reaction through disclosure. By using *literally*, they simultaneously acknowledge the extremity and signal that the claim is nonetheless accurate as stated.

Example (7) operates in a similar way. Here, *literally* collocates with a numerical approximation that locates a number at the large end of a scale:

(7) North Americans are investing literally billions of dollars in fitness clubs and spas, diets, health foods, vitamin and mineral supplements, and rejuvenating cosmetics and surgery (Katz, 1989, p. 84).

In this example, *literally* signals not only that the approximation is accurate in its range, but also that the speaker judges this number to be significant in its largeness. Perhaps the speaker anticipates that the reader will be surprised at the count. More generally, when *literally* collocates with vague quantifying expressions, its use is predominantly evaluative and expressive. It solicits credence for the quantity by emphasizing the speaker's commitment to its significance; that is, the function of *literally* is not to resolve the vagueness, but to affirm the significance of the judgment relative to some norm or expectation (Powell, 1985).

Literally in Dual Readings

In the third category of use, *literally* is used to instruct an interlocutor to a dual reading. The next two examples show that speakers conceive of a literal meaning in relation to some other contextually appropriate meaning that is explicitly or implicitly categorized as nonliteral. These categorizations, however, do not coincide with those a lexical theorist would make, since the nonliteral categorizations in these examples are conventional, formulary constructions. All the same, *literally* is used to designate the conventional, compositional reading.

In example (8), the nonliteral alternative is named:

(8) Ed tried to build the relationship with Paul, hoping to give him the kind of male companionship he had never had, but Paul had slammed the door, literally as well as figuratively, in Ed's face (Green & Provost, 1988, p. 192).[8]

---

[8]Cruse (1986, pp. 37–45) rightly distinguishes among idioms, collocations, and "dead" metaphors. My examples (8), (9), (10), (13), and (14) are either idioms or dead metaphors. Because I can't decide which categorization is appropriate, I hedge by calling them formulary constructions. If they are idioms, then using Fillmore, Kay, and O'Conner's (1988) criteria, they are "grammatical idioms," a "formal" (vs. substantive) type in which "familiar pieces [are] familiarly arranged."

Although the construction, *to slam the door in someone's face,* is formulary, the speaker recognizes it as figurative, if only to distinguish it from the compositional, literal alternative. The linguistic aptness of the dual reading is that the circumstances that may have led to the coining of the metaphor have held on this occasion. Not only was the door actually slammed, but the action was a physical expression of attitudinal rejection. The formulary construction now encodes only the attitudinal meaning; but because both formulary and nonformulary readings are apposite, the speaker calls attention to and intends both.

In example (9), a dual reading is signalled by *literally* when an idiomatic construal is also contextually salient. *Literally* does not override the idiomatic construal; rather it calls attention also to the literal, compositional (nonidiomatic) meaning:

(9) For once, Harald Hardrada was caught napping, literally (BBC 2 Television, 1979).

The collocation, *to be caught napping,* has the formulary interpretation that one has been placed at a disadvantage through lack of attention and that someone else has profited. Here, the commentator employs *literally* to draw the viewers' attention to the truth conditions that also support a nonidiomatic reading. Without this reading, one cannot draw the intended conclusion that Hardrada was, in fact, asleep. But in addition, viewers were also expected to seek the idiomatic construal; otherwise, no point would be made about Hardrada's defeat. Thus both of these readings were required to arrive at the correct, historical fact that he was overcome and defeated while he slept.

In the preceding examples (8) and (9), the conditions of applicability, here truth conditions, are different, yet co-occurrent, for each reading in each of the dual construals. Moreover, one reading provides a linguistic context for the other. One can see, too, that the use of *literally* reveals that speakers are at least unconsciously aware of a point made by Kittay (1987, pp. 79–80), that specificity of meaning rather than multiplicity of meaning is the norm expected by interlocutors. That being so, if a speaker intends a dual reading, an interlocutor may well miss it unless the speaker or context signals it in some obvious way. Kittay (1987) explains that "an utterance in which a single meaning cannot be specified . . . draws attention to itself and thereby captures our attention" (p. 80). This observation may be extended to dual readings in which a single meaning is explicitly not signalled.[9]

---

[9]See Kittay's (1987, pp. 77–82) *General Independence of Applicability Principle* and *The Special Independence of Applicability Conditions Principle (for metaphor and other second-order significations).* These principles operate when more than one construal is required in a given context and when the context itself is not rich enough to yield disambiguation. Since *literally* explicitly cues the reader in my examples, the Principles may or may not be required, depending on the linguistic astuteness of the interlocutor.

Principles of conventionality greatly facilitate specification of meaning, and they are responsible for the heightened effect of dual readings, even in literary contexts where one would expect semantic ambiguity in aesthetic profusion. Formalist literary critics explain the heightening effect by showing how dual readings contribute to linguistic defamiliarization, a process that makes familiar uses of language seem strange (Shklovsky, repr. 1965). Dual readings invigorate ordinary language use through doubly perceived accuracy and aptness of fit.

Literally with Formulary Constructions, as Semantic Innovator

In our fourth subcategory of use, *literally* occurs with formulary constructions and acts in the capacity of semantic innovator. In sentence (10) the speaker achieves linguistic defamiliarization by using *literally* to restructure a formulary construction. The semantic alteration is motivated by a desire to effect a closer fit of the formulary construction to the real-world situation to which it is to apply. However, more than a speaker's commitment to truth is expressed: The semantic restructuring is achieved with linguistic flair.[10] Notice how *literally* serves both truth conditional and aesthetic functions:

(10) Most anthropological theory is based on fragmentary evidence: a femus here, an incisor there. But what Johanson found needed no jigsaw reconstruction. The collection of dozens of bones was literally the skeleton in Homosapiens' closet (Stoler, 1981, pp. 76–77).

A skeleton in the closet is a formulary construction which denotes a situation that has been left largely unexamined and tacitly not spoken of because close scrutiny would result in embarrassment to those involved. Here, the idiom is restructured in two ways. First, it is given the qualifier *Homosapiens,* and then it is deprived of its formulary potential to express a state of embarrassment as a result of restoring the meaning of the lexeme *skeleton* to literal status. The embarrassment for anthropologists has been that their theory of evolution has been postulated upon scanty evidence; but now, upon discovering a new cache of bones, they can construct a far more legitimately constructed skeleton. Its presence eliminates their embarrassment. Yet a new metaphor remains: The classification *Homosapiens* does not literally possess a closet; however, if it did, we might now find an actual skeleton in it. Thus, as Kittay (1987) remarks, the cognitive potential of metaphor "causes us to think about something in a new way, to reorganize the concepts we already have, and to form new conceptualizations" (p. 75). In example (10), a new metaphor reorganizes a formulary construction, and the

---

[10]Cruse (1986, p. 47 n.) calls attention to modifications of idioms and says that the result is that of innovation and semantic intensification.

explicit use of *literally* not only effects the reorganization but also signals a speaker's commitment to accuracy and aptness of expression.

Literally with Nonresonant, Nonliteral Expressions, as Aesthetic Justifier

In the final subcategory of use, *literally* is paired with nonresonant, nonliteral expressions. It is important to see that, in all these examples, the expression being qualified by *literally* is not strikingly original. The function of *literally* is to encode the speaker's aesthetic judgment that the message, as expressed, is not merely warranted by its capacity to satisfy conditions of applicability but is especially tellable—worth displaying because clever (Labov, 1972; Pratt, 1979, pp. 47–50, pp. 136–148). *Literally,* rather than some other closely synonymous lexeme such as *really,* is chosen to encode these impressions because its attitudinal meaning conveys aptness and because the expressive cleverness is appreciated by attending to a literal meaning that the construction or expression trades on for achieving its nonliteral effect. Therefore, even though principles of conventionality are not observed in the final, nonliteral interpretation, a reader is asked explicitly to make use of them as a way of appreciating the nonliteral.

In example (11) *literally* is used to qualify a metaphor:

> (11) Our habits are literally garments worn by our personalities. . . . We have them because they fit us. . . . They are consistent with our self-image and our entire personality pattern. (Maltz, 1960, p. 108)

In the sentences that follow the one in which *literally* occurs, one can see that the writer conceives of the habits-as-garments metaphor as being particularly apt because it is extendible. Using a structural semantic theory of metaphor (Kittay, 1987; Kittay & Lehrer, 1981), one can explain how the metaphor is constructed by the imposition of sense relations from the donor domain, *garments,* to the recipient domain, *habits.* The verb *fit,* taken from the donor field, now also applies metaphorically to *habits,* with its metaphorical meaning being made explicit by the writer: A metaphorical *fit* for a habit is realized by consistency with self-image, and so on. Thus the reader is asked to extend the metaphor in the way in which the literal use of *garments* would allow one to do. Here, the reader is asked to pay attention to the literal while interpreting the nonliteral. The same strategy is used by poets who make implicit use of it, and who employ it even when a figure is resonant. They use it as a means of preventing a reader from turning a resonant figure into a formula (Cunningham, 1976, pp. 253–254; Winters, 1967, pp. xiv–xvii).[11]

---

[11]This fact is not widely recognized in twentieth-century literary theory because of the pervasive view that poetic meaning is essentially different from ordinary meaning and cannot be paraphrased at all.

The next example illustrates the use of *literally* with a lexeme that is to be taken hyperbolically:

(12) The walls were literally paneled with nineteenth-century reproductions and contemporary originals. (MacDonald, 1984, p. 88).

The function of *literally* in this example is to tell the reader that the hyperbolical mode itself is justified by the conditions it applies to and that the lexeme that encodes it is a particularly apt one. In the speaker's judgment, the walls were covered with a very large number of paintings; this being so, and given the literal meaning of *panel,* its choice is perfect for conveying the trope.

Literally is used with the same function in examples (13) and (14) in which a formulary construction is used to convey the hyperbole. These, however, are conventionalized expressions, even though hyperbole itself is not a literal mode. I do not explicate, but I include them because their semantic structure so far as *literally* is concerned is markedly similar to its use in (12):

(13) We've always known that we can literally die of broken hearts and shattered dreams. Laboratory findings are now corroborating that intuitive sense. (Borysenko, 1987, p. 26)

(14) The apprentice is handed the Book at his first Meeting with an Examiner. "From then on you literally eat, sleep and drink it," says Dave Barnes, editor of Taxi magazine. ('Knobbling the knowledge,' *Manchester Guardian Weekly,* May 21, 1989, p. 5)

When speaking of the way in which idioms are used to encode hyperbole, Leech (1983) postulates that a conversational principle that motivates their construction is an Interest Principle, namely to "Say what is unpredictable and hence interesting" (p. 146). And he concludes that there is always a conflict between the Interest Principle and the Maxim of Quality. The use of *literally* in the last three examples illustrates self-conscious effort to redress the tension between the Interest Principle and the Maxim of Quality by signalling that the conditions of application fully justify hyperbolical use.

It is significant that I have found no examples in which *literally* collocates with a resonant and strongly original metaphor or with a strikingly original encoding of hyperbole. In these cases, its presence would simply be redundant: A speaker does not need to intercede explicitly for their tellability because their uniqueness speaks for itself. Furthermore, a hearer has no choice but to process their unintended literal meaning as a way of coming to understand the intended, newly coined expression.

OTHER THEORETICAL IMPLICATIONS: ATTITUDE IN POLYSEMOUS EXTENSION AND SPEECH STYLES

The use of *literally* with nonliteral expressions was noticed by Quirk et al. (1985, p. 619), who illustrate it in a footnote with the following example:

(15) He literally threw his car in the last available space.

and who remark that this use is "absurd." In a similar evaluative vein respecting this use, the *O.E.D.* (1971) observes that *literally* "may be used to indicate that the following word or phrase is to be taken in its literal sense. *Now often improperly used* to indicate that some conventional metaphorical phrase is to be taken in the strongest admissible sense" (s.v. "literally") (My emphasis.). Examples just of these types comprised our last subcategory of use. However, Quirk et al. and the *O.E.D.* notwithstanding, they do not illustrate absurd or improper use. Rather, they illustrate a lexical process that Traugott (1989) describes as a unidirectional tendency in diachronic semantic change, one in which "meanings become increasingly based in the speaker's subjective belief/attitude toward the proposition," the latter meanings "having been licensed by the function of language itself" (p. 35). This subjectification "involves increase in coding of speaker attitude, whether of belief, assessment of the truth, or personal commitment to the assertion" (p. 49).

In the case of *literally,* literal attitudes of linguistic care and aptness were highly appropriate in ecclesiastical uses as early as 1382. In the intervening centuries, these attitudes transferred from this specialized register to others where they also functioned as pragmatic implicatures. Over time, these implicatures strengthened, but not merely through diversification—diversification alone might have weakened, bleached them. Diversification was coupled with a source of strengthening that resulted from the use of *literally* itself to signal literal readings where a speaker anticipated that a hearer would not expect them. The explicit intercession via *literally* conveyed the speaker's attitude of accuracy as one that was especially relevant on these occasions, the intercession succeeding because sanctioned by a standardized use.

The diachronic result has been not so much to weaken the lexeme's capacity to force a literal reading as to strengthen its capacity to convey a literal attitude toward a reading. By 1863, the lexeme was attested in nonliteral contexts; but its application was not incorrect, as the *O.E.D.* maintains; it was appropriate, given strengthened literal attitude. The aptness conveyed in these nonliteral contexts was justified, given the word play that *literally* could effect. Thus it is strengthening of attitude which allows *literally* to function in nonliteral construals where its predominant function is aesthetic: to marshall tellability for a figure that is otherwise unremarkable. This aesthetic potential is also predicted by Traugott's claim that the process of coding formerly pragmatic implicatures results from a speaker's effort to regulate communication with others. In nonliteral readings, communicative regulation may involve not only a negotiation of speaker understanding but also of aesthetic appreciation. I do not know whether this environmental change in the use of *literally* is sufficiently different from other uses to justify independent status as a polysemous sense. Nevertheless, the direction that the change has taken is one that leads systematically to polysemy.

One could advance another, but to my mind, less satisfactory account of how *literally* has come to collocate acceptably with nonliteral expressions. One could posit an homonymous member for *literally* and maintain that its sole function is to intensify meaning. Greenbaum (1969, p. 88) posits such a member, but he provides neither argument for nor examples of it. The theoretical move does give one a solution, but it fails to distinguish between emphasizing and intensifying— *literally* characteristically serves the former function. And even if one were to conflate the two functions, the move would not explain how the effect is achieved. Most important of all, it fails to provide a unified explanation for the manifest similarity in function of *literally* across markedly diverse contexts.[12]

Finally, I draw on what I have said about *literally* along with some additional remarks to comment on a recent statistical study by Biber and Finegan (1988) that uses speaker attitudes for defining speech styles. This study is pertinent in that it takes up six subclasses of stance adverbs and semantically cognate adjectives and nouns. The subclass called *actually* adverbs consists of *actually, actuality, really, realistic, reality, factually,* and *fact.* Even though they did not include *literally* in this subclass, they might have, because in many environments, it is closely synonymous with both *actually* and *really.*[13]

Biber and Finegan (1988) report that these *actually* adverbs mark an emphatic stance, and that when they occur with frequency they define a style that encourages a sense of solidarity, a style they call "Emphatic Shared Familiarity." In their conclusion, the authors stress that "the function associated with the stance style does not correspond to the function suggested by the literal meanings of the adverbials" and that "the relative frequency of the stance markers tends to be

---

[12]I think it well worth our time to begin looking more closely at the ways in which attitudinal meaning becomes incorporated and then used as metalinguistic comment. Brugman (1984) observes that *very* and *real* may collocate with conventionalized nonliteral meanings. These lexemes also closely parallel *literally* in conferring emphasis, in encoding positive attitudinal commitment, in signalling closeness of fit, and in expressing metalinguistic comment via attitude. Brugman does not document their occurrence with nonformulary, nonliteral expressions. Perhaps this extension has not occurred, but it also may be that no one has thought to look for it.

Powell (1992) shows that the lexemes *actually* and *really,* like *literally,* developed an intensifying and/or emphasizing attitudinal and metalinguistic use long after an identifying function was established. I am grateful to Adrienne Lehrer for suggesting that I pursue this line of investigation.

[13]Biber and Finegan did include *literally* in the subclass of *honestly* adverbs. These occurred so infrequently in the corpora that little of statistical significance could be said about them.

associated with more or less specialized functions." These functions are not different from one another but rather are "more or less specialized uses of a common underlying function" (p. 30).

These conclusions are explicable when one takes fully into account the very parameter their study purports to measure: attitude itself. The attitudes conveyed and elicited by *actually* adverbs contribute systematically to their discourse effects in the following ways. First, notice that all the *actually* adverbs signal a close fit between word-to-word and word-to-world, and that they encode a speaker's close commitment to rather than distance from a message. In addition, these attitudinal commitments are conveyed by semantic meanings that also objectify the claim by locating it in the projected realm of the actual, the real, the factual, and the literal—that is, in the communally available realm of intersubjectivity. Since this projected realm is more accessible to an interlocutor than one constituted of a speaker's wholly private experience, the rhetorical effect of invoking this realm is to increase the potential for self-evidence of the message and thereby to facilitate rather than to inhibit communal agreement and disagreement. Biber and Finegan (1988), themselves, observe that these adverbs are "commonly used in situations where the speaker judges the asserted information to be shared with the listener . . ." (p. 21). One can see that, in appealing to actuality, reality, factuality, and literality, a speaker provides the conditions for an exchange whose message is potentially both sharable and familiar.

Contributing further to sharability and familarity as stylistic effects is the discourse potential of these and other stance adverbs that signal a close fit and positive speaker attitudinal commitment to occur as single lexemic utterances meaning, "I agree." One may say, Exactly! Precisely! Definitely! Certainly! Right! True! Really! *Literally* may function in this way as well:

(16) Speaker A: Well, you've just about worked your fingers to the bone.
      Speaker B: Literally![14]

---

[14]Brown and Levinson (1978, pp. 155–156) document a corresponding selection of these lexemes in Tzeltal, a Mayan language spoken in Ciapas, Mexico: *melel,* glossed by English "true" and "really," *bun* meaning "sure," *solel* meaning "really," and *kati* denoting surprise or emphasis are used as rhetorical assurances of sincerity. These, along with two others that derive from Spanish, *puru* and *meru,* "proliferate in any long argument (especially in public speaking by men)." They are regarded as emphatic hedges and pragmatic strengtheners. Brown and Levinson remark that "no clear literal meaning exists for most of these, but in one way or another they all indicate something about the speaker's commitment toward what he is saying, and in so doing modify illocutionary force." It would seem that in these cases, as in the English examples, attitude has very great pragmatic strength.

Black English may use terms from my second list to mean terms from the first. For example, *Unreal!* may mean "You're right; what you have said is extraordinary." *Bad* meaning "good" was used by Cannonball Adderley in an extemporaneous comment at the Seattle Jazz Festival in 1971: "This is a golden oldie from the baaad old days." He was looking back nostalgically to the musicality of these times, and giving freshness to a cliché by reversing it.

A parallel list of oppositional lexemes we do not enlist as single lexemic utterances to mean "I agree" shows how odd it sounds to select those which signal a loose fit and which distance or detach a speaker from a message: *Roughly! Imprecisely! Indefinitely! Uncertainly/Doubtfully! Wrong! False! Unreal!

Both sharing and familiarity develop from a mutual feeling that agreement is at least possible. In conversational structure, agreement and acceptance are preferred categories of response. Levinson (1983) explains that a preferred turn is structurally simpler than a dispreferred turn, the latter being systematically marked by significant delay, or by a particle such as *well* that signals the dispreferred status, or by some explanation as to why the preferred option cannot be offered (p. 307). Moreover, speakers avoid dispreferred responses. Although this conversational notion of preference is a structural one, corresponding to a linguistic conception of markedness (p. 333), it correlates plausibly with an attitudinal stance: Speakers feel more convivial when they can agree, and they feel hurt when they are not accepted.[15] Thus a text that makes frequent use of stance adverbs which may express agreement increases its potential for imparting the stylistic effect which Biber and Finegan define.

Therefore, the overall effect of a speech style that is characterized by "emphatic shared familiarity" is achieved by frequent use of *actually* adverbs because these signal (a) a close fit, (b) a speaker's positive attitudinal commitment to the message, (c) a projected realm of intersubjectively sharable experience, and (d) a potential for expressing agreement. Biber and Finegan also point out that frequent, but judicious, use of *actually* adverbs characterizes a style that emphasizes individual position—a conclusion that is also consistent with what we have learned about *literally*. Only when it is overused is the effect irritating to a hearer.

Finally, Biber and Finegan describe one style that uses these adverbs with unusually great frequency, but, because the results are confined to a single text and speaker, they conclude that the results are idiosyncratic. In a statistical study, this conclusion is warranted. However, such a style may have, as its speaker, someone who is literal minded. In the role of hearer, such a person may miss nonliteral nuance or refuse to accept an intended nonliteral encoding. In the role of speaker, due regard for self-conscious accuracy and aptness may give way to excessive concern for being understood, or to a fear of being misunderstood and rejected. Acceptable degrees of self-conscious care and aptness may succumb to

---

[15]Speakers may also feel linguistically threatened when agreement cannot be reached. In characterizing the nature of wine talk, Lehrer (1983) observes that speakers actively work toward agreement on the meaning and denotation of words even though the function of the exchange is essentially aesthetic and not scientific, where such agreement is especially important. "In our society, there is a strong belief in linguistic correctness. . . . [W]hen there is disagreement about descriptions, then the specter of correctness arises to challenge the linguistic (or possibly perceptual) competence of the speakers" (pp. 173–174).

humorless and pedantic precision. Normal care in specifying an interpretation may yield to an insistence on an interpretation, to an imposition of the linguistic will. In these ways, communicative cooperativeness is subverted by preoccupation with the self.

To conclude: The misuse of conventionally determined linguistic attitudes, even the names we have coined to describe the linguistic offenders, help us to see that principles of conventionality and folk theories of meaning, of which folk theories of reference are a part, *are* informed by these attitudes. In the cued case, a literal attitude signals a speaker who is self-consciously commited to norms of accuracy and aptness of use, both literal and nonliteral. In the uncued case, the commitment may be implicitly present, but it is affected by both occasion of use and register. A literal attitude is an appropriate one to accompany the consistency of lexemic application that is encouraged by principles of conventionality. In turn, consistency of application makes reference possible and successful, irrespective of whether it is rationalized by folk beliefs that are compatible with a Putnam–Kripke or a Fregian folk theory. The implication for lexical theory is clear: A literal attitude is a constituent of literal use and thus of literal meaning.

REFERENCES

Aronoff, M. (1976). *Word formation in generative grammar*. Cambridge, MA: MIT Press.

Berg, R. (1988). *Acquired traits: Memoirs of a geneticist from the Soviet Union*. David Lowe (Trans.). New York: Viking Penguin.

Biber, D., & Finegan, E. (1988). Adverbial stance types in English. *Discourse Processes, 11*, 1–34.

Borysenko, J. (1987). *Minding the body, mending the mind*. Reading, MA: Addison-Wesley Publishing Co.

Brown, P., & Levinson, S. (1978). Universals in language usage: Politeness phenomena. In E. Goody, (Ed.), *Questions and politeness: Strategies in social interaction* (pp. 56–289). Cambridge, England: Cambridge University Press.

Brugman, C. (1984). The VERY idea: A case study in polysemy and cross-lexical generalizations. *Papers from the parasession on lexical semantics* (pp. 21–38). Chicago: Chicago Linguistics Society.

Chafe, W. (1986). Evidentiality in English conversation and academic writing. In Chafe, W. & Nichols, J. (Eds.), *Evidentiality: The linguistic coding of epistemology* (pp. 261–272). Norwood, NJ: Ablex.

Clark, E. V. (1987). The principle of contrast: A constraint on language acquisition. In B. MacWhinney (Ed.), *Mechanisms of Language Acquisition* (pp. 1–33). Hillsdale, NJ: Lawrence Erlbaum Associates.

Cruse, D. (1986). *Lexical semantics*. Cambridge, England: Cambridge University Press.

Cunningham, J. V. (1976). *The collected essays of J. V. Cunningham*. Chicago: The Swallow Press.

Esau, H. (1973). *Nominalization and complementation in Modern German*. Amsterdam: North Holland.

Fillmore, C. (1985). Frames and the semantics of understanding. *Quaderni di Semantica, 6.2*, 222–254.

Fillmore, C., Kay, P., & O'Conner, M. (1988). Regularity and idiomaticity in grammatical constructions: The case of *Let Alone*. *Language, 64,* 501–538.

Foley, D. (Ed.). (1986). With Tarzan as role model, he lost 140 pounds. *Prevention,* December, 102–106.

Green, M., & Provost, G. (1988). *Finder: The true story of a private investigator.* New York: Crown Publishers.

Greenbaum, S. (1969). *Studies in English adverbial usage.* London: Longmans, Green.

Halliday, M. A. K. (1970). Functional diversity in language as seen from a consideration of modality and mood in English. *Foundations of Language, 6,* 322–361.

Halliday, M. A. K. (1979). *Language as social semiotic.* London: Edward Arnold.

Harley, K. (1980). 'Potpourri.' *Homemaker's Magazine,* September, p. 88.

Jackendoff, R. (1972). *Semantic interpretation in generative grammar.* Cambridge, MA: MIT Press.

Katz, S. (1989). How to live to be 80 years young. *Chatelaine,* March, pp. 84–87, 174–175.

Kay, P. (1983). Linguistic competence and folk theories of language: Two English hedges. *Proceedings of the Ninth Meeting of the Berkeley Linguistics Society* (pp. 128–137).

Kiparsky, P. (1981). Lexical morphology and phonology. In *Linguistics in the morning calm. Selected paper from SICOL* (pp. 117–138). Seoul: Hanshin.

Kittay, E. (1987). *Metaphor: Its cognitive force and linguistic structure.* Oxford: Clarendon Press.

Kittay, E., & Lehrer, A. (1981). Semantic fields and the structure of metaphor. *Studies in Language, 5,* 31–63.

Labov, W. (1972). *Language in the inner city.* University Park: University of Pennsylvania Press.

Lakoff, G. (1972). Hedges: A study in meaning criteria and the logic of fuzzy concepts. *Papers from the Eighth Regional Meeting, Chicago Linguistic Society* (pp. 183–228).

Leech, G. (1983). *Principles of pragmatics.* London: Longman Group.

Lehrer, A. (1983). *Wine and Conversation.* Bloomington: Indiana University Press.

Lehrer, A. (1990). Polysemy, conventionality and the structure of the lexicon. *Cognitive Linguistics, 1,* 207–246.

Levinson, S. (1983). *Pragmatics.* Cambridge: Cambridge University Press.

Lyons, J. (1977). *Semantics 2.* Cambridge: Cambridge University Press.

Lyons, J. (1981). *Language, meaning, and context.* Suffolk: Fontana.

MacDonald, R. (1984). *The Zebra-striped hearse.* New York: Bantam Paperback.

Maltz, M. (1960). *Psycho-Cybernetics.* New York: Pocket Books.

Oxford English Dictionary (1971 and supplement). New York: Oxford University Press.

Paul, H. (1889). *Principles of the history of language* (2nd ed.). H. A. Strong (Trans.). New York: Macmillan.

Powell, M. J. (1985). Purposive vagueness: an evaluative dimension of vague quantifying expressions. *Journal of Linguistics, 21,* 31–50.

Powell, M. J. (1992). The systematic development of correlated interpersonal and metalinguistic uses in stance adverbs. *Cognitive Linguistics, 3,* 75–110.

Pratt, M. L. (1979). *Toward a speech act theory of literary discourse.* Bloomington: Indiana University Press.

Putnam, H. (1975). The meaning of "meaning." *Mind, language and reality. Philosophical Papers* (Vol. 2, pp. 215–271). Cambridge, England: Cambridge University Press.

Quirk, R. S., Greenbaum, S., Leech, G., & Svartvik, J. (1985). *A comprehensive grammar of the English language.* London: Longmans Group.

Shklovsky, V. (1965). Art as technique. In L. Lemon & M. Reis (Trans. & Eds.). *Russian formalist criticism.* Lincoln: University of Nebraska Press. First published in 1917.

Stoler, P. (1981). Happy hominid. A review of Johanson, D. and Edey, M. (1981). *Lucy: The beginnings of humankind. Time Magazine,* March 16, 1981, pp. 76–77.

Stubbs, M. (1986). 'A matter of prolonged field work': Notes towards a modal grammar of English. *Applied Linguistics, 7,* 1–25.

Taylor, E. (1989). *Milton's poetry: Its development in time*. Pittsburgh: Duquesne University Press.

Traugott, E. (1989). On the rise of epistemic meanings in English: An example of subjectification in semantic change. *Language, 65*, 31–55.

Winters, Y. W. (1967). *Forms of discovery: Critical and historical essays on forms of the short poem in English*. Chicago: Allan Swallow.

Wren, P. C. (1924). *Beau Geste*. London: John Murray.

14 "Something that Rhymes with Rich"

Keith Allan
Monash University

This chapter was inspired by the text quoted from *Time Australia* (March 6, 1989) as (1).

> (1) To borrow words Barbara Bush once used to describe Geraldine Ferraro, Millie Kerr Bush is something that rhymes with rich. (p. 62)

I have asked about 100 people to demonstrate what they understand from (1) by getting them to complete the following statements in the underscored spaces:

> Barbara Bush was (according to this author) implying that Geraldine Ferraro is _____.
>
> Consequently, Millie Kerr Bush is also _____.

Validated against the rest of text of the original article, the success rate has been 99%. This indicates that readers have little or no difficulty accessing the appropriate lexicon entry cued by the words "something that rhymes with rich" (namely, *bitch*); and the question I pursue in this chapter is just what such a result reveals about the nature of a lexicon entry.

HOW MUCH INFORMATION SHOULD GO INTO A DICTIONARY?

An important question for linguistic semantics is HOW MUCH INFORMATION IS IT NECESSARY TO INCLUDE TO CREATE A COMPLETE SEMANTIC

355

REPRESENTATION IN THE DICTIONARY? The normal practice before the 1980s was to favor parsimonious dictionary knowledge against elaborated encyclopedic knowledge. But then Jackendoff (1983) suggested that information in the lexical entry "shades toward 'encyclopedia' rather than 'dictionary' information, with no sharp line drawn between the two types" (p. 139f). Wierzbicka (1985) developed semantic descriptions very reminiscent of those in an encyclopedia; for example, she quotes the following entry for *tiger* from the *Encyclopedia Britannica,* which is followed by her own lexicon entry:

> TIGER (*Panthera tigris*), a striped carnivore, the largest of the cat family (Felidae), rivaled only by the lion in strength and ferocity, the differences between them lying mainly in their external appearance. The tiger is confined to Asia, and [. . . there follows a detailed account of its distribution.]
>
> The tiger's characteristic stripes and ground colour vary in distinctness and brightness according to the locality and subspecies. [There follows a detailed account of variation between subspecies.] A male may weigh more than 500 lb. (227 kg.), reach a height at the shoulders of 5 ft. (1.5m), and a length of 14 ft. (4.3m.). The tiger has no mane, but in old males the hair on the cheeks is rather long and spreading. (p. 194)

Wierzbicka's lexicon entry is much less detailed as to the appearance, size, weight, subspecies, and range of the tiger; it emphasizes subjective impressions rather than zoological data:

TIGERS
A KIND OF ANIMAL
IMAGINING ANIMALS OF THIS KIND PEOPLE COULD SAY THESE
    THINGS ABOUT THEM
they live in the jungle   *HABITAT*
in places which are far away from places where people live
in parts of the earth where they don't live people can see them in a zoo
they are similar to cats in the way they look and in the way they move   *SIZE*
but they are much bigger than cats
being more like people in size than like cats
they have black stripes on a yellowish body   *APPEARANCE*
they have big sharp claws and big sharp teeth
they attack other animals and people and kill and eat them   *BEHAVIOR*
they can move quickly and without noise like cats
and they can move quickly where other big animals can't
so that they can come close to people without people noticing them, and attack
    people
people are afraid of them, and think of them, and   *RELATION TO PEOPLE*
    think of them as fierce animals
[people also think of them as animals who know what they want and who know

how to get it, and whom one can't help admiring for that] (Wierzbicka's brackets, p. 164)

I have no intention of critically evaluating Wierzbicka's lexicon entry for *tiger;* but I do comment that it has the twin virtues of being anthropocentric and impressionistic, both of which strike me as being relevant to the representation of the lexicon that people carry around in their heads, provided that there is also room for the inclusion of "scientific data."

In school, comprehension of a text is usually tested by having a student summarize the text, or answer questions on it, or both. Attempts in the field of artificial intelligence to program a machine to interpret a text so as to answer questions on it or to provide a summary for it reveal that the project requires input from what Schank and Abelson (1977) call "scripts," Lakoff (1987) "idealized cognitive models," Minsky (1977) and Fillmore (1975, 1982) "frames," which all include encyclopedic knowledge. Langacker (1987) has suggested that the information in a lexicon IS encyclopedic (cf. "The distinction between semantics and pragmatics [or between linguistics and extralinguistic knowledge] is largely artifactual, and the only viable conception of linguistic semantics is one that avoids false dichotomies and is consequently **encyclopedic** in nature" p. 154). All these enterprises just cited attempt to simulate human understanding. If we want a semantic system to be nothing more than a translation from one set of symbols into another set of symbols, it can be as parsimonious as you like; but if the linguist's account of the lexicon is to make any pretense of representing the meaning of an object language expression *E* as what humans (potentially) understand by *E,* then it will need to include what has often been thought of as encyclopedic knowledge. Leech (1981) holds (or held) the contrary view and so he wrote: "The oddity of propositions like 'The dog had eighty legs' is something that zoology has to explain rather than conceptual semantics" (p. 84). Leech is mistaken, or rather he puts the wrong case: whereas we should look to zoology to explain why genera of higher animals have no more than four limbs, we should look to linguistic semantics to recognize that, if the speaker or writer is speaking of a world identical with or similar to ours, the statement *The dog had eighty legs* is either false or identifying an incredibly abnormal creature. If we are interested in properly accounting for discourse coherence (i.e., in the grammar of texts larger than a sentence), then this is surely a matter that an adequate linguistic semantics should recognize—and for exactly the same kinds of reasons that it recognizes the animacy of a dog [but see the postscript].

In a paper entitled "Some English terms of insult invoking body-parts" (Allan, 1990), I examined the semantics of literal and nonliteral uses of certain tabooed body-part terms in several English dialects. The original impetus for the paper was the recognition that certain literal and nonliteral senses of terms for female genitalia have different semantic relations: on a literal interpretation they CONTRAST in meaning with terms for male genitalia (cf. *Your twat/cunt needs a wash* vs. *Your prick needs a wash*); whereas on at least some nonliteral interpretations in some dialects they CAN BE IDENTICAL in meaning with terms for male genitalia (cf. *You twat!*, *You cunt!* and *You prick!*)[1] These semantic relations would need to be specified at the level of sense in any traditional semantics, requiring that the distinction between literal and nonliteral be established at that level. But the distinction between literal and nonliteral is dependent on context; more precisely, it depends on which world is being spoken of,[2] and therefore on pragmatic and not purely semantic data. In Allan (1990) I was able to show that, if we are to say anything worthwhile about the relatedness of literal and nonliteral meanings, the content of a lexicon entry must draw on background information about the entity being denoted; this information may be based on any or all of five things: human experience, convention, custom, myth, and language use (i.e., pragmatics).

UNDERSTANDING "SOMETHING THAT RHYMES WITH RICH"

Now let's get back to (1), repeated here for convenience.

(1) To borrow words Barbara Bush once used to describe Geraldine Ferraro, Millie Kerr Bush is something that rhymes with rich.

For convenient reference in the discussion that follows, I identify two necessary implicata of (1), indicated by '→':

(1) → (2) Barbara Bush once said of Geraldine Ferraro that she "is something that rhymes with rich."
(1) → (3) Millie Kerr Bush is something that rhymes with rich.

In understanding what is Speaker-meant in (1), we need to take into account a whole raft of things that I now examine. I assume that understanding a text requires the hearer or reader to construct a mental model of the world spoken of. I use the expression "mental model" quite literally to denote a construction in the mind, something like (and perhaps in the end identical with) Lakoff's (1987) "cognitive model" or that of Jackendoff (1987), perhaps in a "parent [mental] space" as envisioned by Fauconnier (1985); therefore "mental model" is not intended as a term of art that commits me to the theory expounded by Johnson-Laird (1983)—even though I have some sympathy for that theory. I also use the

---

[1]The dialect differences are discussed in Allan (1990) and Allan & Burridge (1991) but these are of no particular relevance in this chapter.

[2]Some explanation of this notion is given later, but for details, see Allan (1986).

phrase *world spoken of* to include a world WRITTEN of. Evidence for the constructive nature of text understanding is: (a) the proven use of inferences and speculations in the course of language understanding, and people's ability to predict what is likely to happen next in a story (which has a priming effect on understanding); (b) the effect that titles and headings have on the way a text is interpreted; (c) experimental evidence for the realignment of scrambled stories in both summaries and recall, and the replacement of abnormal by normal events but not vice versa in recall situations.[3] A text is judged coherent where the world spoken of is internally consistent and generally accords with accepted human knowledge. The world spoken of is one category of context. "Context" is three ways polysemous: (i) the crucial category of context is the world spoken of, because the other two categories are relevant by reference to it. But in addition, there is (ii), the situation in which the utterance occurs (the world spoken IN), and the situation in which it is heard or read. These identify appropriate denotations for deictics like tense, personal pronouns (*I* = speaker or writer, *you* = hearer or reader, etc.); demonstratives (*this, that, yonder*); and verbs like *come, go, bring*. (iii) The third category of context is co-text (the text surrounding some expression), which is relevant in constructing the world spoken of.

(A) To interpret (1) the reader will have to access the lexicon through the metalinguistic statement "something that rhymes with rich." Although metalinguistic knowledge does not contribute to the sense of an expression, it does undoubtedly contribute to the hearer or reader's understanding on a particular occasion of use by enabling the term to be evaluated against others from the same semantic field, as to the appropriateness of its style in the context, and so forth. So, for instance, the connotations of lexicon items need to be catalogued somewhere: They are necessary to figure out the implications of a speaker choosing one of the terms from the set *geegee, horse, nag, steed, gelding, mare*, etc. rather than any of the others; or choosing to say *lady* instead of *woman, girl, broad*, etc. (see Allan, 1990, for more evidence). The most natural place for such information is the lexicon; which is why it is sometimes found in standard dictionaries. If connotations are not to be included in the lexicon, it is difficult to imagine just whereabouts they ought to be located within a model of language processing.

(B) Text (1) demonstrates that the reader must be able to access the lexicon through rhyme. Although all the evidence indicates that alphabetical organization of phonologic lexicon entries is the norm, there is no doubt that speakers are able to access them through rhyme. The fact that rhyme is valued as a form of

---

[3]For (a) compare Allan (1981, 1986), Black (1984), Charniak (1976), Clark (1977), Graesser & Clark (1985), Johnson-Laird (1983), Lakoff (1987), Rickheit & Strohner (1985), Schank & Abelson (1977), Thorndyke (1976, 1977), Uyl & Oostendorp (1980), Van Dijk & Kintsch (1983). For (b) compare Black (1984), Bransford & Johnson (1972), Kozminsky (1977). For (c) compare Kintsch, Mandel, & Kozminsky, (1977), Schank & Abelson (1977), Thorndyke (1977), Van Dijk & Kintsch (1983).

word play, and that some phonesthemes[4] are rhymes (e.g., the -*ump* and -*ash* sets in English) suggests that the rhyme is important as a constituent of the phonological word; but it is quite possible that rhymes are accessed simply through a string search mechanism analogous to the standard computer search procedure. Given the computational nature of the brain—apparently terrific at parallel processing, but comparatively slow at serial processing—this is an unhappy conclusion.

(**C**) The reader of (1) is seeking a word or phrase that rhymes with *rich*, and which can function as a predicate ranging over both "Geraldine Ferraro" and "Millie Kerr Bush." *Rich* is an adjective but note that the reader is not necessarily seeking another adjective in its stead: What s/he requires is any predicate that will be an appropriate syntactic and functional substitute for "is something that rhymes with *rich.*"

(**D**) Assuming, as indeed we should, that the writer is observing the (neo-Gricean) cooperative maxims of quantity and manner (i.e., offering no more and no less information than is required to make his/her message clear to the reader and also trying to present his/her meaning in a clear, concise manner that avoids ambiguity and avoids misleading or confusing the reader through stylistic ineptitude), then, if there is more than one rhyme available, the writer will try to ensure that there are sufficient contextual cues provided for the reader to successfully select the appropriate item from among the set of possible rhymes.

(**E**) A subset of the words that rhyme with *rich* is: *kitsch, Mich, which, a witch, a glitch, a stitch, a flitch, a switch, a niche, a tich, a twitch, spinach, an itch, a hitch, a pitch, a bitch, a ditch,* etc. (This list mixes dialects; my own dialect is British interlaced with Australian. The author of (1) presumably speaks American.)

(**F**) Consider the contextual clues to selecting an appropriate rhyme for "something that rhymes with rich." A random search is quite possible in theory, but I would reject a method that so blatantly ignores the fact that communication between humans is context sensitive. In (1) the writer assumes that the reader knows who "Barbara Bush" and "Geraldine Ferraro" are, but not who (or, as it turns out, what) "Millie Kerr Bush" is. Even if the reader had never heard of

---

[4]A phonestheme is a cluster of sounds, located at either the onset of a word or its rhyme, which symbolizes a certain meaning (e.g., the *fl*-onset in *flack, flag, flail, fl*a*me, flap, flare, flash, flay, flee, flick, flicker, flinch, fling, flip, flirt, flit, flood, flop, flounce, flounder, flourish, flow, fluent, flurry, flush, fluster, flutter, flux, fly*). In at least one sense of all of them there is a suggestion of "sudden or violent movement"; many verbs with the rhyme *-ash* denote "violent impact" (e.g., *clash, crash, dash, flash, gash, gnash, lash, mash, slash, smash, thrash*). Phonesthemes are typically incomplete syllables, and their meanings are much more difficult to pin down than that of morphemes; furthermore, exactly the same cluster of sounds that constitute the phonestheme will appear in many vocabulary items that have no trace of the meaning associated with the phonestheme! Consequently, phonesthemes are often said to manifest a SUBREGULARITY in the language (all languages seem to have them) (see Allan, 1986, §4.9.3); Bolinger, (1950).

Barbara Bush and Geraldine Ferraro, s/he would know (assuming s/he knows English) that the names *Barbara, Geraldine,* and *Millie* are normally names for female humans and, on that basis, would establish the necessary entities within the world spoken of. Furthermore, like other human names these may be extended to pets and to certain kinds of inanimates. The fact that they are normally names for female humans must be noted in the lexicon.[5] To conclude: the reader filters out the most incompatible predicates from (**E**) on the grounds that "Geraldine Ferraro" and "Millie Kerr Bush" are female animates (if not female humans).

(**G**) The procedure just described in (**F**) leaves the following predicates to substitute for "is . . . rich": *is kitsch, is a snitch, is a witch, is a tich, is a bitch,* and just possibly *is a flitch, is an itch,* and *is a twitch.*

(**H**) To choose between the predicates in (**G**) the reader appeals to another criterion. From implicatum (2) s/he may conclude that Barbara Bush exploited the cooperative maxim of manner in order to present her message as a word play rather than stating her opinion directly and explicitly (I comment later on the writer's reason for borrowing Bush's words). Barbara Bush presumably chose to do that in order to be euphemistic—what other reason could she have had?

Let me digress for a moment to define two terms that I am using in this part of the discussion, namely, *euphemism* and *dysphemism.* These terms and the phenomena that they identify are investigated at great length and in close detail in Allan and Burridge (1991); the definitions we give these terms are as follows:

A **euphemism** is used as an alternative to a dispreferred expression, in order to avoid possible loss of face: either the speaker's own face or, through giving offense, that of the audience, or of some third party.

A **dysphemism** is an expression with connotations that are offensive either about the denotatum or to the audience, or both, and it is substituted for a neutral or euphemistic expression for just that reason.

I am suggesting that Barbara Bush presumably uttered (2) in order to make a

---

[5] I assume this has to be the case because there is no other practical solution to the question of where they are stored. Names like Aristotle and Dante, among thousands of others, are available for use as rigid designators among males in our community. It is a fact that "proper names" have different characteristics from common names, but this is no basis on which to exclude them from the lexicon. The fact that *John broke his arm* is open to the interpretation "John broke his own arm" whereas *John broke her arm* is not indicates that *John* denotes a male almost as surely as *father* does; and such information is expected to be located in the lexicon. Adrienne Lehrer's chapter in this volume offers additional, and novel, evidence that proper names are NOT semantically empty. It may be that the lexicon has different compartments: The effect of Gilles de la Tourette's syndrome seems to show that obscenities are not stored with other lexical material (see Allan & Burridge, 1991 p. 24), though I know of no comparable neurolinguistic evidence relevant to the storage of proper names.

dysphemistic remark in a euphemistic manner. The reader therefore concludes that the rhyming predicate s/he is seeking is dysphemistic.

Note that the reader is utilizing pragmatic criteria in trying to access an appropriate item from the lexicon; and that the procedure is heuristic rather than algorithmic.

(I) Now, all the epithets in (G) are dysphemistic to some degree, so how do we choose between them? Before answering this question we should take into account that there has been 99% agreement in responses to the two questions immediately following (1) at the beginning of this chapter. (The one exception was a choice of *witch,* which appears to be more dysphemistic in American than in my mother dialect; when questioned about his choice, the American respondent reported that, on reflection, *bitch* was more likely.) Ninety-nine percent consistency makes it impossible that a reader chooses just any old dysphemism from among the set in (G). I suggest that the most reasonable procedure must be to select THE MOST DYSPHEMISTIC member of the set, because the less dysphemistic a remark is, the more likely it is to be made directly.

(J) This decision presupposes that degrees of dysphemism are marked in the lexicon, along with degrees of euphemism (see Allan & Burridge, 1991): the unmarked case is taken to be neutral. Allan and Burridge propose a "middle class politeness criterion" (p. 21) to determine degrees of euphemism and dysphemism and characterize it as follows: In order to be polite to a casual acquaintance of the opposite sex in a formal situation in a middle-class environment, one would normally be expected to use the euphemism rather than its dispreferred counterpart(s). A dispreferred counterpart would be a dysphemism. Cases where we are undecided which way the judgment should fall we dub "neutral terms."

(K) When predicated of a woman, such as "Geraldine Ferraro" is, the most dysphemistic member of set (G) is *is a bitch.* My interpretation of the word *bitch* matches the entry in the *Macquarie Dictionary* with a few minor variations:

> **bitch** /bɪč/, *n* **1.** a female dog. **2.** a female of canines generally. **3.** a woman, esp. a disagreeable or malicious one. **4.** *Colloq.* a complaint. *-v.i.* **5.** *Colloq.* to complain. *-v.t.* **6.** *Colloq.* to spoil; bungle.

I have two minor disagreements with the definitions: I am not convinced of a distinction between senses **1** and **2;** and sense **3** cannot be used of a woman without imputing of her that she is disagreeable or malicious. Very shortly I examine the evidence for a semantic correlation between the literal and nonliteral meaning of *bitch* and try to demonstrate why it is so dysphemistic. But first let's reconsider text (1) via (2) and (3) to check out whether the predicate *is a bitch* seems appropriate. The formula 'X ≫ Y' means "Y is an implicature of X":

(2) ≫ (2') Barbara Bush once said of Geraldine Ferraro that she is a bitch.
(2' & 3) ≫ (3') Millie Kerr Bush is a bitch.

This is indeed what *Time* magazine meant. The sentence following (1) reads "The White House staff has confirmed that the First Pooch is expecting in late March"; and the text is located around the photograph of a spaniel.

LEXICON ENTRY

Before looking at what goes into the lexicon to allow the author of (1) to make the word play s/he does, there are two more things of take note of.

Firstly, the term *bitch* itself is not used in (1) to describe Geraldine Ferraro, because it would be regarded by the public as offensive behavior on the speaker's or writer's part to be known to have used such a term publically. I make further comment on this later.

Secondly, likening someone to an animal is normally dysphemistic. Metaphorical uses of animal names take some salient characteristic from the folk concepts about the appearance and or behavior of the animal that is then attributed to the human named or addressed. There are constraints on the application of these metaphors. Names of female animals can normally be used only in naming or addressing women and male homosexuals (e.g., in addition to *bitch*, a *cat* is typically a "vicious and/or scratchy woman"; a *vixen* is a "cunning, perhaps sneaky, woman"; *cow* and *sow* don't differ much, they generally denote a "woman disliked, who is typically doltish"; and there are connotations of being fat, too, cf. the commonly used *fat cow/sow*). Some animal names are typically used of men: a *mongrel* or *cur* denotes a "vicious, nasty fellow, held in contempt" (cf. *cat* and *bitch* of women); a *fox* denotes a "cunning man," cf. *vixen;* a *bull* is for a "big, often rather clumsy, man"; a *goat* or *ram* can be used of a "randy or horny man." Most animal names can be applied to either men or women (e.g., *louse, mouse, dog, coot, turkey, galah, goat, ass, donkey, mule, snake,* etc.). The overwhelming majority of these are dysphemistic to some extent, and I presume that every speaker of English knows this to be the case.

I now turn to the semantic content of the lexicon entry for *bitch,* with the caveat that the schema that follows is meant to be illustrative only. The schema is presented as a set of modules or gates, some of which are necessarily passed through, whereas others are controlled by the nature of the world being spoken of: In particular, they are controlled by the familiarity of the topic and the amount of information apparently required. The reason for this is not just that different degrees of detail are needed for different purposes in normal conversation; it is to offer a way of bypassing potentially infinite loops within the system that could result from the "lookup" function that appears among the ADDITIONAL SEMANTIC INFORMATION section of the sample lexicon entry. I make further brief comments on these and other characteristics later. The system is set up to work as an algorithm of the form shown in Fig. 14.1.

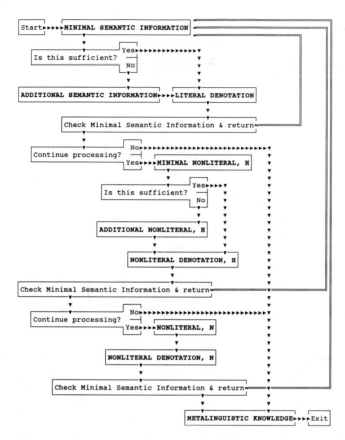

FIG. 14.1. The algorithm for using the proposed lexical entry for *bitch*.

****

MINIMAL INFORMATION

β is a *bitch* → (β is female & (β is a dog xor β is human)
    xor β is nonanimate

> [Symbolically: B → (F & (D xor H)) xor N, where 'X or Y'
> means "either X or Y but not both"]

If this is sufficient information, goto LITERAL DENOTATION

****

ADDITIONAL INFORMATION

[Comment 1: A bitch is significantly different from a male dog in that from time to time she is oestrus, and she has the potential to bear pups and lactate—things that follow from her being a female mammal. What makes a bitch different from other female mammals is that a bitch in heat has the reputation for being unconstrainedly willing to mate, often with several partners, and many dog-owners believe the bitch needs to be protected from male dogs at this time and rather than have all this trouble, they have the bitch spayed. End of comment 1.]

B = F & D. Lookup *female,* lookup *dog.*
(B=F&D) → There are times when β is a bitch in heat.

[Symbolically: (B=F&D) → BIH]

It is widely believed that a bitch in heat is unconstrainedly willing to mate, often with several partners.

[Symbolically: BIH ! FC, where 'X ! Y' means "Given X, it is widely believed and conventionally understood that Y"]

When in heat, a bitch is a nuisance and therefore a cause of complaint to people.

[Symbolically: (BIH!FC)causeTR (therefore TR)]

A bitch that has copulated will probably conceive and bear a litter of pups that she will suckle for several weeks.

[Comment 2: This point is not germane to the present chapter.]

If β is a bitch then there are times when β is in heat and unconstrainedly willing to mate, often with several partners, thereby giving cause for complaint.
(B → BIH!FC) & (B ! FC) & (B → TR)

[Comment 3: These conjuncts will give rise to all the extended uses of *bitch;* thus the nonliteral senses of the word are grounded in the literal sense. For instance, TR gives rise to the *Macquarie Dictionary* sense **4** "a complaint," and also sense **5** the intransitive verb *bitch about something [which causes complaint];* the latter gives rise to the transitive verb *bitch up* "do something which causes complaint". End of comment 3.]

****

LITERAL DENOTATION

β is a *bitch* means that "β is a female dog"; if the world spoken of is consistent with this proposition, then check MINIMAL SEMANTIC INFORMATION, return. If the world spoken of is more consistent with "β is a female dog" than with any other possibility offered in MINIMAL SEMANTIC INFORMATION, goto METALINGUISTIC KNOWLEDGE. Else Lookup *human*: if β is female human goto MINIMAL NONLITERAL, H, else goto NONLITERAL, N.

****

MINIMAL NONLITERAL, H

B = F & H
If this is sufficient information, goto NONLITERAL DENOTATION, H

****

ADDITIONAL NONLITERAL, H

β is female human & β is like a bitch in heat & it is widely believed that a bitch in heat is unconstrainedly willing to mate, often with several partners.
(B=F&H & B!FC) ≫ β is a whore & β is despised

[Symbolically: (B=F&H)&B!FC) ≫ WHR]

If β is a whore and β is despised then β is a cause of complaint

[Symbolically: WHRcauseTR, thus B ≫ TR. But we already know that B → TR: the fact that B is human in the former but a dog in the latter is of no apparent consequence.]
[Comment 4: This sense of *bitch* suggests that Norrick's (1981, p. 84) "Metaphorical Principle 4" is at work. The largely archaic use of *bitch* for "whore" (cf. *O.E.D.* 2) is retained in *son-of-a-bitch* (comparable with Spanish *hijo de puta* and similar expressions in many other languages). It is worth commenting that to call a woman a whore is one of the worst ways to insult her, and one of the commonest. In the case of *bitch,* linking the sexual insult with an animal-name insult is doubly dysphemistic. It can be accounted for in the following way (cf. Allan & Burridge, 1991, pp. 61–63; Ortner, 1974). Because women and not men bear children, and consequently menstruate and lactate, etc., women are perceived to be more closely bound by and to their bodies and body functions than are men, which renders women more like (other) animals and therefore closer to nature than are men. Men, not being physiologically bound in such ways, not only had the opportunity to become politically and economically dominant but furthermore had the time and energy to expend on things of the mind rather than of the body; that is, to control the domain that supposedly distinguishes humans from animals. The association of

women with the animal side of humans, and men with power and intellectual pursuits, has in all societies produced a cultural and social appraisal in which men are superior to women.[6] Two of the effects of this are: (a) the pollution taboos on women's unique physiological processes at certain times; and (b) the downgrading of a man by ascribing to him the characteristics of a woman, in contrast with the converse: A woman is not generally downgraded to a similar degree when ascribed the characteristics of a man. The disadvantage that women's physiology imposes on them has been exploited by men to assert social dominance and even ownership rights over them; it has led to peculiar taboos over women's procreative organs (and often over their entire bodies), which purportedly aim to protect a genealogical investment. There is reason behind this (irrespective of one's moral evaluation of it): Until the advent of *in vitro* fertilization, a woman invariably knew that the child she has borne is genetically her own; whereas a man can only be certain his wife's child is genetically his if he is certain she has not had sexual intercourse with another man. In the interests of self-protection, women have generally accepted and even encouraged the taboos on their bodies and effluvia as measures towards ensuring their personal safety. These taboos have been confirmed by the dominant religions in our culture, and in many others too. Against this background, any question about a woman's sexual behavior has been seen as an offence against a desirable social and religious—and even rational—norm. The consequence is the willingness to condemn a suspected miscreant as a bitch in heat, a whore.

We do not yet have any explanation for why a bitch is "disagreeable" and "malicious," to quote the *Macquarie Dictionary*. The answer is that a number of associative influences seem to be at work. First there is the transformation of B → TR, i.e., "a bitch is someone or something who gives cause for complaint," to "a bitch is someone or something that deliberately causes trouble" (i.e., β **is disagreeable and malicious**). Such a transformation from a passive to an active role is frequently made of humans and other willful beings. Furthermore, this additional meaning would be strengthened by the fact that *bitch* complements the epithets *dog, cur, mongrel* predicated of a man (male human), all of which denote a man not only despised, but also disagreeable and malicious. And there is further contamination of *bitch* from other dysphemisms invoking women's sexuality (for the reasons, see Allan & Burridge, 1991). The most strongly tabooed word in nearly all present-day dialects of the English language is *cunt*, used as a term of abuse to denote "a contemptible, nasty, malicious, despicable person, someone to be avoided"— which makes it a stronger version of *bitch*. *Cunt*, along with a number of other terms for the female pudend, is often used to denote a woman who is unconstrainedly willing to copulate with several partners. There is possibly some backflow to *bitch* from *cunt*, i.e., from "a contemptible, nasty, malicious, despicable person, someone to be avoided"—a meaning that in some English dialects has been extended to other terms of abuse invoking sex organs, cf. Allan (1990). Allan and Burridge (1991) show that many present-day dysphemisms have meanings that

---

[6]Eva Kittay disagrees with this hypothesis but has yet to persuade me that there is any other that comes close to accounting for all the relevant cultural, social, behavioral, historical, and linguistic facts that this hypothesis DOES explain. Note that I do NOT claim that it morally justifies any of them; that's another matter altogether.

derive from no single source, but from the coalescence of a demonstrable network of mutually reinforcing associations: It would now appear that *bitch* should be included among these. End of comment 4.]

β is pejorated to "disagreeable and malicious" by the coalescence of (a) a reevaluation from passive TR to willful maliciousness [Symbolically: TR ! MAL]; (b) by its association with the semantically related terms *dog, cur, mongrel;* and (c) by association with terms for female genitalia and female promiscuousness.

$$(((B!FC) \& (B \gg WHR) \& (B \gg TR)) ! MAL) \to B ! MAL$$

B ! β is disagreeable and malicious

****

NONLITERAL DENOTATION, H

Prototypical nonliteral denotation: β is a *bitch* means that "β is a disagreeable, malicious, despised female human (or homosexual man), and someone to be avoided." If the world spoken of is consistent with this proposition, then check MINIMAL SEMANTIC INFORMATION, else return. If the world spoken of is more consistent with "β is a disagreeable, malicious, despised female human (or homosexual man), and someone to be avoided" than any other possibility offered in MINIMAL SEMANTIC INFORMATION, goto METALINGUISTIC KNOWLEDGE. Else goto NONLITERAL, N.

****

NONLITERAL, N

$$(((B=N) \& (B \to TR)) \to (N \to TR)) \& TR ! MAL$$

[Comment 5: The use of abusive epithets towards inanimate objects that irritate one often results in the use of a term of abuse more applicable to humans (see Allan, 1990). It is as if the object were treated as being capable of malevolent force—a view often disparaged as primitive or animistic, but apparently alive and well in western cultures. End of comment 5.]

****

NONLITERAL DENOTATION, N

β is a *bitch* means that "β, which is not human, is something disagreeable, malicious if animate, the source of harm or injury if not, it is despised or deeply disliked and is something to be avoided." If the world spoken of is consistent with this proposition, then check MINIMAL SEMANTIC INFORMATION, return. If the world spoken of is more consistent with "β, which is not human, is something disagreeable, malicious if animate, the source of harm or injury if not, it is despised or deeply disliked and is something to be avoided" than with any other possibility offered in MINIMAL SEMANTIC INFORMATION, goto METALINGUISTIC KNOWLEDGE. Else stack *bitch* and goto EXIT.

****

METALINGUISTIC KNOWLEDGE

Literal *bitch* is a marked term, *dog* being the term (a) for the genus, (b) for *canis familiaris* used as workdogs and pets, and (c) for male canines.

Nonliteral *bitch* is a term of abuse, and as such is intrinsically dysphemistic. The closest to a neutral counterpart is to predicate the denotatum with one or more of the adjectives used in the prototypical denotation.

Comparable terms of abuse comparing female humans with animals are *cow, sow, old bat, vixen, mouse,* etc. Comparable terms of abuse commenting on the alleged promiscuity of the denotatum are *whore, slut,* etc. Comparable terms of abuse describing the denotatum as disagreeable, malicious, etc. are body-part terms like *asshole, cunt,* etc.

There is a wealth of evidence that where a language expression is ambiguous between a taboo or dysphemistic sense and a nontaboo sense its meaning will often narrow to the taboo sense alone (cf. *accident, coney, cock, ass, gay,* etc.). Many people therefore avoid using *bitch* lest they be misunderstood. [See Allan & Burridge, 1991 pp. 21–25.]

****

EXIT

****

In this schema, the nonliteral interpretation is shown to be based upon semantic information included within the literal sense, a position argued for in Kittay (1987). Like Kittay (p. 92), I do not believe that this rational representation is necessarily a mirror of real cognitive processing for every occurrence of nonliteral *bitch*. Further investigation of the relationship between literal sense and metaphorical extension is needed before this matter can be decided, and it is possible that all possible denotations are always checked via the MINIMAL SEMANTIC INFORMATION module. Furthermore, I make no general commitment on the question of whether or not all metaphor is as literally based as is the nonliteral meaning of *bitch* or of the terms examined in Allan (1990). Nor would I wish to claim that S and H cannot access the nonliteral sense directly: It is conceivable that there is someone who does not know the literal meaning of *bitch;* for such a person *Millie is a bitch* would be taken literally to mean "Millie is disagreeable, malicious, and despised." Note that for such a person this is a literal meaning and not a nonliteral one; his or her vocabulary is different from the standard vocabulary. If there were many such people among whom this was the conventional meaning for *bitch,* their dialect would reflect a semantic change from the standard dialect.

Typical, though not necessarily prototypical, aspects of the denotatum are also drawn upon in the semantic representations given in the schema. These seek to capture the kind of information that will help determine the coherence and internal consistency or normality of the world spoken of as it is being constructed from what is said (assuming the latter includes the word *bitch*); and they are not subject to the general objection against selection restrictions (see Allan, 1986, §5.2.4). Much of the information they include derives from general knowledge, experience, custom, convention, and belief: things that have traditionally been associated with language used in particular contexts (i.e., with pragmatics).

I said earlier that I would tell why the author of (1) did not use the term *bitch* anywhere in the news item. In fact, s/he went so far as to claim to have borrowed the words "something that rhymes with rich": s/he did so in order to disclaim responsibility for any offence to the reader. As I said before, people will avoid using a language expression that is ambiguous between a taboo or dysphemistic sense and a nontaboo sense just in case they may be misunderstood, or inadvertently cause offence. An additional motivation for such avoidance may be the intuition of a well-established fact, namely, that taboo forms are particularly salient in any discourse (cf. Allan & Burridge, 1991 pp. 23–24; McWhinney, Keenan, & Reinke, 1982; Osgood, Suci, & Tannenbaum, 1957).

IN CONCLUSION

A not uncommon use of the dysphemism *bitch* in American includes this form within the phrase *son-of-a-bitch* often remodelled as the end-clipping *son-of-a* or the abbreviation *S.O.B. Son-of-a-bitch* is an idiom requiring its own separate entry in the lexicon: Presumably the syntactic and semantic content of this entry will be shared with its euphemistic clipping and abbreviation in their graphological and phonological forms. These particular euphemistic remodellings have few if any interesting consequences for the nature of the lexicon, but remodellings like *Shoot!* or *Sugar!* for expletive "Shit!" do. To treat these euphemistic expletives as nothing more than homonyms of the noun or verb *shoot* and the noun *sugar* ignores what speakers recognize to be a remodelling of the taboo expletive; it is a remodelling whose force in part derives from copying the word initial voiceless palatoalveolar fricative of the tabooed model (and in the case of *Shoot!* copying the final consonant, too). Together with the circumstances under which the remodelled item is used, this copying is what gives these forms their euphemistic stamp. Such information should be incorporated in the lexicon under METALINGUISTIC KNOWLEDGE; the networking of lexicon entries that would follow from such a solution is an intuitively satisfying result. The existence of word association and certain kinds of speech errors and misperceptions is suggestive of lexical networking, though I know of no specific experimental evidence to confirm the existence of the networks that I have been discussing.

Networking is also implied by the "lookup" function that appears among the ADDITIONAL SEMANTIC INFORMATION section of the sample lexicon entry. Once again, this is intuitively satisfying, but it raises the problem of infinite and vicious loops within the system. That is why there needs to be some heuristic for avoiding the problem by instituting some kind of weighting within the system, controlled by nature of the world being spoken of. The algorithm in Fig. 14.1 shows that MINIMAL SEMANTIC INFORMATION is demanded from every lexical entry, and where more information is required, more gates are opened, more terms looked up. This raises the question of how a processor knows what amount of information is necessary at any point during the processing: I don't have an answer to the question; but the burden of solution does not fall on the lexicon.

At least one lesson from this exercise in semantics is that there is no boundary between semantics and pragmatics (cf. Kittay, 1987, p. 42). This is not to deny that there are clear cases of difference: One can talk about the sense of the expression *the president* (semantics) and contrast that with its reference (pragmatics). But just as the deeper one gets into phonology, the closer one gets to phonetics; so the deeper one gets into semantics, the closer one gets to pragmatics. It has been my intention in this chapter to show that, if we are to say anything worthwhile about their meanings, the contents of the senses of certain words must draw on background information about the entities spoken or written of; this information may be based on any or all of experience, convention, custom, myth, and language use. Therefore, it is no surprise that Allan and Burridge (1991) are able to demonstrate that the meanings of many words do not derive from a single source but show a variety of influences leading to the conventionalization of their meanings: Influence is exerted from a host of imagistic, associative and formal as well as pragmatic factors that coalesce and mutually reinforce one another. It is these kinds of effects on the semantics of lexicon entries that justify Lakoff (1987) championing an "experientialist" analysis of meaning. If semantics is to go beyond translating symbols into yet more esoteric symbols, it must begin to reflect the richness of human experience that is intrinsic to language understanding; that is, semantics should start to represent what intelligent reflective layfolk understand by "meaning" in language. To accomplish such a goal, semantic representations need to be correlated with human experience as it is ordinarily expressed in natural language. The kind of semantic representation I have offered here is a faltering step in that direction; and what it clearly reveals is that senses are abstracted from language use, and from the beliefs and customs of users. It is these pragmatic issues that drive semantics.

ACKNOWLEDGMENTS

Firstly, I would like to thank the editors for organizing the conference that gave birth to this chapter and provided so much stimulation and camaraderie amongst those who attended; and secondly, to thank them both for their help in dispensing with some of the graver infelicities of this contribution. Alas, no one but myself is to blame for the inadequacies you now find in it.

POSTSCRIPT (OCTOBER 1991)

Since writing this chapter, I have done some thinking about proper names and been led to recognize that all proper names are entered in the lexicon and some have senses attached (e.g., **John** *proper name* "bearer of the name *John,* normally male"; **Robin** *proper name* "bearer of the name *Robin,* either male or female"; **Aristotle** *proper name* "bearer of the name *Aristotle;* a Greek name, normally for a male"). I hypothesize that the lexicon is either part of, or closely networked with, the mental encyclopedia (or knowledge base) in which information about name-bearers is stored (e.g. [1]**Aristotle** *proper name* of an ancient Greek philosopher, born in Stagira in C4 BCE. Author of *The Categories, On Interpretation, On Poetry* . . . Pupil of Plato and teacher of Alexander the Great . . . etc.; [2]**Aristotle** *proper name* of Aristotle Onassis, C20 CE Greek shipping magnate . . . etc.) This is what allows a proper name like *Hoover* to become the common name for a class of products, and a proper name like *Boycott* to be extended to the kind of activity intimately associated with someone of the name. The encyclopedia contains information about common name bearers as well as proper name bearers, and presumably about all sorts of temporal phenomena, events and qualities as well. I suspect that the encyclopedia incorporates not only a lexicon, but other linguistically relevant components. In this chapter as in Allan (1990) I have proposed that where the literal meaning of a lexicon item is inappropriate, a nonliteral meaning is sought. The nonliteral meaning often derives from connotation; like any form of semantic extension, it is ultimately based on perceptions (perhaps prejudiced perceptions) of the typical denotatum. I now believe that such information would not be part of the lexicon entry, but would either be stored, or perhaps generated, in some other component of the encyclopedia which abstracts connotations from encyclopedic information. Yet another component that needs to be networked with the lexicon and the encyclopedia is one that stores metalinguistic information about expressions, their stylistic characteristics, and alternatives to them. Further examination of these hypothetical components is needed, and they will be dealt with on another occasion.

REFERENCES

Allan, K. (1981). Interpreting from context. *Lingua, 53*, 151–73.

Allan, K. (1986). *Linguistic meaning* (2 Vols.). London: Routledge & Kegan Paul.

Allan, K. (1990). Some English terms of insult invoking body-parts: Evidence of a pragmatic driver for semantics. In S. L. Tsohatzidis (Ed.), *Meanings and Prototypes: Studies in Linguistic Categorization* (pp. 159–194). London and New York: Routledge.

Allan, K., & Burridge, K. (1991). *Euphemism and dysphemism: Language used as shield and weapon.* New York: Oxford University Press.

Black, J. B. (1984). Understanding and remembering stories. In J. R. Anderson & S. M. Kosslyn (Eds.), *Tutorials in learning and memory: Essays in honor of Gordon Bower* (pp. 235–255). San Francisco: W. H. Freeman.

Bolinger, D. (1950). Rime, assonance, and morpheme analysis. *Word, 14,* 109–149.

Bransford, J. D., & Johnson, M. K. (1972). Contextual prerequisites for understanding: Some investigations of comprehension and recall. *Journal of Verbal Learning and Verbal Behavior, 11,* 717–726.

Charniak, E. (1976). Inference and knowledge I & II. In E. Charniak & Y. Wilks (Eds.), *Computational semantics: An introduction to artificial intelligence and natural language comprehension* (pp. 1–21, 129–154). Amsterdam: North-Holland.

Clark, H. H. (1977). Inferences in comprehension. In D. LaBerge & S. J. Samuels (Eds.), *Basic processes in reading: Perception and comprehension* (pp. 243–263). Hillsdale, NJ: Lawrence Erlbaum Associates.

Fauconnier, G. (1985). *Mental spaces.* Cambridge: MIT Press.

Fillmore, C. J. (1975). An alternative to checklist theories of meaning. *Proceedings of the first annual meeting of the Berkeley Linguistics Society* (pp. 123–131).

Fillmore, C. J. (1982). Frame semantics. In Linguistic Society of Korea (Ed.), *Linguistics in the morning calm* (pp. 111–138). Seoul: Hanshin.

Graesser, A. C., & Clark, L. F. (1985). *Structures and procedures of implicit knowledge.* Norwood, NJ: Ablex.

Jackendoff, R. (1983). *Semantics and cognition.* Cambridge, MA: MIT Press.

Jackendoff, R. (1987). *Consciousness and the computational mind.* Cambridge: MIT Press.

Johnson-Laird, P. N. (1983). *Mental models: Towards a cognitive science of language, inference, and consciousness.* Cambridge, England: Cambridge University Press.

Kintsch, W., Mandel, T. S., & Kozminsky, E. (1977). Summarizing scrambled stories. *Memory and Cognition, 5,* 547–552.

Kittay, E. (1987). *Metaphor: Its cognitive force and linguistic structure.* Oxford: Clarendon Press.

Kozminsky, E. (1977). Altering comprehension: The effect of biasing titles on text comprehension. *Memory and Cognition, 5,* 482–490.

Lakoff, F. (1987). *Women, fire, and dangerous things.* Chicago: University of Chicago Press.

Langacker, R. W. (1987). *Foundations of cognitive grammar.* Stanford: Stanford University Press.

Leech, G. (1981). *Semantics.* Harmondsworth: Penguin.

Minsky, M. (1977). Frame-system theory. In P. N. Johnson-Laird & P. C. Wason (Eds.), *Thinking: Readings in cognitive science* (pp. 355–376). Cambridge, England: Cambridge University Press.

McWhinney, B., Keenan, J. M., & Reinke, P. (1982). The role of arousal in memory for conversation. *Memory and Cognition, 10,* 308–317.

Norrick, N. R. (1981). *Semiotic principles in semantic theory.* Amsterdam: John Benjamins.

Ortner, S. B. (1974). Is female to male as nature is to culture? In M. Z. Rosaldo & L. Lamphere (Eds.), *Woman, culture, and society* (pp. 67–87). Stanford CA: Stanford University Press.

Osgood, C. E., Suci, G. J., & Tannenbaum, P. H. (1957). *The measurement of meaning.* Urbana: University of Illinois Press.

Rickheit, G., & Strohner, H. (Eds.). (1985). *Inferences in text processing.* Amsterdam: North-Holland.

Schank, R., & Abelson, R. P. (1977). *Scripts, plans, goals and understanding: An inquiry into human knowledge structures.* Hillsdale, NJ: Lawrence Erlbaum Associates.

Thorndyke, P. W. (1976). The role of inferences in discourse comprehension. *Journal of Verbal Learning and Verbal Behavior, 15,* 437–446.

Thorndyke, P. W. (1977). Cognitive structures in comprehension and memory of narrative discourse. *Cognitive Psychology, 9,* 77–110.

Uyl, M. den, & van Oostendorp, H. (1980). The use of scripts in text comprehension. *Poetics, 9,* 275–294.

Van Dijk, T. A., & Kintsch, W. (1983). *Strategies of discourse comprehension.* New York: Academic Press.

Wierzbicka, A. (1985). *Lexicography and conceptual analysis.* Ann Arbor, MI: Karoma.

IV COMPUTATIONAL PROCESSES IN THE LEXICON

15 Lexical Retrieval Processes: Semantic Field Effects

Merrill F. Garrett
University of Arizona

My objective is to examine some aspects of patterns in normal word substitution errors for their bearing on claims for psychologically effective semantic fields. By "psychologically effective," I mean to assert an active role in the normal function of a significant part of the communicative system. In so doing, I associate some empirical observations about a particular data base of speech errors with claims for specific processing mechanisms in language production. By way of preliminaries, the nature of the data base is first discussed, and second, the manner of my interpretation of it. Following those remarks, I report results of analyses of several classes of error and discuss their relation to some proposals that have been made regarding semantic fields.

The Data Base

The observations consist of errors made by normal speakers in the course of regular conversational or expository speech. Such data reflect the exigencies of real-time performance systems, for the errors arise while speakers seek to formulate the linguistic expressions that will serve their communicative intention.

The structures so implicated may differ from those based on reflective judgments of the kind used to justify formal analysis of language structure. Note that this possibility raises two complementary concerns about the relevance of the observations for theory: One may worry that the systems based on reflective judgment are artificial constructs with only an indirect relation to mental processes (i.e., one of the conventional performance/competence questions about the relation of linguistic formalisms and language processing systems). The complementary worry is that real-time processing systems may mix representational types that are treated independently (and for good reason) in formal systems, or that processing systems may use structural contrasts that are rough and ready, and of statistical utility for processing, but are not analytically defensible. I am not inclined to struggle with such issues at the outset of this or any similar effort, because I do not think there are useful a priori answers to such concerns. If different structural claims arise, they are best addressed in the context of the independently motivated formal and computational proposals for a given processing task.

The primary data base used for this chapter is a collection of more than 12,000 language production errors of various types, made by many different speakers in normal communicative situations. The collection has been assembled over a period of several years by Stephanie Shattuck-Hufnagel of MIT and me. A diary method was the principal procedure (i.e., written records taken at the time of error occurrence). For some discussion of the collection procedures and limitations of the data, see Shattuck (1975), and Cutler (1982). The errors I rely on from the corpus are those made in normally fluent speech (i.e., variably hesitant, structurally fractured, and topically fluid, but for any given full utterance, underlyingly well-formed and with identifiable interpretive intent). I comment later on some relevant methodological matters in passing.

The objective of our study of these speech errors has been to find distributional patterns that provide evidence for the structure of the general cognitive and linguistic processes that underlie language production. Several distinct processes have been identified that are systematically associated with different types of linguistic structure and with specific error mechanisms. A particularly salient distinction for our current purpose is between errors that involve more than a single location in the intended utterance (e.g., those in 1), and lexical errors that seem to have a single error site (e.g., those in 2)—as when there is a single substitution, deletion, or

(1) (moved elements boldface)
   a. " . . . on a sot **h**oddering iron." (*hot soldering*)
   b. "They get weird_everi**er** day" (. . . *weirder every*)
   c. "It just **sound**ed to **start.**" (*started to sound*)
   d. "We completely forgot to add the **list** to the **roof.**" (*roof to the list*)
(2) (substituted elements boldface)
   a. "It looks as though you're making considerable **process.**" (*progress*)
   b. "I've got whipped cream on my **mushroom.**" (*mustache*)
   c. "He rode his bike to school **tomorrow.** (*yesterday*)
   d. "What I've done here is torn **together** three . . . , uh torn apart three issues that . . . "

addition of an intended element. The former type of error may involve movement of intended elements (i.e., exchanges like 1a,c,d, or shifts like 1b) or some other interaction between two different elements (i.e., anticipations and perseverations). Both types of errors (single or multiple locus) involve most basic element types: sounds, morphemes, words, simple phrases; of these, meaning-based lexical errors of the kind illustrated in (2c,d) provide the primary data relevant to the present discussion.

Interpretation of the Data

Though simple word substitution errors are the focus of later analysis, it is helpful to consider some relations between such errors and the multilocus errors. Briefly: The movement errors provide independent justification for an important distinction to be drawn among the word substitutions, namely, that between form-mediated and meaning-mediated errors (e.g., the contrast between 2a,b and 2c,d).

Movement Errors. The movement errors have provided a basis for claims that sentence planning processes proceed in distinct processing levels, and that lexical and segmental content are significantly dissociated from their phrasal environments in the computational processes that build sentence form. Moreover, the movement errors reveal significant restrictions on the information flow between processing levels and in particular indicate a distinction between processes that build abstract logical and syntactic representations (i.e., phonologically uninterpreted) and those that build prosodically and phonetically interpreted surface phrasal structures. Put simply, the argument is that such assumptions can economically account for a variety of otherwise apparently unrelated constraints on error distributions. For discussion, see Garrett (1975, 1980). The processing levels so motivated correlate well with formal levels of representation in a "generic" contemporary grammar: semantic, syntactic, phonological, and phonetic.

These claims are relevant to the current concern in the following way: The two levels of *sentence* processing indicated by the movement errors correlate directly with two major types of lexical processing implied by the patterns of lexical substitution errors. The two levels of sentence structure motivated by the several types of movement errors may plausibly be associated, respectively, with a conceptually driven process that provides lexical content for abstract syntactic structures, and with a form-driven process that associates the phonological descriptions of words with their phrasal environments. There is, therefore, good empirical reason based on specifically sentence-level processes to assign a two-stage structure to the systems that account for lexical retrieval in language production. This complements and reinforces the patterns seen in the word substitution errors themselves. Following Levelt (1989) and others, I refer to the first of these two retrieval stages as "lemma activation," by which I mean the identification of a specific lexical item with its semantic and syntactic specification, but *without* the specification of its phonological form.

Word Substitution Errors. On the face of it, word substitutions have heterogeneous causes: anticipatory and perseveratory copying (e.g., 3.), discourse and environmental intrusion (e.g., 4.), and those with no apparent discourse or environmental source (e.g., 2,5. and 6.). These latter are the focus of current interest because they are the best candidates for errors of lexical retrieval.

(3) anticipation
   a. "the crazy **idea** who has a good idea, but doesn't have a grant, . . ." (*guy*)
   associative perseveration:
   b. "At ANU, there was a little creek running through the **river**." (*campus*)
(4) conversational intrusions; prior mention:
   a. [immediately prior series of temperature reports] " . . . it's been hot and
   muggy—the kind of weather that shortens **temperatures**." (*tempers*)
   conversational intrusions; topic relevant:
   b. [immediately prior comment on weather; no overt use of word] "I love the
   Cape at this time of **weather**." (*year*)
   environmental intrusions:
   c. "You found your **pen?**" (*bag*) [addressee was waving a pen in speaker's
   face while cleaning it; the question actually concerned a misplaced briefcase.]
(5) form related:
   a. "You'll earn her eternal **grapefruit**" (*gratitude*)
   b. "I gave you my **undevoted** attention." (*undivided*)
(6) meaning related:
   a. "The picture on the front was the **whale** from Jaws." (*shark*)
   b. "**Ask** me whether you think it'll do the job." (*tell*)

I have excluded errors like those in (3) and (4) from the initial data set used for
lexical retrieval analysis, whether form or meaning based. They are ambiguous
as to their source or multiply determined, and there is good indication that some
at least include attentional factors (i.e., the environmental intrusions). The environmental errors in particular seem responsive to several distinct influences,
form, meaning, and situational, where the situational information is as often
topic irrelevant as relevant. The heterogeneous set of lexical and conceptual
relations in the discourse and environmental errors undoubtedly have some interesting relations to lexical recovery processes. But one is in no good position to
say what that relation is at the outset of study, and, accordingly, one would like to
set them aside for future consideration.

There can be difficulty in executing the desired separation if the information
that was recorded about the discourse or the environment of the errors is limited—as it sometimes is in the diary method of error collection for a variety of
reasons. Broad decisions about the likelihood of topical relevance for a given
lexical target may be made on general grounds of the conversational setting but
detailed recording of prior remarks in a discourse or, more difficult still, of
unrelated collateral discussions or events is necessary for a secure assignment to
the environmental errors category. It is essential to make the separation, however, for the structural properties of the clear cases of lexical retrieval error do
differ from those of environmental and discourse errors, and this is particularly
so for the analysis of meaning-related cases. For example, compare the relations
in a set of environmental and discourse intrusions, like (**error/target**): **weath-
er/year, pen/bag, cup/pot, bird/tree, church/train, erotic/exotic, men-**

ace/message, with those in a set for which such environmental confounds are, as best we can determine, absent, as **whale/shark, ask/tell, together/apart, to-morrow/yesterday, lunch/supper, barks/meows, recent/early.** For the former type, lacking the context or background facts leaves one often mystified as to what relation supported the error; but for the latter set, the readily inferable relations are, in fact, the situationally relevant ones. Excluding the environmental and discourse errors from the initial data set provides a structurally more stable set of cases that plausibly bear specifically on lexical retrieval processes during language production. In dealing with this problem for the analyses reported here, I have construed the environmental evidence liberally, preferring to err on the side of excluding some retrieval errors incorrectly than to include some environmental errors incorrectly. That having been said, for the present report, the number of problematic cases is not large and the patterns of these analyses not significantly affected. This issue is, however, quite important for the long run in studies of this kind and will require systematic attention for use of combined error corpora (viz., from different investigators) or for new efforts at error collection focused on the kinds of questions addressed here.

The retrieval errors, such as those of (5) and (6) may be separated, as the relations of target and intrusion suggest, into meaning-determined and form-determined cases. This separation is readily done for the most part because the form-related cases are not commonly related by meaning as well (e.g., the cases in 5. are representative). The argument for a distinction between form- and meaning-based errors is of considerable independent interest (see, e.g., Fay & Cutler, 1977; Garrett, 1988; see Schreifers, Meyer, & Levelt, 1990, for a recent discussion and some related experimental evidence) but concern us here only insofar as it affects analysis of semantic regularities in the discussion of possible semantic field effects (i.e., by providing an alternative account of exceptions to semantic generalizations in those errors that might be also be construed as semantic).

SOME SEMANTIC CONSTRAINTS ON WORD
SUBSTITUTION ERRORS

With the obscuring effects of adventitious processing interactions (i.e., the environmental contaminations) stripped away, we may ask some questions about the data that bear on hypotheses about the effects of semantic structures in lexical retrieval. The presence of semantic field effects is readily apparent and intuitively compelling. A substantial proportion of the word substitution errors that involve meaning-related pairs may be organized into clusters that correspond to natural categories, many of which have independent justification from other kinds of research.

Semantic Substitution Fields

The Body Parts Field. One example that well illustrates two significant points is the field of *body part* terms (see Fig. 15.1). The terms examined in this set are for the most part morphologically simple and are part of the common production vocabulary of ordinary English speakers. This field is developmentally salient and it has received significant attention in aphasia research, where there is evidence for its selective loss and preservation (Dennis, 1976; McKenna & Warrington, 1978).

The relations among the terms may be further specified by subfields within the larger semantic set: head, torso, and limb. Note that the relations illustrated here depend on similarity judgments for pairs sampled from the set of possible pairings of set members and on clustering in a list generation task; the "prominence" of a term in the field is roughly indicated by type size, and it reflects the frequency with which a term was included in the timed list generation task as well as the ordering of items in clusters. No very sophisticated analysis of the clustering is required for present purposes—the subfield effects are robust.

Two questions concerning the integrity of the field may be asked of the word substitution data: How well do the substitution patterns reflect the field boundaries, and for those that do, is there further evidence for the subfield structures? For those errors in which a body part term is supplanted by another word in the MIT/AZ corpus, Table 15.1 shows the frequency with which a target word within the field is replaced either by a word within that field or from outside it; similarly, the rate of within-subfield substitutions and cross-subfield substitutions is given for the errors that are internal to the field. I have included a similar tabulation for the sample of word substitution errors published by Fromkin (1971) and for a corpus of word substitution errors collected by David Fay and kindly made available by him.

The results for this field are straightforward, and they indicate a strong con-

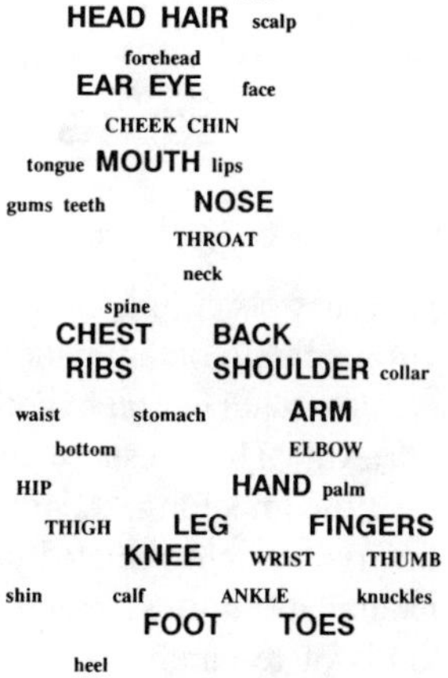

```
                        skull
               HEAD HAIR  scalp
                     forehead
               EAR EYE   face
                 CHEEK CHIN
             tongue MOUTH lips
          gums teeth        NOSE
                         THROAT
                          neck

                   spine
            CHEST        BACK
            RIBS         SHOULDER collar
       waist      stomach     ARM
            bottom          ELBOW
       HIP                HAND palm
          THIGH    LEG        FINGERS
                   KNEE   WRIST   THUMB
      shin     calf     ANKLE      knuckles
                   FOOT    TOES
      heel
```

FIG. 15.1. Relations for body parts terms.

TABLE 15.1
Substitution Pairs in which the target Word is a Body Part Term

	MIT				Fromkin and Fay Corpora			
				Category of Intrusion Word				
Subfield	Head	Torso	Limb	Outside	Head	Torso	Limb	Outside
Head	4	0	1	1	5	0	0	1
Torso	0	2	0	1	0	0	0	0
Limb	2	0	9	0	1	1	3	1

straint of field boundaries on the substitution patterns. There are 28 field internal errors (e.g., **hair/head, nose/hand, shoulder/elbow, finger/toe** and four field external errors (water/waist, soldier/shoulder, mind/mouth, list/lips). All these field external substitutions have plausible alternative accounts. It is very likely that they are not conceptually determined at all but rather are *form-based* substitutions that occur after lemma selection has been accomplished. The field external substitution for "shoulders" is a particularly clear case. This pair of words shows up three times in the word substitution corpus (MIT corpus and Fay corpus combined); only one of the instances is relevant to the tabulation for Table 15.1—that in which "soldiers" displaces "shoulders"; but in the other two instances, the reverse obtains: "Shoulders" displaces "soldiers." The lack of semantic similarity coupled with the bidirectional substitution pattern and the very strong form similarity strongly support an alternative account—either as a word form substitution like those in (5), or perhaps as a sound error (feature exchange). The other three field external cases also show the relevant form similarity (initial segmental overlap) and no plausible semantic base. Subfield effects also seem to be present in the body part substitutions. Though some cross-field errors within the larger field do occur, the dominant pattern reflects the subfields: 6 of 28 errors cross subfield boundaries and the remaining 22 are internal to subfields.

It is worth considering how much of the field and subfield structure might be accounted for in terms of links between specific lexical representations rather than as field effects—as, for example, associative relations between word pairs. Based on free-association performance for each of the target terms in the set reported here, 13 pairs are associates (i.e., the error word is among the first three free associates) and 15 pairs are not directly associated or only weakly associated. On those grounds, the major field effects clearly implicate more than associative lexical relations. The subfield effects are less clearly distinguishable. As might be expected, all the associative pairs are within-subfield errors; the nonassociated cases are roughly split between-within-subfield and cross-subfield cases (6 cross subfield and 9 are within subfield).

We can supplement the associative evaluation of these patterns by considering as well word frequency. On the assumption that the errors reflect the relative availability of lexical *forms*—as opposed the processes that relate conceptual structure to lexical representations—one might expect more frequent forms to displace less frequent ones as a dominant pairwise relation in the errors. But, for the body part errors, (and other meaning related pairs we consider), such an effect is not supported. There is no systematic asymmetry between target and intrusion, and in particular none for higher frequency field members to replace lower frequency ones: In the 28 within-field errors, 10 show a lower frequency for the target than for the intruding word, 14 show the reverse relation, and 4 show about equal frequency. To illustrate more specifically: **Finger (frequency 46)** displaces both **hand (f 431)** and **toe (f 10)** and is in turn displaced by **toe** and by **mouth (f 106); shoulder (f 66)** displaces **arm (f 108)** but is itself displaced by **elbow (f 10).**

Levelt (1989) has suggested a combination of associative and word-frequency tests to assess the causal factors in such errors, namely, that one might distinguish conceptual from lexically specific associative cases in terms of word-frequency effects: The associative cases might be expected to show a frequency asymmetry whereas conceptual cases would not. He reports an analysis of Fromkin's published error cases indicating that associatively related antonyms and cohyponyms show a frequency as symmetry, though nonassociated ones do not. Although this does hold for the Fromkin published corpus, the result may not be representative. For the set of body part terms we have been discussing and for those fields discussed in the following sections, when associated pairs are analyzed separately from nonassociated pairs, the effects do not encourage the view that a frequency bias is a strong factor for the associatively related items (see Table 15.2).

An interesting ancillary point may be made based on the absence of lexically mediated substitution pairs such as *"guns" for "arms," *"coconut" for "palm," or *"inch" for "foot" in, for example, the body part field (and for similar cases in other fields as well). Where the *target* word is clearly a body part term, the intruding form is another body part term rather than a lexically related term from the other sense of the target word. This indicates, if the null result can be relied upon, that the mechanism of these substitutions is the mapping from conceptual representations to lemmas rather than one or another kind of connectedness among the lexical representations themselves. By contrast, we know that, for *comprehension* systems, the response of the processing system to a given lexical form *does* cross semantic field boundaries—multiple activation of lexical interpretations for a word form is the general rule (Seidenberg, Tannenhaus, Leiman, & Bienkowski, 1982; Swinney, 1979). If, in production processes, the activation of a word under semantic/conceptual control had as an immediate consequence the spreading of activation to related word forms, cross-field substitutions for ambiguous words might be expected to occur, though it is

TABLE 15.2
Substitution Pairs for Semantic Categories

Internal		External
Animals 7 (e.g., dog/cat; cat/dog; lion/tiger; whale/shark; squirrel/turtle)		0
Clothing 8 (pants/shirt; pants/shorts; shoes/socks; hat/tie; collar/belt)		3
Color names 9 (pink/green; yellow/red; red/yellow; brown/orange; blue/black)		0
Food & Drink 13 (apricot/asparagus; grapes/oranges; onion/honey; milk/water; beer/wine)		1
Temporals 11 (seconds/minutes; minute/second; year/week; week/month; day/year)		1

difficult to say with what frequency. Another way of expressing this is that interlexical relations among *word forms,* but not among word lemmas, would support such cross-field effects. For unsystematic ambiguity, no salient link between the conceptual content and hence the lemmas for PALM/tree and PALM/hand is available. If only lemma representations are activated by conceptual input, with form activation coming later as a result of separate processing operations, the observed pattern for the terms of the semantic field would be the expected one.

Whatever we may conclude from the seeming lack of cross-field activation for ambiguous terms, or concerning the role of association and word frequency in word substitutions, the general point seems secure: There is a reasonable basis in the available data from the body part field to look for accounts in terms of a mapping from conceptual structure to lemmas.

Some further examples.   One must, of course, ask whether the pattern of semantic constraint illustrated in the body parts field is typical of other plausible fields. Body part terms may be special in some way. Several other fields of commonplace terms have sufficient representation in the corpus to permit a preliminary evaluation of that question, and the results indicate that the effects are general, though there are some reservations that I consider shortly. Table 15.2 lists the frequency of field internal and field external substitutions for several other categories with enough error cases to be of some interest. The indications are similar to those for the body parts field, although these others do not provide a test for internal structures of the field in the same degree.

As with the body parts field, significant frequency effects in the relation between target and intrusion are not observed in any of these fields. Associative relations differ in the degree to which they appear in the various fields—so clothing terms, color terms, and temporal terms each have a number of associatively related pairs, whereas the pairs that are in the other two fields have fewer strong associates. But in any event, the result for associatively related pairs in the various fields is the same as for the fields as a whole—no significant tendency for the target to be lower in frequency than the intrusion word. In these fields, there are a number of examples of pairs that reverse their relation as target and intrusion words, and this seems to happen as readily for word pairs that have a large frequency difference between them as for pairs that are closer to each other in frequency.

But we should note that whereas associative relations do not seem to have an observable relation for the errors that I have been treating as within-field errors, there may be a different tendency for errors that are cross-field errors. There are not many cases, but where they are associated (feet/shoes, head/cap), there is a trend for higher frequency to displace lower frequency items. This may be tested more generally in the pairs that display a different relation than the cocategory one in these noun substitutions, and we return to this question later.

Field integrity is strongly indicated in this data set: When a term is displaced, its replacement is another closely related field term. But what about the reverse error situation (i.e., those cases in which a field term from one of the test sets itself displaces a word that is *not* in the field)? Shouldn't the substitution effects be symmetric?; that is, if every word has a "semantic field home," and if the constraints on substitution are as indicated so far, we shouldn't see any cross-field substitutions. We do see cross-field effects, however, and so must consider that all field effects are not of equal strength or that other factors so far not considered are at work. Consider in this context other errors involving body part terms, but as error intrusions into another field, for example:

(7) "She doesn't want to get her foot off the pavement" (for " . . . her wheel off the pavement").

The "foot" for "wheel" error turns up twice in the MIT/AZ corpus of errors; two other body part examples are "head" for "cap" and "eye" for "light." Errors like these, although not common, do incontestably occur. Some cross-field errors may be associative and others might arguably arise from the environmental contaminant mechanisms discussed earlier, but although there is always some room for doubt, there remain cases that do not have a plausible explanation in such terms.

The "foot" for "wheel" example seems to involve an analogical relation between target and intrusion. There is an interesting relation between such cases and observations that have been made in connection with the study of language disorders. A number of reports of semantically specific lexical losses have been made (Shallice, 1988; Warrington & Shallice, 1984; see Garrett, in press, for a recent discussion). These reports range from cases in which the loss is claimed to be a general compromise of concrete terms when compared to abstract ones, to those in which the loss is for basic level categories, as for example, terms for fruits and vegetables (e.g., Hart, Berndt, & Caramazza, 1985). Of particular interest for our error example are cases in which the contrast is between living and nonliving things (Warrington & Shallice, 1984). The suggestion by Warrington and Shallice is that such cases may be distinguished in terms of featural analyses that include a contrast between "functional" versus "perceptual" descriptions. A crossover from one of these domains to the other might reflect the failure of this high-level classificatory decision in the presence of a partial correspondence for featural descriptions in lower levels. If, for example, one considers the perceptual description of animates within the living things category as including something like [capable of motion], and [limbs/means for locomotion], the extension from "wheel" for automobile to "foot" for a person (particularly, given in this example, the agent relation between the driver referred to in (7) and the vehicle's motion) makes a plausible conflation in terms of the mapping from concept to lemma representation. Many of the cases of cross-field substitutions that have an analogical flavor might be given a description in terms of featural similarities of this kind (e.g., "speed" for "temperature" in an action description for an oven; "awake" for "open" in the description of a restaurant; "years" for "yards" in a measure expression).

These are interesting cases whose best analysis remains to be determined. In any event, they do not compromise the basic point illustrated by the field internal word substitutions: There is a powerful influence of semantic relatedness on word substitution patterns that suggests something more general than pairwise lexical relations.

Some Grammatical Class Effects

The cases we have discussed so far concern nouns. The relation between the target-intrusion pairs is one of common category memberships, with various types of relation between the superordinate category and the terms arrayed under it represented (meronyms in case of the body parts set; simple taxonomies in clothing, animals, etc.). However, the relations we have considered do not exhaust the effective structural relations in noun substitutions. We consider other types of relations that seem to be reflected in substitution patterns for nouns and compare these to relations implicated for other grammatical categories.

Nouns. The relational types for nouns are summarized in Table 15.3. The major influence is the one we have already discussed—one or another kind of taxonomic or part–whole relation. In addition, however, there is a clear case to be made for some role of conceptual oppositions, with contradictories like "end–beginning," "birth–death," "top–bottom," and functional contrasts like "husband–wife," "host–guest," "answer–question" strongly represented. The role

TABLE 15.3
Relations Between Noun Substitution Pairs: N = 181

Common category: (bodyparts, colors, etc., sets; fork/spoon, car/bicycle, vowel/noun, asterisk/italics, symphony/opera)	137
Opposites: (beginning/end, conclusion/opening, today/tomorrow, bottom/top, death/birth, husband/wife, guest/host, harvesting/planting)	26
Analogies and rough synonyms: (foot/wheel, speed/temperature, stairs/bus, velocity/acceleration, aisles-alleys, verge-fringe, sentence/term)	9
Loose associate: (bunk/dorm, cards/tricks, audience/orchestra, requirements/procedures)	6
Other (fingernail/telephone, firecracker/ashtray, television/alarm)	3

of conceptual contrast in substitution errors is, as we see next, significant across all classes of error. Purely associative substitutions (i.e., cases in which that is the *only* significant relation) are not that common in the error set when the discourse and environmental cases are set aside. As our earlier discussion of Levelt's analysis of frequency effects in associatively related cases suggests, it is difficult to evaluate the claim for associative influences because many such substitutions also display other relations.

Here we take explicit notice of the absence of clear synonymic substitutions in the errors. The import of that absence is unclear. It may reflect the fact that it is simply hard to tell when such errors have occurred because the communicative intent will be served in most cases. We consider this matter further in discussion of adjective substitutions and of blend errors. These latter are strongly similar in meaning and provide a useful counterpoint to the substitution errors.

Three ommisions from the treatment of noun substitutions should be noted. I have not discussed substitutions of number names for other number names or letter names for other letter names, though such are frequent and their category boundaries are effective. There is some reason to treat these as special categories—though nothing about their behavior is incompatible with the remarks made about the errors that are discussed. Similarly, I have not discussed proper names, though there are many substitutions that involve them. There is considerable interest in such errors both from the perspective of retrieval mechanisms and the perspective of semantic treatments for proper names. I leave those matters for another occasion, noting only that there is quite good evidence for what might be called field effects in such errors (e.g., substitutions are constrained by kinship [family members substitute for other family members; friends for friends], professional area [politicians substitute for politicians, composers for composers, artists for artists], etc.; see Hotopf, 1980, for some discussion).

Adjectives and Verbs.   Let us turn to some similar questions for substitutions other than nouns. Various suggestions have been made that grammatical classes differ in their lexical structures. One interesting such suggestion is that whereas nouns are characterized by hyponomy and meronomy of the kind we have just been considering, adjectives are organized by antonymy and synonomy. There is some general support for this view in the word substitution patterns. Before examining that point, however, I should note that the word substitution data shows various kinds of oppositions to be a potent factor for all grammatical classes—nouns, verbs, adjectives, and other minor categories. We consider some implications of this after looking at the regularities for adjectives and verbs.

Gross, Fisher, and Miller (1989) have argued that the semantic space for adjectives is organized around basic contrast terms (antonyms) with a field of associated terms (synonyms) at each pole of the basic bipolar pair. So, for example, for the basic pair "wet–dry," their proposal associates a set (damp, moist, soggy, . . .) with the wet pole and a set (arid, parched, dessicated, . . .) with the dry pole. They characterize the synonymic relation within each of the two polar sets as conceptual, and the relation between the members of the bipolar pair as lexical. Thus, contrasts between words that are members of distinct associated sets (e.g., "moist–arid") would, on that view, be mediated by the lexical relation between the members of the bipolar pair at the core. Gross et al. present some experimental evidence for this view based on timed judgments of meaning relatedness.

This way of looking at adjective structure has some implications for word substitution patterns. If the relations that are effective in meaning-based word substitutions are conceptual to lexical mappings, one would expect the dominant patterns of adjective substitution to be antonymic. Substitutions of one member of a synonymic set for another would represent a conceptual error—not at all an impossible event, but by working definition for the Gross et al. hypothesis, not an error of the language processor per se. More particularly, one expects errors to involve core contrast pairs, or pairs in which one member is a core contrast term. So, for example, for a target like "My shirt is completely WET," one might expect to most often find the substitution DRY. If synonomy and conceptual error are functional here, MOIST (a "one step error") might be expected and detected in the target environment. A substitution like ARID for WET or MOIST should be rare (two or more steps). Note that there is an asymmetry of salience for error reporting: Substitutions that don't involve change of polarity may be detected only if circumstances are right. "My shirt is WET," when DRENCHED was intended may go unremarked; but "this cake is certainly WET," when MOIST was intended will likely be noticed.

Adjective substitutions from the error corpus show that they are indeed strongly dominated by antonymy, and that the majority of the errors involve substitutions of one basic term for its polar opposite. Table 15.4 indicates the frequency of subtypes of errors; examples are given in the order error/target.

TABLE 15.4
Relations Between Adjective Substitution Pairs
Antonyms: N = 62

Basic: 29
(cold/hot, warm/cool, short/long, high/low, heavy/light, slow/fast, strong/weak, hard/easy,
easy/difficult old/new, less/more, first/last, dead/alive, fresh/stale, private/public)

Morphological: 15
(impossible/possible, implausible/plausible, unrelated/related, discouraging/encouraging,
allowed/disallowed, appropriate/inappropriate, intelligibly/unintelligibly, meaningful/meaningless)

Functional: 9
(married/single, semantic-syntactic, oral/written, auditory/verbal, blind/deaf)

Analogy: 5
(awake/open, big/wide, narrow/shallow, slower/smaller)

Other: 4
(downstairs/lower, frozen/packaged, thick/sticky, round/long)

There are no cases in the current data set of substitutions that involve polar opposites from the associated fields (e.g., drenched–dessicated). The strongly dominant pattern is for substitution between opposite terms that have substantial semantic overlap, and even those cases that do not have that precise description do occur in environments of functional contrast: "Deaf" is not the opposite of "blind," nor "syntactic" of "semantic," but the discussions in which these errors occurred were ones in which the terms did contrast as incompatible candidates for the intended lexical slot (i.e., the underlying intent carried the implications): "syntactic only, and therefore not semantic"; "deaf only, and therefore not blind"). Where the substitution is not between opposites, the observed cases are not from a synonymy field for a given polar opposition (though recall that these may be hard to detect) but "sideways slips" to a related dimension (e.g., big/wide, narrow/shallow). There are few examples to go on, however.

For the pairs that represent a "marked/unmarked" contrast (e.g., good–bad, happy–sad, hot–cold), there is no significant tendency for bias—marked terms displace unmarked terms and vice versa with roughly equal frequency. And, similarly for the question of a frequency bias: no significant effect. In light of our earlier discussion of association as a possible contributing factor to semantic substitutions, here is where one might well have expected to see such an effect, given the abundance of bipolar adjectives that have strong associative values. But, in the set of basic oppositions, for example, the pattern is 16 (higher replaces lower) to 13 (lower replaces higher). The other subclasses also show no significant frequency bias.

Somewhat surprisingly, for verbs, the pattern is quite similar to that for adjectives. Verb-substitution pairs are summarized in Table 15.5. Thirty of 48 pairs are sensibly viewed as "opposites" (contradictories, contraries, strong

TABLE 15.5
Relationships for Verb and Minor Category Substitution Pairs

Verbs: N = 48

Opposites: 30
(go/come, start/stop, remember/forget, believe/doubt, ask/tell, precede/follow, fill/empty, love/hate, heard/said, taken/given)

Weak functional contrast: 7
(answer/dial, drink/breath, eat/cook, don't like/don't mind, shove/carry)

Related, non-contrastive: 11
(drink/eat, watch/listen, written/published, looks/sounds, smells/sounds)

Minor Categories: N = 19

Opposites: 11
(there/here, now/then, all/none, until/since, without/with, on/off)

Other: 8
(much/well, in/on, from/for, from/of, from/about)

---

function contrast). Several of the remaining cases (drink/breathe, answer/dial) are, whereas not opposites, can be used contrastively, and in the context of the error were quite plausibly being so used. Table 15.5 also includes a tabulation for minor grammatical categories, many of which are also oppositions. NB: Not much weight should be placed on the minor category figures. I am not at all confident that the sample of minor category errors is representative in the way that the major category errors are. I suspect that substitution errors in this class are less detectable than major class errors, particularly those that are not opposed terms.

As with the adjectives, frequency effects for the verb errors are not significant; 28 of the 48 cases have a more frequent word displacing one of lower frequency. Restriction of the test to only the associated pairs does not change the pattern. Moreover, there are several instances here and in the adjectives in which there are bidirectional errors (e.g., remember/forget; forget/remember); these and the nonsignificant trends for frequency bias suggest that if a frequency bias exists for meaning-related word substitutions, it exerts only weak pressure on the error mechanism.

Blend Errors

There is a substantial additional body of word errors of relevance to the questions we have been discussing. These are errors in which, as with the word substitutions discussed in preceding sections, there is "competition" between two lexical items for a single slot in the intended output frame. In the substitution errors, one element, the wrong one, "wins" and intrudes in the stead of its related competitor. In the errors under current examination, neither word wins—parts of each are output and the resulting form is a phonetic compromise. For example (8), (9), (10):

(8) noun blends:
"He can be the umparee. (umpire/referee)
"An athler like . . . " (athlete/player)
"I'll take just a tab of that." (tad/dab)

(9) verb blends:
"you will never evoid that . . ." (evade/avoid)
"do you want to try cussing over?" (cutting/crossing)
"you wanna know how to ooze your mind?" (soothe/ease)

(10) adjective blends:
traffic is all conjammed up (congested/jammed up)
"Isn't that kweird?" (queer/weird)
"I have to back all the way out of here—'cause I don't have any room to turn around in this luttered . . . [yard]." (littered/cluttered)

As the examples indicate, the relation between the competing forms is a strong kind of synonymy, and it sharply contrasts with the kind of relations that were functional in the word substitutions. Table 15.6 provides a summary for a set of 167 blends in the error corpus. Blends are well represented in the three major classes, and in roughly the proportion of their relative occurrence in the language.

The synonymy effect for blends contrasts sharply with the absence of such effects in substitution errors. There are three points to bear in mind: First, synonymy may not be uniformly and readily observable in substitution errors—though there are cases where it is plausible that approximations to it should be detected (e.g., some of the adjective cases illustrated earlier where weaker terms or stronger terms are substituted for their roughly synonymic associate). Although some such cases should surface, they are not in evidence in substitutions. Second, the cocategory pairs so abundant in noun substitutions might be expected to compete in blends—but they don't. Third, the blends involve adjectives and verbs—classes that show powerful contrastive substitution effects and little effect of synonymy broadly construed; yet in the blends these classes appear and with the same type of synonymy effects as in the nouns.

TABLE 15.6
Relations Between Blends in Different Grammatical Categories

Nouns	83		Adjectives	40		Verbs	35
common	77		simple	33		Adverbs	8
proper	6		gerund	3		Determiner	1
			participial	4			

Two ways of looking at the import of the blends suggest themselves for our present interest. First, the lack of synonomy effects in the substitution errors should not be taken as conclusive evidence that synonymic relations do not affect lexical retrieval—clearly, they do for blends. But how? That's the second issue, and its evaluation determines how we view the import of the blend data for semantic organization. The occurrence of blends need not dictate that the target representations in conceptually guided lexical retrieval processes are organized in a way that reflects synonomy relations.

In a recent discussion of lexical selection in language, Levelt (1989) argues for a parallel retrieval process in speaking based on the speed of access performance and on the claim that message elements that dictate lexical selection are simultaneously available in a "stored conceptual structure." The function of the parallelism in Levelt's treatment is normally to permit the simultaneous lexical instantiation of diverse parts of conceptual structures, but, given the mechanism and some degree of latitude in the conceptual/lemma fit, blends may follow. Lexical blend errors might be taken as one of the empirical consequences of parallelism—multiple lemma activation for a given conceptual input rather than multiple lemma activation for distinct conceptual inputs.

Notice that if the occurrence of word substitution errors were taken to be a consequence of the same feature—multiple lexical candidates aroused by the conceptual features they share, with the pruning of that set required—we would then still be left with the question of why the effective relations in blends and substitutions differ. If one considers instead that substitutions actually reflect *errors* in the conceptual to lemma mapping, scope for the differences may be provided. If substitutions arise from conceptual representation to lemma representation matching errors, the organizational character of the lemma space might plausibly emerge. But, when two lemmas match a conceptual relation satisfactorily and set the stage for a blend, that may be simply the accident of the communication being pursued. On this account, blends and substitutions both reflect early stages of the mapping from messages to lemma representations, but in rather different ways.

CONCLUDING REMARKS

The features of the word substitutions reviewed provide a rather clear case for a semantic field constraint at the level of basic categories, such as body part terms, clothing terms, color terms, etc. There are also some cases that might implicate higher order featural contrasts, though the case here is merely suggestive.

The field effects are most evident in the case of noun substitutions, and such relations are a major feature of errors in that grammatical class. There is, however, a strong influence of semantic contrast in the noun substitutions as well, and in this respect they have affinities with the verb and adjective substitutions, for which categories the effect of antonymy is very powerful. Thus, whereas there is a correspondence between the error patterns for adjectives and suggestions independently made for their organization, the generality of such effects across all grammatical categories must temper our interpretation of that correspondence. There may be some feature of the mechanisms that gives rise to the substitution errors that enhances the influence of antonymous relations.

An unsettled general question is: how does the relation between message and lemma representations govern lexical retrieval? Are lemmas in semantic fields? Or, are conceptual relations the underlying cause of the apparent field effects? Clearly, word *forms* are not organized in sets by their semantic relations (malapropisms would be inexplicable, and frequency effects a conundrum). There are some suggestive features of the contrast of blends and substitutions that may be helpful. And on balance, the claim that the substitution effects reflect lemma organization is attractive because it directly explains constraints of grammatical category on the errors. Still, the question will bear much closer attention before one decides which way to bet heavily.

REFERENCES

Cutler, A. (1982). The reliability of speech error data. In A. Cutler (Ed.), *Slips of the tongue.* Mouton: Amsterdam.

Dennis, M. (1976). Dissociated naming and location of body parts after left anterior temporal lobe resection: An experimental case study. *Brain and Language, 3,* 147–63.

Fay, D., & Cutler, A. (1977). Malapropisms and the structure of the mental lexicon. *Linguistic Inquiry, 8,* 505–520.

Fromkin, V. (1971). The non-anomalous nature of anomalous utterances. *Language, 47,* 27–52.

Garrett, M. F. (1975). The analysis of sentence production. In G. Bower (Ed.), *Psychology of learning and motivation. Vol 9.* New York: Academic Press.

Garrett, M. F. (1980). Levels of processing in sentence production. In B. Butterworth (Ed.), *Language production, Vol 1: Speech and talk.* London: Academic Press.

Garrett, M. F. (1988). Processes in sentence production. In F. Newmeyer (Ed.), *The Cambridge linguistics survey, Vol 3: Biological and social factors.* Cambridge, England: Cambridge University Press.

Garrett, M. F. (in press). Disorders of lexical selection. In W. Levelt (Ed.), *Cognition: Special Issue on lexical access in speech production.*

Gross, D., Fisher, U., & Miller, G. (1989). The organization of adjectival meanings. *Journal of Memory and Language, 28,* 92–106.

Hart, J., Berndt, R., & Caramazza, A. (1985). Category specificity naming deficit following cerebral infraction. *Nature, 316,* 439–440.

Hotopf, W. (1980). Semantic similarity as a factor in whole-word slips of the tongue. In V. Fromkin (Ed.), *Errors in linguistic performance: Slips of the tonue, ear, pen, and hand.* New York: Academic Press.

Levelt, W. J. M. (1989). *Speaking: From utterance to interpretation.* Cambridge, MA: MIT Press.

McKenna, P., & Warrington, E. (1978). Category-specific naming preservation: A single case study. *Journal of Neurology, Neurosurgery, and Psychiatrry, 41,* 571–574.

Schriefers, H., Meyer, A., & Levelt, W. (1990). Exploring the time course of lexical access in language production: Picture–word interference studies. *Journal of Memory and Language, 29,* 86–102.

Seidenberg, M., Tannenhaus, M., Leiman, J., & Bienkowski, M. (1982). Automatic access of the meanings of words in context: Some limitations on knowledge-based processing. *Cognitive Psychology, 14,* 489–537.

Shallice, T. (1988). *From neuropsychology to mental structure.* Cambridge, England: Cambridge University Press.

Shattuck, S. (1975). *Speech errors and sentence production.* Doctoral dissertation, Massachusetts Institute of Technology.

Shattuck-Hufnagel, S. (1979). Speech errors as evidence for a serial order mechanism in sentence production. In W. Cooper & E. Walker (Eds.), *Sentence processing.* Hillsdale, NJ: Lawrence Erlbaum Associates.

Swinney, D. A. (1979). Lexical access during sentence comprehension: (Re)Consideration of context effects. *Journal of Verbal Learning and Verbal Behavior, 18,* 645–659.

Warrington, E., & Shallice, T. (1984). Category specific semantic impairments. *Brain, 107,* 829–854.

16 Synonymy from a Computational Point of View

Yael Ravin
IBM Thomas J. Watson Research Center
Yorktown Heights, New York

Until recently, research in computational linguistics has mostly focused on syntactic parsing. As a result of this effort, the syntactic capability of natural language processing (NLP) systems has reached a level of relative maturity and stability, enabling researchers to turn to other linguistic areas, such as semantics and the lexicon, which have so far been neglected. Some systems that are dedicated to syntactic parsing tend to operate with small lexicons, usually manually coded and restricted to a few hundred entries. Others are restricted to narrow semantic domains, where vocabulary is limited and lexical items mostly unambiguous. The few systems that are based on large lexicons restrict the content of their lexicon to syntactic information with minimal semantic information. It has recently become clear, however, that if machines are to "understand" natural language, they must have recourse to extensive lexical databases, in which a wealth of information about the meaning of words and their semantic relations is stored. To create such databases manually is not feasible. The task is too time consuming and labor intensive. Instead, current research in lexical semantics concentrates on the extraction of semantic information from sources available on-line, such as dictionaries and thesauri in machine-readable form (see Walker, Zampolli, & Calzolari, 1987). This information is then being used to create lexical databases for NLP systems.

The goal of the Lexical Systems Group at the T. J. Watson Research Center of IBM is to create such a lexical database, called *Complex,* in which word senses are properly separated and the relationships among them are stored (Byrd, 1989). The project is ambitious and involves several aspects: Criteria should be developed for separating words into senses and for identifying individual senses; heuristics are needed to "map" information found in various on-line sources onto the appropriate word senses in *Complex;* and links among individual senses should be incorporated, to represent lexical relations among lexical items. Within this framework, my colleagues (Martin Chodorow, Howard Sachar, and Michael Gunther) and I have worked on these issues as they relate to synonyms and to the information found in machine-readable thesauri. This chapter describes our work (see also Chodorow, Ravin, & Sachar, 1988, and Ravin, Chodorow, & Sachar, 1988). It focuses on the nature of the synonymy relation found in our on-line sources, its formal characteristics, and the algorithms that manipulate it.

SYNONYMY

The definition of synonymy and the existence of synonyms have long been debated in linguistics. On one hand, there is the extreme position voiced by Quine (1951), according to which it is impossible to define synonyms or to identify synonymous terms. In an attempt to characterize analytic statements such as "bachelors are unmarried," Quine appeals to the notion of synonymy. But he then rejects it when synonymy turns out to be undefinable. According to Quine (1951), synonymy cannot be defined on the basis of sameness of dictionary definitions because "we find that definition—except in the extreme case of the explicitly conventional introduction of new notations—hinges on prior relations of synonymy" (p. 68). Similarly, interchangeability cannot function as a criterion for synonymy. Using interchangeability as a criterion for synonymy involves circularity, because the kind of interchangeability that is relevant is definable only with recourse to analyticity, which is what Quine wishes to explain in the first place, using synonymy. Thus, according to Quine, it is not possible to define synonymy or to establish a noncircular criterion for identifying synonyms. A directly opposite theoretical view is expressed in Katz (1972). Katz argues that Quine's skepticism does not apply to an empirical theory of linguistics such as the one he proposes, in which the meaning of words is defined by theoretical constructs (Katz's semantic markers). "Synonymy relations are affirmed on the basis of sameness of semantic representation, i.e., formal identity between the readings correlated with the two terms or expressions" (p. 245). According to Katz, this formal and theory-internal definition of synonymy is not subject to the danger of circularity noted by Quine.

For opposite reasons, both positions invalidate the synonyms compiled by lexicographers and published in thesauri. Quine (1951) dismisses the lexicographer as "an empirical scientist, whose business is the recording of antecedent facts" (p. 66). Katz would question the accuracy of a thesaurus not based on sound theoretical principles of semantic decomposition. From our computational point of view, however, the lexicographer's work represents a rich source of input data. It embodies lexical information that speakers of the language know and find useful. Therefore, rather than either of the theoretical approaches, we have adopted an operational approach, one that is defined by our on-line sources: *Roget's II, The New Thesaurus* (1980) (henceforth, *Roget's*), and *The New Collins Thesaurus* (1984) (henceforth, *Collins*). In this approach, the relation of synonymy is defined by the properties of the data found in these sources, and the synonyms of a particular word by its entries in these sources.

Roget's and *Collins* differ in the view of synonymy they represent. *Roget's* exhibits what we refer to as a *STRONG* view of synonymy, whereas *Collins* represents a *WEAK* view. The difference is expressed by the words of the editors found in the introductions to the two books. In *Roget's,* the criterion for synonymy is sameness of denotation: Two words are synonyms if they mean the same thing or refer to the same concept or object. "The fact that they share a denotation makes them synonymous and available as substitutes for [each other]" (*Roget's:* p. 6). This strong requirement for identical denotation and substitutability is close to the theoretical notion of synonymy of both Quine and Katz. Quine (1951) stated: "The synonyms of two linguistic forms consists simply in their interchangeability in all contexts without change of truth value— interchangeability, in Leibniz's phrase, *salva veritate*" (p. 68). The editors of *Collins* (1984), by contrast, hold a weaker view: "no synonym is entered unless it is *fully* substitutable for the headword in a sensible English sentence" (p. v). This criterion is a weak substitution criterion: It limits the extent of substitution to some, not *all*, English contexts; and it is stated asymmetrically, requiring that the synonym be substitutable for the headword but not requiring the headword to substitute for its synonym. The two different views of synonymy held by the editors of *Roget's* and *Collins* are reflected in differences in the structure and content of the two sources. We have defined two measures—the degree of symmetry and the degree of transitivity—by which these differences can be quantified and characterized formally, as described in the next section.

Properties of the Thesaurus

Both *Roget's* and *Collins* consist of alphabetized entries. Each entry contains a headword separated into different senses and followed by a list of synonyms for each sense.[1] *Roget's* contains 17,359 headwords, with about 10 synonyms per word on average. In addition to synonym lists, *Roget's* provides short definitions for each synonym group. Our file of *Collins* contains 16,794 headwords and 287,136 synonym tokens, averaging 17 synonyms per word. Having these thesauri on-line enables us to view them as lexical networks rather than as collections of discrete entries, as they appear in print. In the network, word a is linked to word b if a is a headword and b appears in its synonym list. The links in the

---

[1]In the *Collins* publisher's tape headwords were not marked for their part of speech. We have supplemented part-of-speech information from the UDICT computerized lexicon system (Byrd, 1986).

thesaurus can be characterized according to their degree of symmetry and transitivity. We say that the link between a and b is *symmetric* if a points to b and b points to a; that is, if the headword a has b in its synonym list and the headword b has a in its list. We say that the link between a and b is *transitive* if, for every word c, b points to it, then a points to it too; that is, if all the synonyms found in a's synonym list are also found in b's list (with the exception of a and b themselves, of course). In a thesaurus based on the *strong* synonymy criterion, all links throughout the thesaurus are symmetric and transitive, and all words partition into disjoint sets, where each member of the set is a synonym of every other member. This is because if word a has the same meaning as word b, then word b must have the same meaning as a. And if a has the same meaning as c, and b has the same meaning as c, then a and b must also share the same meaning. In a thesaurus based on a *weak* criterion, by contrast, links vary in the degree of symmetry and transitivity they exhibit, and words do not partition into disjoint sets but rather link to each other, often indirectly, via other words.

In *Roget's*, which is based on a strong criterion, all synonyms exhibit completely symmetric and transitive links.[2] In *Collins*, by comparison, there are only 27 sets of words that exhibit completely symmetric and transitive links among their members. According to our criteria, these may be considered to have identical meaning: 26 out of the 27 are word pairs—the 27th is a triple—and all have a single sense and a unique part of speech. These sets are given next.

allocate	= allot
aphorism	= apothegm
astonishing	= astounding
at_times	= from_time_to_time
bystander	= eyewitness
cemetery	= necropolis
congratulate	= felicitate
eatable	= edible
entomb	= inter
everybody	= everyone
exactitude	= exactness
greetings	= regards
insomnia	= sleeplessness
lozenge	= pastille
myopic	= near-sighted
naught	= nought
perk	= perquisite
permeable	= porous
piddling	= piffling

---

[2]In fact, in processing the *Roget's* tape, we found about 1,000 cross-reference errors in the sources, but because partition was the editor's original intent, we were able to correct them.

podium	= rostrum	
prizefighter	= pugilist	
prizefighting	= pugilism	
saw	= saying	
slattern	= slut	
testy	= tetchy	
triad	= trinity	= trio
weal	= welt	

Most of the synonymy links in *Collins* are markedly different from these: 62% are asymmetric (e.g., *part* has *department* as a synonym, but *department* does not have *part*); and 65% are nontransitive (e.g., *part* has *piece* as a synonym; *piece* has *chunk* as a synonym; but *part* does not have *chunk* as a synonym).[3]

The substitutability requirement expressed by the editors of *Collins* would seem to imply symmetry, because, if it is possible to substitute *b* for *a* in a "sensible" English context, then it is always possible to reintroduce *a* into that context as a substitution for *b*. The lack of symmetry we find may be due to other lexicographical considerations, such as usefulness to a human reader, constraints on space, and aesthetic presentation. These considerations often override the substitutability criterion to result in some asymmetry. The particular resolution of this conflict for each entry gives the thesaurus its individual character, but it is also a potential source of inconsistencies. Inconsistencies can be revealed by automatic means, as we show next.

Sense Disambiguation

Because synonymy links occur between senses of words and not between words themselves, we found it necessary to disambiguate the words given in the synonym lists, so that we would be able to refer to a particular sense of each synonym. For *Roget's*, the process was quite straightforward because all synonymous senses share a common definition, as can be seen in the entries for *feel* and *perceive*, given here:

feel (verb)
1. To be physically aware of through the senses: experience, have.
2. To bring into contact, esp. by means of the hand or fingers, so as to give or receive a physical sensation: *touch.
3. . . .
4. To be intuitively aware of: *perceive
. . .

---

[3]The percentage of nontransitive links does not include synonyms that have no entries in *Collins* (see the section on asymmetry and intransitivity later); nor does it include synonyms that could not be disambiguated (see the section on sense disambiguation). Thus 65% is a conservative estimate.

perceive (verb)
1. To be intuitively aware of: apprehend, feel, intuit, sense.
2. To apprehend (images) by use of the eyes: *see
3. To use the power of vision: *look

The subentry for *feel$4*[4] refers to the entry of *perceive,* where all the synonyms of the set are listed. The intended *perceive* sense is easily identified as *perceive$1* by the match of the identical definitions. The intended senses can then be indexed as follows:

feel (verb)
1. . . .
2. . . .
3. . . .
4. To be intuitively aware of: *perceive$1
. . .

perceive (verb)
1. To be intuitively aware of: apprehend, feel$4, intuit, sense.
2. . . .

In *Collins,* however, there are no definitions to match. Thus, sense indexing is more complex. We have tried two automatic methods of sense marking (i.e., sense disambiguation): disambiguation by symmetry and disambiguation by intersection. In some cases an entry *a* may have word *b* listed as a synonym of its nth sense, and entry *b* may have word *a* listed as a synonym of its mth sense. We can mark *b* in entry *a* as the mth sense of *b,* and *a* in entry *b* as the nth sense of *a.* An example of this type of one-to-one mapping in *Collins* is given next:

dense (adj) 1. . . . condensed . . . solid. . . .
            2. . . . dull . . . stupid . . .

dull (adj) 1. dense . . . stupid . . .
            2. . . . callous . . . unsympathetic
            .
            .
            .
            7. drab . . . muted . . .

Here, sense 1 of *dull* is synonymous with sense 2 of *dense.* Thirty-seven percent of the 287,000 synonym tokens show this type of symmetry. Of course, there are also mappings of the one-to-many variety (for example, only the first sense of *feeble* has *faint* as its synonym, whereas both senses 1 and 2 of *faint* have *feeble*), but they account for only .5% of the tokens. By this method of disambiguation-by-symmetry, we could automatically mark the senses of all synonyms in one-

---

[4]We use $ to indicate sense number.

to-one and one-to-many relations. The third type of mapping, many-to-many, accounts for just .5% of the total, but it poses a problem for the strategy outlined previously. This can best be seen by considering an example. Senses 1 and 2 of *institution* list *establishment* as a synonym, and senses 1 and 2 of *establishment* list *institution*. Is sense 1 of *institution* synonymous with sense 1 of *establishment* or with sense 2? The distribution of the terms *institution* and *establishment* cannot answer the question.

The problem of many-to-many mappings and the large percentage of asymmetric synonyms in *Collins* led us to another method. Consider again the case of *dense* and *dull*. Evidence for linking sense 2 of *dense* with sense 1 of *dull* comes from the symmetric distribution of the two words in the entries. There is however another piece of evidence for linking sense 2 of *dense* with sense 1 of *dull*, and that is the co-occurrence of the word *stupid* in their synonym lists. Thus, the intersections of synonym lists serve as the basis for an automatic disambiguation of the many-to-many mappings, and, for that matter, for the disambiguation of the whole thesaurus. This is similar to Lesk's suggestion for disambiguating hypernyms (Lesk, 1986). The intersection method disambiguated more entries than the symmetry method, but it, too, left a certain percentage of ambiguous words. In some cases, the intersection of two words was null. For example: *successful* and *victorious* are symmetric synonyms but none of their other synonyms are shared. Their entries are given next.[5]

SUCCESSFUL:
≫ 0 acknowledged$, at_the_top_of_the_tree$99, best-selling$99, booming$99, efficacious$, favourable$, flourishing$0, fortunate$1.2, fruitful$3, lucky$1, lucrative$0, moneymaking$0, out_in_front$99, paying$99, profitable$1, prosperous$1, rewarding$0, thriving$0, top$, unbeaten$1, victorious$, wealthy$0

VICTORIOUS:
≫ 0 champion$, conquering$99, first$, prizewinning$99, successful$, triumphant$0, vanquishing$99, winning$2

In other cases, there was a tie. For example, *ripe2* has equal-size intersections with both *perfect1* and *perfect4*. In their following entries, ties are indicated by a pair of numbers joined by a period.

PERFECT:
≫ 1 absolute$1, complete$1.3, completed$99, consummate$2, entire$1.3, finished$2, full$1, out-and-out$, sheer$2, unadulterated$99, unalloyed$99, unmitigated$2, utter$99, whole$1
≫ 4 accomplished$2, adept$1, experienced$1, expert$2, finished$1, masterly$0, polished$, practised$0, skillful$0, killed$0

---

[5]The number following the dollar sign indicates the sense number. No number indicates that the intersection is null and therefore a sense number was not picked up. 99 indicates that the word has no entry in *Collins* and consequently no sense numbers. 0 means that there was only one sense given in the entry.

RIPE:
≫ 2 accomplished$1, complete$2, finished$, in readiness$, perfect$1.4, pre-pared$1, ready$1

No disambiguation resulted in either of these cases. The results obtained with each method are shown in the following Fig. 16.1.[6]
The quantitative advantage of the intersection method is evident. To determine the qualitative difference, we studied cases where the symmetry and the intersection methods conflicted. We compared 50 randomly selected entries. Of the approximately 900 synonyms listed in the entries, 337 were disambiguated by both methods. Of these, there were 33 pairs for which the two methods disagreed: 20 were symmetric ties, disambiguated by the intersection method; 5 were intersection ties, disambiguated by the symmetry method. The remaining 8 were given to two human reviewers. In 3 out of the 8, the reviewers could not determine which of the methods provided better disambiguation, as shown in the following example.

FEEBLE:
1. debilitated, delicate, doddering, effete, enervated, enfeebled, etiolated, exhausted, failing, faint, frail, infirm, languid, powerless, puny, shilpit (*Scottish), sickly, weak, weakened
2. flat, flimsy, inadequate, incompetent, indecisive, ineffective, ineffectual, inefficient, insignificant, insufficient, lame, paltry, poor, slight, tame, thin, unconvincing, weak

POOR:
1. badly off, broke (*Informal), destitute, hard up (*Informal), impecunious, impoverished, indigent, in need, in want, necessitous, needy, on one's beam-ends, on one's uppers, on the rocks, penniless, penurious, poverty-stricken, skint (*BritishSlang), stony-broke (*BritishSlang)
2. deficient, exiguous, inadequate, incomplete, insufficient, lacking, meagre, miserable, niggardly, pitiable, reduced, scanty, skimpy, slight, sparse, straitened
3. below par, faulty, feeble, inferior, low-grade, mediocre, rotten (*Informal), rubbishy, second-rate, shabby, shoddy, sorry, substandard, unsatisfactory, valueless, weak, worthless
4. bad, bare, barren, depleted, exhausted, fruitless, impoverished, infertile, sterile, unfruitful, unproductive
5. hapless, ill-fated, luckless, miserable, pathetic, pitiable, unfortunate, unhappy, unlucky, wretched
6. humble, insignificant, lowly, mean, modest, paltry, plain, trivial

The symmetry method linked *feeble2* with *poor3*, whereas the intersection meth-

---

[6]The total of 221,957 represents the number of nonterminal links, as discussed in the section on asymmetry following.

by symmetry:

sense disambiguated:	103,648	(46.7%)
ties:	1,662	(0.7%)
remainder	116,647	(52.5%)

Total number of synonyms available for processing:	221,957

by intersection:

sense disambiguated:	179,126	(80.7%)
ties:	6,029	(2.7%)
remainder:	36,802	(16.6%)

Total number of synonyms available for processing:	221,957

FIG. 16.1.

od linked *feeble2* with *poor2*. The remaining four cases were somewhat clearer. In three, the intersection method performed better; in one, the symmetry method was superior. To conclude, the best disambiguation algorithm would be a combination of the two methods. We are currently studying more cases where the methods disagree in order to determine how they should be combined.

Transitivity

In *Roget's* synonyms fall into discrete groups that bear no relation to each other. In *Collins,* however, there exist indirect links among senses from different entries via senses that they share in common. These indirect links reflect the particular type of relation captured by the *Collins* network: It is a relation of closeness of meaning rather than of strict synonymy. As such, it represents a continuum, from senses that are most closely related to each other to senses that are only marginally related.

Using senses instead of words, we recomputed the number of sets that are symmetric and transitive (see section on the properties of the thesaurus before) and found 86 sets of synonymous *senses* (as opposed to 27 sets of synonymous *words*). Given here are some of the new sets:

adhesive$2	= glue$1	= paste$1	
beak$1	= bill$5		
conservatory$0	= hothouse$1		
draw$11	= tie$7		
grade$3	= gradient$0		
grouch$2	= grouse$2	= grumble$3	
myopic$0	= near-sighted$0	= short-sighted$1	
poison$1	= venom$1		
spectator$0	= witness$1		
well-off$2	= well-to-do$0		
wolf$2	= womanizer$0		

These sets represent the senses most closely related in *Collins*. To find more indirect links we use a program known as SPROUT. It was originally used (Chodorow, Byrd, & Heidorn, 1985) to generate taxonomic trees from the hyponym relation as extracted from *Webster's Seventh Collegiate Dictionary* (1963) (henceforth *Webster's*). SPROUT starts with a root node and retrieves from a designated file (in this case, the *Collins* file) the words that bear the given relation to the root. These words are the first-level descendents (daughters) of the root. SPROUT then applies recursively to each of the daughter nodes, generating their daughters, etc. In this way, the tree is generated in a breadth-first fashion. The process is complete when the only nodes that remain open are either terminals (i.e., nodes that have no daughters) or nodes that appear earlier in the tree, indicating a cyclic structure.

We applied SPROUT to the first sense of *house* in *Collins*. The program reached closure after picking up 85% (!) of the total number of noun-senses in *Collins* (see Appendix 1). Obviously, to relate such a vast number of senses to *house$1* is not very useful or interesting. To reduce the number of senses picked up and to increase their semantic relation to the root node, we have explored ways to automatically prune the sprout tree when a semantically irrelevant branch is generated. Before any synonym is accepted as a node of the tree, its descendents are checked against the immediate descendents of the root node. If their intersection is not null, the node is accepted into the sprout tree. We have experimented with a few variations: choosing either the daughters or both daughters and granddaughters of either the root node or the branch node. We have also varied the size of the intersection that serves as threshold. A promising scheme involves checking the daughters of each node against the daughters and granddaughters of the root, discarding nodes whose intersection is of size 1. When pruned this way, the sprout tree of *house$1* reached transitive closure with a total of 173 noun senses, which constitute 1.4% of the total noun senses in *Collins*. Closure was reached at the 4th level. The first following list includes most of the nodes that were rejected by the pruning method. The second list includes most of the nodes that were accepted.[7]

> 2-home$3, 2-fabric$2, 3-barracks$0, 3-assembly$2, 3-composition$1, 3-erection$1, 3-fabrication$1, 3-figure$3, 3-form$7, 3-formation$2, 3-shape$1, 3-design$4, 3-make$12, 3-making$1, 3-manufacture$3, 3-mould$2, 3-organization$1, 3-production$1, 3-house$2, 3-point$2, 3-orientation$1, 3-quarter$1, 4-chamber$1, 4-framework$0, 4-system$1, 4-anatomy$2, 4-build$4, 4-hull$1, 4-physique$0, 4-rack$1, 4-skeleton$0, 4-arrangement$1, 4-configuration$0, 4-format$0, 4-organization$2, 4-architecture$2, 4-turn$17, 4-conformation$0, 4-constitution$2, 4-method$2, . . ., 4-entourage$2, 4-field$3, 4-aspect$2

---

[7]The number preceding the word indicates the level on which it was encountered in the tree. The number following the dollar sign indicates its sense number.

0-house$1, 1-abode$0, 1-building$1 1-domicile$0 1-dwelling$0 1-edifice$0 1-habitation$1 1-home$1 1-residence$1 1-address$1 1-establishment$4 1-place$5 1-seat$4 2-lodging$0 2-quarters$0 2-lodgings$0 2-mansion$0 2-pile$4 2-structure$2 2-construction$1 2-erection$2 2-household$1 2-pad$4 2-location$0 2-situation$1 2-whereabouts$0 3-accommodation$2 3-billet$1 3-apartment$0 3-frame$4 3-make-up$2 3-structure$1 3-bearings$0 3-locale$0 3-place$1 3-position$1 3-site$1 3-spot$2 3-emplacement$1 3-locality$2 3-seat$2 3-setting$0 3-station$1 3-environment$0 3-scene$2

Asymmetry and Intransitivity

The high degree of asymmetric and intransitive links in *Collins* has prompted us to investigate their nature more carefully. We have identified several different categories of asymmetry and have found automatic ways of sorting asymmetric links into these categories.

The largest source of asymmetry in *Collins* is *terminal* nodes: words that are offered as synonyms but do not occur as headwords. We found about 65,000 terminal nodes, accounting for 36% of the total of asymmetric links; 18,500 of them occur only once, but more than 400 occur 10 times or more. A sample of frequently occurring terminals is given next, with the number of their occurrences and a list of the entries in which they occur:

10 NONPLUSSED(adj): blank$3, confused$1, dazed$0, dumbfounded$0, dumfounded$0, flabbergasted$0, puzzled$0, stuck$2, surprised$0, thunderstruck$0

10 RECKLESSLY(adv): blindly$2, dangerously$1, fast$6, hastily$2, headfirst$2, helter-skelter$1, impetuously$0, incautiously$0, madly$3, pell-mell$1

10 PRIME_MOVER(n): architect$2, author$0, cause$1, creator$0, father$3, instigator$0, mainspring$0, originator$0, prompter$2, protagonist$2

10 PROSECUTION(n): action$6, arraignment$0, enforcement$1, execution$1, furtherance$0, indictment$0, lawsuit$0, litigation$0, pursuance$0, suit$4

12 RIDGE(n): bank$2, bluff$3, crease$2, crest$1, knurl$0, ledge$0, projection$1, seam$3, wave$3, weal$0, welt$0, wheal$0

20 MITE(n): atom$0, bit$1, crumb$0, dot$1, dreg$0, grain$3, iota$0, jot$1, modicum$0, molecule$0, mote$0, particle$0, pennyworth$0, pinch$7, pittance$0, scrap$1, speck$2, tittle$0, tot$1, whit$0

23 RESTRICTED(adj): captive$2, cloistered$0, closed$3, cramped$1, dialectal$0, exclusive$2, exclusive$3, finite$0, hush-hush$0, incommodious$0, inside$5, light$25, limited$1, limited$2, local$2, narrow$1, parochial$0, peculiar$2, qualified$2, reserved$1, scanty$0, straitened$0, topical$2

28 REDUCTION(n): abasement$0, abatement$1, abbreviation$0, abridgment$0, alleviation$0, allowance$3, bargain$2, condensation$3, constriction$0, con-

traction$0, cut$9, cutback$0, debasement$1, decrease$2, deduction$2, deple-
tion$0, diminution$0, discount$3, drain$6, drop$4, fall$11, lessening$0, re-
trenchment$0, saving$2, vitiation$1

28 RUDENESS(n): acerbity$1, audacity$2, awkwardness$1, brass$0, churlish-
ness$0, contumely$0, crudity$2, discourtesy$1, disrespect$0, effrontery$0,
grossness$2, impertinence$0, impoliteness$0, impudence$0, incivility$0,
indelicacy$0, insolence$0, insult$1, lip$2, meanness$2, misbehaviour$0, mis-
conduct$1, mouth$3, pertness$0, ribaldry$0, sauce$0, sauciness$0, vul-
garity$0

35 MAKE_KNOWN(v): advertise$0, advise$2, air$7, announce$1, blazon$0, cir-
culate$1, communicate$0, convey$2, declare$2, disclose$1, divulge$0, ex-
pose$2, express$2, impart$1, intimate$6, introduce$1, leak$5, mention$1,
post$2, proclaim$0, promulgate$0, propagate$2, publicize$0, push$4, re-
lease$3, reveal$1, say$2, show$1, speak$1, spread$3, tell$1, uncover$2, un-
fold$2, unveil$0, ventilate$0

41 REASONABLE(adj): common-sensical$0, considerable$1, credible$1, de-
cent$2, economic$4, economical$3, enlightened$0, equitable$0, fair$3, feasi-
ble$0, inexpensive$0, judicious$0, just$3, justifiable$0, legitimate$2, level-
headed$0, likely$3, logical$1, logical$2, low$10, lucid$4, moderate$1, nor-
mal$2, open-minded$0, plausible$0, presumptive$2, probable$0, rational$1,
respectable$2, restrained$1, right$4, sane$2, sensible$1, sober$2, sound$8,
temperate$2, tenable$0, thinkable$0, warrantable$0, well-balanced$2, wise$1

According to the editors of *Collins,* there are two criteria by which a word is
chosen as an entry: The first is "if it is likely to be looked up as an entry in its
own right." Thus, the editors explain, rare or obsolete words do not appear as
entries although they may be given as synonyms for other, simpler words. The
second criterion is that concrete words are usually not selected as entries, unless
they have "genuine synonyms or give rise to a figurative use." The first criterion
could explain why phrases such as *prime mover* or *make known* do not occur as
entries. The second probably applies to *ridge,* which has only concrete senses.
However, many words in the sample do not appear to fit these criteria. Rather,
our sorting clearly indicates that derived forms often tend to be terminal nodes. If
this is a conscious choice on the part of the editors, it should perhaps be made
explicit in the introduction to the book. If it is not, computer programs that do
manipulation of lexical data of the kind described here may be very useful as an
aid to lexicographers to prevent such inconsistencies.

A small percentage of the terminal nodes in *Collins* is due to vocabulary
inconsistencies. For example, *record* has *annals, archives,* and *diary* as synonyms; whereas *annals* and *archives* have the plural *records;* and *diary* has the
phrase *daily record.* This inconsistency results in both *records* and *daily record*
becoming terminal nodes, whereas it would seem that they should not be because
they are equivalent to the main entry *record.* Identifying this category of termi-

nals is particularly important because its correction involves changes in several entries.

The first category of vocabulary inconsistencies is due to variation in number, that is, cases when the same word-sense is referred to sometimes in the plural and sometimes in the singular. We identified these automatically by running our UDICT morphological analyzer (Byrd, 1986) on all the terminals found in noun entries, and retrieving all terminals that are plural forms of English nouns. Here is a sample of 20 nouns:

```
SAFEGUARDS: security$2
SALES: commerical$1
SALTS: laxative$0
SALUTATIONS: greeting$2, greetings$0, regard$10, regards$0, respect$4, re-
    spects$0
SANDS: beach$0, shore$1
SAWBONES: physician$0
SAWS: lore$1
SAYINGS: lore$1
SCHOOLDAYS: childhood$0
SCIONS: issue$7, posterity$1, progeny$0, seed$3
SCORES: a_lot$0, lot$4, lots$0, many$2, multiplicity$0, myriad$2
SCOURINGS: dregs$1, garbage$2, swill$3
SCRUPLES: conscience$1, hesitation$2, morals$0, principle$3
SEATS: seating$0
SECURITIES: holdings$0
SENSITIVITIES: feelings$0
SERVANTS: retinue$0
SERVICES: liturgy$0, military$2
SHADOWS: darkness$1, obscurity$2, shade$1
SHEETS: bedclothes$0
```

The second step was to check if the singular forms of these plural nouns were *Collins* headwords and, if so, whether their synonym lists included any of the entries that listed the plural forms. From the sample the following five entries were found:

```
SAFEGUARD$2: . . . security$2 . . .
SCORE$3: . . . lots$0 . . .
SCRUPLE $2: . . . hesitation$0 . . .
SERVICE$4: . . . liturgy$0 . . .
SHADOW$1: . . . darkness$1 . . . obscurity$2 . . . shade$1
```

Ten percent of the plural terminal nodes in *Collins* are similar to the five preceding, in that they have corresponding singular entries whose synonyms intersect with the entries in which the terminals occur. We would want to distinguish these cases, where the singular and plural are synonyms (at least, on one sense), from words such as *salts* and *sawbones,* where the singular and the plural differ in meaning. For the synonymy case, a uniform marking convention for both head-words and synonym-tokens will be useful. If the senses in question are written as *safeguard(s)* or *shadow(s),* for example, the synonymy of the two forms is always apparent.

Another type of vocabulary inconsistency is the variation between a single word and a phrase containing the word and a modifier, as in *daily record.* Here we checked all the terminal nodes for two-word phrases composed of a modifier and a head (capitalized) as follows: ADJECTIVE_adverb, adverb_ADJECTIVE, adverb_ADVERB, adjective_NOUN, VERB_prep and VERB_adverb.[8] The following is a sample of 20 combinations retrieved in this search:

SCARED_stiff: frightened$0, panic-stricken$0, petrified$2, terrified$0
slightly_DRUNK: tipsy$0
slightly_WARM: tepid$1
unbearably_HOT: scorching$0
unduly_QUICK: hasty$3
vastly_SUPERIOR: overhwelming$0
scarcely_EVER: rarely$1, seldom$0, uncommonly$1
very_MUCH: awfully$2, by_far$0, by_half$0, considerably$0, dearly$1, far$2,
    far$3, greatly$0, half$4, heavily$7, highly$1, mightily$1, overly$0, well$8
very_NEARLY: practically$1
very_OFTEN: frequently$0
very_WELL: intimately$1, intimately$2, swimmingly$0
sanitary_MEASURES: hygiene$0
scenic_VIEW: panorama$1
secret_MEETING: assignation$1
secret_PLACE: hide-out$0
semiprecious_STONE: gem$1
servile_FLATTERY: adulation$0
sexual_ACT: intercourse$2
SAW_down: cut$3
SCARE_off: intimidate$0

The second step was to check whether the head in isolation was a headword, and if so, whether its synonyms included any of the entries linked to its corresponding phrase:

SCARED$0(adj): frightened$0 . . . panic-stricken$0 . . . petrified$2 . . . ter-
    rified$0
DRUNK$1(adj): . . . tipsy$0 . . .

---

[8]We assumed that combinations of the form noun_NOUN have meanings that are distinct from the meaning of their heads in isolation.

WARM$1(adj): . . . tepid$1.2 . . .
HOT$1(adj): . . . scorching$0 . . .
QUICK$1(adj): . . . hasty$1 . . .
MUCH$2(adv): . . . considerably$0 . . .
NEARLY$0(adv): . . . practically$1 . . .
OFTEN$0(adv): . . . frequently$0 . . .
WELL$5(adv): . . . intimately$1.2 . . .
VIEW$1(n): . . . panorama$1 . . .
MEETING$1(n): assignation$1 . . .
FLATTERY$0(n): adulation$0 . . .
SCARE$1(v): . . . intimidate$0 . . .

Here, too, a more consistent marking convention is needed. Phrases that are synonymous with their heads can be written as *(slightly)_drunk* or *(unbearably)_hot*. Written in this way, the cross-reference to the single-word entry or synonym remains transparent. The use of parentheses can help to differentiate these phrases from others, such as *secret_places* or *sexual_act,* which are not synonymous with their heads.

Many verbal or adjectival phrases (VERB_prep, PARTICIPLE_prep, or ADJECTIVE_prep) in *Collins* occur in run-on entries that themselves consist of the single main-entry word followed by a preposition. Most (but not all) synonyms offered for such run-on entries are phrases, whereas most (but not all) synonyms offered for single main entries are single words. The following entries illustrate this contrast:

UNFAMILIAR:
≫ 1 alien$1, curious$3, different$4, little_known$99, new$1, novel$1, out-of-the-way$2, strange$2, unaccustomed$2, uncommon$1, unknown$1, unusual$0
≫ 2 with *with:* a_stranger_to$99, inexperienced_in$99, unaccustomed_to$0, unacquainted$99, unconversant$99, uninformed_about$99, uninitiated_in$99, unpractised_in$99, unskilled_at$99, unversed_in$99

UNACCUSTOMED:
≫ 1 with *to:* a_newcomer_to$99, a_novice_at$99, green$3, inexperienced$0, not_given_to$99, not_used_to$99, unfamiliar_with$0, unpractised$99, unused_to$0, unversed_in$99
≫ 2 new$1, out_of_the_ordinary$0, remarkable$0, special$1, strange$1.2, surprising$0, uncommon$1, unexpected$0, unfamiliar$1, unprecedented$0, unusual$0,

INEXPERIENCED:
≫ 0 amateur$, callow$0, fresh$7, green$3, immature$1, new$1, raw$4, unaccustomed$1.2, unacquainted$99, unfamiliar$1, unfledged$0, unpractised$99, unschooled$99, unseasoned$99, unskilled$0, untrained$0, untried$0, unused$1, unversed$99, wet_behind_the_ears$0

In our processing of *Collins* we have duplicated run-on entries, so that our version of *Collins* has *unfamiliar$2* also referenced as *unfamiliar_with$0* and *unaccustomed$1* also as *unaccustomed_to$0*.

Let us now examine the synonym lists for these entries. A distinction between the sense of the single adjective and the sense of the adjectival phrase is made, as can be seen from the separate links between *unfamiliar_with* and *unaccustomed-_to* on one hand and *unfamiliar$1* and *unaccustomed$2* on the other. However, the distinction appears inconsistent: the simple *unacquainted* and *unconversant* are given as synonyms for *unfamiliar_with*. (Why not *unacquainted_with* and *unconversant_in?*). Similarly, the phrasal *inexperienced_in* is given as a synonym of *unfamiliar_with,* but the simple *inexperienced* is given as a synonym of *unaccustomed_to*. There are many other such cases, which, again, could be avoided if lexicographers had access to our computational tools.

From a computational point of view, terminal nodes represent incomplete information. In a printed book, considerations of use and of space may force lexicographers to omit entries that they would otherwise include. However, on a computer, differences in space on such a small scale do not matter. We would like to have all terminal nodes turned into entries by automatic means. A trivial way of doing it would be to create links from each terminal node to each of the entries that point to it. This, however, leaves a disambiguation problem as the new entries for the terminal nodes are not separated into senses. To illustrate the difficulty, compare the links of the two following terminals:

10 PROSECUTION(n): action$6, arraignment$0, enforcement$1, execution$1, furtherance$0, indictment$0, lawsuit$0, litigation$0, pursuance$0, suit$4

28 REDUCTION(n): abasement$0, abatement$1, abbreviation$0, abridgment$0, alleviation$0, allowance$3, bargain$2, condensation$3, constriction$0, contraction$0, cut$9, cutback$0, debasements$1, decrease$2, deduction$2, depletion$0, diminution$0, discount$3, drain$6, drop$4, fall$11, lessening$0, retrenchment$0, saving$2, vitiation$1

All the entries that mention *prosecution* are quite closely related in meaning, suggesting that *prosecution* appears in *Collins* in one sense only, and that an entry created for it should consist of one sense. The entries pointing to *reduction,* by contrast, differ in meaning from each other, suggesting that an entry for *reduction* should contain several senses, each pointing back to only some of the entries just mentioned. Whether it is possible to disambiguate terminal nodes automatically, or at least semiautomatically, by comparing various intersection counts among entries pointing to terminal nodes is a question we leave for further study.

There are other asymmetries in *Collins* that do not involve terminal nodes. A small number is caused by 900 headwords that do not occur as synonyms. Here are 10 out of the list:

ABAFT(adv): aft$99, astern$99, behind$

ABDUCTION(n): carrying_off$99, kidnapping$99, seizure$1

ABSENTLY(adv): absent-mindedly$99, abstractedly$99, bemusedly$99, blankly$99, distractedly$99, dreamily$99, emptily$99, heedlessly$99, inattentively$99, obliviously$99, unconsciously$99, unheedingly$99, vacantly$99, vaguely$0

AND(conj): along_with$99, also$, as_well_as$, furthermore$, in_addition_to$, including$, moreover$, plus$, together_with$99

ATHLETE(n): competitor$0, contender$99, contestant$0, games_player$99, gymnast$99, player$1, runner$1, sportsman$99, sportswoman$99

AWE-STRICKEN(adj): afraid$1, amazed$99, astonished$99, awed$99, awe-inspired$99, cowed$99, daunted$0, dumbfounded$0, fearful$1, frightened$0, horrified$99, impressed$99, intimidated$99, shocked$99, struck_dumb$99, stunned$0, terrified$0, wonder-stricken$99, wonder-struck$99

BEDCLOTHES(n): bedding$99, bed_linen$99, blankets$99, coverlets$99, covers$99, sheets$99

FAIR-AND-SQUARE(adj): above_board$99, correct$3, honest$2, just$1.2, on_the_level$, straight$4

FEATURED(adj): given_prominence$99, headlined$99, highlighted$99, in_the-_public_eye$99, presented$99, promoted$99, recommended$99, specially_presented$99, starred$99

FEATURING(adj): calling_attention_to$99, displaying$99, drawing_attention-_to$99, giving_a_star_role$99, giving_prominence_to$99, giving_the_full-_works$99, highlighting$99, making_the_main_attraction$99, presenting$99, promoting$99, pushing$, recommending$99, showing$, showing_off$99, starring$99, turning_the_spotlight_on$99

The reason for their asymmetry is not clear, but they can easily be symmetrized automatically.

About 18% of the nonterminal asymmetries are instances of hypernymy (the superordinate relation) or hyponymy (the subordinate relation).[9] For example, *book* lists *manual* as a synonym, but *manual* does not list *book;* instead special types of books, such as *handbook,* are given. This is because *book* is really a hypernym (not a synonym) of *manual.* Hypernym links are truly asymmetric in nature. Opinions differ about whether such hypernym links should be included in the thesaurus, and, if so, whether they should be separated from or marked differently than genuine synonyms.

In *Collins* hypernym links are not distinguished from other links, and so there

---

is no automatic way to retrieve them. The best we could do was to produce an approximate list of hypernym links by comparing *Collins* synonyms with hypernym and hyponym lists that we have on-line, in our taxonym files. Our taxonym files were built automatically with information extracted from *Webster's*. For a given word *a*, the files contain all the words defining it (that is, the words occurring as heads of its definitions) and all the words that *a* defines (that is, words in whose definitions *a* is the head; Chodorow et al., 1985). Following are some sample results of intersecting the *Collins* synonym lists with our hyponym lists. For each entry on the left, we list the synonyms that were also found to be hyponyms of it. Because this is the result of a comparison between two different sources, each with its own sense separation, no sense disambiguation was possible.

TABLE(n):	bench board
TACK(n):	thumbtack
TACKLE(n):	rig
TAINT(n):	spot stain
TALE(n):	romance yarn
TALENT(n):	ability gift
TALK(v):	blather chat gab gossip harangue jaw palaver
TANGLE(n):	snarl
TAP(n):	touch
TART(n):	tartlet
TASK(n):	business chore duty job mission work
TASTE(n):	decorum palate partiality smack

The following is the result of intersecting the *Collins* synonym lists with our *hypernym* lists:

TABLEAU(n):	representation
TABOO(n):	prohibition
TACK(n):	course direction method nail
TACT(n):	perception
TACTIC(n):	device method
TAG(n):	marker
TAIL(n):	end line
TALE(n):	narrative relation report
TALENT(n):	aptitude endowment power
TALK(n):	discussion negotiation
TANGLE(n):	mass
TART(n):	pie

Unfortunately, these listings do not contain very conclusive data. A word *a* can occur in both the thesaurus entry and the dictionary entry of some word *b* for two very different reasons: Either *a* is a true hypernym and is found in the thesaurus too because it can substitute for *b* in some contexts, or *a* is a true synonym and appears in the dictionary because it helps define *b*. Thus, occurrence on the list does not indicate whether the word is a synonym or a hypernym.

The majority of the nonterminal asymmetries are not instances of possible hypernymy. For example, *assembly* has *throng* listed as a synonym of one of its senses, but *throng* does not list *assembly* as a synonym, although it does give *assemblage, congregation, multitude,* and other related words. Perhaps many of these omissions are due to the fact that rare, very formal, or metaphoric words tend not to be offered as synonyms. This may explain why *conversant, familiar,* and *informed,* for example, are listed as synonyms of *cognizant,* whereas *cognizant* is not listed as their synonym. Another possible reason could be cases when a central sense of one word is synonymous with a very peripheral sense of another. One sense of *say* lists *add,* as in "He added that he would do the demonstration." The entry for *add* does not, however, contain this peripheral sense and deals only with the arithmetic sense *add* and the sense of enlargement. Unfortunately, it is not evident how to automatically produce a list of asymmetries due to these reasons.

Intransitive links form a more complex phenomenon. We observed the existence of many while applying SPROUT: We would often encounter nodes that point back to *different* senses of nodes already encountered. For example, the following branch of the *house$1* tree points to a problem:

house$1 - > building$1 - > construction$1 - > building$2

We have noticed that in most such loops, the problem lies in poor sense separation in the original *Collins* entries. *Building$2,* for example, is a mixture of the act of building, the object built, and its design.

1. domicile, dwelling, edifice, fabric, house, pile, structure
2. architecture, construction, erection, fabricating, raising

We cannot undertake an exhaustive review of all such loops. The task seems too formidable—we found 260 loops in the first 1,000 entries alone—but we did find a way to identify some of the spurious links and ignore them during the sprouting process. For example, the intersection of *building$2* and *erection$1* contains only *construction.*

Erection:
1. assembly, building, construction, creation, elevation, establishment, fabrication, manufacture
2. building, construction, edifice, pile, structure

Intersection of size 1, that is, when the two lists have only one element in common, is good indication of a spurious link. Indeed, by ignoring links with intersections of size 1 we were able to reduce the sprout tree of *house$1* to include only 76% of the total nouns, as opposed to the previous 85%.

CONCLUSION

As our measures of symmetry and transitivity indicate, the two thesauri available to us vary considerably in their content and structure. In fact, they complement each other. *Roget's* contains small sets of lexical items all sharing the same denotation, which is expressed by the short definition accompanying each set. Thus, *Roget's* forms a link between synonym sets and the dictionary. *Collins,* by contrast, lists larger groupings of semantically related items. Because *Collins* can be sprouted, it provides a way of measuring the semantic "distance" between word senses, on the basis of the number of levels and nodes that exist on the path(s) that link(s) them. Both types of lexical relations—strong synonymy and the weaker relation of closeness of meaning should be incorporated into *Complex,* the ultimate lexical database we are building. If information from both sources is successfully incorporated, each word-sense in *Complex* will be linked to all other word-senses that are synonymous with it, as well as to a continuum of other senses that are close to it in varying degrees. Moreover, through the *Roget's* definitions, each sense will also be linked to its dictionary definitions supplied by the monolingual dictionaries that we have on-line, such as *Webster's* and the *Longman Dictionary of Contemporary English* (1978) (henceforth, *Longman*).

As a first step towards the incorporation of the two thesauri into *Complex,* we have begun to map them onto each other. We have developed a metric, which compares the *Roget's* entry for a word to the *Collins* entry for it and determines what senses the two entries share. We have handmapped a random sample of 100 headwords and checked it against our metric. In a comparison of the results, we found that our judgments about the mapping between senses corresponded quite well to the decisions made by the metric. We are now studying ways in which to combine the information found in the two sources into a single file of augmented entries. If the automatic combination of the two sources succeeds, we will next attempt to map the short definitions provided by *Roget's* onto the more detailed definitions found in *Webster's* and *Longman.* Thus, we hope to make significant progress towards our goal of automatically building one comprehensive database out of the various lexical sources at our disposal.

REFERENCES

Byrd, R. J. (1986). Dictionary systems for office practice. *Proceedings of the Grosseto workshop 'On automating the lexicon.'* Also available as IBM Research Report RC 11872. Grosseto, Italy.
Byrd, R. J. (1989). Discovering relationships among word senses. Dictionaries in the electronic

age: *Proceedings of the Fifth Annual Conference of the University of Waterloo Centre for the New Oxford English Dictionary.* Waterloo, Canada.

Chodorow, M. S., Byrd, R. J., & Heidorn, G. E. (1985). Extracting semantic hierarchies from a large on-line dictionary. *Proceedings of the Association for Computational Linguistics* (pp. 299–304). Chicago.

Chodorow, M. S., Ravin, Y., & Sachar, H. (1988). A tool for investigating the synonymy relation in a sense-disambiguated thesaurus. *Proceedings of the Second Conference on Applied Natural Language Processing* (pp. 144–151). Austin, Tx.

Collins. (1984). *The new Collins thesaurus.* Glasgow: Collins Publishers.

Katz, J. J. (1972). *Semantic theory.* New York: Harper & Row.

Lesk, M. (1986). Automatic sense disambiguation using machine-readable dictionaries: How to tell a pine cone from an ice-cream cone. *Proceedings of 1986 SIGDOC Conference.* Canada.

Longman's. (1978). *Longman dictionary of contemporary English.* Harlow, England: Longman.

Quine, W. V. O. (1951). Two dogmas of empiricism. *Philosophical Review, 60,* 20–43. In J. F. Rosenberg & C. Travis (Eds.), *Readings in the philosophy of language.* Engelwood Cliffs, NJ: Prentice-Hall. (1961).

Ravin, Y., Chodorow, M., & Sachar, H. (1988). Tools for lexicographers revising an online thesaurus. *BUDALEX, '88 Papers from the Third Congress of the European Association for Lexicography.*

Roget's. (1980). *Roget's II: The new thesaurus,* Boston: Houghton–Mifflin.

Walker, D. E., Zampolli, A., & Calzolari, N. (1987). *Computational Linguistics: Special Issue on the Lexicon, 13,* 3–4.

Webster's. (1963). *Webster's seventh new collegiate dictionary.* Springfield, MA: G. & C. Merriam.

APPENDIX 1

The following listing shows portions of the sprouting output from sense 1 of *house.* Each node starts a new line. The number to its left indicates its level in the *house1* tree. The words to its right are its synonyms.

0 house$1	abode$0 building$1 domicile$0 dwelling$0 edifice$0 habitation$1 home$1 homestead$99 residence$1 address$1 establishment$3 establishment$4 place$5 property$1 seat$4
1 abode$0	domicile$0 dwelling$0 dwelling-place$99 habitat$0 habitation$1 home$1 house$1 lodging$0 quarters$0 residence$1 address$1 establishment$4 home$3 lodgings$0 mansion$0 place$5 seat$4
1 building$1	domicile$0 dwelling$0 edifice$0 fabric$2 house$1 pile$4 structure$2 construction$1 erection$2 establishment$3 property$1
. . .	
1 establishment$3	building$1 factory$0 house$1 office$ plant$2 quarters$ erection$1 premises$0
1 establishment$4	abode$0 domicile$0 dwelling$0 home$1 house$1 household$1 residence$1

. . .

1 property$1   assets$0 belongings$0 building$1 buildings$99 capital$3 chattels$99 effects$0 estate$2 goods$1 holdings$0 house$1 houses$99 means$2 possessions$0 resources$0 riches$0 wealth$1 asset$2 estate$1 fortune$1 movables$0 place$5 possession$2 premises$0 stock$4 substance$4

. . .

2 habitat$0   abode$0 element$2 environment$0 home$3 home-_ground$99 locality$ natural_home$99 surroundings$0 terrain$ territory$0 ground$2 grounds$0 medium$4

2 lodging$0   abode$0 accommodation$2 apartments$99 boarding$99 digs$99 dwelling$0 habitation$1 quarters$0 residence$1 rooms$99 shelter$ address$1 billet$1 rest$4

. . .

2 structure$2   building$1 building$2 construction$1 edifice$0 erection$2 pile$4

. . .

2 space$4   accommodation$ berth$ place$4 place$5 place$6 seat$2 seat$5 slot$2

2 assets$0   capital$3 estate$2 funds$1 goods$1 holdings$0 means$2 money$1 possessions$0 property$1 reserves$99 resources$0 valuables$ wealth$1 coffers$0 finances$0 possession$2 principal$4 riches$0 stock$1 substance$4 treasury$2

. . .

3 element$2   domain$2 environment$0 field$3 habitat$0 medium$4 milieu$0 sphere$2 home$3

3 environment$0   atmosphere$2 background$0 conditions$0 context$2 domain$1 element$2 habitat$0 locale$0 medium$4 milieu$0 scene$2 scene$3 setting$0 situation$1 surroundings$0 territory$0 entourage$2 field$3 home$3 scene$7 worlds$5

. . .

3 architecture$1   architectonics$99 building$2 construction$1 design$4 planning$99

. . .

4 domain$2   area$3 authority$1 bailiwick$99 concern$2 department$3

. . .

5 concern$2   affair$1 business$4 charge$6 deportment$ field$ interest$7 involvement$1 job$1 matter$2 mission$1 occupation$1 responsibility$1 task$1 transaction$1 domain$2 function$1 importance$1 interests$0 issue$1 lookout$4 part$3 pigeon$3 place$7 province$2 stake$5

. . .
5 orbit$2

ambit$99 compass$1 course$3 domain$2 influence$ range$1 reach$6 scope$0 sphere$2 sphere_of_influence$99 sweep$4 circle$2 jurisdiction$2 province$2 purview$1 realm$2

. . .
5 mood$1

disposition$1 frame_of_mind$0 humour$3 spirit$2 state_of-_mind$99 temper$1 tenor$ vein$3 ambience$0 atmo-sphere$2 attitude$1 climate$2 fit$7 frame$7 nature$4 posture$3 spirit$7 state$3 tone$2 tune$3

5 spirit$2

attitude$1 character$1 complexion$2 disposition$1 es-sence$ humour$3 outlook$1 quality$2 temper$1 tempera-ment$1 ambience$0 atmosphere$2 blood$3 distillation$0 ethos$0 fibre$2 flavouring$0 frame$7 frame_of_mind$0 mood$1 morale$0 odour$2 quintessence$0 strain$10 tone$2

5 spirit$5

atmosphere$2 feeling$6 gist$ humour$ tenor$ tone$2 odour$2 purport$3 quintessence$0 strain$10 style$6

. . .
12 car$1

auto$99 automobile$99 jalopy$99 machine$ motor$99 motorcar$99 vehicle$ coach$1

12 unbeliever$0

agnostic$99 atheist$0 disbeliever$0 doubting_Thomas$99 infidel$0 sceptic$0 doubter$0 freethinker$0 heathen$1 pagan$1

12 freethinker$0

agnostic$99 deist$99 doubter$0 infidel$0 sceptic$0 un-believer$0 atheist$0

. . .
12 puberty$0

adolescence$1 awakward_age$99 juvenescence$99 pubes-cence$99 teenage$ teens$99 young_adulthood$99

12 anchorite$0
12 eremite$0

eremite$0 hermit$0 recluse$1 ascetic$1
anchorite$0 hermit$0 recluse$1 solitary$4

. . .
13 niggard$0

cheapskate$99 cheeseparer$99 churl$3 miser$0 penny-pincher$0 screw$ Scrooge$0 skinflint$0 hoarder$0

17 Developing Computational Lexical Resources

Donald E. Walker
Bellcore
Morristown, NJ

In the last few years there has been a dramatic increase of interest in the lexicon by the research community, publishers, software developers, and industry more generally.[1] People working in the fields of linguistics, computational linguistics, artificial intelligence, psycholinguistics, cognitive science, and information technology are now exploring issues that used to be the sole province of lexicographers and lexicologists. This recognition of the importance of lexical resources can be attributed to a number of converging factors.

On the theoretical side, the major contemporary linguistic theories are assigning to the lexicon an increasingly central role. Similarly, lexical information is a critical component in computational linguistic formalizations of natural language processing models.

On the application side, the availability of lexical resources in machine-readable form is becoming a major concern for what the Europeans in particular call the *language industries* or *language engineering*. This field, which is emerging as an autonomous sector within the information industries, includes both computer assistance to traditional applied linguistics professions (including, among others, lexicography, translation, and language teaching) and the development of computational systems based on natural language processing (as required, for example, in natural language interfaces, speech analysis and syn-

---

[1] A version of this chapter was included in the **Proceedings of the 5th Annual Conference of the UW Centre for the New Oxford English Dictionary.** University of Waterloo Centre for the New Oxford English Dictionary, Waterloo, Ontario (1989, pp. 1–22).

Some material from this section, written with Antonio Zampolli, appeared in the Foreword of Boguraev and Briscoe (1989).

421

thesis, automatic indexing and abstracting, information retrieval, office automation, machine translation, and, more generally, support for communication).

Computational linguists and language industry developers recognize that, for real-world applications, natural language processing systems must be able to deal with tens and even hundreds of thousands of lexical items. Consequently, the development of large lexical knowledge bases has emerged as one of the most urgent tasks they face. Because that work is so human-intensive, it is also expensive and time-consuming.

Computational lexicology and lexicography is beginning to emerge as a discipline in its own right: Witness the number of specialized workshops (*Machine-Readable Dictionaries, Automating the Lexicon in a Multilingual Environment, The Lexical Entry, The Lexicon in Theoretical and Computational Perspective, Lexical Semantics*, the *The Structure of the Lexicon: Semantic Fields and Other Alternatives, The First International Lexical Acquisition Workshop*), conferences (*Advances in Lexicology* [UW Centre for the New OED, 1986], *Standardisation in Lexicography, Electronic Dictionaries*), panel discussions at workshop and conference meetings (*Machine-Readable Dictionaries, The Lexicon in a Multilingual Environment, Words and World Representations* [Wilks, 1987]), specialist ad hoc working groups (*Computational Lexicology and Lexicography, Dictionaries and the Computer*), and publications (**Lexicography in the Electronic Age** [Goetschalckx & Rolling, 1982], **Computational Linguistics** *Special Issue on the Lexicon* [Walker et al., 1987a], **International Journal of Lexicography, Computational Lexicography for Natural Language Processing** [Boguraev & Briscoe, 1989]). It is also appropriate to remark on the fact that four or five papers on the lexicon are included in every conference of the *Association for Computational Linguistics* as well as to note the centrality of lexical issues in the conferences organized by the University of Waterloo Center for the New OED.

At the same time, it is becoming apparent that, even though human users and computer programs emphasize different aspects of lexical information and require different data structures, explicitly formulated and intelligently accessible lexical knowledge bases can greatly improve the quality and the benefits of the human uses of lexicographical data, as well as directly support the work of lexicographers.

In this context, the problem of the "reusability of lexical resources" acquires a dramatic new dimension. This expression, which with increasing frequency appears in the definition of the objectives of national and international projects and, in particular, designates an entry in the *Framework Research Program* formulated by the Commission of the European Communities for 1987–1991, refers to two major complementary issues.

The first concerns the current growing efforts to establish new large lexical knowledge bases as generalized natural language-processing modules, designed so that they will serve, through appropriate interfaces, a wide variety of projects, both research and applications, even when they utilize different linguistic and/or computational frameworks. Work at the University of Pisa (Calzolari, forthcoming; Calzolari & Zampolli, forthcoming) and at the IBM T. J. Watson Research Center (Neff, Byrd, & Rizk, 1988) is illustrative.

The second concerns the ability to reuse existing lexical resources by extracting or converting the data they contain for incorporation in a variety of different language-processing modules. The various kinds of existing dictionaries, and in particular the dictionaries available in machine-readable form, are among the richest and most valuable sources, based, as they are, on a long lexicographical tradition that encompasses a treasure store of data, information, and knowledge. Boguraev and Briscoe's (1989) new book, *Computational Lexicography for Natural Language Processing,* provides substantive documentation for this assertion (see also Boguraev, forthcoming).[2]

Whereas the foregoing remarks have focused on the lexicon, the need for textual resources is becoming increasingly recognized. The development of lexical knowledge bases is critically dependent on the availability of massive text files as sources of lexical information. Similarly, although traditional dictionaries are a rich source of relevant data, they are far from complete. Consequently, the analysis of texts must be recognized as an integral part of a comprehensive research and development program.

As interest in the lexicon began to expand, it became clear that some coordinated effort was needed to bring people together, to establish modes of cooperation, and to define a comprehensive research program. The following sections describe successively my involvement in a series of workshops on the lexicon, some key issues facing lexical and textual research, the establishment of an international initiative to provide an interchange standard for text encoding, the formation of an initiative within computational linguistics to promote the collection of texts that can be shared by the research community, a proposal for the establishment of a consortium for lexical research, and, finally, the identification of a concept, *language ecology,* that I believe will become increasingly important in future research.

THE LEXICON WORKSHOPS:
AN HISTORICAL PERSPECTIVE

Over the past 6 years, I have been involved in the organization of a series of workshops intended to bring people from different disciplines, different backgrounds (academic and commercial, research and applications), and different theoretical persuasions together to discuss the lexicon.

---

[2]Robert Amsler (1989b) has prepared a review of the history of work with machine-readable dictionaries that attempts to put it in a "generational" perspective. He believes we are beginning a third generation of computational lexicology in which reusability will be a central feature and in

The first workshop, "Machine-Readable Dictionaries," which Robert Amsler and I organized, was held in April, 1983, at SRI International in Menlo Park, California.[3] For the first time, publishers, people from the research community, and representatives from the emerging market intermediaries met to discuss issues of mutual interest. What the meeting demonstrated more than anything else was the gulf that existed among what can best be described as protagonists. However, it did initiate a process of communication that has continued to increase significantly both during the subsequent workshops and independently of them.

The second workshop, "Automating the Lexicon in a Multilingual Environment," in May, 1986, in Marina di Grosseto, Italy, had a much broader agenda. This time Antonio Zampolli, Nicoletta Calzolari, Juan Sager, and Loll Rolling joined with me in its organization.[4] The objective of this workshop was to examine research efforts, current practice, and potential developments in work on the lexicon, machine-readable dictionaries, and lexical knowledge bases with special consideration for the problems created by working with different languages. Our intent was to identify the current state of affairs and to recommend directions for future activities.

To help in the realization of its objective, a set of papers was solicited for the workshop under the following general headings: Research Areas, Core Problems, Application Areas, and Developing Research Resources. Comprehensive surveys and evaluations of activities on those topics were prepared as well as reports on national projects in related areas. At the end of the agenda, a "consolidation" session was held to consider the following topics: the lexical entry as a basis for integration, cooperation and communication, priorities for research and development, and the next steps.

The participants in the second workshop were chosen to bring together representatives from the different kinds of areas that we believed were relevant to the various problems associated with the lexicon. This led us to invite linguists, lexicographers, lexicologists, computational linguists, artificial intelligence specialists, cognitive scientists, publishers, lexical software marketers, translators, funding agency representatives, and professional society representatives. It seemed to us critical that this heterogeneous mix of people get to know each other and appreciate the similarities in their interests and the need for cooperation to achieve both shared and separate objectives.

---

which incompatible and overlapping sets of information about language will be integrated into a coherent computational resource.

[3]Sponsored by the U.S. National Science Foundation.

[4]The workshop was sponsored by the European Community, the University of Pisa, and the Institute for Computational Linguistics of the Italian National Research Council. In addition, a number of professional societies lent their support: the *Association for Computational Linguistics,* the *Association for Literary and Linguistic Computing,* and the Commission on Computational Linguistics of the *International Association for Applied Linguistics.*

The papers that were prepared for the workshop did identify the current state of affairs better than any other material currently available.[5] More importantly, though, the discussions led to an extensive set of recommendations for further work, some of which are reflected in later sections.

To pick up immediately on the momentum provided by the Grosseto workshop, a third one, on "The Lexical Entry," was held in July, 1986, in conjunction with the 1986 Linguistics Institute at the City University of New York, less than 2 months after the Grosseto meeting.[6]

Having established the diversity of perspectives and approaches at the prior workshop, the next step was to determine the extent to which people could agree on features of the lexicon. Specifically, the participants were asked to examine in detail how different theoretical frameworks and system implementations influence the format for a lexical entry. A specific goal was to characterize a general representation or "metaformat" that would subsume the specific ones. We did not expect that everyone would agree to share a single model. Rather, we hoped to identify the range of parameters that were being used in different systems in such a way that different approaches might be said to be making a selection from them. In this way, people would appreciate better both what they were including and what they were excluding in the choices they were making.

The group began by examining lexical entries in current dictionaries to establish their parameters and the range of variation associated with them. Then it considered how this information was relevant for current research in morphology, syntax, and semantics, and how it could be included in lexical databases and lexical knowledge bases. The discussions were encouraging, but it was clear that much more time would be needed to reach any kind of agreement about what could be included in a "neutral lexicon."

One of the most promising results of the third workshop was the establishment of a syntax working group. It met in March, 1987, in Pisa for 3 days to examine in some detail and from a variety of theoretical perspectives the subcategorization phenomena associated with a small set of carefully selected verbs. The theoretical approaches represented were the BBN Context-Free Grammar, Dependency Unification Grammar, Generalized Phrase Structure Grammar, Government-Binding, Lexical Functional Grammar, and Systemic Functional Grammar. In spite of the theoretical differences, there was a substantial consensus on the distinctions that need to be made in a lexicon with regard to verbs. Although Government-Binding and Systemic Functional Grammar required more detailed descriptions of semantic information, they shared with the others a core set of syntactically oriented categories. In the course of these discussions an exhaustive

---

[5]The proceedings, long delayed in publication, are expected to appear reasonably soon (Walker, Zampolli, & Calzolari, 1992).

[6]This workshop had support from the Linguistics Institute, the *Sloan Foundation,* the *Association for Computational Linguistics,* and Bell Communications Research (now Bellcore).

set of subcategorization types was developed, and a *template* was prepared that specified the kinds of data necessary to describe a verb. The group also considered the kinds of tests needed to establish equivalence classes. Finally, a beginning was made on comparing English and Italian to test (in an obviously minimal way) the generality of the model. Some of the working papers were gathered in Walker, Zampolli, and Calzolari, (1987b).

The results achieved by the "Pisa Working Group" were sufficiently encouraging to motivate extending the model to other areas. Consequently, a more extensive 2-week workshop was held in July, 1987, during the 1987 Linguistic Institute at Stanford University.[7] The syntax working group continued its efforts to specify the "ideal," shareable properties of verbs in a *polytheoretical* (the term *neutral* having been replaced) and multipurpose lexicon, building on the lexicographic information contained in traditional machine-readable dictionaries. A set of other working groups was convened in the hopes of making similar kinds of progress in the areas of semantics, morphology, and data and knowledge base design. The semantics group explored thematic and case role relations and considered ways of representing real-world knowledge at the lexical level. The morphology group tried to show how morphological data can be used to predict syntactic and semantic properties. The data and knowledge base group explored more effective ways of structuring, storing, and retrieving data from machine-readable dictionaries and corpora so that relevant information can be located. Another group met to examine a particular text and consider what lexical information would be needed for each word. A final group discussed multilingual issues.

Some progress was made on all these dimensions, but the 2 weeks of the workshop were not enough to produce any substantive conclusions. Much time was devoted to providing background because so many new people were involved. In addition, most of the participants attended several working groups, and no one group devoted enough time to its central issue. Of course, each problem addressed was much larger than one could expect to solve even during 2 weeks of intensive work. However, a consensus was reached about the appropriateness of the goals and about the path being followed to reach them.

This consensus is influencing the work of a number of groups, but it has its most clear realization in an ESPRIT project that addresses the "Acquisition of Lexical Knowledge for Natural Language Processing Systems."[8] As described in the proposal (Boguraev et al., 1988):

> The research will draw on and extend current work on extracting data from published MRDs and formalising this data to facilitate the algorithmic processing of

---

[7]The *Association for Computational Linguistics* provided financial support.

[8]Submitted by Bran Boguraev, Ted Briscoe, Nicoletta Calzolari, Arthur Cater, Willem Meijs, and Antonio Zampolli.

language. The main focus of the project will be on extending existing techniques for processing single MRDs in a monolingual (and currently mostly English) context to the extraction of lexical information from multiple MRD sources in a multilingual context with the overall goal of constructing a single integrated multilingual lexical knowledge base. . . .

The emphasis of our research is on identifying the most general and domain-independent aspects of lexical knowledge and expressing this knowledge in a fashion that will make it reusable by a wide variety of NLP systems. The central, long-term, goal of the research programme is the development of a multilingual lexical knowledge base, rooted in a common conceptual/semantic structure which is linked to, and defines, the individual word senses of the language covered and which is rich enough to be capable of supporting a 'deep' processing model of language. The lexical knowledge base will contain substantial general vocabulary with associated phonological, morphological, syntactic and semantic/pragmatic information capable of deployment in the lexical component of a wide variety of practical NLP systems. The functionality of such a knowledge base will be evaluated by assessing its capability of supporting prototype monolingual (e.g., query processing) and multilingual (e.g., machine translation) systems. (p. 1)

TEXTUAL AND LEXICAL ISSUES

A major premise of this chapter is that the development of lexical resources depends critically on the parallel development of textual resources. This same conclusion followed from a "Lexical Research Survey" distributed by the Applied Information Technologies Research Center (AITRC) (Bowers, 1989). It identified needs for supporting three basic activities:

1. The acquisition, development, and management of an extensive array of electronic resources—textual material, machine-readable dictionaries, thesauri, and so forth.

2. The development of fundamental tools and techniques for understanding the wide variety of syntactic and semantic elements of language, and for processing raw textual material in such a way that it can be both further analyzed and used for applications where such understanding is needed.

3. The creation of applications which utilize lexical information either for its own sake (e.g., academic applications) or for support of existing electronic publishing (e.g., commercial applications) (ibid, p. 3).

Although this summary certainly is appropriate, my own analysis of the survey data led me to distinguish the following issues as particularly relevant for consideration in this chapter: database development—insuring the accessibility of resources; standards for representation—guaranteeing accuracy and consistency; lexical units—establishing their adequacy for document collections; other linguistic dimensions—determining their relevance for lexical relations; tools for research—developing algorithms and other processing aids; and ecological parameters—identifying why, how, and where particular forms of language are used.

Database Development entails a number of different issues: (1) acquiring data, that is, determining sources, getting permission for access, resolving copyright issues; (2) insuring coverage either through selecting representative samples or identifying complete collections; (3) making data accessible, which involves storage facilities, management procedures, and access strategies; (4) preprocessing the data to maximize utility, a process that includes formatting, tagging, and classification. Many of these concerns are reflected in the *ACL Data Collection Initiative* described in a later section.

Standards for Representation are intended to maximize shareability. Identifying theoretical and methodological communalities in data collected by different people for different purposes is critical, as the workshop experiences described earlier demonstrate. International standards for capturing textual information, like the Standard Generalized Markup Language, are reasonable places to begin, as the discussion of the *Text Encoding Initiative* that follows demonstrates. Another important aspect is the establishment of common user interface features for systems that support interacting with textual and lexical data.

The determination of *Lexical Units* proves to be a more complicated problem than might seem at first glance. A word cannot be distinguished in text simply by demarcation with blank spaces. What should be considered a single lexical entry may actually contain several words in that simplistic sense. Obviously, much more research must be devoted to the analysis and differentiation of words, phrases, compounds, collocations, and idioms (Ahlswede et al., 1988; Amsler, 1987b, 1989a, forthcoming; Choueka, 1988). In addition, proper nouns, which figure significantly in many kinds of text, must be represented by "dictionaries," just as other words are, although Amsler (1987a, 1989a) points out that proper nouns have a grammatical structure, based on contractions and rearrangements. Their variant forms are sufficiently complicated that it is not always possible to store them under a single entry. Lehrer (this volume) shows how names need to be considered in relation to frames and fields.

Lexical Units interact with other *Linguistic Dimensions,* and there are morphological, syntactic, semantic, pragmatic, and discourse-structural considerations that need to be resolved. In effect, the entire program of computational linguistics is implicated. Work by Boguraev (forthcoming) and by Boguraev and Briscoe (1987, 1989) illustrates the kind of research that is needed, and, indeed, their ESPRIT project referred to before (Boguraev et al., 1988) has a charter to explore the lexical implications of these problems.

Tools for Research is a global category under which many things can be subsumed. Of particular interest from the standpoint of the lexicon are the attempts to develop "tool-kits" as reflected in Boguraev (forthcoming), Boguraev and Briscoe (1987, 1989), Byrd et al. (1987), and Neff and Boguraev (1989). Other work is being done on a variety of different kinds of disambiguation procedures: structural, contextual, and domain-independent. Papers by Lesk (1986) and Hindle (1989) provide interesting research directions.

These last three issues, *Lexical Units, Linguistic Dimensions,* and *Tools for Research,* all figure directly in the research program envisioned for the *Consortium for Lexical Research* discussed later.

A final issue here refers to what I call *Ecological Parameters.* In the survey, the concerns expressed referred to more refined statistical analysis procedures, the collection of preference and probability information, and the establishment of a systematic treatment of sublanguages. However, I believe that ecology is a more encompassing issue. Because of its importance, it is discussed in more detail at the end of this chapter.

The Text Encoding Initiative[9]

The concern with standardizing ways of encoding features of machine-readable text is pervasive. It has led to the development of the Standard Generalized Markup Language (SGML) as ISO Standard 8879 (International Standards Organization, 1986). SGML characterizes the content of a document descriptively rather than procedurally; that is, the markup identifies the logical features of the text rather than specifying a set of procedures that realize a particular representation in print. Bryan (1988) and van Herwijnen (1990) provide eminently readable introductions. European involvement was immediate, and the Commission of the European Community has accepted SGML as a documentation standard. Within the United States, the Association of American Publishers produced SGML tag sets for three basic electronic manuscript types—books, articles, and serials— which have been accepted as Standard Z39.59 of the American National Standards Institute (Association of American Publishers, 1987) and are being submitted to ISO. More recently, the U.S. Defense Department in its Computer-aided Acquisition and Logistics Support Program began requiring all responses to requests for proposals to be in SGML form. Now the U.S. Government has approved SGML as a Federal Information Processing Standard; as a result, all text-processing systems it develops or acquires must conform to it. In response to these and related demands, a number of software companies have developed commercial systems for supporting SGML.

The factors motivating these developments certainly contributed to the creation of the *Text Encoding Initiative (TEI),* but the route was more indirect. The

---

[9]Some material from this section has been derived from documents generated for the *Text Encoding Initiative* by various participants.

TEI is a major international project to formulate and disseminate guidelines for the preparation and interchange of machine-readable texts for scholarly research and to satisfy a broad range of uses by the language industries more generally. Its immediate inspiration came out of the recognition that increasing amounts of grant funds from the U.S. National Endowment for the Humanities (NEH) were being used for the electronic capture of texts, but that these materials were being encoded idiosyncratically so that they could not be shared easily with other research groups. As a result the NEH was responsive to a proposal from the *Association for Computers and the Humanities (ACH)*, written by Nancy Ide, for what became the planning phase for the *TEI*.

Ide organized a conference on "Text Encoding Practices" in November, 1987, at Vassar College to determine the feasibility and desirability of establishing guidelines and to formulate aims and technical specifications for them. She brought together a distinguished group of experts from universities, learned societies, and text archives from Europe, Israel, Japan, and North America. As a result of this conference, three overall goals for the initiative were defined: (1) to specify a common interchange format for machine readable texts; (2) to provide a set of recommendations for encoding new textual materials; and (3) to document the major existing encoding schemes and develop a metalanguage in which to describe them.

After the Vassar meeting, *ACH*, the *Association for Computational Linguistics (ACL)*, and the *Association for Literary and Linguistic Computing (ALLC)* joined as co-sponsors of the project in defining a 4-year work plan to achieve the project's goals. Recognizing the fact that the problems facing humanists are shared by many other groups both in the research community and in industry, the scope of the project was broadened to address the common concerns more generally. The project began officially in June, 1988, with a substantial grant from the NEH. Funding has since been provided by the European Economic Community.[10]

The project is coordinated by a six-member steering committee, comprised of two representatives from each of the sponsoring organizations. Two editors over-

---

[10]In addition to the three sponsoring organizations, the following associations are currently represented on an Advisory Board to the project: the *American Anthropological Association;* the *American Historical Association;* the *American Philological Association;* the *American Society for Information Science;* the *Association for Computing Machinery;* the *Association for Documentary Editing;* the *Association for History and Computing;* the *Association Internationale Bible et Informatique;* the *Canadian Linguistic Association;* the *Dictionary Society of North America;* the *Electronic Publishing Special Interest Group of the Association of American Publishers;* the *International Federation of Library Associations and Institutions;* the *Linguistic Society of America;* and the *Modern Language Association.* Other organizations are likely to become involved. The Advisory Board is intended to ensure that the members of each association are kept informed of work within the *TEI* and that appropriate individuals within each organization are suitably involved in the effort. The Advisory Board will be asked to endorse and promote the guidelines when they are completed.

see the activities undertaken by the project's four Working Committees, each of which is responsible for a distinct part of the work plan.

The *Committee on Text Documentation,* with a membership drawn largely from the library and archive management communities, is establishing procedures for the cataloguing and identification of key features of encoded texts.

The Committee on Text Representation is encoding character sets, layout, and other features physically represented in the source material. It will provide precise recommendations covering those features of continuous discourse for which a convention already exists in printed or written sources.

The *Committee on Text Analysis and Interpretation* is providing discipline-specific sets of tags appropriate to the analytic procedures favored by that discipline, but in such a way as to permit their extension and generalization to other disciplines using analogous procedures.

The *Committee on Syntax and Metalanguage* has determined that the syntactic framework of SGML is adequate for foreseeable applications within the scope of the *TEI* and thus will provide the basic syntax. This committee is now surveying major existing schemes and developing a formal metalanguage that can be used to describe both these schemes and one being developed for the Guidelines. The metalanguage can provide formally specifiable mappings between pairs of schemes.

In July, 1990, the *TEI* issued a public release draft of its "Guidelines for the Encoding and Interchange of Machine-Readable Texts." It is being widely circulated for review, testing, and evaluation.[11] A number of "Affiliated Projects" are currently working with the *TEI,* encoding their textual data to conform to the guidelines. A substantially modified and significantly enlarged 'Final Report' is expected to be issued in June, 1992.

The ACL Data Collection Initiative[12]

Computer-based text archives have been in existence since the late 1940s. Most of them were developed to reflect an interest in a particular body of literature. A few, like the Oxford Text Archive, have collected texts primarily for the purpose of making them available to scholars. Several recent surveys have been conducted: Lancashire and McCarty (1988) in *The Humanities Computing Year-*

---

[11]Requests for copies should be addressed to one of the two editors: C. Michael Sperberg-McQueen, Computer Center (M/C 135), University of Illinois at Chicago, Box 6998, Chicago, IL 60680, USA; u35395@uicvm.cc.uic.edu or u35395@uicvm.bitnet; (+1 312) 996-2477; (+1 312) 996-6896 fax. Lou Burnard, Oxford University Computing Service, 13 Banbury Road, Oxford OX2 6NN, ENGLAND; lou@vax.ox.ac.uk; (+44 865) 273238; (+44 865) 273275 fax.

[12]Parts of this section are based on descriptions prepared jointly with Mark Liberman.

book; Lita Taylor and Geoffrey Leech from the University of Lancaster, and Michael Neuman from Georgetown University. The latter two appeared on the *HUMANIST* Bulletin Board, which can be expected to contain further supplements. However, although some of the archives make material available for research, and there are a few specialized collections on CD–ROM and other media, most scholars have difficulty getting the data they need.

The extent of interest in the humanities is indicated by the recent award by the NEH of a planning grant to explore the possibility of creating a "National Center for Machine-Readable Texts in the Humanities." Rutgers and Princeton Universities are cooperating in this effort. Its goals are to: create an ongoing inventory of machine-readable texts in the humanities; catalog these items in an online database and make their existence known internationally; acquire, preserve, and service humanities textual data files that would otherwise disappear; make the files available to scholars in the most convenient and least expensive manner; and act as a resource center and referral point for humanities scholars to other projects and centers that disseminate humanities textual data.

In computational linguistics, there has been a recent upsurge of interest in computational studies of large bodies of text. The aim of such studies varies widely, from lexicography and studies of language change to automatic indexing methods and statistical models for improving the performance of optical character readers. In general, corpus-based studies are critical for the development of adequate models of linguistic structure and for insights into the nature of language use. However, researchers have been severely hampered by the lack of appropriate materials, and specifically by the lack of a large enough body of text on which published results can be replicated or extended by others.

Recognizing this problem, the *Association for Computational Linguistics* has established the *ACL Data Collection Initiative (ACL/DCI)*. It provides the aegis of a not-for-profit scientific society to oversee the acquisition and preparation of a large text corpus to be made available for scientific research at cost and without royalties. The initial goal was to acquire at least 100 million words, but more than that amount has already been pledged.[13] The material in the *ACL/DCI* text corpus is being coded in a standard form based on SGML. Over time, we hope to be able to incorporate annotations reflecting consensually approved linguistic features like part of speech and various aspects of syntactic and perhaps semantic structure. Both the coding and the annotations will be coordinated with the work of the Text Encoding Initiative *(TEI)*.

Although our initial efforts will concentrate on the collection of American English, we are interacting with groups in other countries with respect to British

---

[13]All materials submitted for inclusion in the collection remain the exclusive property of the copyright holders (if any) for all other purposes. Each applicant for data from the *ACL/DCI* is required to sign an agreement not to redistribute the data or use it for other than research purposes. Special restrictions on some materials are necessary, but that will be done only if the restrictions do not compromise the central objective of providing general long-term access for research.

English and other European languages, and we hope to encourage the establishment of similar initiatives for other language families as well. Our current plan is to try to make available by the end of the summer about 50 million words of English text, which will probably be issued on 6250 bpi 9-track magnetic tape. For this initial release we will not be concerned about the systematicity of coverage. In addition, the data will only reflect a minimal SGML formatting of the descriptive features of the text. The tape would also include some programs, probably in C and LISP, for word concordancing and possibly other kinds of simple manipulations. In the future we hope to be exploring issues in the "ecology of language" more systematically so that we can begin to consider providing representative samples of language usage, as discussed later in this chapter. We also would like to establish some kind of clearing house so that the results of research using the collection can be made more widely available.

The *ACL/DCI* already has some public domain text and commitments from some publishers. Of particular interest as a lexical resource is the offer by Patrick Hanks of the first edition of the *Collins English Dictionary* (Hanks, 1979). However, we are actively soliciting additional material, preferably on magnetic tape, and would appreciate receiving relatively large amounts that are free of copyright restrictions and can be distributed without requiring royalties.

In a related development, Mitch Marcus at the University of Pennsylvania had a grant from the General Electric Corporate Research and Development Center and is receiving funding from the U.S. Defense Advanced Research Projects Agency and the U.S. Air Force of Scientific Research for the initial work on a "Tree Bank of Written and Spoken American English." His intent is to annotate millions of sentences with part of speech assignments, skeletal syntactic parsings, intonational boundaries for spoken language, and other forms of linguistic information that can be encoded consistently and quickly. At the same time, the project can be expected to develop a methodology for annotation that should be of general interest. This body of tagged and annotated materials is expected to derive at least in part from the *ACL/DCI* collection and to be available for distribution through it. The *Tree Bank* project will also be coordinated with the work of the *TEI Committee on Text Analysis and Interpretation,* which will be concentrating initially on developing tag sets for linguistically salient features of texts.[14]

---

[14]Other groups have been developing tagged corpora. The Brown Corpus (Kucera & Francis, 1967) is now available with part-of-speech and parse structure coding (Francis & Kucera, 1982). Garside, Leech, and Sampson (1987) have been analyzing structural features of the Lancaster-Oslo/Bergen Corpus. Beale (1988) describes the development of software used in that project. Spoken material has been prosodically transcribed and tagged in the London–Lund Corpus of Spoken English (Svartvik & Quirk, 1980). These three projects are discussed further in the *Ecology* section following. The hope is that future work in all these and related efforts can be coordinated for the benefit of the research community as a whole.

Consortium for Lexical Research

In recognition of the need for lexical resources, Roy Byrd of the IBM T. J. Watson Research Center has proposed that a *Consortium for Lexical Research (CLR)* be established for the purpose of enabling and encouraging the creation of precompetitive lexical resources for natural language processing. His proposal reflects the fact that the construction of adequate lexical bases is a major problem for the development of large-scale natural language processing (NLP) applications. Existing lexical bases do not encompass the words required, much less the information needed for each word to make it functional. However, as noted earlier, there is a consensus emerging that there are classes of lexical information that can be used for different NLP applications. This has led Byrd to the notion of a "precompetitive lexical resource": The information in the intersection of the requirements for different applications that "each system developer (1) realizes that the others also need and (2) concedes that the others will eventually acquire." He believes that the entire NLP community would benefit by cooperating on their acquisition.

The *CLR* would establish a shared repository of lexical data and lexical tools. Participants would contribute their own tools and data and would have the right to withdraw material in order to carry out specific research projects. The results of the research, in turn, would be contributed to the repository, in the form of data, tools, and theoretical insights. Byrd recognizes a number of issues that would have to be addressed by the *CLR:* technical (e.g., mechanisms for collecting and redistributing data and software in a heterogeneous computing environment), organizational (e.g., choosing a location for the repository; establishing and enforcing distribution policies), and legal (e.g., protecting the intellectual property rights of the owners of data and software).

The following types of lexical data are among those that are of interest: published dictionaries as typesetting tapes and lexical data bases; collections of proper nouns; lists of phrases, collocations, and idioms; and other kinds of word lists incorporating syntactic, semantic, and phonetic information.

The software tools would include: data base management and access procedures for lexical data bases; concordance and related programs for analyzing text corpora; morphological analyzers; and tools for converting and processing SGML data, particularly in the format being developed by the *Dictionary Encoding Initiative*.

Access to material in the repository would be restricted to *CLR* participants. Byrd distinguishes two classes: *contributing participants* who donate lexical data or software tools to the repository; *research participants* who use materials from the repository in their research and who redeposit the results for use by other participants. A given organization could function in both capacities. Withdrawals would require licensing agreements and probably some evaluation to ensure that the research is relevant and likely to be of interest, particularly to the contributing participants.

The *CLR* probably should be located at and administered by an academic or noncommercial research institution to avoid the problems that would result from having one commercial participant place its proprietary material under the control of another commercial institution. The host should also be a research participant, preferably a center of expertise and excellence in lexical research. "Steering" and "Advisory" committees would need to be established to oversee the operations and make sure they serve the participants and the research community as a whole.

Protecting the intellectual property rights of the participants is a critical concern. Unlike the *ACL Data Collection Initiative*, many of the contributing participants are likely to establish limits on access to their materials. License agreements will be required, some of which might want to control derivative products as well. Special agreements could of course be negotiated between contributors and prospective users that would be outside the *CLR* but facilitated by its existence.

Byrd believes that dictionary publishers would have a special role in the Consortium. Including their databases is crucial for its effectiveness, but because those materials cannot be viewed as "precompetitive resources," special arrangements would have to be made to protect them. Nevertheless, the *CLR* should offer an opportunity for publishers to benefit from research done using their data. Fostering separate agreements in sensitive areas is one mechanism that could be exploited.

Basic funding would be needed to support the cost of personnel, space, and computer usage. Recognizing the limited budgets in the research community, the intent is to minimize the financial costs of participation. However, it would be reasonable to charge small fees for creating and shipping tapes. Furthermore, if publishers decide to charge for access to their dictionaries, these costs would probably have to be passed on to recipients.

The *CLR* would not itself be a funding organization. The research must be separately supported, although the Consortium could certify that the proposed project has its approval and that the data and tools requested will be available.

In the summary section of the proposal, Byrd argues that creating a *Consortium for Lexical Research* would benefit the Natural Language Processing Community "by providing a focal point for the creation of an interacting community of lexical researchers, fostering cooperation on the creation of better lexical resources faster, establishing a center of competence in lexical research, encouraging the creation of re-usable lexical tools, techniques, and data, enabling research that has more impact than is possible with simple publication of theoretical results, and removing the necessity to negotiate multiple bilateral joint-study agreements covering this kind of research." It would indeed be a significant development.

The Ecology of Language

Most research in linguistics and computational linguistics has approached language either abstractly by analyzing formal models of linguistic structure, or concretely by selecting a particular instantiation of some linguistic phenomena and studying their specific properties. Phrased in Chomskyan terms, people have tended to focus on competence or on performance, with only occasional concern for the interaction between competence and performance. Recently, though, as an applications dimension has emerged in natural language processing, it has become clear that it is no longer possible to ignore the distributional aspects of language. These aspects become increasingly important as attempts are made to evaluate the computational linguistic systems and programs that are being developed.[15]

People talk and write differently; they are exposed both aurally and visually to many different kinds of language material. Consequently, there is a need to study the *ecology* of language, that is, the relation between particular uses of language and the contexts in which they occur. In order to proceed systematically, it is necessary to have vast amounts of material, appropriately diversified to represent the contexts.

As noted in the discussion of the *ACL Data Collection Initiative*, there are many archives in existence. Most specialize in material of a particular type. Others, like the Oxford Text Archive, accept a variety of kinds of data but are limited by the sources that contribute them. The Brown Corpus (Kucera & Francis, 1967) was one of the first attempts to collect "samples" of published material with the intention of drawing some conclusions about English usage: 500 sets of 2,000 words gathered from a range of media all published in a particular year. Subsequently, other diversified collections of English have been made: the Lancaster-Oslo/Bergen Corpus (Johansson, 1985) and the Birmingham University Corpus (Sinclair, 1987b) for written English, and the London-Lund Corpus (Svartvik & Quirk, 1980) for spoken English being the best known. The Birmingham Corpus is of particular interest because a substantial part of its 20 million words of general British English were used in the development of the COBUILD Dictionary (Sinclair, 1987a). Whereas these and other collections certainly have been "useful," questions of representativeness are raised when "Beowulf" appears 14 times in the Brown Corpus and a surprisingly

---

[15]A "Workshop on Evaluation of Natural Language Processing Systems" was organized by Martha Palmer of Unisys on 8–9 December, 1988. It and subsequent meetings on this topic sponsored by the U.S. Government testify to recognition of the need for being able to judge the relevance of research.

frequent word following "wet" in the Birmingham Corpus is "nappies." It is now clear that collections of hundreds of millions of words are necessary. More important, these collections need to be "representative."

Determining what constitutes a *representative collection* begs the question of what population is being sampled. So the first requirement is the development of a methodology. There are many perspectives from which the population question can be approached. One extreme would be to consider the population to consist of all the language that has ever been written or spoken. Another possibility, of particular interest to psycholinguists, would be all the language to which an individual has been exposed during his or her lifetime. A third would be all the kinds of language to which a particular individual might be exposed at any one time. From a slightly different vantage point, one much more familiar to humanistic research, one could consider all the material in some area, for example, classical Greek or Latin, or epic poetry, although the body of literature on computational linguistics might also be considered. Each of these alternatives entails a different strategy for collection and different levels of confidence in the adequacy of the sample with respect to its population.

Sociolinguists have of course investigated some of these problems. Indeed, the well-established concepts of dialect, genre, style, register, and the like can take on a new and particularly significant perspective in a computational context. Recent work by Biber (1988, 1989) is of particular interest in this regard. He (Biber, 1989) remarks, quite properly, that "a typology of texts is a research prerequisite to any comparative register analysis, whether of speech and writing, formal and informal texts, restricted and elaborated codes, literary and colloquial styles, 'good' and 'bad' student compositions, early and late historical periods, or whatever, to situate particular texts relative to the range of texts in English" (p. 4). His typology, based on a multivariate analysis of sets of lexical and syntactical features that co-occur in texts, results in the identification of eight classes: intimate interpersonal interaction, informational interaction, scientific exposition, learned exposition, imaginative narrative, general narrative exposition, situated reportage, and involved persuasion. These labels do not do full justice to the kinds of materials each subsumes. At the same time, the types themselves are constrained by the particular linguistic features (67) Biber worked with and, of course by the spoken and written texts (481) he selected from the Lancaster-Oslo/Bergen and London-Lund Corpora. Much more work along these lines is needed.

Studies of sublanguages were a subject of considerable interest a few years ago, as Sager's (1981) review of the work of the New York University Linguistic String Project and the proceedings of Kittredge and Lehrberger (1982) and Grishman and Kittredge (1986) demonstrate. Within this context, Walker and Amsler (1986) showed how the subject codes of the *Longman Dictionary of Contemporary English* (Procter, 1978), which characterize different senses of a given word, could be used to identify the topics of stories from the *New York*

Times newswire service. Whereas those codes are useful for "general" English, it is clear that extensive studies of the occurrences of vocabulary in specialized subject areas will be necessary to develop a broader, deeper, and more refined subject-coded scheme.

Ecological studies of language can be expected to have major implications for dictionary design and dictionary content. From the standpoint of selecting lexical entries, it is essential to explore the collocational strategies referred to in the preceding section on *Issues* (Ahlswede et al., 1988; Amsler, 1987b, 1989a, forthcoming; Choueka, 1988) to determine what phrases and compounds need to be added. More knowledge of syntactic structure is also a critical requirement. Parsers that are designed to handle unrestricted text need to be used more extensively. It will be interesting in this context to contrast the results provided by approaches that differ as much as Church's (1988) stochastic parser and Hindle's (1983, 1989) deterministic parser, Fidditch. Also worth exploring is an information theoretic measure of mutual information developed by Church and Hanks (1989) that can be used to identify semantic relations among content words, lexico-syntactic co-occurrence constraints between verbs and prepositions, and estimations of word association norms as well.

As a final note in this section, it is appropriate to call attention to some recent work that Mark Liberman presented in an invited address, "How Many Words Do People Know?" at the 27th Annual Meeting of the Association for Computational Linguistics earlier this year. Explicitly applying a statistical model developed by Fisher to study animal ecology, he was able to establish that in vocabulary acquisition words travel in "herds," and that it may be reasonable to describe sublanguages as "swarms." Here again, selecting the linguistic universe is critical.

CONCLUSIONS

This chapter has ranged broadly. I began by noting the recent increase in interest in the lexicon and the critical importance of cooperation to insure that lexical sources can be shared and reused. Then I reviewed a series of workshops that have resulted in bringing together publishers, software developers, and people from the research community to work toward mutually relevant goals. After considering a set of issues shared by these groups regarding the collateral development of both textual and lexical resources, I describe the *Text Encoding Initiative,* the *ACL Data Collection Initiative,* and a proposal for a *Consortium for Lexical Research.* Finally, I discussed some steps toward establishing an "ecology of language."[16]

---

[16]It was a fascinating experience for me to discover a book on *The Ecology of Computation* (Huberman, 1988) a few months ago, quite some time after I had began working out my own

My perceptions of the progress and coherence among these efforts is, I am sure, more than I have been able to demonstrate. In the context of my own long-term goals, the work described constitutes a bare beginning. What I am aiming for is a global but distributed electronic library that will contain all the world's knowledge. For "knowledge specialists" to be able to access the information contained in the library through computer workstations, it will become necessary to elaborate an equally global "dictionary" that will be adequate for the "electronic age." I see the efforts I have been describing as definite progress toward that end.

There is, of course, a much more near-term goal that is particularly relevant within the context of the present volume. All these activities are contributing to increase the resources that can be used by scholars concerned with elucidating *Frames, Fields, and Contrasts*. The "research enterprise" represented by the other chapters can be dramatically furthered by the availability to the community it represents of machine-readable data, suitably coded in a standard form, and processible by a much broader range of computational tools than we now possess. Given access to these materials, I am confident that the next few years will result in dramatically increased insights into the principles of lexical and semantic organization.

ACKNOWLEDGMENTS

This chapter owes much to my long-time collaborations with Robert Amsler, Antonio Zampolli, and Nicoletta Calzolari. I also am indebted to many other colleagues with whom I have been involved in exploring the dimensions of lexical research, particularly Sue Atkins, Bran Boguraev, Roy Byrd, Bob Ingria, Judy Kegl, Beth Levin, Jonathan Slocum, and Frank Tompa.

My participation in the *Text Encoding Initiative* has brought ne a new set of valued colleagues: Susan Hockey, Nancy Ide, Michael Sperberg-McQueen, and Lou Burnard (as well as providing excuses for working more with Amsler and Zampolli). Their words and ideas have contributed substantively to that section of this chapter.

The *ACL Data Collection Initiative* has increased my interactions with Mark Liberman, Ken Church, and Mitch Marcus, in particular, for which I am grateful. Their ideas, along with those of Bob Amsler, and, as noted, some of Mark's words as well, are reflected in the description in that section.

---

ecological concerns. It takes its point of departure from distributed computational systems that the editor believes are acquiring features characteristic of social and biological organizations. What I found most impressive is that the book ends with a chapter on "The Next Knowledge Medium" (Stefik, 1988) in which the issues of standardization, collection, and reusability figure in the development of knowledge bases and a knowledge medium.

Roy Byrd deserves special thanks for his cogent formulation of the requirements for a *Consortium for Lexical Research.*

More generally, it is appropriate to express my personal gratitude to the organizations that have made resources available for research. For my own research, it is particularly appropriate to thank G. & C. Merriam for the Webster's Seventh Collegiate Dictionary, Longman Publishing Group for the Longman Dictionary of Contemporary English, and Mead Data Central for the New York Times.

Finally, I would like to thank Bellcore, SRI International, the U.S. National Science Foundation, and the *Association for Computational Linguistics* especially for their support of my research.

REFERENCES

Ahlswede, T., Anderson, J., Evens, M., Li, S. M., Neises, J., & Pin Ngern, S. (1988, March 21–28). Automatic construction of a phrasal thesaurus for an information retrieval system from a machine readable dictionary. *Proceedings of the RIAO88 Conference on User-Oriented Content-Based Text and Image Handling.* Cambridge, MA. Paris: Centre de Hautes Etudes Internationales d'Informatique Documentaire.

Amsler, R. A. (1987a, January 16–19). Words and worlds. *TINLAP-3, Theoretical issues in natural language processing 3* (pp. 16–19). New Mexico State University. Morristown, NJ: Association for Computational Linguistics.

Amsler, R. A. (1987b). How do I turn this book on?—Preparing text for access as a computational medium. *Uses of Large-Text Databases: Proceedings of the 3rd Annual Conference of the UW Centre for the New Oxford English Dictionary.* University of Waterloo Centre for the New Oxford English Dictionary, Waterloo, Ontario.

Amsler, R. A. (1989a). Research toward the development of a lexical knowledge base for natural language processing. *Proceedings of the 1989 SIGIR Conference.* Cambridge, MA, 25–28 June 1989. Association for Computing Machinery, New York.

Amsler, R. A. (1989b). Third generation computational lexicology. *Proceedings of the First International Lexical Acquisition Workshop.* Detroit, Michigan, 21 August.

Amsler, R. A. (1992). Deriving lexical knowledge base entries from existing machine-readable information sources. In D. E. Walker, A. Zampolli, & N. Calzolari (Eds.), *Automating the Lexicon: Research and practice in a multilingual environment.* Oxford University Press, Oxford.

Association of American Publishers. (1987). *Standard for electronic manuscript preparation and markup.* Washington, DC: Association of American Publishers.

Beale, A. D. (1988, June 7–10). Lexicon and grammar in probabilistic tagging of written english. *Proceedings of the 26th Annual Meeting of the Association for Computational Linguistics* (pp. 211–216). Buffalo, NY. Morristown, N.J.: Association for Computational Linguistics.

Biber, D. (1988). *Variation across speech and writing.* Cambridge, England: Cambridge University Press.

Biber, D. (1989). A typology of English texts. *Linguistics, 27,* 3–43.

Boguraev, B., & Briscoe, T. (1987). Large lexicons for natural language processing: Utilizing the grammar coding system of LDOCE. *Computational Linguistics, 13* (3–4), 203–218.

Boguraev, B., & Briscoe, T. (Ed.). (1989). *Computational lexicography for natural language processing.* London and New York: Longman.

Boguraev, B., Briscoe, T., Calzolari, N., Cater, A., Meijs, W., & Zampolli, A. (1988). *Acquisition of lexical knowledge for natural language processing systems.* Proposal for ESPRIT Basic Research Actions. Cambridge: University of Cambridge.

Boguraev, B. K. (1992). Machine-readable dictionaries and computational linguistic research. In D. E. Walker, A. Zampolli, & N. Calzolari (Eds.), *Automating the lexicon: Research and practice in a multilingual environment.* Oxford University Press, Oxford.

Bowers, R. A. (1989). *Results of the lexical research survey.* Special Report. Columbus, OH: AITRC.

Bryan, M. (1988). SGML: *An author's guide to the standard generalized markup language.* Wokingham, England and Reading, MA: Addison-Wesley.

Byrd, R. J., Calzolari, N., Chodorow, M. S., Klavans, J. L., Neff, M. S., & Rizk, O. A. (1989). Tools and methods for computational linguistics. *Computational Linguistics, 13* (3–4), 219–240.

Calzolari, N. (1992). Structure and access in an automated lexicon and related issues. In D. W. Walker, A. Zampolli, & N. Calzolari (Eds.), *Automating the lexicon: Research and practice in a multilingual environment.* Oxford University Press, Oxford.

Calzolari, N., & Zampolli, A. (1992). Very large linguistic databases: The problem of the re-usability of lexical resources. *The dynamic text: Proceedings of the 9th International Conference on Computers and the Humanities and the 16th International Association for Literary and Linguistic Computing Conference.* Toronto, Ontario. Oxford: Oxford University Press.

Choueka, Y. (1988, March 21–24). Looking for needles in a haystack or locating interesting collocational expressions in large textual databases. *Proceedings of the RIAO88 Conference on User-Oriented Content-Based Text and Image Handling.* Cambridge, MA. Paris: Centre de Hautes Etudes Internationales d'Informatique Documentaire.

Church, K. W. (1988, February 9–12). A stochastic parts program and noun phrase parser for unrestricted text. *Proceedings of the Second Conference on Applied Natural Language Processing* (pp. 136–143). Austin, TX. Morristown, NJ: Association for Computational Linguistics.

Church, K. W., & Hanks, P. (1989, June 26–29). Word association norms, mutual information, and lexicography. *Proceedings of the 27th Annual Meeting of the Association for Computational Linguistics* (pp. 76–83). Vancouver, British Columbia. Morristown, NJ: Association for Computational Linguistics.

Francis, F. W., & Kucera, H. (1982). *Frequency analysis of English usage: Lexicon and grammar.* Boston: Houghton–Mifflin.

G. & C. Merriam Company. (1963). *Webster's New Collegiate Dictionary* (seventh ed.). Springfield, MA: G. & C. Merriam Company.

Garside, R., Leech, G., & Sampson, G. (1987). *The computational analysis of English: A corpus-based approach.* London and New York: Longman.

Goetschalckx, J., & Rolling, L. N. (Eds.). (1982). *Lexicography in the electronic age.* Amsterdam: North-Holland.

Grishman, R., & Kittredge, R. (Eds.). (1986). *Analyzing language in restricted domains.* Hillsdale, NJ: Lawrence Erlbaum Associates.

Hanks, P. (Ed.). (1979). *Collins English Dictionary.* Glasgow: William Collins Sons.

Hindle, D. (1983, June 15–17). Deterministic parsing of syntactic non-fluencies. *Proceedings of the 21st Annual Meeting of the Association for Computational Linguistics* (pp. 123–128). Cambridge, MA. Morristown, NJ: Association for Computational Linguistics.

Hindle, D. (1989, June 26–29). Acquiring disambiguation rules from text. *Proceedings of the 27th Annual Meeting of the Association for Computational Linguistics* (pp. 118–125). Vancouver, British Columbia. Morristown, NJ: Association for Computational Linguistics.

Huberman, B. A. (Ed.). (1988). *The ecology of computation.* Amsterdam: North-Holland.

International Standards Organization. (1986). *International Standard ISO 8879: Information Processing—Text and Office Systems—Standard Generalized Markup Language (SGML).* New York: American National Standards Institute.

Johansson, S. (1985). Word frequency and text type: Some observations based on the LOB corpus of British English texts. *Computers and the Humanities, 19*(1), 23–26.

Kittredge, R., & Lehrberger, J. (Eds.). (1982). *Sublanguage: Studies of language in restricted semantic domains.* Berlin: de Gruyter.

Kucera, H., & Francis, F. W. (1967). *Computational analysis of present-day American English.* Providence, RI: Brown University Press.

Lancashire, I., & McCarty, W. (Eds.). (1988). *The humanities computing yearbook.* Oxford: Clarendon Press.

Lesk, M. E. (1986, June). Automatic sense disambiguation using machine readable dictionaries: How to tell a pine cone from an ice cream cone. *Proceedings of the 1986 SIGDOC Conference* (pp. 24–26). Toronto. New York: Association for Computing Machinery.

Neff, M. S., Byrd, R. J., & Rizk, O. A. (1988, February 9–12). Creating and querying lexical data bases. *Proceedings of the Second Conference on Applied Natural Language Processing* (pp. 84–92). Austin, TX. Morristown, NJ: Association for Computational Linguistics.

Neff, M. S., & Boguraev, B. K. (1989, June 26–29). Dictionaries, dictionary grammars and dictionary entry parsing. *Proceedings of the 27th Annual Meeting of the Association for Computational Linguistics.* Vancouver, British Columbia. Morristown, NJ: Association for Computational Linguistics.

Procter, R. (Ed.). (1978). *Longman dictionary of contemporary English.* Harlow and London, England: Longman.

Sager, N. (1981). *Natural language information processing: A computer grammar of English and its applications.* Reading, MA: Addison-Wesley.

Sinclair, J. M. (Ed.). (1987a). *Collins COBUILD English language dictionary.* Glasgow: Collins.

Sinclair, J. M. (Ed.). (1987b). *Looking up: An account of the COBUILD project in lexical computing.* Glasgow: Collins.

Stefik, M. J. (1988). The next knowledge medium. In B. A. Huberman (Ed.), *The ecology of computation* (pp. 315–342). Amsterdam: North-Holland.

Svartvik, J., & Quirk, R. (1980). *A corpus of English conversation.* Lund: Gleerup.

UW Centre for the New OED. (1986). *Advances in Lexicology: Proceedings of the 2nd Annual Conference of the UW Centre for the New Oxford English Dictionary.* Waterloo, Ontario: University of Waterloo Centre for the New Oxford English Dictionary.

van Herwijnen, E. (1990). *Practical SGML.* Dordrecht: Kluwer.

Walker, D. E., & Amsler, R. A. The use of machine-readable dictionaries in sublanguage analysis. In R. Grishman & R. Kittredge (Eds.), *Analyzing language in restricted domains* (pp. 69–83). Hillsdale, NJ: Lawrence Erlbaum Associates.

Walker, D. E., Zampolli, A., & Calzolari, N. (Eds.). (1987a). Special issue on the lexicon. *Computational Linguistics, 13* (3–4).

Walker, D. E., Zampolli, A., & Calzolari, N. (Eds.). (1987b). *Towards a polytheoretical lexical database.* Preprints. Pisa: Istituto di Linguistica Computazionale.

Walker, D. E., Zampolli, A., & Calzolari, N. (Eds.). (1992). *Automating the lexicon: Research and practice in a multilingual environment.* Oxford: Oxford University Press.

Wilks, Y. (Ed.). (1987, January 7–9). *TINLAP-3, Theoretical issues in natural language processing 3.* New Mexico State University. Morristown, NJ: Association for Computational Linguistics. To be published in revised form by Lawrence Erlbaum Associates, Hillsdale, NJ.

Author Index

Durrell, M., 306
Dummett, M., 145, 169

E

Edelson, S. M., 27, 71
Embretson, S., 259, 286
Esau, H., 335, 351
Estes, W. K., 23, 69
Evens, M., 277, 287, 428, 440

F

Fauconnier, G., 197, 207, 358, 373
Fay, D., 381, 382, 383, 394
Fehr, B., 69, 255, 286
Fellbaum, C., 264, 286
Fillenbaum, S., 254, 286
Fillmore, C. J., 4, 5, 6, 10, 12, 14, 15,
  16, 17, 28, 70, 85, 102, 211, 226,
  311, 315, 317, 322, 330, 334, 341,
  342, 351, 352, 373
Finegan, E., 335, 348, 349, 350, 351
Fisher, U., 389, 394
Flannigan, M. J., 50, 70
Fodor, J. A., 9, 12, 17, 27, 44, 70, 194,
  195, 196, 197, 198, 205, 206, 207,
  226, 233, 234, 239, 240, 249,
  251, 254, 287
Foley, D., 352
Forbus, K. D., 57, 70
Francis, F. W., 436, 441, 442
Frege, G., 13, 195, 207, 309, 321, 339,
  351
Freko, D., 27, 71
Fried, L. S., 50, 70
Fromkin, V., 382, 384, 394
Frumkina, R., 220, 226

G

Garrett, M. F., 2, 14, 207, 226, 379,
  381, 386, 394
Garside, R., 433, 441
Gellatly, A. R. H., 258, 287

Gelman, S. A., 184, 185, 187, 188
Gentner, D., 27, 70, 72
Geroch, R., 145, 169
Gerrig, R. J., 174, 178, 187
Glass, A. L., 22, 70
Gleik, J., 40, 70
Gleitman, H., 51, 53, 68, 70, 255, 286
Gleitman, L. R., 51, 53, 68, 70, 255,
  286
Gluck, M. A., 23, 70
Glucksberg, S., 22, 71, 116, 121, 258,
  287
Goddard, C., 210, 226
Goetschalckx, J., 422, 441
Goldberg, L. R., 48, 69
Goldberg, R., 186, 188
Goldin, S. E., 255, 287
Goldman, A., 229, 251
Goldstone, R. L., 27, 70, 72
Golinkoff, R. M., 183, 187
Goodman, N., 8, 17, 34, 70, 113, 121
Graesser, A. C., 359, 373
Grandy, R. E., 3, 5, 6, 12, 14, 16, 17,
  25, 63, 70, 104, 121, 229, 239, 251
Gray, W. D., 22, 72, 279, 288
Green, M., 342, 352
Greenbaum, S., 335, 348, 352
Greenspan, S. L., 268, 271, 287
Gregg, V. H., 258, 287
Grice, H. P., 103, 121, 172, 188
Grishman, R., 437, 441
Gropen, J., 186, 188
Gross, D., 389, 394
Guha, R. V., 28, 30, 71

H

Hale, C. R., 54, 69
Halff, H. M., 41, 70
Halliday, M. A. K., 337, 340, 352
Hampton, J. A., 22, 32, 70, 254, 274,
  278, 279, 281, 287
Hanks, P., 433, 438, 441
Harter, K. B., 141
Harkness, A. R., 255, 286

Subject Index

A

acceptability, 15
  of color words, 220
  in craft-bound discourse, 167
  of proper names, 125-142
  semantic contagion and, 148, 156-161, 167
ACL Data Collection Initiative (ACL/ DCI), 428, 432, 433, 435, 436
acquisition, problems of, 194, *see also* language acquisition; concepts, acquisition of
actor category, 83-85, 88, 89, 99, 100
actually adverbials, 348-350
adjectives, representation of by frames, 29
adjective substitution errors, 389-390, 393, 394
adverbs, representation of by frames, 29
affinity, individuation and, 230, 235, 236, 243, 244, 246, 247, 250, 251
  linguistic relativity and, 5, 6
  meaning and, 13
  semantic contagion and, 146-148, 155-157, 160, 161, 165, 168
  semantic fields and, 3, 4, 13, 229, 230, 237, 245
aggregation, 199, 203-206
AI, *see* artificial intelligence
Ainu, 225
ambiguity, 103, 166, 294, 295, 322-326, 385

American National Standards Institute (ANSI), 429
American Publishing House for the Blind, 84
analogy, semantic contagion and, 144, 154
analysis, *see* componential analysis
anaphora, 79, 321, 322
anchoring, 157, 158
animal names, 137, 177, 212, 243, 363, 366, 369, *see also* pet names
antonymy, committed vs. uncommitted, 291, 294, 299, 301, 303, 304
  componential analysis and, 110
  cross-linguistic comparison and, 8
  errors and, 384, 389, 394
  gradable properties and, 289-305
  impartiality and, 291-301, 304-305
  lexicalization and, 265, 266
  polar, 299, 300, 305
  as primitive, 7
  relation elements and, 272
  relation similarity and, 256, 258
  semantic fields and, 3, 5
  sub vs. supra, 298-303, 305
  typicality gradient and, 256-258
aphasia, 382
Applied Information Technologies Research Center (AITRC), 427
aptness, 334, 336, 337, 343, 345, 347, 350, 351
Arabic, 293, 297, 299, 301, 302, 304
argument structure, 199-202
artificial category learning, 23-25

U

UDICT morphological analyzer, 399n,
  409
unification, 309, 310, 322-326
U.S. Air Force of Scientific Research,
  433
U.S. Defense Advanced Research
  Projects Agency, 433
U.S. Defense Department, 429
units of meaning, *see* meaning units
Universal Grammar, 194, 205, 246
universal linguistic force, *see* linguistic
  force
universals, *see* primitives, universal
universal semantic primitives, *see*
  primitives, universal
university building names, 126, 136
University of Waterloo Center for the
  New OED, 422
utility words, 146, 154, 159, 163

V

valance description, 78, 81
value, 336
  constraint, 49
  defined, 30, 31
  linguistic (Saussure), 237-240, 243,
    244, 248, 251
  patterns of, 49
  see also attribute-value sets
valued object category, 82, 87-91, 97-
  100
venery, terms of, 108
verb substitution errors, 389, 390-394
victim category, 82, 86, 99
vocabulary inconsistency, 408-410

W

Webster's Seventh Collegiate Dictionary, 406, 414, 416
weight, gradable property of, 289, 293-
  295, 299
weighted features and dimensions
  view, 119
word frequency, 384-386, 388, 390,
  391, 394
word substitution errors, 1, 2, 14, 377-
  394
workshops, *see* lexicon workshops

X

X-bar theory, 200, 202, 203, 314

Y

Yiddish, 3